Anglistentag

2013 Konstanz

Anglistentag
2013 Konstanz

Proceedings

edited by

Silvia Mergenthal and Reingard M. Nischik

with assistance from
Emily Petermann and Melanie Stengele

wvt Wissenschaftlicher Verlag Trier

Anglistentag 2013 Konstanz
Proceedings
ed. by Silvia Mergenthal, Reingard M. Nischik
Trier: WVT Wissenschaftlicher Verlag Trier, 2014
   (Proceedings of the Conference of the German
   Association of University Teachers of English; Vol. 35)
   ISBN 978-3-86821-561-8

Umschlaggestaltung: Brigitta Disseldorf

© WVT Wissenschaftlicher Verlag Trier, 2014
ISBN 978-3-86821-561-8

Alle Rechte vorbehalten
Nachdruck oder Vervielfältigung nur mit
ausdrücklicher Genehmigung des Verlags

Gedruckt auf alterungsbeständigem
und säurefreiem Papier
Printed in Germany

WVT Wissenschaftlicher Verlag Trier
Bergstraße 27, 54295 Trier
Postfach 4005, 54230 Trier
Tel.: (0651) 41503 / 9943344, Fax: 41504
Internet: http://www.wvttrier.de
e-mail: wvt@wvttrier.de

Proceedings of the Conference
of the German Association
of University Teachers
of English

Volume XXXV

Contents

Silvia Mergenthal and Reingard M. Nischik (Konstanz)
  Preface   XI

Linda Hutcheon (Toronto)
  From Reader Response to Reader Response-Ability   XV

Section 1: Victorian Lives and Minds:
Scientific Cultures in the Nineteenth Century

Nadine Böhm-Schnitker (Erlangen) and Philipp Erchinger (Düsseldorf)
  Scientific Cultures in the Nineteenth Century: Introduction   3

Jochen Petzold (Regensburg)
  It's Not Cruel, It's Science! The Re-Invention of Bird-Nesting
  in Late Victorian Juvenile Culture   9

Joanna Rostek (Passau)
  Female Authority and Political Economy: Jane Marcet's and
  Harriet Martineau's Contradictory Strategy in Disseminating
  Economic Knowledge   21

Stefani Brusberg-Kiermeier (Hildesheim)
  Half Man, Half Machine: Wilkie Collins's and Charles Reade's
  Constructions of Victorian Machine Men   35

Stefanie Fricke (München)
  Scientific Discourses in Late Victorian Fantastic Texts   47

Nora Pleßke (Passau)
  The Object(ivity) of Imperial Thinking   59

Pascal Fischer (Würzburg/Flensburg)
  The "Third Culture Intellectuals" and Charles Darwin   71

Section 2: Historical Media Cultures

Kai Merten (Kiel) and Nicola Glaubitz (Siegen)
  Historical Media Cultures   83

Albrecht Koschorke (Konstanz)
  Social Media 1800   91

Jürgen Meyer (Halle)
  Theatre, Library, Lab: Mediating Knowledge, 1600-1800   105

Gerd Bayer (Erlangen)
    The Broken Letters of Early Modern Fiction   117

Ingo Berensmeyer (Gießen/Ghent)
    Grub Street Revisited: Late Eighteenth-Century Authorship Satire
    and the Media Culture of Print   127

Rainer Emig (Hannover)
    The Visiting Card: A Historical Medium that Bridges Culture and Literature   137

Natalie Roxburgh (Oldenburg)
    Between Property and Propriety: *David Simple* and Social Mediation   145

Section 3: Not Shakespeare: New Approaches to Drama in the Seventeenth Century

Susanne Gruß (Erlangen), Lena Steveker (Saarbrücken), and Angelika Zirker (Tübingen)
    Not Shakespeare: New Approaches to Drama in the Seventeenth Century   153

Stephan Laqué (München)
    Leaving Wittenberg: Faustus, Hamlet, and Early Modern Education   159

Katrin Röder (Potsdam)
    Intercultural "Traffique" and Political Change in Samuel Daniel's
    Philotas (1596-1604) and Fulke Greville's *Mustapha* (1587-1610?)   171

Felix C. H. Sprang (Hamburg)
    Neither Shakespeare Nor the Gilded Monuments:
    Rethinking the Dramatic Impact of Jacobean and Caroline Civic Pageants   183

Matthias Bauer and Martina Bross (Tübingen)
    Character Writing and the Stage in the Early Seventeenth Century   195

Ellen Redling (Heidelberg)
    "From the Top of Paul's Steeple to the Standard in Cheap":
    Popular Culture, Urban Space, and Narrativity in Jacobean City Comedy   207

Section 4: Rhetoric and Poetry

Monika Fludernik and Ulrike Zimmermann (Freiburg)
    Rhetoric and Poetry: An Introduction   223

Jonathan Culler (Ithaca, NY)
    The Strange Present Tense of the English Lyric   229

Wolfgang G. Müller (Jena)
    Is There a Special Use of Language in Poetry? Roman Jakobson's
    Concept of Poeticity and the Relation between Language and Verse   239

Claudia Claridge (Duisburg-Essen)
    George Herbert's *The Temple*: Positioning the Speaker   249

Gero Guttzeit (Gießen)
    From Hearing to Overhearing? Eloquence and Poetry, 1776-1833   261

Alwin Fill (Graz)
    Humanizing Metaphors in the Nature Poems of D. H. Lawrence   271

Eva Ulrike Pirker (Freiburg)
    Language and Agency after Modernism: A Reading of J. H. Prynne's
    "Die A Millionaire (pronounced: 'diamonds in the air')"   279

Marie-Luise Egbert (Leipzig)
    Poetic and Rhetorical Figurations of Touch in Les Murray's
    Fredy Neptune (1998)   291

Section 5: Comparison and Comparability in Language Studies

Klaus P. Schneider (Bonn) and Anne Schröder (Bielefeld)
    Comparison and Comparability in Language Studies: An Introduction   303

Miriam A. Locher (Basel)
    The Relational Aspect of Language: Avenues of Research   309

Bernd Kortmann (Freiburg)
    Comparison and Comparability: The WAVE Perspective   323

Daniela Kolbe-Hanna (Trier)
    The Comparability of Discourse Features: *I think* in Englishes Worldwide   337

Stephanie Hackert (München) and Anne Schröder (Bielefeld)
    Comparing Tense and Aspect in Pidgins and Creoles:
    Dahl's Questionnaire and Beyond   349

Klaus P. Schneider (Bonn)
    Comparability and Sameness in Variational Pragmatics   361

Tanja Rütten (Köln)
    Comparing Apples and Oranges: The Study of Diachronic Change
    Based on Variant Forms   373

Thomas Kohnen (Köln)
    In Search of Faithful Standards: Comparing Diachronic Corpora
    across Domains   387

SILVIA MERGENTHAL AND REINGARD M. NISCHIK (KONSTANZ)

Preface

Thirty years after the University of Konstanz had first hosted the Anglistentag, the annual conference of the German Association of University Teachers of English once again took place at Konstanz in September 2013. It was with particular pleasure that the 2013 organizers welcomed their 1983 predecessor, Jürgen Schlaeger, as well as a few other colleagues who had participated in that memorable event.

The University of Konstanz was founded as a reform university in 1966 and it became one of Germany's "Universities of Excellence" in 2007, a status it defended successfully in 2012, not least on the strength of its humanities departments. Konstanz is unusual in that it does not have a traditional departmental structure. Hence, the local hosts in 2013, Silvia Mergenthal and Reingard M. Nischik, are members of the Department of Literature, Art, and Media Studies, where they hold posts in British Literature and Culture and in American Studies, respectively. Both British Literature and Culture and American Studies at Konstanz have consistently done well in rankings, perhaps precisely because of their interdisciplinary institutional contexts.

One of the founding members of Konstanz University was Wolfgang Iser, arguably one of the most distinguished literary scholars of his generation. After his death in 2007, his successor, Aleida Assmann, was instrumental in establishing an annual commemorative lecture, which is usually scheduled for a date near Iser's birthday in late July. Since 2009 Iser Lectures have been held by Geoffrey Hartman, Hans Ulrich Gumbrecht, J. Hillis Miller, and David Wellbery. For the purposes of the 2013 Anglistentag, the Iser Lecture was rescheduled so as to coincide with the conference. Entitled "From Reader Response to Reader Response-Ability", the 2013 Iser Lecture was introduced by Aleida Assmann and Reingard M. Nischik and delivered by Linda Hutcheon. It provided a brilliant prologue to the Anglistentag, a role it also fills for this volume.

The Anglistentag proper was formally opened on September 19, 2013 with the welcoming addresses by Silvia Mergenthal, who, as one of the Vice-Rectors, also spoke on behalf of the university, and by the then President of the Anglistenverband, Julika Griem, University of Frankfurt. This was followed by two award ceremonies, in the first of which Jan Alber, University of Freiburg, was awarded the 2013 *Habilitationspreis* for his book on *Unnatural Narrative: Impossible Worlds in Fiction and Drama*. In the presence of its sponsor, Franz Karl Stanzel, the second award, the 2013 Helene Richter Award, went to Irmtraud Huber, University of Bern, for her dissertation entitled *Reconstructive Dreams: A Pragmatic Fantastic After Postmodernism*. A few weeks after his ninetieth birthday, Stanzel was the focus of yet another Anglistentag event when, in the session "Franz Karl Stanzel in Dialogue", he presented his recently published autobiography *Verlust einer Jugend*.

The academic programme of the conference comprised three plenary lectures and five parallel sections. The three plenary speakers and their topics were:
- Jonathan Culler (Cornell University): "The Strange Present Tense of the English Lyric".
- Albrecht Koschorke (University of Konstanz): "Social Media around 1800".
- Miriam A. Locher (University of Basel): "The Relational Aspect of Language: Avenues of Research".

The five sections were:
1. Victorian Lives and Minds: Scientific Cultures in the Nineteenth Century (conveners Nadine Böhm-Schnitker and Philipp Erchinger).
2. Historical Media Culture (conveners Kai Merten and Nicola Glaubitz).
3. Not Shakespeare: New Approaches to Drama in the Seventeenth Century (conveners Susanne Gruß, Lena Steveker, and Angelika Zirker).
4. Rhetoric and Poetry (conveners Monika Fludernik and Ulrike Zimmermann).
5. Comparison and Comparability in Language Studies (conveners Klaus P. Schneider and Anne Schröder).

The Annual General Meeting of the Anglistenverband on September 20, 2013 elected a new president, Klaus P. Schneider of the University of Bonn; his predecessor, Julika Griem, took over as Vice-President, whose portfolio includes co-operation with other national associations within the ESSE.

In its new, much more compact format – the Konstanz Anglistentag was only the second annual conference (after the Potsdam conference in 2012) in which the academic programme comprised, effectively, just over one full day – the conference does not leave a great deal of room for explorations of local sites other than the actual conference venue. This year's venue, the university campus, is located a few kilometres outside the historic city centre. For this reason it was decided at an early stage to choose signature sites for the three main social events of the conference, the conference warming, the civic reception, and the conference dinner. Thus, in the run-up to the 600th anniversary of the Council of Konstanz (1414 to 1418), memorably linked to "how the world became modern" in Stephen Greenblatt's *The Swerve* of 2011, both the civic reception and the conference dinner took place in buildings associated with this world-historical event, namely, in the *Konzilgebäude* and in the *Inselhotel*. This former Dominican monastery also witnessed the first lecture of the fledgling university, held on June 21, 1966 by eminent political scientist Waldemar Besson, another of the university's founding members. As for the excursion, the organizers were rather spoiled for choice and after a lengthy decision-making process eventually settled on one of the three UNESCO world heritage sites in the vicinity, namely, on the historic *Stiftsbibliothek* at St. Gallen, Switzerland.

The local organisers in Konstanz are indebted to the many people who have contributed to making the Anglistentag 2013 a success. Melanie Stengele and Martina Thibaut were tremendously helpful during the long preparatory stages for the conference and during the event itself. Their talent for organisation, their reliability, their promptness, and their cheerful attitudes were much appreciated. Anke Waldau and Anne Emmert produced the programme brochure with what seems professional savvy and were also involved in the useful online presentation of the conference. During the conference itself, the local organisers could rely on the helping hands of the following Anglistik and Amerikanistik student assistants (in alphabetical order): Alena Frey, Lisa Gabauer, Romina Heimburger, Ingrid Kaplitz, Valerie Neumann, Srdjan Perko, Julia Schiller, Magdalena Schreiber, Bernadette Schroh, and Anke Waldau. The conference could not have been run successfully without a great number of incredibly helpful and committed people from various university support services such as the facility management, the event management, the computing centre, and media technology services, who worked extra hours and went to great lengths to make Konstanz a hospitable venue.

The prestigious keynote speakers were lured to small but beautiful Konstanz with generous assistance from the Excellence Cluster 16 "Cultural Foundations of Integration" at the University of Konstanz, whose support of the lectures by Linda Hutcheon and Jonathan Culler is gratefully acknowledged here. Last but not least, we thank Theresia Bauer, Baden-Württemberg's Minister of Science, Research, and the Arts, for providing the patronage of our conference.

As to the proceedings volume at hand, we thank Emily Petermann and Melanie Stengele for their conscientious and time-consuming work with the copyediting of the many contributions. We are also grateful to Christine Schneider for producing the camera-ready copy for the publishing house. Without their efficient help, this book manuscript could not have been produced in this manner in a relatively short period of time.

The local organisers of the conference/co-editors of the proceedings volume hope that this books brings back good memories to those who attended the conference and may give those who could not be present an impression of the range of the topics and the papers presented at the Anglistentag 2013 at the University of Konstanz.

Silvia Mergenthal and Reingard M. Nischik   Konstanz and Toronto in June 2014

LINDA HUTCHEON (TORONTO)

From Reader Response to Reader Response-Ability

It is a very great honour to be invited to give the Wolfgang Iser Lecture in Konstanz, the university and the city in which Iser made his home and his reputation. He and Hans Robert Jauss helped put Konstanz on the literary theoretical map – where it has stayed and gone on to become a centre of excellence in so many fields of literary study. Then too, it is a special pleasure to give this talk in the company of Jonathan Culler – because (though he may not know this) he and Iser, between them, changed how I learned, how I thought, how I wrote about literature. Let me explain.

From the start, I have to confess that I have a difficult, not to say a traumatic relationship with reader-response theory in general and Wolfgang Iser's work in particular. The sad but true story of my trauma goes this way: In another century (in fact, in the year 1974), when I was completing my doctoral thesis in Comparative Literature at the University of Toronto, Wolfgang Iser arrived to offer a graduate course. The contents of this extensive course would eventually take the form of the book we know as *The Act of Reading: A Theory of Aesthetic Response* (1978). I had not planned to attend the course. I was in the last throes of writing my dissertation, and I was in an intellectual state that I suspect many readers will recognize: I did *not* want to learn anything new; I just wanted to finish writing. I was wearing what I think of as my "intellectual blinkers" and was pushing onward; the end was in sight. But since everyone was so excited about Iser's course, I went along to the first lecture.

Two hours later, my entire intellectual world had changed. I am making it sound like a miracle, but it felt more like a disaster at the time: Within hours, I knew I would have to rewrite my entire dissertation. Somehow, in what was, at that time, my particular structuralist, formalist mode of "professional deformation", I had drafted an entire study of self-reflexive fiction without ever thinking about the reader or the act of reading. I do not know how I could have ignored the reader in metafiction by everyone from Laurence Sterne to Vladimir Nabokov, from Italo Calvino to John Barth. But I had, though not for much longer. These were fictions, I *now* saw, that self-consciously offered their readers a different relationship – a relationship based on a mirroring of the actual creative process in which their authors had engaged when they wrote: the process of bringing to life the fictive worlds of their imagination in and through language. And as Iser had theorized so cogently, the links between *critical* discourse and contemporary *literary writing* are always strong – or certainly should be (1989, 131).

It was while I was laboriously rewriting my entire thesis to get to this point that I discovered Jonathan Culler's 1975 book, *Structuralist Poetics: Structuralism, Linguistics and the Study of Literature*. It was specifically his theorizing of "literary competence" in that book that reinforced the lesson of Wolfgang Iser. Together they taught me that literature is literature because of the way we *read* it, because, in Culler's words, "potential properties, latent in the object itself, are actualized by the theory of discourse applied to the act of reading" (1975, 113).

These two important theorists came from very different critical formations. Though I generalize here, as I saw it at the time, one came out of a Germanic phenomenological tradition, the other from the exciting new Parisian structuralism. But their combined message to me was a three-part one. First, you cannot ignore the reader and the process by which we "make" sense of what we read. This is why I was busy rewriting my thesis: I had learned this lesson well. The second message was that the act of reading changes us, making us more self-reflexive as what Culler called *homo significans*, "maker and reader of signs" (1975, 130), and as what Iser called "an interpreting animal" (1989, 209). This is what Iser thought of as the transformative power of reading. And this was what would soon lead him to theorize what he called "literary anthropology" as the study of what literature does to us and why we seem to need what he called these "inventions enabling humankind to extend itself" (1989, 265).

The third message from these theorists was perhaps less obvious, but just as powerful for me, and that was that there can be more to literary study than the interpretation of individual texts. It was not that I did not (and do not) enjoy elucidating literary works. I did and do. But it had been a graduate course taught by the Canadian theorist Northrop Frye that had first opened the door to the pleasure as well as the power and function of what came to be called "theory" – or "theorizing", perhaps, would be more accurate. What Culler called "poetics", he said, was "essentially a theory of reading" (1975, 128). Iser, too, was interested in how meaning *is produced*; that is why he constructed a theory that he called a "heuristic model of the activities basic to text-processing" (1980, 71; 61).

In a way, the rest is history – in more ways than one, however. Iser's theory of literary response, along with Jauss's reception aesthetic, together brought the reader into the centre of literary theoretical attention. Far from Konstanz, in the Anglo-American academy, in those same years, Tony Bennett, Stanley Fish, Jane Tompkins, and Norman Holland were among the others who did the same – though from very different critical principles and different ideological positions (see Bennett 1990, Fish 1980, Tompkins 1980, Holland 1968). In Italy, Umberto Eco entered the fray in semiotic armour. It was not long, inevitably, before critical works began to appear that analyzed and synthesized all these different perspectives on reading (see e.g. Holub 1984, Freund 1987, Machor and Goldstein 2001). Equally inevitably, attacks were launched from various directions. For some opponents, to concentrate on the reader was to promote a debilitating relativism (see e.g. Guillory 1993). For others, given the times, reader-response criticism was not oppositional enough, but rather simply reinforced the interpretive (and thus ideological) status quo (e.g. Bové 1992).

Yet, there *was* a major ripple-effect (not to say, tsunami) associated with this new "lector-centric" vision. It affected everything from drama and film studies – newly concentrating on spectatorship and audiences – to emerging fields as they developed – including Cultural Studies and Book History.[1] Ground-breaking work by feminist, Marxist, post-colonial, race, and Queer theorists taught us that many things have an impact on

---

[1] In theatre studies, see Bennett 1990/1997; for film, see Mayne 1993; for cultural studies, see Radway 1984), Dickinson et al. 1998, Hay et al. 1996, Cruz and Lewis 1994; on book history, see Darnton 1986.

reading and reception. To adapt Judith Fetterley's famous title, there were a lot of "resisting readers" out there (1978).

We know all this; that is what I meant by saying that it is now history. We likely do not even think about it all very much anymore. We have gone from a time of "high theory" to a time when many of these theoretical insights have been assimilated and digested, perhaps even unknowingly. We say: Of course, reading is an active process of making meaning and negotiating ideology within a social and cultural context. We have absorbed this much in the same way as we have absorbed the teachings of theorists like Derrida and Foucault. Yet I do not think that the age of theory (including reader-response theory) is really *over*. It is more a case of it now forming the background or perhaps even the ground upon which we work.

Today, however, both the fact and the act of reading may have made their way back onto the academic agenda in a more up-front and conscious way. In recent years, we have seen the publication of books with titles like *The Lost Art of Reading* (Ulin 2010) and *How to Read a Novel: A User's Guide* (Sutherland 2006; see also Foster 2003). In fact, there has been a spate of studies – though some are more pontifications, or correctives, or speculations – but they are all about the impact of digital technologies on reading. The list of concerns is now a familiar one: the shorter attention spans, the non-linear modalities, the compulsive need to be constantly connected, the new speed of communication. (As my own historical corrective to these complaints, however, I offer Walter Bagehot, writing in 1855 about readers of the new English literary reviews in these terms: the "multitude are impatient of system, desirous of brevity, puzzled by formality" [qtd. in Eagleton 1984, 50].) Marshall McLuhan had taught us that literature is a "cool" medium, one high in participation or completion by its audience (McLuhan and Zingrone 1996, 162). But he did not live to see the impact of the new kind of texts created by the immersive, interactive technologies of our digital age.

Wolfgang Iser, too, had seen that, as we read, we immerse ourselves in the imaginative recreation of another's world. But things became more complex and complicated with the advent of electronic technology. Suddenly there were kinesthetic, aural, and visual additions to that immersive literary experience that Iser had theorized in both cognitive and emotional terms (see Baron 2013). But technology and the social practices that accompany it have arguably always changed how we read. Reading a hand-written manuscript is not the same as reading a printed book, complete with index and table of contents. Other things have also changed *who* reads, as well as *how* they read: With mass education came greater literacy and a new and expanding supply of works to read, reading aloud is not the same as reading silently (see Saenger 1997), and reading to others is not like reading to oneself – or reading *with* others, as in a book club or university classroom (see Manguel 1996, 44-47). Still other new modes of reading occurred with the mass circulation of (and greater access to) the sharing of our reading experience that came with the internet (see Collins 2010). In the digital age of media convergence, our iPads and other mobile devices make us into readers of words who are also (often simultaneously) viewers of images and listeners of sound and music.

The reader-response theories of earlier years were based on the print medium. Wolfgang Iser theorized how it is that we read – or perhaps more accurately, he theorized how it is that we have been *taught* to read. It is the dynamic interaction of text and reader that produces the meaning of the text, he argued. Is the same true (in the same way) today, when what we would call the "text" has multiple other media platforms and thus multiple other experiential dimensions? To take just one example, does the genre of hypertext fiction represent a major change in reading practices, or is it really just a "false interactivity", as Lev Manovich has argued (2001, 61). Does it, in effect, restrict our choice to a limited set of narrative threads provided by the author? Yes, as readers of hypertext fiction, we can choose which link to follow – but is our choice really not limited to either obeying or ignoring the possibilities offered us by the author? Or when we experience, on our various mobile devices, a digital remediation of a poem or a story, complete with visuals and sound track, is our imaginative engagement expanded ... or limited? Where, as Iser taught us, we can concretize and visualize for ourselves as we read, we now have that task done for us. And, as is the case with a film adaptation of a novel, it is the director's imagination that dominates, indeed, colonizes our own. Those textual gaps Iser theorized have been filled, but not by us. Has our engagement, then, been expanded or has it been diminished? Or has it simply changed?

In the 1970s, both Iser and Culler thought deeply about the reader's degree of engagement with texts – but not yet with digital texts; that era was still to come. For Iser, it was those difficult works of modernist literature, with their multiple indeterminacies and gaps, that can most deeply engage readers in the process of reading and offer the greatest triggers to our imagination, and thus to our understanding of the limits of our own norms, habits, and expectations.[2] For Culler too, it was, at this time, these "challenging and innovatory texts" that contest "the limits we set to the self as a device or order and [allow] us, painfully or joyfully, to accede to an expansion of self" (1975, 130). But for both theorists, it was the *meaning* of the text – relocated now in the interaction of reader and text – that brought about that challenge and that change. Reader *response* was, in a sense, a way to arrive at textual *meaning*, as Jane Tompkins pointed out in her insightful 1980 essay called "The Reader in History: The Changing Shape of Literary Response" (Tompkins 1980, 201-232).

Tompkins reminded us that there was once a time – starting in the classical period – when people were interested not in the *interpretation* of literature, but in its *effect*. In ancient Greece and Rome, rhetoric was the study of language as a form of power. Language was seen as action, not signification; it was a "force acting on the world", not "signs to be deciphered" (Tompkins 1980, 203). With the breakdown of the patronage system and the rise of commercial publishing, the small but known audience (upon whom literature's language was to work its magic) was transformed into a wider and totally unknown mass, a newly literate mass, for whom the text had to be interpreted and *explained*. Interpretation and meaning won out over effect and impact.

At this precise, democratizing moment of the capitalist eighteenth century, the English book reviewer came into being, precisely to do that explaining and interpreting – with the aim of helping that new reading public choose which of the many new books being published to read and demonstrating how to read them. In other words, the book reviewer began as a professional reader, with the task of being what today we would call a "consumer reporter" for other readers. Reviewers, however, have never been simply what Murray Krieger once called "readers who have recorded their reactions" (1982,

---

2   See, for example, "*Ulysses* and the Reader", (Iser 1989, 131-9).

320). They are readers who have recorded their reactions to a very particular end (or ends), in a very particular context. And that context has changed over time, and with it have changed responses to these specialized readers. In England, the reviewer went from being the Grub Street hack to the Romantic Sage to the Victorian Man of Letters to the modern Professional – to use Terry Eagleton's categories (1984, 33; 45). Jonathan Culler has suggested that we should add another category, since the mantle of public criticism, he has argued, has passed to the academic critic in recent decades (1988, 3). So we must add to the list the postmodern Academic as Public Intellectual (rather than as literary critic).

If I may open a parenthesis here to explain what I mean by that last comment: I am coming to believe that the *reviewer*-as-reader and the literary *critic*-as-reader may feel that they operate with different institutional aims today. Barbara Herrnstein Smith has shown that evaluation was actually exiled from academic literary criticism, first by the historically and philologically inclined within the academy, and then by the interpretively or structurally focused (so, New Criticism, structuralism, and so on) (1988, 17). Others have traced the progress of interpretation as it replaced evaluation as the goal of academic literary criticism. They comment upon how the hermeneutic displaced the axiological, and show how the determination of meaning took the place of the determination of value. Northrop Frye, too, made a distinction between academic literary criticism and what he called "judicial criticism" or reviewing: The university-based literary critic, he said, was "primarily concerned with the expansion of knowledge and sensitivity rather than with evaluation and 'maintaining standards'" – which he saw as the tasks of the reviewer as reader (1982, 33). That evaluating job was what that witty and insightful British book reviewer, Cyril Connolly, once called "the thankless task of drowning other people's kittens" (qtd. In Lewis 1997, 177). But more recent literary theory – from feminist to poststructuralist – has suggested that evaluation is unavoidable in critical discourse because all discourse, in effect, creates and constitutes values and hierarchies, which we tacitly take as criteria even when interpreting meaning (Bové 1990, 56). Like book reviewers, in other words, literary critics evaluate as they read and as they then interpret what they read.

I close my parenthesis about literary critics and reviewers, and return to book reviewers as specialized, guiding readers, but this time in relation to the *readers* of their readings. Why do we read book reviews? Leonard Woolf argued back in 1939 that the function of the book review had not changed since the time of its origins several centuries before. That function "is to give to readers a description of the book and an estimate of its quality in order that he may know whether or not it is the kind of book which he may want to read" (1950, 132). But European and North American culture has a long history of valuing its expert reviewers more than that, of trusting them to do a whole range of other things for us, besides doing Woolf's form of consumer reporting: to inform and describe, of course, but also to explain, elucidate, interpret, teach, archive, and, of course, evaluate what is out there. To these ends, reviewers as readers have taken on various roles over the years. Here is a very short version of a very long possible list: Reviewers have acted as the critical arbiters of taste, the guiding instructors, the witty entertainers, the inspiring enthusiasts, the spokespersons for the values of a community, the recorders and witnesses of culture, the gate-keeping guardians or conscious creators of educated taste.[3]

That is the history of the reviewer as reader. What about the present, for we are arguably at a very different historical and cultural moment? When anyone with an internet connection can become a reviewer, what does "reviewing" mean today? With the digital turn has come a form of commercial – as well as democratic – "customer reviewing." This is said to have its parallel in what has been called the "citizen journalism" that has changed the face of news reporting today. Armed with our smartphones, we can all become reporters. Or can we? We can certainly be witnesses and take photos, but is that the same as researched reporting? Similarly, anyone who can get online can claim the role of (customer) reviewer. To be honest, you would not even have to read the book to have your say about it on the Amazon.com website. (Of course, not all print reviewers have been innocent of this charge of omission, either.) The ideology of participatory democracy rules the internet.

In 1995, when Amazon founder, Jeff Bezos, invented customer reviewing to allow people to offer their commentary on the books he was selling, the sheer number of reviews that began to appear surprised even him. We need to recall the date here, for this was in the days before social networking, and therefore before the web-as-participation; this was the time of the web-as-information. But Amazon's owner saw in book reviewing and in star rating processes an interactive community-building possibility: Here was a chance to provide a virtual town square where customers could come together to discuss books and share advice. In other words, what the company said it wanted to do was simply to provide a neutral and enabling platform for consumer conversation. Yet what it was actually doing, in effect, was harnessing user-generated energy to provide free content for its website, and it was doing it through book reviewing, of all things.

Do we read these unpaid "customer" reviews on Amazon.com differently or for different purposes than we read the reviews of professional reviewers employed *as readers* by the mainstream media? Should these different readers, in other words, be read differently? Whose responsibility is it to figure this out? These are a few of the questions I am asking myself in this brave new (democratized and commercialized) digital world we now inhabit.

One reason I am asking myself these questions is to try to understand why print media outlets, especially in North America, seem to be intent upon getting rid of their expert reviewers. Obviously one motive is economic: Staff reviewers cost money. But the newspapers also claim that it is because they have been told that their readers prefer the opinion of "someone like themselves" to that of a professional reader. Their customers are looking for assessments that are quick, timely, and easily digested. (Three stars? Thumbs up?). They know that we need help to filter and sort through the vast

---

[3] This is not to ignore the other roles reviewers have taken, from star-makers to destroyers of reputations. Though he did not address the subject directly, Michel Foucault might well have seen reviewers as normatively disciplining readers: "The judges of normality are present everywhere. We are in the society of the teacher-judge, the doctor-judge, the educator-judge, the 'social-worker'-judge; it is on them that the universal reign of the normative is based; and each individual, wherever he may find himself, subjects to it his body, his gestures, his behaviour, his aptitudes, his achievements" (1977, 304).

array of available books out there, and feel that one way to do it is by means of a kind of simple taste matching. What concerns me is the fact that they do not seem to care that book reviewing, in the past and arguably in the present, has had not only other functions but also broader social roles – that is, as both a touchstone of cultural values and a space of shared public discourse.

Oscar Wilde agreed with Matthew Arnold that in the nineteenth century criticism created "the intellectual atmosphere of the age" (Wilde 1968/1969, 403). Do we no longer take professional reviewing this seriously? Even those holding a positive view of the potential democratizing of reviewing on the web have feared that the demise of expert reviewing might be a threat to what one calls the entire edifice of any modern democratic society that thrives on "the freeplay of critical intelligence" in the public sphere (Waters 2007). While I do not want to go that far – for it seems to me that there is still much freeplay of critical intelligence, both online and off, in our modern democracies – I am wondering about the consequences of the move away from informed opinion and expertise in the act of reviewing. Are we happy to surrender reviewing's critically informed function to anonymous pundits (or consumers) who may well see themselves as having more rights than responsibilities? Or, is this the wrong tack to take? Is it simply the definition of the reviewer that is changing? Are we redefining the multiple and often contradictory tasks reviewing has done in the past? I admit that these have been jobs that range in ideological impact from opening up space for what is new (and perhaps in need of introduction and even explanation) to its opposite – gate-keeping and thus reinforcing existing values. Because professional reviewing has had the power to work in such opposing political ways, its disappearance will be greeted as either catastrophic or heaven-sent. If the development of the press in earlier centuries was what made the reviewer a permanent fixture of cultural life, is the expert reviewer doomed to be an endangered species in the electronic age? Or have new technologies simply meant a re-defining of the function, task, and qualities of the reviewer?

From its beginnings, the internet has been presented as a transformative democratic space that overcomes the limitations of real space, including its capitalist economics. Whether this is now the case is open to debate. Nonetheless, this new medium has been said to be democratic, to increase access, and widen intellectual horizons for more – or perhaps simply different – people. In terms of reviewing, authority on the web manifestly shifted from expertise (or what I have been calling informed opinion) to simply opinion and, perhaps, experience. Therefore, no longer seeing their function as gate-keepers, these new reviewers, on either commercial websites or in literary blogs, feel that they can concentrate on non-mainstream or overlooked books and thus widen the scope of works reviewed. And this is a real positive, I think. No longer in the pocket of the marketing departments of the big publishing houses (as they argued the print reviewers were), the independent online bloggers and reviewers have seen themselves as free-thinking alternatives. They have claimed to offer fresh perspectives and to do so in a truly interactive and dialogic context.

In other words, the one-way mode of the pronouncements of the hired, professionalized, trained (and remunerated) expert reader is almost incompatible with the current online dialogic fashion of the unpaid, but engaged, consumer reviewer, tweeter, or blogger. Today, power is meant to be shared with what Jay Rosen has aptly designated as "The People Formerly Known as the Audience" (2012). And that unpaid "someone like us" might share our taste more readily than a professional, hired reviewer. As French sociologist Pierre Bourdieu explored at length in *Distinction: A Social Critique of the Judgment of Taste* (1984/2010), what we call taste most often does not operate on the conscious level at all: It is what seems "natural" to us. That taste is, in fact, far from "given" or "natural" is the thesis of Bourdieu's study of the social determination of taste. If taste, then, is a matter of education and family background, as Bourdieu argues it is, then the paid professional readers may have no exclusive claim to good taste, as informed by study and experience. Certainly what Jim Collins calls "taste acquisition" has become an industry, with media celebrities like Oprah Winfrey in the United States taking on the role of taste arbiter who, says Collins, can pass on both refined taste and thus the requisite expertise: It is just a matter of knowing where to access it and whom to trust.

In the past, as we have seen, reviewers as readers had many other roles as well, and while taste entered into those roles, so too did this concept of trust. But how does one establish trust in someone's taste in a digital world? Here, the normal development of interpersonal trust – based on a direct relationship between named/known persons that develops over time – does not happen (see Hardin 2002). The multiple anonymous authors of those short customer reviews on Amazon.com perhaps cannot be trusted personally in the same way that Cyril Connolly reviewing books or Kenneth Tynan reviewing theatre once could. But perhaps they can be trusted to do certain things – for instance, to give a collective, cumulative sense of at least one kind of shared "taste". The fact that their opinions may not be based on any stated reasons may mark the difference between these opinions and those of the expert readers, whose reputations depend on developing a following of people who, from the reasons given in their reviews, have come to trust their informed opinion and thus their taste. But the same need for a following is true for bloggers as responding readers, for their status is directly related to the online community's "reputation economy" (Shay and Pinch 2005, 5).

Literary blogs, like the other new online reviewing sites, do not just offer opinion and evaluation, however. They also implicitly *constitute* and then *acknowledge* the reviewer's existence and dignity – not only as a consumer but also as both a reader and what we might call a "cultural subject." Here I adapt Pierre Bourdieu's idea of what he calls the "political subject" (1984/2010, 446) and make it into the idea of a "cultural subject." This would be someone who is capable of being, if not a subject *of* culture, then at least a subject *of a discourse on* culture. Hence the appeal of blogging, and of much online reviewing: there is rarely any financial gain; the currency is cultural.

And this is where I recall my title and its designated shift from reader response to reader responsibility and response-ability. Here again, I want to talk about the responsibility of two kinds of readers: the reviewer as reader and the reader of those reviews. The reason is that there are ethical as well as political and economic implications – and consequences – to reviewing and there always have been. Think of the early history of book reviewing in the United States. In the nineteenth century, publishers would send review copies of books to magazine or newspaper editors, often accompanied by prepared notices (to save the editor time). Assigned reviews were likely to be laudatory *if* the publisher advertised in the paper (Charvat 1968, 172-174). Nevertheless, it was in the interests of both authors and publishers to keep up the pretense that "reviews were the uninfluenced opinion of critics working in the interest of the public" (*ibid.*, 186). But pretense it was, and that pretense drove Virginia Kirkus in 1933 to set up the *Kirkus Reviews*, a book review company self-consciously situated *outside* the influence and power of the publishers. Her ethically-inspired aim was to offer informed opinion to booksellers and, later, libraries.

Other kinds of ethical concerns have also been part of book reviewing from the start. As Nina Baym has shown in her study of reviews of the novel in nineteenth-century America (where most of the novel-reading population was female), reviewers saw their role as that of moral preceptor, instructing women, especially on their sexual duties and their sexual natures (1984, 183). As she pointedly puts the case: "Talk about morality is so characteristic of and so widely prevalent in novel reviewing in the 1840s and 1850s as to indicate that it was taken as part of the reviewer's job" (173). If a novel was seen to have the potential to form (or deform) the reader's character, the review's function was to "suppress, or direct, or improve, the female reader" (194).[4]

The moral and the ethical enter reviewing in other ways as well, because of the potential power wielded by the reviewer. As World War One broke out in 1914, Rebecca West (1914) chastised the blandness and "faintness of spirit" of British book reviewing practices. She attacked what she saw as the prevalent wartime view of things cultural: that "it is a pity to waste fierceness on things that do not matter." To this she firmly replied: "But they do matter". Reviewers, by their very act of reviewing, have the validating power to make us feel that something matters, that some things are worth fighting about. They also have the power to dismiss and destroy. That they can do both with equal passion is a given. Negative reviews can damage spirits, reputations, and pocketbooks; positive ones can make stars and celebrities out of authors – and make them wealthy. Reviewing is a "*normative* (that is, value-maintaining and value-transmitting activity" (Smith 1990, 182). Reviewers as readers, therefore, have multiple ethical responsibilities: to the work they review and its author, and also to their own readers, in turn.

That said, reviewing by paid, designated, professional readers in the mainstream media does not have the monopoly on quality writing, balanced or insightful analysis, deep contextualizing, or ethical intelligence. All reviews are readings, and specifically readings as "rejoinders" in a dialogue. This is what they might have been called by Mikhail Bakhtin – had that theorist who believed in the active, responsive nature of all understanding written about reviews (he did not). As what I imagine to be Bakhtinian rejoinders, then, reviews would be reader responses that are directed toward someone else whose subsequent rejoinder is expected, desired, perhaps even feared. The only thing more terrible would be a *lack* of response. It is this essential "addressivity" (Bakhtin 1986, 127) or "response-ability" (*ibid.*, 95) that means the review-as-rejoinder can interpret, comment upon, evaluate; it can refute, agree with or support. As a recorded reader response, it also provides at least one means by which, as one critic has put it, authors can know whether the long battle they fought with themselves, their families, and the world "to get the book written, had any point at all" (Curtis 1998, 12).

---

4 Children's books and films, even today, are often reviewed with a didactic or even censoring eye: is this work "suitable" for children?

But reviews may well also induce the author of the book reviewed to respond publicly as well – and in a different way. I am alluding here not only to authors' private or published responses (positive or negative) but also to the inevitable gaming of the online review system, in particular, with its much publicized abuses – from ballot stuffing to self-reviewing.[5] But I would want to argue that these abuses have, in fact, initiated a more open and frank conversation about reviewing practices in recent years. For a few days in February 2004, the Canadian division of Amazon accidently (and I like to believe, subversively) revealed the identities of thousands of theoretically anonymous reviewers. Not too surprisingly, it was found that authors reviewed their own books – both positively and multiply. So too did their family and friends. But we need to remind ourselves that Walt Whitman did the same much earlier and offline, even citing three of them in the preface to the second edition of *Leaves of Grass*. Is that any less ethically questionable? (see Marcus 2004). Some have argued that this self-promoting Amazon practice is benign and not in the last questionable for this is a marketing website, after all.

Readers of reviews, Jonathan Culler has argued, are fully capable of adjusting their impressions and making allowances for the positions of both the venue and the reviewer (Culler 1982, 299). But what is true for any of us who read (or see or hear) a review is that its evaluative verdict (positive or negative) becomes part of what the Konstanz School referred to as our "horizon-of-experience" or horizon of expectation (Jauss 1982, 19), which thus becomes part of our response to and interpretation of what was reviewed. The review, in other words, mediates between us, the addressed readers, and the what is being reviewed. The review becomes for some of us a benchmark against which we may measure our own responses. A review's hostility or its generosity will obviously be experienced differently by different members of the public (See Curtis 1998, 23). But will either a positive or negative judgment really affect our decision to pursue interest in (or purchase) whatever is reviewed?

Virginia Woolf, despite, herself, being a formidable book reviewer, appeared to doubt it. Writing in 1939, she asked: "So why bother to write reviews or to read them or to quote them if in the end the reader must decide the question for himself?" (1930/1950, 122). Yet surely that is the whole point: Reviews, as we know, *do* help people decide the question. Furthermore, surveys even show that those of us who seek out reviews often seek out more than one in order to compare them (Hunt 1972, 149).

Reviewing has clearly meant different things at different times in different places: It depends on *who* is reviewing *what*, and *when, where, how,* and for *whom*. In the end, it is the responsibility of us, as responding readers, to know what we are seeking from reviews, so that we can judge from that personal perspective the assessment and the argument (or lack thereof) of the reviews – professional or customer. It will obviously help if the reviewers openly acknowledge where their opinions as readers are coming from, making transparent their position and power, their biases and preferences. Simply by showing how and why they arrived at their judgments, reviewers can "model" both taste and critical response, or at least offer a "yardstick" to guide readers in

---

5   As in the recent "Historian"/Orlando Figes fraud case. See *The Guardian*, 18 Apr. 2010; *The Independent*, 17 Apr. 2010; *The Telegraph*, 18 Apr. 2010.

weighing the value of the review for themselves.[6] In this way reviews can help readers develop and trust our own tastes, as well as critical faculties.

Professional reviewers have always been held responsible – legally and ethically – for their published opinions. The anonymous or pseudonymous online "customer reviewers" are not. But most bloggers are, and if one participates in *Goodreads*, the online social network for discovering and sharing books to read, one will have to agree to their terms of use: "You are solely responsible for your User Content [...] and you agree that we are only acting as a passive conduit for your online distribution and publication of your User Content" (2014). I would argue that readers of online reviews – indeed readers of all reviews – are also "solely responsible" for deciding what they are seeking, what they gain, and how (and what) they in turn choose to read as a result. As the editors of *The Complete Review* website remind us, reviews are opinions and "you can do with them what you will" (2011). Since we can now so easily compare reviews – across media – we should always do so, they claim, adding: "Always ask yourself why these people are passing these judgments" (*ibid.*). Or, as the editors of the website called *The Omnivore: Criticism Digested* put it: "We ask that you take our ratings with a very large pinch of salt" (2012).

I would like to think that this is the kind of sense of *responsibility* mixed with critical scepticism in your reader's *response* that I hope might be the result of reading about my excursion from the personal trauma of reader-response theory to the ethical thickets of reviewing and its responsibilities. Wolfgang Iser once wrote that "the beginning and the end are paradigms of realities that we can neither experience nor know" (1989, 282) – and that is one of the reasons we need and desire fictions of beginnings and endings. Though this lecture is not fiction, just as it had a beginning, it will indeed – now – have an end, a paradigm of reality you can indeed know and experience.

References

Bakhtin, Mikhail (1986): *Speech Genres and Other Late Essays*. Ed. Caryl Emerson and Michael Holquist, trans. Vern. W. McGee. Austin: University of Texas Press
Baron, Naomi S. (2013): "Redefining Reading: The Impact of Digital Communication Media", *PMLA* 128.1, 193-200
Baym, Nina (1984): *Novels, Readers, and Reviewers: Responses to Fiction in Antebellum America*. Ithaca, NY: Cornell University Press
Bennett, Susan (1990/1997): *Theatre Audiences: A Theory of Production and Reception.* 2nd edition. London: Routledge
Bennett, Tony (1990): *Outside Literature*. New York: Routledge
Bourdieu, Pierre (1984/2010): *Distinction: A Social Critique of the Judgment of Taste*. Abingdon: Routledge
Bové, Paul (1990): "Discourse", in: Lentricchia, Frank; McLaughlin, Thomas (eds.): *Critical Terms for Literary Study*. Chicago: University of Chicago Press, 50
Bové, Paul (1992): *In the Wake of Theory*. Hanover, NH: Wesleyan University Press
Charvat, William (1968): *The Profession of Authorship in America, 1800-1870: The Papers of William Charvat*. Ed. Matthew J. Bruccoli. Columbus: Ohio State University Press

---

6   This is Hermann Hesse's image for the utility of revealing the subjective element in reviewing. See (Hesse 1930/1974, 167).

Collins, Jim (2010): *Bring on the Books for Everybody: How Literary Culture Became Popular Culture*. Durham, NC: Duke University Press

Cruz, Jon; Lewis, Justin (eds.; 1994): *Viewing, Reading, Listening: Audience and Critical Reception*. Boulder: Westview

Culler, Jonathan (1975): *Structuralist Poetics: Structuralism, Linguistics and the Study of Literature*. London: Routledge and Kegan Paul

--- (1982): "*The Uses of Uncertainty* Re-viewed", in: Hernadi, Paul (ed.): *The Horizon of Literature*. Lincoln: University of Nebraska Press

--- (1988): *Framing the Sign: Criticism and Its Institutions*. Norman: University of Oklahoma Press

Curtis, Anthony (1998): *LIT ED: On Reviewing and Reviewers*. Manchester: Carcanet

Darnton, Robert (1986): "First Steps toward a History of Reading", *Australian Journal of French Studies* 23, 5-30

Dickinson, Roger et al. (eds.; 1998): *Approaches to Audience*. London: Arnold

Eagleton, Terry (1984): *The Function of Criticism: From* The Spectator *to Post-Structuralism*. London: Verso

Fetterley, Judith (1978): *The Resisting Reader: A Feminist Approach to American Fiction*. Bloomington: Indiana University Press

Fish, Stanley (1980) *Is There a Text in This Class?: The Authority of Interpretive Communities*. Cambridge, MA: Harvard University Press

Foster, Thomas C. (2003): *How to Read Novels like a Professor: A Jaunty Exploration of the World's Favorite Literary Form*. New York: Harper

Foucault, Michel (1977): *Discipline and Punish: The Birth of the Prison*. New York: Pantheon

Freund, Elizabeth (1987): *The Return of the Reader: Reader-Response Criticism*. London: Methuen

Frye, Northrop (1982): *Division on a Ground: Essays on Canadian Culture*. Ed. James Polk. Toronto: Anansi

Goodreads (2014): "Terms of Use". https://www.goodreads.com/about/terms> [accessed 8 May 2014]

Guillory, John (1993): *Cultural Capital*. Chicago: University of Chicago Press

Hardin, Russell (2002): *Trust and Trustworthiness*. New York: Russell Sage

Hay, James et al. (eds.; 1996): *The Audience and Its Landscape*. Boulder, CO: Westview

Hesse, Hermann (1930/1974): "About Good and Bad Critics: Notes on the Subject of Poetry and Criticism", in: Ziolkowski, Theodore (ed.): *My Belief: Essays on Life and Art*. Trans. Denver Lindley. New York: Farrar, Straus & Giroux, 163-176

Holland, Norman (1968): *The Dynamics of Literary Response*. New York: Oxford University Press

Holub, Robert C. (1984): *Reception Theory: A Critical Introduction*. London: Methuen

Hunt, Todd (1972): *Reviewing for the Mass Media*. Philadelphia: Chilton

Iser, Wolfgang (1976): *Der Akt des Lesens: Theorie ästhetischer Wirkung*. Munich: Wilhelm Fink

--- (1978): *The Act of Reading: A Theory of Aesthetic Response*. Baltimore: Johns Hopkins University Press

--- (1989): *Prospecting: From Reader Response to Literary Anthropology*. Baltimore: Johns Hopkins University Press

--- et al. (1980): "Interview: Wolfgang Iser", *Diacritics* 10.2, 57-74

Jauss, Hans Robert (1982): *Toward an Aesthetic of Reception*. Trans. Timothy Bahti. Minneapolis: University of Minnesota Press

Krieger, Murray (1982): "Theories about Theories about *Theory of Criticism*", in: Hernadi, Paul (ed.): *The Horizon of Literature*. Lincoln: University of Nebraska Press, 319-336

Lewis, Jeremy (1997): *Cyril Connolly: A Life*. London: Jonathan Cape

Machor, James L.; Goldstein, Philip (eds.; 2001): *Reception Study: From Literary Theory to Cultural Studies*. New York: Routledge

Manguel, Alberto (1996): *A History of Reading*. New York: Penguin

Manovich, Lev (2001): *The Language of New Media*. Cambridge, MA: MIT Press

Marcus, James (2004): *Amazonia: Five Years at the Epicenter of the Dot.Com Juggernaut*. New York: New

Mayne, Judith (1993): *Cinema and Spectatorship*. London: Routledge

McLuhan, Eric; Zingrone, Frank (eds.; 1996): *Essential McLuhan*. New York: Basic Books

Radway, Janice (1984): *Reading the Romance: Women, Patriarchy, and Popular Literature*. Chapel Hill: University of North Carolina Press

Rosen, Jay (2012): "The People Formerly Known as the Audience", *Huffington Post*. <http://www.huffingtonpost.com/jay-rosen/the-people-formerly-known_1_b_24113.html> [accessed 11 June 2012]

Saenger, Paul (1997): *Space Between Words: The Origin of Silent Reading*. Stanford, CA: Stanford University Press

Shay, David; Pinch, Trevor John (2005): "Six Degrees of Reputation: The Use and Abuse of Online Review and Recommendation Systems", Cornell University S&TS Working Paper

Smith, Barbara Herrnstein (1988): *Contingencies of Value: Alternative Perspectives for Critical Theory*. Cambridge, MA: Harvard University Press

--- (1990): "Value/Evaluation", in: Lentricchia, Frank; McLaughlin, Thomas (eds.): *Critical Terms for Literary Study*. Chicago: University of Chicago Press, 177-185

Sutherland, John (2006): *How to Read a Novel: A User's Guide*. New York: St. Martin's

The complete review (2011): "Editorial Policy". <http://www.complete-review.com/main/editorial.html> [accessed 15 December 2011]

The Omnivore: Criticism Digested (2012). <www.theomnivore.co.uk/AboutPage.aspx> [Accessed 17 April 2012]

Tompkins, Jane (ed.; 1980): *Reader-Response Criticism: From Formalism to Post-Structuralism*. Baltimore: Johns Hopkins University Press

Ulin, David I. (2010): *The Lost Art of Reading*. Seattle: Sasquatch

Waters, Lindsay (2007): "Poisoning the Well", *Critical Mass*. <http://bookcriticscircle.blogspot.com> [accessed 11 June 2012]

West, Rebecca (1914): "The Duty of Harsh Criticism", *New Republic*, 7 Nov. 1914. <www.tnr.com/book/review/the-duty-harsh-criticism> [accessed 13 April 2012]

Wilde, Oscar (1968/1969): "The Critic as Artist", in: Ellmann, Richard (ed.): *The Artist as Critic: Critical Writings of Oscar Wilde*. New York: Random House, 340-408

Woolf, Leonard (1950): "Note" to Virginia Woolf, "Reviewing" (1930), in *The Captain's Death Bed and Other Essays*. London: Hogarth Press, 131-134

Woolf, Virginia (1930/1950): "Reviewing", in: *The Captain's Death Bed and Other Essays*. London: Hogarth Press, 118-131

Section 1

Victorian Lives and Minds: Scientific Cultures in the Nineteenth Century

Chairs:

Nadine Böhm-Schnitker and Philipp Erchinger

NADINE BÖHM-SCHNITKER (ERLANGEN) AND PHILIPP ERCHINGER (DÜSSELDORF)

Scientific Cultures in the Nineteenth Century: Introduction

In the nineteenth century science became endowed, it has been argued, with a "cultural authority which it had not had before and was not to enjoy in quite the same way again" (Gilmour ²2009, 111). Indeed, by the middle of the century, science seems to have become such a prominent and "integral part of Victorian culture" that "the period from 1850 to 1890" has sometimes even been characterized as an "age of the cult, or worship, of science", as Bernard Lightman points out. "Science was everywhere – in the news, in the monthly and quarterly periodicals, in literature, in the museums, in exhibitions and even in the theatre" (Lightman 2010, 17). Yet even though the label 'scientific' was frequently deployed to authorize particular world views, ideologies and methods, to make them appear objective, justified and generally true (see Böhm-Schnitker 2013, 91), the concept of 'science' was never as undisputed and self-evident as its usage might sometimes suggest.[1] Rather, throughout the century and beyond, the meaning, function, and value of science remained highly volatile and controversial, subject to a continuous process of appropriation and re-appropriation in which the authority of scientific knowledge had to be (re)constituted or defended, again and again, in relation to what science was considered *not* to be.

Such controversies and discussions in and about science have provided, and continue to provide, a rich field of research, not only for cultural historians, but also for literary critics. Whenever these debates were carried out and multiplied through public media and forums of one kind or another, science had to be represented and communicated in writing, by means of texts that may be referred to as 'literature' in the most general sense of the term. As David Amigoni has put it, "science in the public domain was made of symbolic material, and thus always already literary" (Amigoni 2007, 27). What is more, the representation of science could not yet rely on a firmly established discursive formation. In fact, since many texts that nowadays tend to be classified as science – from Lyell's *Principles of Geology* to G.H. Lewes's *Sea-Side Studies* – were addressed to a general rather than a specialist audience, they often made abundant use of images, plot patterns, tropes, and rhetorical devices typically associated with specific forms of 'the literary'. Conversely, the themes and structures of much Victorian literature in a narrow sense of the term were substantially informed by scientific theories and notions as well.

Therefore, since the appearance of the seminal studies by Gillian Beer (1983) and George Levine (1988), the relationship of literature and science has often been con-

---

1   In fact, according to the OED, it may not even have been until the middle of the century that the term science was widely used in the sense in which it is common today: as referring to the physical and experimental sciences only, and excluding the field of the theological and metaphysical (see Postlethwaite 2001, 99).

ceived of in terms of a reciprocal exchange, a "two-way" communication, by virtue of which ideas, concepts, and metaphors travel back and forth between these domains (Beer 1983, 5). Yet, while in this exchange model science and literature still tend to be viewed as separate fields or discourses, albeit with a permeable boundary in between, newer approaches have focused more on the practices of writing and reading through which the parallels and distinctions between these fields were themselves made out and repeatedly drawn afresh (see Erchinger 2012, 796-797). As Adelene Buckland has recently shown, geology, for example, was a discipline that "was written into existence as much as it was found, discovered, collected, mapped, or modelled" (Buckland 2013, 4). Thus, what many Victorian geologists were concerned with, she argues, was to find literary forms that could serve to represent or interpret the forms of the earth in a way that is true to them. "Geologists were keen to experiment with the ways in which different forms of writing could help them see the 'truth' better, and to delimit those kinds of writing [...] that they felt encouraged excessive speculation" (Buckland 2013, 18). Similarly, 'the literary' was shaped into disciplinary outlines by the emerging discourse of criticism, a process that may be illustrated by the mid-century debate about 'sensation fiction'. The labelling of the works by, first and foremost, Wilkie Collins, Elizabeth Braddon, and Ellen Wood as 'sensational' can be described as "a discursive construction invented by the reviewers" (Allan 2013, 92). In short, 'science' and 'literature' were equally contested terms.

Yet, to emphasize how both 'the scientific' and 'the literary' took form through writing is by no means to obliterate all differences between scientific knowledge and literary fiction, something one might all too easily be tempted to do, as several critics have warned (Levine 2008 and Norris 1997). Rather, to focus on practices of writing is to take account of the techniques of sense-making, the activities of drawing lines of connection and distinction, through which literature and science were associated and dissociated in the nineteenth century, made both similar and different, in a continuous process of comparison and mutual "self-definition" (Buckland 2013, 23) that has, in fact, continued until the present day.

In one way or another, most of the contributions to this section can be seen to consider ways in which science, literature, and culture come together in writing and reading. Yet, with the material presented in this section ranging from children's magazines to adventure novels, the world exhibition, and even traces of Victorian thought found among contemporary popularizers of science, the articles assembled here constitute an array of themes and approaches that are as diverse and lively as Victorian culture itself. In this way, this section reflects a general trend in Victorian studies: While earlier research in the field of Victorian literature and science had predominantly focused on biology and the impact of evolutionary theory, in recent years the scope of interest has widened considerably. Thus, in line with this trend, the following articles include not only references to biology and physiology, but also to other domains of interest that are part of what might be called the scientific culture of the age. These include aspects of anthropology and the ways in which it is intertwined with colonialism, technologies of the body and their effects on notions of masculinity, the discursive construction of economics as a science and the concomitant exclusion of women from the field, as well as the after-effects of Victorian science in the twenty-first century.

Jochen Petzold opens up this section with his essay entitled "It's Not Cruel, It's Science! The Re-Invention of Bird-Nesting in Late Victorian Juvenile Culture". He explores a process by which the discourse on bird-nesting gradually changed from a moral vilification of a potentially rather cruel pastime to a respectable activity for boys and – to a lesser degree – girls by way of its representation as scientific. Juvenile magazines such as *The Boy's Own Magazine* or *The Boy's Own Paper* played a vital role in introducing bird-nesting into the everyday practices of youngsters, encouraging them to take up the hobby through competitions and prizes. In addition they provided manuals in order to enable young people to acquire competencies associated with adulthood, or, more precisely, manhood. As Petzold shows, the discourse on bird-nesting can be understood in the context of the debate about education – with Thomas Huxley and Matthew Arnold as its main opponents – and the question of whether there is a place for science in a traditionally humanist curriculum focussing on the classics. The practice of and discourse on bird-nesting illustrate the ways in which natural science and its implementation at schools contribute to cultural formations inculcating new stances towards nature, introducing new concepts of education and constructing new, clearly gendered subjectivities by way of offering young people a means by which they can experience themselves as competent naturalists and empowered explorers of ornithology.

Joanna Rostek, concentrating on Jane Marcet and Harriet Martineau, explores how political economy developed into the science of economics by way of its separation from its roots in moral philosophy as well as the concomitant exclusion of women from the field. To be able to make contributions to political economy as women, both Marcet and Martineau had to find ways that did not stray too conspicuously from the gender ideology of separate spheres so prevalent for nineteenth-century middle-class women. Fashioning themselves as popularizers of male academic achievements, they selected genres that rendered political economy more readily accessible to wider audiences. Marcet presents her findings by way of a Socratic dialogue; Martineau chose to write short narratives to illustrate major insights in the field. These forms were consequently excluded from economics proper, as were women economists. To this day, Elinor Ostrom (1933-2012) remains the only woman to hold the Nobel Prize in economics, a fact that testifies to the successful construction of economics as a male as well as masculine domain. Rostek elucidates the ways in which the emergence of disciplines as sciences frequently entails strategies for distributing powerful subject positions along the gender divide.

The relationship between developments in the sciences and contemporary views on gender is also the subject of Stefani Brusberg-Kiermeier's article "Half Man, Half Machine: Wilkie Collins's and Charles Reade's Constructions of Victorian Machine Men". According to Brusberg-Kiermeier, many Victorian novelists can be seen as engaging with the idea that human beings are "conscious automata" (Huxley), an idea that, although not itself a new one, acquired fresh topicality and persuasiveness through social and industrial developments driven by science. In the writings of Collins and Reade in particular, this idea is not only used, as Brusberg-Kiermeier shows, to cast doubt on the well-established link between mechanical work and masculinity, but also to re-draw the lines of distinction and transition between the natural and the cultural as well as the regular and the deviant.

The question of how fictional texts draw on and respond to the new prominence of scientific work is further investigated in Stefanie Fricke's essay on "Scientific Discourses in Late Victorian Fantastic Texts". More specifically, Fricke analyzes how popular novels by H. Rider Haggard, Richard Jefferies, and H.G. Wells make use of scientific modes of justification and expression to characterize and define their own fictional way of writing. According to her readings, these novels frequently use scientific discourse in order to make their fantastical elements appear more believable while, conversely, they deploy fantastical stories to present scientific approaches in forms that would appeal to a wide readership. In this way, she argues, the novels not only manage to pose a number of topical questions about the constitution, preservation, and transmission of knowledge. They also participate in a search for a method of adequately representing the culture of peoples whose systems of beliefs and customs are (taken to be) substantially foreign to those of the ethnographic observer.

In "The Object(ivity) of Imperial Thinking", Nora Pleßke focuses on the relevance of material culture with regard to the construction of self and other in the nineteenth century. She analyzes the ways in which objects partake of the construction of Britain's colonial mentality, and, conversely, how this mentality's naturalization and seeming 'objectivity' is based on the display of colonial goods and objects. This objectivity, however, is highly dependent on nineteenth-century visual regimes, and Pleßke concentrates on the Great Exhibition as a paradigmatic example of the so-called exhibitionary complex. Museums and exhibitions further inculcate and, in the course of time, popularize the discursive entanglements of ways of seeing, architectural structures, objects, and imperialism. Sciences such as anthropology, ethnology, and evolutionary theory are incorporated into this formation and help to provide scientific justifications of Empire that are further corroborated by the very object(ivity) of the respective exhibits.

Finally, Pascal Fischer's article examines the role that Charles Darwin plays in the self-constitution and self-definition of a contemporary group of scientists that he, following John Brockman, the founder of the Internet community *Edge*, calls "The Third Culture Intellectuals". As Fischer shows in detail, for many of these intellectuals – the most famous include Helena Cronin, Richards Dawkins, and Daniel Dennett – Darwin functions as a kind of ideal scientist, an absolute authority on whom they variously call in order to justify their own theories and world views. More precisely, Darwin, by their account, embodies an integrated culture of knowledge-making in which the sciences and the humanities, as well as all the multiple disciplines subsumed under these two heads, have not yet been torn apart. While Fischer expresses some sympathy with the unifying idea of a 'third culture', he nonetheless criticizes the proponents of this idea for their quasi-religious deification of Darwin as well as for their anglocentrism and their reductionist and essentialist rhetoric that betrays little willingness to engage with the humanities on equal terms.

References

Allan, Janice (2013): "The Contemporary Response to Sensation Fiction", in: Magham, Andrew (ed.): *The Cambridge Companion to Sensation Fiction*. Cambridge et al.: Cambridge University Press, 85-98

Amigoni, David (2007): *Colonies, Cults and Evolution: Literature, Science and Culture in Nineteenth Century Writing*. Cambridge: Cambridge University Press

Beer, Gillian (1983): *Darwin's Plots: Evolutionary Narrative in Darwin, George Eliot and Nineteenth-Century Fiction*. Cambridge: Cambridge University Press

Böhm-Schnitker, Nadine (2013): "Diskurse der (D)Evolution im Fin de Siècle", in: Feldmann, Doris; Krug, Christian (eds.): *Viktorianismus*. Berlin: Schmidt, 91-104

Buckland, Adelene (2013): *Novel Science: Fiction and the Invention of Nineteenth-Century Geology*. Chicago: University of Chicago Press

Erchinger, Philipp (2012): "Nature, Culture and Art as Practice in Victorian Writing", *Literature Compass* 9.11, 786-800

Gilmour, Robin (1993): *The Victorian Period: The Intellectual and Cultural Context of English Literature, 1830-1890*. London/New York: Longman

Levine, George (1988): *Darwin and the Novelists: Patterns of Science in Victorian Fiction*. Cambridge, MA: Harvard University Press, 1988

--- (2008): "Why Science Isn't Literature: The Importance of Differences", in: Levine, George (ed.): *Realism, Ethics and Secularism: Essays on Victorian Literature and Science*. Cambridge: Cambridge University Press, 165-181

Lightman, Bernard (2010): "Science and Culture", in: O'Gorman, Francis (ed.): *The Cambridge Companion to Victorian Culture*. Cambridge et al.: Cambridge University Press, 12-42

Norris, Christopher (1997): *Against Relativism: Philosophy of Science, Deconstruction and Critical Theory*. Oxford: Blackwell

Postlethwaite, Diana (2001): "George Eliot and Science", in: Levine, George (ed.): *Cambridge Companion to George Eliot*. Cambridge: Cambridge University Press, 98-118

"Science, n." *OED Online*. December 2013. Oxford University Press. <http://0-www.oed.com.lib.exeter.ac.uk/view/Entry/172672?redirectedFrom=science> [accessed 5 March 2014]

JOCHEN PETZOLD (REGENSBURG)

It's Not Cruel, It's Science! The Re-Invention of Bird-Nesting in Late Victorian Juvenile Culture

In the twenty-first century, the topic of bird-nesting in connection with 'science' may well seem far-fetched, if not obscure. The term can refer to the act of searching for birds' nests with the intention of merely observing them, but usually refers to the collection of eggs, young birds, or whole nests. The practice itself appears frequently – in passing – in a wide range of nineteenth-century texts. For example, bird-nesting boys are mentioned in Anne Brontë's *Agnes Grey*, in Charles Dickens's *Great Expectations* and *David Copperfield*, in George Eliot's *Scenes of Clerical Life* and *Silas Marner*, in Thomas Hughes's *Tom Brown's School Days*, and in Sir Walter Scott's *Waverley* and *St. Ronan's Well*.[1] Bird-nesting was not only noted in the realms of fiction but regularly made it into the newspapers: A search for the term among the 48 newspapers digitized in the database "19th-Century British Library Newspapers" (Cengage Learning) produces almost 900 hits;[2] the entries range from passing references – somebody observing something while out bird-nesting – to articles explicitly dealing with the practice. For example, in May of 1843, *Lloyd's Weekly London Newspaper* reports at length on the

> amusement [...] afforded for some hours in Hyde-park [...] in consequence of the fruitless attempts of the police to dislodge a couple of men from their elevated situation in one of the trees, which they had climbed with the view of taking bird's nests. ("Police" 1843, 7)

The frequency with which bird-nesting is referred to both in fictional and non-fictional texts of the nineteenth century suggests that it was a common practice, mainly carried out as an enjoyable pastime. Furthermore, despite Frederick Milton's claim that "girls recorded extracting as much enjoyment from impromptu bird-nesting as their brothers" (2008, 57), the extreme infrequency with which girls are mentioned in connection with the activity would suggest that bird-nesting was predominantly carried out by boys: Of the ca. 900 newspaper articles that refer to bird-nesting, fewer than three per cent specifically do so in connection with girls – sometimes explicitly pointing out that bird-nesting is "not generally included in a young lady's accomplishments" ("Woman's Wrongs" 1872, 12).[3] Furthermore, of more than 70 articles in juvenile magazines that

---

1   The full-text search for bird-nesting and its spelling variants was conducted in the online database "Literature Online" (http://lion.chadwyck.co.uk); in total, the search produced 52 hits in 20 poems, 2 plays, and 20 prose works.
2   The actual number of articles dealing with the practice of bird-nesting is somewhat lower, since the search would also include references to one or more "bird(s) nesting" in a particular place. However, sample analysis shows that this is not a frequent occurrence.
3   To calculate the percentage of articles connecting bird-nesting with girls, a search for 'bird-nesting' (in its various spelling variants) and 'girl(s)' was combined, resulting in 291 hits. However, these hits only signify that both search terms occurred within the same article or, more often, within the same page. Of these 291 instances, every fifth was taken for sample-analysis, and of these 59 articles, five actually mentioned girls in direct connection with bird-nesting. This

were examined for this paper, only one presents a girl actively involved in bird-nesting.[4] These numbers provide an indication both that bird-nesting was a common occurrence and that it was predominantly seen as a boys' activity.

However, although it was widespread, bird-nesting was not unanimously approved. A line of argument that goes back to Thomas Aquinas claims that cruelty towards animals in childhood is likely to lead to cruelty towards humans in later life. Particularly John Locke's *Some Thoughts on Education* (1693/1902) proved highly influential in the eighteenth and nineteenth centuries, and it suggests that the behaviour of children towards animals should be monitored and controlled:

> One thing I have frequently observ'd in Children, that when they have got Possession of any poor Creature, they are apt to use it ill: They often torment, and treat very roughly young Birds, Butterflies, and such other poor Animals, which fall into their Hands, and that with a seeming kind of Pleasure. This I think should be watched in them, and if they incline to any such Cruelty; they should be taught the contrary Usage. For the custom of tormenting and killing of Beasts will, by Degrees, harden their Minds even towards Men; and they who delight in the Suffering and Destruction of inferior Creatures, will not be apt to be very compassionate or benign to those of their own kind (100-101).

Bird-nesting was often taken as an example of such ill usage, particularly if it led to the destruction of young birds. Thus, it is not surprising that *A Little Pretty Pocket-Book*, printed and probably written by John Newbery in 1744 and arguably one of the first books specifically written not only for the instruction but also for the entertainment of children (see Thwaite 1966, 2-3), includes criticism of bird-nesting. A woodcut illustration of two boys taking a nest from a tree is accompanied by the following rhyme, entitled "Birds-Nesting":

> Here two naughty boys
> Hard-hearted in jest
> Deprive a poor bird
> Of her young and her nest. (Newbery 1744/1966, 95)

Although this short poem is not very detailed, it encapsulates the essence of condemning bird-nesting. The practice is branded as *cruel* toward the "poor bird" and it constitutes an act of *stealing* ("deprive […] of") and is hence in conflict with God's commandment 'Thou shalt not steal'. The fact that it is worthy of condemnation is made clear by calling the perpetrators "naughty" and "hard-hearted". This basic pattern is repeated again and again in texts that try to teach children appropriate treatment of animals. For example, Sarah Trimmer's *Fabulous Histories Designed for the Instruction of Children, Respecting their Treatment of Animals* (also known as *The History of the Robins*), published in 1786 and reprinted repeatedly throughout the nineteenth century, is a particularly successful case in point. The text offers its readers a bird's point of view on the theft of its young ones and invites children to share the bird's suffering in the loss of the nestlings (see 49-50). To emphasise the point, bird-nesting children are depicted as "rude" and thoughtless (55-56), and one of the 'good' children makes

---

sample-analysis would indicate that some 25 of the 900 articles concerned with bird-nesting (and hence fewer than three per cent) do so in connection with girls.

4 Dorothea Sinclair's "Six Little Robins", published in *The Children's Friend* in 1887, includes a bird-nesting girl who repents after accidentally drowning a young bird.

the moral explicit: "My dear mamma [...] has taught me to think, there is harm in any action which gives causeless pain to any living creature" (57).

Thus, denouncement of bird-nesting as cruel and/or theft forms a frequent motif in early literature for children. When magazines became an increasingly important medium for children during the nineteenth century, the arguments against bird-nesting were often repeated in these magazines. Particularly in publications with a strong Christian agenda, like *The Children's Friend* (1824-1929) or *The Child's Companion* (1832-1932), most articles that mention bird-nesting condemn the practice. However, the last decades of the nineteenth century also saw the rise of two counter-discourses that either praised bird-nesting as an adventurous exploit that emphasised the practitioner's manliness and was hence an important exercise in character-building, or presented bird-nesting as a scientific activity. In this paper, I will look at the latter strand of pro-bird-nesting articles, and I will treat them as a specific example of a much broader trend, namely the widespread inclusion of scientific topics in juvenile magazines.[5] I will argue that, from a magazine editor's point of view, scientific bird-nesting is an attractive topic. It is a popular pastime and hence likely to be of interest to a large number of readers. Furthermore, by offering bird-nesting advice and by holding bird-nesting competitions, magazines can use the topic to strengthen readers' identification with the publication. However, in order to utilise its popularity, magazines needed to defend bird-nesting against the discourse denouncing it, and depicting it as a scientific endeavour was a possible strategy. Before I turn to the topic of 'scientific bird-nesting' in juvenile magazines, however, I will briefly situate my discussion within the broader debates about the role of science in education.

1. Victorian Science Education

In mid-century, the universities of Oxford and Cambridge both introduced honours examinations in mathematics and natural science that "ended the monopoly of classics" and "laid a solid foundation for the more laboratory-based and research-oriented science degrees of the 1880s" (Olby et al. 1990, 952); nevertheless, the ideal of a 'liberal education' was still upheld by most educators. However, the situation in the public schools was slowly beginning to change. Rugby was at the forefront of these changes: As Roderick and Stephens point out, "natural philosophy became a [voluntary] subject of instruction in 1849 [and] in 1859 a science school and a small chemistry laboratory were built" (1972, 32-33). When the Clarendon Commission examining the nine public schools published its report in 1864, it noted that

> [n]atural science is taught at Rugby by an assistant master to those who choose to study it instead of modern languages, and it counts in promotion. Lectures on it are given at Winchester and occasionally at Eton [...]. There is also a Lecturer on Chemistry at the Charterhouse, and there are periodical voluntary examinations in natural science at Harrow (Clarendon Commission Report 1864, 13).

And while the commission was convinced that "the classical languages and literature should continue to hold [...] the principal place in public school education" (*ibid.*, 30), it was equally "convinced that the introduction of the elements of natural science into the regular course of study is desirable" (*ibid.*, 32). When J. M. Wilson, who was the

---

5   For an analysis of bird-nesting as adventure, see Petzold 2012.

assistant master teaching natural science at Rugby mentioned in the Clarendon report, reflected on his teaching experience in the essay "On Teaching Natural Science in Schools" in 1867, he claimed that science has "peculiar merit as a means of educating the mind" (1867, 250), and he pointed out that it was well received by the pupils: "most boys show a degree of interest in their scientific work which is unmistakeably greater than in any other study" (*ibid.*, 244). Thus, when Thomas Huxley gave his famous "After-Dinner Speech" on the role of science in education at the Liverpool Philomathic Society in 1869, he was able to observe that public opinion regarding the "introduction of scientific training into the general education of the country [...] has of late undergone a rapid modification" (1869/1893, 111).

Changes were continuing, also with regard to the actual method of teaching science. While the Clarendon Commission had referred primarily to lectures, Wilson held more progressive views, for he emphasised practical experience as an educational tool – "in educating others you must make them *do* whatever you intend them to learn to do, and select subjects and circumstances in which *doing* is most facilitated" (265). When the *Journal of Education* started a series of "Essays on Science Teaching in our Public Schools" in 1882, most contributors also emphasized the importance of practical work.[6] For example, T. N. Hutchinson pointed out that at Rubgy "a large number of boys will avail themselves of the opportunity of applying their theoretical Chemistry to practice" despite the fact that "laboratory work is voluntary, and must be taken at hours between lessons or on half-holiday afternoons" (1882, 352). However, despite this near-consensus amongst educators, actual practice seems to have been different. In the introductory essay to the series, Sydney Lupton points out that the "present method of teaching physics and chemistry in schools" usually consists of "lectures" (1882, 250). This is not really surprising, given the infrastructure of schools: In the early 1870s, the Royal Commission on Scientific Instruction (Devonshire Commission) had sent out questionnaires to 205 schools; of the 128 schools that responded, only 63 taught science and only thirteen declared that they had a laboratory (see Roderick and Stephens 1972, 36). The situation may have improved somewhat over the next decades, but it remains fair to say that practical experiments were available only to a select few, and Roderick and Stephens conclude that "the cause of science probably suffered as much from indifferent teaching as from its absolute exclusion from the schools" (*ibid.*, 34).

2. Science in Juvenile Magazines

While educators and educational institutions were dragging their feet, publishers were quick to recognise a business opportunity. In the adult market, commercial magazines specifically devoted to science saw a "sturdy growth in the 1830s and 1860s" (Brock 1980, 97), which is both an indication of the popularity of scientific topics and of the growing magazine market in general. Juvenile magazines saw a similar growth, and in the analysis of Diana Dixon, "children's magazines became an important vehicle for the popularisation of science in *England* from the 1850s onwards" (228). More importantly, while the science education that did exist in schools tended to be theoretical,

---

[6] The one exception is Elliot Steel. While he does not negate the importance of practical experiments, he "strongly deprecate[s] placing a boy too soon in a chemical laboratory" (1883, 139).

magazines emphasised a more practical approach. This may at first sound paradoxical, since the printed page is not in itself particularly 'practical', and illustrated articles describing animals, plants, or natural phenomena are arguably the most frequent treatment of scientific topics in juvenile magazines. However, writers soon found a way to encourage their readers to become practically involved. *The Boy's Own Magazine* is an early case in point. Launched in 1855 by Samuel Beeton, it was the first magazine to be explicitly addressed to 'boys', and in Drotner's analysis it "marked the beginning of a change in juvenile papers from religious didacticism [...] toward moral entertainment" (1988, 67). In a kind of mission statement Beeton promised that "the Natural History of Animals, of Birds, and Fishes" would be included, as well as that of "Plants, Trees, Flowers, and all the other beautiful and useful products of creation" ("The Boys Own Magazine" 1855, 2). While science articles in the first issues were mainly descriptive – for example, the second issue included a long article on the boa constrictor ("The Boa") – the magazine soon ran articles that combined factual information on animals with practical instruction on how to keep them, like "Pigeons, Their Choice and Management" or "Rabbits, Their Choice and Management" (all in 1855). Instructions for practical experiments followed soon after: For example, readers were told how to "procure laughing gas" in 1857, noting that "great care should be taken not to inhale too much" ("To Procure...", 128), and in 1858 a "Course on Illustrative Chemistry" was started, which encouraged its readers to carry out their own experiments following the instructions given ("The Mystery of the Crucible" 1858). A few years later, in 1864, a small series of four "Papers on Pyrotechny" was started, and the author employed the programmatic pseudonym "Practicus", insisting that his papers would be "thoroughly practical", with the objective of "showing how exhibitions may be provided at a small cost" (154).

The insistence on practical application is carried even further in *The Boy's Own Paper*, which was first released in 1879. Its very first number included an article by the Rev. John George Wood (who had previously written for the *The Boy's Own Magazine*) called "Out with a Jack-Knife", in which he shows "what could be done in practical Natural History with no other apparatus than a common jack-knife" (3). In this essay the jack-knife is used only for digging out worms, breaking old logs, and opening up the nests of insects – however, *The Boy's Own Paper* did not shy away from more drastic examples of "Practical Natural History". In July 1879, Wood started a seven-part series "On Killing, Setting, and Preserving Insects", and roughly a year later, in October 1880, Gordon Stables began an eight-part series entitled "The Boy's Own Museum: Birds and Beasts and How to Stuff Them". In this series, Stables provides detailed instructions for the preparation of various animals, starting with birds and ending with mammals. It is hard to imagine that boys would actually have attempted to follow his step-by-step instruction to dissecting, cleaning, preserving, and stuffing a dog, but Stables clearly suggests that they *could*, if they wanted to.[7] *The Boy's Own Paper* further encouraged practical experiments in taxidermy by starting a competition for the "best preserved specimen of natural history", claiming that "crows, owls, moles, rabbits, rats, etc. will readily suggest themselves as suitable objects to work

---

7   However, he suggests they should practice on a dead dog obtained from the London Home for Lost Dogs before they attempt to stuff a deceased family pet ("The Boy's Own Museum [vi]" 1880, 134).

upon" ("Taxidermy Competition, 1"). The prize money offered was substantial (more than three pounds for the best two entries), and in December 1881 the editors were pleased to announce that "a goodly number of readers entered this competition, most of them admitting, too, that their whole knowledge of taxidermy had been derived from the illustrated articles in our pages" ("Taxidermy Competition, 2"). In the end, prizes were divided and a total of 13 boys, between 15 and 19 years of age, received monetary rewards or honorary mention.

These examples will have to suffice here; it should have become clear that science, particularly natural history, played a significant role on the pages of children's magazines, especially in magazines aimed at boys. Many of these magazines were commercial enterprises that needed to entertain their readers if they wanted to be successful, and hence it is not surprising that Diana Dixon should conclude that "what emerges from all the boys' periodicals' treatment of science is that it is to be enjoyed" (2001, 234).

3. Re-Inventing Bird-Nesting as Science

Bird-nesting was a topic that could be easily exploited as 'popular science', since it had already been enjoyed by children for centuries – the only problem being that it had also been criticised as cruel theft for decades. Hence, the practice of bird-nesting had to be re-defined in order to justify it, and in the remainder of this paper I will look at attempts of this re-definition in a selection of children's magazines.

Generally speaking, magazines specifically aimed at boys were likely to excuse bird-nesting on the grounds of science. We have already encountered Beeton's *The Boy's Own Magazine* as the first magazine explicitly addressed at boys. Bird-nesting is not a particularly frequent topic in the magazine and it does not appear at all during the first years of its publication history. But when a new series of the magazine was launched in 1863, this was to be the bird-nesting year of *The Boy's Own Magazine*. In February, it offered a prize for "The best collection of birds' nests and eggs" and the competition guidelines already indicate the scientific nature of the task: The collection is to be "properly arranged and labelled", and to be accompanied by an "account of where taken, and when the nests were discovered, and of any incidents occurring in the search of them" ("Prize Models" 1863). In June, the magazine then printed an essay entitled "Birds' Nests and Birds'-nesting" by Capt. A. W. Drayson, which is clearly an attempt at re-defining bird-nesting. The article starts out with the typical condemnation of the practice: "To take a bird's nest is very cruel, and causes much grief to the parent birds", and the initial excuse, "if *we* had not taken it, somebody else would", is hardly convincing. However, the author offers a second justification: "When birds abound, and when eggs are sought for the purpose of making a collection, there may be an excuse for birds'-nesting, and it has not unfrequently happened that a taste for natural history has been induced in consequence of the interesting facts discovered in birds'-nesting expedition" (526). If bird-nesting was frequently condemned because it might lead to cruel behaviour towards humans, it is now condoned, because it might lead to a prolonged interest in scientific matters. Drayson continues to give instructions on how to properly blow eggs for the purpose of putting them in a cabinet, but on the whole, the article is not an enthusiastic justification of egg-collection for scientific purposes. Rather, Drayson insists that "the greatest amount of amusement and instruction is obtained by watching a bird's nest from day to day", and this would argue for a non-intrusive kind of bird-nesting that does not interfere with the nests. In fact, the justification remains strangely undecided, "there *may* be an excuse" (526, emphasis added), as if the author was not himself convinced of its moral soundness. Hence he ends with the rhetorical trick of inventing a straw-opponent:

> Thus even birds'-nesting and egg-hunting, although a comparatively cruel sport, especially if carried to excess, is certainly less to be condemned than are the proceedings of many youths of the present day, whose foul, dirty pipes have long since irrevocably polluted their breath, and who, probably, are under the impression that "one of the slowest things going is a roam in the country" in search of specimens of natural history, or for the purpose of observing the habits of various creatures (532).

This can hardly be called a whole-hearted endorsement of bird-nesting: It is explicitly called a "comparatively cruel sport" and it only becomes acceptable in comparison with smoking boys who take no interest in the natural world at all – clearly a case of *non sequitur*. Even though the article suggests that bird-nesting is a scientific activity, it literally ends on the topic of observing rather than collecting animals.

If the article was intended to inspire prospective young naturalists to send in their collections for the prize competition – no reference to the competition and its approaching deadline is made, however – it was not particularly successful. Only six collections were sent in, and the Rev. J. G. Wood commented on them at length in the August number, giving numerous hints for improvement – even to the winner, who had sent in nests and eggs of 38 different species of birds, ordered "according to modern arrangement" ("Prize for the Best Collection" 1863). The bird-nesting year of *The Boy's Own Magazine* is then rounded off by Wood's detailed instructions (with illustrations) on how to blow and preserve eggs in the September number ("To Blow Eggs" 1863).

Compared to Drayson, Wood is clearly much more convinced that bird-nesting is a worthwhile scientific activity, and he frequently refers to his own collection. Wood's enthusiasm for biological collections becomes even more obvious if we look at *The Boy's Own Paper*. *The Boy's Own Magazine* had stopped publication in 1874, and Wood was among those who continued writing for *The Boy's Own Paper*, launched five years later. As has already been mentioned, to the latter magazine he frequently contributed essays like "Out With a Jack-Knife" or "Pupa digging" or essay series like the seven-part "On Killing, Setting and Preserving Insects" (all 1879). Thus, it is hardly surprising that he should also write on bird-nesting: "Birds' Eggs and Egg Collecting" was published in seven instalments between 24 April and 5 June 1880. While the articles are mainly concerned with providing descriptions of the parent birds belonging to the eggs of a beautifully printed colour display, Wood also provides a detailed justification for the practice itself. Like Drayson he starts with a reference to the supposed cruelty; to this, he responds by re-defining the term 'bird-nesting':

> [My critics] and I attach two different meanings to the term 'bird-nesting.' They fancy that it signifies the destruction of every nest that can be found, the theft of all the eggs, and either the robbery or murder of the young. [...] My idea is totally different. Just as the genuine entomologist is the best friend of the insects, never killing even a noisome insect without just cause, so is the genuine ornithologist the best friend of the birds, even though he should know every nest within miles, and lay them under contribution for his collection of eggs. [...] I assume that the young egg-collector will neither destroy eggs nor meddle with the young birds when hatched,

and that he visits the nests for the sake of studying the habits of birds and enlarging his collection of eggs. (478)

By using specialised discourse, "entomologist", "ornithologist", Wood clearly situates his article in the realm of science, and although he does not make it explicit, scientific knowledge seems to be the 'just cause' referred to with regard to killing an insect. Like Drayson in *The Boy's Own Magazine*, Wood emphasises that the habits of birds should be studied, and like Drayson he argues for a bird-nesting that interferes as little as possible; however, he clearly has no moral qualms about taking eggs: "No bird appears able to count its eggs, and if they are gradually withdrawn, without damaging the nest or alarming the parents, the bird goes on laying without seeming conscious of the loss which she has sustained" (478). Thus, Wood argues, bird-nesting, if done properly, is not cruel. And if it is to be counted as theft, there are clearly mitigating circumstances if the victim is not even aware of it. In a similar vein, George Williamson defended bird-nesting in *The Boy's Own Paper* in 1889, declaring that "the study of this branch of natural history need not be cruel in any way" if carried out sensibly ("On Birds' Eggs and Nests" 1889, 527). Interestingly, Williamson emphasises the scientific nature of proper bird-nesting by linking it to adults: He invites his readers to make their "study of zoology a real science" and hence to "be a man while a boy" (527).

While bird-nesting had always been seen as primarily an activity of boys, it was not only defended in the boys' magazines. For example, *Kind Words: A Magazine for Boys and Girls* encouraged its readers to "make a collection of birds' eggs by all means", provided they did "not *clear* a nest of them" and did not "touch young birds" ("The Young Naturalist Look-out" 1869, 149-150) by the Sunday School Union, an institution that was much more likely to condemn bird-nesting than to condone it. And the magazine *Chatterbox*, aimed at younger children of both sexes, printed Henry Ullyett's "Chapters for Young Naturalists", in which he gives detailed instructions on how to collect and label birds' eggs, encouraging his readers to use not only the English names but the scientific ones, since the latter "gives you information at once as to what class the bird belongs" (1871, 88).

It has become clear that many magazines printed articles on bird-nesting, and if the 'Correspondence' page(s) are any indication, the topic of birds' eggs and their collection was indeed a popular one. Answers to correspondents were a regular feature of most children's periodicals: Readers would address questions to the editors, who would publish brief replies (using initials or a pseudonym of the letter writer for identification). In 1879 and 1880, *The Boy's Own Paper* printed 38 responses that refer to birds' eggs, and the answers suggest that many boys sent in specimens for identification. Ten years later, in 1889 and 1890, the number fell to 29 responses, but requests to identify eggs were still common. This practical interest in egg collection was further encouraged by some boys' magazines through the formation of naturalists' societies. *The Union Jack*, edited by G. A. Henty, was particularly successful in this respect. Its "Union Jack Field Club" boasted of more than 3000 members in 1881, and Archibald McNeill, the "second in command" of the club, deliberately uses militaristic language to encourage the members: "We must be in deadly earnest – that's the best word, I think, for it is a very emphatic one – to make ourselves, within the limits of our spare time, as capable collectors as possible" ("The Union Jack Field Club" 1881, 607). The militaristic language, however, also begs the question if scientific endeavour is really the driving force behind much egg-collecting. The term 'capable collector' may well be defined purely quantitatively so that amassing eggs becomes an end in itself, and the phrase 'deadly earnest' certainly connotes danger and hence marks bird-nesting as an adventurous exploit, reducing the 'scientific' specimens collected to mere trophies.

Thus, it is arguably an indication for the growing importance of science in late Victorian culture that it should be so regularly used as a justification for a pastime which, in many cases, probably had very little to do with actual scientific interest. However, criticism of bird-nesting grew as the century progressed, and in 1900 *The Boy's Own Paper* published an article by Linda Gardiner, in which she specifically denounced the pretence to scientific interest for the justification of bird-nesting. She starts by declaring that many readers of *The Boy's Own Paper* probably see themselves as "a bit of a naturalist", continuing by pointing out that there are different kinds of naturalists, "some of them genuine students and some mere pretenders and humbugs" ("The Bird World" 1900, 310). Later she claims that "not [...] one-fiftieth of the 'collectors' [of birds' eggs] know anything of the sciences of ornithology and oology", and she closes her essay by telling her readers that if they wish to be ornithologists "of the first class", they should "discourage birdnesting among [their] companions, and encourage in its place an intelligent interest in the living birds" (*ibid.*, 312). The hey-day of bird-nesting as a scientific endeavour was drawing to its close.[8]

4. Conclusion

The practice of bird-nesting is not solely a phenomenon of the nineteenth century: It had entertained boys much earlier, and it did not completely disappear at its end. However, the last three decades of the nineteenth century saw an unprecedented interest in the pastime, and an attempt to harness an activity that came 'naturally' to boys to the serious yoke of scientific – or at least proto-scientific – study. This development should be seen in the context of a debate on the role of the natural sciences in (public school) education, which had been going on since mid-century. While science education remained mainly theoretical, juvenile magazines could use the popularity of bird-nesting as a pastime to support their claim that science could be an enjoyable activity – carried out with the help of those magazines. By offering advice to beginners and prize competitions for experts, the practice of scientific bird-nesting could be utilised to strengthen the bond between a magazine and its readership, and hence to increase sales figures. To what extent the practice of bird-nesting really fostered scientific interest in boys is a question that remains beyond the scope of this essay.

---

8   The correspondence pages of *The Boy's Own Paper* provide further evidence of this trend: References to birds' eggs drop to one each for the years 1899 and 1900.

References
Children's Magazines

Since many articles in the magazines were published anonymously, all articles are listed by their titles. Of the series referred to, only the first article is referenced (unless later articles are quoted in the text). The magazines were accessed through the database "19th Century UK Periodicals", GALE Cengage <http://gdc.gale.com> and the Gale Document Number (GDN) is provided in addition to bibliographical data of the printed magazines.

"Birds' Eggs and Egg Collecting." By John George Wood. *The Boy's Own Paper* 2 (1880), 478-9. GDN: DX1901396120

"Birds' Nests and Birds'-nesting." By A. W. Drayson. *The Boy's Own Magazine* 1, New Series (1863), 526-32. GDN: DX1901685981

"Chapters for Young Naturalists." By Henry Ullyett. *Chatterbox* 11 (1871), 87-8. GDN: DX1901314508

"How to form a collection of British Birds' Eggs." By Richard Kaerton. *Chums* (1893), 575. GDN: DX1901956543

"On Birds' Eggs and Nests." By George Williamson. *The Boy's Own Paper* 11 (1889), 527-8. GDN: DX1901387784

"On Killing, Setting, and Preserving Insects." By John George Wood. *The Boy's Own Paper* 1 (1879), 431-2. GDN: DX1901386445

"Out with a Jack-knife." By John George Wood. *The Boy's Own Paper* 1 (1879), 3-5. GDN: DX1901386003

"Papers on Pyrotechny." *The Boy's Own Magazine* 4, New Series (1864), 153-7. GDN: DX1901685599

"Pigeons, Their Choice and Management." *The Boy's Own Magazine* 1 (1855), 186-8. GDN: DX1901793863

"Police" (14 May 1843), *Lloyds Weekly London Newspaper* 7. GDN: BC3205315401

"Prize for the Best Collection of Birds' Eggs and Nests." *The Boy's Own Magazine* 2, New Series (1863), n.p. GDN: DX1901685107

"Prize Models." *The Boy's Own Magazine* 1, New Series (1863), n.p. GDN: DX1901685821

"Pupa Digging." By J.G. Wood. *The Boy's Own Paper* 1 (1879), 163-4. GDN: DX1901386193

"Rabbits, Their Choice and Management." *The Boy's Own Magazine* 1 (1855), 316-8. GDN: DX1901793941

"Six Little Robins." By Dorothea Sinclair. *The Children's Friend* (1887), 91-93. GDN: DX1902015626

Steel, Elliot (1883): "Essays on Science Teaching in Our Public Schools: VII", *Journal of Education* 62, New Series, 138-140

"Taxidermy Competition [1]." *The Boy's Own Paper* 3 (1881), 296. GDN: DX1901385499

"Taxidermy Competition [2]." *The Boy's Own Paper* 4 (1881), 174. GDN: DX1901393465

"The Bird World." By Linda Gardiner. *The Boy's Own Paper* 22 (1900), 310-2. GDN: DX1901390545

"The Boa." *The Boy's Own Magazine* 2 (February 1855), 47-50. GDN: DX1901793803

"The Boy's Own Magazine." *The Boy's Own Magazine* 1 (1855), (2). GDN: DX1901793776

"The Boy's Own Museum; or Birds and Beasts, and How to Stuff Them [i]." By Gordon Stables. *The Boy's Own Paper* 2 (1880), 21-2. GDN: DX1901385239

"The Boy's Own Museum; or Birds and Beasts, and How to Stuff Them [vi]." By Gordon Stables. *The Boy's Own Paper* 2 (1880), 134-5. GDN: DX1901385334

"The Mystery of the Crucible." *The Boy's Own Magazine* 4 (1858), 182-7. GDN: DX1901684946

"The Union Jack Field Club." By Archibald McNeill. *The Union Jack* (1881), 607-8. GDN: DX1901725842

"The Young Naturalist Look-out." By W. H. G. *Kind Words* 176 (1869), 149-50. GDN: DX1901499976

"To Blow Eggs." By John George Wood. *The Boy's Own Magazine* 2, New Series (1863), n.p. GDN: DX1901685140

"To Procure Laughing Gas." *The Boy's Own Magazine* 3 (1857), 128. GDN: DX1901994198

"Woman's Wrongs" (12 October 1872): *Pall Mall Gazette* 12. GDN: BA3207698301

Other Sources

Brock, W. H. (1980): "The Development of Commercial Science Journals in Victorian Britain, in: Meadows, A. J. (ed.): *Development of Science Publishing in Europe*. Amsterdam: Elsevier, 95-122

Clarendon Commission Report (1865): "Report from the Select Committee of the House of Lords, on the Public Schools Bill [H. L.]; together with the Proceedings of the Committee, Minutes of Evidence, Appendix and Index", *House of Commons Papers*, Paper nr. 481, Volume X.263. House of Commons Parliamentary Papers. <http://gateway.proquest.com/openurl?url_ver=Z39.88-2004&res_dat=xri:hcpp&rft_dat=xri:hcpp:rec:1865-041115>

Dixon, Diana (2001): "Children's Magazines and Science in the Nineteenth Century", *Victorian Periodicals Review* 34, 228-238

Drotner, Kirsten (1988): *English Children and Their Magazines, 1751-1945*. New Haven: Yale University Press

Hutchinson, T. N. (November 1882): "Essays on Science Teaching in our Public Schools: IV", *Journal of Education* 57, New Series, 350-352

Huxley, Thomas Henry (1869/1893): "Scientific Education: Notes of an After-Dinner Speech", in: Huxley, T. H.: *Science and Education: Essays*. Collected Essays, Volume 3. London: Macmillan, 111-133

Locke, John (1902): *Some Thoughts Concerning Education* [1693]. Introd. R.H. Quick. Cambridge: Cambridge University Press

Lupton, Sydney (August 1882): "Essays on Science Teaching in our Public Schools: I", *Journal of Education* 54, New Series, 248-250

Milton, Frederick (2008): "Taking the Pledge: A Study of Children's Societies for the Prevention of Cruelty to Birds and Animals in Britain, c. 1870-1914", unpublished Ph.D. thesis. Newcastle University. <http://hdl.handle.net/10443/1583> [accessed 10 January 2014]

Newbery, John (1966): *A Little Pretty Pocket-Book* [1767]. Facsimile edition. Introd. M.F. Thwaite. London: Oxford University Press

Olby, R. C. et al. (eds.; 1990): *Companion to the History of Modern Science*. London: Routledge

Petzold, Jochen (2012): "'The end was not ignoble'? Bird-Nesting between Cruelty, Manliness and Science Education in British Children's Periodicals, 1850-1900", in: McGavran, James Holt Jr. (ed.): *Time of Beauty, Time of Fear: The Romantic Legacy in the Literature of Childhood.* Iowa City, IA: University of Iowa Press, 128-150

Roderick, Gordon; Stephens, Michael (1972): *Scientific and Technical Education in Nineteenth-Century England: A Symposium*. Newton Abbot: David & Charles

"Schools Inquiry Commission Report" [1867-8], in: *The History of Education in England: Documents*. URL: <http://www.educationengland.org.uk/documents/sicr/sicr1-06.html> [accessed 29 August 2011]

Thwaite, M. F. (1966): "John Newbery and His First Book for Children", in: Newbery, John: *A Little Pretty Pocket-Book*. Facsimile of the edition of 1767. Ed. M. F. Thwaite. London: Oxford University Press, 1-49

Trimmer, Sarah (1786): *Fabulous Histories Designed for the Instruction of Children, Respecting their Treatment of Animals*. London, *Eighteenth Century Collections Online*. GDN: CW119954660

Wilson, J. M. (1867): "On Teaching Natural Science in Schools", in: Farrar, F. W. (ed.): *Essays on A Liberal Education*. London: Macmillan, 241-291

JOANNA ROSTEK (PASSAU)

Female Authority and Political Economy: Jane Marcet's and Harriet Martineau's Contradictory Strategy in Disseminating Economic Knowledge

1. Introduction: Women and/on Political Economy

The birth of modern economics is usually traced back to the late eighteenth century and associated, perhaps somewhat ironically, with a professor of moral philosophy: Adam Smith. Smith is seen as the founding father of classical political economy and as a precursor of economic liberalism, while his seminal *An Inquiry into the Nature and Causes of the Wealth of Nations* (1776) is considered "one of the most important works of the millennium" (Otteson 2004, 1). The late eighteenth and early nineteenth centuries saw a rise in other British thinkers scrutinizing and systematizing the principles guiding the production and distribution of individual and, above all, national wealth. In 1805, Thomas Robert Malthus was the first in Britain to be appointed Professor of History and Political Economy at the East India Company College in Hertfordshire. The denomination of his position marked the emergence and institutionalization of a new science that would unfold and solidify throughout the Victorian period. Hilda Hollis observes that "undergirding this organizational and institutional shift was a change in the mass perception of the value and knowledge of political economy" (2002, 380). The nascent science can be viewed as one of many attempts to render understandable and manageable a society increasingly dominated by industrialization, urbanization, social stratification, and international trade.

The names of the period's economic theorists and their principles are known and discussed at universities even today: Thomas Robert Malthus's controversial principle of population, David Ricardo's concept of comparative advantage, or John Stuart Mill's defense of utilitarianism. Nevertheless, the contribution of *female* writers to the formation and dissemination of economic knowledge tends to be overlooked. According to Janet Seiz such negligence is a general problem in the history of economics, the regrettable result being that "we know almost nothing about how many women have worked as economists in the past, what sort of work they did and under what conditions, and how their work was received" (1993, 189). With this article[1] I hope to address this gap by focusing on two women who, in the early nineteenth century, made successful contributions to the emergent science of political economy. I argue that because women at that time were largely denied scientific and economic authority, the two female authors in question chose a contradictory strategy when disseminating economic knowledge in their popularizing publications: one that both confirmed and challenged the traditional and restrictive gender norms.

---

[1] I would like to thank the Institute for Advanced Studies in the Humanities at the University of Edinburgh for granting me a fellowship in the framework of which I could conduct research for this article.

Before substantiating this claim with examples, I wish to highlight a quotation from a recent text, penned in 2009 for an occasion poignant to this article's central thesis and to which I will return at the end of the article. This is how Elinor Ostrom (1933-2012), an acclaimed American economist, recalls the beginnings of her academic career in the 1950s and early 1960s:

> When I started to look for a position after graduation, it was somewhat of a shock to me to have future employers immediately ask whether I had typing and shorthand skills. The presumption in those days was that the appropriate job for a woman was as a secretary or as a teacher in a grade school or high school. [...] My initial discussions with the Economics Department at UCLA about obtaining a Ph.D. in Economics were [...] pretty discouraging. [... T]hey discouraged any further thinking about doing a Ph.D. in economics. Political Science at that time was also skeptical about admitting any women to their Ph.D program [...]. (Qtd. in "Elinor Ostrom – Biographical" 2013)

Ostrom's experience reveals that as late as the mid-twentieth century academic disciplines such as political science or economics were deemed not only inappropriate for women, but also beyond their mental capacity. One could therefore presume that the lot of women with similar ambitions in the early nineteenth century must have been even more stringent. And yet, in 1832, a British reviewer writes in *Tait's Edinburgh Magazine*: "The ladies seem determined to make the science of political economy peculiarly their own" (*Tait's Edinburgh Magazine* 2004, 416). The "ladies" whom the author goes on to mention as worthy of the tribute are Jane Marcet and Harriet Martineau.

The praise bestowed on the two authors was due to their respective publications: In 1816, Jane Marcet had issued a book entitled *Conversations on the Nature of Political Economy, in Which the Elements of That Science Are Familiarly Explained*; Harriet Martineau followed in 1832 with the first volume of her *Illustrations of Political Economy*. From the vantage point of our time, when economics as a discipline is taught at schools and when virtually every university can boast of a School of Business and Economics, the motivation behind Marcet and Martineau's works might at first glance seem astounding. Marcet writes in the preface to her *Conversations*:

> Political Economy, though so immediately connected with the happiness and improvement of mankind, and the object of so much controversy and speculation among men of knowledge, is not yet become a popular science, and is not generally considered as a study essential to early education. (Marcet 2009, xxxvii)

A similar regret is expressed by Harriet Martineau: "Political Economy has been less studied than perhaps any other science whatever, and not at all by those whom it most concerns, – the mass of the people" (Martineau 1834a, iv). Both authors seek to redress the apparent knowledge gap and for that purpose address a non-scholarly readership with the explicit aim of popularizing and explaining the basic assumptions of political economy.

2. Uncommon Women: Marcet's and Martineau's Careers as Political Economist(resse)s

Jane Marcet (1769-1858)[2], whom Bette Polkinghorn rightly terms "an uncommon woman" (1993), was the eldest of ten children of an affluent Anglo-Swiss couple. Her family's close connections to Geneva had important consequences for Marcet's later writing career. Firstly, in accordance with the tradition of the Geneva *salons*, she received a substantial amount of formal education: in mathematics, astronomy, and philosophy, among others. Polkinghorn emphasizes that "[h]er early education had been somewhat unusual in that she and her brothers and sisters were taught by the best available tutors, the subjects being the same regardless of the sex of the child" (Polkinghorn 1993, 4). Secondly, Marcet's family was involved in the banking business: Her father, Antoine Haldimand, was a successful banker, trader, and real estate developer, while her brother William became Director of the Bank of England in 1809. Furthermore, the Marcets were acquainted with some of the leading political economists of that time, including Malthus, Ricardo, and James Mill. Jane Marcet was thus exposed to and familiar with the discussion of complex economic issues within influential intellectual circles. Thirdly, in Genevan families, property was traditionally passed on in comparable shares to male and female offspring. This meant that Marcet eventually inherited a notable portion of her father's sizable fortune, which again arguably attuned her more acutely to the relevance of money matters.

It should be noted that *Conversations on Political Economy* was by no means the only popularizing publication delivered by Marcet. Her first work was *Conversations on Chemistry*, in part inspired by the interests of her husband Alexander Marcet, a medical doctor, which was published in 1805. The book proved immensely popular and went through at least sixteen British and two French editions during Marcet's lifetime. She built upon the formula developed in her first publication while composing her second major work, *Conversations on Political Economy*, in 1816. It relies on what Marcet termed a "didactic composition" (Marcet 2009, xxxix), namely a neo-Socratic dialogue between two fictional characters. Importantly, these characters are female: The young and ingenuous Caroline asks various questions regarding the production and distribution of wealth, while her governess, one Mrs B., patiently explains the basic lessons of political economy to her inquisitive pupil. In such manner, women are explicitly granted the authority to convey and comprehend intricate economic principles. *Conversations* became an immediate success and was reissued, with minor alterations suggested in parts by none other than Malthus and Ricardo, only a year later. Over the next two decades, it went through at least seven editions. In the years to come, Marcet went on to write further didactic texts, the range of which testifies to the impressive scope of her interests. The list of Marcet's publications includes, among others, *Conversations on: Natural Philosophy* (1819), *Mineralogy* (1822), *Evidences of Christianity* (1826), *Vegetable Physiology* (1829), *Nature and Art* (1837), *Chronology* (1837), *Language* (1844), and *Harmony* (1855). She returned to the topic of political economy in 1833 with *John Hopkins's Notions on Political Economy*, a publication aimed at a working-class readership and supported by the Society for the Diffu-

---

2 The biographical information on Marcet and Martineau provided in this subchapter is based on Cicarelli and Cicarelli 2003, Forget 2009, Polkinghorn 1993, Polkinghorn 1995, Webb 1960, as well as on Martineau's *Autobiography* (1877/1983).

sion of Useful Knowledge. This text, however, never matched up to the success of the *Conversations*.

Harriet Martineau (1802-1876), an avid reader and eventual friend of Marcet's, was born into a family of textile manufacturers. As in Marcet's case, her family's Huguenot background meant that she benefited from an uncommonly high degree of education in her youth. In contrast to her predecessor, however, who never suffered from material concerns, Martineau was unexpectedly forced to earn her living in her late twenties when her father's business went bankrupt. It was during that period that *Illustrations* took shape. It is noteworthy that in her *Autobiography* of 1877, Martineau pays direct tribute to Marcet by indicating her, rather than male political economists, as the initial inspiration for *Illustrations*. She writes that their

> view and purpose date from [her] reading of Mrs Marcet's Conversations. During that reading, groups of personages rose up from the pages, and a procession of action glided through its arguments, as afterwards from the pages of Adam Smith, and all the other Economists. (Martineau 1877, 138-139)

Martineau read *Conversations on Political Economy* in 1827, but it was not until 1831 that she embarked in earnest on her own popularizing project. She chose to depart from Marcet's dialogic form and instead to convey the main principles of the nascent science of political economy by way of didactic fictional stories, through which the lessons derived from writers such as Smith, Malthus, and Mill were to be explained to the general public. The daily troubles of doctors and laborers, fishers and farmers, men, women, and children, would be presented in tales of roughly 120 pages each, yielding individual economic lessons. After considerable difficulties in finding a publisher willing to take on such an unusual project stemming from an unknown female author, Martineau saw her first story, "Life in the Wilds", appear in print in February 1832. The enthusiastic reception it met with proved that she was right in her appraisal of popular demand. *Illustrations*, ultimately consisting of twenty-four fictional tales and a comprehensive final summary of the tales' morals, became an overnight success. For two years, between 1832 and 1834, Martineau published one tale per month, attracting the attention of such prominent readers as the young Princess Victoria, Robert Peel, John Stuart Mill, and Edward Bulwer-Lytton. No longer forced to earn her living through needlework, Martineau had now become a respected and financially secure "teacher of the people" (Webb 1960, 91-133). She later contentedly concluded in her *Autobiography* that "any one to whom that happens by thirty years of age may be satisfied; and I was so" (Martineau 1877, 181). Subsequently, Martineau established herself as an influential yet also controversial Victorian writer, journalist, and, as some maintain, the first woman sociologist, publishing on a wide range of topics including slavery, American society, and political economy. In contrast to Marcet, who fulfilled the gender expectations of her time by marrying respectably and giving birth to four children, Martineau remained single for the rest of her life.

3. Staking Out a Claim: Marcet's and Martineau's Contradictory Strategy

Marcet's and Martineau's publications met with immediate and substantial public acclaim. Not only were they popular in America and translated into foreign languages; they also outsold some of those theoretical works whose lessons they sought to popularize (Polkinghorn 1995). This success story might seem surprising in view of the prevalent gender norms at the time: After all, in nineteenth-century Britain, women were hardly credited with knowledge regarding complicated financial issues, and the separate spheres doctrine constituted a further obstacle for women pursuing economic questions (see Bodkin 1999, 62; Dalley 2010, 103-104; McDonagh 1996, 14). Brian P. Cooper avers in this regard that "political economy was, by definition, political and, according to some, scientific as well. Both attributes made it potentially excludable from the acceptable sphere of activities by women" (Cooper 2007, 121). In other words, because of their sex, it was anything but self-evident for female writers to assume authority regarding economic questions.

By way of three examples, I suggest that, faced with such limitations, Marcet and Martineau opted for a contradictory strategy in their texts, which allowed them to stake their claim within the male-dominated economic discourse. This strategy is somewhat comparable to what Elaine Showalter, drawing on Susan Lanser and Evelyn Torton Beck, has famously termed the "double-voiced discourse", i.e., a form of expression "that always embodies the social, literary, and cultural heritages of both the muted and the dominant" (Showalter 1981, 201). Both the dominant and the muted voices can be traced in Marcet's and Martineau's writing: On the one hand, they uphold the gender norms set forth by their times, but on the other, they negotiate and question them.

3.1 More Than Mothers: Accounting for the Relevance of Political Economy for Women

This ambivalent strategy manifests itself when Jane Marcet contemplates the prospective readers of her publication. Already in the preface to *Conversations*, she declares that the book is "especially intended" for the instruction of "young persons of either sex" (Marcet 2009, xxxvii), which calls to mind a central tenet of "the feminist declaration of independence" (Brody 2004, ix), Mary Wollstonecraft's *A Vindication of the Rights of Woman* (1792). Wollstonecraft, whom some critics cite as "[t]he principal inspiration for Marcet" (Cicarelli and Cicarelli 2003, 110), likewise believed that "the first object of laudable ambition is to obtain a character as a human being, regardless of the distinction of sex" (Wollstonecraft 2004, 14) and therefore posited that "day schools, for particular ages, should be established by government, in which boys and girls might be educated together" (Wollstonecraft 2004, 209). Although Marcet does not take up Wollstonecraft's request directly, she nevertheless makes the case for teaching girls the same subjects as boys – for example political economy.

If Marcet departs here from accepted gender divisions, she presently justifies her unconventional demand with a statement that upholds the separate spheres model. She has Mrs B. explain that women should be taught political economy in order to be able to duly perform their most essential duty, namely that of being good mothers:

> If a more general knowledge of political economy prevented women from propagating errors respecting it, in the education of their children, no trifling good would ensue. [...] I would wish that mothers were so far competent to teach it, that their children should not have any thing [*sic*] to unlearn. (Marcet 2009, 9)

One could contend that the progressive strand in Marcet's argumentation is thereby stifled. However, it is worth pointing out that this line of thinking was already put forward in *Vindication* where Wollstonecraft justified her demand for female education with the catchphrase: "Make women rational creatures, and free citizens, and they will quickly become good wives, and mothers" (Wollstonecraft 2004, 222). Marcet, who on the whole is decidedly less radical than her predecessor, adopts this somewhat gendered and conservative line of reasoning, which, however, does not preclude her from placing the intellectual faculties of women on an equal footing with those of men. What is more, putatively domestic feminine tasks, such as rearing and educating children, acquire a public dimension: For Marcet, being a knowledgeable mother results in contributing to national welfare. The impossibility of a neat distinction between a female and private sphere on the one hand, and a male and public sphere on the other, is thereby disclosed.

This separation is subtly challenged on another occasion in the text. When Caroline professes that she finds political economy boring and instead "should at least be privileged to talk about dress, amusements, and such lady-like topics", Mrs B. immediately retorts: "I have heard no trifling degree of ignorance of political economy betrayed in a conversation on dress. 'What a pity', said one lady, 'that French lace should be so dear; for my part I make no scruple of smuggling it: there is really a great satisfaction in cheating the custom-house'" (Marcet 2009, 7). Allegedly unimportant and private feminine topics are thus presented as directly related to questions of national and even international economy. Marcet moreover implicitly accuses her fellow women of intellectual laziness and exhorts them to pay heed to the larger implications of their mundane concerns. This again brings to mind Wollstonecraft, who sought "to persuade women to endeavour to acquire strength, both of mind and body" (Wollstonecraft 2004, 13-14) and railed "against the custom of confining girls to their needle, and shutting them out from all political and civil employments" (*ibid.*, 211).

The young Caroline posits another query which is equally instructive in its regard to whether female readers would profit from the knowledge of political economy:

> Well, after all, Mrs B., ignorance of political economy is a very excusable deficiency in women. It is the business of Government to reform the prejudices and errors which prevail respecting it; and as we are never likely to become legislators, is it not just as well that we should remain in happy ignorance of evils which we have no power to remedy? (Marcet 2009, 9)

Caroline's seemingly guileless question of course risks being answered in the affirmative and dismissed as the naive and unreasonable musings of an ignorant young girl. Hilda Hollis raises an important point when she asserts that "the choice of a girl as a pupil [...] has possibly other, unfeminist, strategic importance", as her arguments can be shoved aside as merely 'feminine'" (Hollis 2002, 386). For Hollis, the rhetorical strategy permeating *Conversations* relies on Mrs B.'s consistent rebuttal of her pupil's counter-queries and on Caroline's continual submission to the governess's superior reason. Yet 'convincing' Caroline does not necessarily mean that the readers are/were convinced as well. In the case quoted above, Caroline draws attention to the limited political agency of women. Once such objections are articulated – even if this occurs only via the "the mind of an intelligent young person [...] naturally imbued with all the prejudices and popular feelings of uninformed benevolence" (Marcet 2009, xl) – they remain on the page and might give food for thought to readers less willing than Caroline to surrender to Mrs B.'s doctrines.

Harriet Martineau pursues a similarly ambivalent course when she indirectly explains why women writers may claim authority with regard to economic questions. The preface to her *Illustrations* contains an extended analogy in which the nation and the state – presumably here the domain of men – are compared to two realms of female activity: the family and the household. Martineau refers to "the nation" as "that larger family" (Martineau 1834a, vi) and regrets that England's "national distresses" prevent her from "go[ing] on to say that civilized states are managed like civilized households, that Political Economy was nearly as well understood by governments as domestic economy is by the heads of families" (Martineau 1834a, viii). These analogies of the household thus provide the female author with a point of entry to the public discourse of political economy. As a woman, she may justly claim expertise in matters of family and household; but if managing these two domains is analogous to managing a state, why should she lack authority to judge on the latter issue?

It appears that Martineau's line of reasoning actually convinced some of her contemporaries. The reviewer from *Tait's Edinburgh Magazine* quoted above affirms:

> After all, we believe that there is something in the female mind which peculiarly fits it for elucidating, in a familiar manner, the intricacies of political economy. The economy of empires is only the economy of families and neighbourhoods on a larger scale. Now woman is eminently the best family manager. [...] She lacks the strength to take an active share in the concerns of an empire, but her experience in the business details of her own miniature state enable her to read lessons worthy of serious attention from all who take an interest in public affairs. (*Tait's Edinburgh Magazine* 2004, 416)

The equivocality of this double-edged compliment points towards the contradictions inherent in Martineau's own argumentation. On the one hand, her analogy – just like the review – refers to essentialist notions of gender and reinforces the association of women with the domestic sphere. On the other hand, it mobilizes and reinterprets the separate spheres doctrine in such a way that women's authority to speak out in "public affairs" is effectively legitimized.

3.2 Founding Fathers: Paying Oblique Tribute to Political Economist(er)s

A second issue worthy of consideration is Marcet's and Martineau's attitudes towards the theories of those male scholars they set out to propagate. When estimating Marcet's contribution to the economic discourse of the early nineteenth century, some present-day critics emphasize that she contented herself with merely popularizing theses that were developed by male authors. James and Julianne Cicarelli, for example, write: "The entire house of classical economics was essentially built during Marcet's long life, yet she did not contribute one doctrinal brick to its edifice" (Cicarelli and Cicarelli 2003, 109). The author of *Conversations* seems to lay the ground for such a view when she avers in her preface:

> As to the principles and materials of the work, it is so obvious that they have been obtained from the writings of the great masters who have treated this subject, and more particularly from those of Dr. Adam Smith, of Mr. Malthus, M. Say, M. Sismondi, Mr. Ricardo, and Mr. Blake, that the author has not thought it necessary to load these pages with repeated acknowledgements and incessant references. (Marcet 2009, xxxviii)

Martineau feels obliged to pay a similar tribute to male authorities in the last volume of her *Illustrations* containing "The Moral of Many Fables" (1834). Significantly, she makes no mention here of Marcet's book, though she does name *Conversations* as a source of inspiration in her *Autobiography*, published more than four decades later. In *Illustrations*, by contrast, Martineau posits that

> great men must have their hewers of wood and drawers of water, and scientific discoveries must be followed by those who will popularize their discoveries. When the woodman finds it necessary to explain that the forest is not of his planting, I may begin to particularize my obligations to Smith and Malthus, and others of their high order. (Martineau 1834b, 143)

At first glance, both quotations conceive of knowledge production as existing within a distinctly male domain. Even so, Marcet and Martineau enter their scientific and economic discourse with palpable aplomb. Although only men authored the groundbreaking economic treatises that they draw upon, as women, their works attest that they are nevertheless perfectly capable of understanding and synthesizing male findings in a methodical and systematic way. Accordingly, Mrs B. informs Caroline at the very outset of *Conversations*: "I must tell you fairly, that I did not commence my studies by opening these works at random, or by consulting Adam Smith on an insulated point, before I had examined his plan, or understood his object[.] I knew that in order to learn I must begin at the beginning" (Martineau 2009, 12). This is a claim to female intellectual thoroughness and credibility.

Hollis argues regarding *Conversations* that "Mrs. B is simply explaining what learned men are responsible for discovering: no glory accrues to her for this popularization" (Hollis 2002, 387). It is true that Marcet and Martineau duly emphasize that their contributions are subordinate to those of the founding fathers of political economy. Still, the seeming homages to the male masters at times appear equivocal. Martineau, for instance, describes the bible of political economy in the following words:

> It is very natural that the first eminent book on this new science should be very long, in some parts very difficult, and, however wonderful and beautiful as a whole, not so clear and precise in its arrangement as it might be. This is the case with Smith's Wealth of Nations, – a book whose excellence is marvellous when all the circumstances are considered, but which is not fitted nor designed to teach the science to the great mass of the people. (Martineau 1834a, x)

The possible defects of Smith's foundational analysis are summed up even more bluntly by the outspoken Caroline:

> Then there is a perpetual reference to the works of Adam Smith, whose name is never uttered without such veneration that I was induced one day to look into this work on political economy to gain some information on the subject of corn, but what with forestalling, regrating, duties, drawbacks, and limiting prices, I was so overwhelmed by a jargon of unintelligible terms, that after running over a few pages, I threw the book away in despair, and resolved to eat my bread in humble ignorance. (Marcet 2009, 5)

Regardless of their obvious respect for political economist(er)s, Marcet and Martineau implicitly suggest that their publications in some way surpass those authored by the founding fathers of that discipline. Martineau confidently states in her preface that "the works already written on Political Economy are very valuable, but they do not give us what we want" (Martineau 1834a, xi). The two women endeavor to fill this gap, evidently trusting in their own faculties: Not only are they capable of unravelling the impenetrable male "jargon of unintelligible terms" (Marcet 2009, 5) and of negotiating difficult subject matter; they also know how to translate complex economic principles into a language that will ensure their intelligibility to and application by the general public. Hence, their works are presented as just as, or possibly even more, useful than those of the male 'masters'. Made in a society permeated by utilitarian principles, this claim should not be dismissed lightly.

3.3 Gender and Genre: Negotiating Science and Literature

The third important point pertains to the negotiation of both literary and scientific discourses which enter Marcet's and Martineau's popularizing projects. Lana L. Dalley asserts that

> within early nineteenth-century print culture, fiction – especially domestic fiction – was regarded as the domain of pleasures and emotions, while more 'serious' works – on such topics as history, politics or economics – were regarded as serving a higher intellectual purpose that contributed to the greater good in ways that fiction did not. (Dalley 2010, 103)

Further, these realms were clearly gendered, with fiction deemed appropriate for female readers and writers, while the 'serious' domain was reserved for male authors.

Marcet's *Conversations* reinforces the differentiation between literature and science. Even if in Marcet's time the latter term had not yet wholly acquired the positivist meaning we attribute to it today (Kelley 2012, 357), it is noteworthy that Marcet clearly positions herself on the side of science, thus belying the conviction that women are unsuitable for that realm. This might not be evident at a first glance, given that *Conversations* abounds in references to literary works. They begin with Caroline reading an excerpt from François Fenelon's *The Adventures of Telemachus*. This is followed by quotations from or references to Oliver Goldsmith, Daniel Defoe, Maria Edgeworth, Greek mythology, and others. Yet, as Hilda Hollis (2002, 388) demonstrates, with the notable exception of Edgeworth (importantly, the only female author), the main function of the literary excerpts is to provide examples of faulty economic reasoning. Mrs B. is at pains to draw a sharp distinction between agreeable, yet unrealistic notions evoked by literature, and the slightly unwieldy, yet credible knowledge yielded by science.

One of Caroline's favorite poems by Goldsmith is accordingly accepted on aesthetic but dismissed on scientific grounds:

> Ignorance of the principles of political economy is to be discovered in some of the most elegant and sensible of our writers, especially amongst the poets. That beautiful composition of Goldsmith, the Deserted Village, is full of errors of this description, which, from its great popularity, are very liable to mislead the ill informed. […] Its intrinsic merit as a poem is quite sufficient to atone for any errors in scientific principles. Truth is not, you know, essential to poetic beauty; but it is essential that we should be able to distinguish between truth and fiction. (Marcet 2009, 9)

Time and again, Mrs B. warns her well-read pupil against accepting at face value the economic principles suggested by literary works. Pastoral adulations of rural life are thus rejected with the brisk comment: "But this picture is drawn by the poet, who paints it, not from the life, but from the enchanting yet delusive image formed by his imagination" (*ibid.*, 69). For Mrs B. – as for Marcet – truth resides on the side of science, not on that of literature. *Conversations*, despite its paradoxically frequent references to literary texts, clearly positions itself on the side of the former.

This offers another instance of the contradictory strategy permeating *Conversations*. On the one hand, Marcet's project aims at popularizing existing rather than generating new knowledge. She thus demurely accepts the role of a female teacher who 'merely' disseminates principles established by male authorities. Yet, on the other hand, Marcet's insistence on the distinction between literature and science and her concurrent claim to the scientific discourse undermine the "gendered understanding of authorship and forms of knowledge" that Dalley diagnoses for the early nineteenth century (Dalley 2010, 103). The title of Marcet's publication captures this ambivalence fairly well: *Political Economy in Which Elements of the Science Are Familiarly Explained*. Whether consciously or not, 'science' and 'family' figure side by side.

A comparably hybrid, albeit textually divergent, strategy emerges in Martineau's *Illustrations*, which deliberately combine fiction with science. By resorting to fictional texts Martineau ostensibly upholds the coupling of gender and genre: As a woman writer she opts for allegedly unimportant sentimental themes and domestic settings that can more easily be found in literature than in science. However, as Dalley points out, the hybrid form of *Illustrations* presents a subversion of prevalent gender norms, because "by employing and reconfiguring economic discourse, Martineau challenges the cultural limits imposed upon women's discursive and economic acts, stretches the boundaries of novelistic discourse, and assigns women writers and fiction greater cultural authority" (Dalley 2010, 115). In addition, two further aspects must be borne in mind: Firstly, Martineau insisted that "Political Economy" should feature in the title of her series. She recalls in her *Autobiography* that certain publishers "wanted to suppress the words Political Economy altogether: but I knew that science could not be smuggled in anonymously" (Martineau 1983, 162). By holding on to that title, Martineau lays direct claim to the male, serious, scientific discourse. Secondly, in the preface to *Illustrations* she professes that she developed the format of didactic short stories not because she thought it more appropriate for a female writer, but because she believed it more appropriate with regard to her objective:

> The reason why we choose the form of narrative is, that we really think it the best in which Political Economy can be taught [...] W]e have chosen this method not only because it is new, not only because it is entertaining, but because we think it the most faithful and the most complete. (Martineau 1834a, xiii)

Martineau evidently does not see herself as a victim of gendered standards of writing, but as a confident author choosing an innovative format that best fits her purpose at hand.

4. Conclusion: A Short-Lived Success

I could conclude by optimistically stating that Marcet and Martineau's clever, contradictory strategy allowed them to become successful writers in spite of the subtle challenge to prevalent gender norms detectable in their works. One important development, however, suggests that we should take their considerable achievements with a grain of salt. As Marcet and Martineau affirm in their individual works, political economy was at the time of their writing not yet an established scientific discipline. It progresses, however, over the course of the Victorian period, and by the late nineteenth century political economy becomes known as economics – the quantitative, empirical science that continues to be taught today. Two influential British publications marking this transition are William Stanley Jevons's *A General Mathematical Theory of Political Economy* (1862) and Alfred Marshall's *Principles of Economics* of 1890 (Jay and Jay 1986, 14-15).

Yet the increasing importance of political economy and, as it was later termed, economics, did not go hand in hand with an increased authority of female economists. In this way, Marcet and Martineau became the tragic victims of their own success. "Through Marcet's work", writes Hilda Hollis – and I believe that the same applies for Martineau – "the ideas of the political economists were given prominence and authority, and these men began to acquire the institutional authority critical to cultural hegemony" (Hollis 2002, 386). In other words: Once the female popularizers achieved their aim and political economy indeed became a scientific discipline of universally acknowledged importance, women found themselves with limited access to that sphere.

One telling example of this development is provided by Alfred Marshall's monumental *Principles of Economics*. The book, though featuring a historical appendix on "The Growth of Economic Science", ignores Marcet's contribution and relegates Martineau to a single, rather denigrating footnote, presenting her as one of "those who cared little for the scientific study of economics […], professing to simplify economic doctrines, [but] really enunciat[ing] them without the conditions required to make them true" (Marshall 1920, 763n1). Led by an apparent misreading of Martineau's *Autobiography*, Marshall proceeds to offer a patronizing and clearly gendered excuse for her alleged economic blunders by stating:

> But Miss Martineau was not an economist in the proper sense of the word: she confessed that she never read more than one chapter of an economic book at a time before writing a story to illustrate economic principles, for fear the pressure on her mind should be too great: and before her death she expressed a just doubt whether the principles of economics (as understood by her) had any validity. (Marshall 1920, 763n1)

As this blatant example of denying economic authority to female popularizers shows, the contradictory strategy of Marcet and Martineau to claim female authority within economic discourse was, unfortunately, only a short-lived success. Disproving the optimistic appraisal of *Tait's Edinburgh Magazine* of 1832 quoted earlier, the Victorian period did not see "ladies […] make the science of Political Economy peculiarly their own" (Anon. 2004, 416).

In light of this development, it is appropriate to give a final short thought to the relevance of Marcet and Martineau's legacy for our times. In writing about the economic discourse of the early nineteenth century, Josephine McDonagh attests that "the conventions of political economy [were] such that there [were] limited ways in which women themselves [could] talk about it" (McDonagh 1996, 14). The examples discussed here indicate that notwithstanding such limitations, women *did* find ways to contribute to the economic discourse of their times. They developed particular strategies and embraced specific textual genres which allowed them not only to adapt to but also to circumvent the presumed opposition between the female sex and economy. It is now tempting to ask: How has this debate developed and changed in today's public and academic circuit?

That the exclusion of women from scholarly debates on economy has lasted for more than a century is made apparent by the example of Elinor Ostrom, in the introductory part of this article. Her case is symbolic in that, as regards economic discourse, gender and issues of authority are even today palpably and problematically entwined: Out of by now more than seventy laureates, Ostrom is the only woman to have received the Nobel Prize for Economic Sciences awarded since 1969. The blatant disproportion was unsurprisingly registered on the occasion of Ostrom's nomination. Immediately after the Nobel Prize Foundation announced its decision, the economist was interviewed by its representative and asked: "Do you think that the ratio of Laureates in Economic Sciences – the gender ratio – is it in any way representative of the ratio of people working in the subject now or has it really changed?" To which Ostrom replied: "It's slowly changed. I've attended economic sessions where I've been the only woman in the room, but that is slowly changing and I think there's a greater respect now that women can make a major contribution" (Qtd. in "Elinor Ostrom – Interview" 2013).

In a peculiar twist of fate – which in a literary text would amount to poetic justice – the man who interviewed Ostrom on behalf of the Nobel Prize Foundation and congratulated her on her success had a more than fitting name: Adam Smith. The namesake of the founding father of political economy thus paid tribute to a female economist. One would assume that Marcet and Martineau, the 'Eve Smiths' of their times, would have been proud of their latter-day colleague. Yet Ostrom's singular success remains precisely that: singular. Given the overbearing influence of economic doctrines on most aspects of our daily existence, the under-representation and undervaluation of women producing knowledge in that field certainly gives pause.

References
Primary Sources

Anon. (August 1832): "Miss Martineau's Illustrations of Political Economy", *Tait's Edinburgh Magazine*, in: Martineau 2004, 416-418
Marcet, Jane (2009): *Conversations on the Nature of Political Economy [1816]*. Ed. Evelyn L. Forget. New Brunswick: Transaction
Martineau, Harriet (1834a): "Preface". *Illustrations of Political Economy*. Volume 1. London: Fox, ix-xviii
--- (1834b): "The Moral of Many Fables". *Illustrations of Political Economy*. Volume 9. London: Fox, 1-144
--- (1983): *Harriet Martineau's Autobiography [1877]*. Volume 1. London: Virago
--- (2004): *Illustrations of Political Economy: Selected Tales*. Ed. Deborah Anna Logan. Peterborough: Broadview
Wollstonecraft, Mary (2004): *A Vindication of the Rights of Woman* [1792]. Ed. Miriam Brody. Oxford: Penguin

Secondary Sources

Bodkin, Ronald G. (1999): "The Issue of Female Agency in Classical Economic Thought: Jane Marcet, Harriet Martineau, and the Men", *Gender Issues* 17.4, 62-73
Brody, Miriam (2004): "Introduction". *A Vindication of the Rights of Woman*. 1792. By Mary Wollstonecraft. Ed. Miriam Brody. London: Penguin, ix-lxxviii

Cicarelli, James; Cicarelli, Julianne (2003): *Distinguished Women Economists*. Westport, CT: Greenwood Press
Cooper, Brian P. (2007): *Family Fictions and Family Facts: Harriet Martineau, Adolphe Quetelet, and the Population Question in England, 1798-1859*. London: Routledge
Dalley, Lana L. (2010): "Domesticating Political Economy: Language, Gender and Economics in the Illustrations of Political Economy", in: Dzelzainis, Ella; Kaplan, Cora (eds.): *Harriet Martineau: Authorship, Society and Empire*. Manchester: Manchester University Press, 103-117
"Elinor Ostrom – Biographical". *Nobelprize.org*. Nobel Media AB 2013. Web. <http://www.nobelprize.org/nobel_prizes/economic-sciences/laureates/2009/ostrom-bio.html> [accessed 23 October 2013]
"Elinor Ostrom – Interview". *Nobelprize.org*. Nobel Media AB 2013. Web. <http://www.nobelprize.org/nobel_prizes/economic-sciences/laureates/2009/ostrom-telephone.html> [accessed 23 October 2013]
Forget, Evelyn L. (2009): "Introduction to the Transaction Edition", in: Forget, Evelyn L. (ed.): *Conversations on the Nature of Political Economy*. New Brunswick: Transaction, vii-xxxvi
Hollis, Hilda (2002): "The Rhetoric of Jane Marcet's Popularizing Political Economy", *Nineteenth-Century Contexts*, 24.4, 379-396
Jay, Elizabeth; Jay, Richard (1986). "Introductory Essay", in: Jay, Elizabeth; Jay, Richard (eds.): *Critics of Capitalism: Victorian Reactions to 'Political Economy'*. Cambridge: Cambridge University Press, 1-26
Kelley, Theresa M. (2012): "Science", in: Faflak, Joel; Wright, Julia M. (eds.): *A Handbook of Romanticism Studies*. Malden, MA: Blackwell, 357-373
Marshall, Alfred (1920): *Principles of Economics: An Introductory Volume*. 1890. Volume 1. London: MacMillan
McDonagh, Josephine (1996): "Infanticidal Mothers and Dead Babies: Women's Voices on Political Economy and Population", *BELLS: Barcelona English Language and Literature Studies* 7, 11-20
Otteson, James R. (2004): "Introduction", in: *Selected Philosophical Writings*. By Adam Smith. Exeter: Imprint Academic, 1-10
Polkinghorn, Bette (1993): *Jane Marcet: An Uncommon Woman*. Aldermaston: Forestwood
--- (1995): "Jane Marcet and Harriet Martineau: Motive, Market Experience and Reception of Their Works Popularizing Classical Political Economy", in: Dimand, Mary Ann et al. (eds.): *Women of Value: Feminist Essays on the History of Women in Economics*. Aldershot: Edward Elgar, 71-81
Seiz, Janet (1993): "Feminism and the History of Economic Thought", *History of Political Economy* 25.1, 185-201
Showalter, Elaine (1981): "Feminist Criticism in the Wilderness", *Critical Inquiry* 8.2, 179-205
Webb, R. K. (1960): *Harriet Martineau: A Radical Victorian*. London: Heinemann

STEFANI BRUSBERG-KIERMEIER (HILDESHEIM)

Half Man, Half Machine: Wilkie Collins's and Charles Reade's Constructions of Victorian Machine Men

This article discusses how novelists like Wilkie Collins and Charles Reade engage with science by constructing male characters whose approach to life and access to society are defined by machines. Mechanical knowledge or mechanical approaches to culture are clearly gendered as male in the novels of these authors. I will argue that their respective constructions of weak or eccentric male characters contribute to a negotiation of notions of masculinity and might even indicate a crisis of masculinity. Although the function of machines and mechanical appliances is primarily presented as a utilitarian one, the moral and aesthetical implications are in fact complex, since the machines are at times assigned 'hellish' qualities or make a character appear grotesque.

The invention of new machines and their impact on the industrial development of the nineteenth century are experienced as twofold: as both a deterioration *and* an improvement of living conditions, for many. Lower-class poverty and health problems resulting from hard working conditions are contrasted with middle-class comforts of railway travel and the use of new mass media. Those who believe in industrial progress can regard machines as potential aids to overcoming a personal lack, either in terms of social standing and financial means or in terms of physical deficiency.

The influence of the Gothic can be discerned in the labyrinthine settings that many Victorian novelists favour to a greater or lesser extent in their texts. The labyrinth is no longer located in the cellar of a castle or monastery, but forms part of everyday life in an industrialized town, and the individual has to find her or his orientation in this alienated space. The industrialist's dream is not the creation of a beautiful human creature with the help of body parts, as Dr. Victor Frankenstein planned, but the invention of machines that ease human life. The Victorian age saw the intersection of the lives of many men and women with machines due to the consequences of industrialization.

1. The Victorian Idea of Human Automata

Not only do machines and factories influence the lives of their owners and workers, but Victorian men also perceive each other more and more in mechanistic terms: as machines that must fulfil the commands of an industrialized society. Reformers fear that man might no longer be seen as a divine creation but rather as an unsatisfactory component of the labour force. The mechanization of working life also influenced scholarly research, especially in the field of biology. The re-positioning of man in a secularized world brought about new approaches, for instance in brain research. Victorian biologist and educationalist Thomas Henry Huxley was particularly interested in the relations between the brain and consciousness. In his 1874 essay "On the Hypothesis that Animals Are Automata", Huxley develops his argument on different levels of consciousness in connection to different levels of animalistic existence. He argues:

> But though we may see reason to disagree with Descartes' hypothesis that brutes are unconscious machines, it does not follow that he was wrong in regarding them as automata. They may be more or less conscious, sensitive, automata; [...].
>
> It seems to me that in men, as in brutes, there is no proof that any state of consciousness is the cause of change in the motion of the matter of the organism. If these positions are well based, it follows that our mental conditions are simply the symbols in consciousness of the changes which take place automatically in the organism; [...]. We are conscious automata, endowed with free will in the only intelligible sense of that much abused term – inasmuch as in many respects we are able to do as we like [...]. (Huxley 1971, 128)

This idea that humans work like automata in various ways influenced many Victorian writers. We find, for instance, humorous mechanical bodies in Edward Lear's limericks. In Lear's limerick no. 121, there is an old man "who said Tick-a-Tick, Tick-a-Tick; / Chickabee, Chickabaw, / And he said nothing more" (Lear 1988, 125). As he is moreover described as "laconic", Lear seems to imply that for a machine man it suffices to make machine noises.

A sinister version of the mechanics of the body can be found in Charles Dickens's *Martin Chuzzlewit*, when the brother of the old Martin Chuzzlewit, Anthony Chuzzlewit, dies while Mr. Pecksniff is visiting his son Jonas Chuzzlewit. They are in the same room together, when Mr. Pecksniff suddenly says to Jonas: "A strange noise that, Mr. Jonas!", and Jonas replies: "Something wrong in the clock, I suppose [...]." When the sound repeats itself, Pecksniff remarks:

> "Upon my word, Mr. Jonas, that is a very extraordinary clock," [...].
>
> It would have been, if it had made the noise which startled them: but another kind of time-piece was fast running down, and from that the sound proceeded. [...] they saw Anthony Chuzzlewit extended on the floor, with the old clerk upon his knees beside him.
>
> He had fallen from his chair in a fit, and there, battling for each gasp of breath, with every shrivelled vein and sinew starting in its place, as it were bent on bearing witness to his age, and sternly pleading with Nature against his recovery. It was frightful to see how the principle of life, shut up within his withered frame, fought like strong devil, mad to be released, and rent its ancient prison-house. (Dickens 1998, 262-263)

Dickens invents a death for Anthony Chuzzlewit that sounds as if a clock comes to a standstill to show, on a metaphorical level, that 'the sands of time have run out for him'. At the same time this kind of "hideous spectacle" and mechanical death can be seen as a comment on the character's understanding of the individual as 'a cog in the works' of capitalist society. Because Anthony Chuzzlewit is such a superficial, greedy character, only his old clerk Mr. Chuffey mourns his death. Since Mr. Chuffey has no family of his own, he is also the only one who feels any sympathy for his master while the latter is still alive: "But this man's enthusiasm had the redeeming quality of being felt in sympathy with the only creature to whom he was linked by ties of long association, and by his present helplessness" (*ibid.*, 158). Earlier in the novel, a tipsy Mr. Pecksniff earnestly applies the understanding of the human body as a machine to the "wonderful works" of digestion:

> "The process of digestion, as I have been informed by anatomical friends, is one of the most wonderful works of nature. I do not know how it may be with others, but it is a great satisfaction to me to know, when regaling on my humble fare, that I am putting in motion the most beautiful machinery with which we have any acquaintance. I really feel at such times as if I was doing a public service. When I have wound myself up, if I may use such a term," said Mr. Peck-

sniff with exquisite tenderness, "and know I am Going, I feel that in the lesson afforded by the works within me, I am a Benefactor to my Kind!" (ibid 1998, 108)

The famous words of Shakespeare's Hamlet – "What piece of work is a man / how noble in reason, how infinite in faculties, in form / and moving how express and admirable [...]" (*Hamlet*, II.ii, 303-305) – are taken to new sarcastic heights in such Victorian texts. Dickens foregrounds the mechanical aspects of human automata, but does not investigate the implications on the characters' consciousness as such, though he raises questions about their sanity.

2. 'Gender Mechanics': Victorian Machine Men and Women

Masculinity and femininity in Victorian fiction are often depicted with the help of parallels that are drawn between human and animal nature and that are negotiated accordingly in terms of ethics and aesthetics. For the construction of Victorian femininity or masculinity other contexts are also crucial, especially the interrelations between human beings and machines. I would suggest that the representation of gender and mechanical occupations is highly unbalanced. On the one hand, we find, in literature, only few female but a great variety of male workers who are closely connected to the machines they have to operate and whose health might be endangered by this work. On the other hand, all factory owners whom I have come across in literary texts are male. They could choose to live in relative distance to the works and to imitate the life-style of the aristocracy.

One of the few texts from the period which presents female workers operating heavy machinery is Herman Melville's short story "The Paradise of Bachelors and the Tartarus of Maids", first published in 1855. In the story the narrator requires a huge number of paper envelopes for professional reasons and travels to a paper-mill to inspect them. He describes his approach to the paper-mill, which is located in an inhospitable remote mountain area:

> Suddenly a whirling, humming sound broke upon my ear. I looked, and there, like an arrested avalanche, lay the large white-washed factory. It was subordinately surrounded by a cluster of other and smaller buildings, some of which, from their cheap, blank air, great length, gregarious windows, and comfortless expression, no doubt were boarding-houses of the operatives. A snow-white hamlet amidst the snows. (Melville 1998, 85)

The paper-mill is called the Devil's Dungeon paper-mill and only employs girls – "maidens" – who have to feed "the iron animal" (Melville 1998, 85). The machinery is represented in organomorphic terms, while the girls are being described with the help of expressions which derive from paper and its characteristics: "At rows of blank-looking counters sat rows of blank-looking girls, with blank, white folders in their blank hands, all blankly folding blank paper" (Melville 1998, 88). Through the work at the paper-mill the girls' faces become "ruled and wrinkled" (*ibid.*).

Melville's short story has been analysed by, among others, Konstanze Kutzbach (2007), who reads it as "Melville's pessimistic vision of society's decline" (Kutzbach 2007, 183). Kutzbach argues that "the girls' insignificance and meaninglessness culminates eventually in their final absorption and annihilation through the machines themselves" (2007, 185). This becomes obvious especially in the narrator's comments on the relation between the girls and the machines: "The girls did not so much seem accessory wheels to the general machinery as mere cogs to the wheels" (Melville 1998,

88). This again can be read as an expression of the anxiety that the individual might end up as 'a cog in the works' of capitalist society.

As Robert Milder explains in the introduction to the Oxford World's Classics edition, Melville's paper-mill found models in countless New England factories (Milder 1998, xvi). They employed farm girls whom they supervised with "a paternalistic attention to their moral and religious health" (xvii). As Milder argues, Melville illustrates how machinery has become humanity's enslaver: "female victims [are] sacrificed on the male altar of capitalist productivity" (*ibid.*).

3. Charles Reade's 'Adaptable Man'

Like Melville, many authors of industrial tales combine novelistic with humanitarian purposes and write with the wish to make labour unrest less unsettling and more understandable for the reader (see Adams 2005, 60). Elizabeth Gaskell's *Mary Barton* (1848) and other social problem novels often depict the industrial worker, especially the unemployed one, as sufferer and the entrepreneur as a self-made man whose humble origin enables him to understand and ease the workers' hard fate. Both Charlotte Brontë's Robert Moore in *Shirley* and Charles Reade's Henry Little in *Put Yourself in His Place* are men of humble social origin who rise to power as self-made men. But while Moore, a character from the late 1840s, asserts the equality of men, Little, a character of the early 1870s, stands for the rights of the new manufacturers to rule their labour force. The Brontë sisters famously combine both views in their novels and present contradicting ideas: equality and democracy alongside authority and obedience (see Gordon 1989, 66). For instance, in *Agnes Grey*, Anne Brontë has Agnes's mother say: "there are bad and good in all classes" (Brontë 1988, 112). Despite the industrial novel's sympathy for the working classes the genre still gives prominence to middle-class life, just as the Victorian novel on the whole shows a tendency towards the representation of more affluent modes of life (see Adams 2005, 52).

Charlotte Brontë's *Shirley* and Charles Reade's *Put Yourself in His Place* display aspects of the ugliness of the new industrial culture. But while *Shirley*, published in 1849, focuses on the consequences of industrialization for human relationships, *Put Yourself in His Place*, published in 1870, is interested more in the interrelations between man and machine. As Eckart Voigts-Virchow has argued, Reade uses "personified ugliness" for his presentation of industrial towns and hardware works (Voigts-Virchow 2002, 154). Harking back to descriptions of industrialized towns in Benjamin Disraeli's *Sybil* (1845) or Charles Dickens's *Hard Times* (1854), Reade introduces his town as a human hell (Reade 1896, 1).

For his description of Hillsborough Reade employs a special technique of 'class-ification', i.e., he contrasts rural beauty and nature, which can in effect be regarded as upper-class, with industrialization, the effects of which are closely connected with the lower classes. The importance of environmental influences on temporary or permanent physiognomical changes is a recurring theme in nineteenth-century fiction. Here, one of "the loveliest sites in England" has become an industrial town which is "pockmarked" and belches forth black smoke, like a worker who smokes and is marked by illness (Reade 1896, 1). Reade takes up this technique again when he introduces his protagonist as a gentleman-worker and contrasts him with a 'low type' of a worker.

Like the whole town Hillsborough, its factories are described with the help of metaphors of the human body and physical illness that verge on the monstrous. For instance, the "hardware work" that houses the grindstones looks "like a gigantic polypus with its limbs extended lazily, and its fingers holding semicircular claws" (Reade 1896, 104). Interestingly, Reade mixes metaphors, i.e., he transfers images of the human body and animals onto the factories and in turn uses similes peculiar to industrial work for the description of his characters. Such a mixture of organomorphic and mechanomorphic imagery can already be found in René Descartes's writing, which juxtaposes the human mind and spirituality with the mathematical laws of mechanics and optics.

What is important for my argument is that metaphors typical of the grotesque, which usually amalgamate human and bestial features, are here enlarged so as to encompass machines. On the one hand, in Reade's description the hideousness of the works becomes personified ugliness: "In these hardware works the windows seldom or never open: air is procured in all the rooms by the primitive method of breaking a pane here and a pane there; and the general effect is as unsightly as a human mouth where teeth and holes alternate" (Reade 1896, 50). On the other hand, Reade introduces the journalist Mr. Holdfast, who carries a whole journal "on [his] head", and also characterises him with a description of his mouth: "an agreeable face, with one remarkable feature, a mouth full of iron resolution" (74). Thus Reade expands the scope of metaphors in the industrial novel with a combination of organomorphic and mechanomorphic imagery and establishes a grotesque aesthetics that is clearly influenced by the writings of Herbert Spencer.

A good example of Reade's tendency towards a post-Darwinian grotesque is Billy, 'the Anomaly'. The doctor of entrepreneur Henry Little, Dr. Amboyne, first helps him to recover from a horrible accident that he meets with in the works as a result of the workers' abuse of gunpowder. Later he introduces Little to a young man, who is to help Little when he inspects the working conditions in the hardware works. This young man is generally taken for an idiot and called 'Silly Billy' by the townspeople, but the doctor realizes that Billy has a special kind of intelligence that might help Little. Dr. Amboyne therefore calls Billy 'the Anomaly', an expression that is later taken up by the narrator as well. The doctor and Henry are presented as members of the middle-class, who claim for themselves the privilege of classifying members of the lower-class according to their typologies of deviance. Billy is one of many examples of lower-class characters in industrial novels who illustrate that the poor are rarely objects of close acquaintance and remain a class apart in Victorian fiction (see Adams 2005, 60). The reader first encounters Billy through Henry's eyes:

> On Little's entrance the pupil retired from his uphill work, and glowered with vacillating eyes. The lad had a fair feminine face, with three ill things in it: a want, a wildness, and a weakness. To be sure Henry saw it at a disadvantage: for vivid intelligence would come now and then across the mild, wild, vacant face. Like the breeze that sweeps a farmyard pond. (Reade 1896, 96)

"Mild" and "wild", with a "vacant face" and "vivid intelligence" at the same time, Billy becomes 'the noble savage' of the narrative, who helps Little to inspect the works and the workers' health. His strange kind of intelligence turns out to be an instinct that enables 'the Anomaly' to sense that a defective grindstone needs repair. I would suggest that Henry Little not only refers to middle-class typologies of deviance but is moreover disturbed by Darwin's concept of natural selection and Herbert Spencer's vision of the survival of the fittest. By adopting the doctor's name, 'the Anomaly', for Billy, Little 'others' and distances himself from Billy. At the same time he uses it to cover up his fear that what he sees as "a want" in Billy might actually be a want that he suffers from himself, a lack of instinct and understanding. Little wishes to distance himself from Billy in terms of class, as he is afraid of appearing shabby or vulgar himself, as well as in terms of Spencer's 'fitness'.

The part of the novel in which Little meets Billy is also interesting insofar as it can be understood as criticism of the working conditions in the hardware factories. Reade makes clear that the grinders in particular suffer under extreme health risks:

> They were also subject to a canker of the hands, and to colds, coughs, and inflammations, from perspiration checked by cold draughts and drenched floors. These floors were often mud, and so the wet stagnated and chilled their feet, while their bodies were very hot. Excellent recipe for filling graves. (Reade 1896, 101)

This description compares well with Melville's of the paper-mill, also with regard to the authors' preference for alliteration: While Melville describes "blank paper, blank girls, wrinkled brows", Reade confronts us with "canker, colds, and coughs". Yet whereas in Melville's imagery the colour white and dryness are predominant, Reade sketches a picture of darkness and wetness.

Little represents an interesting mixture of upper-class sensitivity, lower-class honesty and manual skill, and middle-class work-ethics and capitalism (see Voigts-Virchow 2002, 157). As Reade shows, Little's mixed descent finds expression in a special combination of views and abilities that turns out to be a fortunate one for a man at that time and place. By presenting Little as a kind of worker-artist Reade links aestheticism with morality and both transgresses and reinstates class stereotypes at the same time. Henry Little is a feminized and genteel workman who brings together the virtues of human warmth and craftsmanship that are constructed as lower-class with an artistic talent that is constructed as feminine and aristocratic. His mixed ancestry is accordingly detectable from his body.

What becomes clear here is that the new ideal of the self-made man poses an enormous challenge to traditional norms of inherited rank and also upsets people's ability to 'read' and 'interpret' strangers. Samuel Smiles's best-selling *Self-Help* (1859) is the most famous exponent of a whole new range of conduct books, which "celebrated the possibilities for social advancement and self-determination that awaited those with sufficient talent, initiative, and self-discipline" (Adams 2005, 57). Reade's Henry Little can be regarded as the apotheosis of this bourgeois ethos, as a character who combines these middle-class virtues with the fantasy of perfect autonomy.

Reade contrasts Henry Little, the worker turned entrepreneur, with the workers in the hardware works. There is one man in particular who is presented as a worker turned animal and who Reade therefore calls "the greyhound-man" (Reade 1896, 43):

> a workman who had heard the raised voices, and divined the row, ran out of the works, with his apron full of blades, and his heart full of mischief. It was a grinder of a certain low type, peculiar to Hillsborough, but quite common there, where grinders are often the grandchildren of grinders. This degenerate face was more canine than human; sharp as a hatchet, and with fore-

head villainously low; hardly a chin; and – most characteristic trait of all – the eyes, pale in colour, and tiny in size, appeared to have come close together, to consult, and then to have run back into the very skull, to get away from the sparks, which their owner, and his sire, and his grandsire, had been eternally creating. (Reade 1896, 42)

This example makes clear how Spencer's interpretation of Darwin's *On the Origin of Species* has changed the use of physiognomic and phrenological ideas in the industrial novel. The "greyhound-man" is the product of adaptation of several generations to their working conditions. This adaptation is necessary for survival and forms part of the process of selection (see Richardson 2005, 212). As Angelique Richardson explains, under the influence of Darwin's writing Spencer coined the phrase "the survival of the fittest", "perhaps the most frequently evoked of nineteenth-century phrases" (Richardson 2005, 203).

4. Wilkie Collins's 'Perfectible Man'

From the 1870s onwards, England increasingly feared the competition of continental industries and experienced economic stagnation. Interestingly enough, from around that time nature is often presented as potentially a 'nature that errs' and that therefore must be corrected by man. Novels of these decades represent an ideological shift from 'goodness' to 'fitness'. When Victorian novels allude to what should happen to the 'unfit', the other, the 'anomalies' of society, the reader is confronted with the presentation of sublimation: Sublimation develops from 'the faith in the perfectibility of humankind' into 'the need for the perfectibility of humankind'. This leads, on the one hand, to the development of a criminal anthropology which may result in racism or euthanasia. Cesare Lombroso's notion of atavism, his cause-and-effect connection of biology with criminality, had a strong impact on anthropological thinking for a long time (Becker 1996, 185-186). On the other hand, belief in the perfectibility of man is combined with technical inventions, in which case machines are regarded as making it possible to overcome a personal lack and to compensate for the 'unfitness' of a physically deficient body.

In 1875, Wilkie Collins presents a more extreme mixture of organomorphic and mechanomorphic imagery, but also a more humane and tolerant discussion of social Darwinism, because he does so under the viewpoint of eccentricity. His novel *The Law and the Lady* is especially interesting regarding the enrichment of characterization with the help of mechanical appliances. While Reade describes his deficient figures as industrialized, abnormal, bestial or, in a post-Darwinian way, grotesque on the level of metaphor, Collins combines all these aspects on the level of actual character construction. With his Miserrimus Dexter, Collins created, as Jenny Bourne Taylor describes his invention, "his most bizarre and contradictory image of insanity" (Taylor 1988, 221).

The oddity of Miserrimus Dexter starts with his name. As the reader learns through the report of Eustace Woodville's trial, when Dexter appeared as a witness during the trial the calling of his name produced "a burst of laughter from the public seats" (Collins 1999b, 172) – to which he reacted with the remark: "People generally laugh when they first hear my strange Christian name" (173). Thus the name takes over the function of comic relief for the other characters even before Dexter appears, but increases the readers' suspense and shock when they finally 'set eyes' on the handicapped man in a wheelchair. In his other novels, Collins uses contradictions within the body itself or between the body and its clothing for his 'fashioning' of gender. In *The Law and the Lady* his portrayal of contradictions within the body includes the mechanical. Dexter is half man, half chair, "the trunk of a living human being: absolutely deprived of the lower limbs" (173). The lower stratum of his body – the part which would actually prove his manliness – is replaced by a mechanical appliance. The implications of Dexter's handicaps are made explicit in reference to his restricted mobility, but are only alluded to with regard to his sexual impotence. Nature in *The Law and the Lady* is far removed from a nature that cannot err, it is a nature that mixes all kinds of characteristics in a human being and makes the mistake of mixing features that cannot easily be brought into harmony with each other:

> To make this deformity all the more striking and all the more terrible, the victim of it was – as to his face and his body – an unusually handsome, and an unusually well-made man. [...] Never had Nature committed a more careless or a more cruel mistake than in the making of this man! (Collins 1999b, 173)

But Dexter is not only a strange composite of 'man' and mechanical appliance. As in his presentation of Frederick Fairlie in *The Woman in White*, Collins tries to overcome traditional gender boundaries with his description of Dexter. I would argue that Dexter is the most grotesque of Collins's characters, because he is a combination of contradictory ideas and therefore transgressive in many respects, morally as well as aesthetically. He is supposed to reconcile discourses on self-control and madness, on aesthetics and deviance, on truth and criminality. For his *blazon* description of Dexter's body Collins mixes traditionally male and female aspects:

> His long silky hair, of a bright and beautiful chestnut colour, fell over shoulders that were the perfection of strength and grace. His face was bright with vivacity and intelligence. His large, clear blue eyes, and his long, delicate white hands, were like the eyes and hands of a beautiful woman. He would have looked effeminate, but for the manly proportions of his throat and chest: aided in their effect by his flowing beard and long moustache [...] (Collins 1999b, 173)

As in the figure of Marian Halcombe, in Miserrimus Dexter strange composite physical features and astonishing mental qualities are presented as analogues. Major Fitz-David says about Dexter: "The man's mind is as deformed as his body. [...] He is a mixture of the tiger and the monkey. At one moment, he would frighten you; at the next, he would set you screaming with laughter" (Collins 1999b, 191). What we find here is the fascinating concept of a mixed and fractured body with a mixed gender, which in consequence produces a mixed and fractured identity.

Dexter's fractured identity is especially clear in his approach to humour and performance. When we first encounter this weird character through the eyes of Valeria in the chapter "Miserrimus Dexter – First View", he is in a state of mania, moves around quickly in his wheelchair, and impersonates Napoleon, Nelson, Shakespeare, and King Lear. While Valeria coolly uses her masquerade for a special purpose, Dexter enjoys playing with his identity for the sake of playing and can be described as a kind of 'theatrical dandy'. With the help of these performances Collins assigns Dexter a special quality of changeableness and attractive fascination. As Taylor explains, the name "Dexter" is Latin for 'right', suggests deftness and mental agility, and can also be understood as a pun on 'writer' (Taylor 1988, 424, n. 174) – and on 'playwright', I would add. Dexter's processes of transformation have the quality of an "extraordinary delicacy and dexterity", and they therefore produce a special admiration and sympathy on Valeria's side. When she sees him again shortly afterwards, Valeria notes: "but I could see nothing mad in him, nothing in any way repelling, as he now looked at me" (Collins 1999b, 213). The reader is invited to look at Dexter through Valeria's eyes and to follow her statement and feelings of empathy.

Dexter's progression from madness to sanity and back from sanity to madness is also expressed in his muddling up of sense and nonsense. Valeria's mother-in-law remarks on Dexter: "You would have been either very much disgusted with him, or very much amused by him [...]. He mixed up sense and nonsense in the strangest confusion" (Collins 1999b, 199). Collins repeatedly emphasizes Dexter's 'impish' quality, which becomes most grotesque when he plays "leapfrog" and hops down the room on his hands (259). For the creation of Dexter's game of "leapfrog" Collins might have been inspired by a real-life model. Harvey Leech, a North American acrobat, had very short legs and impersonated all kinds of strange creatures in London freak shows in the 1840s. In one show he appeared in a cage in hairy dress as a "Baboon Man" or "Ourang Outang Man", in another as an enormous bluebottle fly (see Altick 1978, 265-266). For Dexter, Collins seems to have adapted Leech's ability to "waddle along" with his hands touching the ground "in the manner of higher primates" (Altick ibid, 266).

Dexter's mixed approach to humour consists of a wide variety of performances and amusements. Collins's reference to William Shakespeare is illuminating here, since, like Falstaff, Dexter could boast that "[he is] not only witty in [him]self, but the cause of that wit is in other men" (*Henry IV, Part 2*, I.ii, 8-9). Dexter himself repeatedly laughs about Valeria's "exhibitions of human folly" (Collins 1999b, 237-238), just as she laughs about him. At one point in the narrative Dexter embarrasses Valeria by asking her to pity him. Although she generally does pity him, she cannot produce the feeling at request, cannot 'perform' it. When he asks her to express her pity by patting his hand she bursts out laughing (233). Dexter is obviously not hurt by her reaction, but amused: "'Do it again,' he said [...]'. Merry Mrs Valeria, *you* have a musical laugh—*I* have a musical ear. Do it again'"(233). Here he reminds one of Count Fosco in *The Woman in White*, whose excessive sentimentalism has a strong ridiculous quality as well: "At the ripe age of sixty, I make this unparalleled confession. Youths! I invoke your sympathy. Maidens! I claim your tears" (Collins 1999a, 612).

With the invention of Dexter's mixed and fractured identity Collins also raises questions about the possibility of authentic emotions and expressions. When a body is a mixture of elements that cannot be brought into harmony and when an identity is constituted by performances, Collins seems to imply, feelings and mind become fractured, too. As long as Dexter can control himself, his humour and performances can still go by the name of 'eccentricity'. Whenever he addresses Valeria, she asks herself: "What new piece of eccentricity was he about to exhibit?" (Collins 1999b, 233). This question harks back to the famous passage in Shakespeare's *Hamlet*, which starts "What piece of work is a man" and which was already mentioned above (*Hamlet*, II.ii, 303). While Collins negotiates such an understanding of man with all his character constructions, the eccentricity of Dexter is certainly his most extreme variation of this humanist ideal.

When witnesses for the defence are required, Valeria is not sure whether to include Dexter among them, because of his "eccentricity" (Collins 1999b, 281). Therefore she asks a doctor to examine him. The doctor prophecies that Dexter will lose the control of his will and "end in madness" sooner or later (281). On the doctor's written statement Jenny Taylor comments: "The doctor's report hovers, as the figure of Dexter does, on the boundary between self-control and degeneration, finally collapsing into the latter" (Taylor 1988, 226). In Chapter XL, the reader witnesses Dexter's sudden transgression from sanity to madness, which Collins presents as a quick change from excessive laughter to crying: "'Why don't you laugh? Funny, funny, funny, funny. Aha-ha-ha-ha-ha— —' He fell back in the chair. The shrill and dreadful laugh died away into a low sob" (Collins 1999b, 346). Interestingly, Dexter's journey from sanity to madness is reminiscent of the development that the illness of William Makepeace Thackeray's wife Isabella took. After having tried out all kinds of treatment in England, France, and Germany, Thackeray placed her in private care in Camberwell in 1845 and visited her less and less after 1847. In one of his letters he refers to her apathetic behaviour and remarks that she does not care "2^d for anything but for her dinner and her glass of porter" (in a letter to Mrs. Brookfield, 14 Oct. 1858, quoted from Small 1996, 180). Collins constructs a similar image of imbecility when he writes about Dexter: "He showed an animal interest in his meals, and a greedy animal enjoyment of eating and drinking as much as he could get – and that was all" (Collins 1999b, 350).

Valeria's endeavours as a detective finally bring forward proof that Eustace's first wife, Sara Macallan, committed suicide: Sara's farewell letter to Eustace is found in a dustheap. The letter states that she was driven to suicide by her husband's evident distaste of her, which he also made clear in his notorious diary. It also comes out that Dexter knew about the suicide and the reasons for it, but refused to reveal them out of malice towards Eustace and because he had always admired Sara and wished to marry her himself. Throughout the whole plot, Valeria oscillates between her resolute self-determination, which even leads her to subversive scheming, and her self-fashioning as the ideal, honourable Victorian wife. But although she presents her function as a detective as that of 'Nemesis' to recover Eustace's honour, for the reader the verdict remains 'not proven', since Eustace obviously drove his first wife to her suicide with his sexual abhorrence for her. As Taylor has noted, Sara Macallan is a disturbing character because she – like Rosanna Spearman in *The Moonstone* – represents passionate female sexuality that is not itself the object of male desire (Taylor 1999, xxii).

The ending of the novel neither achieves nor aims at a complete containment of the subversive tendencies of the text. Valeria's constant self-fashioning is much too close to one of Dexter's performances, and Eustace is much too weak and dubious a husband to restore patriarchal order and a clear gender divide. Like *The Woman in White* and *Armadale*, *The Law and the Lady* negotiates the definition of gender and gender roles and achieves a balance between the social and the sexual drives of the characters at the end of the novel, but only on the surface of the narrative. Dexter finally becomes insane, so his fate is tragic, and the perfectibility of human beings through the help of medical knowledge or machines remains questionable. Collins's novel can partly be read as a treatise in favour of eccentricity and against the standardization of human beings. Like John Stuart Mill in his essay *On Liberty*, Collins seems to argue for adapting norms to human beings instead of adapting human beings to norms. Published in the same year as Darwin's *On the Origin of Species*, Mill's essay offers an alternative reading of the obligations of a normative ruling class in terms of progress as well as in terms of ideology: "Human nature is not a machine to be built after a model, and set to do exactly the work prescribed for it, but a tree, which requires to grow and develop itself on all sides, according to the tendency of the inward forces which make it a living thing" (Mill 1924, 57). Moreover, the idea of fixed gender roles and especially the authority of the husband have been reduced to absurdity. Eustace's sexual abhorrence of his first wife and his inability to disguise it mark a crisis of male self-control and gentlemanly self-fashioning.

My literary examples illustrate the complex dynamics between 'life', 'mind', and 'culture' vividly, because their machines not only play a practical or financial role in the characters' lives, but moreover control their states of mind. Consequently, the characters' approaches to and conceptions of any form of culture are likewise established in accordance with their conviction that a life without their machines is not conceivable, worth living, or even possible at all. The consequences for the 'subject' are substantial and far-reaching, and of alarming topicality as well.

While Darwin's and Spencer's theories made obvious that nature might err – that creations might be 'imperfect' and even 'grotesque' – culture may make up for nature's deficiencies with the help of man-made inventions. 'Imperfect' man may be 'perfected' in particular with new technologies or appliances that transform the idea of a 'natural evolution' into a 'cultural evolution'. Accordingly, concepts of what is 'natural' or 'normal' on the one hand and of what is 'beautiful' or 'good' on the other hand are being renegotiated by Collins and Reade and as a result the whole understanding of what is human and in what shape or moulding life should be allowed to exist.

References

Primary Sources

Brontë, Anne (1847/1988): *Agnes Grey*. London: Penguin
Collins, Wilkie (1860/1999a): *The Woman in White*. London: Penguin
--- (1875/1999b): *The Law and the Lady*. Oxford University Press
Dickens, Charles (1843-1844/1998): *Martin Chuzzlewit*. Oxford University Press
Huxley, Thomas Henry (1874/1971): "On the Hypothesis that Animals Are Automata", in: *T.H. Huxley on Education*. Ed. Cyril Bibby. Cambridge University Press, 126-129
Lear, Edward (1988). *Sämtliche Limericks*. Englisch/Deutsch. Stuttgart: Reclam
Melville, Herman (1855/1998): "The Paradise of Bachelors and the Tartarus of Maids", in: Melville, Herman: *Billy Budd, Sailor and Selected Tales*. Ed. Robert Milder. Oxford University Press, 74-96
Mill, John Stuart (1859/1924): *On Liberty*. Bielefeld/Leipzig: Velhagen und Klasing
Reade, Charles (1870/1896): *Put Yourself in His Place*, London: Chatto and Windus
Shakespeare, William (1980): *Complete Works*. Ed. W. J. Craig. Oxford University Press

Secondary Sources

Adams, James Eli (2005): "'The Boundaries of Social Intercourse': Class in the Victorian Novel", in: O'Gorman, Francis (ed.): *A Concise Companion to the Victorian Novel*. Malden, MA/Oxford/Melbourne: Blackwell, 47-70
Altick, Richard D. (1978): *The Shows of London*. Cambridge, MA/London: Harvard University Press

Becker, Peter (1996): "Physionomie des *Bösen*: Cesare Lombrosos Bemühungen um eine präventive Entzifferung des Kriminellen", in: Schmölders, Claudia (ed.): *Der exzentrische Blick: Gespräch über Physiognomik*. Berlin: Akademie Verlag, 163-186

Gordon, Felicia (1989): *A Preface to the Brontës*. London/New York: Longman, 1989

Kutzbach, Konstanze (2007): "The Two-...One-...None-Sex Model: The Flesh(-)made Machine in Herman Melville's 'The Paradise of Bachelors and the Tartarus of Maids' and J.G. Ballard's *Crash*", in: Kutzbach, Konstanze; Müller, Monika (eds.): *The Abject of Desire: The Aestheticization of the Unaesthetic in Contemporary Literature and Culture*. Amsterdam: Rodopi, 181-196

Milder, Robert (1998): "Introduction", in: Melville, Herman: *Billy Budd, Sailor and Selected Tales*. Ed. Robert Milder. Oxford University Press, vii-xxxix.

Richardson, Angelique (2005): "'The difference between human beings': Biology in the Victorian Novel", in: O'Gorman, Francis (ed.): *A Concise Companion to the Victorian Novel*. Malden, MA/ Oxford/Melbourne: Blackwell, 202-231

Small, Helen (1996): *Love's Madness: Medicine, the Novel, and Female Insanity, 1800-1865*. Oxford: Clarendon

Taylor, Jenny Bourne (1988): *In the Secret Theatre of Home: Wilkie Collins, Sensation Narrative, and Nineteenth-Century Psychology*. London/New York: Routledge

--- (1999): "Introduction", in: Collins, Wilkie: *The Law and the Lady*. Oxford University Press, vii-xxiv

Voigts-Virchow, Eckart (2002): "From Greyhound Man to Iron Man: Charles Reade's *Put Yourself in His Place* and the Rhetoric of Labour in the Industrial Novel", in: Drexler, Peter (ed.): *Nice Work? Critical Perspectives on the Changing Nature of Labour, Leisure, and Unemployment in Britain*. Trier: WVT, 149-163

STEFANIE FRICKE (MÜNCHEN)

Scientific Discourses in Late Victorian Fantastic Texts

In his autobiography, H. Rider Haggard wrote about his first bestseller *King Solomon's Mines* [1885]:

> [N]o book that I have written seems to have conveyed a greater idea of reality. At this moment I hold in my hand at least a dozen letters […] anxious to know whether or not the work is a record of fact. Even the great dealer in precious stones, Mr. Streeter […] approached me on the subject. I believe he actually sent an expedition to look for King Solomon's Mines, or at any rate talked of doing so. (Haggard 1926, 242)

This seems surprising when one considers the fantastic nature of the story told in the novel, namely, how three English adventurers use a centuries old map to find Kukuanaland, a hidden, Eden-like country in the African interior, which not only contains the fabled diamond mines of King Solomon, but also an unknown tribe tyrannized by an apparently immortal witch. In spite of these fantastic elements, however, many readers obviously believed that the story could at least potentially be true.

This was due not only to a yearning for exotic adventures or the belief that anything was possible in the wilds of Africa, but also to the way in which Haggard told his story, which included the use of scientific discourse in the narration and plot of the novel. As this paper will show, this is characteristic for many late-Victorian fantastic texts. Focussing on a number of novels from the 1880s and 1890s – H. Rider Haggard's *King Solomon's Mines* [1885], *Allan Quatermain* [1887] and *She* [1887], Richard Jefferies's *After London* [1885], and H. G. Wells's *The Time Machine* [1895]), all of which describe alien surroundings and peoples, this paper will analyse how these often hugely popular texts not only used scientific elements to lend credibility to their fantastic stories, but in addition mediated new scientific theories for a wide audience. As will become apparent, they also ultimately drew attention to the problem of how to transmit knowledge over time and to some extent questioned the validity of describing alien peoples and cultures by using one's own systems of reference.

1. Constructing Africa: H. Rider Haggard

Haggard's novels belong to a subgenre of the imperial romance, the so-called Lost World-stories, in which Western explorers discover a previously unknown or forgotten civilisation in an isolated part of the planet. Accordingly, in *Allan Quatermain* the heroes of *King Solomon's Mines* return to Africa in search of the kingdom of Zu-Vendis. And in *She* the narrator Horace Holly, a Cambridge don and man of science, travels to Africa with his ward Leo Vincey to find the immortal white queen Ayesha, who lives in the ruins of the forgotten civilisation of Kôr and who had killed one of Leo's ancestors 2000 years earlier. Lost World-stories became popular in an age when most of the unknown reaches of the world had been explored and distances seemed to shrink rapidly due to modern networks of communication and travel. At the same time, however, there were also a number of spectacular archaeological discoveries, such as Troy or long-lost cities hidden in the American jungle, which captured the public's imagination and were incorporated into the new genre. Lost World-stories provided the readers with a sense of wonder in a world that was ever more thoroughly measured, explored, and explained. They did this, however, by drawing on scientific trappings and discourse, incorporating into the fantastic voyages of earlier centuries the new theories and discourses of disciplines like biology, geology, anthropology, and archaeology (see Pringle et al. 1995, 735).

Looking at Haggard's *King Solomon's Mines* and its sequel *Allan Quatermain*, this narrative strategy becomes readily apparent. Haggard goes to great pains to create authenticity, the most important element of this strategy being his use of a specific first-person narrator, the old hunter Allan Quatermain. Quatermain is an unassuming narrator, and in the introduction to *King Solomon's Mines* he excuses himself for his "blunt way of writing. I can but say in excuse of it that I am more accustomed to handle a rifle than a pen, and cannot make any pretence to the grand literary flights and flourishes which I see in novels" (Haggard 1998a, 6). It is however exactly this simple way of telling his story that stresses its proclaimed authenticity, for "I venture to hope that a true story, however strange it may be, does not require to be decked out in fine words" (*ibid.*, 6).

Quatermain has been living in Africa for decades and knows its peoples, cultures, and landscapes intimately. *King Solomon's Mines*, *Allan Quatermain*, and *She* are filled with descriptions of African flora and fauna, customs, and geography, which create Barthes's 'reality effect' (Barthes 1968). African terms are also frequently used, sometimes with a translation or explanation in parentheses (see Haggard 1995, 93, 150). References to the real African surroundings are mixed with detailed descriptions of the fantastic societies and places Haggard's heroes encounter; these fantastic sites are depicted with the same level of geographical, biological, archaeological, and anthropological detail as the African reality, and are reminiscent of reports of Victorian expeditions. Contemporary travel narratives like Joseph Thomson's bestseller *Through Masai Land* (1885) were indeed used by Haggard in the writing of his stories (see Haggard's Afterword in Haggard 1995 and Dennis Butts's Introduction in Haggard 1998a, xiv-xv), but more important were his own experiences in Africa where he lived from 1875 to 1881, working first on the staff of the Governor of Natal in South Africa and later running an ostrich farm (see Higgins 1981, 15-38, 42-52).

The supposed authenticity of Haggard's stories is further stressed by footnotes which give additional information or comment on what is told in the main body of the text. These footnotes are allegedly written by either the narrators themselves, or by editors (see Haggard 1998a, 5, 11; Haggard 1995, 22, 99; Haggard 1998b, 61, 99), which provides a scientific, sometimes critical frame to the fantastic stories (see Haggard 1998b, 5; Haggard 1998a, 11). Additional material proof of the authenticity of *She* as well as of *King Solomon's Mines* is given by pictorial depictions in the novels of ancient maps, documents, and other relics. In *King Solomon's Mines* the readers are presented with the reproduction of the map which shows the way to the fabled diamond mines; *She* includes a facsimile of the so-called Shard of Amenartas on which Greek and Latin inscriptions tell the story of Leo's ancestor, as well as further facsimiles of these inscriptions that Haggard had made by experts (see Haggard 1926, 251-252). For both the map and the shard real models were manufactured by Haggard's sister-in-law, which he put on display at his house together with his collection of Egyptian art, and of whose convincing appearance he was very proud (see Arata 1996, 99; Haggard 1926, 248).

The great success of Haggard's stories testifies to his readers' fascination not only with his exciting tales, but also with their African setting, which, due to the scramble for Africa, was gaining in public interest (see Higgins 1981, 84-85). As has often been noted, Haggard's fantastic adventure stories were an important part of late-Victorian imperial discourse on Africa[1], and the descriptions and interpretations he gave and the attitudes expressed in them – in short the knowledge produced in his novels – helped shape attitudes towards Africa, its people and British imperialism.

The imperialism expressed in Haggard's stories is, among other things, characterised by its supposed long history. A major motif in *King Solomon's Mines* and *She* is the English explorers' discovery of the material remnants of ancient cultures. Haggard himself was very interested in archaeology and especially Egyptology (see Pocock 1993, 69), and in his works the African wilderness seems to be littered with the ruins of ancient empires.[2] With the help of western knowledge and systems of classification, however, Haggard's heroes have no problems coming to terms with these discoveries. In *King Solomon's Mines*, the three English explorers, none of whom is an archaeologist, come to the conclusion that the Egyptians were the first to build in and exploit Kukuanaland, followed by King Solomon, probably together with the Phoenicians (see Haggard 1998a, 108 and "Explanatory Notes"). When Quatermain and his friends arrive at the mines, which are guarded by three large, ancient stone figures, they do not have to search long for an explanation:

> Whilst I was gazing and wondering, it suddenly occurred to me (being familiar with the Old Testament) that Solomon went astray after strange gods, the names of three of whom I remembered—"Ashtoreth the goddess of the Zidonians, Chemosh the god of the Moabites, and Milcom the god of the children of Ammon"—and I suggested to my companions that the three figures before us might represent these false divinities.
> "Hum," said Sir Henry, who was a scholar, having taken a high degree in classics at college, "there may be something in that; Ashtoreth of the Hebrews was the Astarte of the Phœnicians, who were the great traders of Solomon's time. Astarte, who afterwards was the Aphrodite of the Greeks, was represented with horns like the half-moon, and there on the brow of the female figure are distinct horns. Perhaps these colossi were designed by some Phœnician official who managed the mines. Who can say?" (259)

Drawing on the Bible and some classical knowledge, these ruins present no problems for the European interpreters. Moreover, by means of references to the Bible they can be integrated into the explorers' own, European culture. The otherness and exoticism of the ruins are consequently tamed in this as well as in Haggard's other works.

In all three novels it is stressed that the impressive material remains encountered by the characters are most likely the work of either Egyptians, Jews, or Phoenicians – that is, more or less white cultures and emphatically not black ones. Similarly, the culturally advanced society discovered in *Allan Quatermain* in a secluded part of Africa is

---

[1] This is discussed in Katz 1987, Sandison 1967, Etherington 1984, Brantlinger 1988 and Chrisman 1990.
[2] For the further significance of the ruins in *She*, as well as in Jefferies's *After London* and Wells's *The Time Machine*, see Fricke 2009.

white and its citizens are presented as the descendants of either Jewish, Persian, or Phoenician ancestors (see Haggard 1995, 155-156). In *She* the origin of the civilization of Kôr is more mysterious, but again its long-dead people are described as fair and sometimes blond (see Haggard 1998b, 97, 111). Africa is thus rendered as the subject of exterior domination and exploitation that reach back thousands of years. Haggard presents the ancient colonizers as forerunners of the Europeans now ruling over Africa, thereby tapping into the discourse in which Britain constructed itself as the heir to ancient empires like the Roman Empire[3], and also legitimizing the ongoing European exploitation of the continent.

Haggard's depiction of the African past is in keeping with contemporary trends in archaeology, as the discourse on the ruins of Great Zimbabwe shows. Since the sixteenth century there had been theories that these impressive buildings had been erected either by King Solomon, the Phoenicians, or the Queen of Sheba (see Higgins 1981, 75-76; Pocock 1993, 178).[4] It was only in the twentieth century that black Africans were acknowledged as the builders of Great Zimbabwe, and even then this truth was taboo while Rhodesia was ruled by a white minority (see Frederikse 1983, 10-13).

Haggard's detailed description of the exotic African environment and his characters' euro-centric, scientific interpretations of the ruins and the people they encounter can also be seen as a strategy to exert a semblance of control over these vast and alien spaces. As Thomas Richards argues in *The Imperial Archive: Knowledge and the Fantasy of Empire* (1993), the gathering and ordering of facts was an important element of "controlling territory by producing, distributing, and consuming information about it" (Richards 1993, 17) – even if this was often no more than a virtual form of control (see *ibid.*, 3-4). The urge to make the alien familiar and thus ultimately manageable is also present in Haggard's tendency to describe the world of *King Solomon's Mines* by constructing analogies to Europe, and especially to the European past, for example when a Kukuana warrior who has just thrown a spear is likened to a Greek statue (see Haggard 1998a, 111), or the execution of a great number of Kukuanas is compared to Roman gladiatorial games (see *ibid.*, 165). The narrator moreover uses references to English literature (Shakespeare, Dryden, Dickens; see *ibid.* 183, 231, 165) to comment on the events in Kukuanaland. For Haggard's English heroes, their explorations into the African hinterland thus become on many levels journeys into their own past, and Africa is constructed as a space in which different stages of European history are still present, if in a somewhat warped way. In doing so, Haggard takes up a discourse noticeable in much of eighteenth- and nineteenth-century travel writing, namely the linking of geo-

---

3 See Vance 1997 for the Victorians and Ancient Rome.
4 With the publication of *King Solomon's Mines,* Haggard himself became part of this rather literary discourse on actual ruins. Not only was Great Zimbabwe often seen as the model for Haggard's mines, but in the "Post Scriptum" to the *New Illustrated Edition* (1905) Haggard identified the Kukuanas with the Matablee tribe who lived in Zimbabwe (Haggard 1998a, Explanatory Notes to 5, 20). When Haggard finally visited the ruins of Zimbabwe in 1914, he found that they were presented to tourists as "the original of Kôr and the abode of She; two hills had been named Sheba's Breasts after the mountains in *King Solomon's Mines* and a road after Allan Quatermain" (Pocock 1993, 178). In 1896 Haggard himself wrote a Preface to A. Wilmot's *Monomotapa (Rhodesia): Its Monuments, and its History from the most Ancient Times to the present Century*, which stresses the claim that Great Zimbabwe was Phoenician (Haggard 1896, xvii.).

graphical with historical distance, and the perception of alien societies as embodying earlier periods of European history. Friedrich Schiller claimed in 1789:

> Die Entdeckungen, welche unsre europäischen Seefahrer in fernen Meeren und auf entlegenen Küsten gemacht haben, geben uns ein ebenso lehrreiches als unterhaltendes Schauspiel. Sie zeigen uns Völkerschaften, die auf den mannigfaltigsten Stufen der Bildung um uns herum gelagert sind, wie Kinder verschiednen Alters um einen Erwachsenen herumstehen und durch ihr Beispiel ihm in Erinnerung bringen, was er selbst vormals gewesen, und wovon er ausgegangen ist. Eine weise Hand scheint uns diese rohen Völkerstämme bis auf den Zeitpunkt aufgespart zu haben, wo wir in unsrer eignen Kultur weit genug würden fortgeschritten sein, um von dieser Entdeckung eine nützliche Anwendung auf uns selbst zu machen, und den verlornen Anfang unsers Geschlechts aus diesem Spiegel wiederherzustellen. (Schiller 1789, 754)

Accordingly, anthropologists used such societies to formulate theories about Europe's past (see Bowler 7, Gilmour 59). Just as in Haggard's novels, constructing the other as part of or analogous to the European past made it more comprehensible while at the same time retaining a certain distance and superiority to it.

However, making the European and African systems analogous may, as in Haggard's construction of Africa in King Solomon's Mines, also serve to at least partly collapse the dichotomy between them. This is most obvious in Haggard's depiction of the leader of the expedition, Sir Henry, and the rightful king of the Kukuanas, Ignosi. The similarities these two men share are stressed again and again, both being described as particularly 'manly' (see Haggard 1998a, 48-49, 200).[5] It becomes clear that there is a very thin line between the 'barbaric' Kukuanas and the 'civilized' English explorers who, by entering Kukuanaland, to some extent regress to former stages of civilization and, for example, eat raw meat (see *ibid.*, 103) and fight clad in ancient chain mail (see *ibid.*, 200). As Quatermain tells the readers in *Allan Quatermain*: "It is a depressing conclusion, but in all essentials the savage and the child of civilization are identical" (Haggard 1995, 10).

Surprisingly enough, this is not necessarily seen as negative. Sir Henry, who is presented as the model of Anglo-Saxon and consequently English manliness (see Haggard 1998a, 11), ironically needs the primitive society of the Kukuanas to express his true, manly and warlike nature, for this is no longer possible in 'civilized' English society. In Haggard's novels Africa is constructed as a space in which men can be 'real' men, pitting their prowess against wild animals, deadly natural conditions, and warlike natives (see Haggard 1998a, 199-200). Ultimately it seems that the only thing that really differentiates Africans and Europeans is the latter's modern scientific knowledge and superior technology. In *King Solomon's Mines*, Gagool describes the ancient colonizers as "skilled in magic and all learning" (149), and the English adventurers take up this connection of knowledge and 'magic' and use advanced technology together with native superstition to assert their power over the Kukuanas. While their superior knowledge gives the English explorers a clear advantage, however, both in *King Solomon's Mines* (see Haggard 1998a, 306) and in *Allan Quatermain* it is also seen as ambivalent, making it ultimately necessary to shield secluded countries from the influence of European civilization and scientific and technological advance. As Sir Henry claims at

---

5   A similar kinship between Sir Henry and a heroic Zulu warrior is constructed in *Allan Quatermain* (Haggard 1995, 76).

the end of *Allan Quatermain*, in which he becomes the king of the fantastic country of Zu-Vendis,

> I am convinced of the sacred duty that rests upon me of preserving to this, on the whole, upright and generous-hearted people the blessings of comparative barbarism. [...] I cannot see that gunpowder, telegraphs, steam, daily newspapers, universal suffrage, &c., &c., have made mankind one whit the happier than they used to be, and I am certain that they have brought many evils in their train. (Haggard 1995, 281-282)

In Africa Haggard's heroes are not only confronted with the historical past, however, but also with the much larger time frames of geology and biology. Both *She* (see Haggard 1998b, 287) and *Allan Quatermain* (see Haggard 1995, 117-118) feature extensive journeys into the depths of the earth where the heroes encounter strange pillars of flame. And in *King Solomon's Mines* the explorers are led to a large stalactite cave where the slow growth of the rock awes the narrator with its intimation of the contrast between geological deep time and human time (see Haggard 1998a, 262-264). Both are merged in a memorable image when Quatermain detects that after their death the former kings of the Kukuanas are brought to this cave where the dropping water slowly turns them into stone:

> A look at the white forms seated on the stone bench that ran round that ghastly board confirmed this view. They were human forms indeed, or rather had been human forms; now they were stalactites. This was the way in which the Kukuana people had from time immemorial preserved their royal dead. They petrified them. What the exact system was, if there was any, beyond placing them for a long period of years under the drip, I never discovered, but there they sat, iced over and preserved for ever by the siliceous fluid. (*ibid.*, 268)

In *She*, the focus is not so much on geological time as on evolution and degeneration. Taking up contemporary discourses such as Victorian fears of degeneration through miscegenation, Haggard presents the Amahagger (a people his heroes encounter when they discover Ayesha) as the descendants of the white people of Kôr and Arabs or black Africans (see Haggard 1998b, 181). As a 'bastard' people they are not able to continue the high standard of civilization established by their 'pureblood' forefathers (see *ibid.*, 89-90, Greenslade 1994, 22) and – with a few exceptions – are presented in a very negative way as "swarthy demons" (Haggard 1998b, 103), a description which seems to be justified when they turn out to be cannibals (see *ibid.*, 107). Human degeneration is situated not only in the safe distance of Africa, however, but also in Europe. According to the narrator Holly, the modern Greeks cannot hold a candle to their illustrious ancestors (see *ibid.*, 147), and the narrator himself suffers from bodily degeneration and is described as:

> shortish, rather bow-legged, very deep chested, and with unusually long arms. He had dark hair and small eyes, and the hair grew right down on his forehead, and his whiskers grew right up to his hair, so that there was uncommonly little of his countenance to be seen. Altogether he reminded me forcibly of a gorilla [...]. (2)

Holly's ugliness and his likeness to a monkey or ape are stressed several times (see *ibid.*, 7-8, 108, 110), drawing attention to contemporary debates about the origin of man. When, at the end of the story, Ayesha again enters the mysterious fire that gave her immortality hundreds of years ago, this time the effect is to the reverse, and she degenerates into an ape-like creature in a kind of backward evolution (see *ibid.*, 293-294). It is interesting that both Holly and Ayesha, who are presented as the characters with the greatest intellectual powers and scientific knowledge, are linked to apes, thereby stressing that all the achievements of civilisation cannot eradicate the human-animal connection and the threat of degeneration.

Haggard here again takes up contemporary discourses that saw the British themselves, and especially the lower urban classes, who often suffered from horrible living conditions, as at risk of degeneration. As James Anthony Froude wrote in 1886:

> It is simply impossible that the English men and women of the future generations can equal or approach the famous race that has overspread the globe, if they are to be bred in towns such as Birmingham and Glasgow now are, and to rear their families under the conditions which now prevail in those places. Morally and physically they must and will decline. (Froude 1886, 342)

Part of this discourse was the drawing of analogies between life in the jungle and England. In 1883 George Sims described his work *How the Poor Live* as a journey "into a dark continent that is within easy walking distance of the General Post Office" (quoted in Driver 2001, 181), and in 1890 William Booth, the founder of the Salvation Army, published a work of social criticism, *In Darkest England and The Way Out*, which in its title as well as in quotes makes references to the bestseller *In Darkest Africa* by Henry Morton Stanley, also published in 1890 (see Arata 1996, 16-17; Driver 2001, chapter 8; Eldridge 1996, 144-145).

2. Searching for Answers: H. G. Wells and Richard Jefferies

This collapse of the seemingly secure distance between the worlds described in the novels and developments in Britain itself is also implied in two other fantastic novels, H. G. Wells's *The Time Machine* [1895] and Richard Jefferies's *After London* [1885].

Wells's time 'traveller' never alters his geographical location, but when he arrives in the year 802,701 the changes effected by time make the England he encounters utterly alien to him. Consequently, the traveller finds himself in the position of an explorer trying to make sense of an alien, exotic country and its people. To order, explain, and rationalise what he encounters, he falls back on the knowledge and theories of the late nineteenth century. Thus when the traveller discovers impressive but dilapidated statues dotting the pastoral landscape that has replaced London, he processes and describes them by likening them to his own world and, more specifically, to antiquity, describing them as a sphinx, obelisks, a faun, and griffins' heads (see Wells 1995, 19, 27, 54). The large palaces he encounters are also reminiscent of ancient models, and he believes "I saw suggestions of old Phoenician decorations as I passed through" (*ibid.*, 23). The time traveller can only absorb and describe the buildings of the future by reverting to known models from the past of his own culture. For him – as for Haggard's protagonists – the archaeological remains he finds in an alien setting seem to be merely echoes of European antiquity.

In contrast to Haggard's heroes, however, who, faced with the most fantastic phenomena still manage to integrate them within their European frames of references – or, if they cannot do that, are not overly troubled by it – the time traveller has more problems with the interpretive models he applies to the future. Again and again he has to qualify his theories (see Wells 1995, 26-27, 29-30, 36-37, 45, 70) until he can no longer be sure of them: "Very simple was my explanation, and plausible enough – as most wrong theories are!" (*ibid.*, 30).

Most of the traveller's theories centre on the people he meets in the future. At first he encounters the Eloi, a beautiful but small and frail people who live a seemingly utopian, hedonistic life in the dilapidated large buildings. As the traveller soon notices, however, not only their bodily powers, but also their intellect seems to be diminished (see 20, 24-25). The descendants of the Englishmen turn out to be very similar to primitive and degenerate savages squatting in the ruins of a former high culture – very similar, in fact, to the Amahagger in Haggard's *She*. From childhood on Wells had been interested in theories of biological evolution and degeneration, and for one year he studied biology under Thomas Huxley (see Wells 1934, 201-205, 208, 227). In 1891 he published an essay titled "Zoological Retrogression", in which he stated: "The zoologist demonstrates that advance has been fitful and uncertain; rapid progress has often been followed by rapid extinction or degeneration [...]. There is, therefore, no guarantee in scientific knowledge of man's permanence or permanent ascendancy" (Wells 1891, 253). According to the time traveller's interpretation, the Eloi are the victims of biological degeneration, which is ironically the result of their utopian surroundings and the lack of hardship they experience (see Wells 1995, 27-29, 45). As it turns out, however, the Eloi are not the 'worst' result of human evolution, for the traveller comes across a race of subterranean creatures that has retained only scant traces of its former 'humanity'. When he visits their subterranean living space, he draws the conclusion that their development is the result of social developments already apparent in his own time, and, like Haggard, takes up contemporary discourses on the alleged degeneration of the lower urban classes due to their living and working conditions:

> At first, proceeding from the problems of our own age, it seemed clear as daylight to me that the gradual widening of the present merely temporary and social difference between the Capitalist and the Labourer, was the key to the whole position. [...] even now there are existing circumstances to point that way. There is a tendency to utilize underground space for the less ornamental purposes of civilization; [...] Evidently, I thought, this tendency had increased till Industry had gradually lost its birthright in the sky. I mean that it had gone deeper and deeper into larger and ever larger underground factories, spending a still-increasing amount of its time therein, till, in the end – ! [...] So, in the end, above ground you must have the Haves, pursuing pleasure and comfort and beauty, and below ground the Have-nots, the Workers getting continually adapted to the conditions of their labour. (Wells 1995, 43-44)

The de-humanization of the Morlocks is furthered by what the traveller interprets as cannibalism, i.e., his conclusion that they eat the Eloi (see *ibid.*, 55-56), "mere fatted cattle, which the ant-like Morlocks preserved and preyed upon – probably saw to the breeding of" (*ibid.*, 56). Repeated comparisons of both Morlocks and Eloi to animals (see *ibid.*, 40, 42, 46) again draw attention to evolutionary theory. The degeneration of the human race seems to be completed when the time traveller moves on to an even more remote future in which he comes across creatures that remind him of "rabbits, or some small breed of kangaroo" (*ibid.*, 86), but which still show a "faintly human touch" (*ibid.*, 87).[6]

In contrast to Wells's novel, Richard Jefferies's *After London* [1885], which John Fowles calls "the strangest book that Richard Jefferies ever wrote, if not the strangest from any considerable writer of his period" (Introduction in Jefferies 1980, vii), is

---

6   This scene was included when the novel was originally serialized but was omitted when it was published as a novel in 1895 (Lawton, Introduction to Wells 1995, xxxiii, note 14).

hardly known today. It consists of two self-contained parts that are very different with regard to their length and genre. The first part, titled "The Relapse into Barbarism", encompasses about a fifth of *After London* and is a scientific text written by a historian in an unspecified future. In it he describes the historic, cultural, and biological features of a future England which has relapsed into quasi-medieval times. The second part, titled "Wild England", is a novel narrating the story of a young man living in this setting. It culminates in a visit to the site of London, which has turned into a poisonous swamp where no life can exist. Drawing on contemporary discourses on moral corruption, environmental pollution, and the fear of leaking gas pipes[7], Jefferies here creates a memorable apocalyptic image of the end of the capital that also becomes the end of British culture as we know it.

Like Wells, Jefferies combines a biological-Darwinistic vision of the future with pessimistic social prophecy, which here is linked to the contemporary agricultural depression in England (see Grimble 2004, 14, 80, 101; Korte 2003, 143). The reason for the relapse into barbarism is the unexplained disappearance of a large part of the British population. Consequently, the land quickly turned into a wilderness: Fields and roads were overgrown until finally nearly all of England was covered by dense woods. Abandoned domestic animals relapsed into a wild state and most of the different races of dogs, cattle, etc., were lost. Not only the landscape and animals changed, but also society. The severe reduction of the populace led to a brain drain, which, together with the fact that people were long isolated from one another and busy ensuring their basic survival, meant that much knowledge was lost. At the time the story is set, things like the railway or the telephone are only fairy tales. Regarding the English themselves, the changes have led to a social differentiation into three fundamentally different groups: the farmers and those living in the cities, the "Bushmen" and the "Romany/Zingari". The Bushmen are at the lowest end of the social ladder and are said to be the descendents of beggars and tramps. They live under primitive conditions in the woods and are described as savages and "human wild beasts" (Jefferies 1980, 95) who eat their meat raw and often fall into a murderous frenzy. The "Romany/Zingari" are the descendants of the gypsies. Like the Bushmen, the narrator depicts them as bloodthirsty and a danger to 'normal' Englishmen (see *ibid.*, 19-24). Though he doesn't go as far as Wells, Jefferies describes how the social structure of late Victorian Britain and the marginalization of certain groups of its population will in the future lead to the development of wholly different peoples that continually fight each other.

Both Wells's and Jefferies's narrators try to explain the future worlds they describe in as much detail and with as much scientific accuracy as they can, but, as stated earlier, in these novels this is presented as far more difficult than in Haggard's stories. In *After London* no one seems to know what actually led to the catastrophic loss of population. Thus, while the historian depicts all the resulting changes in great and convincing detail, he can merely guess at the trigger for these changes. Since most records have been destroyed, he can only rely on oral tradition and freely admits that "nothing is certain and everything confused. None of the accounts agree, nor can they be altogether reconciled with present facts or with reasonable supposition" (Jefferies 1980, 15). The fact that without written sources knowledge can only be attained and history only writ-

---

7   For the latter see Schivelbusch 1983, 38-43.

ten by relying on oral tradition had already been discussed by Jefferies in 1877 in a short manuscript called "Three Centuries at Home":

> The thought occurred to me: suppose the written records of English history were swept away and an inquiring spirit like Herodotus went about collecting from popular tradition and national monuments the story of the past, what a strange and interesting work it would be! Imagine Clarendon and Macaulay, Bacon and other great authors, quite extinct, or retained only in unreadable hieroglyphics, and our Herodotus gravely stepping into Westminster Abbey, listening, half credulous, half critically, to the attendants' tales of the Richards, and Edwards and Henrys [...] It was something in this way that history was first written; and it is not difficult to believe that our own would be as full of demi-gods and heroes and marvellous exploits as that of the Trojan war, were the same method pursued at this day. (Jefferies 1948, 135)

In *After London*, Jefferies draws further attention to the transitoriness of knowledge when he describes how averse to learning and reading future English society is. Moreover, only few books have survived, most of them very old (see Jefferies 1980, 46-47). Of the nineteenth century, all knowledge and literature seems to have been lost:

> so many English writers, once famous, had dropped out of knowledge and disappeared. [...] The books which came into existence with printing had never been copied by the pen, and had consequently nearly disappeared. Extremely long and diffuse, it was found, too, that so many of them were but enlargements of ideas or sentiments which had been expressed in a few words by the classics. It is so much easier to copy an epigram of two lines than a printed book of hundreds of pages, and hence it was that Sophocles had survived while much more recent writers had been lost. (Jefferies 1980, 114)

The problem of how to preserve knowledge in a changed world is also addressed by Wells in the episode of the time traveller's visit to the "Palace of Green Porcelain", a museum[8] presumably built by the ancestors of the Eloi and Morlocks. Like everything else the traveller encounters, it is falling into ruins:

> Only ragged vestiges of glass remained in its windows, and great sheets of the green facing had fallen away from the corroded metallic framework. [...] along the face of it I saw an inscription in some unknown character. I thought, rather foolishly, that Weena might help me to interpret this, but I only learned that the bare idea of writing had never entered her head. (Wells 1995, 57)

The traveller hopes to find information on the future there or at least a weapon he can use against the Morlocks, but he cannot decode the messages left in the museum, nor make sense of the futuristic machines he finds, and his Eloi-friend lacks the knowledge, intellectual power, and motivation to do so (see *ibid.*, 58-59). The problem of how to transmit and preserve knowledge over time is cast in sharp relief when the traveller finds a library within the museum:

> I went out of that gallery and into another and still larger one, which at the first glance reminded me of a military chapel hung with tattered flags. The brown and charred rags that hung from the sides of it, I presently recognized as the decaying vestiges of books. They had long since dropped to pieces, and every semblance of print had left them. But here and there were warped boards and cracked metallic clasps that told the tale well enough. (Wells 1995, 60)

Wells, like Jefferies, here draws attention to the materiality of knowledge. While in theory language, writing, and books can preserve knowledge over time, this of course only works if later recipients can still read the scripture and language, and if the me-

---

8 For the role of museums and libraries in Science Fiction literature see Crossley 1990.

dium on which the text is written survives in the first place. The purpose of the museum – to preserve culturally important works and knowledge for posterity – here fails because of posterity's lack of interest. Finally, the only weapon the time traveller can take with him is a lever he uses as a mace, along with a box of matches (see *ibid.*, 60). He leaves this vast array of the future's advanced knowledge and technology with the most primitive weapons imaginable.

As this analysis has hopefully shown, late-Victorian fantastic texts engage with contemporary scientific discourses in a multifaceted way that encompasses all levels of narration and plot. Moreover, while at first glance these texts often seem to present simplistic versions of reality, their engagement with the use, creation, and dissemination of knowledge, as well as the question of how to preserve knowledge and apply it to alien worlds and societies, is often more complex than expected.

References

Primary Sources

Froude, James Anthony ([1886]; 1887): *Oceana: Or England and Her Colonies.* Leipzig: Bernhard Tauchnitz

Haggard, H. Rider (1896): "Preface", in: Wilmot, A.: *Monomotapa (Rhodesia): Its Monuments, and Its History from the Most Ancient Times to the Present Century*. London: T. Fisher Unwin, xiii-xxiv

--- (1926): *The Days of My Life: An Autobiography*. 2 vols. Volume 1. Ed. C. J. Longman. London: Longmans, Green & Co

--- (1995): *Allan Quatermain* [1887]. Ed. Dennis Butts. Oxford: Oxford University Press

--- (1998a): *King Solomon's Mines* [1885]. Ed. Dennis Butts. Oxford: Oxford University Press

--- (1998b): *She* [1887]. Ed. Daniel Karlin. Oxford: Oxford University Press

Jefferies, Richard (1948): "Three Centuries at Home [1877]", in: Looker, Samuel J. (ed.): *The Old House at Coate and Other Hitherto Unpublished Essays*. Cambridge, MA: Harvard University Press, 135-143

--- (1980): *After London or Wild England [1885]*. Ed. John Fowles. Oxford: Oxford University Press

Schiller, Friedrich ([1789]; 2004): "Was heißt und zu welchem Ende studiert man Universalgeschichte? Eine akademische Antrittsrede", in: Alt, Peter-André et al. (eds.): *Friedrich Schiller: Historische Schriften (Sämtliche Werke*, Volume. 4). München: Carl Hanser, 749-767

Wells, H. G. (1891): "Zoological Retrogression", *The Gentleman's Magazine* 271, 246-253

--- ([1895]; 1995): *The Time Machine: The Centennial Edition*. Ed. John Lawton. London: Everyman

--- (1934): *Experiment in Autobiography: Discoveries and Conclusions of a Very Ordinary Brain (since 1866)*. 2 vols. Volume 1. London: Victor Gollancz

Secondary Sources

Arata, Stephen (1996): *Fictions of Loss in the Victorian Fin de Siècle*. Cambridge: Cambridge University Press

Barthes, Roland ([1968]; 1989): "The Reality Effect", in: *The Rustle of Language (La Bruissement de la Langue)*. Transl. Richard Howard. Berkeley: University of California Press, 141-148

Bowler, Peter J. (1989): *The Invention of Progress: The Victorians and the Past*. Oxford: Blackwell

Brantlinger, Patrick (1988): *Rule of Darkness: British Literature and Imperialism, 1830-1914*. Ithaca, NY: Cornell University Press

Chrisman, Laura (1990): "The Imperial Unconscious? Representations of Imperial Discourse", *Critical Quarterly* 32.3, 38-58

Crossley, Robert (1990): "In the Palace of Green Porcelain: Artefacts from the Museum of Science Fiction", *Essays and Studies* 43 *(Fictional Space: Essays on Contemporary Science Fiction.* Ed. Tom Shippey), 76-103
Driver, Felix (2001): *Geography Militant: Cultures of Exploration and Empire.* Oxford: Blackwell
Eldridge, C. C. (1996): *The Imperial Experience: From Carlyle to Forster.* Basingstoke: Macmillan
Etherington, Norman (1984): *Rider Haggard.* Boston: Twayne Publishers
Frederikse, Julie (ed.; [1982] 1983): *None but Ourselves: Masses vs. Media in the Making of Zimbabwe.* London: Heinemann
Fricke, Stefanie (2009): *Memento Mori: Ruinen alter Hochkulturen und die Furcht vor dem eigenen Untergang in der englischen Literatur des 19. Jahrhunderts.* Trier: WVT
Gilmour, Robin (1993): *The Victorian Period: The Intellectual and Cultural Context of English Literature, 1830-1890.* Harlow: Longman
Greenslade, William (1994): *Degeneration, Culture and the Novel 1880-1940.* Cambridge: Cambridge University Press
Grimble, Simon (2004): *Landscape, Writing and "The Condition of England": 1878-1917, Ruskin to Modernism.* Lewiston, NY: Edwin Mellen
Higgins, D. S. (1981): *Rider Haggard: A Biography.* New York: Stein and Day
Katz, Wendy R. (1987): *Rider Haggard and the Fiction of Empire: A Critical Study of British Imperial Fiction.* Cambridge: Cambridge University Press
Korte, Barbara (2003): "*After London* – Die Metropole als Zukunftsruine bei Richard Jefferies (1885) und Ronald Wright (1997)", in: Seeber, Hans Ulrich; Griem, Julika (eds.): *Raum- und Zeitreisen: Studien zur Literatur und Kultur des 19. und 20. Jahrhunderts.* Tübingen: Max Niemeyer, 139-155
Pocock, Tom (1993): *Rider Haggard and the Lost Empire.* London: Weidenfeld and Nicolson
Pringle, David et al. (1995): "Lost Worlds", in: Clute, John; Nicholls, Peter (eds.): *The Encyclopedia of Science Fiction.* New York: St Martin's, 734-736
Richards, Thomas (1993): *The Imperial Archive: Knowledge and the Fantasy of Empire.* London: Verso
Sandison, Alan (1967): *The Wheel of Empire: A Study of the Imperial Idea in Some Late Nineteenth and Early Twentieth-Century Fiction.* London: Macmillan
Schivelbusch, Wolfgang (1983): *Lichtblicke: Zur Geschichte der künstlichen Helligkeit im 19. Jahrhundert.* München: Carl Hanser
Vance, Norman (1997): *The Victorians and Ancient Rome.* Oxford: Blackwell

NORA PLEßKE (PASSAU)

The Object(ivity) of Imperial Thinking

1. Introduction

In 2013, the 119th Proms at London's Royal Albert Hall introduced an Urban Night of soul, hip-hop, and rap, and its Last Night was, for the first time in history, conducted by a woman. Nevertheless, according to tradition, the program still featured Thomas Arne's *Rule Britannia!* (1740). Both the pomp and circumstance of the Last Night of the Proms and the jingoist content of the song's lyrics nostalgically preserve the perceived glories of Great Britain's imperial past in the nation's cultural memory. Today, the performance stands as one of the most audible remnants and visible displays of Britain's Empire mentality.

In 1895, when the first indoor Promenade Concerts took place, Britain experienced a high tide of jingoism. This political and cultural patriotism particularly materialized in imperialist writing towards the end of the nineteenth century. In their introduction to *Fictions of Empire*, Ansgar and Vera Nünning elucidate the constructive role of literature in the making of imperialist mentalities (see Nünning and Nünning 1996, 7-8). These collective standardizations of thinking, imagining, feeling, and acting (see Pleßke 2014, 71-72) are characterized by specific preconceptions, beliefs, values, and epistemological habits summarily based on the conviction of British superiority in opposition to the inferiority of colonized peoples (see Nünning and Nünning 1996, 12-13). This essential notion, manifest in various discursive practices, produced knowledge about the 'Other' and extended metropolitan control over the colonial periphery. Importantly, however, according to Edward Said's *Orientalism* (1978), this 'objective' historical reality of imperial superiority presents but a discursive "system of ideological fictions" (Said 2003, 321; see Nünning and Nünning 1996, 16).

In the present contribution, I will approach this idea by underlining the significance of objects in constructing the seemingly objective world-view of Britain's Empire mentality. The British Empire was not only built on colonial objects, such as cotton, sugar, tea, china, gems, ivory, etc., which served as an economic motivation for further expansion, subjugation, and exploitation, but this "*Empire of Things*" (Myers 2001) also represented a manifestation of the imperial idea itself. On the one hand, their concrete materiality and presence made exotic things less 'fictional' and thus more 'objective' or scientifically evident. On the other hand, due to the versatility of objects, their meaningfulness was just as easily adopted by as adapted for the developing taxonomies of the sciences in the Victorian age, most notably in anthropology. The following analysis centers on the nineteenth-century exhibitionary complex, which illustrates this object(ivity) of imperial thinking by laying bare the dynamics between knowledge and power, visual and material culture, as well as the rise of science and the expansion of Britain's Empire mentality.

The article will first elaborate on Tony Bennett's initial definition of the nineteenth-century exhibitionary complex, particularly by concentrating on the construction of its specific visual knowledge system. Based on extractions from Bennett's article, the present study, using the central example of the Great Exhibition, will then analyze the visual, spatial, and narrative constructions of material taxonomies that furthered imperial stereotypes of the colonial 'Other' as primitive. Because it was formative for the expanding exhibitionary complex as a whole, the Great Exhibition's influences on other media of display will be addressed in a fourth section. Finally, the paper will comment on the consequent manifestations and objectifications of imperial thinking.

2. The Nineteenth-Century Exhibitionary Complex and Its Object(ives) of Knowledge

A key term for the nineteenth-century, the exhibitionary complex encompasses the idea of display both as a reflection of ideology and a form of social control. This concept helps to enlarge the understanding of Victorian knowledge systems and institutional power as well as the connections between visual culture, cultural politics, nationalism, and imperialism. It also provides a useful shorthand for national and international exhibitions, history and natural science museums, panoramas and dioramas, arcades and department stores (see Bennett 1988, 73). These spaces of the exhibitionary complex served as central sites for the development and circulation of new disciplines, such as history, biology, art, anthropology, and their concomitant discursive formations of the past, evolution, aestheticism, and man (see Bennett 1988, 73).

Tony Bennett, first in his influential essay of 1988 and later in his book *The Birth of the Museum* (1995), offers the most extensive definition of "The Exhibitionary Complex". He asserts that in the beginning of the nineteenth century, older forms of display, such as cabinets of curiosities, were moved from the private realm to the public arena (see Bennett 1988, 73). This change had three aspects: First, an engagement with the public through pleasure created new types of power and knowledge (see Bennett 1988, 74). Second, the public access to displays played a pivotal role with regard to ethics, education, and civilization (see Bennett 1988, 76). Third, the permanent display of power and knowledge served as a claim to be able to command, order, and control objects and bodies alike (see Bennett 1988, 79). Bennett thereby shows how the visual strategies of containment and control transform the visitor into a self-regulating citizen who disciplines his behavior and internalizes civil norms and values (see Bennett 1988, 76). In order to explain these relations between visuality, knowledge, power, and control Bennett borrows from Foucauldian surveillance theory: Whereas the carceral system functions through punishment, the exhibitionary complex produces a self-administered disciplinary system through the civilizing pleasures of entertainment (see Bennett 1988, 81). Yet, the exhibitionary complex cannot simply be seen as a reversal of the panopticon, but must rather be considered to incorporate its spatial, social, and mental axioms (see Bennett 1988, 81). Bennett argues that "[r]elations of space and vision are organized not merely to allow a clear inspection of the objects exhibited but also allow for the visitors to be the objects of each other's inspection" (Bennett 2009, 52). In this way, people become the agents of their own subjection and the social body is rendered amenable to collective regulation (see Bennett 1988, 77).

This specific epistemology of vision constitutes a central paradigm of nineteenth-century visual culture. Fascinated by the act of seeing and the human eye, Victorians struggled with two contradictory models of visual perception: on the one side, the mere appearance of things and subjective organizations of vision; on the other side, realist modes of representation and the positivist certainty of visual facts (see Brosch 2008, 21-22, 55-57). The latter casts the eye as the organ of 'truth', thus feeding notions of objective observation. Under the slogan 'seeing is believing' the visual was endowed with the quality of evidence, which in turn enhanced the primacy of the visual as a conduit of scientific knowledge (see Ogata 2010, 200; Müller-Scheessel 2011, 157). The nineteenth-century concept of 'object lesson' suggested that every material object, which is available for inspection, has the power to educate its viewers (see Müller-Scheessel 2011, 158). Because all sectors of the exhibitionary complex heavily depended on the widespread appeal of visuality, the 'show and tell'-attitude linked the nineteenth-century exposition visitor, the museum viewer, department-store shopper, and freak show spectator alike, lending each of them the power to see and to know. Visitors were enabled, in Bennett's words, "to become the subjects rather than the objects of knowledge" (Bennett 1988, 76). Hence, the scientific imperative of making things visible was, in connection with practices of codification and classification, associated with attaining knowledge and control over the world: The visible was perceived as governable. With regard to exotic objects within the exhibitionary complex, this meant that a combination of visual colonialism and visual consumerism sustained the hegemony of 'Self' versus 'Other', while the visual taxonomy of exhibitions and museums played a growing role in stabilizing and structuring imperial orders of knowledge. The emergent exhibitionary complex of the nineteenth century therefore created possibilities for objectifying imperialist mentalities by both ordering colonial objects for public inspection and ordering the public that inspected them.

3. The Great Exhibition and the Visual Logics of Imperial Thinking

The Great Exhibition of the Works of Industry of All Nations (1851) is paradigmatic for the development of the nineteenth-century exhibitionary complex because it brought together a number of disciplines as well as techniques of display that had been established within previous sites of exhibition and, in its turn, translated these into formations of order and surveillance that were to have a lasting influence on the subsequent expansion of museums and expositions (see Bennett 1988, 74). With respect to its legacy John Davis argues that "a shared belief in the 'objectivity' of the Exhibition and its scientific methods" resulted in the promotion of various scientific, economic, or nationalist causes on the grounds of the "so-called 'evidence' of the Great Exhibition" (Davis 2002, 26). Thus, with its international scope, the Great Exhibition was relevant for both highlighting colonial manufactures and for manifesting an imperialist mentality. Taking place in Hyde Park from 1 May to 11 October 1851, the Great Exhibition displayed more than 100,000 objects by nearly 14,000 exhibitors from 94 countries (see Mergenthal 2008, 66; Ogata 2010, 201). It was a major spur to the expansion of an open-door policy of exhibitions, attracting over six million visitors to its venue, the Crystal Palace, which offered new relations of sight, vision, and display that were so formative for the exhibitionary complex (see Bennett 1988, 85-86).

Probably the most iconic exhibit, the exposition building of the Crystal Palace itself, was often seen as standing metonymically for the Great Exhibition and set the frame for the show; thereby it came to dominate not only the display but also the viewers' perception of objects. Designed by Joseph Paxton after his greenhouse constructions, the Crystal Palace was the largest glass structure of its time. Its visual effects, which tended toward both bedazzlement and control, underline the architectural problematic of spectacle and panopticon alike. The new visual world order of majestic illumination was described from Queen Victoria's vantage point in the following way:

> The galleries are finished, and from the top of them the effect is quite wonderful. The sun shining in through the Transept gave a fairy-like appearance. The building is so light and graceful, in spite of its immense size. (Queen Victoria's *Journal*, 18 February 1851, 17)

Similarly, *The Times* wrote on the opening ceremony of the Great Exhibition:

> In a building that could easily have accommodated twice as many, twenty-five thousand persons [...] were arranged in order round the throne of our SOVEREIGN. Around them, amidst them, and over their heads was displayed all that is useful or beautiful in nature or in art. Above them rose a glittering arch more lofty and spacious than the vaults of even our noblest cathedrals. On either side the vista seemed almost boundless. (*The Times*, 2 May 1851 qtd. in McNab and Mackenzie 1982, 171)

The borderless appearance, the missing reference of distance, and the lack of shadow and light contrasts lent the interior of the Crystal Palace a kaleidoscopic effect, which proffered optical illusions or even visual disorientations (see Haltern 1971, 73; Gieger 2007, 93-94; Mergenthal 2008, 69-70; Ogata 2010, 201-202). Thus, on the one hand, the spectacle of the building itself was one of perceptual shock, leaving the impression of magical creation. On the other hand, the building offered a pragmatic approach to, and comprehensive overview of, the assembled displays:

> The Crystal Palace reversed the panoptical principle by fixing the eyes of the multitude upon an assemblage of glamorous commodities. The Panopticon was designed so that everyone could be seen; the Crystal Palace was designed so that everyone could see. (Davison qtd. in Bennett 1988, 78)

Underlining these new principles of vision with respect to the exhibitionary complex, Bennett, however, counters Davison's notion by stressing that "while everyone could see, there were also vantage points from which everyone could be seen, thus combining the functions of spectacle and surveillance" (Bennett 1988, 78). Referring to the Queen's diary and the newspaper article quoted above, we find that the galleries and the center of the transept offered a panoptic subject-position for the observer from which the actions of others could actually be scrutinized. Arndt Mersmann exemplifies in his analysis of various prose texts on the Great Exhibition how this static perspective of the onlooker creates a vision of an ideal and governable world (see Mersmann 2001, 52). In this context, the spatial order of the Crystal Palace represents global stage, panopticon, museum, and factory of knowledge at once.

Prince Albert's vision, extolled at one of his speeches on the Great Exhibition, was to bring together peacefully the industry of all nations and "to give us a true test and a living picture of the point of development at which the whole of mankind has arrived in this great task" (Prince Albert 1850, 112). However, instead of a holistic image of the earth's manufactures, the structure suggested by the administrative organizer, Henry Cole, was one of national divisions: The western half of the Crystal Palace was completely occupied by Great Britain and its colonies, while the eastern wing offered room for all other participants. Thus, for one thing, Britain as a nation not only hosted, but the Empire's section visibly housed the world. For another thing, the Crystal Palace, as Britain's largest exhibit and emblem of technological success, acquired connotations of a secular cathedral in which the industrious progress of peoples could be displayed 'objectively' by rendering all the things it contained into miniatures. Yet in contrast to eighteenth-century cabinets of curiosities, the architecture of the Crystal Palace's iron columns created a linear order of rooms or compartments that were allotted to the different countries (see "Supplement Gratis" 1851, n. pag.; "A Guide to the Great Exhibition" 1851, 361). Hence, the Great Exhibition provided a space in which the superiority of Great Britain was visually staged by the arrangement of objects from around the world (see Mersmann 2001, 45).

This form of collectible control becomes particularly apparent with the inclusion of colonial courts in the British section. The largest share of the public attention was certainly drawn to the later 'Jewel in the Crown': metaphorically, the Indian Court and, literally, its center piece the Koh-i-Noor (see "The Koh-i-Noor" 1851, 5-7). Sitting in a golden cage with a crown on top, the diamond symbolized the Motherland's domination and served as an objectified reminder of British imperial power (see Kriegel 2013, 166-167). In this way, the colonial courts allowed Britain to display the riches of the Empire (see Benedict 2002, 82-85; Kriegel 2013, 150; Ogata 2010, 206), while simultaneously appropriating its produce for an imperialist ideology. These material invocations of empowerment and disempowerment are also apparent in other gifts handed to the Queen on the occasion of the Great Exhibition, such as the throne and footstool offered by the Maharajah of Travancore (see "Carved Ivory Throne" 1851, 65; Prince Albert 1854, n. pag.). Made of carved ivory, gold, diamonds, emeralds, gilt bronze, and embroidered silk velvet, this symbol of power was intended to advertise the skills of southern India, but in the exhibitionary order of the Crystal Palace it became enshrined in an orientalist composition (see Prince Albert 1854, n. pag.).

A Canadian commissioner noted how the Great Exhibition's Indian bazaar and its models transported the visitor "into the midst of the scenery [...] and caused minds to wander within the Tales of thousand and one nights" (qtd. in Hoffenberg 2001, 150). The spectator became an imaginary traveler inside the stylized oriental image, which was not only richly decorated with raw materials, but also enlivened through the 'civilized' enactment of 'primitive natives' in the process of manufacturing. Consequently, for example by contrasting their manual work on the weaving stools with the mechanical steam engines of English manufacture, the Indian production sector was reduced to a stage of stasis, justifying Britain's ongoing colonial involvement in South Asia. Ironically, the classification of exhibited objects from raw materials, manufacturing goods, and machinery to the "'highest' forms applied in fine arts" (Davison qtd. in Bennett 1988, 93; see Mergenthal 2008, 74), which was supposed to overcome national boundaries, enforced the perceived contrast between colonizing and colonized countries. Above all else, this economic and ideological principle of organization transformed the display of objects into signifiers of progress (see Bennett 1988, 80): The spatialities of the Great Exhibition turned the exhibits into a means of conveying popular object lessons in the material and moral development of civilizations from the primitive to the advanced, with Britannia ruling at the top of the scale. The comprehensive aspirations, comparative method, and exacting taxonomy of its amazing visual exposition of goods, resources, commodities, and oddities from around the world particularly furthered conceptions of primitiveness and Orientalism. However, these spectacular representations not only turned the displayed colonial objects into commodities, but the visitors-observers into consuming subjects of exotic Otherness.

With respect to the exhibitionary complex as a new instrument of moral control, particularly of the working class, it was variously acknowledged that the Great Exhibition successfully regulated the crowd as a potentially dangerous 'Other' into an ordered public. For instance, the *Illustrated London News* emphasized the self-regulating effects of the exhibitionary complex, remarking that "the doors of the Crystal Palace have been opened to many thousands of industrious, grateful, well-behaved, and admiring people" ("A New Result" 1851, 607). In other words, the panoptical mechanism of this international spectacle exerted visual control over the exotic 'Other' in order to regulate the 'Other' within the British 'Self'. The British public, through their dominating gaze onto foreign objects, the staged object lessons on the exotic 'Other', and the power of knowledge conferred therewith was stylized into a visible and objective example of its own stage of development. Within the Great Exhibition, this process of objectification, defined as the "concrete embodiment of an idea" (Tilley 2005, 60), again helped to (re)form the exhibitionary complex to such an extent that the display of colonial objects was perceived as scientific proof of British superiority and 'peripheral' inferiority. Hence, foreign exhibits, by objectifying theories of race, strengthened the conceptual opposition between colonial subject and colonial object and consequently justified the imperative for an ongoing colonization in the name of Britain's civilizing mission. Moreover, British visitors hereby became both observers and consumers of an imperial ideology. This cementation of a certain order of things and the principle of visual knowledge developed within the exhibitionary complex of the Crystal Palace thus led to a further objectification of Britain's Empire mentality.

4. The Imperial Object(ivity) in Victorian Museums and Expositions

The Great Exhibition of 1851, according to Yanni, "left a complex legacy that affiliated nature and commerce, science and showmanship, and education and entertainment" (Yanni 2002, 122). It brought together an ensemble of disciplines and techniques of display that greatly influenced the subsequent development of the exhibitionary complex in museums, galleries, international expositions, theme parks, panoramas, arcades, and department stores. Concerning the objectivity of imperial thinking, two direct consequences of the Great Exhibition on the exhibitionary complex are of particular relevance: museums and expositions.

Museums are amongst the most Victorian of institutions; between 1860 and 1900 their number rose from 50 to 200 in Great Britain (see van Keuren 1984, 171-172; Bennett 1988, 84). Private collectors transferred their cultural and scientific property to newly built museums that opened their doors to the public. With their collections, museums contributed to bringing order to a presumably controllable world and thus served as major realms of power and knowledge: They offered forms of classification and typologies of display that complemented the standardized picture of Britain's progress. Beyond that, museums served an educational function as they endeavored to cultivate the collective mind. After the Great Exhibition, most of its collections were transferred to the Natural History Museum, the Science Museum, and the South Kensington Museum, which reflected the three categories of products at the exhibition (see Mergenthal 2008, 77). As the world's greatest museum of art and design, the South Kensington Museum (today's Victoria and Albert Museum) assembled objects like furniture, fashion, china, etc., which illustrated the lives of many different cultures from around the world. Although the primary use of the institution was to educate the taste of designers and reform the visiting public into consumers, it also served to demonstrate national pride in British civilized modes of production. At the time, *The Graphic* magazine commented on the underlying imperial mission of the museum:

> No alien, of whatever race he may be – Teuton, Gaul, Tartar or Mongol – can walk through the marvellous collection at South Kensington and look at the innumerable variations of our national Union Jack, without feeling the enormous influence that England has had, and still has, over every part of the globe. (*The Graphic* qtd. in Barringer 1998, 23)

Timothy Barringer argues that the museum decontextualized and appropriated colonial artefacts into strategies of display, which mirrored the development of British imperialism during the second half of the nineteenth century (see Barringer 1998, 12). First, from 1852-1870, the formal qualities of Indian objects were promoted in order to improve national economic performances (see Barringer 1998, 12-17). Second, until 1885, the museum followed the principle of academic imperialism to exert authority over non-Western objects (see Barringer 1998, 17-21). Third, the years until the end of the century were marked by an imperialist triumphalism (see Barrringer 1998, 21-26) – and perhaps even a standardized (pseudo-)scientific victory over unfamiliar objects.

These phases of constructing display narratives can also be detected in other anthropological museums that focused on colonial exhibits, such as the collections by the army officer, archaeologist, and ethnologist Augustus Henry Lane Fox Pitt-Rivers or the tea-trader-cum-compulsive-collector Frederick John Horniman. The founding of the Pitt Rivers Museum (1887) falls into the second period of academic imperialism. In the late 1870s, Pitt Rivers had given about 10,000 objects to the South Kensington Museum for public display, but only a few years later he sought a more permanent home for his collection of archaeological and ethnographic objects (see Petch 2005, n. pag.). He thus decided to donate 20,000 pieces to Oxford University on the condition that it would build a museum and appoint a lecturer in anthropology (see Petch 2005, n. pag.). The person chosen, namely the renowned Edward B. Tylor, had already published his account on *Primitive Culture* (1871), which outlined the differences between 'primitive' and 'civilized' mentalities. Likewise, Pitt Rivers insisted on a particular exhibitionary narrative for his museum, which would illustrate this exact view: The classification by series of objects had to correlate material development with socio-cultural evolution (see van Keuren 1984, 181-182). Earlier, he had elaborated on this taxonomy:

> For this purpose ordinary and typical specimens, rather than rare objects, have been selected and arranged in sequence, so as to trace, as far as practicable, the succession of ideas by which the minds of men in a primitive condition of culture have progressed from the simple to the complex, and from the homogenous to the heterogeneous. (Lane Fox 1875, n. pag.; see Bennett 2009, 43)

Similarly, in 1896, a newspaper article commented on the collectables of London's Horniman Museum:

> Although these have very little fascination from a picturesque point of view, yet they are attractive to us because they portray the vast difference that exists between the civilised and uncivilised races of the world. The dress, the weapons used, the domestic utensils and other articles seem so peculiar to the Western eye that it is almost impossible for us to imagine that at one time in the annals of Great Britain a similar state of affair existed. (*Examiner* qtd. in Coombes 1994, 117)

Yet, back then, Horniman's collection of approximately 30,000 items, encompassing many artificial colonial artefacts bought from the Great Exhibition, were still, without any storyline or sequence, arranged according to geographical area and material category into "oriental panoramas" (Levell 2000, 313). But with the transformation from private to public hands, the collection had to be integrated into a larger standardized exhibitionary narrative and the systematic of its display shifted to illustrate the 'laws' of cultural evolution. When the collection passed to the London County Council, the two new curators, A.C. Haddon and H.S. Harrison, oversaw the rationalization and reclassification into comparative displays based on the Pitt Rivers system (see Levell 2000, 316-317). Hence, once more material culture was linked to stages of evolution and served as visual evidence of the development 'from savagery to civilization'. Colonial exhibits within nineteenth-century anthropological museums thereby helped to consolidate the hierarchy between the imperial subject and the exotic object. They were considered proof of Britain's cultural superiority and therefore used as objectifications of authoritative knowledge.

This official cultural logic, however, from the Great Exhibition onwards, expanded its influence on further spaces of exhibition: for example, on mass entertainment and its popular displays of science. First, the exhibitionary architecture of the Crystal Palace was employed as a template for all subsequent exposition buildings (see Mergenthal 2008, 66; Ogata 2010, 202). Most notably, in 1854, the palace itself was relocated to Sydenham Hill. Dedicated to the entertainment and education of the public, it housed a school of art, science, and literature as well as entertainment spaces, but most prominently historical courts, natural, and ethnological departments (see Yanni 2002, 121). These included large Egyptian, Indian, and Chinese courts (see Levell 2000, 29-46). Moreover, the exhibition at Sydenham not only represented colonial arts and manufactures, but within its natural history courts also objectified the colonial in life-sized ethnological specimens (see Levell 2000, 46). Second, by offering an overview of different nations and by presenting various things from the colonies, the Great Exhibition had encouraged an interest in Britain's overseas territories. In the following decades, this led to the organization of further expositions, which demonstrated colonial commercial and artistic production in particular (see Haltern 1971, 314-315), such as the Colonial and Indian Exhibition (1886), the Empire of India Exhibition (1895), and the Greater Britain Exhibition (1899). The Colonial and Indian Exhibition, opening with *Rule Britannia* at the Royal Albert Hall, must be considered a product of neo-imperialist strategies for displaying materials from the youngest colonies (see Levell 2000, 63-111). Next to the territorial possessions, such as the courts of India and Ceylon, Australia, British New Guinea, Fiji, Canada, New Zealand, and the recently scrambled African colonies, the exposition also presented the Empire's colonized peoples to the London crowd (see *Illustrated London News* 17 July 1886, n. pag.).

This inclusion of peoples, already on display at the Great Exhibition (see "The Great Exhibition" 1851, 404), is even more central to the exhibitionary complex as race theory becomes an intrinsic element to uphold the hegemonies of the Empire. For the Greater Britain Exhibition, director Imre Kiralfy imported about 200 "Matabeles, Basutos, Swazis, Hottentots", etc., to enrich the display of the exhibition with "a vivid realistic and picturesque representation" of "Savage South Africa" (*Daily Programme, Greater Britain Exhibition* qtd. in Shephard 1986, 97) through the reconstruction of a native village, dance performances, and the ostentatious use of 'primitive' tools. This re-enactment was mostly designed to appeal to the public's growing taste for circus-like attractions. Nineteenth-century ethnological show business capitalized on the objectification of the colonial 'Other', for example, in histories of habitation, human showcases, freak shows, and *Völkerschauen* (see Shephard 1986, 92-112; Ogata 2010, 206-207; Müller-Scheessel 2011, 166-170). The bodily spectacle entailed physical regulation and objectification in differentiating the 'freak' or 'Other' from the social 'norm', i.e., the white English man. Additionally, it was also a form in which new sciences, such as evolutionary theory, anthropology, and ethnology, found their way into the entertainment zones.

Although, as Bennett argues, fairs and their displays of so-called monstrosities had rather been perceived as impediments to the rationalizing influences of the Victorian age, the restructured exhibitionary complex, via the display of bodies, finally reached urban popular cultures (see Bennett 1988, 96). These sites indeed served as a buffer zone between official high and popular low culture, combining pleasure with control. Bennett suggests:

> In their interrelations, then, the expositions and their fair zones constituted an order of things and of peoples which [...] rendered the whole world metonymically present, subordinated to the dominating gaze of the white, bourgeois, and [...] male eye of the metropolitan powers. (Bennett 1988, 96)

The exhibitionary complex thereby helped to subject the ideological theme of popular entertainments to the official rhetoric of progress. The influence of the visual logics of the exhibitionary complex thus consolidated notions of imperial thinking in the wider public mind.

5. Conclusion

This paper has elucidated the function of the nineteenth-century exhibitionary complex in objectifying Britain's imperial thinking. It has shown that the combination of visual colonialism and visual consumerism – particularly with respect to exotic objects – sustained the hegemony of 'Self' versus 'Other' by encoding, reifying, reproducing, circulating, and recontextualizing ideas of the colonial 'Other'. The constructions of these visualized and objectified knowledge systems reinforced the power of the Empire and established scientific discourses in order to rationalize the very same cultural preconceptions. The visual taxonomy of museums and expositions thus paves the way for objectifications of knowledge in which the recurrent and standardized arrangement of colonial objects set Western technical sophistication apart from what was perceived as non-European primitivism. This process of reframing objects stresses how colonial products were turned into epistemic things and appropriated as visual proof of theoretical conceptions. Conversely, the exhibitionary complex also helped to spur the development of the sciences: Whereas a progressive sequence of display as a principle of classification was still alien to the eighteenth century (see Bennett 1988, 88), towards the end of the Victorian age, the emergence of a historicized framework within the exhibitionary complex had spread throughout the sciences. In the context of nineteenth-century imperialism, the employment of anthropology proved most central to its ideological goal of differentiating the imperialist power from colonial inferiority (see Bennett 1988, 91-92). The versatility of objects and their salient nature made them amenable to incorporation into hegemonic strategies within the exhibitionary complex. By reducing cultural complexities of meaning through standardized classification, by employing visible things as an objective proof of inferiority, by displaying exotic objects in order to construct a narrative of difference between 'Self' and 'Other', by justifying further colonization in an 'objective' or scientific way, colonial objects served as a material base for the popularization of hegemonic, imperialist attitudes that shaped fictional conceptions of Britannia's superior rule and hence the construction of the Empire mentality during the nineteenth century.

References
Primary Sources

"A Guide to the Great Exhibition of Industry" (1851), in: *The Illustrated London News*, 3 May 1851, 359-372

"A New Result of the Great Exhibition" (1851), in: *The Illustrated London News*, 28 June 1851, 607-608

"Carved Ivory Throne, &c, Exhibited by Her Majesty" (1851), in: *The Crystal Palace, and Its Contents; Being an Illustrated Cyclopaedia of the Great Exhibition of the Industry of All Nations of 1851 Embellished With Upwards of Five Hundred Engravings, With a Copious Analytical Index*. London: W. M. Clark, 65

Fox, A. H. Lane (1875): "On the Principles of Classification Adopted in the Arrangement of His Anthropological Collection, Now Exhibited in the Bethnal Green Museum", *Pitt Rivers Museum*, n. pag. <http://www.prm.ox.ac.uk/Kent/musantob/display4.html.> [accessed 13 January 2014]

Prince Albert (1850): "Speech at the Banquet Given by the Right Hon. Lord Mayor Thomas Farncombe, to Her Majesty's Ministers, Foreign Ambassadors, Royal Commissioners of the Exhibition of 1851 and the Mayors of the One Hundred Eighty Townes, at the Mansion House, 21st March 1850", in: Prince Albert, Prince Consort of Victoria, Queen of Great Britain (1862): *Principal Speeches and Addresses of His Royal Highness the Prince Consort*. London: Murray, 109-114

--- (1854): *Dickinson's Comprehensive Pictures of the Great Exhibition of 1851, from the Originals Painted for H. R. H. Prince Albert by Messrs. Nash, Haghe, and Roberts, R.A.* London: Dickenson Brothers, Her Majesty's Publishers

Queen Victoria (1851): "Extracts from Queen Victoria's Journal, 1851", in: Gibbs-Smith, Charles H. (1981): *The Great Exhibition of 1851*. London: H.M.S.O, 17-20

"Supplement Gratis to the Illustrated London News" (1851), in: *The Illustrated London News,* 8 March 1851, n. pag.

"The Great Exhibition" (1851), in: *The Illustrated London News*, 31 May 1851, 487-496

The Illustrated London News, 17 July 1886, n. pag.

"The Koh-i-Noor – Ancient and Modern History" (1851), in: *The Crystal Palace, and Its Contents; Being an Illustrated Cyclopaedia of the Great Exhibition of the Industry of All Nations of 1851 Embellished With Upwards of Five Hundred Engravings, With a Copious Analytical Index*. London: W. M. Clark, 5-7

Secondary Sources

Barringer, Timothy J. (1998): "The South Kensington Museum and the Colonial Project", in: Barringer, Timothy J.; Flynn, Tom (eds.): *Colonialism and the Object: Empire, Material Culture and the Museum*. London: Routledge, 11-27

Benedict, Burton (2002): "Ethnic Identities at the Great Exhibition", in: Bosbach, Franz et al. (eds.): *Die Weltausstellung von 1851 und ihre Folgen: The Great Exhibition and Its Legacy*. München: K. G. Saur, 81-88

Bennett, Tony (1988): "The Exhibitionary Complex", *New Foundations* 4, 73-102

--- (2009): *The Birth of the Museum: History, Theory, Politics*. London: Routledge

Brosch, Renate (2008): "Victorian Challenges to Ways of Seeing: Everyday Life, Entertainment, Images, and Illusions", in: Brosch, Renate (ed.): *Victorian Visual Culture*. Heidelberg: Winter, 21-64

Coombes, Annie E. (1994): *Reinventing Africa: Museums, Material Culture, and Popular Imagination in Late Victorian and Edwardian England*. New Haven, CT: Yale University Press

Davis, John R. (2002): "Introduction", in: Bosbach, Franz et al. (eds.): *Die Weltausstellung von 1851 und ihre Folgen: The Great Exhibition and Its Legacy*. München: K. G. Saur, 23-30

Gieger, Etta K. (2007): *Die Londoner Weltausstellung von 1851: Im Kontext der Industrialisierung in Großbritannien*. Essen: Blaue Eule

Haltern, Utz (1971): *Die Londoner Weltausstellung von 1851: Ein Beitrag zur Geschichte der bürgerlich-industriellen Gesellschaft im 19. Jahrhundert*. Münster: Aschendorff

Hoffenberg, Peter H. (2001): *An Empire on Display: English Indian and Australian Exhibitions from the Crystal Palace to the Great War*. Berkeley: University of California Press

Kriegel, Lara (2013): "Narrating the Subcontinent in 1851: India at the Crystal Palace", in: Purbrick, Louise (ed.): *The Great Exhibition of 1851: New Interdisciplinary Essays*. Manchester: Manchester University Press, 146-178

Levell, Nicky (2000): *Oriental Visions: Exhibitions, Travel, and Collecting in the Victorian Age*. London: Horniman Museum and Gardens

McNab, Colin; Mackenzie, Robert (1982): *From Waterloo to the Great Exhibition: Britain 1815-1851*. Edinburgh: Oliver & Boyd

Mergenthal, Silvia (2008): "'The Realisation of the Unity of Mankind'? The Great Exhibition of 1851 and the South Kensington Museum", in: Brosch, Renate (ed.): *Victorian Visual Culture*. Heidelberg: Winter, 65-82

Mersmann, Arndt (2001): *"A true test and a living picture": Repräsentationen der Londoner Weltausstellung von 1851*. Trier: WVT

Müller-Scheessel, Nils (2011): "To See Is to Know: Materielle Kultur als Garant von Authentizität auf Weltausstellungen des 19. Jahrhunderts", in: Samida, Stefanie (ed.): *Inszenierte Wissenschaft: Zur Popularisierung von Wissen im 19. Jahrhundert*. Bielefeld: transcript, 157-176

Myers, Fred R. (ed.; 2001): *The Empire of Things: Regimes of Value and Material Culture*. Santa Fe, NM: School of American Research Press

Nünning, Ansgar; Nünning, Vera (1996): "Fictions of Empire and the Making of Imperialist Mentalities: Colonial Discourse and Post-Colonial Criticism as a Paradigm for Intercultural Studies", *Anglistik & Englischunterricht* 58, 7-31

Ogata, Amy F. (2010): "'To See Is to Know'. Visual Knowledge at the International Exhibitions", in: Kromm, Jane (ed.): *A History of Visual Culture: Western Civilization from the 18th to the 21st Century*. Oxford: Berg, 200-210

Petch, Alison (2005): "Augustus Henry Lane Fox Pitt-Rivers and the Founding Collection of the Pitt Rivers Museum", *Pitt Rivers Museum*. <http://www.prm.ox.ac.uk/pdf/Pitt_Rivers.pdf> [accessed 13 January 2014]

Pleßke, Nora (2014): *The Intelligible Metropolis: Urban Mentality in Contemporary London Novels*. Bielefeld: transcript

Said, Edward W. ([1978] 2003): *Orientalism*. London: Penguin Books

Shephard, Ben (1986): "Showbiz Imperialism: The Case of Peter Lobengula", in: MacKenzie, John M. (ed.): *Imperialism and Popular Culture*. Manchester: Manchester University Press, 94-112

Tilley, Chris (2005): "Objectification", in: Tilley, Chris (ed.): *Handbook of Material Culture*. London: SAGE, 60-73 van Keuren, David K. (1984): "Museums and Ideology: Augustus Pitt-Rivers, Anthropological Museums, and Social Change in Later Victorian Britain", *Victorian Studies* 28.1, 171-189

Yanni, Carla (2002): "The Crystal Palace: A Legacy in Science", in: Bosbach, Franz, et al. (eds.): *Die Weltausstellung von 1851 und ihre Folgen: The Great Exhibition and Its Legacy*. München: K. G. Saur, 119-126

Pascal Fischer (Würzburg/Flensburg)

The "Third Culture Intellectuals" and Charles Darwin

1. Introduction

In his recent article "The Closing of the Scientific Mind" David Gelernter complains about a growing tendency of the natural sciences to become dogmatic and intolerant. As an example of this mental inflexibility, he mentions the unhealthy reverence for Charles Darwin among scientists: "Attacking Darwin is the sin against the Holy Ghost that pious scientists are taught never to forgive" (2014, 18). It must be emphasised that this criticism does not emerge from creationist circles, where sneering at a supposed "Darwin cult" is commonplace, but from an eminent computer scientist at Yale who, albeit favourably to religion, has no sympathy for fundamentalism. While it is widely known in continental Europe that the controversy between proponents of creationism and evolutionism continues to constitute a defining feature of American life, it is largely overlooked that Darwin also functions as an important figure of identification and a central reference point for several other debates in the Anglo-American sphere today. He is, for instance, regularly invoked in discussions of the relationship between the natural sciences and the humanities, of the universality of human nature, and – by extension – of the validity of certain tenets of postmodernism. The nineteenth-century scholar, as well as the scientific and philosophical culture of his day, assumes a disportionately greater cultural presence in Britain and the United States than in other countries of the West.

My paper approaches this phenomenon by looking at a movement that has been particularly instrumental in incorporating Darwin into these discussions: the "Third Culture Intellectuals". This is a loose organisation of scientists and writers who have attained an enormous authority in the interpretation of social, cultural, and philosophical matters today. Their honouring of Darwin's heritage demands closer scrutiny, not just because it can reveal the internal mechanisms with which Darwin serves as connecting element for the group, but because such an analysis may illuminate the wider cultural ramifications of the orientation towards Darwin. In their relationship to the Victorian naturalist, several problematic aspects of their world view, and thus of an extremely influential portion of the science community in Britain and the United States, become apparent.

The structure of my article arises quite naturally from my topic: First I will introduce the "Third Culture Intellectuals" in a general way. The second part of my study will then focus on Charles Darwin and the question of why he is so important to the movement. In a third step, I will critically examine some of the key ideas of the "Third Culture Intellectuals" that are related to Darwin.

2. The "Third Culture Intellectuals"

So who are the "Third Culture Intellectuals"? The term "Third Culture" was first used by British physicist and novelist C.P. Snow. After he had lamented the rift in British society between the two cultures, i.e., the natural scientists and the "literary intellectuals", in 1959, the second edition of his book *The Two Cultures* (1964) opened up the prospect of a "Third Culture" in which these groups could communicate with each other. The suggestion was seized upon by the American literary agent, publisher, and author John Brockman in his article "The Emerging Third Culture" (1991), and then elaborated on in a collection of essays entitled *The Third Culture*, which was edited by Brockman in 1994. While Brockman borrows Snow's phrase, its meaning does not exactly correspond to the original concept. Snow's intention of bridging the gap between the natural sciences and the arts is not relinquished in the new project, but the "Third Culture Intellectuals" Brockman has in mind are mainly scientists who speak a plain language to communicate with a wider public (1991, 18), and it is his explicit aim to recapture the designation "intellectuals" for them: "The third-culture thinkers are the new public intellectuals" (19).[1]

According to Brockman's own account, the "Third Culture" movement began in the early 1980s with a group of people who also called themselves the "Reality Club" (2001). After having met in informal places in New York up to the mid-90s, the Reality Club moved to the internet to Brockman's homepage "edge.org". On this website the expressions "Third Culture", "Reality Club", and "Edge" are used almost interchangeably.

Brockman's claim that "here you will find a number of today's sharpest minds" (2001) can hardly be disputed. Several of the contributors have held professorships at top universities in America and England and some have been awarded Pulitzer and Nobel Prizes. Eileen Joy and Christine Neufeld comment: "The list of members of Edge (http://www.edge.org/) and Brockman's 'Third Culture' collective reads like a 'who's who' of the leading scientists, philosophers of science, and social scientists of our times" (2007, 184). In an article in *The Observer* John Naughton is hardly less enthusiastic: He calls Edge "the world's smartest website" and "a salon for the world's finest minds" (2012, 12). The impact of the "Third Culture" is equally impressive. Karl Giberson comments: "For millions of readers and viewers, their pronouncements constitute science" (2002, 121).

As the Edge homepage lists several hundred "members", no strict disciplinary, thematic or ideological limitations can be expected. It is nevertheless evident that there is an inner circle that defines the core interests of the "Third Culture". Many of those who most vocally express the ideals of the movement and regularly participate in "Edge dinners" and "special events" organised under the banner of Edge are in some

---

1 This article is exclusively concerned with thinkers who are connected to John Brockman's movement. It should be mentioned, though, that the term "Third Culture" has also been used by other scholars who work at the interface between the sciences and the humanities outside of the framework described here. The most noteworthy application of the expression without any connection to Brockman's circle can be found in Elinor S. Shaffer's collection of essays *The Third Culture: Literature and Science* (1998). That Shaffer entirely ignores Brockman's book in the explication of the term "Third Culture" in her introduction emerges as an unfortunate attempt to pass over the fact that the term has already been appropriated by others.

way concerned with evolutionary theory. Whereas the biological concept according to which species change over time and the variety of life on earth has developed in the course of hundreds of millions of years is their main focus, "Third Culture Intellectuals" frequently transfer elements of that theory to fields of knowledge outside of biology.

Brockman's original collection *The Third Culture* already shows the priorities: The book has five parts and the first one, which lays out the parameter of the project, bears the title "The Evolutionary Idea". Part Four has the heading "What Was Darwin's Algorithm?", and also deals with evolution. In the other parts evolution looms large as well. In view of this emphasis, it is quite apposite that Jonathan Gottschall and David Sloan Wilson, Edge members themselves, refer to Brockman's "stable of evolutionary authors" (xxi).

However, it is not only the abstract concept of evolution that ensures coherence within the group, but to a remarkable extent Charles Darwin himself, who contributed the principle of natural and sexual selection to evolutionism.

3. The Role of Charles Darwin for the "Third Culture Intellectuals"

The importance of the nineteenth-century naturalist for the phenomenon is really amazing. Many "Third Culture Intellectuals" have written books about Darwin's life and thought; several have shown a respect for Darwin bordering on adoration. Here, I can only introduce the most central figures. Probably nobody has formed the image of Charles Darwin today as much as the evolutionary biologist Richard Dawkins of Oxford University. The author of several books on Darwinism and creator of the three-part television documentary on Channel 4 "The Genius of Charles Darwin" is extremely central to the "Third Culture". Asked how he adds names to Edge, Brockman explained that there are some people who usually give him recommendations. Dawkins is one of them (Naughton 2012, 12). Another one is Steven Pinker, Harvard Professor of Psychology. Very much influenced by evolutionary theory, Pinker has also constantly been involved in debates about Darwin. Some of the personalities on Edge head institutions particularly concerned with Darwinism. The philosopher Helena Cronin runs the Darwin Centre at the London School of Economics and Political Science (LSE), and is co-editor of the Yale University Press series Darwinism Today. One of the most active members of Edge is the American philosopher Daniel C. Dennett, co-director of the Center for Cognitive Studies at Tufts University and the author of *Darwin's Dangerous Idea: Evolution and the Meanings of Life*, 1995.

The close ties that exist between the leading figures of the movement very often have to do with Darwin. Dawkins's documentary on Darwin features interviews with Pinker and Dennett. Dawkins, Pinker, and Dennett have participated in events at Cronin's Darwin Seminars at the LSE, have written endorsements for her book series, and so forth. That the exchange between the Darwinians regularly takes place under the umbrella of Edge shows to what extent the "Third Culture" is defined by the Darwin connection. At the Darwin bicentennial in 2009, and in order to celebrate the three hundredth edition of Edge, eight of its contributors attended the Darwin Seminar in Santiago de Chile entitled "Darwin's Intellectual Legacy to the 21st Century", and then went on a boat trip through the "Beagle Channel" to commemorate Darwin's journey (www.edge.org/events/darwin-in-chile). Helena Cronin and Daniel Dennett participated, Stephen Pinker took the pictures, and the British novelist Ian McEwan was also on board, another Edge "member". The example of this trip can illustrate that the turn to Darwin involves a great esteem for his individual ingenuity, exploratory spirit, and determination.

What is related to this perspective on Darwin is a general orientation towards the nineteenth century as a time when the individual, driven by a zest for adventure, could still make a great difference. Reflecting on Darwin's genius and the immensity of his findings, today's Darwinians often imaginatively transport the reader into the Victorian era. The year 1859, which saw the publication of Darwin's principal book on evolutionary theory, *On the Origin of Species*, is singled out as the greatest watershed in history. After having commented on the "awesome gulf [that] divides the pre-Darwinian world from ours" (1991, xi) at the beginning of her book *The Ant and the Peacock*, Helena Cronin opens the second chapter with the date "1859" and the following lines: "Imagine a world without Darwin. Imagine a world in which Charles Darwin and Alfred Russel Wallace had not transformed our understanding of living things" (*ibid.*, 7). Richard Dawkins also repeatedly points to that moment in time. The following example is from his popular book *The Blind Watchmaker*: "Simple as the theory may seem, nobody thought of it until Darwin and Wallace in the mid-nineteenth century, nearly 300 years after Newton's *Principia*, and more than 2,000 years after Eratosthenes measured the Earth" (1986, xi). And a bit further on, Dawkins, the avowed atheist and fierce critic of religion, remarks: "I once discussed the matter at dinner. I said that I could not imagine being an atheist at any time before 1859, when Darwin's *Origin of Species* was published" (5). Helena Cronin (1991, 7-40) and Daniel Dennett (1995, 35-83) recapitulate the debates that were contemporaneous with Darwin's research activity. And many "Third Culture" writers are quick to bolster up their explanations with anecdotes from Darwin's life. A sound familiarity with Darwin's biography and time is taken for granted within the inner circles of the "Third Culture". Even though the Victorian age is not explicitly mentioned as an inspiration for Edge in the "About" section of the homepage, the somewhat earlier Lunar Society of Birmingham (with Erasmus Darwin, Josiah Wedgwood, and Joseph Priestley) is given as the major model (www.edge.org/about-us). The turn towards the British past is ingrained in the movement.

Of course, many of the "Third Culture" authors feel the need to defend the insights of evolutionary theory against the onslaught of creationism and intelligent design, particularly in the United States. Indefatigably explaining the fundamentals of Darwinism, they often go back to the original discussions in the Victorian age. In analogy to the most stalwart defender of Darwinism in the nineteenth century, T. H. Huxley, who was known as "Darwin's Bulldog", Richard Dawkins has in turn been called "Darwin's Rottweiler", e.g. by the *Discover* magazine (Hall 2005), owing to his aggressive stance against biblical literalism.

But in order to comprehend the reasons for Darwin's centrality to the "Third Culture", as well as the implications of his prominence, further aspects have to be considered. In keeping with the general aim of the movement to close the gap between the natural sciences and the humanities, Darwin is highly esteemed as the embodiment of an integrated culture that stands in sharp contrast to our present diversification of disciplines. In their collection *The Literary Animal*, American literary scholar Jonathan Gottschall and American evolutionary biologist David Sloan Wilson honour Darwin in the following way:

> His ability to function as an extreme integrationist was due partially to his personal genius but also to his theory, which provides a common framework for studying all things animate and their productions, therefore all things human. We might not share Darwin's personal genius, but we can make use of his theory to reverse the trend of extreme specialization of knowledge that has taken place in the absence of a unifying conceptual framework. (Gottschall and Wilson 2005, xvii)

The passage expresses a longing for a time when the disciplines still spoke a common language. And it also reveals a nostalgic yearning for a coherent model of world explanation. The "unifying conceptual framework" that has been lost and which Darwin's theory is supposed to replace is, quite obviously, Christianity.

It is characteristic of "Third Culture" publications that it is not only Darwinism that serves as the link between the various fields of knowledge, but also Darwin the man. In his article in the same collection, Ian McEwan takes a similar line of reasoning. Reflecting on the difficulties literary people face in comprehending greatness in science, he mentions Darwin as the positive counter-example (2005, 6). Apart from commenting on the accessibility and relevance of Darwin's theory, McEwan approaches his personality through his biography (7-10).

In spite of the rhetoric of reconciliation with the humanities that permeates "Third Culture" writing, its adherents also fiercely criticise the direction Literary and Cultural Studies have taken. Again, it is Charles Darwin's authority that is invoked. Edge scholars chiefly attack "social constructivism" or "cultural determinism", the theory that humans are primarily formed by their social and cultural surroundings. For Edge members John Tooby and Leda Cosmides (both from the Center for Evolutionary Psychology at the University of California, Santa Barbara), who refer to "social constructivism" as the "Standard Social Science Model" (1992, 24-32), Darwinism proves that we are not first and foremost the products of our culture, but that there are universals, common characteristics in our biology, that define human nature (21). Joe Rose, the narrator in Ian McEwan's novel *Enduring Love*, sums up the "Third Culture" position:

> Biologists and evolutionary psychologists were re-shaping the social sciences. The post-war consensus, the Standard Social Science Model, was falling apart and human nature was up for re-examination. We do not arrive in this world as blank sheets, or as all-purpose learning devices. Nor are we the 'products' of our environment. [...] The word from the human biologists bears Darwin out. (1997, 60-70)

At the same time, McEwan also presents us with the opposite view in the person of Joe's wife Clarissa, a literary scholar who calls "neo-Darwinism" the "new fundamentalism" (79). So we certainly should not reduce McEwan to a simplistic position within the controversy.

That "Third Culture Intellectuals" use Darwin to distance themselves from the humanities also becomes evident in another respect: They frequently show their aversion to the idea that reality is a subjective category and that truth can never be entirely reached. It is indeed a core conviction of large parts of the humanities that our knowledge of reality must of necessity be limited. In contrast to that, the scientists involved in Edge claim that these doubts are misguided. With the designation "Reality Club" they want to show that they accept reality as a given fact. In their publications it is sometimes mentioned that the return to Darwin can help to overcome scepticism about truth. Edge member Dylan Evans, for example, describes his own acceptance of "Truth and Evidence" as his personal journey "From Lacan to Darwin" – as the title of his article puts it (2005). Positioning himself against "deconstructionism, postmodernism, and other relativist doctrines" (2002, 208), Stephen Pinker does not only insist upon an objective reality (in the chapter "In Touch with Reality" of his book *The Blank Slate*, 197-218), but also on the idea that our brains are well equipped to identify it, and that our language is fit to describe it. It is an important element of the "Third Culture" historical narrative that there had been a general belief in the accessibility of reality before "social constructivism" began to dominate the intellectual landscape in the twentieth century. Darwin and his time are seen as an antidote against the postmodernist way of thinking. Frederick Crews writes in the foreword to *The Literary Animal*: "Darwin conducted himself like a member of a disciplinary community held together by a common regard for truth. We can do the same, and it is in that spirit that I salute the authors of the essays that follow" (2005, 15). Again we see the desire to emulate Darwin and his time.

4. Criticism of the "Third Culture Intellectuals"

In the third part of my paper I will now point to aspects of the "Third Culture" worldview in connection with Darwin's heritage that appear to be problematic and deserve to be critically assessed. In Europe we usually shake our heads at the literalist readings of the Bible by some Christian fundamentalists in the United States, for instance at the claim that the world was created some 6,000 years ago. It therefore seems only logical that we side with those who defend the scientific consensus on evolution. That, however, does not exempt Edge scholars from criticism. Cultural Studies in particular provide the intellectual and methodological resources to throw a critical light on "Third Culture" doctrines, most notably where they affect the relationship between the sciences and the humanities. Considering the variety of voices within the "Third Culture", I can, of course, only address certain tendencies and do not necessarily mean to implicate everyone who has ever contributed to Edge.

That there is a large distance between Cultural Studies and the "Third Culture" has already been shown in an article from 2012 by Slovene philosopher Slavoj Žižek entitled "Cultural Studies versus the 'Third Culture'". While offering a critique of the movement, Žižek does not comment upon the significance of Charles Darwin for the "Third Culture Intellectuals", the focus of my attention here.

My first point of criticism, in fact, concerns the adoration that is shown for Darwin. In principle, there is nothing wrong with a high regard for personal achievements, and Darwin certainly merits our esteem. Yet, in this group, Darwin is often exalted to super-human proportions. Daniel Dennett writes:

> Let me lay my cards on the table. If I were to give an award for the single best idea anyone has ever had, I'd give it to Darwin, ahead of Newton and Einstein and everyone else. In a single stroke, the idea of evolution by natural selection unifies the realm of life, meaning, and purpose with the realm of space and time, cause and effect, mechanism and physical law. [...] My admiration for Darwin's magnificent idea is unbounded [...]. (1995, 21)

As the initiator of a new coherent pattern of world explanation, Darwin is elevated to a position similar to that of a spiritual leader or prophet. That this desire for a totalizing *weltanschauung* is projected onto an individual, who thus assumes the role of the originator of something entirely new, is not without irony. The notion that one man can change the course of intellectual history all of a sudden is at odds with the belief in the slow process of evolution. Dennett's portrayal of Darwin as a super-human being creating with "a single stroke" may even remind us of the God of Genesis. However, the theory of evolution by natural and sexual selection was not a *creatio ex nihilo*; Darwin did not found evolutionary theory from scratch, but built upon the research of others.[2] Somewhat paradoxically in view of the passage quoted above, Dennett later admits that the "idea of natural selection was not itself a miraculously novel creation of Darwin's but, rather, the offspring of earlier ideas that had been vigorously discussed for years and even generations" (40).

Still, it is typical of the "Third Culture" to spotlight individual agency and great men who make history, rather than structural and cultural contexts. John Cartwright's and Brian Baker's assessment of "Third Culture" authors is very relevant to the exalted image of Darwin in the group: "It is as if the institution of science itself approves stories of heroic discovery and the transforming power of science as part of its own means of justification" (2005, 304). Cultural Studies, in contrast, stress that the individual can only act within cultural boundaries. That the "myth of individual autonomy" or "individual agency" is particularly widespread in the Anglo-American sphere is common knowledge in Cultural Studies. The "Third Culture" adoration of Darwin is furthermore based on considerable elitism, as John Brockman's article "The Emerging Third Culture", the very founding document of the movement, shows: "Throughout history, intellectual life has been marked by the fact that only a small number of people have done the serious thinking for everybody else" (1991, 19). Conversely, Cultural Studies have argued that the intellectual life of a nation is not limited to the select few (Assmann 2012, 20-21).

My next point of criticism relates to the supposed reconciliation with the humanities. It is certainly the case that some "Third Culture" scholars do indeed pursue the aim of diminishing the humanities-science divide, but on closer inspection it becomes clear that this should chiefly be done on terms set by the natural sciences. Again it is worth looking at Brockman's manifesto, in which he belittles literary people, for instance when he writes: "Unlike previous intellectual pursuits, the achievements of the third culture are not the marginal disputes of a quarrelsome mandarin class: they will affect the lives of everybody on the planet" (1991, 19). The idea that their colleagues in the philosophy departments are unfit to contribute to the larger philosophical questions is quite characteristic of the "Third Culture". Consequently, insights that do not suit the scientists' positions can simply be brushed aside.

Take the issue of "human nature": Several Edge scholars claim that Literary and Cultural Studies have given up on the concept of "human nature" in favour of a radical version of "cultural determinism". It may be true that some in the humanities have conveyed this impression, but the field on the whole does not reject the idea that there are some things common to humanity.

---

2   Without mentioning Daniel Dennett, Sally Shuttleworth provides a critique of the present glorification of Darwin that perfectly fits the passage at hand: "The Darwin industry, in its populist forms, has created a heroic image of an individual who almost single-handedly changed the fundamental framework of Western human thought, redefining psychological, social and religious understanding. He stands as an image of a man who has defeated history by conferring his own lasting order. Such deification then stands in direct contrast to our own age where no such human agency seems at work, and individuals appear as slaves to their own technological productions" (1998, 260).

While the people involved in Edge generally pride themselves on a balanced view of the interaction between "nature" and "nurture", for instance Denis Dutton, author of the book *The Art Instinct: Beauty, Pleasure, and Human Evolution* (2009a; see Dutton 2009b, "Art and Human Reality"), they frequently downplay the role of culture in their insistence that it is the biological heritage of our species that decides who we are. This is most evident in their view of gender. In her talk "Why Sex Differences Matter: The Darwinian Perspective" (2009), Helena Cronin explains the differences between men and women largely by evolutionary theory. The 'fact' that, according to one study, male vervet monkey babies prefer toy cars over dolls and female babies dolls over cars, is passed off as sufficient evidence that gender-specific behaviour is innate *in general*. Simply disregarding all the discussions of gender studies, Cronin makes statements about what is typically male and female that could hardly be more clichéd. To prove that "men notoriously find any arena to be the first, the biggest, the most, the best", she shows pictures of men doing rather extreme things, like cycling backwards while playing the violin (Cronin 2009). She even postulates that "women prefer people" and "men prefer things" (*ibid.*). Attributing her dubious insights to a male and a female "human nature", Cronin does not realise (or will not admit) that her supposedly objective scientific methods merely reproduce stereotypes. It would be easy for Cultural Studies to show the origins of these stereotypes. That men are at their most masculine when alone, is, for instance, a notion that was developed in Romanticism and later cultivated in hard-boiled fiction and countless Western movies.

What must furthermore be addressed is the "Third Culture's" unshaken belief in the attainability of truth and their use of Darwin to support that conviction. Literary and cultural critics have questioned the scientists' claim to an objective reality by pointing out the dependency of their theories on literary models, narrative patterns, and metaphors. Since the way we perceive reality is always structured and filtered by language, we only have access to a construct of reality. Darwin, for instance, continuously personifies "Nature" with the feminine pronoun "she". The very concept of natural selection is based on the metaphor of nature as a person. Metaphors are an indispensable means of conceptualizing scientific findings, but at the same time they also hide certain aspects of reality. One of the central texts in the study of scientific discourse, Gillian Beer's *Darwin's Plots* (first published in 1983), explains that Darwin himself was very sceptical about the possibility of describing the full range of reality: "His theory deconstructs any formulation which interprets the natural world as commensurate with man's understanding of it. It outgoes his powers of observation and is not coextensive with his reasoning" (2009, 90). It is therefore misleading when "Third Culture" authors use Darwin to testify that truth is simply there to be discovered.

My final critique has already been hinted at in the article by Slavoj Žižek. For him the "Third Culture Intellectuals" are so preoccupied with the "ultimate enigmas" (2002, 23) of our existence that they silently pass over the burning questions of today's societies, for instance racism, multiculturalism, and Eurocentrism (*ibid.*, 22). I doubt that these authors are indifferent to racism, as they continuously reject all varieties of Social Darwinism as based on logical fallacies (see e.g. Pinker 2002, 15-16; McEwan 2005, 10, 16). Where Žižek really has a point, though, is in his observation that the phenomenon is Eurocentric. Yet we should be more precise and specify that it is Anglocentric. While Edge is registered in the United States as a nonprofit organisation, the people who are associated with it make it a predominantly Anglo-American project. In the aforementioned article on "The World's Smartest Website", John Naughton remarks: "Edge seems biased towards the Anglo-Saxon world; at any rate, there are surprisingly few continental Europeans or Asians. Brits, on the other hand, figure prominently" (Naughton 2012, 12). And in an interview about his relationship to Darwin, Ian McEwan explains that the Anglo-Saxon publishing world has been blessed with "superb interpreters of science" whereas "it's not quite the same in, say, France, Germany, Spain" (2009). The exalted image of Darwin must be understood in relation to this Anglocentricity. Darwin does not only strengthen the professional identity of these scientists, but their Anglo-Saxon identity as well. With their frequent references to Victorian scientific culture they can assure themselves of a common heritage. As much as Darwin may unite people from different disciplines, his prominence can, at the same time, have an exclusive effect, as it defines intellectual culture as Anglo-American in the first place. The focus on Darwin and the idealization of a male-dominated Victorian culture also indirectly affects the categories of race and gender. The recurrent turn to Darwin and his time shows that Edge's model of a "universal human nature" may be connected to a white and male norm. Scholars in Cultural and Postcolonial Studies have rightly remarked that the insistence on the universality of human nature has often been used to disguise Western predominance. When human nature is chiefly defined from an Anglo-American perspective, cultural practices from widely different regions may even appear to be at odds with human nature.

5. Conclusion

I have shown that Darwin holds a very prominent position in the "Third Culture" and that the causes, functions, and implications of that are diverse. The last part of my paper has exposed some problematic aspects of the phenomenon: the idolization of Darwin, the glorification of individual agency, the ridicule for scholars in the humanities and the disregard for their research, the one-sided insistence on a biologically determined human nature, and the rather simple-hearted confidence in our ability to recognise truth objectively. Finally, I have tried to explain why the portrayal of Darwin as the embodiment of scientific culture may help to construct an Anglo-Saxon identity – with the consequence of shutting out others. Taken together, these elements may illustrate that there is a tendency towards dogmatism and intolerance in the movement. This is regrettable, as the basic idea behind the term *Third Culture*, the aim of reducing the distance between the natural sciences and the humanities, is a very laudable one. But this can only be achieved if both sides acknowledge the limitations and the strengths of their fields and enter into a real dialogue. Cultural Studies have much to offer in this respect.

References

Assmann, Aleida (2012): *Introduction to Cultural Studies: Topics, Concepts, Issues*. Berlin: Schmidt
Beer, Gillian (^{3}2009): *Darwin's Plots: Evolutionary Narrative in Darwin, George Eliot and Nineteenth-Century Fiction*. Cambridge: Cambridge University Press
Brockman, John (^{1}1991): "The Emerging Third Culture", in: Brockman, John (ed.; 1994): *The Third Culture: Beyond the Scientific Revolution*. New York: Simon & Schuster, 17-37

--- (2001): "Edge: The Reality Club", <http://www.edge.org/discourse/about.html> [accessed 05 January 2014]
--- (ed.; 1994): *The Third Culture: Beyond the Scientific Revolution*. New York: Simon & Schuster
Cartwright, John H.; Baker, Brian (2005): *Literature and Science: Social Science and Interaction*. Santa Barbara, CA: ABC-CLIO
Crews, Frederick (2005): "Foreword from the Literary Side", in: Gottschall, Jonathan; Wilson, David Sloan (eds.): *The Literary Animal: Evolution and the Nature of Narrative*. Evanston, IL: Northwestern University Press, xiii-xv
Cronin, Helena (1991): *The Ant and the Peacock: Altruism and Sexual Selection from Darwin to Today*. Cambridge: Cambridge University Press
--- (2009): "Why Sex Differences Matter: The Darwinian Perspective", <http://www.edge.org/conversation/why-sex-differences-matter-the-darwinian-perspective> [accessed 05 January 2014]
Dawkins, Richard (1986): *The Blind Watchmaker: Why the Evidence of Evolution Reveals a Universe without Design*. New York: Norton
Dennett, Daniel C. (1995): *Darwin's Dangerous Idea: Evolution and the Meanings of Life*. London: Penguin
Dutton, Denis (2009a): *The Art Instinct: Beauty, Pleasure, and Human Evolution*. New York: Bloomsbury
--- (2009b): "Art and Human Reality: A Talk with Denis Dutton", <http://www.edge.org/conversation/art-and-human-reality> [accessed 05 January 2014]
Evans, Dylan (2005): "From Lacan to Darwin", in: Gottschall, Jonathan; Wilson, David Sloan (eds.): *The Literary Animal: Evolution and the Nature of Narrative*. Evanston, IL: Northwestern University Press, 38-55
Gelernter, David (2014): "The Closing of the Scientific Mind", *Commentary*, January 2014, 17-25
Giberson, Karl (2002): *Species of Origins: America's Search for a Creation Story*. Lanham, MD: Rowman and Littlefield
Gottschall, Jonathan; Wilson, David Sloan (2005): "Introduction: Literature – a Last Frontier in Human Evolutionary Studies", in: Gottschall, Jonathan; Wilson, David Sloan (eds.): *The Literary Animal: Evolution and the Nature of Narrative*. Evanston, IL: Northwestern University Press, xvii-xxvi
Hall, Stephen S. (2005): "Darwin's Rottweiler: Sir Richard Dawkins: Evolution's Fiercest Champion, Far Too Fierce", *Discover*, 26.09 <http://discovermagazine.com/2005/sep/darwins-rottweiler> [accessed 05 January 2014]
Joy, Eileen A.; Neufeld, Christine M. (2007): "A Confession of Faith – Notes Toward a New Humanism", *Journal of Narrative Theory* 37.2, 161-190
McEwan, Ian (1997): *Enduring Love*. London: Cape
--- (2005): "Literature, Science, and Human Nature", in: Gottschall, Jonathan; Wilson, David Sloan (eds.): *The Literary Animal: Evolution and the Nature of Narrative*. Evanston, IL: Northwestern University Press, 5-19
--- (2009): "Ian McEwan on Darwin", *ABC Radio National - The Science Show*, Aug. 1, 2009, <http://www.abc.net.au/radionational/programs/scienceshow/ian-mcewan-on-darwin/3063744#transcript> [accessed 05 January 2014]
Naughton, John (2012): "John Brockman: The Man Who Runs the World's Smartest Website", *The Observer*, 08 January 2012, 12-15
Pinker, Steven (2002): *The Blank Slate: The Modern Denial of Human Nature*. New York: Viking
Shaffer, Elinor S. (1998): "Introduction: The Third Culture – Negotiating the 'Two Cultures'", in: Shaffer, Elinor S. (ed.): *The Third Culture: Literature and Science*. Berlin/New York: de Gruyter, 1-15
Shuttleworth, Sally (1998): "Natural History: The Retro-Victorian Novel", in: Shaffer, Elinor S. (ed.): *The Third Culture: Literature and Science*. Berlin/New York: de Gruyter, 253-68
Snow, C.P. (1964): *The Two Cultures: And a Second Look*. Cambridge: Cambridge University Press
Tooby, John; Cosmides, Leda (1992): "The Psychological Foundations of Culture", in: Barkow, Jerome H. et al. (eds.): *The Adapted Mind: Evolutionary Psychology and the Generation of Culture*. New York: Oxford University Press, 19-136
www.edge.org/events/darwin-in-chile ["Darwin's Intellectual Legacy to the 21st Century"]
Žižek, Slavoj (2002): "Cultural Studies versus the 'Third Culture'", *South Atlantic Quarterly* 101.1, 19-32

Section 2

Historical Media Cultures

Chairs:

Kai Merten and Nicola Glaubitz

KAI MERTEN (KIEL) AND NICOLA GLAUBITZ (SIEGEN)

Historical Media Cultures

History, media, and culture are terms whose discussion no longer requires justification in the context of English Studies. The "cultural turn" has long been productively registered by German Anglistik, and media like film, television, and games are routinely studied by now. Yet the terms 'history', 'media', and 'culture' are far from self-evident and demand explanation.

They can be most productively considered as work in progress, we would argue: Even a superficial survey of the research that has been done in the last decade will be evidence enough that history, media, and culture can still enter into new configurations. What we had hoped for when we planned the section, and what our contributors have in fact done with surprising consistency, is to expand media studies into periods before the advent of the so-called new media of modernity (photography, sound recording, and moving pictures). Applying the concept of media, media theories, and a range of epistemological questions from the present to the remote past admittedly involves risks, but it also has advantages, allowing us to detect media debates *avant la lettre*, and in (perhaps) unlikely places.

We will briefly sketch a few areas of study in which media of the past have moved into the focus of interest: Early Modern Studies, Romantic Studies, Nineteenth-Century Studies, and Modernist Studies. In Early Modern Studies, two recent trends in media and media debates of the past should be mentioned: One is represented by Michael Bristol's and Arthur Marotti's book *Print, Manuscript, Performance: The Changing Relations of the Media in Early Modern England* (2000), which analyses Early Modern media constellations in the light of the two central media inventions of the period, namely the printed text and the public theatre. This kind of research into the relation of the page to the stage is also a productive field in Shakespeare Studies at the moment (see Orgel and Macmillan 2006 as well as Weimann and Bruster 2008). Another, equally interesting approach is represented by James Kearney's *The Incarnate Text: Imagining the Book in Reformation England* (2009), which studies media and mediality in the European Reformation debates beginning in the early sixteenth century. The Reformation attack on the idea that images or any other object could mediate the Holy Spirit was countered by the Catholic argument that the Holy Bible, elevated by the Reformers, was just another such mediator. This discussion and comparison of images, books, and other liturgical objects is undoubtedly a media debate from today's perspective because it negotiated human objects as carriers of data outside themselves, which is a classical definition of "medium" (Engell 2002, 127; Wiesing 2008).

In Romantic Studies, Clifford Siskin and William Warner (2010) argue that the Enlightenment must be conceived of as an event in the history of what they call "mediation" and linked to both technical and symbolic media. They have extended this argument to the period of Romanticism in their keynote to the 2010 NASSR Annual Conference *Romantic Mediations*, an event wholly dedicated to exploring Romantic media cultures.

It is perhaps less of a surprise to find a host of studies on the media cultures of the nineteenth and early twentieth centuries. The study of Modernism in particular has profited from media-historical perspectives. One important trend in "New Modernist Studies" (see Mao and Walkowitz 2008, 738; 742) is media archaeology and its focus on the media technologies around 1900 (Trotter 2009). Media ecology is another approach that has brought about a re-examination of past cultural periods: It enquires into the artificially created worlds of perception that affect bodies and fashion subjects (Armstrong 1998).

These studies are concerned with the origins of still familiar media like photography, film, sound recording, and radio. Their very familiarity can obscure media-historical developments, however, when contemporary concepts of media are taken for granted. Jonathan Crary's influential study *Techniques of the Observer* (1990), for example, reconstructs a history of vision in the nineteenth century with respect to visual technologies (chiefly stereoscopy). Taking into account the interrelatedness of scientific and aesthetic discourses on seeing, and the impact of metaphors on the epistemology of vision, Crary nevertheless subscribes to the idea of technological innovations as driving forces behind cultural developments.[1] One of the arguments derived from this premise is that the invention of stereoscopy amounts to a major rupture in the tradition of perspectival representation and its epistemological underpinnings (Crary 1990, 36). This claim is difficult to support, since, on the one hand, other modes of constructing perspective were in use and continued to be so. On the other hand, photography – another important visual technology of the nineteenth century – continues to produce a perspectival, *camera obscura* type of image (see Schröter 2014, 8). Julian Murphet argues that even though the idea of media determinism (as represented by Kittler or Crary) is not a viable systematic perspective, it still needs to be studied as a historical phenomenon. Writers and artists of the Anglo-American avant-garde "behaved as if new media and technologies were 'causing' the series of formal and technical breaks internal to their work", and "relations among the media governed the material complexities of modernist forms" (Murphet 2009, 2). Literary history can therefore be rewritten as a history of competing media institutions, and no longer as "literature within a field of technology" (Murphet 2009, 2-3). The transfer of modern media concepts to the past can be problematic, as Crary's example shows, but it can also sharpen awareness for the historicity of media concepts themselves. This transfer can also reveal, as Murphet demonstrates, how technological inventions *become* media; how discourses, metaphors, institutions, and practices contribute to the creation of functional equivalents to present-day media configurations. Paying attention to media cultures is thus of vital importance. The general trend towards an awareness of technological and material aspects of literary production that we have described already involves a closer scrutiny of their institutional frameworks, and of their practical dimensions – dimensions captured by the term "cultures".

---

1   See Crary 1990, 29-30. Lisa Gitelman outlines the problem of media histories that tend to naturalize and essentialize media in a more general sense in *Always Already New* (2006).

Talking about media cultures (in the plural) means to rethink the idea of media as artefacts, or as technologies with fixed properties, with fixed functions, and with intrinsic differences. Noel Carroll has pointed out the difficulties involved in arguments "that the new media have a range of aesthetic effects peculiar to them whose exploitation marks the proper avenue of artistic development within the medium in question" (Carroll 1984, 127). Carroll here refers to a crucial assumption of modernist aesthetics and art theory, namely the idea that media such as painting, sculpture, or language have specific properties, whose foregrounding and reflection is the prime task of the artist. Transferring this assumption to technical media such as film or video merely consecrates and ennobles such media as art and turns them into legitimate objects of study, Carroll holds. If this objection has lost some of its relevance for present-day discussions, another observation of Carroll's is still to the point: "If media have essences, which is itself a controversial issue, it is far from clear that an ostensible essence [...] has any directive force regarding how the medium is used, let alone how it should be used" (Carroll 1984, 139). Looking at media cultures instead of specific media implies looking at unstable, changing configurations, embedded in and shaped by media discourses. Media discourses perform as scripts that tell us how to use media correctly or incorrectly, routinely or creatively, and inform media practices without determining them.[2] Such configurations are highly contingent and need to be reconstructed historically as changes in media practices and media definitions.

Media cultures also open up new aspects of cultural history for discussion. Some of the trends we have presented are motivated by dissatisfaction with New Historicism, a leading paradigm of the last 20 years. As Rita Felski observes, treating "works of art only as cultural symptoms of their own *moment*" (Felski 2011, 575; our emphasis) fails to account for continuities. Felski's objection is as old as historicism itself: historicism is, paradoxically, not historical enough – it fails to account for the interplay of continuities and discontinuities over longer periods of time. If the New Historicism could be seen as a turning away from the grand historical narratives provided by theories of modernisation or a history of ideas, it is still open to debate which histories remain to be reconstructed, and along which lines. The return to aesthetic issues that has recently stepped into the place of New Historicism, Felski warns, "conspicuously fails to answer the question of how texts resonate across time" (Felski 2011, 575). Here, a closer look at the media of cultural and literary history (the media configurations, including those underpinning academic practice, that render history intelligible in the first place) could offer new perspectives (see Gitelman 2006, 5). Another alternative is the history of media practices and media cultures; it could be written as a history of continuing problems such as mediated sociality or social media. Rainer Emig's contribution is an example for such an approach; the visiting card, an apparently simple and ephemeral medium, is shown to occupy and bridge a gap between public and private

---

2 Albert Kümmel and Petra Löffler show, for example, that the invention and diffusion of communication technologies at the beginning of the twentieth century can be observed as a media-historical event (and became a point of reference for later media developments) because technologies were described as media: They were embedded in discourses problematizing their mediality, that is, their functions of transmission, storage, and circulation of information. Even though the term "medium" only began to shed its spiritualist connotations at the turn of the century, the period between 1888 and 1933 is characterised by debates on the use and functions of what would later be called "media" (see Kümmel and Löffler 2002, 14-15).

spheres in the nineteenth century, and can function as a means of both intimate and official communication as well as a commodity indicating prestige or status. The visiting card as an early example of social media further exemplifies the productivity of a deliberate and controlled use of anachronism: Approaching historical periods "through the conscious election of a media paradigm from a different era", Alan Liu argues, is a mode of remaining committed to the past while still being able to follow the complex web of historical trajectories connecting a past moment to the present (Liu 2008, 25). One such past moment that features prominently in contributions to this section is the eighteenth century. In his keynote, Albrecht Koschorke studies how the distance medium of writing gained prevalence in eighteenth-century Europe, and how this development shaped the culture of sensibility as a concomitant mediatization of the body to bridge temporal and spatial distance as well as to enable the communication between private and mutually anonymous individuals. What this media-historical development implied for the history of the British novel is explored in Natalie Roxburgh's chapter. The novel of sensibility, she argues, experiences its own mediality as a paradox, so that the ruin of the sentimental hero, a stock element of the genre, should be read as conveying the novel's uneasiness with the very culture of distance mass media that both enables and shapes it. In a similar vein, Gerd Bayer analyses the discontents of the epistolary novel within eighteenth-century media culture. He argues that eighteenth-century epistolary fiction, while harking back to a medium developed before the period, explores the letter not as facilitating transparency and realism but as a form of potentially misfiring and deceptive communication; the epistolary novel thus ultimately inserts a destabilising self-reflexivity into the nascent genre. Ingo Berensmeyer cautions us that it is important to study the role of authorship conceptions in the eighteenth-century media culture of written communication and to keep in mind contemporary differentiations between autonomous and heteronomous authors. Interestingly, the literary example that he explores is an epistolary novel, which, if perhaps not quite constituting deceptive communication, nevertheless reminds its readers to take the authorial position of the letter writer himself into account as a further option in the culture of authorship as explored in the novel.

What connects these contributions is that they all follow the history of mediated sociality while also being inspired by the controlled anachronism of the notion of social media. If we want to trace this history somewhat further back while staying alert to the continuing challenge of mediating individuality, the early modern period offers itself as another, if somewhat understudied, transitional moment in the history of media. The media-historical implications of the Reformation have already been mentioned. If we relate the Reformation to the history of social mediation, an interesting prehistory to the problems explored in our contributions arises.

In mid-seventeenth century Britain, radical reformers cast doubt on the institution of God-given monarchy and demanded that rulers be humbler while at the same time legitimated by their individual deeds and religious inspiration. One of the most prominent examples for this is John Milton's 1649 pamphlet *Eikonoklastes*. Milton argues that an abstract but divine "Truth", defended by "Justice" (583), is the supreme power over humanity. In the face of this authority, all human beings, monarchs included, are identical, just as they are individually exposed to it. Political leaders are therefore legitimated not by being earthly representatives of God (as was claimed in absolutism) but because they are particularly strongly inspired by divine Truth and hence entitled to provide for its earthly implementation. Importantly, this inspiration can befall anybody; in principle, everybody can be called to rule the country. This is a political version of the Protestant, and in particular Puritan, belief that everybody stands in the same relationship with God, and that priests (or monarchs) as mediators supposedly closer to the Lord are not needed. Against the anointed and inherited body politic Milton holds the notion of the invisible but inspired single soul. Altogether, in this argument Milton attempts to legitimate Oliver Cromwell's military dictatorship from a theological perspective. On the other hand, this is also an example of an Early Modern advocacy of individualism as a social and political principle.

Particularly important to us, the context of Milton's argument is also a media-theoretical one, in that *Eikonoklastes* reacts to a pamphlet titled *Eikon Basilike* ("The Kingly Image"). This text, written by a close confidant of the imprisoned – and later executed – King Charles I, features a frontispiece that shows the praying monarch as a martyr in the succession of Jesus Christ. Milton's antimonarchical argument rests considerably on a refutation of the media Charles uses to establish and defend his power, and he attacks the frontispiece in particular. He refers to it as a "conceited portraiture […] drawn out to the full measure of a Masking Scene, and sett there to catch fools and silly gazers" (342). According to Milton, the King's text is headed by a theatrical image with strongly material, sensual, and therefore manipulative qualities. Already by its title, literally "the image breaker", his own text stylises itself as a kind of de(con)-struction of the *Eikon Basilike*'s "Idolatry", which is both of a "religious" and a "civil kinde" (343). According to Milton, images and other material objects representing monarchical power (as well as divinity in Catholic liturgy) distract the British people, some of them unfortunately an "image-doting rabble" (601), from the invisible Truth, which is both the spiritual foundation of the world and its highest political power. Milton nowhere reflects on the mediality of his own text, let alone on his own reliance on (verbal) imagery in many passages. However, his position implies an endorsement of the textual medium, which, although potentially also assailable as idolatrous, still gives his own argument a somewhat safer medial grounding in – or near – Reformist scripturalism. Altogether, in the 1640s in Britain, Protestant media scepticism became connected to an attack on the governmental as well as cultural style of monarchy with its reliance on image, ornament, and performance, against which it held the unillustrated text as the more suitable medium for communicating the "Truth" to the people, who were all individuals in equal relation to it.

While the Reformation appears thus as another important media-historical transition, the outcome of this media battle was of course not a straightforward victory of the Protestant and individualist medium of the printed text over the collective, performative, and iconic media of Catholic monarchy but rather a complicated merging of different medialities. As can for example be glimpsed from British pamphlets dating back to the seventeenth century , which freely combined images and texts, both now based on printing, the use of particular media now became loaded with political and religious significance (see Sharpe 2010). This meant that any media usage suggested a particular ideological position was therefore vulnerable to attack; it also meant, however, that media became more expressive and hence themselves contributed to the increasing public communicability, typical of the period, of different individual positions and voices. To a certain extent, the Restoration in the 1660s rehabilitated the visual and collective medialities of absolutist monarchy, such as architecture and the theatre, and therefore somewhat reversed this development. However, the (temporary) textualization and individualisation of British media culture in seventeenth-century Britain must be seen as a prehistory of what Albrecht Koschorke and others in this section explore as the overwhelming importance, from the eighteenth century onwards, of a media culture of private individuals communicating in writing.

What debates on mediation and mediality before and leading up to 1800 alert us to is that material media and media technologies often unfold their potential only in combination with overarching cultural, religious, and political processes, i.e., as *media cultures* in specific, and shifting, constellations of discourses and materialities. The restructuring of epistemological orders in the seventeenth century (as Jürgen Meyer's contribution shows) leads to a re-examination of existing media configurations such as the library and the theatre and their realignment with laboratory practice. Such reconfigurations are difficult to describe in terms of media history but can appropriately be approached in terms of a history of mediation, or as "historical media culture". By contrast, the sociocultural impact of audiovisual media and "media of inscription" (Kittler 1999, 5-6) around 1900, and the impact of digitization in the twentieth century are usually perceived as results of technological innovations (Glaubitz et al. 2011, 27; 33-35). In the light of these considerations, and against the backdrop of the contributions to this section, the prominent role assigned to media technologies bears re-examination as another historically contingent position that may not be applicable to earlier periods. While these are moments and media of the past, there is also the kind of historical trajectory to the present that Alan Liu speaks of. Even if the media we use are rapidly changing right now and past technologies are sometimes soon forgotten, the idea that a society is mediatized – that its members position themselves in it by text, image, and sound – is much older. In this sense, a shared assumption of the contributions to this section is that it is important to both historicise media and to study the culture of their usage because these media cultures have life periods independent of and sometimes radically different from the changing technical means of communication.

References

Armstrong, Tim (1998): *Modernism, Technology, and the Body: A Cultural Study*. Cambridge: Cambridge University Press

Bristol, Michael; Marotti, Arthur (eds.; 2000): *Print, Manuscript, Performance: The Changing Relations of the Media in Early Modern England*. Columbus: Ohio State University Press

Carroll, Noel (1984): "Medium Specifity Arguments and Self-Consciously Invented Arts: Film, Video and Photography", *Millennium Film Journal* 14/15, 127-153

Crary, John (1990): *Techniques of the Observer: On Vision and Modernity in the Nineteenth Century*. Cambridge, MA; London: MIT Press

Engell, Lorenz (2002). "Zur Einführung. Wege, Kanäle, Übertragungen", in: Pias, Claus et al. (eds.): *Kursbuch Medienkultur: Die maßgeblichen Theorien von Brecht bis Baudrillard*. Stuttgart: Deutsche Verlagsanstalt, 127-133

Felski, Rita (2011): "'Context Stinks!'" *New Literary History* 42, 573-591

Gitelman, Lisa (2006): *Always Already New: Media, History, and the Data of Culture*. Cambridge, MA/London: MIT Press

Glaubitz, Nicola et al. (2011): *Eine Theorie der Medienumbrüche 1900/2000*. Siegen: universi

Kearney, James (2009). *The Incarnate Text: Imagining The Book in Reformation England.* Philadelphia: University of Pennsylvania Press

Kittler, Friedrich (1999): *Gramophone, Film, Typewriter.* Stanford: Stanford University Press

Kümmel, Albert; Löffler, Petra (2002): "Einleitung", in: Kümmel, Albert; Löffler, Petra (eds.): *Medientheorie 1888-1933: Texte und Kommentare.* Frankfurt: Suhrkamp, 9-18

Liu, Alan (2008): *Local Transcendence: Essays on Postmodern Historicism and the Database.* Chicago, London: University of Chicago Press

Mao, Douglas; Walkowitz, Rebecca (2008): "The New Modernist Studies", *PMLA*, 123.3, 737-748

Milton, John (1649/1962): *Eikonoklastes,* in: Milton, *Complete Prose Works. Volume III, 1648-1649,* New Haven: Yale University Press, 337-601

Murphet, Julian (2009): *Multimedia Modernism: Literature and the Anglo-American Avant-Garde.* Cambridge: Cambridge University Press

Orgel, Stephen; Holland, Peter (eds.; 2006): *From Performance to Print in Shakespeare's England.* Basingstoke: Palgrave Macmillan

Schröter, Jens (2014): *3D: History, Theory and Aesthetics of the Transplane Image.* New York/London: Bloomsbury

Sharpe, Kevin M. (2010): *Image Wars: Promoting Kings and Commonwealths in England, 1603-1660.* New Haven: Yale University Press

Siskin, Clifford; Warner, William (eds.; 2010): *This Is Enlightenment.* Chicago: University of Chicago Press

Trotter, David (2009): *Modernism and the History of Media.* Oxford: Blackwell

Weimann, Robert; Bruster, Douglas (2008): *Shakespeare and the Power of Performance: Stage and Page in the Elizabethan Theatre.* Cambridge: Cambridge University Press

Wiesing, Lambert (2008): "Was sind Medien?" in: Münker, Stefan; Roesler, Alexander (eds.): *Was ist ein Medium?* Frankfurt: Suhrkamp, 235-248

ALBRECHT KOSCHORKE (KONSTANZ)

Social Media 1800*

1. Introduction

It is well known that the German Enlightenment was accompanied by a comprehensive program of spreading literacy. Above all in the second half of the eighteenth century, written forms of communication became increasingly widespread.[1] Writing, previously limited to certain professions and widely practiced only by specialists, became an everyday phenomenon among the enlightened elite. Beyond the expanded technical need for written information, this was manifest in a private use of script that was becoming habitual – either in diaries and other similar activities or in the burgeoning practice of correspondence. The same process was at work in relation to printed material, with improvements in the postal service and the expansion and commercialization of the book market here forming the material foundation. In many contemporary polemics, we read of a "rage for reading" and "addiction to authorship"; these texts confront what is viewed as a threat to traditional familial and social structures.

Literacy was no longer tied to privilege. Traditional Christianity offered a paragon of a privilege-centered approach to the letter: At the center of faith stood the Book itself, the Bible, surrounded by a concentrically ordered hierarchy of interpreters, while communication with ordinary people was the preacher's responsibility and took place in oral form. Starting with the Reformation, we find an increased reading of the holy texts – a process determined by printing – and the repression of Latin that had been the scholar's prerogative, together with a gradual shift from edifying writing to the *belles lettres* that Gellert and Klopstock would come to represent in Germany. This development was closely tied to a steady decline of the authorities mediating between book and recipient, that is, to a decentralization of book-knowledge. Importantly, the letter's move beyond a framework of oral interaction is not only evident in the religious context, but in the literary realm itself. Thereby, an older discursive paradigm was rendered obsolete, one that – codified in the old European universal science of rhetoric – tied verbal expression to specific contexts and the identity of those being addressed; in doing so, it had represented a communicative practice divested of validity step by step as typographical forms of reproduction prevailed (see Ter-Nedden 1988, 171-190). Where classical rhetoric had treated writing as an inferior resource, it now emerged

---

*   Parts 1-3 of this text are basically a translation from my book *Körperströme und Schriftverkehr* (2003), making some of its findings accessible to an English-speaking audience. In parts 4 and 5 I add some new aspects that I had not sufficiently taken into consideration at the time I wrote the book.

1   See Wegmann 1988, 15: "Among all the details and individual trends, what is most striking is the rapid growth of the alphabetization of communication". (All translations from the German are by Joel Golb and Eric Hounshell unless indicated otherwise.) On the difficulties of statistically verifying such processes while confirming the general tendency, see Hinrichs 1980, 100-106.

with growing strength to compete with spoken discourse while imprinting it with its own structures. We can sum up this drawn-out process as follows: The relation of literary communication to oral interaction was now more and more substitutive, no longer only subsidiary.

On the side of reception, this produced new habits. In a study by Erich Schön, we learn that the silent, individual reading of books with an immobilized body – a practice modeled on the discipline of the academy – now increasingly repressed the delivery of artful speech and live recitation, together with the rhetoric-anchored collective forms of reception to which it was tied (see Schön 1987, 63-72). The emergence of this type of reading was connected with a turn away from a traditional model of public space in favor of a new valorization of private life and private spaces. To this extent, the new literacy indeed contained an element dangerous to the old social structures – just as the critics of reading-addiction had feared: It annulled corporate group formation and consensual pressures; it released an individualizing potential that could not be assimilated into the established social code.

In this manner, the formation of a modern concept of interiority was a phenomenon that accompanied the spread of literacy.[2] In an oral culture – and even in a script-supported rhetorical culture – the utterance "I'm alone" is, strictly speaking, impossible, since it presumes the presence of the same addressee it denies. Inwardness here has no discursive locus, precisely because there is no medium for the individual's turn away from the interactions determining his or her life. Only literacy in its pure form allows non-communication to communicate, thus laying the groundwork for fundamental literary paradoxes since the mid-eighteenth century. The paradoxes may be authorial, related to the idea of the solitary genius, producing without a context; or they may be thematic, related to the sensitive soul's enthused longing and to romantic love – conveyed as basically isolated feelings, withdrawn from the world.

Consequently, there was apparently a close relation between the surge of literacy that imbued the generation of sensibility (in German: *Empfindsamkeit*) in particular and the questions of affective modeling that were glossed in the age's excessive correspondence. The two phenomena had a shared root: the growing social interdependence dissolving the old estate-dominated network of relations between individuals and prevalent cognitive-corporative structures; and its replacement with a complex system of multi-leveled communication at a distance.

Generally speaking, every society produces a certain quantity of "absence" within its communicative network. With every new level in the communicative process, there is a higher degree of abstraction – of its portion of virtual absences. With increasing abstraction, new possibilities of integration have to be provided for on both the medial

---

2   See Schön 1987, 99-122. "With the abandonment of reading out loud, reading is taken inside from the outside. And with this, it contributes its share to creating this 'inside', as we conceive it, in the first place" (Schön 1987, 114). In the English context, Stone sees the process as already underway in the seventeenth century: "At the same time, there developed a series of almost wholly new genres of writing, the intimately self-revelatory diary, the autobiography and the love letter. [...] these products were the result of a shift from an oral to a written culture among the laity. Literacy is probably a necessary precondition for the growth of introspection" (Stone 1977, 226). On the connection between the rise of literacy and individualization in the late eighteenth century see Jäger 1990.

and psychological level. The most important technology for rendering absence communicable is writing. But in order to impose literacy, a new affective instrument is needed. With the extension of social interdependence, pressure emerges on the subjective side to conform to the corresponding intensification of psychic mobility. The affective cathexis involved here has to cover ever greater distances over ever longer chains of mediation. In this manner, it becomes detached from the realm of close interaction that is typical of a pre-industrial economy, hence of essentially oral and physical contact between kin or clan-members or those in the same productive group; it now attaches itself to the wide-reaching mediations of the network of distant relationships (see Osterloh 1976).

The extension of its mental reach is purchased with a weakening of its ties to the present. The cathexis restructures itself: More than before, pleasure and distance enter into a kind of symbiosis. The affects that adapt themselves to the new forms of communication gain a more fleeting, intellectual-spiritual quality. This process is, then, for the most part not determined by a shift in moral premises (whatever its basis), but rather reflects a structural shift in the communication system.

In the course of the eighteenth century, two tendencies are manifest that, when examined closely, appear to be mutually determining: on the one hand, the final emergence of a culture ruled by techniques of knowledge processing and mediation based on literacy – a development mirrored in a highpoint of bourgeois socialization; on the other hand, the intensification of affects at a remove from the body and their incorporation into daily life, as we can especially observe in the literature of *Empfindsamkeit*. Put briefly: Increasing bourgeois literacy and sensibility are two dimensions of a single process.

2   Deprivation of the Body

As the title suggests, Joachim Heinrich Campe's *Neues Abeze- und Lesebuch* (*New ABC-book and Reader*, 1807/1973) was a primer, intended to motivate children to learn to read. To that end, under a heading that could be translated as "A Means to Speak with Your Friends a Hundred Miles Away", the children are told a story. It is centered on August and Christel, who "were always very good friends". Because of a move, they have been torn apart. The pain of separation is great, but Father knows how to help:

> You must get hold of a speaking tube, said August's father, in order to be able to continue speaking with each other from a distance.
> Ah, *is* there such a speaking tube, both boys called out, letting us speak from a hundred miles apart?
> Not yet, answered Father; but you need to try to see if you can't yourselves invent something like that.
> August and Christel lowered their eyes and again began to cry.
> Listen, children, Father now said, you don't need such an invention; for a long time we've known about a sure way for you to speak very clearly with each other when you're not together. If you feel like it, I'd like to teach it to you.
> Oh please teach us, please! called out both boys while they coaxingly hung to his arms.
> You've already heard about this method, continued Father; it is the fine art of *writing* and *reading*.

As soon as you've learned it, you can fix all your thoughts on paper and mail them to each other week by week.
Then you'll know as well as if you've just spoken with each other what each of you has been thinking and how you're doing. (Campe 1979, 120-121)

This little story imparts a double lesson. Its main didactic goal is to present the reading training that the children undergo as something desirable. Those who can read and write can avoid a certain form of pain: the pain of separation. Through the mediation of thoughts fixed on paper, as Campe precisely if awkwardly puts it, separation can be overcome. The lesson's second part thus affirms that friendship is not based on being neighbors. To the extent that oral contact is needed for the sake of exchanging thoughts, it is medially replaceable.

Yet media are never simply substitutes. They alter what they appear to replace. The intrusion here underway takes place without ever being fully seen through by those affected. In this context Campe's fable can serve as a paradigm, presenting written communication as a kind of prosthetic extension of acoustic understanding. As the children quickly grasp, this is impossible by oral means: No hearing tube can carry the spoken word over hundreds of miles; to "speak very clearly with each other when you're not together", recourse is needed to a different medial level – this of course being script. But in the apparently effortless replacement of speech's function by writing, what the medium *fails* to replace is passed over in silence. Campe presents the children as satisfied with a continuation of their friendship as an exchange of thoughts. His story thus has a deeper meaning: The function of writing not only consists of mediating intellectual substrates but also of by-passing the previous vehicle for ties of friendship – the bodies.

In its medial form, written communication defines the body as something absent. It activates the division of human beings into spirit and body that emerged in Plato's time together with the alphabet's formation, removing the body from the stage and letting the spirit wander. The alphabet (whatever Derrida has to say on the matter) functions Platonically.

The primal scene of writing, as described by Campe in his child-centered adaptation, corresponds fully to the epoch's general understanding. First published in 1742, Gellert's treatise on letter writing – a determining influence in the turn from professional epistolary rhetoric and the emergence of letter-writing as an everyday form of communication – programmatically took up (with merely stylistic limitations) the antique formula of the letter as a conversation between absent parties.[3]

But the norm of the letter as conversation that Gellert reactivated and enforced on behalf of the medium's broad privatization and against the officiousness of formal German is not simply relevant to the history of style. Rather, it determined the imaginative field in which all writing-related acts would henceforth belong. In contrast to humanistic penmanship, in the eighteenth century the simulation of orality developed into the

---

3   See Gellert 1751/1971, 2-3.: "The first thing that strikes us with a letter is that it takes the place of a conversation. This concept is perhaps the surest. A letter is no ordinary conversation; hence in a letter not everything will be allowed that is allowed in informal society. Nevertheless it takes the place of oral language, and for this reason must become closer to the way of thinking and speaking at work in conversation than to a careful and polished sort of writing".

prevalent literary ideal. And paradoxically, this "mimesis of orality" (Vellusig 1991), which Gellert demanded for letter-writing and which took on an extreme, literary stamp in the invective style of the *Sturm und Drang*, occurred simultaneously with the fading of the primacy of traditional rhetoric.

The phantasm of conversation thus suppressed the practice of discourse. To the extent that written communication freed itself from the task of supplementing rhetorical conversational techniques, it took on a quasi-oral character. Notably, this secondary oralization of writing was linked to a growing propensity for staged sentimentality. Not only did oral behavioral fictions attach themselves to the literary techniques requiring realization, which is to say letters 'spoke', were 'devoured', kissed, pressed to one's body, and so forth. Also, scarcely a single act of writing took place that was not intended, despite all paths of mediation, as a form of intimate interaction with the addressee; and scarcely an emphatic reading was unaccompanied by corresponding fantasies.

We can see how the phantasm of epistolary conversation was enacted in a scene composed by Gellert's confidant Rabener as something like an introduction to Gellert's treatise: "I imagine that you are sitting next to me and that everything I say is being imparted to you orally" (quoted in Brockmeyer 1961, 55). Writing, considered secondary to speaking, was thus accompanied by the necessary self-deception of the addressee being present. This impossible presence prevailed even when the fact of separation was emphasized – just as in the age's correspondence sorrow over physical separation and celebration of a compensating spiritual proximity generally mixed, in various tonalities, without any noticeable contradiction. "I wish", Klopstock thus writes to Maria Sophia Schmidt, the "Fanny" of his poetry, "with your permission to write long & frequent letters to you. To be sure this will function as if I knew you to be in an adjoining room & addressed you through a closed glass door without seeing you & without your answering. But meanwhile for a few moments you would be in the adjoining room and I would be addressing you".[4] Here as well, writing is a form of speaking that moves the addressee into the writer's direct proximity. At the same time the medial displacement is preserved – it is captured in the oxymoronic image of the opaque glass door; however intensely proximity is imagined, this displacement leaves the poetic character of love secure.

In the wake of such imagined immediacy a fetishism with myriad dimensions attaches itself to the acts of reading and writing. For already on the basis of its *medial* structure, writing creates precisely the conditions from which, on a *semantic* level, the fetishes dear to the era of sensibility emerge: distance that suggests proximity and releases a language of lack of distance; a cutting off of the body, which is compensated for by an unhampered meeting of spirits; a stripping away of the external, allowing the unsheathed inner essences to flow together.

In this manner, mediatization spurred a new mythology of immediacy. Its name was sensibility or *Empfindsamkeit*, its stage and field of practice being correspondence, whether biographical or fictional – and, in a broader sense, all forms of written communication. Structurally analogous procedures are manifest in other realms as well, for instance in the reception history of the graphic arts and the theater. On the one hand,

---

4 Klopstock 1979, 146. For the sake of readability, editorial markings have been eliminated.

then, there was separation and immobilization of the body; on the other hand a play of fantasy as a central aesthetic capacity, now brought into service to restore what had been severed – a restoration taking place, to be sure, on an imaginary plane.

What Campe exemplifies as young friends torn apart by their fathers' professional circumstances thus represents a collective process. Growing social mobility made altered forms of communication necessary. On the level of semiotic transmission, the media took on a special role, conveying a promise to fill in the absence experienced through growing social distance. This was tied to a shift of affective controls. In a certain way, the correspondence of *Empfindsamkeit* offered a continuation of Campe's story, which turns friendship into a literate relationship. It searched for possibilities of finding truth not guaranteed by corporeal signs, for trust lying beyond the reach of direct personal interaction, for intimacy not dependent upon sensual contact.

In this framework, the literature of *Empfindsamkeit* emerges as something like a medial rehearsal enacted under the existential conditions defined by the spread of literacy. What the characters in the novels do in a particularly paradigmatic way, negating their corporeality through emotively charged gestures, corresponds to what is imposed on sensitive readers – prototypes of a new manner of lonely and wordless book reception – through their readership status alone. The novels semanticize a medial effect; they narrate the corresponding psychodramatic processes. They transpose the new affective culture, bound to the deepening social interdependence and mediatization, into the old interactive zones: into the familial and erotic relationships that now, with the progressive limitation and devaluation of corporeal language, press for verbalization, in the process increasingly adapting themselves to the expressive forms of written culture – the most semantically developed level of verbality.

All key concepts of the age of sensibility – virtue, soulfulness, sympathy, tenderness, friendship – that unfolded in the context of the new bourgeois sociability were symbolically tried out mainly in written form, whether in printed literature, in correspondence, or through written introspection. Writing is here by no means a neutral medium, simply a bearer of content. Rather, it cultivates a close complicity with the ideology of virtue and disembodiment for which it furnishes the forum.[5] Expressed more generally: Writing is the correlate in communication technology of the discursive phenomenon 'soul'.

3   Spiritual Compensation

To this extent, literacy has first of all a privative character. It forms an armature against sensual temptations, for reading renders the body latent. "The soul", writes Hemsterhuis in his "Letter on Longing", is

> eternal in its essence and contrary in nature to all we place in a spatial and temporal context, inhabits a body that appears to be very different in its nature from that of the soul. Its tie to this body is thus very incomplete. For during the time you read these lines, you have, if I do not remind you of them, no imagination, no idea, of your legs, arms, or other parts of your body. The non-existence of all these parts would have produced no change whatsoever in the ego that thinks within you. (Hemsterhuis 1912, 54-55)

---

5   On this connection see Müller 1991, 290.

Reading is here a kind of self-awareness that makes manifest the disunity and mutual divergence of body and soul. Undergoing something like a temporary amputation, the reading individual approaches the ideal of a purely intellectual form of existence, his or her moral task being to stabilize this condition of corporeal distance. In the eighteenth century, it was common knowledge that the education to be gained through books brought with it a heightened degree of sensitivity, hence of spiritualization. The loneliness so fundamental to the reading experience initiated a finer nuancing of the soul's life, at the same time promoting resistance against external, sensual stimuli.

Both the heroes of *Empfindsamkeit* and the authors themselves draw all their spiritual strength from their capacity to withdraw into reading or writing and, as mirrored in the immutability of the written word, to form a personal identity away from fleeting daily life. Reading and writing is a proof of virtue; it means privacy, ascetic life, resistance to seduction. In sentimental novels starting with Richardson's *Pamela*, the border between seducers and the virtuous is broadly identical to that between individuals who waste themselves in spreading conviviality and those who educate themselves with books.

This appeal to asceticism is only one part of the story, however. The cult of the literary not only requires abstinence from fleshly pleasures, but also rewards its adherents in a copious way. As in the teachings of St Paul, so in eighteenth-century writing culture: The letter's death is followed by the resurrection of the spirit. "Your absence from us", Bodmer writes to Sulzer in 1747, "and ours from you, would not be better than bitter death if we were not reborn and live in letters" (Bodmer 1804, 70-71). I have already described how the classical eighteenth-century letter reader translated the formula of the letter as conversation into an ensemble of phantasms. At first glance, we can understand the metonymic intercession of writing for the writer in the conventional sense: written testimony as compensation – albeit certainly insufficient – for the author's absence. Within the contemporary epistolary topic, such announcements of incompletion are commonplace; and if we take them literally, the new literary communication appears to consist essentially of expansive resentment against written communication itself. But writing, the substitute, does not limit itself to this subservient role. Rather, it accumulates fetishistic energies that, like every fetish, are no longer derivable from what they replace. The medial present develops its own valences and intensities. "I received your letter", writes St. Preux to Julie in Rousseau's *Nouvelle Heloise*, one of the epoch's models of both epistolary love and physical renunciation, "with the same delight your presence would have caused me; and in the tumult of my joy a mere sheet of paper served as a replacement for you".[6] And a little later:

> But how can I not know you in reading your letters? How could I assign such a touching tone and tender sentiments to another figure than yours? With each sentence, can we not see the sweet look of your eyes? With each of your words, can we not hear your charming voice? Who else but Julie has ever loved, thought, spoken, acted, written like she? Thus do not be surprised if your letters, which show you so clearly, sometimes have the same effect on your adoring beloved as even those exerted by your presence! When I read them over and over, I lose my reason, my thought become confused in enduring delirium, I am penetrated by devouring fire, my blood plunges into tumult and foams, a wild fervor makes me tremble. I believe I am seeing you before me, am touching you, pressing you to my breast – devotion-worthy being! Entrancing

---

6   For this and the following citation see Rousseau 1997, 194-201 (part 2, letter 15 and 16).

girl! Fountain of delight and voluptuousness! When I see you, how can I not see the houris destined for the blessed? (Rousseau 1997, 194-201)

Physical distance is here not at all conceived as a defective state. Before the eyes of the imaginative capacity, that which is removed from reality emerges anew and in no less strength. In his autobiographical texts, Rousseau will defend the particularity of imaginary experience and thus touch on the paradox of the irreplaceability of the substitute. Writing thus materializes a separation that appears to continuously dissipate into the metaphorical subplots accompanying its usage. Writing here allows voice, figure, and body of the beloved to reemerge not instrumentally, but according to the old topos of the soul as mirror: a nearly identical double, but removed from the *Urbild* precisely through the fact of doubling.

Again and again, the various volumes of late eighteenth-century letter writing fuse pleasure with agony in a play on the borders or transitions between text and body. "Come here, my sweet girl", Johann Heinrich Voß writes to Ernestine Boie, his bride, "and sit on my lap; I want to tell you a little story" (Voß 1774/1988, 158). Especially in regards to the expanding genre of bride letters, we can speak of a fully developed lap-centered mystique. "What is it, dearest friend, that you could perhaps tell me on my lap?" Herder asks at one point in his correspondence with Caroline Flachsland. "For aren't you sitting on my lap while writing? Oh, heavens. One word from your heart, is it not just as if I heard it, kissing heard it?" (Herder 1771/1926, 287). In other letters, the image of such intimacy surfaces as deeply felt fantasies of penetration: "Allow me to continue from time to time with the diary of my curiosities, and pour them into the lap of the only female friend with whom I presently speak in the world" (Herder 1771/1926, 211). "Allow me to cry into your lap and small, innocent bosom, my good F" (Herder 1771/1926, 334).

It becomes clear that medial substitution transfers bodies into another register. They re-emerge as *symbolic* entities. When Herder speaks of his bride's "small, innocent bosom", the two adjectives suggest that he means not the female sexual feature but the seat of feelings; similarly the wetting of her lap is not connected to sexual secretions, which to the contrary were the object of rigorous containment in just this period, but to the liquids in which sensitivity circulates – ink and tears: "Let me cry silent tears of sorrowing doubt into your lap", Lavater exclaims to Herder (Lavater 1773/1856-1857, 44). Despite the extent to which writing in the age of sensibility expresses itself in gushing, flowing, and pouring gestures, at times with an orgiastic tenor, it nevertheless transports spiritual substance. The fusing of souls that the correspondence induces is no inferior replacement but stands in clear competition to physical interaction.

For this Platonic mode of communication, the use of letters and the resulting mutual absence of the communicating parties was less a deficit than a precondition. A year-long correspondence like that between Caroline Flachsland and Herder took on the role of the test of virtue that was one of the chief motifs in older amorous romances and their trivialized contemporary offshoots. All the hugging, kissing, outpouring, and melting only corresponded to the morality of *Empfindsamkeit* for one reason: because it took place via medial channels and by means of a displacement that transferred all the stimulated affects into a higher, spiritually aggregate condition. The moral training of literacy consisted of conforming to the structurally determined level of spiritualization – of subjectively assimilating the negation of the body and affirmation of its absence, as soul. This spiritualization intensified to the extent that the writer abandoned him- or herself unreservedly and with an open heart and streaming soul to the transformations of literacy. This represented the antipode of court culture's diplomatic *billets d'amour* – still conceiving of writing as a detour in a relational circle of rhetorical persuasion, hence attacked in bourgeois morality as the mendacious opposite to the authenticity of the writing of the heart.[7]

4 Sensibility, Nationalism, *Bildung*

Let me add three aspects to this structural analysis of sensible communication in order to round out the picture. First, it should be emphasized that the sensible phantasms of nearness served not only the exclusive communication between lovers but also the long-range construction of friendship networks. The formation of intellectual communities across social strata and political borders was, as is well known, a core concern of the eighteenth century. Indeed, the social networks in the age of sensibility distinguished themselves from preexisting group formations – from circles of scholarly correspondence, clubs of urban notables, societies for the promotion of virtue and enlightenment, convivial associations proximal to princely courts, and not least the flourishing orders of Freemasons and Illuminati – through their emphasis on empathy and emotionality. But in fact they amounted to a similar networking fostered by improved postal traffic, especially since the various circles multiply overlapped with one another. Single personalities even made a life's work out of being in the central position of relationship brokers: One could mention, aside from the Anacreontic poet characterized as "Vater Gleim", a bustling figure (who was in any case viewed by his contemporaries with suspicion) such as Franz Michael Leuchsenring, whom Goethe lampooned as an apostle of *Empfindsamkeit* because he supposedly wanted to found an order of the sensible (*Orden der Empfindsamen*) (see Leuchsenring 1976; Markner 2012,173-205).

A second perspective is related to this contribution of sensibility to the "structural transformation of the public sphere" (Habermas). Language of the heart, communication of the souls, friendship between the like-minded who are physically separated from one another and do not even know each other: All of these maxims serve not only as a Platonic eroticization of private exchange. Beyond this, as a means of the production of *imagined communities*, they have a political dimension, for the authors in question here also became significant forerunners of a literary patriotism (and later, nationalism) in Germany. From the circle of the Anacreontics around Johann Wilhelm Ludwig Gleim, who were concerned in particular with a cult of friendship, collections of patriotic songs arose that also came into military use as soldier songs in the Seven Years War (see Blitz 2000, 275-280.). In the spirit of *Empfindsamkeit*, a discourse of death for the fatherland emerged, associated above all in German-speaking areas with the name of Thomas Abbt (Abbt 1761). Abbt's invocation of a death wish in the service of the Fatherland that takes on the character of "orgiastic scenarios of union" (Burgdorf 2000, 168) would influence the lyric poetry of the war of liberation against Napoleon in which Pietistic-mystical notions of blood sacrifice fuse with the senti-

---

7   An example of this might be the letter in Schiller's *Kabale und Liebe*. On the general problem of deceit undermining all authenticity strategies, see the insightful book by Manfred Schneider, *Liebe und Betrug* (1992).

mental idea of the nation as a collective soul (see Kaiser 1973). What was at first only the expression of literary joy in writing and a communicative experiment within a small intellectual elite that detached itself from the modes of communication of the old sort of corporatist (*ständisch*) erudition, stiff and ponderous in style, became, in the course of the nineteenth century, the model of a national, wholly militarized public sphere. It thereby contributed to the transposition of loyalties still imprinted socially with the forms of a small-scale society of presence and politically with dynastic devotion to particular persons onto the abstract collective of the Nation as a totality. For he who communicates in a sentimental manner is no longer the person from a corporatist estate but rather 'man'; modern nations are composed of men, which is why national ideologies need a humanistic substructure.

The third aspect that is important in this context deals with the situation of the history of knowledge in the late eighteenth century. Here, we find ourselves in a period of rupture of the world of perception and memory that could hardly be more profound. This rupture has its *locus classicus,* at least for German-speaking literature, in Herder's *Journal of My Travels in the Year 1769.* This text, a protocol of a crisis that is as much biographical-vocational as epistemological, makes use of the actual situation of a sea voyage as a topos of self-orientation. In the face of a horizon that is empty in all directions, in a situation of sensory deprivation as much as intoxication, in which everything "adds wings to one's thoughts, gives them motion and ample sphere" (Barnard 1969, 65), Herder sees himself confronted with the task "to philosophize from nature without books and instruments" (*ibid.,* 67). He thereby dreams himself into a favorite fantasy of the *Sturm und Drang* writers, namely to leave behind the "student's chair in a musty study", the "pulpit", and the "lecture-desk" (*ibid.,* 65). In hundreds of variations, such escapist impulses are not merely the expression of a generational revolt. Rather, they reveal the collective exodus of the young bourgeois from a world of savants still influenced by Old Europe along with its institutions, which appear as sites of the hypertrophy of dead knowledge. The condition of cognitive deprivation, as Herder experiences the sea voyage, becomes for him a welcome occasion for a general inventory that, in the style of philosophical idealism, validates only that which originates from subjectivity alone:

> Where is the solid land on which I stood so solidly, and the little pulpit, and the armchair, and the lecture desk at which I used to give myself airs? Where are the people of whom I stood in awe, and whom I loved? O soul, how will it be with you when you leave this little world? The narrow, firm, restricted centre of your sphere of activity is no more; you flutter in the wind or float on a sea – the world is vanishing from you – has vanished beneath you! What a changed perspective! But such a new mode of looking at things costs tears, remorse, the extrication of one's heart from old attachments, self-condemnation! (Barnard 1969, 66)

This search for an epistemic state of nature does not hinder Herder from dwelling for the most part in his *Journal* on future plans of encyclopedic magnitudes. In these future plans, the books from which Herder as philosopher 'out of nature' had just wanted to free himself reinvade in force. It is a general characteristic of the scientific revolutions of modernity, beginning with Descartes, that their willful demolition of established stores of knowledge goes hand in hand with a restorative countermovement that ensures continuity. In this way, Herder's sea voyage into uncertainty in the end reveals itself to be a journey "between two libraries" (see Stockhammer 1991). Nevertheless, his draft of a "universal history of the education (*Bildung*) of the world" (Herder 1983,

17) distinguishes itself fundamentally from the older form of erudite universal history. In an enthusiastic tone, punctuated with excited dashes and exclamation points, Herder outlines a reform project of gigantic dimensions[8] that he expands to novel curricula in which everything should be "vitally felt, explained", "vitally savored, celebrated" (Barnard 1969, 71) instead of, in the manner of the extant cram schools, learning "to death and loathsomely" (*ibid.*, 69). The excessive manner by which Herder emphasizes the Pauline opposition between vital spirit and dead letter makes his educational program appear as part of an (incidentally thoroughly Protestant) revival movement.

What induced the bourgeois intellectuals around 1770 to make such a massive break with scholarly conventions and, in its wake, to exhibit such a zeal for reform? A detailed answer would far exceed the confines of this paper. Put briefly, one could argue that it was the development of written culture and the book market itself that led to the collapse of the old system of knowledge production that was still rooted in the rhetorical traditions of memorization. Even the burly Baroque polyhistors were no longer capable of processing accumulated knowledge in a digestible way. To cope with the increased communicative and scientific demands, a new pragmatics needed to be developed – taxonomical, semantic, and habitual. This involves the reorganization of the great reference works from a systematic to an alphabetical order; the introduction of a new, still largely unused dimension of knowledge, namely its historical dimension – history understood as system and living totality, no longer as aggregate of piled-up facts and dates[9]; and finally a change to the intellectual habitus, denoted by the fashionable term of the era – namely, the concept of the original genius. In every sense, the genius is the opposing figure to the corporatist savant. His appropriate place is nature, not the study. He creates on his own terms in soulful solitude instead of inserting himself into a long line of predecessors. In order to be capable of novelty in such a way, he must free himself from existing mental constraints. In short, in this understanding, genius is based not on the art of memory but rather on forgetting and the break from tradition. The reality the genius creates of his own accord is forward-looking, unifies mind with life, and should, though borne of solitude, benefit the education or cultivation (in the sense of the German concept of *Bildung*) of humanity in general.

5 Conclusion

The stylistic transformation of literary communication in the decades before 1800, it should have become clear, transpires in a much broader context, involving society as a

---

8   In the German original this reads as follows: "Welch ein Werk über das Menschliche Geschlecht! den Menschlichen Geist! die Cultur der Erde! aller Räume! Zeiten! Völker! Kräfte! Mischungen! Gestalten! Asiatische Religion! und Chronologie und Policei und Philosophie! Aegyptische Kunst und Philosophie und Policei! Phönicische Arithmetik und Sprache und Luxus! Griechisches Alles! Römisches Alles! Nordische Religion, Recht, Sitten, Krieg, Ehre! Papistische Zeit, Mönche, Gelehrsamkeit! Nordische asiatische Kreuzzieher, Wallfahrter, Ritter! Christliche Heidnische Aufweckung der Gelehrsamkeit! Jahrhundert Frankreichs! Englische, Holländische, Deutsche Gestalt! – Chinesische, Japonische Politik! Naturlehre einer neuen Welt! Amerikanische Sitten u. s. w. – – Grosses Thema: das Menschengeschlecht wird nicht vergehen, bis daß es alles geschehe! Bis der Genius der Erleuchtung die Erde durchzogen! Universalgeschichte der Bildung der Welt!" (Herder 1983, 17).

9   This distinction was introduced by universal historian Schlözer and later adopted by Immanuel Kant (see Schlözer 1772/73/1990, 18).

whole. The growing circulation of books, especially of novels, produced in ever-greater quantities and accessible to ever-broader circles, brings a new type of reader to the fore, for whom real life and literary fiction converge to the degree that they serve as models for each other. The increasing familiarity with the everyday use of writing brings along an intensified encroachment of literary experiences into the everyday authorship of the readers themselves, be it with respect to their own literary attempts, in autobiographical texts of self-assurance, or in letters. Thus, a new user profile for literature emerges that conservative contemporaries register with great concern, for here, especially among adolescents, they sense the danger of addiction, pathological isolation, and decline of social cohesion.[10]

In contrast to these anxieties, the mass production of writing brings about, above all, strong community-forming effects. In various forums, but above all in the abundant private letter exchange of the time, new readers and writers experience themselves as a strong and inclusive community whose members, though bodily separated from each other by spatial distance and multiple obstacles to mobility, find one another through communication that is enabled by writing. The overcoming of physical separation through mental proximity thereby gains, instead of being perceived as a mere makeshift, the trait of a novel anthropological disposition. This media-historical transformation goes hand in hand with a fundamental reconstruction of the physiological models that predetermined the image of the body in that period. Furthermore, the practice of an intimacy free of corporeality fulfills moral-pedagogical functions. At this point, sentimental writing culture takes on a religious, or more precisely, a Christian imperative in a dual sense: The mortification of the flesh is reciprocated by a *jouissance* of spiritual fulfillment that one could locate within the tradition of Christian mysticism.

Beyond such often excessive fantasies of a spiritual erotics in the medium of script, writing appears in the late eighteenth century as an activity that isolates, yet, on the other hand, leads the lone writer into a densely woven communicative fabric that, paradoxically exaggerated, establishes a *sociality of the solitary*. It is precisely here that the abundant exchange of letters between educated people becomes a cultural model. And this is not only because it constitutes far-reaching friendship networks that no longer require the formation of communities among those present but rather because it also represents an early form of mass-medial integration that would be indispensable for the establishment of the nation-state. The nation is based, one could say, on a poetic-sentimental foundation. It is, in Benedict Anderson's famous formulation, an *imagined community*: More precisely, it draws on the force of a religious or sentimental emotional bond (depending on its origin) that develops precisely in the medium of an anonymous communication of virtually all with all.

It should be kept in mind that such novel forms of mass media community-building react to a crisis of knowledge. Most incisive in this context is Ernest Gellner's description of the conversion of the still predominantly agrarian culture of old Europe into a modern national culture around 1800 – a national culture that creates the basis for the introduction of the industrial mode of production through a sweeping reorganization of the education system. In this often ruthless process, great stores of traditional

---

10 Another relevant aspect on which I cannot expand here is the linkage of campaigns against 'reading addiction' with those against masturbation.

knowledge are deactivated, so to speak, or demoted in importance, such that they henceforth play only a marginal, essentially folkloric role (Gellner 1983).

If all of this seems somehow familiar – adolescents and young elites who let themselves be wholly captivated by a new media technology, show symptoms of addiction, lose themselves in the virtual seductions of a 'second life', and establish networks and communities there that they value more highly than the prevailing social forms in the physical world – my paper has fulfilled its purpose. That the introduction of the respectively newest medium regularly triggers culture-critical fears that conform to an unchanging template is well known by now. So is the fact that the respective older medium, as soon as it loses its dominance, becomes the object of nostalgic idealization: the book, cinema, even the public television that after all once synchronized the whole nation, while nowadays each individual consumes his shows individualistically at whatever time. Nevertheless, it is worth analyzing the exact structure and scope of such ruptures in media. If one extends the analogy between the revolution in writing of the eighteenth century and today's internet revolution, at least two questions remain. First, what is today's correlate to the extensive anthropological consequences entailed in the implementation of a written everyday life? What does communication in the digital age do to bodies, souls, and desires? Second, what will happen to the stock of knowledge of the culture of the book in the age of electronic media if it is threatened by a similar loss of importance as that of the knowledge stored in the system of rhetoric after 1800?

Translated by Joel Golb and Eric Hounshell

References

Abbt, Thomas (1761): *Vom Tode für das Vaterland*. Berlin: Friedrich Nicolai

Barnard, F.M. (1969) (ed.): *J.G. Herder on Social & Political Culture*. Cambridge: Cambridge University Press

Blitz, Hans-Martin (2000): *Aus Liebe zum Vaterland. Die deutsche Nation im 18. Jahrhundert*. Hamburg: Hamburger Edition

Bodmer, Johann Jakob (1747/1804): "Brief an Sulzer (12 Sept. 1747)", in: Körte, Wilhelm (ed.): *Briefe der Schweizer Bodmer, Sulzer, Geßner: Aus Gleims litterarischem Nachlasse*. Zurich: Geßner, 70-71

Brockmeyer, Rainer (1961): *Geschichte des deutschen Briefes von Gottsched bis zum Sturm und Drang*. Münster: PhD Thesis

Burgdorf, Wolfgang (2000): "'Reichsnationalismus' gegen 'Territorialnationalismus': Phasen der Intensivierung des nationalen Bewußtseins in Deutschland seit dem Siebenjährigen Krieg", in: Langewiesche, Dieter; Schmidt, Georg (eds.): *Föderative Nation: Deutschlandkonzepte von der Reformation bis zum Ersten Weltkrieg*. München: Oldenbourg, 157-190

Campe, Joachim Heinrich (1830/1979): *Sämmtliche Kinder- und Jugendschriften, Volume 1: Abeze- und Lesebuch*. Braunschweig 1830. Reprint Dortmund: Harenberg.

Gellert, Christian Fürchtegott (1751/1971): *Briefe, nebst einer praktischen Abhandlung von dem guten Geschmacke in Briefen*. Leipzig 1751, in: Gellert: *Die epistolographischen Schriften: Faksimiledruck nach den Ausgaben von 1742 und 1751*. Stuttgart: Metzler

Gellner, Ernest (1983): *Nations and Nationalism*. Ithaca, NY: University of Cornell Press

Hemsterhuis, François (1912): "Über das Verlangen", in: Hemsterhuis, *Philosophische Schriften*, ed. Julius Hilß. Vol. 1. Karlsruhe/Leipzig: Dreililien, 45-70

Herder, Johann Gottfried (1926/1928): *Briefwechsel mit Caroline Flachsland*, 2 vols. Ed. Hans Schauer. Weimar

--- (1983): *Journal meiner Reise im Jahr 1769*. Historisch-kritische Ausgabe, ed. Katharina Mommsen. Stuttgart: Reclam

Hinrichs, Ernst (1980): *Einführung in die Geschichte der Frühen Neuzeit*. München: Beck

Jäger, Georg (1990): "Freundschaft, Liebe und Literatur von der Empfindsamkeit bis zur Romantik: Produktion, Kommunikation und Vergesellschaftung von Individualität durch 'kommunikative Muster ästhetisch vermittelter Identifikation'", *Spiel* 9.1, 69-87

Kaiser, Gerhard (1973): *Pietismus und Patriotismus im literarischen Deutschland: Ein Beitrag zum Problem der Säkularisation*, 2nd edition. Frankfurt a. M.: Athenäum

Kittler, Friedrich (1990): *Discourse Networks 1800/1900*. Stanford, CA: Stanford University Press

Klopstock, Friedrich Gottlieb (1979): *Werke und Briefe: Historisch-kritische Ausgabe, Volume 1*. Ed. Horst Gronemeyer et al.: Abteilung Briefe. Berlin/New York: De Gruyter

Koschorke, Albrecht (1999/2003): *Körperströme und Schriftverkehr: Mediologie des 18. Jahrhunderts*. München: Fink

Lavater, Johann Caspar (1773/1856-1857): "Brief an Herder (14 March 1773)", in: Düntzer, Heinrich; Herder, Ferdinand Gottfried v. (eds.): *Aus Herders Nachlaß, Volume 2*. Frankfurt a. M.: Meidinger Sohn und Co., 44

Leuchsenring, Franz Michael (1976): *Briefe von und an F.M. Leuchsenring*. Ed. Urs Viktor Kamber. Stuttgart: Metzler

Markner, Reinhard (2012): "Franz Michael Leuchsenring, 'Philosoph ambulant' in Berlin und Zürich", *Aufklärung* 24, 173–205

Müller, Lothar (1991): "Herzblut und Maskenspiel: Über die empfindsame Seele, den Briefroman und das Papier", in: Jüttemann, Gerd et al. (eds.): *Die Seele: Ihre Geschichte im Abendland*. Weinheim: Psychologie Verl.-Union, 267-292

Osterloh, Karl-Heinz (1976): "Die Entstehung der westlichen Industriegesellschaft und die Revolution der Interaktionsweisen: Europäischer Kulturwandel als psychosoziales Problem", *Archiv für Kulturgeschichte* 58, 340-370

Rousseau, Jean-Jacques (1997): "Julie, or the New Heloise: Letters of two Lovers who Live in a Small Town at the Foot of the Alps", in: Masters, Roger D.; Kelly, Christopher (eds.): *The Collected Writings of Rousseau, Volume 6*. Hanover, NH/London: University Press of New England, 194-201

Schlözer, August Ludwig v. (1772/73/1990): *Vorstellung seiner Universal-Historie*. Ed. Horst Walter Blanke. Hagen: Rottmann

Schneider, Manfred (1992): *Liebe und Betrug: Die Sprachen des Verlangens*. München/Wien: Hansa

Schön, Erich (1987): *Der Verlust der Sinnlichkeit oder Die Verwandlungen des Lesers: Mentalitätswandel um 1800*. Stuttgart: Klett-Cotta

Stockhammer, Robert (1991): "Zwischen zwei Bibliotheken: J. G. Herders 'Journal meiner Reise im Jahr 1769' als Beitrag zur Diätetik der Lektüre", *Literatur für Leser* 3, 167-184

Stone, Lawrence (1977): *The Family, Sex and Marriage in England 1500-1800*. London: Weidenfeld and Nicolson

Ter-Nedden, Gisbert (1988): "Das Ende der Rhetorik und der Aufstieg der Publizistik: Ein Beitrag zur Mediengeschichte der Aufklärung", in: Soeffner, Hans-Georg (ed.): *Kultur und Alltag*. Göttingen: Schwartz, 171-190

Vellusig, Robert H.(1991): "Mimesis von Mündlichkeit: Zum Stilwandel des Briefes im Zeitalter der technischen Reproduzierbarkeit der Schrift", in: Elm, Theo; Hiebel, Hans H. (eds.): *Medien und Maschinen: Literatur im technischen Zeitalter*. Freiburg: Rombach, 70-92

Voß, Johann Heinrich (1771/1988): "Brief an Ernestine Boie (11 May 1771)", in: Wieckenberg, Ernst-Peter (ed.): *Einladung ins 18. Jahrhundert: Ein Almanach aus dem Verlag C.H. Beck*, München: Beck, 211

--- (1771a/1988): "Brief an Ernestine Boie (5 Oct. 1771)", in: Wieckenberg, Ernst-Peter (ed.): *Einladung ins 18. Jahrhundert: Ein Almanach aus dem Verlag C.H. Beck*, München: Beck, 334

--- (1774/1988): "Brief an Ernestine Boie", in: Wieckenberg, Ernst-Peter (ed.): *Einladung ins 18. Jahrhundert: Ein Almanach aus dem Verlag C.H. Beck*, München: Beck, 158

Wegmann, Nikolaus (1988): *Diskurse der Empfindsamkeit: Zur Geschichte eines Gefühls in der Literatur des 18. Jahrhunderts*. Stuttgart: Metzler

JÜRGEN MEYER (HALLE)

Theatre, Library, Lab: Mediating Knowledge, 1600-1800

1. Introduction

In 1704, Jonathan Swift's persona in "The Introduction" to *A Tale of the Tub* designed a triad of "wooden Machines; for the Use of those Orators who desire to talk much without interruption. These are, the *Pulpit*, the *Ladder*, and the *Stage-Itinerant*". The speaker continues by sardonically excluding the legal "*Bar*" and the parliamentary "*Bench*" (Swift 2010, 25) since one does not necessarily associate either the legal or the political systems with sites of uninterrupted orations, let alone cohesive knowledge transfer ('indoctrination', i.e., the top-bottom transmission of knowledge). Swift's series of images recounts predominantly theatrical stages for disseminating spectacular insights. His obvious target are those physical *loci* serving as instruments of mediation by those loud speakers who always claim a share in the dissemination of 'modern' knowledge, yet divulge ignorance instead. Indeed, apart from verbal/visual *topoi*, epistemic transfer may surface also by different *logoi* expressed, for example, in nonnatural linguistic notation systems, such as arithmetic, algebra, and calculus (see Krämer 2003). In this paper, I shall survey the representation of knowledge, defined by particular spatial and discursive arrangements which, however, depend on technical equipment informed by other factors than scientific ones, such as social and economic ones (see Bennett 2002; Stewart 2008; Shapin 2010). Knowledge transmission is always denoted by a complex relational system of integration and exclusion, of exotericism and esotericism. Thus, wherever epistemic polarities such as "knowledge" and "ignorance", "belief" and "certainty", "orthodoxy" and "heterodoxy", "normality" and "eccentricity" are at stake either by degree or by opposition, the respective world view with its historically determined background norms itself is made an object of social circulation and material transformation.

The three key terms in my title designating different locations seem to require a narrative with a chronology faithful to history, including a shift from the human being to a high degree of scientific complexity. However, my argument rather follows the successive states of knowledge generation, knowledge transmission, and knowledge storage that they represent. For this reason, I shall move along the order of functional differentiation, beginning with the "Laboratory" and ending with the "Library". I shall address the different degree to which the design of the respective locations is public. Needless to say that, in terms of social function, technical equipment and architectural design, each of these locations has changed significantly, both conceptually and physically, in the course of the past 400 years, as much as they did in the 200 years before 1800. Given this historicist *caveat*, however, it is equally necessary to point out that each of these spaces used to epitomize, and continue to do so in their respective ways, functional, hierarchical, and social connections reaching beyond the specific scientific communities and into several groups of informed or ignorant outsiders. Empirical social scientist Bruno Latour, in particular, has focused on the descriptions of internal processes within scientific structures occurring in a modern laboratory (see Latour and Woolgar 1986). Far from considering the lab as a chamber in the figurative Ivory Tower, inhabited by an exclusive community of scientists, Latour views the sciences as dependent on social, indeed anthropological, and especially hierarchical interaction. In the more recent and more generalizing actor-network theory, to which he contributed a significant share of insights, he considered the sciences as part of an almost rhizomatic structure. In my own approach, I shall apply Latour's social scientific tools of analysis to those contexts reconstructed by historians of science such as Steven Shapin, who have presented a variety of examples of natural philosophic research in the eighteenth century and its socio-cultural embedding. In my survey I will present the mediating and interrelating processes occurring in different sites of producing, transmitting, and storing knowledge between the sixteenth and the eighteenth centuries.

2. Laboratories

A brief survey of laboratories may help us to follow various approaches of science historians in their attempts at explaining the phenomenon of the "laboratory" as such. Generally, Shapin reminds us that the "(e)laboratorium" was originally a site where non-intellectual "work" was carried out (2010, 63), whilst the intellectual work ("ora et labora") was done in the "scriptorium", the place where books were kept and copied. Only after the seventeenth century did the term acquire a new meaning, increasingly implying systematic empiricism and complex experimentation. Furthermore, Shapin points out that it was the chemist-physicist Robert Boyle who had a large part in "defin[ing] the nature of a space in which experimental work might be practically situated and in which experimental knowledge would be seen as authentic. Such a space did not then clearly exist" (Shapin 2010, 69). Since Boyle and his erstwhile assistant Robert Hooke, the experimental laboratory has become an increasingly important space with internal patterns of action and mediation, which necessarily underwent significant changes in semiotic design, technological equipment, and social hierarchies since the late middle ages. The difficulties Boyle met were particularly visible in the lack of a public experimental space, for even the newly founded Royal Society was located and relocated in various buildings over the first decades and from one place to another whenever experimentation was impossible. Instead, for public experiments, the researchers performed in private lodgings, or in neighbouring coffee-houses (77), which were open to invited as well as incidental guests who, however, had to testify to what they saw. In the public 'trial' of examining natural laws, autopsy of educated witnesses of high social standing was as equally important as that of simple spectators in the ascription of authenticity in the experiment (73). Because of the different values in private and public experiments, Shapin has distinguished between those that served to present a "demonstration" of novel results that had been carried out previously in privacy by "trial and error", and others with a relatively open end, leading to either success or failure (83).

Moran offers a different, more technical reading of the laboratory interior. In his study of the disciplinary process undergone by rationalist, empiricist chemistry in its transformation from traditionally 'magic', obscure alchemy during the seventeenth and eighteenth centuries, Moran (2006) highlights the description of a laboratory by the

Utrecht-based chemist Johann Conrad Barchusen in his treatise on exothermic reactions utilized in medicine, physics, chemistry, pharmacy, and metallurgy, titled *Pyrosophia: Examining Concisely and Briefly Iatrochemical and Metallic Matters as well as the Business of Making Precious Metals* (1698). Barchusen distinguishes, in his assessment of the equipment used in this laboratory, between "active" and "passive" instruments, meaning that the passives ones "only allowed something to happen", such as a pair of scales, or a filter.[1] Surprisingly, and much in contrast to Latour's view that the laboratory was a place of viral "contagion" and thus a knowledge "agency", Barchusen considered the laboratory a passive place, whereas active instruments in it worked as physical catalysts, i.e., furnaces or test tubes, whose "purpose was to force things to occur". Moran concludes that "Barchusen's 'passive' laboratory was designed as a space in which to show how chemistry could change the situation of [elementary] bodies, rearrange their parts, and, by doing so, provide a special kind of knowledge about how nature herself was put together" (Moran 2006, 130-131). Many of the new insights depended wholly on reliable technology. The laboratory grew into a complex apparatus and needed more space than a mere coffeehouse. Thus, in the course of the eighteenth century, Berwick Street, Soho, "was not only becoming fashionable but [...] was soon also an area riddled with schools of natural and experimental philosophy. Here electrical fire and anatomical displays competed for audiences by way of the practical and the theatrical" (Stewart 2008, 19). However, in contrast to Shapin's all too reductive view of the insurmountable class distinction separating the gentlemanly knowledge community from those who assisted them (see Shapin 2010, 79), Stewart insists:

> There were many in the eighteenth century who thought these distinctions to be both unnecessary and harmful to the philosophical enterprise. Evading such social or intellectual boundaries proved critical to the knowledge economy that characterizes both enlightenment and industry. Here the dramatic did the job. (19)

Tracing the example of a particularly well-established network between Humphrey Davy, the Wedgwood family, and Oxford manufacturers, whose workshops could provide the biologist with high-quality electrical devices, Stewart argues: "Instrument makers held the key [to successful demonstrations of experiments]. [...] Such practical approaches to apparatus argue strongly that the boundaries between medical practice and experimentation were greatly eroded at the end of the century" (Stewart 2008, 17).

In sum, professionalization of knowledge production went hand in hand with the need for internal classification, and with the debate over the question of whether or not the ex-laboratory environment's hierarchies were suspended in that space. Stewart's argument for an almost symbiotic interdependence of laboratories and manufacturers seems convincing. Although there was a rather close circle of experimenters with inside knowledge, they depended on a more loosely involved group of common-sense

---

[1] This binary division of technical equipment ties in, of course, quite well with the dualistic remodelling of the elementary world in correspondence to the cosmos, and features, moreover, in the (vain) attempt to order the chemical-physical foundation of the world into "alkaline" and "acids" (Moran 2006, 120). Following the principal Cartesian dichotomy of *res extensa* and *res cogitans*, the rationalistic, mechanical approach also materialized in the lab by moving away from the holistic explanation to a more reductionist view; devaluing the significance of the four Aristotelian elements in their sympathetic, Neo-Platonic interpretation of the cosmos, which was now derided as "alchemical".

people who would, as it were, confirm the events in a public demonstration experiment: Scientific proof went together with a social stamp that sealed the result as truth. Most importantly, laboratories did not solely serve as the production site of novelty, but they were also a location whose internal action was scripted according to dramaturgical protocols.

3. Theatres

Like the term "laboratory", the term "theatre" invites a brief consideration of its etymology and semantic value. Early modern visual culture provides a wide range of different types of theatre, including, most famously, the emerging institution of public theatre, which served as, and was suspiciously viewed as, competition for previously established locations of (spiritually contextualized) knowledge transfer: the pulpit in church and the lecture theatre at university. The term – in its wider early modern sense – denoted a semiotic channel of visual signs and iconic rhetoric triggering cognitive and emotional responses, famed as well as feared for its ambiguities in knowledge delivery, affirmative or subversive. However, "theatres" were built not only for spectacle as entertainment in our largely reduced modern sense, but also for other kinds of show whose meaning survives today in lexical phrases such as the "lecture theatre" just mentioned, the "operation/anatomy theatre",[2] or – synonymous with the term "battlefield" – the "theatre of war".[3] The theatre-image, the universal metaphor "theatrum mundi", was so attractive and popular because it seemed so inclusive:

> Theatrical settings, with the audience sitting around a stage upon which experiments were performed or models exhibited, were supposed to display nature itself. It was of no consequence that the stage was covered with artefacts such as vessels, instruments, or wax models. This apparatus simply helped to unveil nature, to magnify its aspects or emphasize its processes. (Bensaude-Vincent and Blondel 2008b, 7)

Especially the anatomy theatre was a semiotically charged site of knowledge transfer. Its main function was a dramaturgically designed demonstration of medical dissection after the Roman Catholic Church had first given permission for human dissections in 1482. In its public enactment, usually located in a university dissection room, it was a succession of parallel actions carried out according to a particular script. Involved in the performance were, as Lembke reminds us, a professor who kept his hands clean,

---

2 Stockhorst (2005) lists the scope of analogies in the "anatomy theatre" and the actors' stage: a temporal as well as spatial distinction from everyday life (by special appointment as well as by separating spectacle from spectators); publicity and accessibility; ceremonial progress; symbolic over-determination in the signified, with the performance as signification in its own right; co-presence of essence and appearance (see 276). Carlino (2011) reminds us that it was necessary to obtain and display tickets in order to gain access to both anatomical dissections and stage plays (134).

3 There is a host of other forms of theatre, all dealing less with physical performance around a narrative plot, but rather with the transformation of three-dimensional space into two-dimensional pictures. Again, this implied much more than a simplistic visual representation of knowledge. Abraham Ortelius' *Theatrum Orbis Terrarum* (1570) preceded Gerard Mercator's still more innovative *Atlas sive cosmographicae meditationes de fabrica mundi et fabricati figura* (1595) by a quarter of a century, but cartographers continued to refer to their maps as "theatres" for quite a while. For its greater success as well as for its better usefulness in mercantile and military navigation, the model of the *Atlas* eventually eliminated the outdated mode of chorographical charts and "theatres".

reading from the (ancient) canon of anatomical literature: During the professor's *lectio*, a barber or surgeon did the dirty work of cutting open the human corpse in the *sectio*, and an assistant had to point, in the *demonstratio*, at the organs and those physical phenomena the professor was commenting upon (see Lembke 2005, 19-20). It was anatomist Andreas Vesalius who, at least ideally, unified these three parallel acts in the dissection, as he points out in his "Preface" to the revolutionary anatomical work *De humani corporis fabrica septem libri* (1543), as well as in his bold self-representation in the title image, which shows Vesalius himself in the centre of a motley crew of spectators, representing not only a 'section' of the whole human society by featuring a crowd of men and (presumably) a woman, young and old, gentlemen and beggars, but also the animal world, displaying a monkey and a dog as potential subjects of vivisection. Obviously, the illustration serves as satire and admonition, and like many other depictions within the book, it transports not a naturalistic (scientific) representation, but their symbolic (semiotic) and programmatic (ideological) values – with a clear intention towards the anonymous reading public, much more than towards those individual witnesses present at a dissection.[4]

A dissection might last for three or four days, until the natural decay of the organic tissues stopped the enterprise, for, as Nicholas Udall (1553) reminds us in his "Letter to the ientill readers and Surgeons of England" prefacing the pirated English edition of Vesalius's books and particularly their illustrations (Thomas Geminus, *Compendiosa totius Anatomie Delineatio*) that the "putrefaccion soone commynge in" rendered the dissection a "peinfull labour" for the "woorkman". In the activity as such, considered by Andrea Carlino as a "social drama" (2011, 129), the regular professor literally stood on a higher level in relation to the surgeon and the assistant, and in this spatial distinction we may envision the social strata inscribed into this action, insofar as the professor would usually be a gentleman, much higher in status, intellect, and education than the surgeon, a commoner and mere artisan who would inevitably be considered primitive and morally unsound. As is well known, the dissection material would usually be the corpse of a pauper, a stranger, or a criminal. With such precarious co-presences of high and low, moral and immoral, pure and rotten, authority and illegitimacy, a specifically appointed clerical supervisor (the custodian) monitored the ceremonial script of the dissection, yet if all went well in the "open public", the professor would gain in estimation and prestige, whilst the remnants of the corpse would be, after the ordeal of post-mortem dissection, re-membered as part of the body politic (*ibid.*, 143). In contrast to the relatively short duration of the first steps in the dissection under the eyes of the public, the students and fellows who would witness the slow decomposition of the corpse as a medical enterprise down to its elementary constituents needed to be more patient. Effectively, there were two different plays performed simultaneously in a pub-

---

4   For a brilliant reading of the narrative frontispiece of Vesalius's *Fabrica*, see Sawday (1995), 66-73. Sawday isolates three different theatrical codes: the anatomical (in the central action around Vesalius and his table), the social (in the marginal plots that distract the viewer's attention from the centre), and the spatial (in the architectural design, which is reminiscent of the interior of the San Pietro in Montorio, Rome). Sawday concludes that the image shows "a drama of life and death", since it challenges the contemporary discussion about the cosmos, rather wittily concluding about the meaning of the image: "The world is neither geocentric, nor heliocentric, but uterocentric: the womb is our point of origin, hence its central place in the image." (71) – See also the valuable remarks by Kusukawa (2006).

lic dissection, for the general public did not see the performance of a *scientific demonstration* but of a *moral exemplum*: The long arm of justice, both secular and ecclesiastical, was waved as a warning at least to the commoners and non-professionals among the spectators who were reminded that it was powerful enough to even reach beyond life, but yet forgiving enough to pardon the individual by applying public cruelty (*ibid.*, 144).

Apart from these performative, physical forms of "theatre" staging different kinds of knowledge simultaneously in the parallel arrangements of appropriate discursive formations, we must not overlook the two-dimensional, textual devices supporting the action, not least in the shape of maps, illustrations, and anatomical preparations.[5] Like mountebanks in a marketplace performing their political news-reels, Vesalius was famous for using large scale images during his public dissections: "In the sense that these works aimed to communicate something about [...] medicine to an academic audience, their pictures can be called didactic" (Kusukawa 2006, 76). But if Kusukawa continues to argue that "this should not be confused with the didactic function frequently associated with Gregory the Great, namely the use of images in order to teach or remind the illiterate what they cannot read in words" (76-77), she forgets the motley crew of bystanders watching the dissection (see Carlino 2011, 143). Udall is quite clear about this double focus in the *Compendiosa* by Geminus. In his prefatory "Letter" Udall finds it impossible to decide who "dooeth more effectuallye helpe toward the knowledge of the premises [i.e., locations of the organs]":

> Whether he that by his high learning and profound science of natural thynges dooeth sette it foorthe in writing, or els he that by playn figures and pictures oeeth proporcion out euerye thing to the yie [eye] of the vnlearned. For some haue we knowen, whiche beeyng vnlettred haue been hable to sette in again any member that by anye violent iniuste hath bene broken or sette out of ionict. (Udall 1559).

In the early modern dispositive of the (anatomical) "theatre", the deployment of illustrations ('posters') as well as, since the seventeenth century, 3-D preparations ('props' and pop-ups), served both as an optical magnification of minute anatomical detail for the educated and as a visual aid for the illiterate (who each could claim the reputation of a professional within their own social class, as we know from academically educated gentleman-physicians and their lower trained colleagues, ranging from surgeons to barbers and quacks). But the story does not end here. Due to the overlap of secular (scientific) and spiritual (moral) implications for the different groups in one and the same audience, a dissection – like the demonstration experiment in a public laboratory – must be attributed a highly ambiguous semiotic function. In Latour's terms, the agents and actors performing in the anatomy theatre established a network that unified them with the crowd of spectators, but which must be divided into various and heterogeneous in-groups (i.e., the medical professionals of various sorts, representatives of

---

5   For a detailed discussion of anatomical preparations in their different subjects, categories, and classes, see Rheinberger (2006). They had a multifaceted semiotic and dramaturgical function as well as representational value as items suggesting a co-presence of authentic as well as illusory features. Depending on the spectators' degree of knowledge, anatomical preparations also served both as objectifying pieces of rationalist visualisation (*Anschauung*) and as sensationalist, sentimental items triggering emotional responses. See the case study of the French anatomy-performer Fragonard (Simon 2002).

the legal and church systems) and out-groups (i.e., the commoners, accidental spectators).

Apart from this multi-levelled mediation by action or image, it is no wonder that many writers, who welded their dramatised hands-on practical knowledge into treatises, considered rhetorical and dialogic performativity a particularly attractive representation strategy for their subjects. Therefore we find many essentially theatrical and dramaturgical devices in the super-abundant, hyper-determined mediation of early modern knowledge, in which authors set imaginary combatants upon one another and have them discuss their particular issues. Innumerable imaginary "dialogues" upon controversial natural philosophical topics circulating in the early modern age are eventually complemented by books such as Robert Boyle's *Sceptical Chymist*, which (as Shapin and Shaffer have put it) rather "took the form, not of a Socratic dialogue, but of a *conference*", involving four interlocutors who deal with one another very respectfully and thus perform "a piece of theatre that exhibited how persuasion, dissensus and, ultimately, conversion to truth ought to be conducted" (Shapin and Schaffer 1985, 74-5). Books provided the scripts of demonstrative experiments and thus literally 'contained' (enclosed) them; deriving from what Latour and Woolgar have called "literary inscriptions", or "constituent diagrams and figures" (1986, 88; see also Latour 1987, 68). Books keep a record of experimental results (transforming them into data) and were designed to defend the researcher's supremacy in terms of analytical interpretation. Finally, in their textual shape as books and maps, these publications provided an illustrated inventory of the multifarious fabrics, and fabrications, of body and world.

4. Libraries

The historically relatively recent institution of circulating libraries is only one storage place of knowledge, chosen here for its particularly medial nature. Before libraries became for enlightened and post-enlightened users a rigidly ordered marketplace designed for enabling the trading, trafficking, and "traducing" of epistemic change and exchange, book collections were wholly dependent on the individuals who ran them in a more or less idiosyncratic fashion, recording more or less reliably the holdings and new entries. Often they served as supplement to, and culmination of the curiosity cabinets, which were collections and thus a materially limited site of object and experiential knowledge, whilst the book collections allowed, potentially, a verbal extension into theoretical knowledge. Essential, however, is the ordering of the collection by means of registers and catalogues – at the same time, the curiosity cabinet illustrates the theoretical knowledge locked away in books. Libraries and curiosity cabinets reflect upon one another as mirrors (Roth 1998, 196-197).

According to Martin Davies's entry on "catalog" in the *International Dictionary of Library Histories*, the first Cambridge University Library catalogue dates back to "[a]s late as 1424", recording "122 donated volumes [...] in nine subject divisions, but the one for poetry and chronicles is a heading and no more. Religion, theology, and canon law account for three quarters of the collection". Davies has also pointed out that, from the Middle Ages well into early modern times, "[t]he common libraries of convents and colleges would usually be kept locked, the key in possession of the librarian, who could be variously called the *armarius, cantor* or *precentor, libraries, custos librorum, or bibliothecarius*" (Davies 2001, 107). Thus, libraries must not be considered a public place in the modern sense, despite the fact that catalogues existed and that individual sections were kept for manuscripts and prints according to the subject. No book in these libraries, however, had its individual signature, and the catalogue would only serve the library keeper as a tool for the annual process of inventory. For the majority of chained books, the question of position was obviously not such a problem as for collections of loose manuscripts. Less a 'search-machine' for users, the pre-enlightenment catalogue was more likely a monitor, instrumental for the registration of new entries or losses and thus negligent of any public function as we know it (see Umstätter and Wagner-Döbler 2005, 29).

The Renaissance brought, first, no significant change to these locations. As Nelles emphasises, "[t]he standard classification system accorded scripture pride of place, followed by works of the church fathers, theology, sermons, and other religious works. Canon law and civil law followed, then medicine. Next came philosophy, history, poetry, rhetoric, and grammar (the latter subject encompassing dictionaries, encyclopedias, and many works now considered works of literature)". Thus, Nelles sees the most important innovation in the Renaissance library signalled by the "relatively large number of collections in the secular domain, the great number and size of personal collections, and the emergence of a distinct, professional bibliographical literature" (Nelles 2001, 154).[6] In the latter, Nelles includes such reference works as Conrad Gessner's *Bibliotheca universalis* (1545) and Gabriel Naudé's *Advice for Establishing a Library* (1627). Originally composed in French and in 1661 translated into English by John Evelyn, one of the founding members of Gresham College (the later Royal Society), Naudé's treatise became a significant document for the Restoration period and the discussion about a National Library in the eighteenth century. The author points at the "vital importance" of the idea of a newly defined institutionalised public library, "precisely because libraries represented both quantitative measurements of knowledge and the means by which this knowledge was disseminated" (McDayter 2003, 11). Similar to John Dury's reflections on the utopian image of the "Reformed Library-keeper", which gave the title to his little treatise, published in a collection of bibliographical letters edited by Samuel Hartlib in 1651, Naudé's book changed the function of the library and those who work in it or with it. Whereas Naudé emphasises the cultural, national significance of a well-stocked library with a transparent and efficient catalogue system, Dury focuses on the office of a specifically educated and well-remunerated librarian, who, regardless of religious or political issues, must perform as and embody the centre of a globally extended educational trade-network: "The proper charge then of the Honorarie Librarie-Keeper in an Universitie [...] is then to bee a Factor and Trader for helps to Learning, and a Treasurer to keep them, and a dispenser to applie them to use, or to see them well used, or at least not abused" (Dury 1650, 18). Dury sketched this mercantile exchange of knowledge in similar terms as Francis Bacon had imagined the "Merchants of Light" (Bacon 2002, 487) in the *New Atlantis* (1627):

---

6   Nelles's focus on continuity with the Middle Ages seems too narrow, neglecting the impact of print technology for the ordering of a catalogue. As book-historians insist, the printed title page with its information on author, title, publisher, print shop, and publication year had become a convention no earlier than 1520 (in Germany), with consequences for the rules in cataloguing derived from this page, mounting in the necessity of deciding "what information was essential, what was dispensible?" (Umstätter and Wagner-Döbler 2005, 31-32)

> Thus hee should Trade with those that are at home and abroad out of the Universities, and with those that are within the Universitie, hee should have acquaintance to know all that are of anie parts, and how their vein of Learning doth lie, to supplie helps unto them upon the keeping of correspondencie vvith men of their ovvn strain, for the beating out of matters not yet elaborated in Sciences; so that they may bee as his Assistants and subordinate Factors in his Trade and in their own for gaining of knowledg: Now becaus in all publick Agencies, it is fit that som inspection should bee had over those that are intrusted therewith, therefor in this Factorie and Trade for the increas of Learning, som tie should bee upon those Librarie-keepers to oblige them to carefulness. (Dury 1650, 20-21)

An important position within Dury's imagined library network is given to the complex communication system in which the holdings of each library are registered, and exchanged, in an inter-library catalogue and its annual updates (21-22).[7] A sound catalogue is indispensable, since Dury separates library shelf from magazine, in which those books not meant for the public are stored. They must remain, however, accessible and retrievable by means of an author/title-catalogue, "with a note of distinction to shew the Science to which they are to bee referred" (Dury 1650, 24).

The gap between Dury's ideological dream and the real world was considerable. Two interrelated facts may suffice to illustrate this. On the one hand, we may refer to the holdings of the Bodleian library, which had been severely neglected since the first half of the seventeenth century and slipped, by the early eighteenth century, into a "somewhat somnolent period; no books at all were purchased between 1700 and 1703" (Tyack 2000, 9).[8] On the other hand, the political call for a national public library became ever louder in London, accompanied by the demands for parish libraries elsewhere in the country.[9] For example, Sir Richard Bentley, one of the 'modern' targets of Swift's vituperative satire in the *Battel of the Books*, had published a pamphlet in 1697 in which he deplored the downfall of St. James's Library, whose original "flourishing condition, well stored with all sorts of good Books has gradually gone to Decay [...]. The Room is miserably out of Repair; and so little, that it will not contain the Books that belong to it." Adding that "[t]here has been no supply of Books from abroad for the Space of Sixty years last", he concludes: "It is therefore proposed, as a thing that will highly conduce to the Publick Good, the Glory of His Majesty's Reign, and the Honour of the Parliament" (Bentley 1697) to raise a new library building. Thus, Bentley presents himself as well-suited competitor for the position of a 'reformed' librarian, and he appears to have been genuinely ashamed of the present state in which he found

---

7   Hardly surprising, Hartlib's edition gives two German examples of good and bad librarianship: The 'bad' one is located at Heidelberg, where "the keeping of that Librarie made it an Idol, to bee respected and worshipped for a raretie by an implicit faith, without anie benefit to those who did esteem of it a far off" (Dury 1650, 27). The 'good' example is the ducal library at Wolfenbüttel (Herzog August Bibliothek), a detailed Latin description of which is appended to Dury's two English letters, and another epistolary reflection by John Pell on a (mathematical) library in the same volume (47-65).
8   Tyack concedes that this period also saw hectic building activity in Oxford, with the foundation of many small college libraries and, not least, the Radcliffe Camera under construction. The no-purchase period may be due to the expenses spent on new library buildings.
9   The *Overture for Founding & Maintaining Bibliothecks in every Paroch of this Kingdom* (Kirkwood 1699), is no less enthusiastic in scope than Dury's design. Apart from promising to propel learning into the province, the author also envisions an increase in local employment, because a library in the parish will attract book-binders and other manufactures (9).

the library of St. James Palace, rather than embodying the hoarding "kind of miser" depicted in contemporary caricatures (McDayter 2005, 10). According to Howard Weinbrot, however, one must consider that in Bentley's case, once again, the social distinction is important in these assessments. Here, he features as a socially inferior creature to a gentleman such as William Temple or the nobleman Charles Boyle, two supporters of the 'Ancients', who referred to Bentley in their own writings as "an uppity servant, a thieving tradesman, a dishonest bookseller, and a shoplifter" (Weinbrot 2003, 244).

5. Conclusion

Like the historical anatomy theatre, which shared the functions of an experimental laboratory and a place for storing "curiosities" (as we may see in the famous depictions of the Leyden School of Anatomy), the imaginary super-library system designed by John Dury functions literally as a "Factorie" and thus as a "publick Agencie" (Dury 1651, 22). As Shapin points out, the Ashmolean Museum, Oxford, with its origins in the Tradescent family's collection of curiosities and their comprehensive register, even contained an experimental laboratory in its basement (Shapin 2010: 63). The narrow view on medial practises alone, without the analysis of their underlying epistemic functions, makes it impossible to draw clear-cut boundaries that define each of these sites. Laboratory, theatre, and library were, not only as textual systems, embedded in their own respective contexts; they became their own holistic contexts in which "[e]xperiments do words with things and things with words through instruments, inscriptions and controversies" (Latour 1990). Other places activating knowledge, including the dramatic scenes in a classroom, the universal dramas stored in curiosity cabinets, or the careful designs of gardening as a display of botanical (and cosmic) knowledge, had to be ignored in this paper.[10] Therefore, combined with its companion term borrowed from mercantile exchange, trade, and with implications of epistemic competition, value, and credit, the historically determined activity of knowledge "tradition" is worth further scrutiny, as is a shift in attention from those means located outside the human mind to those epistemic *topoi* inside it. This brings us conveniently back to the beginning. Almost eight decades after Swift's derision of the loud speakers defending their modern learning, Frenchman Louis-Sebastian Mercier boldly declared in his *Tableau de Paris* (1781) that "[t]he reign of humanities is over, physicists replace poets and novelists, the electrical machine takes the place of a theatre play" (qtd. in Bensaude-Vincent and Blondel 2008b, 6). However, it was William Wordsworth who, in his "Preface to *Lyrical Ballads*" (1802), regarded the brain as the internal site of empirical knowledge and emphatically (though vainly) commended it as instrument to generate innovative subjects in poetic diction:

> The remotest discoveries of the Chemist, the Botanist, or Mineralogist, will be as proper objects of the Poet's art as any upon which it can be employed, if the time should ever come when these things shall be familiar to us, and the relations under which they are contemplated by the followers of these respective Sciences shall be manifestly and palpably material to us as enjoying and suffering beings. (Wordsworth 1984, 607)

---

10   On the courtly and private curiosity cabinets and later the public museums, see Roth 1998; Heyl 2006; Schramm 2005. On gardens, see in particular Mosser and Teyssot 2000.

Even in this brief sequence of three quotes by very different writers, we can witness a double shift, spatial as well as discursive: It takes us from the orator's pre-enlightened but de-centred and elevated position across to the radically enlightened idea of a physicist's electrical apparatus, which values empirical analysis higher than a purely imaginary activity, and leads ultimately into the individual Romanticist mind. The latter's creative cognitive ability shifts scientific discoveries into an epistemic system with a spatial order, distinguishing a centre from its periphery, as Wordsworth's use of the adjective "remotest" implies. Knowledge *per se*, in all these cases, is liminal, multi-discursive, and sways between the active and the passive as well as between the individual and the social. The true drama of making knowledge transfer happen, then, lies always in the question of how a super-individual episteme allows the multitude of textual information and data to be converted into personal knowledge, achieved by negotiation and evaluation.

References

Bacon, Francis (2002): "*The New Atlantis,*" in: *Francis Bacon: The Major Works, Including "New Atlantis" and the "Essays."* Ed. Brian Vickers. Oxford: Oxford University Press, 457-489

Bennett, James A. (2002): "Shopping for Instruments in Paris and London", in: Smith/Findlen (eds.), 370-395.

Bensaude-Vincent, Bernadette; Blondel, Christine (eds.; 2008a): *Science and Spectacle in the European Enlightenment.* Aldershot: Ashgate

--- (2008b): "Introduction: A Science Full of Shocks, Sparks and Smells", in: Bensaude-Vincent/ Blondel (eds.), 1-10

Bentley, Richard (1697): *A Proposal for Building a Royal Library, and Establishing it by Act of Parliament.* London (Wing B 1943)

Carlino, Andrea (2011): "Leichenzergliederung als soziales Drama im Europa der Frühen Neuzeit", in: Schramm, Helmar et al. (eds.): *Spuren der Avantgarde: Theatrum anatomicum: Frühe Neuzeit und Moderne im Kulturvergleich.* Berlin: de Gruyter, 129-146

Davies, Martin (2001): "Medieval Libraries", in: Stam (ed.), vol. I: 104-108

Dury, John (1650): *The Reformed Librarie-Keeper.* London: William DuGard (Wing D 2882)

Findlen, Paula (2002): "Inventing Nature: Commerce, Art, and Science in the Early Modern Cabinet of Curiosities", in: Smith/Findlen (eds.), 297-323

Heyl, Christoph (2006): "*Lusus Naturae* und *Lusus Scientiae* im ältesten öffentlich zugänglichen Kuriositätenkabinett Englands", in: *Cardanus: Jahrbuch für Wissenschaftsgeschichte* 6, 25-44

[Kirkwood, James] (1699): *Overture for Founding & Maintaining Bibliothecks in every Paroch of this Kingdom.* sine locus (Wing K648)

Krämer, Sybille (2003): "Textualität, Visualität und Episteme: Über ihren Zusammenhang in der frühen Neuzeit", in: Lachmann, Renate; Rieger, Stefan (eds.): *Text und Wissen: Technologische und anthropologische Aspekte.* Tübingen: Narr, 17-27

Kusukawa, Sachiko (2006): "The Uses of Pictures in the Formation of Learned Knowledge: The Cases of Leonhard Fuchs and Andreas Vesalius", in: Kusukawa, Sachiko; Maclean, Ian (eds.): *Transmitting Knowledge: Words, Images, and Instruments in Early Modern Europe.* Oxford: Oxford University Press, 73-96

Latour, Bruno (1987): *Science in Action: How to Follow Scientists and Engineers Through Society.* Cambridge, MA: Harvard University Press

--- (1990): "The Force and Reason of Experiment", in: LeGrand, H. E. (ed.): *Experimental Inquiries: Historical, Philosophical and Social Studies of Experimentation in Science.* Dordrecht/Boston/ London: Kluwer, 49-80

---; Woolgar, Steve (1986): *Laboratory Life: The Social Construction of Scientific Facts.* 2nd edition. Princeton, NJ: Princeton University Press

Lembke, Sven (2005): "Wie der menschliche Leichnam zu einem Buch der Natur ohne Druckfehler wird: Über den epistemologischen Wert anatomischer Sektionen im Zeitalter Vesals", in: Schirrmeister/Pozsgai (eds.), 19-49

McDayter, Mark (2003): "The Haunting of St. James' Library: Libraries, Librarians, and the 'Battle of The Books'", *Huntingdon Library Quarterly* 66, 1-26

Moran, Bruce T. (2006): *Distilling Knowledge: Alchemy, Chemistry, and the Scientific Revolution.* Cambridge, MA: Harvard University Press

Mosser, Monique; Teyssot, Georges (eds.; 2000): *The History of Garden Design: The Western Tradition from the Renaissance to the Present Day.* London: Thames and Hudson

Naudé, Gabriel (1661): *Instructions Concerning Erecting of a Library.* Transl. John Evelyn. London: G. Bedle, T. Collins, J. Crook (Wing N247)

Nelles, Paul (2001): "Renaissance Libraries", in: Stam (ed.), vol. I: 151-155

Rheinberger, Hans-Jörg (2006). "Die Evidenz des Präparates", in: Schramm, Helmar et al. (eds.): *Spektakuläre Experimente: Praktiken der Evidenzproduktion im 17. Jahrhundert.* Berlin: de Gruyter, 1-17

Roth, Harriet (1998): "Die Bibliothek als Spiegel der Kunstkammer", in: Assmann, Aleida et al. (eds.): *Sammler – Bibliophile – Exzentriker.* Tübingen: Narr, 193-210

Sawday, Jonathan (1995): *The Body Emblazoned: Dissection and the Human Body in Renaissance Culture.* London: Routledge

Schirrmeister, Albert; Mathias Pozsgai (eds.; 2005): *Zergliederungen: Anatomie und Wahrnehmung in der frühen Neuzeit.* Frankfurt: Klostermann

Schmidgen, Henning (2011): *Bruno Latour zur Einführung.* Hamburg: Junius

Schramm, Helmar (2005): "*Kunstkammer*, Laboratory, Theater in the 'Theatrum Europaeum': On the Transformation of Performative Space in the 17th Century", in: Schramm, Helmar (ed.): *Collection, Laboratory, Theatre: Scenes of Knowledge in the 17th Century.* Berlin: de Gruyter, 9-34

Shapin, Steven (2010): *Never Pure: Historical Studies of Science as if It Was Produced by People with Bodies, Situated in Time, Space, Culture, and Society, and Struggling for Credibility and Authority.* Baltimore, MD: Johns Hopkins University Press

---; Schaffer, Simon (1985): *Leviathan and the Air-Pump: Hobbes, Boyle, and the Experimental Life.* Princeton, NJ: Princeton University Press

Simon, Jonathan (2002): "Honoré Fragonard, Anatomico Virtuoso", in: Bensaude-Vincent/Blondel (eds.), 141-158

Smith, Pamela H., Findlen, Paula (eds.; 2002): *Merchants & Marvels: Commerce, Science, and Art in Early Modern Europe.* New York/London: Routledge

Stam, David H. (ed.; 2001): *International Dictionary of Library Histories.* 2 vols. Chicago/London: Fitzroy Dearborn

Stewart, Larry (2008): "The Laboratory, the Workshop, and the Theatre of Experiment", in: Bensaude-Vincent/Blondel (eds.), 11-24

Stockhorst, Stefanie (2005): "Unterweisung und Ostentation auf dem anatomischen Theater der Frühen Neuzeit: Die öffentliche Leichensektion als Modellfall des *theatrum mundi*", in: Schirrmeister/Pozsgai (eds.), 271-290

Swift, Jonathan (2010): "A Tale of the Tub", in: *The Essential Writings of Jonathan Swift.* Ed Claude Rawson, Ian Higgins. New York: W. W. Norton, 4-92

Tyack, Geoffrey (2000): *The Bodleian Library, Oxford.* Oxford: Oxford University Press

Udall, Nicholas (1559): "A Letter to the ientill Reader and the Surgeons of England", in: Thomas Geminus, *Compendiosa Totius Anatomiae Delineatio.* London, s. pag. (^{2}STC 11715.5)

Umstätter, Walther; Wagner-Döbler, Roland (2005): *Einführung in die Katalogkunde: Vom Zettelkatalog zur Suchmaschine.* 3rd edition. Stuttgart: Anton Hiersemann

Weinbrot, Howard (2003): "'He will kill me over and over again': Intellectual Contexts of the Battle of the Books", in: Real, Hermann J.; Stöver-Leidig, Helgard (eds.): *Reading Swift: Papers from the Fourth Münster Symposium on Jonathan Swift.* München: Wilhelm Fink, 225-248

Wordsworth, William (1984): "Preface to *Lyrical Ballads, With Pastoral and Other Poems (1802)*", in: Gill, Stephen (ed.): *William Wordsworth.* Oxford/New York: Oxford University Press, 595-615

GERD BAYER (ERLANGEN)

The Broken Letters of Early Modern Fiction

The eighteenth century stands as a major turning point in the history of the novel. In the complex and dense genealogy related to the genesis of this genre, epistolary writing can claim a prominent place. As I will argue in this essay, rather than contributing a sense of factuality, truthfulness, and overall sense of realism to the early novel, the literary letter in fact presented a more complex gift at the novel's nativity. Far from offering a remedy for the ailing novel-to-be, it inserted into the nascent form some of the formal corrosiveness that, in the shape of ironic metafictionality, would seek from the inception of the form to dismantle its shape and nature. The letter as a poisonous gift, a risky remedy, a pharmakon: It is remarkable how easily a look at the early eighteenth century evokes antiquity and the Platonic dialogues. Before returning to a small selection of textual examples of this almost Bakhtinian dialogic as it plays itself out in the tempestuous relationship between the letter and the novel, I would like to remain with Plato for a little longer. Far from wanting to rehearse Jacques Derrida's argument about speech, writing, logos, myth, or the pharmakon in his discussion of "Plato's Pharmacy" early in *Dissemination* (Derrida 1981, 61-172), I would nevertheless like to return to this text, and in particular to Socrates's statements about the nature of writing and the absence of speech.

In this dialogue, the fatherly Socrates advises Phaedrus about the right uses of language, speech, and rhetoric, amongst other things. In the passage that concerns us here, Socrates draws on an Egyptian story about an inventor, Theuth, addressing an Egyptian god, Thamus, about his art:

> It would take a long time to repeat all that Thamus said to Theuth in praise or blame of the various arts. But when they came to letters, Theuth said: O king, here is a study which will make the Egyptians wiser and give them better memories; it is a specific both for the memory and for the wit. Thamus replied: O most ingenious Theuth, the parent or inventor of an art is not always the best judge of the utility or inutility of his own inventions to the users of them. And in this instance, you who are the father of letters, from a paternal love of your own children have been led to attribute to them a quality which they cannot have; for this discovery of yours will create forgetfulness in the learners' souls, because they will not use their memories; they will trust to the external written characters and not remember of themselves. (Plato 1953, 184)

The word 'letters' in this passage clearly refers to writing, to the invention of script, but as so often, as modern readers we also hear in the word the invention of printing, of movable letters; and especially in the present context, Plato's letters resonate with the epistolary form. In tracing the history of the novel back into antiquity, Margaret Anne Doody has shown that in prose fictions written during antiquity, letters in fact featured prominently, indicating the shift from spoken to written language also discussed in Socrates's discussion with Phaedrus. While her work shows that the notorious appearance on Europe's literary scene of the anonymous *Lettres Portugaises* (1669) did not invent a new style of writing fiction (Doody 1996, 154), the different media environments before and after the print revolution offer a different context for epistolary moments in antiquity when contrasted to the seventeenth century. And, as Elizabeth Eisenstein (1979, 1; 33) has convincingly demonstrated, almost a full century went by after the invention of movable letter printing for its cultural impact to be felt across Europe.

Building on these observations I would like to argue that at epistolary moments, Early Modern fiction resurrects the half-buried ghost of the print revolution, when movable type in letter cases provided the technological and severely materialist basis for the production of books. As Lucien Febvre and Henri-Jean Martin have shown in *The Coming of the Book* (2010, 78-83), the early history of the development that would lead to the dominant lettering system, namely the Carolingian Roman font, already speaks to how media revolutions are marked by hybrid formats. The anonymous form of print production, with its lack of aura (Benjamin 1999, 217) such as is associated with the erstwhile artisans of manuscript illumination, is evoked, belatedly, at moments when narrative fictions turn to letters, to the epistolary avatars of personal speech and the presence of a voice. My argument thus somewhat departs from Joy Bray's argument in *The Epistolary Novel: Representations of Consciousness*, which sees literary letters as primarily lending novels a psychological enrichment of characterization, similar to what Miriam Nandi (2012) has analysed for the emotionality of early modern diaries. In more recent research, however, Bray (2013) also seems to take a more sceptical view of the role played by letters in early modern fiction.

Epistolary fiction existed during the Early Modern age as a narrative form of material memory, as an uncanny return of an earlier media innovation. In thus addressing the print revolution in highly sceptical tones, Early Modern epistolary fiction echoes Plato's distrust of any form of memory machines. Much critical writing on early forms of the novel simply ignores this tendency within epistolary moments, streamlining the argument for the form's ever-closer approach to an intimate form of realism. Patricia Meyer Spacks, for instance, falls for this flawed genealogy when she suggests that for writers and readers alike "personal letters, assumed to be intimate communication, could plausibly express their writers' hidden thoughts and deep feelings" (2006, 92). A more detailed look at Early Modern forms of epistolary writing reveals that a rather sophisticated understanding existed at the time, which at least intuited how letter-writing, both within literary and real-world contexts, allows authors to dissemble or conceal their true intentions. Terry Eagleton obliquely points to this aspect in his discussion of Richardson's contribution to *The English Novel*: He discusses the epistolary form in *Pamela*, which created an effect that was "immediate and transparent" and, simultaneously, reminded readers that this "kind of anti-writing" only emphasizes the mediating nature of any sign system (Eagleton 2005, 69 and 70), what Walter Ong (2002, 128) has described as the effect of "closure" created by print textuality. What might strike modern readers as a highly ambiguous (even poststructuralist) attitude towards epistolary writing, Early Modern readers clearly took in stride. Even Goethe's *The Sorrows of Young Werther* (1774/1787), often portrayed as one of the archetypal examples of epistolary writing, invites its readers to question the veracity of what Werther expresses through his intimate letters (see Bayer 2009). This aspect of epistolary writing coexisted comfortably, for early modern readers and writers, alongside the realist notion of the form. While literary history seems to insist on the letter having worked in singular fashion, the textual trace in fact belies such a straight line of development. It rather follows the kind of principled hybridity that Wolfram Schmidgen (2013) has recently made out as an important intellectual tradition throughout the seventeenth century; and that David Duff (2009) has described as the belated and even retroactive effect of a Neo-Classical process of turning antiquity into a generically pure and unambiguous sphere.

1. **Restoration Lettering**

English Restoration fiction, which existed in a kind of generic limbo (see Bayer 2011), is in fact filled with textual examples where the letter works not so much in a revelatory mode but instead is marked by its deceptive quality. The medium of the letter, far from inviting readerly trust in a text's veracity, instead alerts us to the fact that any medium's lack of immediacy breaks up all claims of total mimesis. If and when letters appear on the pages of these mostly romance-based fictions, they all too often function as a means of delaying the reunification of the lovers, of trying to set up one lover against the other, through lies and fabrications, or of failing to appear, as when they are intercepted by plotting rivals. Rather than put the individuals who make up all these complex love triangles against each other in face-to-face conflict, something that usually only happens during a grand finale, Restoration fiction frequently prefers to have the lovers and their ill-meaning rivals communicate with each other indirectly, through the epistolary forms of mediated, long-distance communication.

One novel where this occurs rather frequently is Mary Davys's *The Amours of Alcippus and Lucippe*, published in London by James Round in 1704 and later known by the title *The Lady's Tale*. It was her first novel and came out four years after the young widow had to leave Ireland and tried to make a living in London. It may not have been her first published prose fiction, as I have argued elsewhere (Bayer 2012), but it was certainly the book that people associated with her name through the early stages of her career, before she became a successful playwright, novelist, and proprietoress of a very popular coffee house in Cambridge (see Backscheider 2004 and Bowden 1999). In her first novel, Davys prepares her readers for the complex textual relationship to reality right in her preface. It opens by dismissing the whole tradition and closes as follows:

> But as it would look very ridiculous for a Person to exclaim against late hours, when he himself sits up all Night; So would it be the very Abstract of Impertinence, in me to say I dislike a Preface, and at the same time Write a very long one: To prevent which and the Censure of the Criticks, I shall only with Sancho Pancho give you an Old Proverb, viz. Little Said soon Amended, and so have done with the Preface. ([A5^r-A6^r] italics reversed)

What Davys in effect tells her readers is that she has both written a preface and refused to do so. The same elusive referentiality also marks her use of the epistolary moments in the novel to follow. For instance, relatively early in the text, soon after the two protagonists have met for the first time and have of course fallen for each other, Lucippe receives a letter from Adrastus, the man chosen by her parents, much to her chagrin, to become her husband. She refuses to read his missive, angry that he dares address her so directly and convinced that she has given him no encouragement to do so. In the end her maid, Mariana, reads out the letter to her. They find out that Adrastus is in effect taking dictation from Alcippus, Lucippe's beloved, who has broken his arm and therefore cannot write in person. Adrastus in fact pleads his case, thereby indicating to

Lucippe that he has given up on his own love interest and is now championing his rival's case. In reality, Adrastus has by no means fallen out of love, and the novel in fact has to kill him off soon, during a short struggle with highwaymen in order to remove him from the love triangle. When Alcippus, a little later, also has to go into hiding, having stabbed a servant while defending Lucippe's father, she tries to send him another letter giving him instructions about how to weather the storm. But her servant, Mariana, falls ill and as a consequence fails to deliver the letter. Alcippus eventually flees to the continent in order to avoid trial and lives there feeling miserably betrayed by Lucippe until the two finally meet face-to-face and the novel ends with their wedding.

As this short summary indicates, the novel relies substantially on how letters transport information, or rather, how they spread dis-information, how the dissemination of letters displaces their supposedly truthful content. Like Davys's other novels, it engages explicitly with questions of form and, as Victoria Joule (2010) has suggested, the role played by realism. The first of the two letters I have just mentioned, where Adrastus supposedly withdraws his claims for Lucippe's love, almost succeeds in getting Lucippe's defences down, and it is only his subsequent death that foils his plan to destroy the love between Lucippe and Alcippus. The letter, though coming disguised in the most intimate tones of amorous conversation, is nevertheless filled with falsehood. The second letter I mentioned would have informed Alcippus that Lucippe will in fact patiently wait for his return from exile, but since it never reaches him, he feels abandoned and betrayed. The absence of the much-desired letter almost ruins the fledgling love between the novel's protagonists. Davys's novel thus employs these epistolary moments not in a manner that draws on their factuality, truthfulness, or trustworthiness, but instead suggests to her readers, already well prepared for such two-faced rhetorical gestures by the work's preface, that letters rarely manage to communicate to their readers something truthful, valuable, or beneficial. If we view her novel in its entirety as a very long sort of letter by Davys to her readers – as the kind of rhetorical gesture outlined by Wayne Booth in *The Rhetoric of Fiction* (1961) and described by Irene Kacandes in *Talk Fiction* (2001) as a typical feature of twentieth-century fiction – it takes on an air of self-deprecation, of belittling its own nature as a written and printed representation of reality that may or may not have a truthful relationship with reality.

2. Behn's Epistolary Genre-Bending

Authors and readers in fact seemed to have been in a certain state of disagreement over the uses made of epistolary and other formal properties during the formative state of the novel, early in the very long eighteenth century. For this reason, paratextual poetics plays a significant role during that time, allowing authors to discuss the formal choices they have made to their generically untutored readers. Aphra Behn's dedication in the first part of her *Love-Letters Between a Nobleman and His Sister* (1684-87) works in the same fashion. Behn's protonovelistic *roman-à-clef* most dramatically demonstrates that dedications, readerly addresses, and generic self-fashioning frequently merged within the actual written text, thus putting in play also the distinctiveness of the literary letter and its supposed existence at some sort of ontological remove from the main body of the text. Her whole project serves to undermine the literary convention that assigns to letters a special quality of facticity.

Neither the title page of the original 1684 edition of the first part of the book, nor the dedication, nor indeed the other paratextual material – consisting mainly of "The ARGUMENT", which reads like the stage directions to a play (see Behn 1996, 9-10) – addresses questions of genre: The mention of the word "letters" in the title, one can assume, was supposed to speak for itself. The first volume, consequently, included almost exclusively the missives that went back and forth between the nobleman and his sister, and as such it constitutes an example of epistolary fiction that almost observes the conventions of factuality later ascribed to it.

In the first volume the prefatory text called "Argument" only uses the first person parenthetically - for instance, coyly adding "(whom we will call Caesario)", thereby creating the sense of an editorial act (9) - and ends with a highly passive phrase that obscures the active writing done by Aphra Behn: "After this flight, these Letters were found in their Cabinets, at their house at St. Denice, where they both liv'd together for the space of a year, and they are as exactly plac'd in the order they were sent, and were those supposed to be written towards the latter end of Amours" (10). Behind the "found" and the "plac'd" Behn hides her active process of invention and storytelling. The tone of this first "Argument" also betrays the unwillingness of a narratorial voice to intervene between content and reader, evoking the elusive nature of Early Modern narrators as audible voices (see Jajdelska 2007). The following excerpt from the much longer description of the heroine, Mertilla, reveals Behn's intention not to introduce a narrative voice into the representation of the love letters. Mertilla is said to have

> Charms enough to engage any heart, she has all the advantages of Youth and Nature, a Shape excellent, a most agreeable stature, not too tall and far from low, delicately proportion'd, her face a little inclined to round, soft, smooth and white, her Eyes were blew, a little languishing, and full of Love and Wit [etc]. (9)

The rather impersonal tone of this passage avoids direct reference to either narrator or implied reader and offers a character description that fully subscribes to the conventional format of romance writing. In as far as the blazon was a ubiquitous trope in chivalric writing, it does not require or evoke the presence of an individual authorial voice.

The second volume, published in 1685, somewhat changed the direction. The title page adds the phrase "Mixt With the HISTORY OF THEIR ADVENTURES", the word "history" appearing in bold (Behn 1996, facing 116). The suggestion here is that issues of genre nevertheless had to be addressed. The dedication of the second book is signed with the initials A.B. (120). The role of the author or editor is furthermore stressed on the title page by the added phrase "The Second Part by the same Hand" (facing 116). The "Argument" inserted into the second part also employs different strategies. By repeating the phrase from the title page, "by the same hand" (121), this paratext emphasizes the role of the author. The "Argument" itself speaks from a decidedly more authorial perspective, introducing a strong first person pronoun and a clear narrative voice: "At the end of the first Part of these Letters, we left Philander impatiently waiting on the Sea shore for the approach of the lovely Silvia; who accordingly came to him drest like a youth, to secure herself from a discovery" (121). The introductory text also, tongue-in-cheek, reveals that some of the adventures described "are well worthy, both for their rarity and comedy to be related intirely by themselves in a Novel" (127). Ironical asides like this only worked when readers were already prepared to accept that epistolary fiction had always already relied on the power of invention.

Whereas the first "Argument" appeared in italics, thus separating the "editorial" comments in the paratext from the actual epistolary material, the second "Argument" abandons this practice, appearing in the same non-italicized Roman font as the main body of the book. The transition between paratext and the bulk of the second volume thus denies any diegetic difference between the two discourses. The level of addressivity conventionally reached in dedicatory epistles is here extended to the body of the text. The paratext accordingly ends with the description of a short note received by one of the characters, the variously spelled Phillander: "When he was alone he open'd it [the Billet], and read this" (128). The deictic pronoun also places the text of the letter that follows in close proximity to the writer of the "Argument". The narrative voice, now, frequently interrupts the textual flow of letters, creating what Susan Wright in an essay on the language of letters has called "narrative interludes" (Wright 1989, 576). These ruptures provide additional material that covers the thoughts and feelings of the protagonists not expressed in their messages, thereby making an important contribution to the early stages of the novel (see Fludernik 2011). In Behn's *Love-Letters* these interruptions frequently take the form of linking one letter to the next:

> As soon as she had dismist the Page, she hasted to her business of Love, and again read over Philanders Letter, and finds still new occasion for fear; she had recourse to pen and paper for a relief of that heart which no other way cou'd find it; and after, having wip'd the tears from her eyes, she writ this following Letter. (Behn 1996, 143)

By conflating dedicatory addressivity with the kind of deictic involvement of her readers, Behn offers a creative and critical commentary on the status of paratextual reader involvement. The manner in which the author intermingles generic guidance with narratorial passages reveals that her literary audience was by no means settled in fixed discursive practices. Given the overall frame of her narrative, generically identified in the title as an epistolary work, Behn's on-going re-fashioning of the formal and fictional properties of her love-letters indicates that Restoration readers were by no means easily fooled by the supposed factuality of the letter format. Instead, her creative and critical use of the epistolary form speaks to the noticeable scepticism with which Early Modern readers approached this form of mediated communication.

3. Romantic Returns of the Letter

Inevitably, I have passed over numerous other examples of epistolary writing published during the Restoration period and at other historical moments. In the context of the paratextual poetics that have surfaced repeatedly in this essay, one could, for instance, have said much about one of the most influential theoretical works about literary form, Horace's *Ars Poetica* (18 BC), which in the original bears the telling subtitle "Epistula ad Pisones", and thus amply demonstrates that the notion of the book, at least in the pre-print age, was understood as some variety of epistolary communication between an author and his or her readers. Living up to this dialogic assumption, Horace frequently addresses his readers directly in the second person. The second sentence already begins with "You may take it from me, my friends" (Horace 1965, 79), openly soliciting an epistolary reading strategy. But as Horace's title also indicates, the letter essentially assumed a personal relationship between author and reader that, at least in the post-Gutenberg era, was no longer a given, and on which Restoration writers were hence less able to rely. On the contrary, the lack of personal involvement that the mass-produced printed book had inserted into literary communication brought with it a certain degree of distrust and even dislike, making of many of the early epistolary novels examples of an almost Luddite aversion to newly invented forms of technology. The book as commodity, while allowing Restoration readers to eke out a living from their literary fictions (see Hammond 1997), came loaded with negative connotations, following very closely the logic presented around two thousand years earlier in Plato's Socratic dialogue with Phaedrus and its strict indictment of the negative impact that newly invented writing would have on human culture in general, and the arts in particular.

As the long eighteenth century moved on, literary culture seemed to have made its peace with its underlying media ecology. Printed forms of communication had long become omnipresent, at least amongst the somewhat affluent and urban social spheres that were also the consumers of novels (see St Clair 2004). The journalistic output by Addison and Steele, the various bestsellers like Defoe's *Robinson Crusoe* (1712), Richardson's *Pamela* (1740), or Sterne's *Tristram Shandy* (1759-1767) all made of the book the kind of companion that people had come fully to embrace. It is not surprising, then, that epistolary moments, with their spectral reminder of the process of printing in the post-Gutenberg age, also found their way into bookish culture – and that they did indeed do so with such great panache that, especially after Richardson, the letter could claim for itself a chief role in the history of the making of the novel, in particular with respect to the kind of reality effect it was able to produce.

Whereas Restoration fiction was replete with the kind of textual moments I have discussed through Aphra Behn and Mary Davys as scenes of failure and betrayal, Richardson's employment of the epistolary format makes do without any such subterfuge, and in fact in his work the betrayal is removed once again to the level of actors (Watt 1957, 228-229). The amorous pursuit that Pamela is made to experience is communicated through the fake intimacy of the private letters she sends to her parents, and later through her journal entries. Richardson sees no need to question his generic format, and readers seem to have been happy to oblige him by not expecting otherwise. The letter had indeed become what twentieth-century literary history has made of it: an almost iconic token for literature's referential relationship to reality.

Yet the memory remains, and traces of letterly discontents appear in innumerous later fictions, evoking the belatedness of print. I would like to close with a few comments on another text that really only belongs to the eighteenth century if we take a very expansive view. Published in 1818, Mary Shelley's *Frankenstein* nevertheless can serve as a capstone for the kind of generic development I have sketched here. Belonging to that other great literary movement, Romanticism, Shelley's work closely engages the kind of factual rationality that Enlightenment authors had promoted, and to which the early novel was deeply committed ever since it crossed paths with the rhetorical programme developed by Royal Society authors (see Markley 1983). Shelley's Preface opens with an unadulterated first-person I, in which a young author seemingly situates herself between the scientific rigour of a "Dr Darwin" and also "the physiological writers of Germany", both of whom, she informs her readers, were willing to approach the medical and scientific inventions of her work "as not of impossible occurrence" (Shelley 1996, 1). The Preface quickly dismisses such claims, dwelling on terms such as "fancy", "supernatural", "enchantment", and "imagination". Rather than present factual accounts of reality, the very project in which the inventors of the novel were supposedly invested, Shelley's preface redirects its readers' attitude to the book, inviting them to reflect about "the truth of the elementary principles of human nature" (1).

All this positioning of course belongs to the larger disenchantment with which Romantic authors approached their intellectual forefathers and what they considered to have been misplaced trust in the power of Cartesian rationality. By turning to the supernatural, the fantastic, even the celestial, Romantic writers like Mary Shelley engaged in an extensive debate with some of the pillars of their own social reality. In the light of this project, it is only appropriate that Shelley's novel opens by reminding its readers of how gullible they have become, of how willing they are to succumb to the literary opiate of epistolary reality. The book, hence, begins thus:

> Letter 1
> To Mrs Saville, England
>
> St Petersburgh, Dec. 11th, 17—.
> You will rejoice to hear that no disaster has accompanied the commencement of an enterprise which you have regarded with such evil forebodings. I arrived here yesterday; and my first task is to assure my dear sister of my welfare, and increasing confidence in the success of my undertaking. (Shelley 1996, 7)

Written by R. Walton, this epistolary frame narrative quickly moves to the background, to make room, during the fourth letter, for the first-person account of his new acquaintance, Victor Frankenstein, whose biographical tale of the creation of some sort of homunculus from various body parts obtained from graveyards and elsewhere is only too well known to the modern reader and cineast. The epistolary frame is eventually and briefly picked up at the novel's conclusion, thus delicately embracing Shelley's horrific tale. The generic choice by Shelley was indeed brilliant, since no other literary fictional genre could look back on a similarly prominent role played in the history of realist writing. Yet, as my earlier examples showed, Shelley's move was not so much original as restitutory: It returned to the letter its earlier sense of scepticism and social critique. It reconnected Shelley's novel with Behn, Davys, and many other Restoration writers, all of whom appeared unconvinced of the extent to which print had been able to efface its status as a form of representation removed from actual reality. In the closing decades of the seventeenth century, when printed material in the shape of chapbooks was printed in numbers sufficient for every single household in England (Chartier 1987, 240), many a writer mildly faulted the letter by pointing to its potential for betrayals. In the light of this tradition, Shelley's novel has to be read as an all-out attack on the foundations of her society's belief-system. As such, it behooves us well to take her advice to heart and approach the word, in its epistolary, printed, or simply written reification, with caution and care.

References

Primary Sources

Behn, Aphra (1996): *Love-Letters between a Nobleman and His Sister*. 1684-87. Ed. Janet Todd. London: Penguin
Davys, Mary (1704): *The Amours of Alcippus and Lucippe*. London: James Round
Shelley, Mary (1996): *Frankenstein*. Ed. J. Paul Hunter. New York: Norton

Secondary Sources

Backscheider, Paula R. (2004): "Davys, Mary (1674-1732)", in: Mathew, H.C.G.; Harrison, Brian (eds.): *Oxford Dictionary of National Biography*. Oxford: Oxford University Press
Bayer, Gerd (2009): "Deceptive Narratives: On Truth and the Epistolary Voice", *LiLi: Zeitschrift für Literaturwissenschaft und Linguistik* 39.154, 173-187
--- (2011): "Early Modern Prose Fiction and the Place of Poetics", *Anglia* 129.3/4, 362-377
--- (2012): "A Possible Early Publication by Mary Davys and Its Swiftian Afterglow", *Notes & Queries* 59.2, 194-197
Benjamin, Walter (1999): *Illuminations*. London: Pimlico
Booth, Wayne C. (1961): *The Rhetoric of Fiction*. Chicago: University of Chicago Press
Bowden, Martha F. (1999): "Introduction", in: Davys, Mary: *The Reform'd Coquet, or, Memoirs of Amoranda; Familiar Letters Betwixt a Gentleman and a Lady; and The Accomplish'd Rake*. Lexington: University Press of Kentucky, ix-xlvi
Bray, Joe (2003): *The Epistolary Novel: Representations of Consciousness*. London: Routledge
--- (2013): "Epistolary Narrative and Point of View", paper presented at the International Conference on Narrative, Manchester
Chartier, Roger (1987): *The Cultural Uses of Print in Early Modern France*. Trans. Lydia G. Cochrane. Princeton, NJ: Princeton University Press
Derrida, Jacques (1981): *Dissemination*. Trans. Barbara Johnson. London: Athlone Press
Doody, Margaret Anne (1996): *The True Story of the Novel*. New Brunswick, NJ: Rutgers University Press
Duff, David (2009): *Romanticism and the Uses of Genre*. Oxford: Oxford University Press
Eagleton, Terry (2005): *The English Novel*. Malden, MA: Blackwell
Eisenstein, Elizabeth (1979): *The Printing Press as an Agent of Change: Communications and Cultural Transformations in Early-Modern Europe*. 2 vols. Cambridge: Cambridge University Press
Febvre, Lucien; Martin, Henri-Jean (2010): *The Coming of the Book: The Impact of Printing, 1450-1800*. (*L'Apparition du Livre*, 1958.) Trans. David Gerard. London: Verso
Fludernik, Monika (2011): "The Representation of Thought from Chaucer to Aphra Behn", in: Bayer, Gerd; Klitgård, Ebbe (eds.): *Narrative Developments from Chaucer to Defoe*. New York: Routledge, 40-59
Hammond, Brean (1997): *Professional Imaginative Writing in England, 1670-1740: Hackney for Bread*. Oxford: Clarendon
Horace (1965): *Ars Poetica*. In: *Classical Literary Criticism*. Ed. and trans. T. S. Dorsch, T.S. London: Penguin
Jajdelska, Elspeth (2007): *Silent Reading and the Birth of the Narrator*. Toronto: University of Toronto Press
Joule, Victoria (2010): "Mary Davys's Novel Contribution to Women and Realism", *Women's Writing* 17, 30-48
Kacandes, Irene (2001): *Talk Fiction: Literature and the Talk Explosion*. Lincoln: University of Nebraska Press
Markley, Robert (1983): "Objectivity as Ideology: Boyle, Newton, and the Languages of Science", *Genre* 16, 355-372
Nandi, Miriam (2012): "Narrating Emotions, Narrating the Self? Representation and Regulation of Emotions in Early Modern Diaries", in: Fludernik, Monika; Kohlmann, Benjamin (eds.): *Anglistentag 2011 Freiburg: Proceedings*. Trier: WVT, 135-146

Ong, Walter J. (2002): *Orality and Literacy: The Technologizing of the Word*. London: Routledge
Plato (1953): *The Dialogues of Plato, Volume III*. Trans. B. Jowett. Oxford: Clarendon
Schmidgen, Wolfram (2013): *Exquisite Mixture: The Virtues of Impurity in Early Modern England*. Philadelphia: University of Pennsylvania Press
Spacks, Patricia Meyer (2006): *Novel Beginnings: Experiments in Eighteenth-Century English Fiction*. New Haven, CT: Yale University Press
St Clair, William (2004): *The Reading Nation in the Romantic Period*. Cambridge: Cambridge University Press
Watt, Ian (1957): *The Rise of the Novel: Studies in Defoe, Richardson and Fielding*. Berkeley: University of California Press
Wright, Susan (1989): "Private Language Made Public: The Language of Letters as Literature", *Poetics* 18, 549-578

Ingo Berensmeyer (Gießen/Ghent)

Grub Street Revisited: Late Eighteenth-Century Authorship Satire and the Media Culture of Print

The distressed poet is a well-known commonplace of eighteenth-century literary culture. It combines a sense of the cultural aspirations of poetry with a critical view of the poet's economic reality – a reality often marked by poverty, as the professionalization of literature and the competition among poets in the literary marketplace transformed a writer's life into a career path paved with insecurity. In the history of authorship (and not only of poetic authorship), this period marks an important turning point away from traditional concepts and models of patronage, of writing as an élite pastime, or other forms of "social authorship" (Ezell 2003) not intended for commercial gain. In the visual culture of the eighteenth century, Hogarth's painting *The Distrest Poet* (1739) is an early example of this changed condition, the continuity of which is attested to by Spitzweg's Romantic painting *The Poor Poet* exactly a century later (1839) and its numerous modern (and popular) revisions.[1] The typical attic setting of these paintings indicates the impoverished living conditions of the starving writer. The Grub Street garret has since become a pathosladen formula of the self-exploitation of an artistically autonomous but economically disadvantaged starving artist.

It is hardly surprising, then, that the distressed poet is also a topos of eighteenth-century literature, especially in the latter half of the century. Its major generic domain is satire, a mode of writing that is particularly well-suited to express what Hans Ulrich Gumbrecht, in a different context, has aptly called "pathologies in the system of literature" (1992, ch. 10). By way of example, consider the beginning of George Keate's little-known "serio-comic poem" *The Distressed Poet,* published in 1787:

> Say, why should POVERTY'S prediction
> O'ercloud the sprightly scenes of Fiction?
> Wherefore so long entail'd its curse,
> On all the numerous sons of Verse?
> Who scarce possessing from their birth
> A legal settlement on earth,
> Exalted to a garret story,
> Live on imaginary glory.
>
> Ah! much I grieve to think how hard
> The lot of an *Aerial Bard!*
> Compelled, himself so ill at ease,
> To force a smile, and strive to please;
> With nothing but bare walls in view,
> To picture scenes he never knew! (Keate 1787, 1-2)

---

1   The author wishes to thank Christoph Heyl for pointing out the relevance of Hogarth to this visual tradition during the discussion in Konstanz. The prevalence of Spitzweg's image in popular cultural memory can easily be demonstrated by an internet search, which reveals the existence of numerous parodies and photographic re-stagings.

Taking the *Distressed Poet* as a starting point, this essay revisits the historical media culture of print in the late eighteenth century, in which Grub Street is not merely a spatial setting but the metonymy for a key mode of literary production in an evolving media configuration. Recent approaches to book history and historical media studies have had a notable impact on the way scholars now approach eighteenth-century literature, no longer predominantly as a monument of 'great works' of literary history or a parade of canonical authors (see St Clair 2004) but as a shifting and changing network of writers, texts, printer-publishers, readers, and critics engaged in textual production as a form of (more or less intellectual) labour, engaged in what Clifford Siskin has famously called "the work of writing" (1998). In recent years, there has been an intense discussion in the field about practices of reading and readerly engagement, from John Klancher's *The Making of English Reading Audiences* (1987) and Adrian Johns's *The Nature of the Book* (1998) to William St Clair's *The Reading Nation in the Romantic Period* (2004) and David Allan's *A Nation of Readers* (2008). The public, social, and political function of literature in the eighteenth century have been explored under the headings of *Print Culture and the Public Sphere* (Keen 1999) or *Print Politics* (Gilmartin 1996), often in connection with investigations of the role of literary magazines (Christie 2009; Higgins 2005; Parker 2000) and/or the rise of literary criticism (Domsch 2009).

How does a focus on print and the agencies connected with print culture under the aegis of a historical media perspective change our view of London's late eighteenth-century key site of literary production, Grub Street, which is traditionally regarded as the stereotypical embodiment of professional, popular, and often (in a Marxist sense) 'alienated' writing, a form of literary labour as opposed to the élite forms of writing, gentleman authorship, and publishing as practised by Pope and Swift? Grub Street was a "literatory", to use Saunders and Hunter's term (1991), rather than literature: a literary laboratory in which writers and printers were busy experimenting with new forms under new conditions of production and reception. In the course of a re-evaluation of Grub Street's opprobrium of the popular, the exploitative, and the manipulative, which has become part of its cultural legacy, it is time to see Grub Street not only as a crucial part of eighteenth-century (popular) media culture but also as a highly significant period in the media history of literary communication.

In particular, I would like to revisit the discourses of professionalization (the hack) and of inspiration (the genius) as crucial cultural-historical sites of debate for the emerging formal autonomy of literary fiction. In order to do this, I shall apply a theoretical perspective on authorship in combination with a historical investigation of eighteenth-century print culture. My principal object of analysis is an example of the ephemeral periodical, a type of publication whose role in the "battle of the books" and in processes of creating and mediating new forms of authorship and new ways of reading cannot be overestimated. These writings were heavily invested and involved in debates about the genius vs. the hack and about inspiration vs. transpiration as essential forms of authorial labour; they also engaged in debates about the extent to which the medium (of print) is conducive to, or constitutive of, certain positions in this debate itself (especially with respect to questions of social class as a factor of authorial distinction).

More specifically, my sample text is a virtually unknown satirical narrative from the late eighteenth century that proposes or contains, at least implicitly, a theory of literary production and its pathologies. This text is "The Brain-Sucker: Or, the Distress of Authorship", published in *The British Mercury* in 1787. Before turning to this text and its relation to the historical media culture of Grub Street, however, I will clarify some theoretical assumptions and prerequisites.

In recent years, there has been a re-awakening of interest in authorship as a literary and cultural phenomenon – not only in the domain of critical theory but also in more traditional fields of historical studies, for instance, on Shakespeare and collaboration (Vickers 2002), on copyright and transatlantic exchanges (e.g. Adams 2011), or on the marketing of authors in modern media (Demoor 2004). In the field of theory, the return of the author may be one of the key developments of the past twenty years, replacing Roland Barthes's radical proclamation of the "death of the author" (2008 [1978]) with detailed studies of authorship from antiquity to post-postmodernism, drawing on and triggering numerous controversies about (*inter alia*) intentionalism, subjectivity, poetics, and rhetoric. It is a field that still seems divided and divisive, with positions ranging from the radical anti-authorialism of Franco Moretti's "distant reading" (2013) or those prophets and practitioners of the digital humanities who believe in a technological realisation of authorless *écriture*, to various re-statements of authorship as individual creativity, as the origin of value, responsibility, and intellectual property.

In this context I am not concerned with evaluating these contrastive positions and taking sides; rather, I would like to propose a model of authorship as a historical configuration of individual activities and social ascriptions, based on the theory of authorship as cultural performance, as proposed in a collaborative research project at Ghent University by Gert Buelens, Marysa Demoor, and myself (see Berensmeyer et al. 2012). This project aims to combine a theoretical with a historical perspective on authorship in English and American literature from the Renaissance to the early twentieth century. The challenge that we try to rise to in this project is to allow for a combination of first- and third-person perspectives on authorship, 'inside' and 'outside' views. Not only for this project, authorship is a key element in theory and criticism because it constitutes an important link between texts and the world in which they are produced and circulated. Yet despite the recent prevalence of context-oriented literary criticism, the dimension of production has remained under-explored outside the specialist circles of book history. Finally, there has been too little contact between theoretical pronouncements on authorship and historical research.

For this reason, literary research needs to embark on a dual course: On the one hand, it needs to investigate historical manifestations of *empirical* authorship; on the other hand, it needs to analyse these manifestations in connection with different *concepts, models*, and *frameworks* of authorship. For the first part of this dual course, it is advisable to follow the lead of Harold Love, who has developed a highly useful taxonomy of 'authemes', of different and distinct acts of authorship that can occur in isolation or in combination with one another (precursory, executive, declarative, and revisionary authorship; see Love 2002, 39-49; Berensmeyer et al. 2012, 13). Such actual performances of authorship, however, also need to be aligned with socially and culturally performative *ascriptions* of authorial agency. For the latter, Berensmeyer et al. (2012) propose a taxonomy of author functions distinguished according to their degree of autonomy or heteronomy, both of which can be strong or weak (or anything in between).

	heteronomy	autonomy
weak to moderate	author as originator and communicator of texts, tied to rules and conventions	author as creator of immaterial 'work' that is materially presented in the text
strong	writer as merely a textual function, a compiler; a genius inspired by higher powers	author as absolute ruler over the work and its meaning; a genius who creates out of his or her own self

Table 1. Taxonomy of author functions (adapted from Berensmeyer et al. 2012, 14)

It may be worth emphasising that these extreme positions and their possible actualisations are based not only on what authors themselves practise or believe but also on the expectations of readers and other agents in the communications circuit (Darnton 1982). A meaningful historical account of this can only be given by linking empirical situations of writing and strategies of publication to wider historical, social, economic, and epistemological developments, in order to understand authorship as cultural performance.

For the eighteenth century, this abstract matrix allows us to distinguish between several available options; first and foremost, between two different conceptualisations of genius: that of genius as taking dictation from the Muse or another higher power (strong heteronomy) and that of the genius who creates out of nothing but his or her own ingenuity (strong autonomy). Both of these stand in contrast to the Grub Street hack as an embodiment of a moderately heteronomous authorship: a writer who is inspired but who has to exploit his creativity for the market or for a particular printer-publisher, subordinating his ingenuity to the commercial and/or political interests of another. One of the ways to investigate the historical media culture of authorship in the eighteenth century is to read literary works that explicitly stage and comment upon acts of authorship, and to read these works as performative realisations of historical possibilities – as revealing what usually remains concealed or implicit. Eighteenth-century authorship satire, then, stands out as a genre that is particularly fruitful and merits closer scrutiny in this respect.

In the subgenre of authorship satire, the cultural and ideological conflict between these positions escalates. The more traditional literary canon has preserved mainly an élite perspective on this struggle, evidently in Pope's and Swift's satires such as *The Dunciad* and the *Tale of a Tub*. Yet it is frequently the case that minor works are equally if not better equipped to serve as an illustration of pathologies in the system of literature, and to show us literature as a 'literatory', a set of emerging practices.

One of these minor works originating from Grub Street has only recently been rediscovered in the context of the Ghent authorship project.[2] This text is "The Brain-

---

[2] A version of it can be found in the ECCO database; we owe the recognition of its significance to Alise Jameson, who has also written about it in her doctoral dissertation, "Constructing Authorial Personae" (Jameson 2012). Jameson, Gero Guttzeit, and myself have prepared a critical annotated edition of this text which awaits publication. I gratefully acknowledge their contributions to my perspective on this text, which I also presented at the annual meeting of the Flemish Association for Comparative Literature in 2012, at the Catholic University of Lisbon, and dur-

Sucker: Or, the Distress of Authorship", published in the ephemeral journal *The British Mercury* in 1787. It gives us three key positions in the constitution of authorship in the late eighteenth century, shifting between autonomy and heteronomy: the genius, the hack, and the brainsucker. Despite the title, it is not a horror story about extraterrestrial invaders who turn writers into zombies by sucking their brains out, but rather a story about the possible horrors of authorship, about genius turning the wrong way, towards madness and starvation. This story puts the much-circulated eighteenth-century genius theory to a reality test by including a greedy printer-publisher-exploiter in the equation: The brain-sucker of the title is a ruthless employer of down-at-heel, hardworking hacks in Grub Street garrets. The story's most likely real-life author is John Oswald, the editor of the short-lived *British Mercury,* a Scottish Radical who died a few years later fighting for the French Revolutionary Army.[3] This "serio-comic caricature" (subtitle) appears to pit the genius against the marketplace, but the question is, what or who is the object of this caricature: the "brainsucker"-bookseller as a capitalist exploiter of creative labour, or the ingenious *ingénu*, the natural-born writer who has a talent for poetry but no education that might have saved him from a Grub Street existence?

"The Brain-Sucker" is narrated in epistolary form by a farmer, named Homely, who addresses an "absent friend". In his letter, he relates the story of his unfortunate son Dick. Dick's brain has become "infected" by reading and composing poetry; this "disorder", as the story calls it (22), makes him abandon his native Yorkshire for London and end up a Grub Street hack and the starving slave of a ruthless bookseller, the "Brain-Sucker", who profits from the young man's literary creativity. After his father has rescued him from imminent demise, the humbled author returns to a life of subsistence farming. The satire addresses, on the one hand, the notion of poetic authorship as the result of inspiration without formal education and, on the other hand, the working conditions of professional writers in the late eighteenth century. It is thus based on a contrast between two kinds of authorial heteronomy: on the one hand, the genius's inspiration that comes from somewhere else, untainted by nurture, and that operates like a disease turning the poet into a victim of poetry; on the other hand, the excruciating labour conditions of professional authors who have to survive in a cut-throat market by selling their intellectual property. Both positions are distinct from the élite notion of the autonomous and economically self-sufficient author, which is celebrated, for instance, in the works of Alexander Pope or in Edward Young's 1759 *Conjectures on Original Composition*, one of the key documents of eighteenth-century genius discourse.

As an authorship satire, "The Brain-Sucker" takes part in the polemic about professional authorship. In an implicit contrast to the cultural ideal of the autonomous gentleman author, it presents the world of literary labour as dangerous, contaminated and contaminating, and it portrays poetic inspiration as a disease. Yet the characters of

---

ing the IAUPE conference at Tsinghua University Beijing in 2013. On the notion of a 'minor' literature, see Deleuze and Guattari 1983.

3   For a brief biography, see Henderson 2004. There is no space here to discuss this attribution in detail, but it was not unusual at the time for editors of minor periodicals to do most of the writing themselves. "The Brain-Sucker" comes with an illustration by Thomas Rowlandson, which also cannot be discussed here.

young Dick and of his father are not drawn without sympathy. The story is told in the letter-writing voice of Dick's father, whose rural viewpoint immediately deflates any metropolitan pretensions to literary fame and whose literal, English-empiricist mindset counteracts Dick's literary metaphors. This distinguishes "The Brain-Sucker" from most known authorship satires, which either show a marked class bias or are told from the point of view of the writer himself, as in Keate's *The Distressed Poet.* Furthermore, there is no competitor from a higher class in the story. Because "The Brain-Sucker" is narrated from a socially inferior position, it could be taken as arguing for a more moderate view on authorial professionalism – it is better to be an autonomous professional, then, than a poor heteronomous genius who is nothing but the slave of a bookseller and the puppet of market forces. Most notably, in terms of generic boundaries, "The Brain-Sucker" is a satire in prose rather than verse; this seems fitting for its unpretentious narrator, Farmer Homely, but it also places this text outside of the much-discussed and well-researched genre of English verse satire from Dryden to Pope and Swift. Its subtitle, "A Serio-Comic Caricature", can perhaps be taken to emphasize the serious (empirical) background of the actual situation of Grub Street hacks, and also to link this "mixed satire" (Engell 2007, 233) to the novel and its claims to contemporaneity and realism.

In practice, despite the pervasive genius discourse of the later eighteenth century, authors were forced to rely on commercial viability, on the market, or on patronage and literary connections. In "The Brain-Sucker", genius discourse is found only in a debased form, as the pathology of authorial creativity, nourished by reading without the necessary education (or, one might add, social status) to flourish as a professional author. The text teems with images of parasites, insects, and diseases connected with reading and writing, and of course with London and in particular with Grub Street. At the beginning, Dick is described as displaying "the strongest symptoms of insanity" (15), which include a dualistic personality and mood swings ranging from anger to melancholy: "Sometimes he looked up, with a contumacious countenance, towards heaven, shaking, with impious audacity, his clenched fist; at other times his arms were folded on his breast, his eyes fixed melancholy on the ground, and the tears trickled down his cheek" (15). He also begins to exercise his creativity in poetically renaming everyday objects. From Farmer Homely's point of view, these are useless activities, even harmful as opposed to the practical, honest activity of farming. Dick's illness and insanity grow as he lives increasingly in his fantasies, occasionally staying out all night. It is revealed that the seeds of this "distemper" (21) were in fact planted by a fellow farmer's son, George: "This youth, who had been educated at Cambridge, communicated to my son all the learned *maggots* with which his own brain was *infected*. At his departure he left with my son a few books, which served to nourish and increase the *disorder*" (21-22, italics added). Homely resorts to burning these books, thereby hastening Dick's departure for London and his career as a hack writer. This equation of reading and writing poetry with disease, infection, and disorder forms part of a long history of criticizing (literary) fiction – going at least as far back as Plato – but it can also be read more concretely against the background of contemporary debates about the value and the dangers of poetry (recalling, for instance, the empiricist stance of Locke and Hume).

Some of the comedy in "The Brain-Sucker" directly results from Farmer Homely's literalist and empiricist mindset, which leads him to misread the literary allusions in his son's correspondence as implying sexual activities with 'Nine Sisters' (= the Muses). This is what makes him decide to travel from rural Yorkshire to London in order to save his son. At the story's end, young Dick is saved from the perversions of literature to return to the 'real', rural life as a farmer's son and a monogamous lover:

> The dreadful distemper that made such woeful havoc in his brain is radically exterminated. He has abandoned forever the heathenish worship of Apollo, swears that he would not exchange a single smile of his lovely Nancy for the last favours of the *Nine Sisters*, and that he would rather plant cabbages on his paternal estate than cultivate with Homer, Ossian, and Virgil the very summits of Parnassus (47-78).

The pathological condition of authorship has been overcome. Ridiculing not so much the brain-sucking publisher but the writer Dick, the satirical caricature literally deflates the aspirations of an uneducated author, yet paradoxically it also inflates the distress of authorship by invoking the reader's empathy with the poor hack, the lowest point of whose career is reached when he is forced to compose an *Apology for Mr. Hastings,* the impeached Governor of Bengal.

"The Brain-Sucker" explores eighteenth-century literary authorship on several levels, emphasising the economic reality of professional writers who were dependent on bookseller-publishers. But it not only comments on (and perpetuates) the stereotype of the poor poet and victimised hack; its manner, as distinct from the urbane authorship satire of Pope or Swift, is more directly urban and realistic in an almost (proto-) Dickensian or Poe-esque way, fusing the material reality of the "distress of authorship" with imaginary and conceptual resources such as the inflated idea of the Romantic genius. Yet perhaps its most interesting character is neither the cruel "Brain-Sucker" nor the young writer, but Farmer Homely, from whose perspective the story is narrated (as if in a mini-epistolary novel). Homely is also a writer, after all, if only a letter-writer. But for him, writing has a literal, not a literary, function of communication; his mindset is thoroughly empiricist. By bringing his son back to the farm – which may not be as humble as his name suggests[4] – he not only saves him from the mad excesses of literary creativity, he also returns the prodigal son to the fold of the real in its socially accepted form (meaning Christianity, as opposed to "the heathenish worship of Apollo", and heterosexual monogamy: "his lovely Nancy") where he can put his talents to more profitable use: to grow cabbages and, probably, to procreate.

This is now the point where conclusions are appropriate. Which of the above-mentioned author functions are realized in "The Brain-Sucker"? I would suggest the following taxonomy, adapting the model given in table 1. Implicitly, the story has mapped almost the entire range of possibilities from strong autonomy (in this case, available only to the Brain-Sucker himself as an exploiter of literary genius and perhaps a declarative author in Love's sense) to strong heteronomy (young Dick), but it also shows an example of weak to moderate heteronomy in the case of Dick's father, Farmer Homely (whose letter-writing is bound to socially accepted conventions and

---

[4] The text refers to it as an "estate", which might of course be ironic. Yet the fact that a neighbour's son was able to study at Cambridge perhaps indicates that these are not lowly subsistence farmers but quite well-to-do landowners; my thanks go to Aleida Assmann for pointing out this possibility in conversation at the Anglistentag in Konstanz.

does not pretend to 'literary' qualities or imagination). For completeness' sake, I have included the empirical/executive author of "The Brain-Sucker", John Oswald (whose authorship can only be inferred from his editorship of *The British Mercury*) as an example of weak to moderate autonomy. (It should be clear by now that moderate autonomy and moderate heteronomy may prove difficult to distinguish; some might claim that they amount to the same. But I would maintain that the distinction matters and is more than just a nuance.)

	heteronomy	autonomy
weak to moderate	FARMER HOMELY (author as communicator, tied to rules and conventions; narrator as letter-writer)	ANON. (JOHN OSWALD) (extratextual empirical/executive author)
strong	DICK (writer as untaught genius, exploited by the bookseller-publisher: executive author of *An Apology for Mr Hastings*, etc.)	THE BRAIN-SUCKER (declarative author, absolute ruler over Dick's work, exploiter of genius)

Table 2. Taxonomy of author functions in "The Brain-Sucker"

A focus on such pathologies of literary culture or literary production, between the genius and the brain-sucker, may help us to gain a more differentiated perspective on the familiar story of the combined emergence of the professional author and the autonomy of fiction. What appears so liberating about "The Brain-Sucker" may be the fact that it provokes laughter, not by ridiculing the impoverished hack from an aristocratic perspective, but by managing simultaneously to mock authorial pretensions to genius and to depict with some sympathy (and presumably from first-hand experience) the poor working conditions of the hack in the printer-publisher's sweat shop. The result is a minor work that nevertheless sheds light on the conditions of its own production and thus also appears to be 'doing theory' in a somewhat recursive and self-referential or self-enlightening fashion. John Oswald's "The Brain-Sucker" is more than a clever, entertaining authorial performance and an intervention in the Grub Street debate about the "distress of authorship" (which deserves to be read, discussed, and taught); it is a piece of "minor literature" (Deleuze and Guattari 1983) that aspires to a level of reflection and generalisation that is not always present in literary fiction even in major works. As a fictional staging of authorial possibilities and constraints towards the end of the eighteenth century, it can serve as a historical illustration of the material conditions of professional authorship (largely unfiltered by the class bias of Pope) and also as an important corrective to mere theoretical abstraction. Its most significant contribution to literary studies and literary theory may be to show how literature is simultaneously embedded in historical contexts and yet can become the force of its own disembedding.

References

Adams, Amanda (2011): "Performing Ownership: Dickens, Twain, and Copyright on the Transatlantic Stage", *American Literary Realism* 43.3, 223-241
Allan, David (2008): *A Nation of Readers: The Lending Library in Georgian England.* London: British Library
Barthes, Roland (2008): "The Death of the Author", 1978. In: Lodge, David; Wood, Nigel (eds.): *Modern Criticism and Theory.* 3rd edition. Harlow: Pearson, 313-316
Berensmeyer, Ingo et al. (2012): "Authorship as Cultural Performance: New Perspectives in Authorship Studies", *ZAA* 60, 5-29
Böker, Uwe (1987): "'The Distressed Writer': Sozialhistorische Bedingungen eines berufsspezifischen Stereotyps in der Literatur und Kritik des frühen 18. Jahrhunderts", in: Blaicher, Günther (ed.): *Erstarrtes Denken: Studien zu Klischee, Stereotyp und Vorurteil in englischsprachiger Literatur.* Tübingen: Narr, 140-153
Christie, William (2009): *The Edinburgh Review in the Literary Culture of Romantic Britain: Mammoth and Megalonyx.* London: Pickering and Chatto
Darnton, Robert (1982): "What Is the History of Books?" *Daedalus* 111.3, 75-78
Deleuze, Gilles; Guattari, Félix (1983): "What Is a Minor Literature?" Trans. Robert Brinkley. *Mississippi Review* 11.3, 13-33
Demoor, Marysa, ed. (2004): *Marketing the Author: Authorial Personae, Narrative Selves and Self-Fashioning, 1880-1930.* Houndmills: Palgrave Macmillan
Detering, Heinrich, ed. (2002): *Autorschaft: Positionen und Revisionen.* Stuttgart/Weimar: Metzler
Domsch, Sebastian (2009): "Attacks and Authority: Forging Literary Criticism in 18th-Century Britain." Postdoctoral dissertation. LMU Munich
Engell, James (2007): "Satiric Spirits of the Later Eighteenth Century: Johnson to Crabbe", in: Quintero, Ruben (ed.): *A Companion to Satire.* Malden, MA: Blackwell, 233–256
Ezell, Margaret (2003): *Social Authorship and the Advent of Print.* Baltimore: Johns Hopkins University Press
Foucault, Michel (2008): "What is an Author?" 1969, in: Lodge, David; Wood, Nigel (eds.): *Modern Criticism and Theory.* 3rd edition. Harlow: Pearson, 281-293
Gilmartin, Kevin (1996): *Print Politics: The Press and Radical Opposition in Early Nineteenth-Century England.* Cambridge: Cambridge University Press
Gumbrecht, Hans Ulrich (1992): *Making Sense in Life and Literature.* Trans. Glen Burns. Minneapolis: University of Minnesota Press
Henderson, T.F. (2004): "Oswald, John (c. 1760-1793)", *Oxford Dictionary of National Biography.* Web
Higgins, David (2005): *Romantic Genius and the Literary Magazine: Biography, Celebrity, Politics.* London/New York: Routledge, 2005.
Jameson, Alise (2012): "Constructing Authorial Personae: Case Studies Illustrating the Conceptualizations, Myths, and Critiques of Eighteenth-Century Authorship." Doctoral dissertation. Ghent University
Johns, Adrian (1998): *The Nature of the Book: Print and Knowledge in the Making.* Chicago: University of Chicago Press
Keate, George (1787): *The Distressed Poet: A Serio-Comic Poem, in Three Cantos.* London: J. Dodsley
Keen, Paul (1999): *The Crisis of Literature in the 1790s: Print Culture and the Public Sphere.* Cambridge: Cambridge University Press
Klancher, Jon P. (1987): *The Making of English Reading Audiences, 1790-1832.* Madison: University of Wisconsin Press
Love, Harold (2002): *Attributing Authorship: An Introduction.* Cambridge: Cambridge University Press
Moretti, Franco (2013): *Distant Reading.* London: Verso
Oswald, John (1787): "The Brain-Sucker, or the Distress of Authorship", *The British Mercury* 1-2, 14-27, 43-48

Parker, Mark (2000): *Literary Magazines and British Romanticism.* Cambridge: Cambridge University Press

Saunders, David; Hunter, Ian (1991): "Lessons from the Literatory: How to Historicise Authorship", *Critical Inquiry* 17.3, 479-509

Siskin, Clifford (1998): *The Work of Writing: Literature and Social Change in Britain, 1700-1830.* Baltimore, MD; Johns Hopkins University Press

St Clair, William (2004): *The Reading Nation in the Romantic Period.* Cambridge: Cambridge University Press

Vickers, Brian (2002): *Shakespeare, Co-Author: A Historical Study of Five Collaborative Plays.* Oxford: Oxford University Press

Young, Edward (1968): *Conjectures on Original Composition: In a Letter to the Author of Sir Charles Grandison.* 1759. *The Complete Works: Poetry and Prose, Volume 2.* Ed. James Nichols. London 1854. Rpt. Hildesheim: Olms, 547-586

Rainer Emig (Hannover)

The Visiting Card: A Historical Medium that Bridges Culture and Literature

Our view of historical media is often geared towards the obvious: public monuments and their inscriptions, manuscripts, and – after the invention of movable type – printed books. In the private sphere the historical medium that has been most thoroughly investigated is certainly the letter.[1] This is true for Literary Studies as well. A quick search for letters in novels in English Literature in the MLA Bibliography currently (as of 14 January 2014) yields 796 hits. The object that I will propose as a historical medium in the present essay, the visiting card, however, only returns two results. Nonetheless, I will investigate the visiting card as an interesting historical medium because it fulfils the following criteria: It is a medium in both the narrow and the broader sense of the definition of the term, a technical device that enables communication, but it also enters a complex network of signification (Briggs and Cobley 1998, 1-13; Faulstich 2004, 11-16). Moreover, it traverses eras with the help of technical innovations, from the manually created to the industrially produced paper card to, eventually, a virtual electronic form. It also connects historical, cultural, and literary investigations, since it features in everyday customs, both in the public sphere of business and in the private one of the family, and also plays an important symbolic role in fictional texts. In the present essay I will concentrate on its heyday in the eighteenth and nineteenth centuries, while also including a brief glimpse at its seeming demise in the late nineteenth century.[2]

The visiting card probably emerged in China in the fifteenth century (Design Float 2012). This makes sense, since Chinese culture made use of paper and paper products much earlier than its Western counterparts, although the only historical examples I have managed to locate in this context are from the eighteenth century and after. What we do know about their career in the West is that visiting cards first became popular in seventeenth-century Italy and France.[3] There, playing cards were often used as early visiting cards, with messages scribbled on them by hand (Schoberer 2013). Like many Continental fashions, the visiting card crossed over to Britain, where it became widely used in the eighteenth century.[4] Once again, early cards were hand-written. Moreover,

---

1 A laudable example is the Historical Media Project at Trinity College, Hartford, CT. See Historical Media Project, n.d.
2 That the real as well as fictional use of the visiting card does not end there is shown, for example, in its pivotal role in E. M. Forster's novel *Howards End* (1910).
3 The history of the visiting card (or calling card) is difficult to establish, since it has been researched mainly by amateurs or by businesses working in the field. Sources range from stamp collectors and their societies to print shops (see von zur Westen 1919; American Stationary 2012).
4 The earliest specimens in the collection of visiting cards in the British Museum date from the eighteenth century. See British Museum Collection Online n.d.

there was also an early split into business cards and private ones, a division that continues to this day.

While business cards did not become surrounded by overly difficult rules (although there are important cultural differences in their use), private visiting cards entered the complex interplay of gender and class in Britain very quickly.[5] Their main function was to establish social connections between individuals and families, and for this reason their use had to follow a set of sometimes almost absurdly complicated conventions. For example, if a person wanted to establish connections with a household to which he or she was not related, a card was first left with a servant of that household (if the interested party could afford it, this card would not be delivered in person, but also by a servant). Admission to the house would only be granted once that card had been inspected and its sender approved by the head of the household. Indeed, a personal encounter would often not be expected for days or even at all, if the point was simply social acknowledgement. Visiting cards as tokens of interest by others – and therefore as proof of one's social standing – were also proudly displayed in the household, usually on specially designed trays in the hall, which were often ornate (Banfield 1989). The visiting card was therefore private and public at the same time.

If instant admission was not the aim of having a card delivered, the expectation was nonetheless that a card would arrive in return. This signalled that social intercourse was approved or even desired. Failure to have a card returned meant that the household did not wish to know the sender, or at least was not keen on closer ties with him or her.

Although this seems straightforward, the simple paper medium of the visiting card also permitted modifications that were used for more complex messages. If the upper right-hand corner was folded, the card's owner's visit was meant for all female members of the household. A card folded in the middle signalled that it was meant for all members of the household. Folding the bottom-right corner meant that the card had been delivered in person. Adding letters to the bottom-left corner of cards could, for instance, make them congratulatory ("p.f." [*pour féliciter*]) or condolence cards ("p.c." [*pour condoler*]). French abbreviations then as now signalled refinement. A modern example is the continued use of "r.s.v.p." (*répondez s'il vous plaît*) on invitations. It is easy to see that such codes also facilitated the employment of visiting cards for courting, which is, of course, a major theme in the literature of the time (McKay and McKay 2008).

The complexity of such social codes often intimidated those who wished to rise in the world but came from a background in the middle or lower middle class that was alien to the initially upper-class refinement of the visiting card. As a consequence, conduct books quickly picked up the theme. Sometimes also called "etiquette books", they were issued by publishers such as Debrett's (Carré 1994). A massive bestseller in this field that continued to be sold in revised editions until the twentieth century is the anonymous *Manners and Rules of Good Society Or Solecisms to be Avoided by a Member of the Aristocracy*. The British Library catalogue lists as the latest edition one from 1955. The earliest dated one I could find dates from 1879, admittedly rather late

---

5   When a business card was delivered to a private household in full view of the neighbours, this signalled that there were unpaid bills.

in the career of the visiting card. It still gives a poignant idea of what was at stake in employing this medium for social advancement:

> Cards should always be returned within a week if possible, or ten days at latest, after they have been left, but to do so within a week is more courteous. And care must be taken to return the "call" or "cards" according to the etiquette observed by the person making the call or leaving the card; that is to say, that a "call" must not be returned by a card only, or a "card" by a "call." This is a point ladies should be very punctilious about.
>
> Should a lady of higher rank return a card by a "call," asking if the mistress of the house were "at home," her so doing would be in strict etiquette; and should she return a "call" by a card only, it should be understood that she wished the acquaintance to be of the slightest; and should a lady call upon an acquaintance of higher rank than herself, who had only left a card upon her, her doing so would be a breach of etiquette. (Anonymous 1916, 13-14)

Two things are striking here: Much of the communication undertaken with the help of visiting cards is placed in the hands of women. Here, the emerging separate spheres show a surprising level of permeability when it comes to establishing social relations, something that would certainly also be seen as important for the men in the household. Paying visits was not merely a pastime, but an important social task of women in the eighteenth and nineteenth centuries (Emig 2010). At the same time, of course, the admonition to "ladies" implies that men would sometimes violate the codes attached to cards and visits – and go unpunished.

Secondly, the rules show that class structures were strict, and their hierarchy was still largely unchallenged. The upper ranks were allowed to ignore the rules of tit for tat; breaking rules was their prerogative, and it emphasised rather than endangered their superiority and authority.

The fashion for visiting cards peaked in the 1820s – and their complicated employment was already considered passé by the 1890s: "As to card-leaving after dinners or parties, the youth who is up-to-date considers it a perfectly exploded relic of the past", is a reviewer's summary of the message conveyed in *The Gentlewoman in Society* by Beatrice Violet Greville, Countess of Warwick, a socialite and mistress of the future Edward VII, in 1892 (Anonymous 1892, 5). Nonetheless, as late as 1916 *Manners and Rules of Good Society* told its readers:

> The etiquette of card-leaving is a privilege which society places in the hands of ladies to govern and determine their acquaintance-ships and intimacies, to regulate and decide whom they will, and whom they will not visit, whom they will admit into their friendship, and whom they will keep on the most distant footing, whose acquaintance they wish further to cultivate and whose to discontinue. (Anonymous 1916, 19)

What is interesting for a Literary and Cultural Studies investigation emerges once again from such statements. How can one situate the visiting card in the supposedly emerging separate gender spheres of the eighteenth and nineteenth centuries? How does it feature in the class system, especially with regard to the upwardly mobile middle class and an upper class that is economically and politically in decline, but still appears to call the shots in cultural terms? Here Pierre Bourdieu's concept of "cultural capital" is evidently appropriate for the visiting card and its related rules of etiquette (Bourdieu 1986, 241-258). In cultural materialist terms, it is interesting to investigate the material shifts of the cards – from hand-written via mechanically or even mass produced (in the case of business cards) to their present-day electronic forms as e-mail appendices or indeed the "pokes" on social networks such as Facebook (Cronin and Rogers 2003).

In the present essay I will only pursue one of these investigations, namely the fictional uses of the visiting card in selected novels from the eighteenth and nineteenth century. I cannot avoid being selective, for there is hardly a novel of the time that does not feature a calling of visiting card. The samples I will use will help me to show once again the dialectic of the card as a cultural phenomenon. The use of visiting cards in fiction doubles but also critically highlights the fictions surrounding visiting cards. These fictions, as Michel Foucault tells us, form part of discourses and these have effects (for instance on social positions, advancements, careers, wealth, and power) that by far exceed the realm of the bourgeois novel, a medium that is ideally suited for the visiting card (Hall 2001, 72-81).

Frances Burney's *Cecilia, or, Memoirs of an Heiress* (1782) is a typical example of a late eighteenth-century novel. Its long and convoluted plot centres around the inheritance and marriage prospects of an heiress, who in her obstacle course to happiness, social standing, and stabilising her assets encounters male and female members of all the classes of her time. A kaleidoscope of late eighteenth-century culture is thereby presented to the reader and the visiting card looms large in it.

At the start of the tale, Cecilia is a newcomer to the social rules of the London upper class (it is important that the visiting card unfolds its strongest power in the urban centres). Thus when she first overhears a reference to it in the form of "a ticket", she displays a telling degree of ignorance:

> "A ticket?" repeated Cecilia, "does Lady Nyland only admit her company with tickets?"
>
> "Oh, lord," cried Miss Larolles, laughing immoderately, "don't you know what I mean? Why a ticket is only a visiting card, with a name upon it; but we all call them tickets now." (Burney 2008, 24)

Cecilia confuses the rules of polite society with those of commercial pleasure gardens, such as Ranelagh, which had opened in 1741, and Vauxhall, which followed suit in 1785. An easy mistake to make, since the reasons for attending either were strikingly similar: to be entertained, but also to make and deepen important acquaintances – and of course to impress others with them (Greig 2012). The visiting card with its dialectic of private and public functions was perfect in this regard, and this makes it credible that "we all", the hegemonic upper-class society in the know, the *bon ton*, would use the same word for entry tickets to amusement parks and private invitations.

Among men, visiting cards can also be used for more serious social concerns than attending a ball, however, as is shown in *Cecilia* when young Mr Belfield, with whom Cecilia briefly believes herself to be in love, uses it to challenge another suitor, Sir Robert, to a duel:

> Then, walking up to Sir Robert, he put into his hand a card with his name and direction, saying, "With you, Sir, I shall be happy to settle what apologies are necessary at your first leisure;" and hurried away. (Burney 2008, 138)

The staunchly middle-class miser Mr Briggs, one of Cecilia's guardians, clearly has no time for all the upwardly mobile frippery associated with visiting cards. This is how he complains about this (for him) newfangled mode of inviting people to a meal: "Invited me once to his house; sent me a card, half of it printed like a book! t'other half a scrawl could not read; pretended to give a supper [...]" (Burney 2008, 453). As I indicated above, fiction is used both to depict the social and cultural developments of the time – and to provide varying perspectives on them, including highly critical ones that might be shared by the largely middle-class readership of the novels. Indeed Burney's novel is also replete with the verb "to discard", literally "to throw away a card" – and once again this indicates both social acceptance or lack of it and the specifically female role in negotiating it, but also the strain that this places on women:

> "You are right, then, madam," cried he, resentfully, "to discard me! to treat me with contempt, to banish me without repugnance [...]" (Burney 2008, 629-630)

> Henceforth let hysterics be blown to the winds, and let nerves be discarded from the female vocabulary [...] (Burney 2008, 659)

In nineteenth-century novels, the function of the visiting card appears largely unchanged. In Charles Dickens's *Bleak House* (1852-53), a novel about middle-class aspirations thwarted by aristocratic malice, we find the following scene:

> "I went to the hall-door, and told them it was the wrong day, and the wrong hour; but the young man who was driving took off his hat in the wet, and begged me to bring this card to you."
>
> "Read it, my dear Watt," says the housekeeper. [...]
>
> "Mr. Guppy" is all the information the card yields. (Dickens 1991, 86)

Mr Guppy is, as his grotesque name already implies, an untrustworthy figure, a dubious lower middle-class character who dares to propose to the novel's heroine Esther Summerson. As a social climber he has internalised the rules of employing visiting cards: Being a man, he can insist that the delivery of his card be followed straightaway by an admission to the family circle. Yet his invasion of social space does not yield the desired reward, and the novel makes him stand out as unsuitable already by the colloquial style of his subsequent introduction:

> "Much obliged to you, ma'am!" says Mr. Guppy, divesting himself of his wet dreadnought in the hall. "Us London lawyers don't often get an out, and when we do, we like to make the most of it, you know." (Dickens 1991, 86)

His presence is clearly as undesirable as that of the wet patches left by his rubberized outdoor coat, a garment associated with the countryside, not the city.

But there are more welcome visitors employing the same strategy:

> We were all assembled shortly before dinner [...] when a card was brought in, and my guardian read aloud in a surprised voice:
>
> "Sir Leicester Dedlock!"
>
> The visitor was in the room while it was yet turning round with me, and before I had the power to stir. (Dickens 1991, 600)

Again, social class determines whether the rules attached to visiting cards are considered to have been violated or not.

Yet, as was stated earlier, the nineteenth century also developed a more critical view of visiting cards and what they stood for, all the way to declaring them to be relics of a bygone age at its very end. Frances Trollope's *The Vicar of Wrexhill* is earlier than Dickens's *Bleak House*. It was first published in 1837 and is, to my knowledge, the first English novel featuring an evil Anglican clergyman. It also depicts visiting cards humorously and even ironically, probably because its rural setting foregrounds the inappropriateness of such a medium in its plot even more strongly. Here is a scene in which a visiting card is used not to prepare a man-to-man combat, but to conclude it:

> Colonel Harrington having given the attorney exactly the quantum of flogging he intended, stuck his card, with his name and address both in town and country, into the groaning man's pocket, laid him down very gently on the grass, and departed. (Trollope 1996, 331-332)

The men in question are not aristocrats or members of the gentry, but a military character and a middle-class one, and the deposition of the card here serves the same function as leaving one's address after having dented someone else's car today, that is, a legal one.

For women, visiting cards and their related gadgets are still indispensible when it comes to signalling, if only to themselves, social standing or aspirations. Thus, the widow Mrs Simpson, who has succumbed not only to the masculine charms, but also to the Low Church habits of the Vicar Mr Cartwright (see Pollard 1982), is accused by the narrator of "turning her little girl into a methodist monkey; her card-boxes, into branch missionary fund contribution cases" (Trollope 1996, 245). Several chapters before, the same Mrs Simpson had already boasted to her female acquaintances: "Look at me, look at my child, look at my albums, look at my books, look at my card-racks, look at my missionary's box on one side, and my London Lord-days' society box on the other" (Trollope 1996, 167). The irony here of course emanates from the unthinking equation of the worldly card-racks with the supposedly religious missionary's and Lord's Day Observation Society boxes, all of which are nothing but genteel accessories of an aspiring – and highly competitive – middle-class feminity.

The visiting card turns out to be both a medium with which class-bound and gendered communication is effected and a means with which social standing and advancement are engineered. At the same time, as a cultural phenomenon, it enters both literary and non-literary discourses, here predominantly that of the bourgeois novel and that of conduct or etiquette books. In these, its standing is ambivalent. While conduct books pretend to aid their readers in performing well in the social sphere, they of course also serve to cement cultural – and here most importantly again class and gender – norms and clichés. The literary representations of visiting cards also display a telling ambivalence. While some texts use them for dramatic or comical purposes without, however, challenging their function and the validity of the rules attached to them, other texts (and it is perhaps no coincidence that the example I presented came from a female author) more drastically expose the limitations that an unthinking hegemonic employment of the medium of the visiting card inevitably creates. In Frances Burney's, Charles Dickens's, and Frances Trollope's novels the visiting card is a powerful social medium. In all of them its realms of discursive effect are those of class and gender. But it is in Trollope's novel (and Frances Trollope is not often ranked among the great writers of her time) that the use of the visiting card as a cultural commodity, as a tool for aggrandising one's cultural capital, is most drastically exposed.

References

Primary Sources

Anonymous (1892): "English Society: Lady Violet Greville on British 'Friskles', Maids, and Boors", *The Argonaut*, 30:4 (15 January 1892), 5

Anonymous (1916): *Manners and Rules of Good Society, Or, Solecisms to be Avoided by a Member of the Aristocracy*. 38th edition. London: Frederick Warne & .

Burney, Fanny [Frances] (2008 [1782]): *Cecilia, Or, Memories of an Heiress*. Ed. Peter Sabor and Margaret Anne Doody. Oxford et al.: Oxford University Press

Dickens, Charles (1991 [1852-1853]): *Bleak House*. New York: Alfred A. Knopf

Forster, Edward Morgan (2000 [1910]): *Howards End*. Ed. David Lodge. London: Penguin

Greville, Beatrice Violet (1892): *The Gentlewoman in Society*. London: Henry

Trollope, Fanny [Frances Milton] (1996 [1837]): *The Vicar of Wrexhill*. Stroud: Alan Sutton

Secondary Sources

American Stationary (2012): "The History of the Calling Card", <http://www.americanstationery.com/blog/the-history-of-the-calling-card/> [accessed 14 January 2014]

Banfield, Edwin (1989): *Visiting Cards and Cases*. Trowbridge: Baros

Bourdieu, Pierre (1986): "The Forms of Capital", in: Richardson, John G. (ed.): *Handbook of Theory and Research for the Sociology of Education*. New York: Greenwood, 241-258

Briggs, Adam; Cobley, Paul (1998): *The Media: An Introduction*. Harlow: Longman

Carré, Jacques (ed.; 1994): *The Crisis of Courtesy: Studies in the Conduct-Book in Britain, 1600-1900*. Leiden: Brill

Cronin, B.; Rogers, Y. (2003): "From Victorian Visiting Card to vCard: The Evolution of a Communicative Genre", *Journal of Communication Science* 29.1, 65-68

Design Float Blog (2012): "A Brief History of Business Cards." <http://www.designfloat.com/blog/2012/04/02/history-business-cards/> [accessed 14 January 2014]

Emig, Rainer (2010): "The 1900 House: Squeezing Late-Victorian Life onto the Small Screen", in: Böhnke, Dietmar et al. (eds.): *Victorian Highways, Victorian Byways: New Approaches to Nineteenth-century British Literature and Culture*. Potsdamer Beiträge zur Kultur-und Sozialgeschichte 8, Berlin: Trafo, 363-384

Faulstich, Werner (2004): *Medienwissenschaft*. UTB Basics. Paderborn: Wilhelm Fink

Greig, Hannah (2012): "'All Together and All Distinct': Public Sociability and Social Exclusivity in London's Pleasure Gardens, ca. 1740-1800", *Journal of British Studies* 51.1, 50-75

Hall, Stuart (2001): "Foucault: Power, Knowledge and Discourse", in: Wetherell, Margaret et al. (eds.): *Discourse Theory and Practice: A Reader*. London/Thousand Oaks, CA/New Delhi: Sage

McKay, Brett; McKay, Kate (2008): "The Gentleman's Guide to the Calling Card." <http://www.artofmanliness.com/2008/09/07/the-gentlemans-guide-to-the-calling-card/> [accessed 14 January 2014]

Pollard, Arthur (1982): "Trollope and the Evangelicals", *Nineteenth-Century Fiction* 37.3. Special Issue: Anthony Trollope, 1882-1982, 329-339

Schoberer, Marc-Michael (2013): "Die Geschichte der Visitenkarte", gutenbergblog.de. <http://www.gutenbergblog.de/offsetdruck/die-geschichte-der-visitenkarte-4032.html> [accessed 14 January 2014]

The British Museum Collection Online (n.d.) <http://www.britishmuseum.org/research/collection_online/search.aspx?searchText=visiting+card> [accessed 14 January 2014]

Trinity College (n.d.): Historical Media Project. <http://www.trincoll.edu/UrbanGlobal/CUGS/Faculty/Historical/Pages/default.aspx> [accessed 14 January 2014]

von zur Westen, Walter (1919): "Zur Geschichte der Besuchskarte", *Mitteilungen des Exlibris-Vereins zu Berlin* 29.1-2, 1-14

NATALIE ROXBURGH (OLDENBURG)

Between Property and Propriety:
David Simple and Social Mediation

To discuss historical media cultures is also to talk about transformations in which direct communication between people is supplanted (or supplemented) by virtual connectedness through systems and technologies that mediate interpersonal interaction. Mediation, therefore, simultaneously enables communication and requires a network of signification. If we accept such a broad formulation, it is perhaps unnecessary to worry about succumbing to anachronism when we think of media or media cultures existing and even shaping the eighteenth century. The title of this paper refers to J. G. A. Pocock's *Virtue, Commerce, History*, in which he argues for the necessity of distinguishing between two terms that had been conflated in the seventeenth century (Pocock 1985, 56). The separation of property and propriety corresponds to changing conceptions of the former: from land, which guaranteed civic virtue, to mobile forms of property, which required a system of value that hinged on buyers and sellers in a marketplace. In what follows, one might note the ongoing difficulty of studying historical media cultures apart from changing economic structures, a difficulty that historians, theorists, and literary critics share when attempting to grapple with the radical changes that took place in this period.

One starting place for talking about key transitions lies in the work of those who have helped us to understand the history of print. Theorists such as Benedict Anderson (1983), Jürgen Habermas (1991), and Charles Taylor (2004) have emphasized the importance of print media in producing a public sphere or a national imaginary. What is significant about print is that it allows for the distancing of the producers of writing from the many readers encouraged by it, creating through mass circulation a virtual, rather than an actual, collectivity.

Clifford Siskin's and William Warner's *This is Enlightenment* (2010) argues for consideration of the Enlightenment as a media event, one which united symbolic and technical media (print being instrumental to this process). It is probably no coincidence that Warner's earlier work, *Licensing Entertainment* (1998), discusses the process by which the novel became a respectable form of new media, at least for the rising middle class. The emergence of the novel is central to a discussion of historical media cultures, as the mediating capacity of print allowed readers to be transported into fictional worlds whose existence need not have an analog in the real world. Print media opened up a space for taking pleasure in the text; the reader could be entertained and perhaps even be edified through fictional worlds.

Novel reading, a pleasurable activity that also served something of a didactic function, became a cultural practice that is still with us today. However, just as today some of us worry about the impact of social media, eighteenth-century contemporaries worried about the effects of novels. Warner emphasizes this point throughout *Licensing Entertainment* (Warner 1998, xi). Critics worried, for example, that novels had the capacity to inflame the (usually female) reader's passions or to create expectations about life that could not be met in the real world. Novels could have the effect of producing readers with a sense of propriety gone astray. But as the century progressed, Warner suggests, the novel came to be seen as morally respectable, primarily through being regarded as more masculine, nationalist, and literary (Warner 1998, 39). Another way to track the history of this more respectable novel is to examine how it imagines itself within the contemporary sea of emergent new media, and for this it helps to examine the novel of sensibility in particular.

Sarah Fielding's *David Simple* (1744) and its sequel *Volume the Last* (1753), both of which can be categorized as novels of sensibility, are chock-full of new media. The novel (or "moral romance") and its sequel allow us to mark a paradox about media and social mediation that still faces us today. On the one hand, media provide us with new rules and opportunities for engaging with others. The flip-side is that when we use media, we do not engage with others directly, and thus mediation inevitably transforms the way we experience other people. This, I hope to show, is part of what is at stake in the novel of sensibility, whose didactic function is to train readers to sympathize with the fictional characters it presents, often eschewing a system predicated on new rules from new media while simultaneously *being one of these media*. The novel of sensibility tries to get the reader to empathize as if the reader were there as a tangible person, despite the fact that the novel (as a medium) precludes this very possibility.

David Simple, set in London, begins when David's brother Daniel attempts to cheat him out of an inheritance. He makes a journey from east to west, from Fleet Street in the City to the Strand to Westminster, and meets various people along the way from different stations in life, people who disappoint him in his attempt to befriend them. He finally meets Cynthia, and then later a pair of siblings, Camilla and Valentine, who have also been deceived or forsaken by others, usually for financial reasons. After David hears their respective stories, the four form a family and share a household: David marries Camilla and Cynthia marries Valentine. The novel ends happily with David having found friends and having created a family, at last. But in *Volume the Last*, a reversal of fortune takes place. Members of David's family lose their fiscal security and thus the capacity to remain together in one household. A relative makes a legal claim on an estate left to David, one which drains him of necessary money. He is no longer able to support his family without outside assistance and becomes financially dependent on creditors. Valentine must get a job in the West Indies, and Cynthia accompanies him. David's house burns down and the family's property is destroyed. All but one of the children die of various illnesses. The sequel ends with David's death.

Many of the mediating devices shown to be dangerous for David's community have origins in new virtual forms of property and reflect a financial transformation that contemporaries faced, one that featured a more regular use of paper money backed by the State. For Patrick Brantlinger, the fiction of the State as such is dependent on paper money and the way it mediates citizens through circulation (Brantlinger 1996, 40). The medium of paper money connected people through intricate (but abstract) trust relationships with rules set by creditors (such as the Bank of England, established in 1694) and Parliament. This is perhaps related to the way new modes of property impinge on characters in a novel so invested in cultivating a mode of propriety based on true sympathy for other human beings. In Gillian Skinner's reading, both the novel and its sequel present multiple economic problems whose elusive solutions are true feeling and communal sensibility (Skinner 1998, 31). Richard Terry argues that the sentimental (or the capacity for characters to sympathize with others) is overtaken by the commercial (Terry 2004, 532). In my doctoral dissertation, I too emphasized the way new types of economic property, such as bank notes, stocks, and other products of a new system of finance challenged social relationships (Roxburgh 2011, 136). Like many critics, I read the novel as taking to task a corrupt commercial system and its underlying contradictions. But this view is limited because it fails to ask the question of what social stakes the novel has in launching such a critique of finance. The critique has more to do with new rules than with the new system that we now call *capitalism*.

By using 'historical media cultures' as an alternate lens for re-reading the novel, one gets a bit closer to what it must have been like to take part in social relationships in a time of such technological change. *David Simple* distinguishes between good media and bad media in an attempt to cultivate propriety that is not tied to virtual forms of property – what it seems to lament about new forms of social mediation is that their rules are designed for a new form of society, one at odds with the more traditional notion of friendship David pursues through a notion of property that harkens back to the household economy.

Before his family sets up house, David finds people coming together to engage in new systems whose rules mediate interactions but do not facilitate the friendship he is looking for. Just after his brother attempts to cheat him by forging their father's will, David sets out on a quest for a real friend, but soon suffers disappointment. At the Royal Exchange, David watches one man luring another into buying massive quantities of a stock that the former immediately thereafter sells:

> The first place he went into was the *Royal-Exchange*. [...] He could not have gone any where to have seen a more melancholy Prospect, or with the more likelihood of being disappointed of his Design, than where Men of all Ages and all Nations were assembled, with no other View than to barter for Interest. The Countenances of most of the People, showed they were filled with Anxiety: Some indeed appeared pleased; but yet it was with a mixture of Fear. (Fielding 1969, 28)

This passage makes a connection between the pursuit of individual interest through insider trading and unbearable social anxiety, but the setting helps us to imagine a system (one with its own rules) that makes it possible or even desirable for people to congregate at the Exchange in the first place.

David's experience at the Royal Exchange might be compared with the players of whist he encounters later on. Whist, a trick-taking card game invented in the seventeenth century, had become popular by the middle of the eighteenth century, perhaps signified by the publication of Edmond Hoyle's *A Short Treatise on the Game of Whist* in 1742, a manual which helped the reader learn the basic arithmetical skills to ascertain probabilities as well as learn the very complicated rules of play. This sort of entertainment, a purported reason for bringing people together in a social setting, ultimately has a negative outcome:

> Those very People, who, before they sat down to play, conversed with each other in a strain so polite and well-bred, that an *unexperienced* Man would have thought the greatest Pleasure they could have had, would have been in serving each other, were in a moment turned into *Enemies*, and in the winning of a Guinea, or perhaps five, (according to the Sum played for) was the only Idea that possessed the Minds of a whole Company of People, none of whom were in any manner of want of it. (Fielding 1969, 79)

In this setting, players are overtaken by the game's structure; they are obsessed with the rules and ignore each other's company in order to win. Less pecuniary than the stock market, the game nonetheless uses a system of rules proliferated by the medium of print. Obsessed by objects of uncertainty in the form of playing cards, the feeling of friendship between each player is undermined by the desire to win.

In these scenes, the intense focus on individual interest leads people to acts of duplicity, creating the need for distinguishing between 'true' and 'false' friendship alluded to in the subtitle. Both cases feature the coming together of people through an apparatus that mediates, uniting people under the umbrella of the same project. What is striking about these passages is that Fielding depicts deep ambivalence in the affects of the participants at the stock exchange and at the gaming table. The calculation of individual interest, while seeming to benefit individual people, divides individual advantage from collective pleasure. I would add, however, that looking out for one's interest is not the simple culprit of the novel – these new systems of mediation with their new rules pose the bigger threat.

What helps people to look out for their pecuniary interests is the legal system, which is an example of a set of rules that divides David from what he desires. From very early on in *Volume the Last*, we learn that David is involved in a chancery suit over his estate. His opponent's attorney knows all the "Tricks of the Law", leading David to eventually lose the suit (Fielding 1969, 318). David's community is then forced to take a smaller house. For a simple person like David, the system of law is incomprehensible. It mediates disputes, but because he does not possess knowledge of the system, it literally breaks up his household. In this case, not knowing how to play the game means that David loses his property. And what David loses in *Volume the Last* is one of the most precious social forms in the novel: the household.

One of the values Fielding repeatedly and exuberantly extols is that of household economy, or looking after the property of the household for the sake of meeting the needs of the family. David's family members, even after they lose their home and must live in a smaller one, practice a diligent household economy: "For every thing in this small Cottage, tho' poor and plain, yet was preserved in so neat a Manner, as visibly proved that the owners of it could not think themselves debarred of every Comfort, whilst they enjoyed each other's Company" (*ibid.*, 372). An emphasis on the visual here is a poignant antonym to the invisible rules governing other projects in the novel. Fielding's text emphasizes taking care of the household for the well-being of those occupying it.

The novel seems not to oppose interest *per se*, because David wants to promote his family's interest (which they achieve through the household). The house is managed so as to ensure the household's common benefit: "Therefore in our little Family of Love, each Day was employed in Endeavours to promote its common Welfare. *Camilla* and her eldest Daughter were industrious in their pursuit of Household Business; not groaning or repining under their Labour, but looking cheerfully forward to their principle Aim" (*ibid.*, 372). Again, the focus is on what is right in front of them. Speaking in the first person plural, encouraging the reader to feel part of the household, Fielding continues to teach the reader about the propriety of investing in this form of property. However, the practice of household economy, valued because it insures subsistence and comfort for the immediate members of the family unit, is not enough to hold the community together when the world outside increasingly privileges individual interest as granted through the new rules and new mediating forces. Household economy falls apart, as do other traditional cultural practices in the novel.

David Simple also explores older media and, in so doing, shows that the rules have changed. When David attends a play, for example, he is taken aback by the chatter of the critics in the audience, who are unable to watch the play "owing to Envy and Anger at another's Superiority of Parts" (*ibid.*, 68). It is telling that the critics fail even to watch the actors on the stage. David, trying to enjoy what the theatre company presents, is distracted by whistles, cat calls, groans, bellowing, beating with sticks, and clapping with hands from members of the audience, critics who are not there to enjoy the play but rather use the occasion to compete with one another. This turns into a larger attack on critics in general a few pages later (*ibid.*, 88), when Fielding weighs in on contemporary proliferation of criticism like many before her (such as Pope, Addison, and Swift). In the case of criticism, the primary medium seems not the problem: David seeks to enjoy the actual performance at the theatre, after all. Rather, the fact that the medium allows people to come together to once again barter for their interests (this time through the rougher but nonetheless rule-governed terrain of criticism) ruins the experience David desires to have.

The use of the older forms of media begs the question of how the novel articulates good and bad media cultures through its conservative stance – it does not write off all media as being problematic in the end. Letters from loved ones, for example, are most welcome to David. Furthermore, how does the novel *as a medium* exempt itself from the very problems it poses? It is, after all, itself a product of the mass media. The answer lies, at least in part, in the sacrifice of David in the end. The brave new world with its new markets and mechanisms is no place for the quixotic David Simple. The world destroys David, but in the end we do not find ourselves believing that seeking friendship is a matter of tilting at windmills (to use the idiom quite precisely). We have sympathized with David, and David does not survive. But the novel survives, precisely because of the nature of the new mass media.

When David dies, Fielding encourages readers to "use their own Imaginations, and fancy David Simple still bustling bout the Earth" (*ibid.*, 432). After all, David is no purportedly real figure but rather an explicit product of fiction. This call for the reader to imagine characters, or even to help the author through the use of his or her imagination, gets reiterated in various places throughout the first novel (*ibid.*, 303; 326). And, like many novels of sensibility, the novel asks the reader to put him or herself in the position of the main character to restore a sense of social belonging that has been lost. One might look a decade into the future – to Harley in Mackenzie's *Man of Feeling* (1771), to Yorick in Sterne's *A Sentimental Journey Through France and Italy* (1768), or to the Reverend Dr. Charles Primrose in Goldsmith's *The Vicar of Wakefield* (1766) – to see how later novels engage with the reader's imagination in order to directly engage with other human beings, usually suffering ones, but ones that are nonetheless fictional.

By accounting for one didactic project of the novel of sensibility, we are perhaps here allowed to break out of our historicism and take the liberty of indulging in anachronism. *David Simple* worries about what certain forms of mediation do to social relationships, and it offers several examples of the dark side of new media. Perhaps what is at stake here is not so far removed from conservative perspectives on what we now call social media, the world of Twitter and Facebook. The American writer Rebecca Solnit, in her recent piece in the *London Review of Books*, wrote:

"I think of that lost world, the way we lived before these new networking technologies, as having two poles: solitude and communion. The new chatter puts us somewhere in between, assuaging fears of being alone without risking real connection. It is a shallow between two deep zones, a safe spot between the dangers of contact with ourselves, with others" (Solnit 2013, 32-33).

Perhaps, though, like all longings for bygone times, Solnit fails to consider that the past was similarly wrought with social anxieties and dubious proprieties, ones the somewhat reactionary novel of sensibility did its best to repair.

The City, its anxious denizens doomed perpetually to haggle and bargain for their conflicting interests in a community mediated by something as fragile as paper adorned with an official stamp, was at some point transformed from a geographical location into a way of life. But we are nonetheless enabled to form communities through media, to imagine ourselves in collectivities, and these virtual collectivities create potentialities of their own. The paradox of media cultures seems to be that, like many features of the modern world, the very problems they produce can also be remedied by them. After all, I recently found Solnit's article by using Twitter, a corporation with a political economy of its own.

References

Primary Sources

Fielding, Sarah (1969): *The Adventures of David Simple and Volume the Last* [1744, 1753]. Oxford: Oxford University Press

Goldsmith, Oliver (1986): *The Vicar of Wakefield* [1766]. London: Penguin

Hoyle, Edmond (1742): *A Short Treatise on the Game of Whist*. London

Mackenzie, Henry (2001): *The Man of Feeling* [1771]. Oxford: Oxford University Press

Sterne, Laurence (2008): *A Sentimental Journey Through France and Italy and Other Writings* [1768]. Oxford: Oxford University Press

Secondary Sources

Anderson, Benedict (1983): *Imagined Communities: Reflections on the Origin and Spread of Nationalism*. London: Verso

Brantlinger, Patrick (1996): *Fictions of State: Culture and Credit in Britain, 1694-1994*. Ithaca, NY: Cornell University Press

Habermas, Jürgen (1991): *The Structural Transformation of the Public Sphere: An Inquiry into a Category of Bourgeois Society*. Trans. Thomas Burger. Cambridge, MA: MIT Press

Pocock, J.G.A (1985): *Virtue, Commerce, and History: Essays on Political Thought and History, Chiefly in the Eighteenth Century*. Cambridge: Cambridge University Press

Roxburgh, Natalie (2011): "The Rise of Public Credit and the Eighteenth-Century English Novel." Diss. Rutgers University

Siskin, Clifford; Warner, William (2010): *This is Enlightenment*. Chicago: University of Chicago Press

Skinner, Gillian (1998): *Sensibility and Economics in the Novel: The Price of a Tear*. New York: Palgrave Macmillan

Solnit, Rebecca (2013): "Diary: In the Day of the Postman", *London Review of Books* 35.16, 32-33

Taylor, Charles (2004): *Modern Social Imaginaries*. Durham, North Carolina: Duke University Press

Terry, Richard (2004): "*David Simple* and the Fallacy of Friendship", *SEL* 44.3, 525-544

Warner, William B. (1998): *Licensing Entertainment: The Elevation of Novel Reading in Britain 1684-1750*. Berkeley: University of California Press

Section 3

Not Shakespeare: New Approaches to Drama in the Seventeenth Century

Chairs:

Susanne Gruß, Lena Steveker, and Angelika Zirker

SUSANNE GRUß (ERLANGEN), LENA STEVEKER (SAARBRÜCKEN), AND ANGELIKA ZIRKER (TÜBINGEN)

Not Shakespeare: New Approaches to Drama in the Seventeenth Century

1. Not Shakespeare: Broadening the Canon of Seventeenth-Century Drama

For critics and theatre audiences alike, Shakespeare has long been the towering figure of Early Modern English drama. This year's events held in honour of 'the Bard's' 450th birthday[1] once more reflect on the central position that has been ascribed to him in western cultural memories. In recent years, however, Shakespeare's prominence has been increasingly challenged as the dramatic output of other authors and their impact on and popularity in Early Modern literary culture has been more widely acknowledged. Within academia, critical editions have been an influential factor in this development. As Kathleen McLuskie has pointed out with regard to the predominance of Shakespeare in Early Modern studies, the centrality of authors in the Early Modern canon taught at schools and universities and, by extension, analysed by academics, is strongly linked to the availability of edited texts:

> The texts which are most commonly discussed and performed are materially 'available' in the form of accessible editions, because they are part of an established canon of 'Shakespearean drama' and are thus granted a status removed from their original conditions of production. (McLuskie 1993, 217-218)

Beginning with the publication of the first complete edition of Thomas Middleton's works in 2007, an increasing number of dramatic texts by both Jacobean and Caroline playwrights has become available in critical editions. The Oxford Middleton (edited by Gary Taylor and John Lavagnino) was followed by the *Dramatic Works in the Beaumont and Fletcher Canon* (ed. Fredson Bowers) in 2008 and the *Cambridge Edition of the Complete Works of Ben Jonson* (eds. David Bevington, Martin Butler, and Ian Donaldson), published in 2012. A new edition of the works of Fulke Greville is currently in the making. The *Richard Brome Online Project*, edited by an international team of scholars, has made the work by this Caroline dramatist available on the Internet (*Richard Brome Online* 2010) and services such as *Early English Books Online* have made a variety of texts – not only from the seventeenth century – easily accessible. Critical editions such as those mentioned here have not only broadened the canon of Early Modern drama; they have also triggered a renewed and more comprehensive academic interest in non-Shakespearean drama of the seventeenth century, as

---

1 See, for example, the celebratory events planned in cooperation by the Shakespeare Birthday Trust and the Royal Shakespeare Company, which will "include plenty of pageantry, pomp and performance" ("Shakespeare's Birthday Celebrations"). The Deutsche Shakespeare-Gesellschaft and the Société Française Shakespeare are hosting major conferences in Weimar and Paris, respectively, to mark the anniversary ("Shakespeare Feiern – Celebrating Shakespeare", Weimar 2014; "Shakespeare 450", Paris 2014).

an increasing number of publications testify.[2] Shakespeare's contemporaries and successors have also begun to return to the stage. In its 2013 season, the Royal Shakespeare Company performed Thomas Middleton's *A Mad World My Masters* in Stratford-upon-Avon, a trend it continues in 2014 with productions of *The Arden of Faversham*, John Webster's *The White Devil*, and Thomas Middleton and Thomas Dekker's *The Roaring Girl*. The opening season of the Sam Wanamaker Playhouse in London (2014) stages Francis Beaumont's *The Knight of the Burning Pestle*, John Marston's *The Malcontent*, and John Webster's *The Duchess of Malfi*, which was also performed at the Old Vic to huge critical acclaim in 2012.

Both stage productions and critical editions indicate a fresh critical impetus in seventeenth-century non-Shakespearean drama. Thus, the study of Early Modern drama "is leaning ever less heavily on the pillar of Shakespeare as it finds its own foundations and stability" (Aebischer 2010, 158). Taking its cue from this new momentum, the present section aims to reflect the current restructuring of the Early Modern canon and to contribute innovative perspectives on the period. The title of this section[3] begins with a phrase that is both a deliberate gesture of negation and an acknowledgement: "Not Shakespeare". The "not" is meant to shift the general attention away from Shakespeare to the rich repertoire of other dramatists and dramatic genres the seventeenth century has to offer, and to collaborative writing as well as the 'one-author-play' that Shakespeare's name (falsely, of course) always seems to imply. The name "Shakespeare", however, re-inscribes what we seek to marginalize and is therefore proof of the predicament which scholars of the Early Modern age who attempt to enlarge the Early Modern canon are faced with. In Early Modern criticism, as Emma Smith highlights:

> Shakespeare is the elephant in the room. Aren't these other writers ultimately also-rans, the not-Shakespeares: Salieris in the age of Mozart, daubers in the shadow of Leonardo? Everything in our institutional culture, from course syllabi to theatre scheduling to politicians' rhetoric, is invested in Shakespeare's superiority to and separation from other writers of his own time and since, and thus implicitly in the corresponding derogation of these other writers. (Smith 2010, 132)

The perceived 'singularity' of Shakespeare is not as self-evident for the Early Modern period as it seems to be for twenty-first-century audiences, readers, or academics. Al-

---

2   See, for instance, Gary Taylor; John Lavagnino (eds.), *Thomas Middleton and Early Modern Textual Culture* (2007); Pascale Aebischer, *Jacobean Drama: A Reader's Guide to Essential Criticism* (2010); Julie Sanders, *Ben Jonson in Context* (2010); Emma Smith; Garrett A. Sullivan, Jr. (eds.), *The Cambridge Companion to English Renaissance Tragedy* (2010); Suzanne Gossett, *Thomas Middleton in Context* (2011); Ton Hoenselaars (ed.), *The Cambridge Companion to Shakespeare and Contemporary Dramatists* (2012); Gary Taylor and Trish Thomas Henley (eds.), *The Oxford Handbook of Thomas Middleton* (2012).

3   In its genesis, this section is indebted both to the recently renewed interest in non-Shakespearean drama we have outlined above and to other panels at preceding conferences of the Deutscher Anglistenverband. The Anglistentag 2010 in Saarbrücken hosted a panel on "Language, Literature and Culture in the 17th Century: New Perspectives on an Under-Rated Period"; for the following year, in Freiburg, another panel was formed that also focused on the seventeenth century: "Early Modern Narratives and the Genesis of Genre". We were excited by this development, but also thought that, after a more general panel on the 'underrated' seventeenth century and one that focused on narrative and questions of genre, a panel on the drama of the period was in order.

so, as our panel has shown in both papers and discussions, it is impossible (and, one might add, undesirable) to escape Shakespeare completely, after all. In the contributions to this section, he repeatedly serves as a point of orientation or of contrast to the authors, plays, and topics in question. With Shakespeare both absent from and, at the same time, present in this section, the "elephant in the room" is used very much as "a reference point rather than an unexamined ideal", as the editors of *The Cambridge Companion to English Renaissance Tragedy* put it (Smith and Garrett 2010, x).

2. Contributions

"Not Shakespeare: New Approaches to Drama in the Seventeenth Century" covers a wide range of literary, historical, cultural, and political contexts. Some of the individual articles are, however, also connected to each other, which may lead to further insights and help us see links with regard to generic questions as well as literary fashions in the early seventeenth century. The first contribution to this section, by Stephan Laqué, guides us from the late sixteenth into the early seventeenth century and openly addresses the "elephant in the room" that is Shakespeare. In "Leaving Wittenberg: Faustus, Hamlet, and Early Modern Education", Laqué re-evaluates the 'education revolution' that would redraw the intellectual and academic map of Britain between 1560 and 1640. In focusing on Christopher Marlowe's *Doctor Faustus* (1594) and Shakespeare's *Hamlet* (1603?), he argues that different attitudes towards schooling and education were a major factor in the formation of Early Modern theatre. Faustus moves from a regular university curriculum to the 'school' of Mephistophilis, but remains, as Laqué notes, indebted to the structures he has forsaken, and Hamlet leaves (or is forced to leave) Wittenberg and eventually replaces formal university education with his quasi-academic interest in theatre.

The next article, by Katrin Röder, is concerned with the political implications of drama: in "Intercultural 'Traffique' and Political Change in Samuel Daniel's *Philotas* (1596-1604) and Fulke Greville's *Mustapha* (1587-1610?)", Röder discusses political debates as put forward in two plays by Daniel (1562-1619) and Greville (1554-1628) with regard to notions of political change and tyranny. In both plays, *Philotas* and *Mustapha*, traditional generic forms such as French Senecan drama are taken up and combined with references to intercultural contact, while, at the same time, concepts of cultural alterity are negotiated, albeit in different ways. In the case of *Philotas*, Röder argues, political change subsequent to the conquest of Persian territory does not result in the elimination of treason or resistance against tyranny. The tragedy therefore ends with the fear of revolt after the execution of Philotas. Greville, by contrast, leaves his tragedy open-ended: Revolt after the murder of Mustapha is a possibility, but it can more likely be avoided. Intercultural exchange between the Christian culture and the Ottoman Empire may have led to tyranny under Solyman, but it has also brought about a new understanding of the contingency of hierarchy and forms of government.

Felix Sprang's essay takes up this section's title. In "Neither Shakespeare Nor the Gilded Monuments: Rethinking the Dramatic Impact of Jacobean and Caroline Civic Pageants", he focuses on a dramatic form that has often escaped critical attention, the Lord Mayor's Show and the annually performed civic pageants in London, which were partly planned and thought through by acclaimed dramatists of the period, among them George Peele, Thomas Dekker, Anthony Munday, Thomas Heywood, and Thomas

Middleton. Sprang emphasizes the aesthetic as well as the programmatic nature of the Lord Mayor's Shows and analyses their impact on Jacobean and Caroline stage performances in close readings of Munday's *Chruso-thriambos: The Triumphs of Golde* (1611) and Heywood's *Londini Status Pacatus: Or, Londons Peaceable Estate* (1639). Their emblematic nature and staging practice might also, he suggests in the final part of his essay, serve as a starting point for a re-evaluation of Shakespeare's late plays.

The dramatic works of Ben Jonson, one of the canonic figures of early seventeenth-century drama, are at the centre of interest in the following two articles. Matthias Bauer and Martina Bross make a connection between "Character Writing and the Stage in the Early Seventeenth Century", based on the revival of character writing in the early seventeenth century with publications by Joseph Hall (1608) and Thomas Overbury (1614) that followed the model of Theophrastus, whose characters were published with Latin translations at the end of the sixteenth century. Character writing, they argue, directly influenced the stage, especially the comedy of humours. In plays of Ben Jonson, in *Every Man Out of His Humour* (1599/1600) and *Cynthia's Revels* (1600/01) in particular, the play texts are supplemented with paratexts, prose descriptions of specific traits of characters, which leads to both compression and redundancy of information that can be linked to the notions of (performance on) the stage and (reading of the play on) the page. Bauer and Bross also demonstrate how quickly and to what extent the character genre had become a part of drama after the first decade of the seventeenth century, and show to what extent the genre developed away from abstract concepts and toward professions as well as social groups.

Ellen Redling, finally, takes up the focus on Jonsonian drama. In "'From the Top of Paul's Steeple to the Standard in Cheap': Popular Culture, Urban Space, and Narrativity in Jacobean City Comedy", she explores city comedies by Ben Jonson, John Marston and Thomas Middleton and reads these Early Modern plays as predecessors of London prose narratives of the twenty-first century. Redling argues that, in spite of generic and historical differences, these two genres are linked to each other through their strategies of representing urban spaces. According to her reading, both Jacobean city comedy and twenty-first-century London narratives juxtapose familiar and unfamiliar places in the city and use narrativity in order to make urban spaces accessible for their audiences and readers, respectively. According to Redling, the two genres not only share plot lines, character representations and what she sees as an interplay between dramatic and narrative modes. They also negotiate the cultural anxieties of their particular historical contexts as each revolves around morally ambiguous images of London as a financial centre.

3. New Approaches to Seventeenth Century Drama

The articles in this section lead to some new insights into Jacobean and Caroline drama that take into account how plays during this period function as spaces of contact between different writers, genres, and cultural practices. As we have illustrated in the preceding outlines of each of the articles, the contributions to this section interact in negotiating similar topics, in referring to earlier as well as contemporary texts and genres, and in engaging with contemporary socio-cultural practices. The essays assembled here cover a wide variety of authors, ranging from Shakespeare to Greville, Daniel, and Jonson, from Munday and Heywood to Marston and Middleton. The concern of finding new approaches to seventeenth-century drama is not restricted to plays written for the stage but includes dramatic interactions with character writing and narrative prose, as well as with other dramatic forms such as pageants and Senecan drama. The section furthermore extends into the present day – to current critical approaches, but also to contemporary literature.

"Not Shakespeare: New Approaches to Drama in the Seventeenth Century" illustrates how seventeenth-century drama impacts other modes of writing as well as socio-political and cultural discourses. Cultural contexts, the politics of the day, theories of kingship and leadership come as much into play as contemporary interaction between the stage and the audience, audience reaction and didactic strategies. As our section shows, non-Shakespearean drama of the seventeenth century has manifold resonances, and academia is still in the process of acknowledging this potential.

References

Primary Sources

Beaumont, Francis; Fletcher, John (2008): *Dramatic Works in the Beaumont and Fletcher Canon*. Ed. Fredson Bowers. Cambridge: Cambridge University Press

Brome, Richard (2010): *Richard Brome Online*. Ed. Richard Cave <http://www.hrionline.ac.uk/brome/home.jsp> [accessed 27 February 2014]

Early English Books Online: <http://eebo.chadwyck.com> [accessed 27 February 2014]

Jonson, Ben (2012): *The Cambridge Edition of the Complete Works of Ben Jonson*. Ed. David Bevington et al. Cambridge: Cambridge University Press

Middleton, Thomas (2007): *The Collected Works*. Eds. Gary Taylor ; John Lavagnino. Oxford: Oxford University Press

Secondary Sources

Aebischer, Pascale (2010): *Jacobean Drama: A Reader's Guide to Essential Criticism*. Basingstoke/ New York: Palgrave Macmillan

Deutsche Shakespeare-Gesellschaft (2014): "Wir feiern Geburtstag – Feiern Sie mit!" <www.shakespeare-gesellschaft.de> [accessed 27 February 2014]

Gossett, Suzanne (ed.; 2011): *Thomas Middleton in Context* (2011). Cambridge: Cambridge University Press

Hoenselaars, Ton (ed.; 2012): *The Cambridge Companion to Shakespeare and Contemporary Dramatists*. Cambridge: Cambridge University Press

McLuskie, Kathleen (1993): "Politics and Dramatic Form in Early Modern Tragedy", in: Mulryne, J.R.; Shewring, Margaret (eds.): *Theatre and Government Under the Early Stuarts*. Cambridge: Cambridge University Press, 217-236

Sanders, Julie (ed.; 2010): *Ben Jonson in Context*. Cambridge: Cambridge University Press

Shakespeare Birthday: <http://www.shakespearesbirthday.org.uk> [accessed 27 February 2014]

Shakespeare Anniversary: <http://www.shakespeareanniversary.org> [accessed 27 February 2014]

Smith, Emma; Sullivan, Garrett A. Jr. (2010): "Shakespeare and Early Modern Tragedy", in: Smith, Emma; Sullivan Jr., Garrett A. (eds.): *The Cambridge Companion to English Renaissance Tragedy*. Cambridge: Cambridge University Press, 132-149

--- (eds.; 2010): *The Cambridge Companion to English Renaissance Tragedy*. Cambridge: Cambridge University Press

Taylor, Gary; Henley, Trish Thomas (eds.; 2012): *The Oxford Handbook of Thomas Middleton*. Oxford: Oxford University Press

STEPHAN LAQUÉ (MÜNCHEN)

Leaving Wittenberg: Faustus, Hamlet, and Early Modern Education

The sixteenth century in England saw an unprecedented surge in higher education. Between 1560 and 1640 what has come to be known as the "Educational Revolution"[1] had a massive impact on assumptions about higher education in England and on its institutions. Intake of undergraduate students into the Universities of Oxford and Cambridge rose sharply from about 1560 to reach a first peak in the early 1580s, and by the outbreak of the Civil War the number of entrants reached figures which would not be seen again until the 1860s (Stone 1964, 48-49). At the time, grammar schools saw a similar development. One reason for the mounting interest in formal education was that in this period of an ever increasing and accelerating mobility of culture and knowledge there simply was a lot to be taught and studied. A stream of foreign scholars, foreign texts, and foreign thinking poured into the still largely medieval institutions and rendered them newly relevant and attractive. However, reactions to the wide-ranging revolution that this new learning was triggering in formal education were not invariably straightforward in their enthusiasm. One arena where probing and sceptical voices were heard was the theatre of the time – a most auspicious platform for forms of educational debate and critique by virtue of its close affiliation with institutions of higher education, which looked toward drama as a place of philological imitation and moral instruction and, moreover, often served as venues for performances.[2] I would like to consider two closely related plays as examinations of the flowering of formal education: Christopher Marlowe's *Doctor Faustus* and William Shakespeare's *Hamlet*.[3] Both plays were written at the height of the educational revolution between the two peaks of university admission and, as I will be arguing, they both offer explorations of the reach and relevance of formal education.

By the time Marlowe and Shakespeare were writing their tragedies, the educational revolution was in full swing to the extent that it was destined to become the object of critical scrutiny and even parody. The background to both plays is the University of Wittenberg where Faustus is a teacher and where Hamlet is a student. Wittenberg was "the epicentre of northern humanism" (Stein 2007, 56), but it is chiefly known as the university where Martin Luther and Philip Melanchthon lived and taught in the sixteenth century. Even though it is debatable whether the majority of the audience in

---

1   The phrase was established by Lawrence Stone, who maintained that revolutionary changes in education were an important factor leading up to the "English Revolution" of the Civil Wars and the Commonwealth in the seventeenth century (Stone 1964, *passim*).
2   According to the title page of Q1, *Hamlet*, for example, had been performed in the City of London and at the Universities of Cambridge and Oxford.
3   This paper, then, does not seek to exclude Shakespeare from its scope. However, it falls within the remit of this section entitled "Not Shakespeare" by taking the discourse of education as a space of contact between Shakespeare and his contemporaries, a space where drama and the social practice of education intersect and where Shakespeare should be considered in the context of his peers.

Early Modern London were aware of the full significance of Wittenberg, its relevance for the plays surely exceeds that of being a mere generic place of learning. The reformation in Wittenberg was centrally concerned with man's salvation, and both Faustus and Hamlet have encounters with creatures from the beyond – characters whose salvation is an important topic and whose punishment after death affects the respective protagonists. In *Doctor Faustus* that figure is Mephistophilis, who is in hell though (paradoxically) walks the earth: "Why, this is hell, nor am I out of it" (Marlowe 1986, 1.3.76). After Faustus has demanded that the unkempt devil get changed into "the holy shape" of "an old Franciscan Friar" (*ibid.*, 1.3.26-27), he is willing to follow Lucifer's henchman in quest of intellectual, material, and sensual satisfaction. Hamlet is confronted with the ghost of his father who is, as it were, on an uneasy excursion to his old home:

> Doom'd for a certain term to walk the night,
> And for the day confin'd to fast in fires,
> Till the foul crimes done in my days of nature
> Are burnt and purg'd away.
>
> (Shakespeare 1993, 1.5.10-13)

The prince is determined to follow the ghost, though it may turn out to be his very own Mephistophilis – "be thou a spirit of health or goblin damn'd" (*ibid.*, 1.4.40), as Hamlet says. Unlike Faustus, he does not demand that the "questionable shape" (*ibid.*, 1.4.43) be coated with pious and pleasing attire, but he is keenly aware that the devil himself may be hiding underneath the ghost's paternal appearance:

> The spirit that I have seen
> May be the devil, and the devil hath power
> T'assume a pleasing shape, yea, and perhaps,
> Out of my weakness and my melancholy,
> As he is very potent with such spirits,
> Abuses me to damn me.
>
> (*ibid.*, 2.2.594-599)

Faced with these eerie apparitions, both Faustus and Hamlet could really do with a sound Wittenberg education. However, it is just when they meet with the personified questions of redemption and salvation[4] that they both turn their backs on Wittenberg and on their alma mater.

In the case of Faustus, his turning away from Wittenberg takes the form of a comprehensive rejection of the academic curriculum; thus his first lines in the play: "Settle thy studies, Faustus, and begin / To sound the depth of that thou wilt profess" (Marlowe 1986, 1.1.1-2). Needless to say, Faustus finds that the university does not offer training in his 'profession':

> Philosophy is odious and obscure.
> Both law and physic are for petty wits.
> Divinity is basest of the three,
> Unpleasant, harsh, contemptible and vile.
> 'Tis magic, magic that hath ravished me.
>
> (*ibid.*, 1.1.105-109)

So Faustus turns from the university to a new, but decidedly 'extra-curricular' topic:

---

4   The two "dire supernatural visitants", as Robert Fleissner describes them (Fleissner 1986, 16).

> These necromantic books are heavenly, [...]
> Oh, what a world of profit and delight,
> Of power, of honour, of omnipotence,
> Is promised to the studious artizan!
>
> (*ibid.*, 1.1.49-54)

Faustus may be still studious, but as an "artizan", that is, as someone who claims to manufacture or create; an "artisan", moreover, in the 'dark arts', who aspires to the creative power of the godhead, he situates himself outside the *artes liberales* which were taught at universities. However, once outside the university, he proceeds to mockingly arrogate to himself an academic 'degree', a *laurea*: "Such is the force of magic and my spells. / Now, Faustus, thou art conjuror laureate" (*ibid.*, 1.3.31-32). Thus Faustus's career under the tuition of Mephistophilis everywhere bears the marks of formal education.

Once Faustus has turned his back on the University of Wittenberg and the constraints of its curriculum, he returns to the status of a student. The teachers he seeks are the two Germans Valdes and Cornelius, who are experts in magic and, as Faustus indicates, are looking for young (or old, as the case may be) professionals to join them in their trade:

> Vales, sweet Valdes and Cornelius!
> Know that your words have won me at the last
> To practise magic and concealed arts.
>
> (*ibid.*, 1.1.99-101)

Valdes and Cornelius see and practise magic as an obscure but ultimately conventional discipline – as a kind of master discipline that would crown the established curriculum. As Cornelius points out, the time that Faustus spent at university was therefore not wasted:

> He that is grounded in Astrology,
> Enriched with tongues, well seen in minerals,
> Hath all the principles magic doth require.
>
> (*ibid.*, 1.1.137-139)

Ultimately, then, magic is just another degree course and Valdes wants to send Faustus off to study:

> Then haste thee to some solitary grove,
> And bear wise Bacon's and Albanus' works,
> The Hebrew Psalter and New Testament;
> And whatsoever else is requisite [...].
>
> (*ibid.*, 1.1.152-155)

The "solitary grove", I would suggest, is the Grove of Academe, the site where Plato established the congregation of scholars that would provide the model for the early university. Valdes therefore has in mind a form of learning that is fully in keeping with the tradition – though not exactly with the proprieties – of the university. But academic study is too conventional and too time-consuming for the greedy and enthusiastic Faustus: "ere I sleep, I'll try what I can do. / This night I'll conjure, though I die therefore" (*ibid.*, 1.1.164-165). Like the bumbling amateur he is, Faustus gives magic a try and carefully prepares the basic spells the two Germans have taught him over dinner and wine: "Faustus, begin thine incantations / And try if devils will obey thy hest" (*ibid.*, 1.3.5-6). He succeeds, but the newly appeared Mephistophilis puts a damper on any academic pride the self-proclaimed 'conjurer laureate' may hold:

> *Faustus*: Did not my conjuring speeches raise thee? Speak.
> *Mephistophilis*: That was the cause, but yet per accidens; [...]
> Therefore the shortest cut for conjuring
> Is stoutly to abjure all godliness
> And pray devoutly to the prince of hell.
> *Faustus*: So Faustus has already done.
>
> (*ibid.*, 1.3.46-54)

From academic discipline to simple incantation to even more simple blasphemy: In the hands of the childishly eager Faustus, black magic is reduced from the academic discipline that Cornelius and Valdes practise to a field that can hardly live up to any conceivable academic standards.

Faustus is only too happy to take shortcuts and simplifications, and Mephistophilis finds him a somewhat unfocused academic student. After some questions about hell, the answers to which Faustus is unable and unwilling to comprehend, he turns the power and knowledge Mephistophilis places at his disposition to far more mundane purposes: "But leaving this, let me have a wife, the fairest maid in / Germany, for I am wanton and lascivious, and cannot / live without a wife" (*ibid.*, 1.5.144-146). This is the disposition on which Mephistophilis is going to build. He teases Faustus by offering him a thinly disguised and repulsive succubus for a wife in order to goad him to engage in more extravagant and refined erotic fantasies:

> I'll cull thee out the fairest courtesans
> And bring them every morning to thy bed.
> She whom thine eye shall like, thy heart shall have,
> Be she as chaste as was Penelope,
> As wise as Saba, or as beautiful
> As was bright Lucifer before his fall.
>
> (*ibid.*, 1.5.155-160)

Faustus and Mephistophilis are here reminiscent of two truant schoolboys leafing through a top-shelf magazine behind the cycle-shed and this juvenile erotic interest will go a long way towards displacing Faustus's academic ambitions. When in Act 5 Faustus eventually returns to Wittenberg after his long journeys with Mephistophilis, he agrees to regale the scholars who come to him with a vision of Helen of Troy. This is the kind of teaching he now has to offer. Wanting to see her and to enjoy her beauty is, as he says, a "just request" (*ibid.*, 5.1.21) and it is a request which he himself will repeat at the end of the scene. No longer content with illusions, he now desires Helen for his lover:

> To glut the longing of my heart's desire,
> That I may have unto my paramour
> That heavenly Helen which I saw of late [...].
>
> (*ibid.*, 5.1.89-91)

Shared schoolboy fantasies now become real, and when Helen appears, Faustus greets her with some of the most poetic and celebrated lines in the play – but with lines which ultimately only rehearse his schoolboyish grammar school training:

> Was this the face that launched a thousand ships,
> And burnt the topless towers of Ilium? [...]
> I will be Paris, and for love of thee
> Instead of Troy shall Wittenberg be sacked.
>
> (*ibid.*, 5.1.97-105)

He is again a schoolboy behind the cycle-shed – one who flaunts the fact that he has paid attention to his classics tutor.

Faustus is reduced to the stature of an unfocused schoolboy. As his interests degenerate, his academic work is increasingly superseded by pranks, and he and Mephistophilis become the class clowns of the play. At the palace of the Pope in Act 3, Faustus asks Mephistophilis to make him an actor in a pitiable exercise in slapstick: "let me an actor be, / That this proud Pope may Faustus' cunning see" (*ibid.*, 3.2.76-77). Made invisible by Mephistophilis, he snatches food and wine and even slaps the Pope – the lowest level of comedy. This, then, is the highest extent to which Faustus is capable of scripting the plays he acts in. For the rest of the play, he is a passive receiver of demands that he passes on to his erstwhile instructor Mephistophilis. The Duke and Duchess of Vanholt, whom Faustus treats to one of his insubstantial request programs – "erecting that enchanted castle in the air" (*ibid.*, 4.7.3), as the Duke remarks – astutely assess the trajectory which Faustus has taken:

> *Lady*: We are much beholden to this learned man.
> *Duke*: So are we, madam, which we will recompense
> With all the love and kindness that we may.
> His artful sport drives all sad thoughts away.
>
> (*ibid.*, 4.7.130-133)

From being a "learned man", Faustus has been reduced to the status of a comedian. The liberal arts of the university – the preserve of 'free men' – he has renounced in favour of his "artful sport" he performs while in thrall to Lucifer.

On his descent from the seat of learning to the pits of hell, Faustus traverses different forms of education and the different roles they offer: teacher, student, teacher's pet, class clown. However, he never leaves the structure and terminology of formal education. From "conjuror laureate" to "artful sport", his decadence is modelled on the institutions of learning. The famous presentation of the seven deadly sins in Act 2 is also a scene taken from the classroom, where Lucifer assumes the role of a schoolmaster offering the Early Modern equivalent to a slide presentation. At this point Faustus is not yet firmly resolved to give up his soul to the devil, and Lucifer and Belzebub put on a special show for his delectation and introduction to the questionable pleasures of hell:

> *Belzebub*: Faustus, we are come from hell in person to show thee some pastime. Sit down and thou shalt behold the seven deadly sins appear to thee in their own proper shape and likeness.
> *Faustus*: That sight will be as pleasant to me as Paradise was to Adam the first day of his creation.
>
> (*ibid.*, 2.2.104-109)

Faustus's reference to Adam is telling in this context. As the sins enter, Belzebub asks Faustus to question them: "Now, Faustus, question them of their / names and dispositions" (2.2.113-114). Faustus duly asks the right questions and is given some rather obvious answers. However, he is nowhere granted Adam's prerogative to name the things that are placed before him. In this pageant, he is not an actor, let alone the stage director. He is content to ask and learn, the scene becoming a rehearsing of hell's vocabulary by the teacher's favourite pupil until, after the seven sins have left, Faustus gets his lines wrong: "*Faustus*: Oh, this feeds my soul. / *Lucifer*: Tut, Faustus, in hell is all manner of delight" (*ibid.*, 2.1.176-177). Faustus's mention of his soul is a manner of speaking, but it is, of course, highly inappropriate in the context of a display of sins. It indicates the student's lack of diligence in studying hell. Having left behind the academic world of Wittenberg, Faustus has become a mediocre pupil in the school of Lucifer – he is given his assignment and is reprimanded as soon as his concentration lapses. Whether as "conjuror laureate" or as bumbling schoolboy to Lucifer, Faustus's academic degeneration takes place within the structures and constellations of the Early Modern education system. It parodies the structures of formal education, which it ultimately renders as irredeemable as Faustus himself.

Faustus's academic descent follows as a countermovement to his earlier rise up the rungs of the social ladder, a movement that has taken place before the action of the play begins. According to the prologue, Faustus was

> born of parents base of stock,
> In Germany, within the town of Rhodes.
> At riper years to Wittenberg he went,
> Whereas his kinsmen chiefly brought him up.
>
> *(ibid.*, prologue, 11-14)

This modest social background places him with the majority of Early Modern university students who tended to come from poor, 'plebeian' families. The Early Modern university was primarily an institution for those who were not well off, for the sons of artisans, farmers, and families "mediocris fortunae".[5] At Oxford, their number had formed as much as 55% of matriculants in 1577-1579, but by the middle of the seventeenth century, these figures had dropped below 40%, and by 1810 had dwindled down to a mere 1% (see Sharpe 1997, 267). What caused the number of plebeian students to drop was an increased desire on the part of the gentry and nobility to send their sons to university.

Unlike Faustus, Hamlet is anything but "base of stock" – he is a prince, no less, which, to quote Elizabeth Hanson, gives us "the odd fact that Hamlet is a university student at all" (Hanson 2011, 225). The Royal Court of Denmark is teeming with all kinds of university wits: Polonius recollects his modest acting career at university, in Act 1; Laertes returns to Paris, whose university, as Curtius argues, is even older than that of Bologna and was much-frequented by English and German students since the end of the twelfth century (see Curtius 1993, 64); Rosencrantz and Guildenstern are fellow students of Hamlet at Wittenberg as is, of course, Horatio.

Hamlet's presence at Wittenberg is made remarkable by his social standing, but right at the outset (with the fourteenth line he speaks in the play), he agrees to follow the wishes of his uncle and mother to put an end to it. Claudius has just given Laertes leave to return to France when he asks Hamlet to stay away from Wittenberg:

> For your intent
> In going back to school in Wittenberg,
> It is most retrograde to our desire,
> And we beseech you bend you to remain
> Here in the cheer and comfort of our eye.
>
> (Shakespeare 1993, 1.2.112-116)

Like Faustus, Hamlet leaves Wittenberg. But why is Claudius so eager to keep him away from university? His impetus is not in any way remarkable or extraordinary

---

5 For the exact figures at St John's College and Gonville and Caius College, Cambridge, see Stone 1964, 66.

since most members of the nobility chose to keep their offspring unschooled. In *The Scholemaster*, Roger Ascham therefore fervently upbraided the nobility for this neglect:

> The fault is in your selves, ye noble mens sonnes, and therefore ye deserve the greater blame, that commonlie, the meaner mens children cum to be the wiesest councellors, and greatest doers, in the weightie affaires of this Realme. And why? for God will have it so, of his providence: bicause ye will have it no otherwise, by your negligence. (Ascham 1863, 40)

But Claudius is too calculating, and the play is too closely knit for Hamlet's removal from Wittenberg to be explained simply as a faithful representation of the low esteem in which the nobility held higher education. A central and far more dramatically relevant motivation may be Claudius's depriving Hamlet of the crown, i.e. of his land.[6] As Lawrence Stone writes in his seminal paper on "The Educational Revolution in *England*":

> Just at this time land was changing hands at an unprecedented speed [...]. For many purchasers, giving their sons a higher education was one way, perhaps the only way, of obtaining for them the social status commensurate with their wealth. [...] the rise and fall of higher education closely follows that of the land market. (Stone 1964, 70-71)

Landownership and the bequeathing of land were seen as a strong motivation for providing one's offspring with a thorough education – and landownership is something that Claudius is withholding from Hamlet. Even though social status was hardly an issue for the royal son, university life would have exposed him to an environment where owning and acquiring land was a central concern. Having dispossessed his nephew of the realm, sending him back to university and thereby equipping him with the academic background requisite for landownership might indeed be "retrograde" to Claudius's desire. But whatever the reasons: Hamlet's removal from Wittenberg is a countermove against the trend of the educational revolution, against the late but forceful addition of wellborn students to the universities and against the exhortations of Ascham and many others who saw a need for a well-educated nobility.

Hamlet leaves Wittenberg, the cradle of the Reformation, where he might have found some answers to the questions of salvation that the ghost raises on the battlements. However, the ghost is alone in being haunted by these questions, while Hamlet's contortions end up centring on such unstable and untheological issues as memory, the imagination, mortality, decay, and cultural determinism. The situation of the ghost and its theological repercussions are brushed aside: "Well said, old mole. Canst work i'th' earth so fast?" (Shakespeare 1993, 1.5.170). While Marlowe's Doctor Faustus is centrally concerned with the theology of Wittenberg (with the question of his own damnation, repentance, and potential salvation) throughout the play, Hamlet dispels the academic interests of his alma mater along with the doctrines and stereotypes of the educational revolution. Unlike Marlowe's Doctor before him, Hamlet is therefore free to experiment with alternative forms of education and with new, heretofore non-academic, curricula.

Hamlet's close friend Horatio, the rational scholar, is a foil to the prince, who turns his back on Wittenberg and is forced to seek new forms of instruction. Like Faustus,

---

6   Margreta de Grazia has elaborated on Hamlet's loss of land in Hamlet *without Hamlet* (2007).

Horatio hails from a poor family and is representative of the majority of students at Oxford and Cambridge. Hamlet greets his friend:

> *Ham.* I am glad to see you well.
> Horatio, or I do forget myself.
> *Hor.* The same, my lord, and your poor servant ever. [...]
> *Ham.* But what in faith make you from Wittenberg?
> *Hor.* A truant disposition, good my lord.
>
> (*ibid.*, 1.2.160-169)

There is the indication here that Horatio is in fact earning his keep at university by acting as Hamlet's servitor, as a servant to one of the wellborn students – at the time a very common occupation for students without money to pay their way through higher education. Horatio, then, might quite literally be Hamlet's "poor servant". He is a university stereotype of the time and remains firmly established at Wittenberg – his absence can at the most indicate a "truant disposition" rather than a genuine turning away from the university.

Since Horatio is not only loyal, but trained in the arts and in philosophy, Hamlet decides to use him as an instrument for recording and reconfirming the results of his cleverly arranged murder-detector experiment, which is "The Murder of Gonzago" in Act 3. But when the King jumps at the speech Hamlet has the player speak, calls for light, and storms out of the theatre, this impressive display of reactions leaves Horatio signally unimpressed as his soberly noncommittal replies to the triumphant Hamlet show:

> *Ham.* O good Horatio, I'll take the ghost's word for a
> thousand pound. Didst perceive?
> *Hor.* Very well, my lord,
> *Ham.* Upon the talk of the poisoning?
> *Hor.* I did very well note him.
>
> (*ibid.*, 3.2.280-284)

Horatio was observant, but he obviously failed to understand. The report that Horatio will give to Fortinbras after the comprehensive stabbing and poisoning in Act 5 will be equally precise, but it will, again, be woefully inadequate in giving a bare summary of a conventional revenge tragedy – without a single word about Hamlet's emotional and intellectual contortions, his flights of madness, without a word about the ghost. Horatio may have "very well noted" the tragedy of Hamlet, but being the prototypical scholar he is, he is also a useless theatregoer, incapable of doing justice either to the Mousetrap or to the tragedy of Hamlet.

Horatio fails woefully in the field of theatre – as does Polonius, whose stabbing behind the Arras in the closet scene is a parody of the role of Julius Caesar, which he had played as a university student. Rosencrantz and Guildenstern equally fail, when Hamlet mercilessly exposes their incompetent playacting under the direction of Claudius: "You would play upon me, you would seem to know my stops [...] do you think I am easier to be played on than a pipe?" (*ibid.*, 3.2.355-361). While all the steadfast university wits thus prove to be incompetent actors and playgoers, it is precisely in this field that Hamlet excels – and it is this field that he transforms into a new quasi-academic discipline. During his first entrance and before Claudius asks him not to return to Wittenberg, the inky-cloaked Hamlet professes an aversion to playacting:

> I know not 'seems':
> 'Tis not alone my inky cloak, good mother,
> Nor customary suits of solemn black,
> Nor windy suspiration of forc'd breath,
> No, nor the fruitful river of the eye,
> Nor the dejected haviour of the visage,
> Together with all forms, moods, shapes of grief,
> That can denote me truly. These indeed seem,
> For they are actions that a man might play;
> But I have that within which passes show,
> These but the trappings and the suits of woe.
>
> (*ibid.*, 1.2.76-86)

But soon after this speech, Hamlet agrees to end his university education and, once he meets the ghost, he has to come up with a non-academic method to handle the epistemological and ethical challenge which is foisted upon him. He points out to his friend Horatio that the university curriculum has nothing to offer that might explain this strange phenomenon and seamlessly moves on to the new method he is going to employ, which is playacting:

> There are more things in heaven and earth, Horatio,
> Than are dreamt of in your philosophy.
> But come,
> Here, as before, never, so help you mercy,
> How strange or odd some'er I bear myself –
> As I perchance hereafter shall think meet
> To put an antic disposition on [...].
>
> (*ibid.*, 1.5.174-180)

The aversion to acting and make-believe which Hamlet professed in his first exchange with his mother has given way to an openness towards an "antic disposition". It is the stage rather than the university that is going to be a central site of his development, of his education.

Hamlet's "antic disposition" is so masterfully acted that, onstage as in the world outside the theatre, his audiences and critics are often at a loss to determine to what extent this madness is feigned or factual. Unlike the largely passive doctor-turned-schoolboy Faustus, Hamlet is an eminently active presence on stage, one who is fully in command. He is actor, stage director, and playwright all in one person – and, what is more, from being a student at Wittenberg, he rises to being a teacher in the art of acting at Elsinore:

> Speak the speech, I pray you, as I pronounced it to you, trippingly on the tongue; but if you mouth it as many of your players do, I had as lief the town-crier spoke my lines. Nor do not saw the air too much with your hand, thus, but use all gently [...]. I would have such a fellow whipped for o'erdoing.
>
> (*ibid.*, 3.2.1-13)

Hamlet decides on the play that is to be staged, he pens some of the lines, he acts the part he has written before the players, and he instructs the players on the art of playacting.

Hamlet teaches acting to the actors, and he teaches Ophelia and Horatio how a theatre production is supposed to be observed. The players as well as Ophelia and Horatio are his students. In his *Passions of the Mind in General* of 1601, Thomas Wright remarked on the pedagogical potential of the theatre:

> Looke upon other men appassionat, how they demeane themselves in passions, and observe what and how they speake in mirthe, sadnesse, ire, fear, hope &c, What motions are stirring in their eyes, hands, bodie &c. And then leave the excesse and exorbitant levitie and other defects, and keepe the manner corrected with a prudent mediocritie. And this may be marked in the stageplayers who act excellently; for as the perfection of their exercise consisteth of imitation of others, so they that imitate best, act best. (quoted in Grantley 2000, 5)

Wright's demand for moderation is reminiscent of the instruction that the Danish prince gives to the players – only that he reverses Hamlet's strategy: Wright asks students as theatregoers to tone down the gestures and manners they see on stage. Hamlet, on the other hand, asks the actors to be moderate in their action, while at the same time he teaches one part of the audience to be attentive and hopes for an excessive reaction from the other part, i.e. from his uncle Claudius. Hamlet is a new form of theatre teacher: His instructions address every aspect of a play and aim much further than Harvey's notion of using the theatre in order to teach proper social behaviour. Thomas Heywood in his *Apology for Actors* makes further reference to the presence of theatre at universities:

> Do not the Vniversities, the fountaines and well-springs of all good Arts, Learning and Documents, admit the like in their Colledges? and they (I assure myself) are not ignorant of their true vse. (quoted in Grantley 2000, 75)

If we are to believe the title page of the first quarto, the tragedy of Hamlet was performed at both Oxford and Cambridge. But whatever the "true use" of the theatre in higher education might be, it is safe to assume that Hamlet's teaching of theatre-skills and his development of the play into an epistemological method went far beyond Heywood's wildest dreams.

The two plays I have looked at, then, both take Early Modern higher education, which was expanding and changing as they were hitting the stage, as raw material for moulding their protagonists. Faustus degenerates as he proudly leaves the university curriculum behind while remaining very closely indebted to the frame and structure of formal higher education and maintaining a keen and, indeed, pressing interest in the theological concerns of Wittenberg. Hamlet, by contrast, is forced out of university by his uncle and mother and, as a result, ends up moving beyond Wittenberg and beyond the limitations of the other Wittenberg students in the play. He goes on to turn his interest in the theatre into a new, quasi-academic field; he expands its reach, and he shapes it into an epistemological tool. By leaving Wittenberg and by continuing their academic lives outside the academe, both Doctor Faustus and Hamlet, in their different ways, demonstrate that the "educational revolution" would go far beyond changes in the numbers and social backgrounds of students.

References

Primary Sources

Marlowe, Christopher (1986): *The Complete Plays*. J.B. Steane (ed.). London: Penguin
Shakespeare, William (1993): *Hamlet*. Harold Jenkins (ed.). The Arden Shakespeare. London: Routledge

Secondary Sources

Ascham, Roger (1863): *The Scholemaster*. London: Bell and Daldy
Curtius, Ernst Robert (1993): *Europäische Literatur und Lateinisches Mittelalter*. Tübingen/Basel: Francke
de Grazia, Margreta (2007): Hamlet *without Hamlet*. Cambridge: Cambridge University Press
Fleissner, Robert (1986): *The Prince and the Professor*. Heidelberg: Winter
Grantley, Darryll (2000): *Wit's Pilgrimage: Drama and the Social Impact of Education in Early Modern England*. Aldershot: Ashgate
Hanson, Elizabeth (2011): "Fellow Students: Hamlet, Horatio, and the Early Modern University", *Shakespeare Quarterly* 62.2, 205-229
Sharpe, James A. (1997): *Early Modern England: A Social History 1550-1760*. London: Hodder
Stein, Suzanne H. (2007): "Hamlet in Melanchthon's Wittenberg", *Notes and Queries* 252, 55-57
Stone, Lawrence (1964): "The Educational Revolution in England, 1560-1640", *Past and Present* 28, 41-80

KATRIN RÖDER (POTSDAM)

Intercultural "Traffique" and Political Change in Samuel Daniel's *Philotas* (1596-1604) and Fulke Greville's *Mustapha* (1587-1610?)

1. Introduction

The following analysis seeks to demonstrate that Samuel Daniel's *Philotas* (1596-1604) and Fulke Greville's *Mustapha* (1587-1610?) discuss notions of political change and of resistance against tyranny in connection not only with the subject of intercultural contact, but also with conceptions of cultural alterity. It places the tragedies of Daniel and Greville in the context of political debates which proved central for historical developments in *England* during the seventeenth century.

Philotas and *Mustapha* follow the tradition of French Senecan drama as exemplified by the works of Robert Garnier, whose tragedy *Marc-Antoine* (1578) was translated and adapted by Mary Sidney (*The Tragedie of Antonie* 1590/1592).[1] Daniel's and Greville's tragedies share many features that are typical of the French Senecan drama in the tradition of Robert Garnier: They abstain from depictions of on-stage actions and from cases of providential intervention[2]; they are entirely made up of long speeches; they put their focus on declamatory presentation; and they make use of the devices of choruses and of the Nuntius (Kastner and Charlton 1921, xx). It is important to note that the focus on *oratio* in these tragedies does not exclude the possibility of performance, let alone of performative readings. The staging of Daniel's *Philotas* (1605) is a case in point. Greville's *Mustapha* was printed in 1609 but there is no evidence that it was ever performed.

Another important aspect of the Senecan tragedies which were influenced by Robert Garnier's and Mary Sidney's dramatic works is their discussion of philosophies of sovereignty and of the subjects of kingship and tyranny. They negotiate Eastern and Western philosophies of sovereignty as well as Eastern and Western practices of government and discuss the consequences of their encounter in the context of imperial expansion.

---

[1] On Mary Sidney and her literary influence see Lamb (1981). The story of Antony and Cleopatra, which is part of Plutarch's *Lives of the Noble Greeks and Romans*, was a central subject of several tragedies, i.e. of Daniel's *The Tragedy of Cleopatra* (published in 1594) and of Greville's tragedy *Antony and Cleopatra*, which was in existence at the time of the Essex rising in February 1601, before its author destroyed it because of its topicality (Greville 1986, 93). The story of Antony and Cleopatra, with its focus on the political consequences of the intercultural contact between East and West, constitutes a thematic link between Mary Sidney's, Daniel's, and Greville's dramatic works and Shakespeare's famous tragedy *Antony and Cleopatra* (1606-1608).

[2] Greville emphasises that the purpose of his tragedies is not "to point out God's revenging aspect upon every particular sin, to the despair or confusion of mortality" (Greville 1986, 133.7-8).

2. Samuel Daniel, *Philotas* (1596-1604)

Daniel's tragedy was written between 1596 and 1604 and performed in 1605 by the Children of the Queen's Revels. Criticism has connected *Philotas* and *Mustapha* chronologically and thematically with the Essex rising, but the political significance of both tragedies goes far beyond this historical event (see Michel 1949, 36-94; Rebholz 1971, 101-103).

Philotas is set in the classical period, in Macedonia during the rule of Alexander the Great and his conquest of the Persian Empire (around 334 BC), whereas Greville's *Mustapha* is set in the Ottoman Empire during the rule of Suleiman the Magnificent. Daniel's tragedy depicts the fate of Philotas, Alexander's talented officer. Although Philotas is highly estimated among the Greeks, he is also accused of pride and prodigality. When he fails to inform Alexander of a conspiracy that was revealed to him, Alexander accuses him of being part of the conspiracy. Philotas obtains the King's pardon but is arraigned for the same crime shortly afterwards. He is tortured, is said to have confessed his guilt, and is then executed.

The subject of imperial conquest is central to both *Philotas* and *Mustapha*. Both tragedies discuss the possible effects of imperial expansion on the practice of government. In Daniel's tragedy, characters and chorus speakers state that Alexander displays traces of a theocratic ruler. In both *Philotas* and *Mustapha*, the Eastern theocratic state (that is the Persian Empire and the Ottoman Empire, respectively) is shown to be distinct from Western monarchies. However, the two tragedies also show that both Eastern and Western rulers abuse their power by neglecting the common good and by using laws only to serve their "private ends" (Daniel 1949, 5.1799-1800).[3]

Philotas covers several alleged cases of political transgression: Alexander the Great's act of "drawing a Pedigree from Heaven", which is said to have turned "feeble Maiestie" (Daniel 1949, 1.1.70) into an idol as well as Dymnus's[4] and Philotas's alleged acts of conspiracy. Daniel's tragedy not only discusses Philotas's ambitions but also the "engin closely laid / Against his grace and greatnesse with the King" (*ibid.*, 1.427-428), that is, the techniques through which he is turned into a traitor by his rivals (Alexander's counsellors) and eventually by Alexander himself. The tragedy's topicality became evident when Daniel had to answer questions before the Privy Council in 1605. His "Apology" appended to the text suggests that it was above all the play's alleged references to the Essex affair which were central subjects of the inquiry.

In his dialogue with Chalisthenes at the beginning of the tragedy, Philotas complains about Alexander's style of government, which produces idols of authority:

> I cannot plaster and disguise m'affaires
> In other colours then my heart doth lay.
> Nor can I patiently endure this fond
> And strange proceeding of authoritie;

---

[3] All quotations from *Philotas* follow Michael Laurence's edition. In *Philotas*, Daniel uses the title "sacred Maiesty" (Daniel 1949, 2.549) for Alexander the Great, but the title was also used to address rulers like James I who held their power by the Grace of God, e. g. in the "Epistle Dedicatory" to the authorized Version of the *King James Bible* (1611).

[4] Dymnus appears on stage only as a corpse (4.2), his confession of guilt is reported. He is said to have committed suicide (see Daniel 1949, 820-821).

> That hath ingrost up all into their hand
> By idolizing feeble Maiestie,
> And impiously doe labour all they can
> To make the King forget he is a man,
> Whilest they divide the spoyles, and pray of power,
> And none at all respect the publicke good [...]. (Daniel 1949, 1.65-74)

In this passage, Philotas presents himself as a champion of political virtues. He criticises the King's neglect of the "publicke good", and he accuses Alexander's sycophants of supporting this abuse of power as well as of promoting the transformation of kings into idols. This imperial cult is a central point of political critique in *Philotas*, which it shares with contemporary tragedies such as Ben Jonson's *Sejanus His Fall* (1605) and Sir William Alexander's *Darius* (1604?). In *Philotas*, both Alexander and Philotas are accused of having betrayed their cultural origins: The Persian chorus speaker argues that Alexander's practice of government resembles that of a Persian king (*ibid.*, 5.1767-1863) whereas Alexander maintains that Philotas "disdaines" his native tongue through his use of "the Persian language" in the trial[5], thereby slighting the Macedonian judges (*ibid.*, 4.2.1372-1380).

Alexander leaves the trial and lets his councillors carry out the inquiry. The Persian chorus speaker interprets this gesture as a sign that Alexander rules like a Persian god-king because he disdains to preside over the trial as superior judge (see *ibid.*, 5.1805-1814). Philotas speaks Persian when he criticises Alexander's practice of government in the ruler's absence, and he uses the Persian tongue to make himself understood by the Persians who attend the trial and to invoke the classical tradition of *parrhesia*, a rhetorical device that comprises not only freedom of speech but also the obligation to speak truly and boldly in defence of the common good, even at personal risk (see Daniel 1949, 4.2.1577-1584; Foucault 2001, 11-19).

Some passages later, Philotas, faced with the court's prejudgment, attempts to downplay his critique of Alexander's title "the sonne of *Iove*", and uses this title to address Alexander at the end of the trial (*ibid.*, 4.2.1739). Although Philotas tries to reduce his criticism to a passionate use of "words unkinde" (*ibid.*, 4.2.1588-1610), Craterus (one of the judges) regards Philotas's speech as "the tinder of sedition" (*ibid.*, 4.2.1615).

The Chorus in Act 5 consists of a dialogue between a Graecian and a Persian speaker. It compares the political traditions of both cultures and comes to the conclusion that Alexander's conquest of Persia has induced a subversion of the Greek tradition of "free governments" (*ibid.*, 5.1769; see also 1767-1782, 1797-1816). According to the Graecian chorus speaker, the growing expansion of Alexander's empire and the "base adorings" (*ibid.*, 5.1819) of the Persian subjects (slaves in their majority) have provoked changes in his style of government (see *ibid.*, 5.1826). Alexander's "gaine" (*ibid.*, 5.1820-1825) of the Persian Empire has led to a loss of political freedom among his Greek subjects (*ibid.*, 5.1819). From the perspective of the Graecian chorus, imperial expansion and tyranny are closely connected (see *ibid.*, 5.1819-1863). At the end of the dialogue, the Persian chorus speaker comments on Alexander's adoption of Persian practices of power, mentioning the "Persian tricke" through which he has Philotas's father killed as well as the hasty "publike triall" of Philotas, which resembles a mock trial and "makes / No doubtfull noise, but buries clamor quick" (*ibid.*, 5.2.1952-1955).

---

5   See 4.2.1374. Daniel's text, however, remains monolingual, that is, English.

In response, the Graecian chorus speaker argues that "now *Persia* hath no cause to rue, / For you have us undone, who undid you" (*ibid.*, 5.2.1956-1957).

Daniel's tragedy is ambiguous with regard to Philotas's guilt: Whereas we are directly confronted with Alexander's problematic behaviour during Philotas's trial, the latter's guilt appears less obvious. The audience may wonder whether or not they can trust the Nuntius's report of Philotas's confession which is said to have "marre[d] all his act of life and glories past" (*ibid.*, 5.2.2017). As Philotas's alleged confession is not shown on stage but reported by the Nuntius (*ibid.*, 5.2.2049-2085), the play remains ambiguous with regard to the question of whether Philotas criticises Alexander's government in order to argue for a free style of government and the common good or whether he selfishly seeks to usurp Alexander's throne. In the second case, Philotas is a traitor not only because he wants to overthrow the ruling monarch but also because he betrays central notions of political liberty.

Daniel's tragedy is also ambiguous in its evaluation of the results of intercultural contact: On the one hand, it suggests that this contact has transformed a free government into a tyrannical one that relies on servile flattery (see *ibid.*, 5.1826). On the other hand, the tragedy shows that intercultural contact does not necessarily extinguish opposition and resistance to tyranny: The Graecian and Persian chorus speakers in Act 5 are cases in point, as is Philotas himself, who utters his impressive critique of Alexander's government in the "Persian language" before downplaying the force and relevance of his criticism in his attempt to save his life (*ibid.*, 4.2.1374).

3. Fulke Greville, *Mustapha* (1587-1610?)

Greville's *Mustapha* depicts a historical event in the rule of Sultan Suleiman the Magnificent, namely his execution of Mustapha (his son and successor) at the instigation of his wife Roxolana. Greville's tragedy shows how Mustapha's and Solyman's guards rise against the Sultan after Mustapha's death. The late versions of the tragedy[6] discuss the Sultan's practices of government in connection with intercultural contact between Ottomans and Christians, which developed in the course of the imperial expansion of the Ottoman Empire and its relations with the Christian world. In these late versions of Greville's *Mustapha*, the speakers of Chorus Secundus see the "traffique" between Christianity and the Ottoman Empire as an important cause for the development of tyrannical practices in the Ottoman government (Greville 2008, 1: Chorus Secundus 85), but they also suggest that this development generates concepts of political opposition, especially notions of resistance against tyranny.

Recent criticism describes *Mustapha* as an Early Modern text that portrays Muslims in a differentiated way and that expresses both religious and political tolerance in its depiction of the Ottoman Empire and its government (see Burton 2005, 193). Greville's nuanced portrayal of Muslims may in part be explained by his access to a great number of diverse texts about the Islamic world, including theological and historical sources as well as government documents. There is considerable evidence about English political, military and mercantile connections with the Ottoman Empire in the sixteenth and early seventeenth centuries: Elizabeth cultivated an alliance with the Otto-

---

6   On the problem of a dating of the different text versions see Wilkes 2008, 1: 182-183 and 1:411-414.

mans after her excommunication in 1570; she achieved the privilege of free passage for English ships in Ottoman waters after 1580; and she started a relationship with the Ottoman Empire that incorporated military cooperation (see Dimmock 2006, 4-5). Richard Hakluyt published the correspondence between Elizabeth I and Murad III[7] (the grandson of Suleiman the Magnificent) under the title *Principall Navigations, Voiages and Discoveries of the English Nation* in 1589, as did Thomas Nelson in *The Blessed State of England* in 1591 (see Matar 1999, 123-24).[8] Although James I changed British policy by turning against the Ottoman Empire, Greville's *Mustapha* (published in 1609) retained its differentiated representation of the Ottomans.[9] In choosing a story from recent Ottoman history, a story about the events leading to and resulting from Suleiman the Magnificent's murder of his son and designated successor Prince Mustapha in 1553, Greville selected a subject that was distant enough from English domestic policy and, at the same time, close enough to raise questions at the heart of contemporary debates about Eastern and Western philosophies of sovereignty and practices of government.

Greville's *Mustapha* represents the Ottoman Empire as an expanding superpower and as an intercultural space formed through regular interaction with Christian nations, above all in the context of the Ottoman conquest of Christian territory. The speakers of Chorus Secundus (defined as "Mahometan Preists", see Greville 2008, 1: 245)[10] reflect on the history of this conquest of territory that had been and partly remained populated by Catholics and members of the Greek Orthodox Church (Greville 2008, 1: Chorus Secundus, 23-36).[11] The religious, political, and cultural borders negotiated in *Mustapha* are permeable and fluid. *Mustapha* contains characters and chorus speakers who are defined by both cultural and social mobility, such as the speakers of Chorus Quartus (introduced as "Converts to Mahometisme", see Greville 2008, 1: 279) and Achmat, Solyman's Pasha, who was selected from the bottom of the social hierarchy and raised to its top – to the "seconde slipperie place of honors steepe" – on the basis of his merit and obedience (*ibid.*, 2.1.27). Although Greville is not very specific about the cultural mobility of his Muslim characters, the sources he used contain information about the Christian origin of many members of the Ottoman military and administrative leadership. Knolles's *Generall Historie* and Georgijević's *The Ofspring of the House of Ottomanno* acknowledge the fact that the Ottoman Empire tolerated Christian subjects, and both texts refer to the Ottoman practice of blood tax.[12] Chorus

---

7   On Queen Elizabeth's letter to Mustafa Beg from October 25, 1579 see Skilliter (1977, 73-75).
8   Elizabeth's friendly relations with parts of the Islamic world and her acknowledgment of Islam's rejection of idolatry in her letters may have impressed Greville, whose texts, as Freya Sierhuis has demonstrated, express a strong Calvinist reaction against idolatry (Sierhuis 2011, 627; see also Schmuck 2010, 551).
9   Tricomi sees the later versions of *Mustapha* as a "profound indictment of Jacobean political life" (Tricomi 1989, 67).
10 The terms "Preists" and "Preisthode" used by Greville are misnomers because Islam has no priesthood.
11 All references to *Mustapha* are to the later versions of the tragedy, see Wilkes (2008, 1).
12 On contemporary discussions of *devşirme* and the promotion of former Christians to political and military offices see Knolles (1603, 645-655) and the entries on "Visier Bassae" and on "Of the unmerciful tributes extracted at the Christians handes" in Georgijević (1569?, sig. Bviii, Hix-Iiii).

Secundus in *Mustapha* also alludes to this practice: "So that we suffer their fonde zeale to pray, / That it may well our Conqueringe armies pay" (*ibid.*, 165-166).

The speakers of Chorus Secundus argue that the Ottoman Empire was a theocracy before its sultans' practices of government became tyrannical (see *ibid.*, 13-14, 37-48). In the following passages, the speakers of Chorus Secundus relate these changes in their government to the intercultural "traffique" with Christianity:

> Yet by our traffique with this dreaminge Nation,
> Their Conquer'd vice hath stayn'd our Conqueringe State,
> And brought thinne Cobwebbes into reputation
> Of tender subtilitie, whose stepmother fate
>   So inlayes courage with ill shaddowinge feare,
>   As makes it much more hard to doe, then beare.
>
> And as in Circles, who breakes anie parte,
> That perfect forme doth utterlie confound:
> Or as amongst the feigned lines of arte,
> Our onely right is, all else crooked found:
>   So from our *Prophets* sawes when *Sultans* stray,
>   In humane witte Power findes perplexed way.
>
> Hence, though we make no Idolles, yet we fashion
> God, as if from Powers Throne he tooke his beinge;
> Our *Alchoran* as warrant unto passion;
> Monarches in all lawes but their owne will seeinge.
>   He whom God chooseth out of doubt doth well:
>   What they that choose their God doe; who can tell?
>
> (Greville 2008, 1: Chorus Secundus 85-102)

The Mahometan "Preists" argue in accordance with William Tyndale's, William Rainolds's, and Queen Elizabeth's descriptions of Islam that they are not guilty of making "Idolls" of worldly power; at the same time they reveal that they have created a secular religion that serves as a political expedient and thus supports blasphemous and tyrannical practices of government (see Tyndale 1940, 184; Dimmock 2004, 119; Raynolds 1597, 123-124; Skilliter 1977, 73-75).

According to the speakers of Chorus Secundus, the "thinne Cobwebbes [...] Of tender subtilitie" and "ill-shaddowinge feare" that were produced in the Ottomans' "traffique" with Christians have not only caused in Solyman "that feare, / Which torrid zones of Tyrannie must beare" (Greville 2008, 177-178), but they have also inspired Mustapha to enact "misplac'd duties" towards Solyman and have "helpe[d] power to disfashion" (*ibid.*, 191-192). Greville's tragedy suggests that the influence of Christian culture on the Ottomans resulted mainly from the conquest of formerly Christian territory, but the influence also seems to be related to trade ("traffique") and above all to an exchange of ideas. Chorus Secundus emphasizes that the Christian influence led to a tyrannical practice of government that is exemplified by Solyman's "fearfull" reaction to Mustapha's greatness (*ibid.*, 103-108). The contention that the crisis in the Ottoman Empire (around 1553) was in part caused by the influence of Christian political culture and religion (which is explicit only in the late versions of the play) is not based on historical facts; instead, it exemplifies Greville's talent for conjecture as well as a bit of Christian wishful thinking, which might be related to the Jacobean policy towards the Ottoman Empire.

Greville's Chorus Secundus elaborates on the differences between Ottomans and Christians and argues that the Christians reward the "wealthy" whereas the Ottomans "grace the active". The Ottomans are associated with "doing" and "force", their empire is defined as a "Conqueringe State". The Christians, by contrast, are associated with "rest", that is, with weakness and tenderness as well as with "lacke of power", "modesty" and "Conquer'd vice" (Greville 2008, 1: Chorus Secundus 81-84, 123-168). Although Richard Knolles does not use the word "active" in his description of the Ottomans in the "Preface to the Reader" that is part of his *Generall Historie of the Turkes* (1603), he uses the related term "vigilancie" (Knolles 1603, sig. Av) in his description of the martial nature of the Ottomans.

In his reading of *Mustapha*, Jonathan Burton has argued that the chorus's criticism of a government that uses laws only to serve the sovereign's will and through which the people's rights are suppressed is levelled at the Islamic theocratic state (Burton 2005, 190-191). However, the criticism is so general that it seems to be directed against Solyman's tyranny as well as at tyrannical governments in general, and it resembles the comparison between Greek and Persian styles of government in the Chorus of Act 5 in Daniel's *Philotas* (Tricomi 1989, 66). At the end of their comparison of Christian and Ottoman practices of power, the speakers of Chorus Secundus conclude: "*Both* being trappes alike us'd, to entice / The weake, and humble into prejudice" (Greville 2008, 1: Chorus Secundus, 131-150, my emphasis).

In the following quotation, the speakers of Chorus Secundus reflect on the changes in the Ottoman government that resulted from the intercultural contact between the Ottoman Empire and Christianity:

> Nay hence mankinde, by craftie power opprest,
> Where it hath given parte, still gives the rest;
> And thinking Thrones in all their practyse true
> Dare not of their owne Creatures aske their due
> But rather, like milde earth with weedes o'ergrowne,
> Yeldes to be plough'd, manur'd, and overthrowne.
> Lastlie, thus Scepters fall with their owne weight,
> When climbinge Power, once risen to her height,
> Descends to make distinction in her lust,
> Which grauntes that absolute may be unjust;
> And so subjectes to censure what should raigne;
> Steppes to bring Power to People backe againe.
> Whence I conclude: Mankinde is both the forme,
> And matter, wherewith Tyrannies transforme.
> For Power can neither see, worcke, or devise,
> Without the Peoples handes, hartes, witte, and eyes:
> So that were man not by himselfe opprest,
> Kinges would not, Tyrants could not, make him beast.
>
> (Greville 2008, 1: Chorus Secundus 191-210)

According to the chorus speakers, the intercultural contact between Ottomans and Christians has not only led to a blasphemous and tyrannical government but has also generated insights into the contingency of the forms of government and of the social and political hierarchy in the Empire.

In the penultimate scene of *Mustapha*, Achmat faces the revolt against his sovereign that is carried out by Mustapha's "Campe" and Solyman's "guarde" after Mustapha's death (see Greville 2008, 1: 5.3.18, 20). In pondering what might be the adequate reaction to the people's revolt, Achmat negotiates notions of violence (connected with "force" and martial action, see *ibid.*, 5.3.116) and non-violence (implying rhetorical strategies of "counsayle" and appeasement, see *ibid.*, 5.3.117). In contrast to Chorus Secundus, these notions are attributed neither to Christianity nor to Islam or the Ottoman Empire (see *ibid.*, 5.3.65-120). Achmat momentarily considers supporting the revolting guards and then reflects on the strategies which could help him to prevent them from deposing Solyman, yet Greville suspends any representation of Achmat's actions as well as any form of denouement in his tragedy. Greville's portrayal of Solyman's Pascha contradicts Richard Knolles's description of the Ottomans as being either militant or servile (Knolles 1603, sig. Av): Achmat decides to repress violence, yet he is not guilty of servile, uncritical obedience.[13]

In his soliloquy, Achmat first supports the revolt on the basis of a classical theory of natural law that is part of the justification of active resistance expressed in the Huguenot treatise *Vindiciae contra tyrannos* (see 1579, 19, 22-24, 46-48, 116-119). His line of argumentation is in accordance with his earlier position[14] that the monarch's power resides in the people and their voluntary submission, a position that closely resembles Étienne de la Boétie's notion of voluntary servitude as expressed in his *Discourse of Voluntary Servitude* (1552?). In the following quotation from the second scene of Act 5, Achmat comments on the people's voluntary submission to kings as well as on their right to depose tyrants:

> Tyrantes! Why swell you thus against your makers?
> Is rays'd equalitie so soone growne wilde?
> Dare you deprive your People of succession,
> Which Thrones, and Sceptres, on their freedoms build?
> Have feare, or love, in Greatnesse no impression?
> Since People, who did rayse you to the Crowne,
> Are ladders standinge still to let you downe.
>
> (Greville 2008, 1: 5.2.1-7)

In his soliloquy from the penultimate scene of the tragedy, Achmat expresses a position of appeasement based on the notion of voluntary servitude because he abhors the "violence" of the people's "mutenie" as well as the irrationality and disorder of a people's government (*ibid.*, 5.2.104, 119). David Norbrook[15] has commented on the relevance of natural law and contract theory in Achmat's soliloquy,[16] but he maintains that Greville's flirt with contract theory ends in "self-protective stutter" and a repression of dissident positions (Norbrook 1989, 159, 171-173). However, Achmat's decision to

---

13   It is important to emphasize that Greville's tragedy includes central characters who exemplify contemporary stereotypes of cruel and lascivious Muslims: Sultan Solyman and his seditious wife Rossa are represented as slaves of their passions and vices (of fear, cruelty, and lust in Solyman's case and of lust, cruelty, and ambition in Rossa's case). However, Achmat, Mustapha, Camena, and Zanger are characters in the tragedy who contradict the stereotypes of militant or servile Muslims that are evoked in the "Preface to the Reader" of Knolles's *Generall historie of the Turkes*.
14   See Greville 2008, 2.1.75-78. For a similar position see *Vindiciae* 1648, 46-48.
15   Jonathan Dollimore has also made similar observations (see Dollimore 1989, 121-124, 133).
16   In the earlier versions of Achmat's soliloquy, Greville even uses the phrase "dutyes to Kinges they be conditionall / When they from god, then wee from them may fall" (Greville 2008, 2: 5.2.185-186).

save Solyman's throne neither retracts his former defence of contract theory nor his justification of resistance against tyranny. According to Achmat's point of view, the people should resist injustice and tyranny, but they must not rule.

Greville's dramatic representation of a political event in Ottoman history enables him to discuss notions of resistance against tyranny which would have provoked severe criticism in a tragedy with a Christian setting. Nevertheless, the most volatile passages in *Mustapha* seem to have caused irritation, and they are absent from the 1609 print version of the tragedy.[17] In the historical context of Greville's depiction of a political crisis in the Ottoman Empire, the disintegration of the empire of the 'Antichrist' might be understood as a piece of evidence of the workings of Christian providence. Although some characters, above all Rossa (see Greville 2008, 1: 5.4.113-126), and some choruses (see *ibid.*, Chorus Quartus 107-124 and Chorus Tertius 121-150) allude to a denouement that implies the deposition of Solyman and the disintegration of his empire, the tragedy does not represent any of these conflict solutions and thereby resists closure. In contrast to contemporary justifications of active resistance against tyranny, as for example in the *Vindiciae contra tyrannos* (1579), and also in contrast to Knolles's *Generall historie of the Turkes*, Greville's tragedy remains ambiguous about the notion of a divine retribution of tyranny.

Richard Knolles's *Generall historie of the Turkes* and Nicholas Moffan's version of the story of Suleiman the Magnificent's act of filicide[18] contain a historical moment of *parrhesia* or fearless speech, in which the sultan, encircled by the enraged Janissaries, has to answer their questions and even has to give in to their demands concerning the choice of pashas and viziers (see Knolles 1603, 764-765; Painter 1890, 413-414). A short time later, however, he revokes these concessions and reverts to his old style of government. Although Greville's tragedy does not contain this historical moment of *parrhesia*, it nevertheless seems to point to it because it affirms the people's right to "question" and to challenge the power of tyrants (Greville 2008, 1: 5.2.92).

4. Conclusion

By reflecting on the political consequences of the intercultural "traffique" between East and West, Daniel's and Greville's tragedies allow insights into the complex practices of signification which generate notions of cultural identity, but also notions of sovereignty and of resistance against tyranny. Both tragedies give similar explanations for the changes in the government of the expanding empires they depict (although *Philotas* discusses the conquest of the East through the West and *Mustapha* the conquest of the West through the East). In *Philotas*, the conquest of Persian territory, that is, the expansion of the empire in itself, was an important cause for the changes in Alexander's government. In addition, the Graecian and Persian chorus speakers in *Philotas* argue that the changes result from the influence of Persian theocracy. In a

---

17 In the 1609 quarto version of *Mustapha*, which was printed for Nathaniel Butter, Achmat's soliloquy in Act 5 with its defence of the people's rights to resist tyrants is missing. In his edition of the early text versions, G. A. Wilkes writes that "the text is broken off and subscribed *Desunt pauca*" (Wilkes 2008, 2: 462).

18 Nicholas Moffan's version of the story was translated by Hugh Gough and published as a part of Bartolomej Georgijević's *The ofspring of the house of Ottomanno* as well as in William Painter's *The Second Tome of the Palace of Pleasure* (1575).

similar way, the speakers of Chorus Secundus in *Mustapha* explain the change in the Ottoman government with the enormous expansion of the empire as well as with the cruelties and vices this expansion entailed (see Greville 2008, Chorus Secundus, ll. 49-78). The speakers of Chorus Secundus also suggest that this change results from the intercultural contact between Ottomans and Christians. *Philotas* shows that the political developments connected with the conquest of Persian territory have not erased notions of resistance against tyranny, and the tragedy ends with the expression of the fear of "fresh treacheries" that might follow on Philotas's execution (Daniel 1949, 5.2.2130). Greville's *Mustapha* suggests that the intercultural contact between Ottomans and Christians has not only led to a blasphemous and tyrannical Ottoman government but has also generated insights into the contingency of the forms of government and of the social and political hierarchy in the empire.

Daniel's and Greville's tragedies are closely related to more popular contemporary dramatic texts about the subjects of tyranny, conspiracy and resistance against tyranny, for example to Jonson's *Sejanus* and Shakespeare's *Julius Caesar*. In addition, both tragedies are related to contemporary plays about the East and the Islamic world[19], which project differentiated, fluid, and ambiguous notions of intercultural contact as well as of cultural and political alterity[20] or change.

References

Primary Sources

Daniel, Samuel (1949): *The Tragedy of Philotas*. Michael Laurence (ed.). New Haven, CT: Yale University Press

Georgijević, Bartolomej (1569?): *The Ofspring of the House of Ottomanno*. Trans. Hugh Gough. London: printed by Thomas Marshe

Greville, Fulke (1986): "A Dedication to Sir Philip Sidney", in: Gouws, John (ed.): *The Prose Works of Fulke Greville*. Oxford: Clarendon

--- (2008): "Mustapha", in: Wilkes, G. A. (ed.): *The Complete Poems and Plays of Fulke Greville, Lord Brooke (1554-1628) in Two Volumes*. Lewiston/Queenston/Lampeter: Edwin Mellen

Hakluyt, Richard (1927): *The Principal Navigations, Voyages, Traffiques and Discoveries of the English Nation. The Original Writings and Correspondence of the Two Richard Hakluyts, Vol. IV*. Intro. E. G. R. Taylor. London: Dent

Knolles, Richard (1603): *The Generall Historie of the Turkes*. London: printed by Adam Islip

---

19 On the intercultural contact between East and West and its political consequences see also Shakespeare's *Antony and Cleopatra*. The Islamic world and Muslims are represented in Shakespeare's *Othello*, in Thomas Heywood's *The Fair Maid of the West, Part I and II* (1600/1601 and 1625-1625-1630), in Thomas Dekker's *Lust's Dominion* (1600), William Percy's *Mahomet and His Heaven* (1601), John Mason's *The Turk* (1609), Robert Daborne's *A Christian Turn'd Turk* (1612), and Thomas Goffe's *The Raging Turk, or Bazazet II* (1613-18) and *The Courageous Turk, or Amurath I* (1618).

20 Linda McJannet, Patricia Parker, Jonathan Burton, and Ania Loomba have shown that the images of Muslims represented in Early Modern English comedies and tragedies about the Islamic world were "far more nuanced, fluid, and ambivalent than previously reported" and more fluid and ambiguous than in later Orientalist discourse; see Parker (2002), McJannet (2009, 186) and Loomba (1999).

La Boétie, Étienne de (1997): *Discours de la servitude volontaire ou le Contr'un. The Politics of Obedience: The Discourse of Voluntary Servitude*. Trans. Harry Kurz, intr. Murray Rothbard. Montréal/New York/London: Black Rose Books
Nelson, Thomas (1591): *The Blessed State of England [...]*. Printed for William Wright
Painter, William (1890): *The Palace of Pleasure, Volume 3*. Ed. Joseph Jacobs. London: David Nutt
Rainolds, William (1597): *Calvino-Turcismus*. Ed. William Gifford. Antverpiae: Bellerus
Vindiciae contra Tyrannos. A Defence of Liberty against Tyrants (1648): London: Matthew Simmons, Robert Ibbitson

Secondary Sources

Burton, Jonathan (2005): *Traffic and Turning. Islam and English Drama, 1579-1624*. Newark: University of Delaware Press
Carroll, Robert; Prickett, Stephen (eds.; 1997): *The Bible: Authorized King James Version*. Oxford: Oxford University Press
Dimmock, Matthew (2004): "'Machomat Dyd Before as Luther Doth Nowe': Islam, the Ottomans and the English Reformation", *Reformation* 9, 99-130
--- (2006): "Introduction", in: Dimmock, Matthew (ed.): *William Percy's "Mahomet and His Heaven": A Critical Edition*. Aldershot: Ashgate, 1-58
Dollimore, Jonathan (1989): *Radical Tragedy: Religion, Ideology and Power in the Dramas of Shakespeare and his Contemporaries*. Brighton: Harvester
Foucault, Michel (2001): *Fearless Speech*. Ed. Joseph Pearson. Los Angeles: Semiotext(e)
Kastner, E.; Carlton, H. B. (1921): "Introduction", in: Kastner, E.; Charlton, H. B. (eds.): *The Poetical Works of Sir William Alexander*. Manchester: Longmans, Green & Co
Lamb, Mary Ellen (1981): "The Myth of the Countess of Pembroke: The Dramatic Circle", *The Yearbook of English Studies* 1, 194-202
Loomba, Ania (1999): "Delicious Traffic: Alterity and Exchange on Early Modern Stages", *Shakespeare Survey* 52, 201-214
Matar, Nabil (1999): *Turks, Moors and Englishmen in the Age of Discovery*. New York: Columbia University Press
McJannet, Linda (2009): "Islam and English Drama: A Critical History", *Early Theatre* 12.2, 183-193
Michel, Laurence (1949): "Introduction", *The Tragedy of Philotas by Samuel Daniel*. New Haven, CT: Yale University Press, 3-94
Norbrook, David (1984): *Poetry and Politics in the English Renaissance*. London: Routledge & Paul.
Parker, Patricia (2002): "Preposterous Conversions: Turning Turk, and Its 'Pauline' Rerighting", *Journal for Early Modern Cultural Studies* 2.1, 1-34
Rebholz, Ronald (1971): *The Life of Fulke Greville*. Oxford: Clarendon
Schmuck, Stephan (2010): "England's Experiences of Islam", in: Hattaway, Michael (ed.): *A New Companion to English Renaissance Literature and Culture*, 2 vols. Oxford: Wiley-Blackwell, 1: 543-555
Sierhuis, Freya (2011): "The Idol of the Heart: Liberty, Tyranny, and Idolatry in the Work of Fulke Greville", *Modern Language Review* 106.3, 625-646
Skilliter, Susan (1977): *William Harborne and the Trade with Turkey, 1578-1582*. London: Oxford University Press
Tricomi, Albert H. (1989): *Anticourt Drama in England 1603-1642*. Charlottesville: University Press of Virginia
Tyndale, William (1940): *An Answer to Sir Thomas More's Dialogue*. Ed. Henry Walter. Cambridge: Cambridge University Press
Wilkes, G. A. (ed.; 2008): *The Complete Poems and Plays of Fulke Greville, Lord Brooke (1554-1628), in Two Volumes*. Lewiston/Queenston/Lampeter: Edwin Mellen

FELIX C. H. SPRANG (HAMBURG)

Neither Shakespeare Nor the Gilded Monuments: Rethinking the Dramatic Impact of Jacobean and Caroline Civic Pageants

A sum of £ 1,300 was spent on the Lord Mayor's Show in 1613, arguably the prime dramatic event of that year.[1] When we think of seventeenth-century drama we still tend to ignore the annual civic pageants that were hugely popular with Londoners, who lined the streets and the Thames to catch glimpses of the spectacle. It is estimated that in the early 1600s about 20,000 Londoners and some visitors viewed the annual procession, meaning roughly one in every ten inhabitants witnessed the festivities. A glimpse of the crowd and the festive spirit that prevailed on the day of the Show is visible on the title page of *The Excellent and Renowned History of the Famous Sir Richard Whittington, Three Times Lord Mayor of the Honourable City of London*, which depicts the crowd waving fireworks and throwing hats.[2] Some of the excitement that undoubtedly came with Early Modern pageants, both civic and royal, was felt during the procession on the occasion of the Queen's Diamond Jubilee in June 2012. It is thus no coincidence that the Lord Mayor's Show, still performed every year in November, has increasingly been marketed as a London event.[3] It thus comes as a surprise that both urban area studies and performance studies have marginalised this dramatic form.[4] However, as Richard Dutton has pointed out,

> to ignore the civic pageants of the Tudor and Stuart period is to ignore the one form of drama which we know must have been familiar to all the citizens of London, and thus an important key to our understanding of those times and of the place of dramatic spectacle in Early Modern negotiations of national, civic and personal identity. (Dutton 1995, 7)

Even if the first pageant was performed as early as 1535, civic pageants were decisively shaped in the Jacobean and Caroline period. From 1585 onwards acclaimed dramatists were asked to oversee the entertainment, among them George Peele, Thomas Dekker, Anthony Munday, Thomas Heywood, and Thomas Middleton. Shakespeare's contemporaries, who, as playwrights, were at the heart of the playhouses in the second and third decade of the seventeenth century, all contributed to these entertainments. Shakespeare, curiously enough, was either never asked by any of the Livery Companies to devise a pageant or he may have declined to do so. Be that as it may, Shakespeare scholarship is undoubtedly to blame for the continued marginalisation of pageants as a dramatic form. As Tracey Hill has pointed out, "it is very likely that

---

1   The social context and the history of the Lord Mayor's Show have been extensively discussed by David M. Bergeron (1971, 1986), Richard Dutton (1995), and Frederick W. Fairholt (1843, 1844).
2   For a detailed discussion of the title page see Hill 2004, 130-131.
3   See www.lordmayorsshow.org.
4   There are some laudable exceptions, for example Anne Lancashire, who has pointed out that "the more we know [about pre-Elizabethan London civic theatre], the more we realize the complexities of the civic theatrical past in London, and how much we do not know about it" (Lancashire 2002, 184).

Shakespeare's absence from the civic scene is one of the main reasons why the Shows [...] have so often been overlooked" (Hill 2004, 21).[5]

I think that speculating why Shakespeare was never actively involved in this hugely popular dramatic form serves little purpose. At the same time, raising our awareness of the aesthetics and the programmatic nature of the Lord Mayor's Show has implications for our understanding of Shakespeare's dramatic art. Furthermore, looking at these pageants can facilitate our understanding of theatrical performance in the Early Modern period more generally. In the following I will focus on issues of staging and character in two of these Shows and argue that the emblematic nature of the Lord Mayor's Show brings dramatic techniques to the fore that are still poorly understood by Shakespeare scholars. In the end I will turn to the last scene from Shakespeare's *The Winter's Tale*. Bearing in mind that this section focuses on 'not Shakespeare' I will not discuss the scene in detail. It will serve as a sounding board for bringing into focus the questions that the performative practice of civic pageants pose with respect to our understanding of Early Modern staging practices and character. By 'character' I do not refer to character studies but the technique of establishing a character on stage, that is, creating a histrionic illusion.[6] However, I should like to stress that looking at pageants can open our eyes to Shakespeare's dramatic art as well, in particular with respect to scenes that verge on the emblematic.

Even though more eyewitness records for the Lord Mayor's Show have survived than for all the plays performed in the Early Modern playhouses together, most of what we can say about performative practices must remain speculative. Before we launch into unchartered territory, however, we should remind ourselves of the nature and aesthetics of the Lord Mayor's Show. Traditionally performed on the 29th of October, the pageant marked the inauguration of the Lord Mayor. He left Guildhall in the morning, made his journey to Westminster to take his oath of office before representatives of the Monarch at midday, and returned to the City for a service and blessings in St. Paul's Cathedral. The ritual thus demonstrated the Lord Mayor's allegiance to both the Crown and the Church while also exhibiting his position as *primus inter pares* in the City of London. The procession, as Hill reminds us, was an "eclectic mixture of extravagantly staged emblematic tableaux, music, dance and speeches, together with disparate crowd-pleasing effects such as fireworks and giants on stilts" (Hill 2004, 1). Planning the Show and overseeing its execution was "a complex and expensive business" (*ibid.*, 53). The guild to which the elected Lord Mayor belonged commissioned the pageant and paid for all the expenses. The Show, a formal act of inauguration, was thus always a display of the Livery Company's splendour and wealth.

While the route of the procession varied over time, the arrangement remained largely the same: The procession passed several stations, usually symbolic locations like the conduits, where it came to a halt. At these stations the Lord Mayor was presented with emblematic tableaux that included speeches and songs, quite often staged with the help

---

5 Hill's magisterial study re-conceptualizes many of the issues discussed in the seminal monographs by David M. Bergeron, who has pointed, for example, at the "interrelationship of street and court entertainments" and stressed the Masque-like qualities of the pageants (Bergeron 1986, 4).

6 For a systematic approach to the technique of establishing characters, albeit with a psychological bias, see Pfister 1988, 160-195.

of devices such as floats or chariots. These devices – comparable to movable pieces of scenery – were crafted by artists and artisans who collaborated to create complicated 'innovations', as they were called by contemporaries. For example, Munday's record of the second emblematic show, presented to the Lord Mayor in 1611 as part of Munday's *Chruso-thriambos: The triumphs of golde*, explains:

> ON a Quadrangle frame, of apt constructure, and answerable strength, we erect a Rocke or Mount of Golde, in such true proportion, as Art can best present it; with clifts, crannies, and passable places, such as may best illustrate the inuention, and expresse the persons therein seated, according to their seuerall Carracter and Office. (Munday 1611, A4)

As the bills for and some drawings of these devices have survived, we have a fair idea of their splendour (see Hill 2004, 118-127). The rock described here supported at least twelve actors, who presented the whole process of mining gold, purifying it, testing the quality of the alloy, and of coining or making jewelry. This is a typical design in that it presents a series of interconnected actions as a sequence of snapshots: Audiences can simultaneously see the miner and the goldsmith at work, even if the invention represents actions and actors that may in reality be divided by space and time.[7]

The actors then dismount the rock and other actors climb the invention: Terra, her eldest daughter Chrusos, gold, and her youngest daughter Argurion, silver, introduce themselves. Then, a show (arguably, a play within a play) is performed in honour of the eldest daughter: Mother and daughters as well as the spectators are presented with the story of king Midas, who turned everything he touched into gold. Contrary to the legend and its account in Ovid, Midas is turned into stone himself in this pageant; he is "metamorphozed into a Stone" (Munday 1611, A4). A speech explains that fragments of that stone are now used by goldsmiths as touch-stones to prove the quality of gold. A piece of Midas-turned-stone is then picked up with one hand by Chrusos, while, with the other hand, holds a scale. While witnessing these events, the audience is told that now Chrusos "represents her owne sacred person in Iustice" (Munday 1611, B1). The audience is thus instructed to accept that the emblematic tableau reflects the truth that fortune results from both wealth and justice, a truth exemplified with the motto *Iusitia Virtutum Regina*. Terra links both daughters fast to her chair with a chain of gold to safeguard them from the "insatiable world", which aims to rob them. Finally, the three are attended by "two beautiful ladies", Antiquity and Memory, who "make discovery of Empeiria, or grave Experience in the Golde-Smith profession" (*ibid.*, B1v). That experience is also evoked by "the imagined Carracter [sic] of learned *Dunstane*", the tenth-century Archbishop of London who "had no little delight in the Art of Gold-Smithery" (*ibid.*, B1v).

The effect created when one tries to narrate the events and the staging is striking: What we have here is a cascade of images, a sequence of emblems or speaking pictures – a sequence that is not a development in the sense of a plot line. Presenting myths, history and the present state of the craft, the invention brings to the fore the peculiar dramatic nature of the Lord Mayor's Show. Historical figures, for example Bishop Dunstane, and mythological characters, like Midas, stand side-by-side, and Munday's textual record of the Show explicitly addresses the cognitive effort to conceptualize the

---

7 Mining for gold, for example, had become a new world-affair by 1611 so that this show also evokes a colonial perspective.

scene. What is most striking in the present context is that spectators are asked to behold the "imagined Carracter of learned *Dunstane*". Imagination, Munday seems to suggest, does not begin when audiences construe absent characters or far-away places – this is not an instance of "Think when we talk of horses, that you see them" (Shakespeare 1995, Prologue 26). Imagination, here, is needed to bring emblematic devices and characters to life, and to endow them with meaning, while they are actually present.

Is it that professional playwrights like Munday or Heywood did not trust their ability to manipulate their audience and to set their audience's imagination working when devising pageants? How is it possible that Middleton the playwright, for example, trusts his pen when creating, in collaboration with Dekker, a character like Moll Cutpurse in *The Roaring Girl* (1611) but not when creating Sir Francis Drake in the Show of 1626, *The Triumphs of Health and Prosperity*? One explanation for the insistence on creating an illusion and the urge to control it in the realm of pageantry is certainly found in the fact that much more is at stake here. If we conceptualize the Lord Mayor's Show as a ritual, imagination has an ontological status that differs markedly from imagination in the playhouse. As Angela Stock has explained with respect to the differences between civic pageantry and plays performed at playhouses, "the fundamental difference between ritual and theatre is precisely that ritual precludes interpretation, whereas theatre depends upon it" (Stock 2004, 136). However, categorizing the civic pageant as a ritual falls short of acknowledging the mixed bag of performative and histrionic elements at play here. The Lord Mayor's Show, as Gervase Rosser, among others, has argued convincingly, is located somewhere between ritual and theatre in that it is an extension of political customs and ceremonies into the realm of drama: "The creative uses of language and imagery in these dramatic occasions show that they were regarded not as occupying a sphere separate from that of political life but, indeed, as the continuation of politics by other means" (Rosser 1996, 17).

However, that "continuation of politics by other means", the blending of ritual and theatre, calls for a particular aesthetic and dramatic form. The complexity and erratic nature of this form means that the emblematic pageants presented in this Show require interpretation in order to function. Explicitly stating who and what are shown may thus be a generic necessity to prevent the crowd from making false assumptions. Eyewitness accounts, for example by the Dutch traveller Abraham Booth, reveal that audiences saw or understood things in a manner that differs markedly from the printed text (see Hill 2004, 122-125). It was undoubtedly necessary to direct spectators' gazes and assist them in their interpretation of what they saw and heard. Characters must be over-determined, and staging must be executed in such a way that the connection between the tableaux is explicit. As a result, characters continuously comment on themselves and the staging business.[8]

In *Chruso-thriambos* the liminal status between ritual and theatre is particularly marked in the tableau performed in front of Baynard's Castle, the Earl of Pembroke's

---

[8] Hill explains that "some writers – Munday in particular – were keen to assist their audiences and readers in comprehending the allegories and emblems the Show used" (Hill 2004, 170), and she discusses the function of a running commentary in the context of the pageants. I would like to suggest that not only the allegories and emblems but also the characters are brought to life in this meta-dramatic fashion.

mansion on the river side of Blackfriars.[9] After disembarking from his barge, the Lord Mayor is greeted by the actor John Lowin[10], who impersonates Leofstane, the first Mayor of London who, as legend has it, was also a goldsmith.[11] In an ensuing dialogue between Time and Leofstane the two elaborate on the "Foure hundred years & three, the L. Maiors sway / Hath held in London" (Munday 1611, B3v). In their journey through time they arrive at the tomb of Nicholas Farringdon, a goldsmith by profession who was elected Lord Mayor four times in the mid-fourteenth century. At this point the dialogue takes the shape of an interlude:

>Time. Arise, arise I say, good Faringdon,
>For in this triumph thou must needs make one.
>
>Time striketh on the Tombe with his Siluer wand,
>and then Faringdon ariseth.
>
>Faringdon. Astonishment and frightfull wonder,
>Shakes and splits my Soule in sunder.
>Cannot Graues containe their dead,
>Where long they haue lien buried;
>But to Triumphs, sports, and showes
>They must be raisde? Alacke, God knowes,
>They count their quiet slumber blest,
>Free from disturbance, and vnrest.
>Time. I know it well good man. Yet looke aboute,
>And recollect thy spirits, free from feare,
>Note what thou seest.
>Faringdon. How? Whence, or where
>May I suppose my selfe? Well I wot,
>(If Faringdon mistake it not)
>That ancient famous Cathedrall,
>Hight the Church of blessed Paule.
>And that this Warde witnesse can,
>Once thereof I was Alderman,
>And gaue it mine owne proper name.
>I built these Gates, the very same.
>But when I note this goodly traine,
>(Yclad in Scarlet) it should sayen
>(And soothlie too) that these are they:
>Who watch for London night and day,
>Graue Magistrates; Of which faire band,
>(When second Edward swayed this Land;)

---

9 Baynard's Castle, referred to by Pepys, among others, was destroyed in the Great Fire. The site is now occupied by a BT office called Baynard House, but the castle is commemorated in Castle Baynard Street and the Castle Baynard ward of the City of London.

10 John Lowin was one of the leading actors of the King's Men appearing alongside Richard Burbage and Henry Condell, for example in the induction to John Marston's *The Malcontent* (1603). He is also mentioned in surviving cast lists for productions of Ben Jonson's *The Alchemist* (1610) and *Catiline* (1611), and as having played the leading role in *Volpone* (1605). He played parts in John Fletcher's *Bonduca* (1613) and *Valentinian* (1613) as well as John Webster's *The Duchess of Malfi* (1614). There can be little doubt, then, that he was known as one of the foremost actors in 1611 (see Butler 2004; Hill 2004, 166).

11 Henry fitz Ailwin (de Londonestone) (1135-1212) was the first (the office known as Lord Mayor of London from 1347 and then Lord Mayor of the City of London from 2006). Londonestone held office from 1189 until his death in 1212 (Keene 2004).

> Foure seuerall times the chiefe was I,
> And Lord of Londons Maioraltie.
> As by the bearing of that Sword,
> It seemes that you are Londons Lord:
> To whom becomes me loute full low,
> Old duty yet (me thinkes) I know.
> Turne now thy Glasse to instant day,
> And let old Faringdon thee pray: (*Chruso-thriambos*; B3v-B4v)

The character Farringdon establishes a connection between past and present in acknowledging the buildings and the territory, the ward, as well as the Lord Mayor, Sir John Pemberton. The gesture of bowing ("loute") in which Farringdon pays his respect to the later-born Pemberton is at odds with a tradition of honouring the past. What we see here, then, is a concept of progress and independence brought about by staging the current Lord Mayor's triumph in space and time. He can point to a line of Lord Mayors stretching back for more than four centuries but ancestor worship is outweighed by the authority that the office holds in the here and now.

Space and time are evoked and construed in this scene in order to create an image of present-day London as the pinnacle of a historic process.[12] According to the historian John Astington we see in this and in similar scenes the emergence of London as a self-confident metropolis: "renowned in London culture, the show formed one of the central icons by which London was memorialised in European civilisation at large" (Astington 1999, 74; also quoted in Hill 2004, 4). There can be no doubt that civic pageants can serve as privileged sources for probing into the political and social situation of Early Modern *England*. Lord Mayor's Shows like Heywood's *Londini Status Pacatus* can also facilitate our understanding of the emergence of the City vis-à-vis the Court: They elucidate the strategies used by aldermen and city merchants to conceptualize London as a leading metropolis in Europe. Their display of wealth and civic pride was paired with an evocation of London's "Peaceable Estate", a state explicitly cited in the title of Heywood's pageant, and Lord Mayor's Shows thus contributed to the construction of London as a free city built on guild crafts and honourable trade.

Munday's Show of 1611 praises London as being "peacefull to all her friendly lovers" (Munday 1611, B2). Heywood's pageant of 1639 bears the programmatic title *Londini Status Pacatus* and points to historical cities like Troy and contemporaneous cities on the continent, rampaged in the conflict we have come to term the Thirty Years' War. "Domesticke War", we are reminded in this pageant, "is the over-throw and ruine of all Estates, and Monarchies, and the incendiary of whatsoever is most execrable, begetting contempt of God, corruption of manners, and disobedience to Magistrates" (Heywood 1639, C2r). Staging is used in Heywood's show to evoke and conjure this peaceable state. The text lists six devices; among them (the fourth) is a "Chariot drawne by two Cammells, upon either back an Indian mounted" (*ibid.*, B4r). With the Drapers' Company celebrating their Mayor and their craft, industry and foreign trade are foregrounded throughout the Show: "Concord and Unity" reign when trade establishes a "Plantation of rest, ease and security" (*ibid.*, C2r). What we see here, then, is an at-

---

12 Ernst Kantorowicz has argued that all pageants are ultimately modelled on the entry into Jerusalem on Palm Sunday (see Bergeron 1971, 93).

tempt at constructing a "common weale" in a climate that had increasingly shown signs of religious conflicts and colonial aspirations.

While the socio-political importance of the Lord Mayor's Shows is widely acknowledged, their dramatic art is hardly ever seriously addressed. Undoubtedly, some of the poetry is mediocre – and the speech by Farringdon seems to prove that point. The rhyming couplets in iambic tetrameter sound hollow in comparison with the elaborate blank verse in iambic pentameter that was common in the period. Yet the lines spoken by Time demonstrate that it is not Munday's incompetence that we witness here, but his ingenuity. Farringdon speaks in tetrameter and rhyming couplets because he is a contemporary of Chaucer – his prosodic teint and his antiquated lexicon are part of an attempt to establish the character as a historical figure actually *present* in the here and now. Shakespeare's Cleopatra masters Elizabethan idioms, Hamlet is a virtuoso with respect to Elizabethan conceits, even Gower is more Shakespeare's contemporary than his prologue would have us believe – but this Farringdon has truly risen from the dead. We have to acknowledge, at least, that this scene cautions us not to judge the poetic quality of the pageants unfairly. More importantly, it cautions us to take illusion and imagination seriously: Within the logic of the pageant men are not merely players.

The function of the pageant in consecrating the city – and I am deliberately using a liturgical term here to refer to a civic practice[13] – is only conceivable if we use categories to describe characters like Farringdon that differ from the categories we usually apply to characters on the Early Modern stage. And the same is true for staging scenes and the use of scenery. We must construe characters as an integral part of the pageant's aesthetic and dramatic qualities that stage abstract ideas such as domestic peace. However, the documents that can tell us something about these practices are even scarcer than those that could help reconstruct notions of character. While the nature and the socio-political function of the procession arguably changed very little in the Jacobean and Caroline periods, the texts produced to document the Shows underwent fundamental changes. Munday describes the devices in detail, but Heywood only briefly explains at the end of the text:

> Concerning these two excellent Artists, Master *Iohn*, and Master *Mathias Christmas*, brothers; the exquisite contrivers of these Triumphall Models; I can onely say thus much: their workeman-ship exceeds what I can expresse in words, and in my opinion their performance of what they undertake, is equall at least, if not transcendent over any's who in the like kind shall strive to parralell them. (Heywood 1639, C4r)

Passages like this call our attention to stage business that "exceeds what [one] can expresse in words". While Heywood refers to the unspeakable splendour and ingenuity of the "Triumphall Models", the printed text of the last Lord Mayor's Show performed before the outbreak of the Civil War also reflects a general awareness that dramatic art is performative rather than textual. Consequently, Heywood prints the speeches that were delivered in 1639 but he does not attempt to describe the devices built by the brothers Christmas. Instead, he briefly guides our interpretation by telling us what they represent, and how they should be read: The first Show by water, for example, "is a person representing Nilus", and the river Nile strikes an "alliance with his brother Thames" (*ibid.*, A4v). Staging peace as a fraternity between two rivers is something

---

13   As I will explain in the following, these acts of consecrating the city are ritualistic and evoke spiritual and liturgical associations.

far removed from what we know took place in the playhouses. While the *imagery* may have been exploited by playwrights such as Webster or Shakespeare, with respect to *stage business* there is more contact here between the masque and the pageant.

Exploring possibilities of how to stage and present ideas, the Lord Mayor's Show was far more experimental than is usually acknowledged. Replete with epic elements and thus verging on the non-dramatic, pageants reinvigorated Jacobean dramatic form. So far the critical focus has been on parodies of the Lord Mayor's Show in city comedies.[14] Angela Stock has traced the "undercurrent of political satire that was created by parodic allusions to the Lord Mayor's Show" (Stock 2004, 128) in plays such as Beaumont's *The Knight of the Burning Pestle* (1607). But the impact of the Shows is not confined to satirical appropriations. Stock accepts too easily that Jacobean playwrights looked down on the dramatic self-fashioning of an emerging civic community. I think we still need to consider more carefully the impact that pageants may have had on Jacobean and Caroline stage performances beyond satirical derision: The episodic nature of Shakespeare's late plays, the growing interest in myths during the Jacobean period, and the development of the city comedy itself can all be seen in the light of the civic pageant. My point is that Munday, "our best plotter" (Meres 1598, Oo3v) according to Francis Meres, and Heywood, author of *An Apology for Actors* (1612), contributed decisively to a fascinating cross-pollination between pageants and stage plays that resulted in a depth of character and a variety of staging practices found across theatrical performances in the period.

In order to discuss the nature of the cross-pollination between pageants and stage plays I would like to return to the reanimation of Farringdon in Munday's *Cruso-thriambos*. Angela Stock has argued that the paradox, the *explicatio* of the ritual which by definition warrants no explication, made the pageants easy prey for satirical predators such as Beaumont or Jonson. The fault with these performances, she claims, is that characters constantly explain the elements of the ritualistic performance and sideline it metatheatrically with commentary (Stock 2004, 133). I am not so sure that Munday's and Heywood's contemporaries would have agreed and I should like to turn to Shakespeare to make my point.

We do not know whether Shakespeare was among those bystanders at the Lord Mayor's Shows who lighted fireworks, but we have no reason to believe that he would miss a theatrical spectacle in which many of his fellow actors and playwrights took part. Some of the peculiarities of his late plays undoubtedly seem less idiosyncratic if we accept that dramatic and aesthetic principles at work in the pageants may have inspired Shakespeare when writing his dark comedies. It is not on the level of genre, though, that this cross-pollination takes place; pageants – also referred to as triumphs at the time – are neither comic nor tragic. As rituals they are affirmative, and they are designed to situate the present moment in a sequence of events that connects the happy past with an even happier future.

It is on the level of character and staging that I think we can learn a lot from these pageants. Let us consider the ending of *The Winter's Tale* in order to examine the impact of the pageant tradition, which I think is still poorly understood.

---

14 For a discussion of epic elements that emphasises peculiar structural parallels between pageants and city comedies, see Ellen Redling's contribution to this volume.

PAULINA	Music, awake her; strike!
	[*Music*]
	[*To* HERMIONE] 'Tis time. Descend. Be stone no more. Approach.
	Strike all that look upon with marvel. Come,
	I'll fill your grave up. Stir. Nay, come away.
	Bequeath to death your numbness, for from him
	Dear life redeems you.
	[*To* LEONTES] You perceive she stirs:
	[HERMIONE *slowly descends*]
	Start not. Her actions shall be holy as
	You hear my spell is lawful. Do not shun her
	Until you see her die again; for then
	You kill her double. Nay, present your hand.
	When she was young you wooed her. Now in age
	Is she become the suitor?
LEONTES	O, she's warm!
	If this be magic, let it be an art
	Lawful as eating.
POLIXENES	She embraces him.
CAMILLO	She hangs about his neck.
	If she pertain to life, let her speak too.
POLIXENES	Ay, and make it manifest where she has lived,
	Or how stolen from the dead.
PAULINA	That she is living,
	Were it but told you, should be hooted at
	Like an old tale. But it appears she lives,
	Though yet she speak not. Mark a little while.
	[*To* PERDITA] Please you to interpose, fair madam. Kneel
	And pray your mother's blessing. – Turn, good lady,
	Our Perdita is found.
HERMIONE	You gods, look down,
	And from your sacred vials pour your graces
	Upon my daughter's head. – Tell me, mine own.
	Where hast thou been preserved? Where lived? How found
	Thy father's court? For thou shalt hear that I,
	Knowing by Paulina that the oracle
	Gave hope thou wast in being, have preserved
	Myself to see the issue.

(*The Winter's Tale*; 5.3.123-155)

Shakespeare sidelines the reanimation of Hermione with a running commentary by Paulina, Leontes, Polixenes and Camillo, so that the reanimation resembles the dramatic form of a pageant. That resemblance is also evoked by Paulina's remark "Were it but told you, should be hooted at / Like an old tale", which brings to the fore that it is precisely the combination of the telling and the enactment – in its peculiar static and solemn fashion – that renders the reanimation plausible as a dramatic scene. In 1932 Lancaster argued convincingly that in the final scene of Shakespeare's play, with Hermione as a statue coming to life, allusions to the Pygmalion myth are "too vague to have much significance", and that both *The Winter's Tale* and Alexandre Hardy's *L'Inceste supposé* (1616) share a common but unknown source for the play's plot (Lancaster 1932, 233, 235). Lancaster admits, however, that intertextual references that can explain the staging of the scene "remain to be discovered, as well as the source of the statue motif" (*ibid.*, 237). I think that ideas for staging the reanimation of

Hermione may have been imported from Munday's pageant. We know that *The Winter's Tale* was performed in front of King James at Whitehall on 5 November 1611, less than two weeks after the Lord Mayor's Show. Shakespeare's play ends with an emblematic tableau: Hermione standing on top of the pedestal, and the other characters arranged at her feet. On the stage at Whitehall all the actors would have probably faced the audience, adding to the effect of stasis, and they would, arguably, not have left the stage at the end of the scene.

Why are we so reluctant to accept that Shakespeare's characters and his staging practice in the dark comedies may owe a lot to the pageants? Iden's speech in 4.9 of *2Henry VI* is arguably a set piece modelled on the pageant tradition. Following Bruce Smith, Janette Dillon explains that "'To introduce a pageant into the middle of the play is to confront actors and audience alike with an aesthetic challenge'; and it is one that modern productions and audiences do not easily rise to, as it is so unfamiliar" (Dillon 2012, 15; quoting Smith 1985, 221). Dillon convincingly argues that

> in modern performances it is all too easy to misread Iden within the terms of assumed realism and hence to dismiss his position as 'smug self-esteem' or 'bourgeois complacency'. But these readings are based on the misguided assumption that Shakespeare's characters are continuously realistic and that we see in them developing psychologies, and that any one scene or part of a scene is to be viewed in the same way as any other. This is quite simply not the case [...]. (Dillon 2012, 15)

According to Dillon, we can learn a lot if we acknowledge "how much our current assumptions about theatre differ from those in place in Shakespeare's time" (*ibid.*, 15). In a world populated by characters framed in the predominant Hollywood/Branagh-style of psychological realism and method acting, it may be difficult to appreciate pre-modern facets of Shakespeare's characters. Dillon cites Mark Rose, who has argued that "the presentation of character in Shakespeare is perhaps less like a modern film in which the figures are in constant motion than an album of snapshot stills to be contemplated in sequence" (*ibid.*, 15; Rose 1972, 9). Pageants can teach us that lesson if we are willing to engage with them in an open-minded fashion. Focusing on the involvement of playwrights and artisans who designed the devices for the pageants allows for a new appreciation of plays performed at the playhouses in general and of Shakespeare's dramatic art in particular. As Frederick Kiefer explained in *Shakespeare's Visual Theatre* (2003), obscure references to stage designs – such as the five senses in *Timon of Athens*, for example – are informed by the practices employed by dramatists when working for the Livery Companies (Kiefer 2003, 129). We should more readily embrace the idea that Shakespeare, who regularly collaborated with Munday, for example when writing *Sir Thomas More* (1596), imported many stylistic and rhetorical devices typical of the pageants when writing his late plays.

The shaping of London as a civic metropolis took place in the streets of London and on the Thames on the basis of the Lord Mayor's Show, with Shakespeare, most likely, as a bystander and spectator, rather than as a dramatist. Nevertheless, our understanding of Shakespeare's dramatic art will benefit from probing into practices of staging and presenting characters as explored in these pageants. There are still real treasures for Shakespeare scholars to be unearthed in these pageants, and there can, in my mind, be no doubt that the aesthetic and dramatic qualities of the Lord Mayor's Show – in particular with respect to staging practices and characterization – are still undervalued and warrant further investigation. Pageants can teach us that Early Modern staging may have been more emblematic and less dynamic than we have commonly assumed to be and characters may have been less 'psychologically real', perhaps even expressionistic *avant la lettre*.

References

Primary Sources

Heywood, Thomas (1639): *Londini Status Pacatus: or, Londons Peaceable Estate*. London: John Okes
Munday, Anthony (1611): *Chruso-thriambos: The Triumphs of Golde*. London: William Jaggard
Shakespeare, William (1988 [1611]): *The Winter's Tale*. Ed. J. H. P. Pafford. The Arden Shakespeare. London: Routledge
--- (1995 [1599]) *King Henry V*. Ed. T. W. Craik. The Arden Shakespeare. London: Routledge

Secondary Sources

Astington, John (1999): "The Ages of Man and the Lord Mayor's Show", in: Ostovich, Helen et al. (eds.): *Other Voices, Other Views: Expanding the Canon in English Renaissance Studies*. Newark: University of Delaware Press, 74-90
Bergeron, David M. (1971): *English Civic Pageantry: 1558 – 1642*. London: Edward Arnold
--- (ed.; 1986): *Thomas Heywood's Pageants*. New York: Garland
Butler, Martin (2004): "Lowin, John (*bap.* 1576, *d.* 1653)", in: *Oxford Dictionary of National Biography*, Oxford University Press <http://www.oxforddnb.com/view/article/17096> [accessed 13 January 2014]
Dillon, Janette (2012): *Shakespeare and the Staging of English History*. Oxford: Oxford University Press
Dutton, Richard (ed.; 1995): *Jacobean Civic Pageants*. Staffordshire: Keele University Press
Fairholt, Frederick W. (1843; 1844): *Lord Mayor's Pageants, being collections towards a history of these annual celebrations*, 2 vols. London: Percy Society Publishers
Hill, Tracey (2004): *Anthony Munday and Civic Culture*. Manchester: Manchester University Press <http://www.lordmayorsshow.org> [accessed 13 January 2014]
Keene, Derek (2004): "Henry Fitz Ailwin (*d.* 1212)", in: *Oxford Dictionary of National Biography*, Oxford University Press <http://www.oxforddnb.com/view/article/9526> [accessed 13 January 2014]
Kiefer, Frederic (2003): *Shakespeare's Visual Theatre: Staging the Personified Characters*. Cambridge: Cambridge University Press
Lancashire, Anne (2002): *London Civic Theatre: City Drama and Pageantry from Roman Times to 1558*. Cambridge: Cambridge University Press
Lancaster, Henry Carrington (1932): "Hermione's Statue", *Studies in Philology* 29, 233-238
Meres, Francis (1598): *Palladis Tamia: Wits Treasury*. London: Peter Short
Pfister, Manfred (1988): *The Theory and Analysis of Drama*. Cambridge: Cambridge University Press
Rose, Mark (1972): *Shakespearean Design*. Cambridge, MA: Belknap
Rosser, Gervase (1996): "Myth, Image and Social Process in the English Medieval Town", *Urban History* 23, 5-25
Smith, Bruce (1985): "Pageants into Play: Shakespeare's Three Perspectives on Idea and Image", in: Bergeron, David M. (ed.): *Pageantry in the Shakespearean Theater*. Athens: University of Georgia Press, 220-246
Stock, Angela (2004): "'Something done in honour of the city': Ritual, Theatre and Satire in Jacobean Civic Pageantry", in: Mehl, Dieter et al. (eds.): *Plotting Early Modern London: New Essays on Jacobean City Comedy*. Aldershot: Ashgate, 125-144

MATTHIAS BAUER AND MARTINA BROSS (TÜBINGEN)

Character Writing and the Stage in the Early Seventeenth Century

Joseph Hall's 1608 collection *Characters of Virtues and Vices* and the Overbury collection *Characters or Witty Descriptions of the Properties of Sundry Persons*, written around 1607 and first published in 1614, sparked a keen interest in the genre of Character writing in *England*, which led to the publication of over twenty Character books and many single Characters before the century was over (Smeed 1985, 25). Hall and Overbury modelled their Characters on those of Theophrastus, which had been edited and published with a Latin translation by Casaubon in 1592 and re-issued in 1599. However, as Boyce and Smeed have pointed out, the forerunners of the English seventeenth-century Characters cannot only be found in the Theophrastan Characters with their vivid descriptions of actions, gestures, and expressions typical of each vice represented but also in classical Roman verse-satire, medieval allegory, epigrams, commonplace books, and the literature of the Estates (Boyce 1967, 55-100; Smeed 1985, 1-19).

It seems no coincidence that a genre that depicts human representatives of virtues and vices, occupations, and stations in life should rise to popularity at a time when drama, and in particular the comedy of humours, features characters dominated by a particular character trait or vice. This raises the question of the influence of drama on the Character genre and vice versa. This article will pursue three aims: first, to address the relationship between drama and the genre of the Character in *England* in the early seventeenth century. In doing so, we take up hints provided by the writers themselves; for example, Joseph Hall presents his collection as "this stage", on which he wishes the "amiable virtue" of Wisdom "to lead" (Hall 1924, 54). Conversely, the first of the vices, Hypocrisy, is regarded as "the worst kind of player, by so much as he acts the better part" (*ibid.*, 71). Secondly and more specifically, we consider the Character as a genre of very short texts, few of them exceeding more than two pages: In which way are its concision and brevity (including its succinct use of metaphors and comparisons) related to and used in the dramatic representation of character? Hall, for instance, points to a principle of economy that serves to bring about a moral effect when he states in his preface: "I desired not to say all, but enough" (A6^r, 1608 edition quoted in Hockenjos 2006, 37). This economy of the prose Character helps the dramatist to bring together the reader's and the spectator's perspectives. Our third aim is to address the nature of characters thus conceived by considering the function of prose Characters inserted into dramatic texts. At this point, it may also become clear why such an inquiry has its place in a section called "not Shakespeare": Ben Jonson's early satirical comedies, for example, are much more closely related to the Character books than most plays by Shakespeare.

Drama and Character Writing: "Hybridisation" of Genre

Our focus will be on Jonson's comical satires *Every Man Out of His Humour*, first performed in 1599 and printed in 1600, and *Cynthia's Revels*, first performed sometime between September 1600 and May 1601 and printed in 1601 (see Donaldson 2012, xciv-xcv). Even though *Every Man Out of His Humour* has been regarded as a case of "generic engineering" (Watson 1986, 337)[1] for "reformulating [...] the conventional genres of its day" (Ostovich 2001, 14), the part played by the Character books in this "engineering" has not yet been fully explored. This is surprising, for in both plays satirical comedy is quite obviously fused with the Character genre. Some critics have at least noticed its presence. Baldwin, for example, argues that the short character descriptions in *Every Man Out of His Humour* are in fact the earliest English Characters based on the Theophrastan model as they are, "except for their brevity, exactly like those of Theophrastus" (Baldwin 1901, 386).[2] Smeed, however, declares that "such prefatory sketches have nothing to do with the possible invasion of the play proper by Theophrastan character-writing; their function is to establish the various personalities in advance of the dramatic action. The character-sketches which come in *Cynthia's Revels* ([1600/]1601) have been more confidently labelled Theophrastan" (Smeed 1985, 201-202). We rather think that the prefatory sketches establish personalities by referring to Character writing, and that the plays are very much about the unfolding and interrelation of characters conceived in the vein of that genre. Perhaps even more interesting than the question whether these Characters are specifically 'Theophrastan' is the mere fact that, a few years before the genre of Character writing would gain popularity in *England*, Jonson chooses to enrich his plays by means of prose descriptions of specific traits that together form a particular character. The plays thus become hybrids of drama and narrative or expository prose.

In *Every Man Out of His Humour* the Character descriptions are part of the paratext, which was added for the printed edition. They can be regarded as explanations of the hints given by the characters' names.[3] The list begins with "Asper, his character": "He is of an ingenious and free spirit [...]" (Jonson 2012, *Every Man Out of His Humour*, Characters 1-2). Of course, one could argue that this is the characterisation of a figure in the play, whereas the Character by, or in the manner of, Theophrastus is the personification of a quality or habit. Theophrastus's "Chatterer", for example, begins with a definition of the quality to be personified: "Chattering is the mania of talking hugely without thinking" (Theophrastus 1924, 30). There is clearly a difference to the description in Jonson. Instead of the description of a person we get the definition of a human weakness. But then Theophrastus goes on: "The Chatterer is the sort of man who sits down beside someone he never saw before and begins by praising his wife" (*ibid.*, 30). This is not an abstract quality defined, this is the imitation of life, "*imitatio vitae*", and accordingly evokes the nature of comedy (of which Jonson reminds us in *Every Man Out of His Humour* 3.1.415). Another link between the two genres is established by

---

1 Watson's phrase refers to all of Jonson's comedies, especially *The Alchemist*.
2 Martin notes that the brief insertions were influenced by Theophrastus in the *Cambridge Edition of the Works of Ben Jonson* (Jonson 2012, *Every Man Out of His Humour* 250n9).
3 Meier lists several of the characters from *Every Man Out of His Humour*, e.g. Carlo Buffone, Asper, and Fastidious Brisk, as representatives of a group of Jonsonian characters who are named after habits (Meier 1964, 91-92).

the fact that, in the English Character books, we find beginnings that are exactly like those of Jonson's paratextual descriptions, for example in Hall's "The Envious": "He feeds on others' evils; and hath no disease, but his neighbours' welfare" (Hall 1924, 92).

Accordingly, we see that the Character genre is itself a mixed one. Even though it is essentially discursive – frequently close to the essay, as suggested by the title of Nicholas Breton's *Characters upon Essays* (1615; see the chapter in Boyce 1967, 190-219) – and strives to define qualities, virtues, and vices with a moral purpose, it also participates in drama by making the characters act and speak in a "characteristic" manner. The moral purpose is part of Jonson's comedy anyway, "accommodated to the correction of manners" (Jonson 2012, *Every Man Out of His Humour* 3.1.416-417). Moreover, Jonson creates 'humour' characters, which are based on the observation of nature but are nevertheless (or for that very reason) representatives of certain qualities, vices, etc., as well.[4] As Asper explains to Mitis and Cordatus in the Induction of *Every Man Out of His Humour*: "As when some one peculiar quality / Doth so possess a man, that it doth draw / All his affects, his spirits, and his powers, / In their confluctions, all to run one way, / This may be truly said to be a humour" (*ibid.*, Induction 103-107).

In *Cynthia's Revels* the fusion of the 'essayistic' Character and dramatic representation is even more obvious, as the descriptions of dramatic characters given by Mercury and Cupid in Act Two are part of the play proper. The diegetic process of characterisation is thus consciously integrated into the play and becomes part of the mimesis. One might even say that, in this play, Jonson more fully amalgamated the Character genre and made quite economic use of it.

Economy: Compression and Redundancy

Jonson's addition of the Character descriptions preceding *Every Man Out of His Humour* for the printed edition of 1600 was a novelty at the time (Jonson 2012, *Every Man Out of His Humour* 250n9).[5] One function of these descriptions can be seen in

---

4   Doran sees a difference between the Theophrastan technique, which "reveals a class of moral behavior (like flattery, boasting [...]) through the behavior of an imaginary individual" (Doran 1954, 230), and the humour technique, which "starts with the person and makes an individual excess [...] the essence of the character" (*ibid.*, 230). For her, the humour characters in *Every Man Out of His Humour* are not types but individualized to the extreme (see *ibid.*, 230) because they are not representatives of a general disposition but represent a "particular departure from the norm" (*ibid.*, 231). It is this distortion of the term 'humour' that Asper criticises at the beginning of *Every Man Out of His Humour* (*ibid.*, 230): The term has come to denote eccentricity rather than a general disposition (see Jonson 2012, *Every Man Out of His Humour*, Induction 100-113).
5   Jonson later added descriptions of the characters to his less successful comedy *The New Inn* (first performed in 1629 and first published in 1631). "The Persons of the Play. With some short characterism of the chief actors" are placed between "The Argument" and the Prologue and give a short account of the respective character's biography, his role in the play, and his relation to other characters in the play. Although the descriptions reveal character traits and dispositions for some of the characters, e.g. for Lovel, who is identified as a "melancholy guest in the inn" (Jonson 2012, *The New Inn*, The Persons of the Play 6-7), or Ferret, who is deemed "a fellow of a quick, nimble wit, [who] knows the manners and affections of people, and can make profitable

providing orientation for the readership of a play that is primarily aimed at presenting characters. The paratextual descriptions have a similar function to the names that Jonson gives his characters. In the printed edition there are four steps of characterisation: the characters' names, which already appear in the paratext; the description of each Character in the paratext; the description of the characters by other characters in the play's Induction, which lies on the boundary between the world of the reader and the world of the play[6]; and the actions and interaction of the characters in the play proper. It may seem utterly redundant to repeat characterisations on the layers of paratext, Induction, and play proper, but we suggest that there are reasons for this that have to do with the literary genre of the Character.

Macilente's name, for example, derives from the Latin word *macilentus* meaning 'lean' or 'thin', thus giving the reader an idea of the character's appearance. The leanness signalled by the name "is the traditional physical attribute of envy, and both qualities are associated with the contemporary stereotype of the malcontent" (Jonson 2012, *Every Man Out of His Humour* 252n10). The paratextual description, then, spells out Macilente's envious trait for the reader and gives possible explanations for it: he feels he does not hold the station in life he merits (see Jonson 2012, *Every Man Out of His Humour*, Characters 6-9). The aspect of envy is then again pointed out by Mitis in the Induction (*ibid.*, Induction 330) and later expressed by Macilente in his soliloquies, which comment on other characters' behaviour throughout the play. Thus envy is established as the trait by which Macilente is to be defined and recognised.[7] This dominance of one streak is of course linked to the notion of the humours, but it is also a feature of the Character genre.

At the beginning of a play, an audience would usually see the actor playing the part before they hear the name of the character; similarly, the prominent placement of the name in the paratext followed by the description also serves the function of putting the Character before the reader's eyes. Macilente's case is a special one, however. When he appears at the end of the Induction, his name is mentioned before he speaks in such a way that the audience is supposed to know all about him: "Oh, this is your envious man, Macilente, I think" (*ibid.*, Induction 330). Jonson here quite economically handles the two media of the stage and the page at once: The experienced theatre audience immediately identifies the lean actor as an envious character, which is confirmed by Mitis's words; for the readers (who do not see the figure coming), the stage direction

---

and timely discoveries of them" (*ibid.*, 12-14), they differ from the descriptions preceding *Every Man Out of His Humour* in that their primary function is to locate each character's role in the play, explain their situation, and summarize what happens to them in the course of the dramatic action rather than to enable and challenge the reader to get an idea of their character.

6   The Induction of *Every Man Out of His Humour* fuses different levels of communication. A fictional author enters and addresses the audience directly (Jonson 2012, *Every Man Out of His Humour*, Induction 49-70), several characters quarrel over the question of whose task it is to deliver the Prologue (*ibid.*, Induction 269-316), and Carlo Buffone enters to talk about the author and the play he is a part of (*ibid.*, Induction 302-12). Thus, the Induction is undoubtedly part of the theatrical performance (or, for the reader, part of the imaginary theatrical performance), yet represents an intermediary stage that is one level removed from the conventional Prologue, whose function it highlights.

7   Doran describes Macilente as belonging to the general class of melancholics but as being individualized by the humour of envy (Doran 1954, 231).

"*Enter* MACILENTE, *solus*" (Jonson 2012, *Every Man Out of His Humour* Induction 329) and Mitis's words serve as a reminder of the Character description that they have perused in the paratext. The redundancy on the page is thus the equivalent of the multiple (verbal and non-verbal) codes realised in the live performance. Moreover, Jonson's technique helps readers in that it enables them to refer back to the descriptions and to keep track of who is who. A theatre audience would have the visual help of costumes, props and particular gestures. Accordingly, the insertion of the narrative genre of Character descriptions into drama might be motivated by a shift from performance towards print, or it may conversely underline the literary[8] origin of stage performance. It also suggests that Jonson's decision to add the brief descriptions is based on the belief that a Character can be unfolded from a name or conversely be observed and then described in a nutshell. (It is important to keep in mind that the description of the paratext was added after the play had been performed, and that Jonson and his audiences had indeed been able to observe these characters.) The Characters by Theophrastus and the Character books that were published a few years after Jonson's play was acted and published rely on the same assumption.

How does this condensation of a dramatic Character into a brief description work, and what effect does it create for the reader? A closer look at the Character descriptions in the paratext of *Every Man Out of His Humour* shows that they differ in what they tell us about each character. The shorter descriptions, such as that of Macilente, provide explanations for motives or a particular view of the world, which might cause certain actions or reactions to particular situations. The descriptions also raise expectations in the reader as to how a Character will respond when confronted with other characters during the play. Of course, they also enable the reader to recognise the actions performed by the characters in the play as caused by their attitudes and particular dispositions.

The longer descriptions in the paratext present typical actions, utterances, and situations the characters might find themselves in. The paratextual description of Carlo Buffone is an example of this. He is described as "a public, scurrilous, and profane jester" (Jonson 2012, *Every Man Out of His Humour*, Characters 19), and this links him to a Character familiar from classical comedy, especially as eating and drinking are set up as his main concerns.

In the Induction, the second layer of characterisation, Carlo immediately calls for drink (*ibid.*, Induction 292). Cordatus then delivers a description of Carlo to Mitis:

> He is one, the author calls him Carlo Buffone, an impudent common jester, a violent railer, and an incomprehensible epicure. One whose company is desired of all men, but beloved of none. He will sooner lose his soul than a jest, and profane even the most holy things to excite laughter. No honourable or reverend personage whatsoever can come within the reach of his eye but is turned into all manner of variety by his adulterate similes. (*ibid.*, Induction 318-324)

---

8   The term "literary" here serves to characterise plays that were not solely conceived to be performed but also written with publication in mind. The title page of the 1600 quarto of *Every Man Out of His Humour* mentions Jonson as the author of the play, and the publication of Jonson's *Workes* in 1616 indicates that he was eager to be perceived as an author of dramatic literature (Martin 2012, 241).

Again we find interplay between the paratext made for readers and the stage performance, which, in spite of certain duplications and amplifications, is not merely redundant. As regards the nature of the jester, the paratext adds "public, scurrilous, and profane" to Cordatus's "impudent" and "common". But the main difference is that the paratext, by means of comparison and metaphor, puts the jester before the reader's eye. Whereas Cordatus in the Induction just says that "honourable or reverend personage[s]" are "turned into all manner of variety" by Carlo, the profound, almost violent effect of the jester's similes is more visibly evoked by the literary comparison to Circe in the paratext (who turned Ulysses's companions into swine): "more swift that [sic] Circe, with absurd similes [he] will transform any person into deformity" (Jonson 2012, *Every Man Out of His Humour*, Characters 19-20). Similarly, Cordatus's brief statement that Carlo is "an incomprehensible epicure" (*ibid.*, Induction 320) is made more concrete in the paratext by means of metaphor when Carlo is presented as a dog, a "feast-hound or banquet-beagle, that will scent you out a supper some three mile off" (*ibid.*, Characters 20-21). Again comparison serves to flesh him out before the reader's mental eye: he "will swill up more sack at a sitting than would make all the guard a posset" (i.e., a drink of milk spiced up with alcohol) (*ibid.*, Characters 23-24). The difference between the two descriptions has to do with the fact that the paratext, added in print, helps the reader visualise a character, whereas Cordatus's description in the Induction comes when Carlo has already presented himself and given an example both of his drinking habits and his simile-making ("A well-timbered fellow, he would ha'made a good column an he had been thought on when the house was a-building", *ibid.*, Induction 297-298). Cordatus interprets, sums up, and identifies the Character that we have seen, whereas the paratext presents the Character to our mental eyes before we read what he says. All these features can be regarded as a productive exploitation of the genre of the Character, comprising both the unfolding of a concept and the analysis of social observation.

The insertion of Characters in Act Two of *Cynthia's Revels* achieves a similar effect in terms of putting characters before the reader's eyes and highlighting the process of characterisation. For example, Mercury expressly introduces his description of Amorphus as a presentation of his "character" (Jonson 2012, *Cynthia's Revels* 2.3.65); this means that he both depicts him as a Character, i.e., that of "a traveler" (*ibid.*, 2.3.66), and characterises him as a 'humorous' individual. In accordance with his name, Amorphus is defined and described as "one so made out of the mixture and shreds of forms that himself is truly deformed. He walks most commonly with a clove or pick-tooth in his mouth" (*ibid.*, 2.3.66-68). As this is part of the play, Mercury may take up aspects the audience is already familiar with, such as costume or props (the pick-tooth) carried by the actor playing the part. This insertion would, however, not be redundant for a reader who must rely on words alone in order to have an idea of Amorphus's appearance. The notion of putting characters before a reader's eyes by picking out striking external features again links the genre of comedy with the Character. Overbury's "Affectate Traveller", who bears a close resemblance to and is believed to be based on Jonson's Character Amorphus (Boyce 1967, 104, 139-140), for example, carries a "pick-tooth" which "is a main part of his behavior" (Overbury 1924, 102). This item identifies the Character described and serves a similar function to a theatrical prop carried by an actor on stage.

There is yet another interplay of stage and page to be seen in the Character of Amorphus, one that has to do with the paradoxical fact that he is a man of no form and yet many forms. By the time Mercury presents his Character, we have been repeatedly introduced to him. In the Induction (or "Praeludium"), the Third Child calls him "Amorphus, or the deformed, a traveller that hath drunk of the fountain [of Self-Love]" (Jonson 2012, *Cynthia's Revels*, Induction 48-49); upon first entering the stage in 1.3, he characterises himself negatively: "I am neither your minotaur, nor your centaur, nor your satyr, nor your hyena, nor your baboon, but your mere traveller, believe me" (*ibid.*, 1.3.4-5). This absence of a specific form may make it difficult for a reader to imagine him, but then he is also made for readers since he is a bookish Character in more senses than one. This becomes clear when Mercury's description in 2.3 continues: "He's the very mint of compliment; all his behaviours are printed, his face is another volume of essays, and his beard an Aristarchus" (*ibid.*, 2.3.68-70). The "essays" may even be a reference to Character books, just as his beard "is imagined as a classical commentary attached to the text of his face", as Rasmussen and Steggle point out in their annotation to *Cynthia's Revels* 3.2.70. This is quite fitting, for Amorphus is many Characters in one and, as it were, in need of annotations. Amorphus is also a creature of the stage, however, the quintessential actor who can assume all sorts of forms. Immediately before Mercury's characterisation, Amorphus has presented a whole set of characters, imitating as well as describing their faces: "First, for your merchant's, or city-face, 'tis thus [*He makes a face*]: a dull, plodding face, still looking in a direct line forward, there is no great matter in this face. Then you have your student's, or academic face, which is here [*He makes a face*], an honest, simple, and methodical face, but somewhat more spread than the former" (*ibid.*, 2.3.216-220). Readers, even though they have to make do without the actor's art, are able to imagine the various professions imitated, as they get hints through Amorphus's Character-like descriptions.

Apart from catering economically for page *and* stage, Jonson's interplay of description and presentation (i.e., the interplay of genres) serves a further purpose. In *Cynthia's Revels* the insertion of the Character descriptions in Act Two also has the function of providing the reader with an alternative view of a character.[9] In Act One, Amorphus, who has drunk from the Fountain of Self-Love, has given a rather favourable description of himself as the "essence so sublimated and refined by travel, of so studied and well-exercised a gesture, so alone in fashion, able to make the face of any statesman living, and to speak the mere extraction of language" (*ibid.*, 1.3.24-27). Mercury depicts him in a different light: "He speaks all cream, skimmed, and more affected than a dozen of waiting women. He's his own promoter in every place; the wife of the ordinary gives him his diet to maintain her table in discourse, which indeed is a mere tyranny over her other guests, for he will usurp all the talk – ten constables are not so tedious" (*ibid.*, 2.3.70-74). Apart from the fact that Amorphus is a Character without specific form, then, his moral evaluation is a matter of perspective.

---

9   One might argue that plays frequently offer alternative views on a character provided by different authorities/characters. What is special in the cases discussed here is that, due to the insertion of the long character descriptions influenced by Character writing, conflicting views on the character are highlighted and lead the audience or reader to reflect on the process of piecing together a character.

In *Every Man Out of His Humour*, Mitis's remark on Cordatus's description of Carlo Buffone, "You paint forth a monster" (Jonson 2012, *Every Man Out of His Humour* Induction 325), underlines the impression that the Character description given in the Induction might not be impartial. For example, the description in the paratext picks up on similar aspects of Carlo's Character as Cordatus does in the Induction. But it leaves out some aspects mentioned by Cordatus, namely that Carlo "will prefer all countries before his native, and thinks he can never sufficiently, or with admiration enough, deliver his affectionate conceit of foreign atheistical policies" (*ibid.*, Induction 326-328). It is left to the reader to piece together the information provided by different authorities. The different layers of characterisation work as a challenge for the reader to reconcile the different versions of a Character with the action displayed by the Character in the play. Carlo, for example, is indeed shown to jest at the expense of other characters; however, compared to Macilente, who poisons another character's dog and helps to seal Carlo's lips with hot wax, he seems rather less of a monster. The addition of the descriptions in the paratext of *Every Man Out of His Humour* and their insertion in *Cynthia's Revels* both advance the notion that a Character can be presented in a nutshell and simultaneously challenge that notion by offering the audience different layers of characterisation and conflicting views on the same character, or by replacing a conceited self-definition with a 'true' view of the character.

The multiplication of perspectives on a Character created by the insertion of a Character book-like description can also be found in John Webster's *The White Devil* (1612), one of the few non-Jonsonian plays of the early seventeenth century in which the genre is used in a dramatic text.[10] The Jonsonian examples have shown that the two genres may be aligned with the transition from the world in which the play is performed (or read) to the world shown in the play (*Every Man Out of His Humour*) and that a Character book-like description may become part of a character's speech (*Cynthia's Revels*). Webster's technique is somewhat different: He has a Character expressly create a Character as a distinct genre on the internal level of communication. This shows that the Character genre, by 1612, had become so popular that it could be evoked without further explanations in a play.

In *The White Devil* 3.2, Cardinal Monticelso is both plaintiff and judge of Vittoria, who is to be put on trial for adultery (and the possible murder of her husband). When he refers to her in court as "this whore" (Webster 1996, 3.2.77) and she replies incredulously "Ha? Whore – what's that?" (*ibid.*, 3.2.77), he starts expounding what a whore is: "I'll give their perfect character. They are, first / Sweet-meats which rot the eater" (*ibid.*, 3.2.79-80). What follows is "a series of bitter metaphors […] of ruin, disease, hellfire, and falsehood" that "is intended to produce a feeling of horror at Vittoria's corruption" (Smeed 1985, 220) at a moment when there is no hard evidence of her guilt. Through openly referring to the Character genre, Vittoria is strategically to be identified with a class of women "worse / Worse than dead bodies, which are begged at gallows" (Webster 1996, 3.2.95-96). She rejects this by responding "This

---

10   According to Smeed (1985, 24), 32 sketches in the 1615 edition of Overbury's *Characters* are attributed to Webster. The Characters of "A Whore" and "A very Whore" (Overbury 1924, 115-17), which are quite different from what we find in *The White Devil*, are apparently not by Webster.

Character 'scapes me" (*ibid.*, 3.2.101), meaning both that she finds this form of characterisation unintelligible and that it does not concern her.[11] Obviously the fashion and mode of Characters have not yet fully reached her.

The effect is an ambiguous one.[12] On the one hand, apart from the Cardinal's ostensible purpose of disparaging Vittoria, the Character serves to entertain the audience by evoking a fashionable genre; it shows the Cardinal's wit (for example in calling a whore "worse than the tributes i'th'Low Countries paid", *ibid.*, 3.2.86) and reminds the audience of the moral evaluation of characters, familiar from Hall's Character book. On the other hand, the insertion of the Character will make the audience see the difference between the wholesale vituperation of this class of women and the Character of Vittoria, who immediately before the Cardinal's speech could garner some sympathy by pointing out his "poor charity" (*ibid.*, 3.2.70); moral evaluation is made more difficult rather than easier by the Character. While the insertion of the Character may provide some sort of comic relief and serves to raise the question of whether it is perhaps just 'character' that makes people act in such a universally evil way in this tragedy, it also points up the limitations of the genre in coming to terms with human life, at least as long as it stays confined to virtues and vices.

Concept of Human Character: Not Shakespeare?

The extensive mingling of Character genre and drama is peculiar to Jonson's early comedies, and the proximity of the plays to the 1592 and 1599 editions of Theophrastus's Characters suggests a direct influence of the Theophrastan Character on Jonson. Obviously it helped him to establish his plays as literary, i.e., written with a publication and readership in mind, as well as theatrical works. Once he had done so, he resorted to the technique much more sparingly. As Smeed points out, it is to be found, for example, in Quarlous's account of Zeal-of-the-land Busy in *Bartholomew Fair* (Jonson 2012, *Bartholomew Fair*, 1.3.106-115; first performed in 1614 and first printed in 1631) or in Compass's description of Parson Palate in *The Magnetic Lady* (Jonson 2012, *Magnetic Lady*, 1.2.15-33; 1632; see Smeed 1985, 206-207).[13]

---

11   See John Russell Brown's note on 3.2.101 (Webster 1996, 80).
12   Ellis (2006, e.g. 64) points out that Vittoria eludes the various (gendered) characterisations of her in the course of the play.
13   Clausen claims that the "first tangible allusions" to Theophrastus's *Characters* can be found in *Volpone* (Clausen 1946, 32-33). He detects an echo of Theophrastus's "Superstitious Man", who, after a weasel has crossed his path, will not go on unless someone else will cross before him or before he has thrown three stones over the way (*ibid.*, 39), in Jonson's Sir Politic Would-Be's diary entry: "A rat had gnawn my spur-leathers; notwithstanding, I put on new, and did go forth; but first I threw three beans over the threshold" (Jonson 2012, *Volpone* 4.1.136-38; Clausen 1946, 38n30). Dutton draws attention to this similarity in the Cambridge edition and comments: "The real point is surely to draw attention to his doubtless prominent spurs, the lame symbol of his knighthood" (Jonson 2012, *Volpone* 135n136-38). The traces of Hall's "Good Magistrate", which Aggeler (1995) points out in Justice Overdo in *Bartholomew Fair*, show that, apart from adopting the technique of presenting a character in a short prose account, Jonson also took up some of the features he found in the English Character books in constructing his characters. Another example of a dramatic character based on a description from a Character book is Shakerley Marmion's Veterano in *The Antiquary* (c. 1635, published 1641), who is clearly based on Earle's "Antiquary" (Boyce 1967, 312-14; Smeed 1985, 202-03).

Jonson's fusion of the genres, however, had implications for the concept of Character as the representation of human life. Although the genre of the Character is often thought to present categories of people rather than individuals (Smeed 1985, 2; Hockenjos 2006, 26), the Characters found in Character books are not merely types. Nor are the figures in the Jonson plays we have considered. Both the plays and many of the texts in Character books rather combine definition and observation. They show, for instance, what is quintessentially "A Child" (as in Earle, who thus gives us the ideal nature of childhood; Bauer 2011, 67-76), "An Excellent Actor" (Overbury), or "The Flatterer" (Hall). But this is frequently done by exemplary features and actions and utterances observed in life, and, as Coleridge says about Bunyan's allegorical characters, "we go on with the characters as real persons, who had been nicknamed by their neighbours" (1830, quoted from Sharrock 1976, 53).

The underlying principle of observation of everyday life is also reflected in a development in Character writing away from the depiction of abstract concepts such as vices as we find them in Theophrastus, or virtues and vices, as in Hall, towards a depiction of professions and social groups, as for example in Overbury and Earle. This observation and depiction of everyday life links the Character genre with the genre of comedy, which is, after all, meant to imitate everyday life. The tendency to depict these professions and social groups is certainly also influenced by drama and its inventory of characters, which is in turn influenced by Characters found in the Character books.

With regard to the Aristotelian dramatic categories of action (*mythos*) and Character (*ethos*), we might claim that drama affiliated with Character books is void of action. Jonson, as a reader of Theophrastus and a forerunner of English Character books, seems to have thought otherwise, for in the paratext descriptions in *Every Man Out of His Humour*, he says about Mitis: "It is a person of no action, and therefore we have reason to afford him no character" (Jonson 2012, *Every Man Out of His Humour*, Characters 90). This statement confirms our view that this is action generated by the Character descriptions. It is neither plot-driven nor the kind of action propelled by the functional types of New Comedy.[14] The plays rather unfold the activity inherent in the Character descriptions, as in the case of Amorphus in *Cynthia's Revels*, who "is his own promoter in every place" (Jonson 2012, *Cynthia's Revels* 2.3.71-72). The fact that action may consist in characters falling "out" of their humours does not contradict this concept.

This will also take us to our last point: Most of the Character book characters and those in the Jonson plays discussed are 'not Shakespeare'. What we mean by this is that, as stated in the Induction to *Every Man Out of His Humour*, "the property of the persons" (Jonson 2012, *Every Man Out of His Humour* Induction 250) must be clearly defined and provides the fixed starting point of the action. Even when there are conflicting views on the same character, the notion of definable Characters prevails. Interplay primarily consists in the meeting and collision of these characters (who are for example railed against by others whose Character is raillery).

---

14 This goes along with Jonson's desire to produce "a particular kind by itself, somewhat like *Vetus Comoedia*" (Cordatus in Induction; Jonson 2012, *Every Man Out of His Humour*, Induction 226).

Characters and their interaction are, as a rule, quite different in Shakespeare's plays. This has to do with what Jeremy Tambling has described quite fittingly as "a hidden organic unity existing between characters" in Shakespeare, whereas "nothing organic" connects the characters in Jonson (Tambling 2012, 12). They are conceived individually, derived from, and held together, by predominant and defining features and occupations. *In toto* they present a social, psychological, and moral cosmos, but they are just like a collection of Theophrastan Characters set to talk to each other and to interact, without being transformed by their relationships. The only way for a Character to change is to fall out of his humour as Asper does in *Every Man Out of His Humour* when he encounters Queen Elizabeth: "Envy is fled my soul at sight of her, / And she hath chased all black thoughts from my bosom, / Like as the sun doth darkness from the world. / My stream of humour is run out of me" (Jonson 2012, *Every Man Out of His Humour* 5.6.85-88).[15] And when this happens, the play is over.

References

Primary Sources

Breton, Nicolas (1924; 1615): *Characters upon Essays*, in: Aldington, Richard (ed. and trans.): *A Book of Characters*. London: Routledge, 169-177

Earle, John (1924; 1628): *Microcosmography*, in: Aldington, Richard (ed. and trans.): *A Book of Characters*. London: Routledge, 191-260

Hall, Joseph (1608): *Characters of Virtues and Vices*. London

---: *Characters of Virtues and Vices*, in: Aldington, Richard (ed. and trans.): *A Book of Characters*. London: Routledge, 53-93

Jonson, Ben (2012): *Every Man Out of His Humour*. Ed. Randall Martin, in: Bevington, David et al. (eds.): *The Cambridge Edition of the Works of Ben Jonson*, 7 vols. Cambridge: Cambridge University Press, 1: 233-428

--- (2012): *Cynthia's Revels, or, The Fountain of Self-Love*. Ed. Eric Rasmussen; Matthew Steggle, in: Bevington, David et al. (eds.): *The Cambridge Edition of the Works of Ben Jonson*, 7 vols. Cambridge: Cambridge University Press, 1: 429-547

--- (2012): *Volpone* Ed. Richard Dutton, in: Bevington, David et al. (eds.): *The Cambridge Edition of the Works of Ben Jonson*, 7 vols. Cambridge: Cambridge University Press, 3: 23-187

--- (2012): *Bartholomew Fair*. Ed. John Creaser, in: Bevington, David et al. (eds.): *The Cambridge Edition of the Works of Ben Jonson*, 7 vols. Cambridge: Cambridge University Press, 4: 269-420

--- (2012): *The New Inn*. Ed. Julie Sanders, in: Bevington, David et al. (eds.): *The Cambridge Edition of the Works of Ben Jonson*, 7 vols. Cambridge: Cambridge University Press, 6: 177-313

---

15 Jonson added a different version of this ending to the printed edition of 1600 alongside the original ending quoted here and a defence of the original ending in which he objects to criticism the 1599 ending had received (Martin 2012, 239-40). While Macilente's running out of humour is clearly caused by his encounter with the Queen in the original ending, the revised version shows his transformation "after he simply runs out of gulls to humiliate" (Martin 2012, 241): "Why, here's a change! Now is my soul at peace. / I am as empty of all envy now / As they of merit to be envied at" (Appendix B 82-84). Jonson added another two different versions of the ending to the 1616 folio text of *Every Man Out of His Humour*. One of them is a shortened version of the revised ending printed in the quarto of 1600 and does not feature an appearance by the Queen while the other once more attributes Macilente's running out of humour (see Appendix C l 88) to the Queen's presence.

--- (2012): *The Magnetic Lady, or Humours Reconciled*. Ed. Helen Ostovich, in: Bevington, David et al. (eds.): *The Cambridge Edition of the Works of Ben Jonson*, 7 vols. Cambridge: Cambridge University Press, 6: 413-540

Overbury, Thomas (1924; 1614): *Characters or Witty Descriptions of the Properties of Sundry Persons*, in: Aldington, Richard (ed. and trans.): *A Book of Characters*. London: Routledge, 95-167

Theophrastus (1924): *Ethical Characters*, in: Aldington, Richard (ed. and trans.): *A Book of Characters*, London: Routledge, 27-52

Webster, John (1996): *The White Devil*. Ed. John Russell Brown, Revels Student Editions. Manchester: Manchester University Press

Secondary Sources

Aggeler, Geoffrey (1995): "Ben Jonson's Justice Overdo and Joseph Hall's Good Magistrate", *English Studies* 78.5, 434-442

Baldwin, Edward Chauncey (1901): "Ben Jonson's Indebtedness to the Greek Character-Sketch", *Modern Language Notes* 16, 193-198

Bauer, Matthias (2011): "Die Entdeckung des Kindes in der englischen Literatur des 17. Jahrhunderts", in: Bauer, Matthias et al. (eds.): *Sprache, Literatur, Kultur: Translatio delectat*. Münster: Lit Verlag, 65-88

Boyce, Benjamin (1967): *The Theophrastan Character in England to 1642*. London: Frank Cass

Clausen, Wendell (1946): "The Beginnings of English Character-Writing in the Early Seventeenth Century", *Philological Quarterly* 25, 32-45

Donaldson, Ian (2012): "Life of Ben Jonson", in: Bevington, David et al. (eds.): *The Cambridge Edition of the Works of Ben Jonson*, 7 vols. Cambridge: Cambridge University Press, 1: lxxxvii-cxv

Doran, Madeleine (1954): *Endeavors of Art: A Study of Form in Elizabethan Drama*. Milwaukee: University of Wisconsin Press

Ellis, Anthony (2006): "The Machiavel and the Virago: The Uses of Italian Types in Webster's *The White Devil*", *Journal of Dramatic Theory and Criticism* 20.2, 49-74

Hockenjos, Katrin (2006): *Frauenbilder in englischen Charakterskizzen des 17. Jahrhunderts*. Tübingen: Narr

Martin, Randall (2012): "Introduction to *Every Man Out of His Humour*", in: Bevington, David et al. (eds.): *The Cambridge Edition of the Works of Ben Jonson*, 7 vols. Cambridge: Cambridge University Press, 1, 235-247

Meier, T. (1964): "The Naming of Characters in Jonson's Comedies", *English Studies in Africa*, 7, 88-95

Ostovich, Helen (2001): "Introduction", in: Ostovich, Helen (ed.): *Every Man Out of His Humour*. By Ben Jonson. Manchester: Manchester University Press, 1-95

Sharrock, Roger (ed.; 1976): *Bunyan*, The Pilgrim's Progress: *A Casebook*. London: Macmillan

Smeed, J. W. (1985): *The Theophrastan 'Character': The History of a Literary Genre*. Oxford: Clarendon

Tambling, Jeremy (2012): "Dickens and Ben Jonson", *English* 61, 4-25

Watson, Robert N. (1986): "*The Alchemist* and Jonson's Conversion of Comedy", in: Kiefer Lewalski, Barbara (ed.): *Renaissance Genres: Essays on Theory, History, and Interpretations*. Cambridge, MA: Harvard University Press, 332-365

ELLEN REDLING (HEIDELBERG)

"From the Top of Paul's Steeple to the Standard in Cheap": Popular Culture, Urban Space, and Narrativity in Jacobean City Comedy

The majority of Jacobean city comedies were first performed at private London theatres such as Blackfriars, which catered to moneyed audiences[1], rather than at more public venues such as the Fortune or the Red Bull.[2] However, this does not mean that only an 'elite' audience attended these plays or that the dramas themselves had no part in 'popular' culture. As Theodore B. Leinwand makes clear, the spectators at the private theatres consisted not only of the nobility, but also of "merchants and successful retailers, military officers and clerics, lawyers and gentry [...] as well as [...] teachers" (Leinwand 1986, 45). In the first part of this paper, I will look at the way this mixture of social groups among Early Modern audiences is reflected in city comedy.[3] Using Ben Jonson's *The Alchemist* (1610), John Marston's *The Dutch Courtesan* (1604), and Thomas Middleton's *A Mad World, My Masters* (1605), I will demonstrate that no easy definition of the 'popular' can be applied to the plays and that twenty-first century readings of these dramas need to take into account the complex meanings of the 'popular' inherent in them.

In the second section, I will focus on the London settings of city comedies, which serve to bring a variety of characters together: from rascal to gentleman, from courtesan to lady, from Anabaptist to alchemist. These settings mirror the actual spaces outside the theatres where encounters between different classes and cultures occurred, such as taverns and marketplaces.[4] The images of London in these plays are varied, thus shedding a new light on the complexity of the cultural meetings portrayed in the plays. All the plays depict the opening up of urban spaces, as in each case the city is becoming inclusive rather than exclusive. This change reflects London's development into a vibrant capital city and growing economic centre in the Early Modern age. The plays show, on the one hand, that old notions of an orderly structure of society have become difficult to uphold in the light of this development. On the other hand, they satirise and thereby strongly criticise the downsides of growing capitalism. The depic-

---

1   The price of admission was "at least 6d" (Leinwand 1986, 45).
2   As Wendy Griswold makes clear, "city comedy took shape in the so-called private theatres, in which most of the genre's early productions were concentrated" (Griswold 1986, 26).
3   The term 'popular culture' is a difficult one to use with regard to city comedies since it could imply something completely distinct from a so-called 'elite culture.' Most of the early comedies were presented at private theatres. However, the differences between the private and the public theatres should not be seen as clear-cut, as there was an intersection of various classes and cultures among the audiences in both types of theatres. Furthermore, some city comedies, such as Thomas Middleton's *A Chaste Maid in Cheapside* (1613), were first shown at public theatres. Theodore B. Leinwand points out that "city comedies were not unique to the private theatres" (Leinwand 1986, 44).
4   Regarding these meeting places outside the theatres, see also Burke 2001, 28.

tion of trickery taking advantage of greed prevails in all of these works. Centred on the market aspects of London, the plays not only portray an overall increase in pride, greed, hypocrisy, and deception, but also characterise them as particularly urban vices. The figure of Iniquity in Ben Jonson's *The Devil Is An Ass* (1616) could be read as being eager to embrace such a transformation of London society, for example, when he announces that he will leap from "Paul's steeple" (Jonson 2008, *Devil Is An Ass* 1.1.56) – which quite literally belongs to the past, having been destroyed by fire in 1561 (see Kidnie 2000, 476) – towards the "Standard in Cheap" (Jonson 2008, *Devil Is An Ass* 1.1.56), a crucial part of Cheapside, an increasingly influential marketplace.

The third aspect of these plays under consideration in this paper, namely the narrativity evident in them, often establishes the visuality as well as the vividness of the London settings. As I will demonstrate, the use of narrativity for the purpose of evoking images of London links seventeenth-century city comedy to twenty-first-century London narratives. Parallels between Early Modern city comedies and twenty-first-century city narratives extend to themes, plot lines, and characterisations and are based on an interplay between narrative and dramatic modes in both genres. This paper will show that these similarities between the city comedies and modern-day London narratives point to a common emphasis on London as a vibrant, but also problematic financial centre in both the seventeenth and the twenty-first centuries. Finally, it will be argued that modern-day works not only emulate the tradition of the city comedies but modify it in order to adapt it to the twenty-first century.

1. Popular Culture in City Comedies by Ben Jonson, John Marston and Thomas Middleton

The elements that critic Alexander Leggatt postulates as typical for plays presented at the public theatres and as pertaining to a "'popular' [...] taste" (Leggatt 1992, 28) often apply equally to those shown at private playhouses. Leggatt lists, for example, a strong visual element, clarity (symmetry, balance, and opposition), an episodic principle, fixed patterns, stock characters, and a side-by-side existence of contradictions (e.g., comedy and seriousness; *ibid.*, 33-38). These features are indeed present in each of the three city comedies examined here. First of all, the costume changes of all of the trickster figures create visual appeal. The cheaters slip into different roles in order to outwit the gulls. Fixed patterns and clear oppositions are perceivable in the contrasts between the tricksters and the tricked. All of the figures of city comedy are to some extent stock characters, since they represent greedy city types that appear repeatedly in the plays belonging to this genre: dyed-in-the-wool male rogues and prostitutes, young gallants in search of money or adventure, avaricious merchants, ladies looking for rich husbands, wealthy, gluttonous lords, and hypocritical Puritans.[5] The plots are episodic, structured around the recurring meetings between the tricksters and their gulls. Contradictory impulses appear in diverse forms. In *The Alchemist*, the quarrel between the two main cheaters at the beginning of the play has a comical side to it, particularly

---

5   See also Leinwand 1986, 7f. and Griswold 1986, 17f. Importantly, Leinwand draws attention to the constructed nature of these types. He argues that "the 'radical critique' [...] consists not in their satire of [...] greedy merchants and idle gentry, but in their self-conscious staging of the clearly inadequate roles and types which Londoners tolerated for the purposes of identifying one another" (Leinwand 1986, 18).

when the two men curse each other (Jonson 2008, *Alchemist* 1.1.106f.). On a more serious note, their quarrel indicates how quickly a personal bond can break in an age marked by greed. As the third, female trickster makes clear in an exaggerated way: "Gentlemen, what mean you? / Will you mar all? [...] Will you undo yourselves with civil war?" (*ibid.*, 1.1.80-82). In Marston's *The Dutch Courtesan*, Malheureux first admonishes his best friend Freevill for visiting brothels, only to become promptly obsessed with the titular Dutch Courtesan himself. In Middleton's *A Mad World, My Masters* the subplot stands in contrast to the main plot: In the former, the character of Penitent Brothel becomes penitent after having committed adultery with a jealous merchant's wife. In the latter, a young gallant marries a whore, reconciling himself to his marriage due to the gold he receives for this union.[6]

There are, however, at least two features of city comedies that do not fit into Leggatt's pattern: their lack of morally good characters and their unresolved moral ambiguity. Leggatt mentions a black-and-white arrangement of oppositions regarding the characters (Leggatt 1992, 33). Yet none of these highly satirical city comedies displays a morally ideal character that could be pitted against a despicable one. All the figures are avaricious, albeit to varying degrees. Furthermore, at the end of the city comedies the clever tricksters often come out triumphant, which indicates that wit – not virtue – can help the individual to both survive and thrive in a morally questionable, market-oriented world. The tricksters also serve as mouthpieces of social criticism in showing up the greed and gullibility of the other characters.

The mixing of different traditions in the city comedies destabilises any easy conception of the 'popular'.[7] Sue Wiseman's reading of the 'popular' in the Early Modern age takes into account this ambiguity when she argues that "for a literary scholar, perhaps, the popular names an aim to track cultural frames as fully as a text allows or invites" (Wiseman 2009, 28). In other words, the popular need "not [be] located in one sphere of culture but rather draws and plays on the way different ideas encounter and overlay one another" (*ibid.*, 28). This encounter of cultures and literary traditions fits the spirit of Early Modern London and its increasingly mixed society.

2. Urban Space in the City Comedies

As the prologue of Jonson's *The Alchemist* famously announces, "Our scene is London" (Jonson 2008, *Alchemist* 5). It is this particular setting that distinguishes the city comedies from Shakespearean comedies, and suggests immediacy and direct relevance to a London audience. During the Early Modern age, London emerged as a capital city, undergoing rapid growth "from an estimated 50,000 in 1530 to 120,000 in 1600 and nearly 300,000 in 1660" (Hebron 2008, 25). An increase in the mercantile economy attracted a large variety of people such as apprentices wishing to join the guilds, but also criminals, vagabonds, and thieves (see *ibid.*, 25). Ian Munro speaks of a "cul-

---

6   In the case of Middleton, P. K. Ayers explains such contradictions by arguing that "one of the [...] primary ends would seem [...] to be to probe the limits to which comic inclusiveness can be pushed and the degree to which an audience can, to its peril, be lured into wilfully rejecting such an inclusiveness in the name of its own indolent comfort" (Ayers 1986, 18).

7   As the third part of this paper will point out, there is a great number and variety of precursors of city comedies.

tural explosion" (Munro 2005, 4), and Giulio Carlos Argan analyses the effects of such a fast, diversified development as follows:

> In the capital city, modern man does not live in familiar, unchanging surroundings; he is caught up, rather, in a network of relations, a complex of intersecting perspectives, a system of communications, a ceaseless play of movements and counter-movements. (Argan 1964, 37)

With its new and complex ways of interconnecting people and new surroundings, London could have easily evoked a feeling of insecurity in its inhabitants. On the one hand, city comedies seem to counter such a sense of unease by providing references to specific parts of the city or fixed landmarks in order to create a feeling of familiarity and communality between the players and the audience. For example, in Marston's *The Dutch Courtesan*, the rascal Cocledemoy announces in his general talk about bawds: "'tis / most certain [the bawds] must needs both live well and die well, / since most commonly they live in Clerkenwell and die in / Bridewell" (Marston 1997, 1.2.53-56). With Clerkenwell a red-light district and Bridewell a London prison, the two places represent social and moral as well as geographical markers. Such jokes also appear in Middleton's *A Mad World, My Masters* and Jonson's *The Alchemist*.[8] On the other hand, London is also 'defamiliarized' in the city comedies and thus appears unstable. The trickery of the cheaters is usually accompanied by role and costume changes and by a sense of magic and the unknown within the 'real' space of London.[9] *The Alchemist*, for instance, portrays a house that becomes the site of strange occurrences: experiments[10] and confidence games.[11]

One of the most famous patterns used in the city comedies is the cheater-cheated formula, which divides the urbanites presented on stage into trickster figures and the tricked. Both fit into the city context since 'urban' vices such as pride, greed and hypocrisy are laid bare by the cheater figure who observes these vices in his gulls and dupes them. The trickster is, of course, greedy himself, but his mind is not completely overpowered by the vices – which distinguishes him from his gulls. He keeps his wits about him and is successful in the end. In *The Alchemist*, there are three tricksters: Subtle, an older cheater who mainly plays the role of the eponymous Alchemist; Face, who changes his 'face' often in the play; and Doll, a prostitute. Face is the cleverest of the three: He has new ideas that the other cheaters adopt as well as the ability to quickly adapt to new circumstances. Together, the three tricksters in turn cheat a lawyer's clerk, a tobacco shop owner, a rich glutton, two Anabaptists, and a young heir

---

8   See, for instance, 5.2.257f. in *A Mad World, My Masters*, with its comic allusion to Bedlam, the lunatic asylum, and 1.1.90-98 in *The Alchemist*, where Face threatens to hang a poster of Subtle in St. Paul's and thereby to openly accuse him of trickery and bawdry.
9   As Ian Donaldson states in *Jonson's Magic Houses*, "the fixed setting of *The Alchemist* [...] creates an air of mystery. [...]. The house in Blackfriars is capable of being whatever people most want it to be: it is a shell within which their fantasies may be projected, a sounding-board for the imagination" (Donaldson 1997, 76-77).
10 See, for example, John Shanahan's article on "Ben Jonson's *Alchemist* and Early Modern Laboratory Space" (2008).
11 Consequently, direct place references only superficially convey a sense of authenticity. As Brian Gibbons points out, the urban setting of city comedy should not be understood in terms of 'photographic' realism but in a metaphorical way (Gibbons 1968, 16). He argues that the realism lies in "transforming typical elements of city life into meaningful patterns, expressing consciously satiric criticism but also suggesting deeper sources of conflict and change" (*ibid.*, 17).

and his sister, a young widow. They promise to each of them that the Alchemist's power or, more specifically, his philosopher's stone, will provide them with exactly the things they want most. The characters and their telling names (e.g. Sir Epicure Mammon, Tribulation Wholesome, and Dame Pliant) serve to satirise the society of the time, which is strongly influenced by money, superstition, religious zeal, the leisure of gentlemen and the marriage market. In each case, the gulls are lured by Face into a house located in Blackfriars, where the Alchemist is supposed to work his miracles for them. The house actually belongs to Face's master Lovewit, who has left London because of the plague. When Lovewit returns early, Face eventually comes out triumphant since he has tricked both Subtle and Doll and has put Lovewit into a generous frame of mind by arranging a marriage between him and the rich young widow Dame Pliant. Lovewit loves Face's wit and protects him from the gulls, the constables and the perturbed neighbours who arrive at the door. Wit and the exposure of vices are thus celebrated above propriety and the law.

As this brief plot outline illustrates, the urban space of London evoked in city comedy represents the greediness of its fictional inhabitants and, by implication, its real-life population. Yet there are other facets of how space is used. *The Alchemist* appears to portray a simple space – a house in Blackfriars in London; the unity of space is adhered to, as are the unities of time and action.[12] The action revolves around the trickery initiated by Subtle, Face, and Doll. The house thus appears to be cut off from city life, following its own rules instead. However, the complication developing from Act 3, Scene 4 onwards arguably introduces a sense of quasi-postmodern "space-time compression" in David Harvey's sense (Harvey 1990, 284-307).[13] Time seems to speed up and space appears to lose its former borders: From this scene onwards the gulls no longer arrive in a strict order but come at unforeseen times and in groups. City life, represented by a large group of people, crowds in on the tricksters as forty neighbours gather outside the house and try to explain to Lovewit that they have seen frequent comings and goings of people.

At this point in the play the conception of the house changes from a closed to an open sphere. It now resembles a marketplace and thus is in effect similar to the 'carnivalesque' space that Jonson introduces in *Bartholomew Fair* (1614).[14] As a place where the cheaters are putting on a show for the gulls, the house in Blackfriars can also be

---

12 These three unities famously became attributed to Aristotle's writings on tragedy in his *Poetics*. However, the only 'oneness' that Aristotle directly refers to is the unity of action – and he does so in a descriptive rather than prescriptive way. He writes about an "action that is one and entire, the parts of it being so connected that if any one of them be either transposed or taken away, the whole will be destroyed or changed" (Aristotle 1955, 20).

13 By "space-time compression" Harvey is referring to the idea that the "history of capitalism has been characterised by speed-up in the pace of life, while so overcoming spatial barriers that the world sometimes seems to collapse inwards upon us" (Harvey 1990, 240). The Early Modern age, which saw the rise of capitalism, represents to some extent a similar epoch of "rapid change, flux and uncertainty" (*ibid.*, 124).

14 According to Mikhail Bakhtin's terminology, a 'carnivalesque' place is one where, for example, no strict order determined by social hierarchies is present. As he writes, "Carnival is the place for working out [...] a new mode of interrelationship between individuals, counterpoised to the all-powerful socio-hierarchical relationships of non-carnival life" (Bakhtin 1984, 123). Jonson's marketplace in *Bartholomew Fair* creates such a space by bringing together people from various social backgrounds.

seen as a theatre space, an eerie double of Blackfriars Theatre itself, where the first spectators of *The Alchemist* were sitting[15], and thus a house-within-the-(play)house. While watching the play, the audience might therefore not only increasingly get the sense of being the equivalents of the deceived gulls on stage (Donaldson 1997, 83); they might also feel that they are confronted with vibrant and uncontrollable city life pushing in from outside the theatre walls. At the end of the play, Lord Lovewit just manages to keep the people at bay who are attempting to enter the house, thereby protecting not only his own reputation but also Face's 'face.' The union between the clever trickster and the lord suggests a mixing of classes and might mirror Ben Jonson's own in-between position.[16] A parallel between the Early Modern age and postmodernity can be drawn here.[17] To use Raymond Williams's terminology, the play displays a shift in the "structure of feeling"[18] regarding the experiences of the characters and perhaps those of the Early Modern spectators. A transition is depicted from an ordered and comprehensible, closed space to an open city space that is full of energy and also poses a potential threat owing to its instability and insecurity.

A complex new city feeling is also palpable in Marston's *The Dutch Courtesan*, albeit in a different way. In this play, the viewer gets a sense of a 'coarse' space, a tavern feeling, which is conveyed by the characters of Cocledemoy and Mulligrub in particular. Cocledemoy is a rascal and trickster. He has stolen a set of valuable goblets from the greedy tavern owner Mulligrub. Throughout the play Mulligrub tries to get back at Cocledemoy, but is only 'fleeced' over and over again – until he is hanged at the end of the play. Right at the beginning of the drama, Freevill, the play's protagonist and another trickster figure, uses so much detail in his description of Cocledemoy's theft that he vividly evokes a tavern atmosphere:

> Freevill: In most sincere prose, thus: that man of much money, some wit, but less honesty, cogging Cocledemoy, comes this night late into mine host's Mulligrub's tavern here, calls for a room. The house being full, Cocledemoy, consorted with his movable chattel, his instrument of fornication, the bawd Mistress Mary Faugh, are imparloured next the street. Good poultry was their food: blackbird, lark, woodcock; and mine host here comes in, cries 'God bless you!' and departs. A blind harper enters, craves audience, uncaseth, plays. The drawer, for female privateness' sake, is nodded out, who, knowing that whosoever will hit the mark of profit must, like those that shoot in stone-bows, wink with one eye, grows blind o'th'right side and departs. [...] Cocledemoy, perceiving none in the room but the blind harper (whose eyes heaven had shut up from beholding wickedness), unclasps a casement to the street very patiently, pockets up three bowls unnaturally, thrusts his wench forth the window, and himself most preposterously, with his heels forward, follows. (Marston 1997, 1.1.11-34)

---

15 See also Donaldson 1997, 82: "Lovewit's house [...] is irresistibly like that other house – situated, in all probability, in Blackfriars too – where this very play was first presented in 1610 by the King's Men."
16 He grew up in poor circumstances, but later sought patronage from aristocratic families and the Court; see Sara van den Berg 2000, 1-14.
17 Michel Foucault's dictum regarding simultaneity seems to apply to this play: "We are in the epoch of simultaneity: we are in the epoch of juxtaposition, the epoch of the near and far, of the side-by-side, of the dispersed" (Foucault 1986, 22).
18 This is Raymond Williams's term for "meanings and values as they are actively lived and felt, and the relations between these and formal or systematic beliefs are in practice variable (including historically variable)" (Williams 1977, 132).

Freevill's descriptions conjure up images of a pub that also serves as a boarding house, of the criminals assembled in the almost empty tavern and of their food, as well as of Cocledemoy's stealing of the goblets. This rather crude atmosphere constitutes a backdrop to both the philosophical and the prosaic discussions between the well-to-do, educated characters Freevill and Malheureux. They are best friends but very different from each other. Freevill has led a wild life and frequented brothels. The prostitute he visits regularly is the titular Dutch Courtesan. Now that he is about to get married – to the honest and virtuous Beatrice – he wants to visit the Dutch Courtesan again, convinced that marriage and the brothel go very well together or even need each other. Malheureux is shocked and warns him of the sinfulness of prostitution. Irony is established when Freevill truly falls in love with Beatrice and subsequently abandons the idea of prostitution, but Malheureux is smitten by the Courtesan and obsessed with the idea of sleeping with her. Freevill wants to 'cure' his friend through trickery, and, in the end, the Courtesan is – perhaps conveniently – sent off to jail and Malheureux freed from his obsession. One might claim that Malheureux simply goes on an exotic journey into the world of the lower classes in the course of the play, an adventure that parallels the experience of the audience watching the dangers of rough life on stage and leaving the theatre with a sense of security. However, there could be more to this journey than simple sensationalism. It is crucial to note that the discussions between the two friends are frequently based on Montaigne's liberal arguments[19]: Freevill and Malheureux discuss the idea of a prostitute selling her body but not her mind and free will as if they were lawyers at one of the Inns of Court.[20] A reason for the coupling of philosophy and coarse life can be found in Montaigne's ideas themselves, since – as a crucial, but easily overlooked quotation in the play makes clear – power should be underpinned by the knowledge of human difficulties.

> Freevill: [...] consider / man furnished with omnipotency, and you overthrow him. (Marston 1997, 3.1.242f.)

> Montaigne: Conceive man accompanied with omnipotency, you overwhelm him: he must in begging manner crave some empeachment and resistance of you. (Montaigne 1908, 3.7.188)

Thus, Malheureux needs to acquire a sense of what it is to be human and to grapple with obstacles – by entering the world of Cocledemoy, Mulligrub, and the Courtesan – before he is truly ready to discover and display his identity and power. The lofty, abstract ideas that Malheureux presents at the beginning of the play have to be brought up against and changed by real-life, down-to-earth experience. Like Jonson's play, Marston's drama thereby opens up the door to bustling city life, where various cultures meet and an old order cannot be upheld.

Instead of focussing on a 'coarse' tavern atmosphere, Middleton's *A Mad World, My Masters* is centred on London wealth. In his play, the main trickster is not a lower-class rogue, but a young gallant, Follywit, who is in search of money. Follywit's major dilemma is that his rich grandfather, Sir Bounteous Progress, wants him to inherit his wealth, but refuses to give him any money while he is still alive. Instead, Sir Bounteous spends his money lavishly in order to impress the members of the aristocracy who

---

19 Regarding parallels between Montaigne's words and Marston's play see also William M. Hamlin 2012.
20 In 1594 John Marston joined his father, a lawyer, at the Inns of Court (David Crane 1997, xi) and therefore was familiar with the conventions of argumentation prevalent there.

visit his estate. Follywit is not supposed to work in order to earn money himself and therefore resorts to trickery. He uses his knowledge of Sir Bounteous's weaknesses and plays the role of a lord and, later, a thief, thus managing to obtain a large amount of his grandfather's money. The grandeur of his grandfather's house in London is invoked when Sir Bounteous questions a footman outside of the house as to whether the rich lord, who is really Follywit, indeed intends to stay at his imposing estate:

Sir Bounteous:	Art sure he will alight here, footman? [...]
	Did he name the house with the great turret a'the'top?
Footman:	No, faith, did he not, sir. [*Going*]
Sir Bounteous:	[...] Did he speak of a cloth o'gold chamber?
Footman:	Not one word, by my troth, sir. [*Going*] [...]
Sir Bounteous:	Was there no talk of a fair pair of organs, a great gilt candlestick, and a pair of silver snuffers?
Footman:	'Twere sin to belie my lord; I heard no such words, sir. [*Going*] [...]
Sir Bounteous:	Was there no speech of a long dining room, a huge kitchen, large meat, and a broad dresser board?
Footman:	I have a greater maw to that, indeed, an't please your worship.
Sir Bounteous:	Whom did he name?
Footman:	Why, one Sir Bounteous Progress.
Sir Bounteous:	Ah, a, a, I am that Sir Bounteous, you progressive round-about rascal.

(Middleton 2009, 2.1.22-50)

Sir Bounteous is a braggart, and these descriptions may of course be exaggerated. However, this passage creates a picture of London wealth and snobbery. In comparison to the endings of Jonson's and Marston's plays, which question complacency in the face of a changing London society, the outcome of *A Mad World, My Masters* is, on the surface, more conservative: Follywit himself is duped when he marries Sir Bounteous's courtesan, who plays the role of an innocent virgin; yet he still receives Sir Bounteous's kindness and financial support and can thus stay at his rich grandfather's estate. However, the rise of the courtesan signals that morality is often compromised in the city, that social mobility is unstoppable, and that London society is increasingly in a state of flux.

3. Narrativity in the City Comedies and Its Influence on London Narratives of the Twenty-First Century

Visuality and vividness of space are often evoked in the narrative passages of city comedy, since word-scenery frequently replaces the actual creation of settings. The technique of word-scenery is used in city comedy for a specific purpose, namely to 'narrate' London settings, e.g., in Freevill's description of the tavern in *The Dutch Courtesan* and in Sir Bounteous's praise of his own house in the city, which outwardly takes the form of the elicitation of a specific answer (see Middleton 2009, 2.1.22: "Art sure he will alight here, footman?"), but really consists of a number of rhetorical questions designed to describe and show off his richness. Thus, categories traditionally used for the analysis of narrative works can be applied to these plays: Freevill's and Sir Bounteous's stories are diegetic narratives because they are not recounted with mimetic means but through "verbal transmission of narrative content" (Nünning / Sommer 2011, 206); they are intradiegetic narratives told by characters in the plays. However, the narrations are also dramatic in the sense that they are what Barbara Hardy terms "performance[s] of telling" (Hardy 1997, 62) – after all, the characters present their stories on stage. Sir Bounteous's story even constitutes an instance of turning narrative content into dialogue (see *ibid.*, 15). 'London' in these city dramas is, then, created through a complex interplay of narrative and dramatic modes.[21]

A third example of intradiegetic storytelling can be found in the vision of immense wealth invoked by the rich glutton Sir Epicure Mammon:

> Mammon: Those [court and town stallions] will I beg to make me eunuchs of,
> And they shall fan me with ten ostrich tails
> Apiece, made in a plume to gather wind.
> We will be brave, Puff, now we ha' the medicine.
> My meat shall all come in in Indian shells,
> Dishes of agate, set in gold, and studded
> With emeralds, sapphires, hyacinths and rubies.
>
> (Jonson 2008, 2.2.68-79)

Sir Epicure Mammon here paints a fantasy picture of a place in London that largely resembles an oriental palace. Dramatic storytelling is therefore not only able to depict the "actual storyworld of the play" (Nünning / Sommer 2011, 201) but also "other possible worlds" (*ibid.*). Sir Epicure's vision is indicative of London's immense growth at the time and the megalomaniac dreams of individuals connected to this development.

The mixture of modes in city comedy can be attributed to the fact that the genre has its roots in both dramatic and narrative works. Among its antecedents are Plautus's comedies, the medieval mystery and morality plays, and revenge dramas on the one hand, and cony-catching pamphlets, jest books, and rogue tales on the other. The idea of several different characters gathering in the same place (and telling stories) can be found in Boccaccio's *The Decameron* (c. 1349-1353) and Chaucer's *The Canterbury Tales* (c. 1387-1400). Regarding the characterisation of urban types, city comedies also draw on the tradition of the Theophrastan character sketch[22]; in *The Dutch Courtesan*, for example, Cocledemoy describes the character of the bawd as follows:

> List, then; a bawd: first for her profession or vocation, it is most worshipful of all the twelve companies; for as that trade is most honourable that sells the best commodities – as the draper is more worshipful than the pointmaker, the silkmaker more worshipful than the draper, and the goldsmith more honourable than both, little Mary – so the bawd above all. Her shop has the best ware, for where these sell but cloth, satins, and jewels, she sells divine virtues, as virginity, modesty, and such rare gems, and those not like a petty chapman, by retail, but like a great merchant, by wholesale. Wa, ha, ho! (Marston 1997, 1.2.30-40)

The trickster, acting as a mouthpiece of social criticism, is mocking the fact that goodness is no longer connected to virtue, since it is now increasingly valued in terms of a market rationale, and that the spiritual concept of virtuousness has thereby become

---

21   Research in the field of narration in drama has been growing in recent years, as the following selection of publications shows: Richardson (1988, 2000a, 2000b, 2001, 2007); Fludernik (1996, 2007); Jahn (2001); Nünning / Sommer (2002, 2006, 2007, 2011); Sommer (2005); Tönnies / Flotmann (2011); Nünning / Schwanecke (forthcoming 2014); Redling (forthcoming 2014). This increase is largely due to the seminal work of Manfred Pfister on Brechtian 'epic' narration (see Pfister 1988, 71-76 and 120-131) and that of Brian Richardson, who pointed out that "the history of the theater is replete with representations of consciousness" (Richardson 1988, 204) and that the two genres – drama and narrative – are closer to each other than is generally believed (*ibid.*, 212).

22   See also Bauer / Bross in this volume.

replaced by an objectification. As Cocledemoy argues, virtues themselves are sold by the bawds, powerful businesswomen who market their 'wares' without the use of any intermediaries and in their entirety (the 'whole' bodies of the prostitutes).

Blurring the boundaries between drama and narrative, many features of city comedy regarding setting, topics, characterisations, and plot structures live on in London narratives of the twenty-first century. In addition, these elements are modified to make them fit into a modern-day context, which shows that the tradition of London works is not only still alive but is also undergoing creative developments.[23] In Craig Taylor's *Londoners* (2011)[24] and Zadie Smith's *NW* (2012)[25], we are presented with a panoply of characters reflecting the problems of London society, each of them caught up in (un)usual situations and spaces. In one of the plot lines of Smith's *NW* we can, for example, see the survival of the descriptions of urban types. The drug addict Shar (as depicted by the main protagonist and focaliser Leah) is such a character:

> The face is familiar. Leah has seen this face many times in these streets. [...] [F]aces without names. The eyes are memorable, around the deep brown clear white is visible, above and below. An air of avidity, of consuming what she sees. Long lashes. Babies look like this. (Smith 2012, 6)

Furthermore, the plot involving Shar and Leah resembles the most crucial element of city comedies' 'mimetic narration,' i.e., their "representation of a temporal and/or causal sequence of events" (Nünning / Sommer 2011, 206).[26] It displays the sequence of a trickster cheating a gull. Dialogic passages are employed in this episode (Smith 2012, 5ff.), which also establishes a connection to the mode of drama. In this part of the novel, Leah, a white woman living in a largely black council estate neighbourhood in London, is gulled by a black woman, Shar, into giving her 30 £. The story has a grim twist; certain elements of city comedy are modified in this novel. Leah and Shar used to go to school together, and Shar has now ended up as a drug addict. Shar's wit, which she demonstrates in her deception of Leah, does not help her to get very far in this world; this stands in direct contrast to a belief in cleverness as a means to 'make it' in the city comedies. Furthermore, Shar is not really the outsider in this trickster-tricked constellation. In fact, instead of a black drug addict or, as in the seventeenth-century city comedies, a courtesan representing someone who is in Tim Cresswell's

---

23 Links to Early Modern city comedy can also be found in nineteenth-century London novels. For example, Dickens's *Oliver Twist* (1837-39) displays cheater figures (e.g. Fagin, Artful Dodger) as well as passages describing places in London. Unlike city comedies, however, where social criticism is largely achieved through distancing techniques such as satire, Dickens's works often use the evocation of sympathy to draw the reader's attention to a social problem – in the case of *Oliver Twist* by, for instance, providing details about the plight of the children in Saffron Hill.
24 The complete title of Taylor's work is *Londoners: The Days and Nights of London Now – As Told by Those Who Love It, Hate It, Live It, Left It and Long for It.*
25 Other twenty-first century London novels could also yield interesting parallels, for example, Nick Hornby's *A Long Way Down* (2005) and Sebastian Faulks's *A Week in December* (2009).
26 Importantly, Brian Richardson points out that "from the outset, theories of drama and theories of narrative have been closely linked [...]. The topics [Aristotle] covers [in his *Poetics*], including character, plot, beginnings and endings, poetic justice, and the goals of representation, are as relevant to narrative theory as to a poetics of drama" (Richardson 2007, 142). Regarding the connections between narratology and Aristotle's *Poetics*, see also Fludernik 1996, 333.

sense "out of place" (Cresswell 2004, 103)[27], we here find a white woman, Leah, who is "out of place," albeit in a different way. She could fit into her middle-class surroundings but does not wish to do so. In contrast to her boyfriend and most of the people around her, she rejects the notion of starting a family and thereby being part of a "bourgeois" society[28], and she does not believe in the idea of moving up in the world.[29] This lack of interest in advancement sets her off from the courtesan character in the city comedies, who is clearly a social climber. However, just like the courtesan, Leah is a challenge or even threat to her surroundings since she refuses to play along with a common conception of a middle-class idyll and therefore repudiates an attitude of complacency in society. Forms of social criticism that are linked to London society are present in *NW* just as they were in the city comedies, but they take on a bleaker dimension.

Like *NW*, Craig Taylor's *Londoners* also portrays the problematic sides of the city. It depicts the hardships of people such as poor artists and squatters (Taylor 2011, 225-232). In addition, Taylor's work sheds light on the "toxic" environment (*ibid.*, 15) that renders a life – especially a life with children – extremely difficult (*ibid.*, 228). The author himself describes in the prologue, where he tells the story of his relocation to London in 2000, how he was tricked by a young prostitute (who looked like a schoolgirl) into giving her money (*ibid.*, 3f.). This episode to some extent resembles the trickery of courtesans in cony-catching pamphlets and city comedies. However, *Londoners* mostly foregrounds a sense of the vibrant energy felt by many people living and working in London: A woman working as the 'voice' of the London Underground, for example, speaks about the marvellous opportunities given to her by this job (*ibid.*, 45-49), and a female plumber loves to think about the history of plumbing in London (*ibid.*, 89). This largely positive emphasis is due to the fact that Taylor is himself fascinated by the city. In contrast to the disbelief in progress depicted in Smith's *NW*, Taylor maintains that "London is propulsion, it rewards people who push forward" (*ibid.*, 7), a notion which recalls the possibility of moving up in society depicted in the city comedies.

Taylor's work consists of first-person narratives by many different *actual* people who are either still living in London or spent a period of time there in the past, including the author's own story. It is thus a collection of personal narratives (or life-writings) told by urban 'figures.' The concept of urbanites telling stories and describing their views of London is thus certainly present in *Londoners*. The large number of urban 'characters' (over 80 Londoners) depicted in this text, who are mostly characterised through their various occupations, greatly exceeds, however, that found in the city comedies or in *NW*. The large variety of their subjective, 'real' stories leads to an increased subjectivisation of urban 'types.'

---

27   By someone who is "out of place" Cresswell refers to a person who transgresses socio-cultural boundaries (Cresswell 2004, 103).

28   When Leah watches her friend Natalie taking care of her child, she asks her boyfriend Michel: "Who is she? Who is this person? This bourgeois existence!" (Smith 2012, 58).

29   For example, when Leah's boyfriend Michel tries to improve his financial and social situation with the help of online trading, Leah shows a lack of understanding – upon which he asks her, annoyed: "Why don't you get on with your own things?" (Smith 2012, 43).

As in the city comedies and in Smith's novel, the interplay between narrative and dramatic modes in *Londoners* is highly complex. Taylor regards his work as "a collage of voices that together would draw a picture of the city" (*ibid.*, 8). On the one hand, the use of the term 'voices' points to the fact that the stories in his work are based on underlying 'dramatic' situations, i.e., on real-life dialogues between Taylor as the interviewer and one or more people as interviewees. *Londoners* sometimes even presents the speeches of the urbanites as part of an interview situation.[30] On the other hand, the questions posed by Taylor are generally not included in his work. Furthermore, the stories of the urbanites cannot really be read as faithful transcriptions of the actual tape recordings of spontaneous speeches; they rather represent carefully structured first-person narratives.

In its depictions of the city *Londoners* displays noteworthy modifications when compared to both the seventeenth-century precursors and *NW*. Urban space is opened up to an even greater extent than in the city dramas and in Smith's novel. While both the dramas and *NW* use meeting places to bring together various different people – a house and a marketplace, a council estate and the Tube – such a 'place' does not exist in *Londoners*. Here, the 'places' are the voices, arranged together first in the mind of the author and then in the work itself. Moreover, single conceptions of urban space are also extended almost infinitely in Taylor's work, which begins and ends with the view of a commercial airline pilot arriving and leaving London. He looks at London from above and the voices from the city follow him up to the sky via the London radio channel. The pilot adores London's energy and this is the note upon which the work finishes (see *ibid.*, 422).

As narratives such as Zadie Smith's *NW* and Craig Taylor's *Londoners* show, works dealing with London are still very much alive and kicking. They can be linked to seventeenth-century city comedies through common plot lines, characterisations and the interplay between narrative and dramatic modes. Just like their Early Modern predecessors, twenty-first-century London narratives are also very much occupied with the city as a financial centre, which is full of vitalizing activity and open spaces, but which, conversely, can also point to dreams that are cynically exposed. As has been demonstrated, works from the twenty-first century even experiment with images of London spaces and characterisations of urbanites. In doing so they continue as well as modify the tradition of Jacobean city drama, adapting it to our contemporary day and age.

References
Primary Sources

Dickens, Charles (1966): *Oliver Twist*. Ed. Tillotson, Kathleen. Oxford: Clarendon
Jonson, Ben (2000): *The Devil Is an Ass*, in: Kidnie, Margaret Jane (ed.): *Ben Jonson: The Devil Is an Ass and Other Plays*. Oxford: Oxford University Press, 223-330
--- (2008): *The Alchemist*, in: Campbell, Gordon (ed.): *Ben Jonson: The Alchemist and Other Plays*. Oxford: Oxford University Press, 211-326

---

30 See Taylor 2011, 199-214, where interview situations are depicted. The names of those involved are followed by colons – just as is usually the case in drama.

Marston, John (1997): *The Dutch Courtesan*. Ed. Crane, David. London: A & C Black
Middleton, Thomas (2009): *A Mad World, My Masters*, in: Taylor, Michael (ed.): *Thomas Middleton: A Mad World, My Masters and Other Plays*. Oxford: Oxford University Press, 1-65
Montaigne, Michel de (1908): *The Essayes of Michael Lord of Montaigne done into English by John Florio*. Ed. Seccombe, Thomas. Volume 3. London: Grant Richards
Smith, Zadie (2012): *NW*. London: Hamish Hamilton
Taylor, Craig (2011): *Londoners: The Days and Nights of London Now – As Told by Those Who Love It, Hate It, Live It, Left It and Long for It*. London: Granta

Secondary Sources

Argan, Guilio Carlos (1964): *The Europe of the Capitals: 1600-1700*. Geneva: Albert Skira
Aristotle (1955): *Aristotle's Poetics and Rhetoric*. Trans. Thomas Twining. London: Dent
Ayers, P. K. (1986): "Plot, Subplot, and the Uses of Dramatic Discord in *A Mad World, My Masters* and *A Trick To Catch The Old One*," *Modern Language Quarterly* 47.1, 3-18
Bakhtin, Mikhail (1984): *Problems of Dostoevsky's Poetics*. Trans. Caryl Emerson. Minneapolis: University of Minnesota Press
Burke, Peter (2001): *Popular Culture in Early Modern Europe*. Aldershot: Ashgate
Crane, David (1997): "Introduction", in: Crane, David (ed.): *John Marston: The Dutch Courtesan*. London: A & C Black, xi-xxx
Cresswell, Tim (2004): *Place: A Short Introduction*. Malden, MA: Blackwell
Donaldson, Ian (1997): *Jonson's Magic Houses: Essays in Interpretation*. Oxford: Clarendon
Fludernik, Monika (1996): *Towards a 'Natural' Narratology*. London/New York: Routledge
--- (2007): "Narrative and Drama", in: Pier, John; Landa, José Ángel García (eds.): *Theorizing Narrativity*. Berlin/New York: De Gruyter, 355-383
Foucault, Michel (1986): "Of Other Spaces", Trans. Jay Miskowiec, *Diacritics* 16, 22-27
Gibbons, Brian (1968): *Jacobean City Comedy: A Study of Satiric Plays by Jonson, Marston and Middleton*. London: Rupert Hart-Davis
Griswold, Wendy (1986): *Renaissance Revivals: City Comedy and Revenge Tragedy in the London Theatre, 1576-1980*. Chicago: The University of Chicago Press
Hamlin, William M. (2012): "Common Customers in Marston's *Dutch Courtesan* and Florio's Montaigne", *Studies in English Literature 1500-1900* 52.2, 407-424
Hardy, Barbara (1997): *Shakespeare's Storytellers: Dramatic Narration*. London/Chester Springs, PA: Peter Owen
Harvey, David (1990): *The Condition of Postmodernity: An Enquiry into the Origins of Cultural Change*. Oxford: Blackwell
Hebron, Malcolm (2008): *Key Concepts in Renaissance Literature*. Basingstoke: Palgrave Macmillan
Jahn, Manfred (2001): "Narrative Voice and Agency in Drama: Aspects of a Narratology of Drama," *New Literary History* 32.3, 659-79
Kidnie, Margaret Jane (ed.; 2000): *Ben Jonson: The Devil is an Ass and Other Plays*. Oxford: Oxford University Press
Leggatt, Alexander (1992): *Jacobean Public Theatre*. London: Routledge
Leinwand, Theodore B. (1986): *The City Staged: Jacobean Comedy, 1603-1613*. Madison, Wisconsin: University of Wisconsin Press
Munro, Ian (2005): *The Figure of the Crowd in Early Modern London: The City and its Double*. Basingstoke: Palgrave Macmillan
Nünning, Ansgar (2006): "Die performative Kraft des Erzählens: Formen und Funktionen des Erzählens in Shakespeares Dramen," in Schabert, Ina; Schülting, Sabine (eds.): *Shakespeare Jahrbuch* 142, 124-141
--- (2007): "Diegetic and Mimetic Narrativity: Some Further Steps towards a Narratology of Drama," in Pier, John; Landa, José Ángel García (eds.): *Theorizing Narrativity*. Berlin/New York: de Gruyter, 331-354

--- (2011): "The Performative Power of Narrative in Drama: On the Forms and Functions of Dramatic Storytelling in Shakespeare's Plays," in: Olson, Greta (ed.): *Current Trends in Narratology*. Berlin/New York: de Gruyter, 200-231

---; Schwanecke, Christine (forthcoming 2014): "The Performative Power of Unreliable Narration and Focalisation in Drama and Theatre: Conceptualising the Specificity of Dramatic Unreliability", in: Nünning, Vera (ed.): *(Un)reliable Narration and (Un)trustworthiness: Intermedial and Interdisciplinary Perspectives*. Berlin: de Gruyter

---; Sommer, Roy (2002): "Drama und Narratologie: Die Entwicklung erzähltheoretischer Modelle und Kategorien für die Dramenanalyse," in Nünning, Vera; Nünning, Ansgar (eds.): *Erzähltheorie transgenerisch, intermedial, interdisziplinär*. Trier: WVT, 105-128

Pfister, Manfred (1988): *Theory and Analysis of Drama*. Trans. John Halliday. Cambridge: Cambridge University Press

Redling, Ellen (forthcoming 2014): "Ein Mörder als 'Superman'?: Sympathielenkung und unzuverlässiges Erzählen in Martin McDonaghs Drama *The Pillowman* (2003)," in: Lusin, Caroline (ed.): *Empathie, Sympathie und Narration: Strategien der Rezeptionslenkung in Prosa, Drama und Film*. Heidelberg: Winter

Richardson, Brian (1988): "Point of View in Drama: Diegetic Monologue, Unreliable Narrators, and the Author's Voice on Stage", *Comparative Drama* 22.3, 193-214

--- (2000a): "Narrative Poetics and Postmodern Transgression: Theorizing the Collapse of Time, Voice, and Frame", *Narrative* 8.1, 23-42

--- (2000b): "Recent Concepts of Narrative and the Narratives of Narrative Theory", *Style* 34.2, 168-175

--- (2001): "Voice and Narration in Postmodern Drama", *New Literary History* 32.3, 681-694

--- (2007): "Drama and Narrative", in: Herman, David (ed.): *Cambridge Companion to Narrative*. Cambridge: Cambridge University Press, 142-155

Shanahan, John (2008): "Ben Jonson's *Alchemist* and Early Modern Laboratory Space", *Journal for Early Modern Cultural Studies* 8.1, 35-66

Sommer, Roy (2005): "Narrative and Drama", in: Herman, David et al. (eds.): *Routledge Encyclopedia of Narrative Theory*. London/New York: Routledge, 119-124

Tönnies, Merle; Flotmann, Christina (eds.; 2011): *Narrative in Drama*. Trier: WVT

Van den Berg, Sara (2000): "True Relation: The Life and Career of Ben Jonson", in: Harp, Richard; Stewart, Stanley (eds.): *The Cambridge Companion to Ben Jonson*. Cambridge: Cambridge University Press, 1-14

Williams, Raymond (1977): *Marxism and Literature*. Oxford: Oxford University Press

Wiseman, Sue (2009): "'Popular Culture': A Category for Analysis?," in: Dimmock, Matthew; Hadfield, Andrew (eds.): *Literature and Popular Culture in Early Modern England*. Farnham: Ashgate, 15-28

Section 4

Rhetoric and Poetry

Chairs:

Monika Fludernik and Ulrike Zimmermann

MONIKA FLUDERNIK AND ULRIKE ZIMMERMANN (FREIBURG)

Rhetoric and Poetry: An Introduction

Why a session on "Rhetoric and Poetry"? The choice of this topic relates both to current developments in the field of literary studies and literary theory and to the politics of Anglistentag meetings. Proposing a session that links the study of poetry with that of rhetoric was a result of recent attempts to provide a forum for literary and linguistic studies to meet within a thematically focussed session providing points of contact between these often disparate areas of our discipline. We gratefully acknowledge that linguistics scholars have indeed come forward to participate in the session by offering papers (see the contributions by Claudia Claridge and Alwin Fill below) and through their presence at the meeting in Konstanz. The lyric, analysed from a linguistic perspective by Jonathan Culler's examination of the present tense in English and in poetry in particular, yields a happy ground of communality between literary and linguistic concerns that are relevant from rhetorical, linguistic, and poetic perspectives.

The second motive for proposing a session on the conjunction of poetry and rhetoric relates to recent developments in literary theory, particularly that of the so-called "New Formalism" (which takes a variety of different forms). Discussed most incisively in a 2007 *PMLA* article by Marjorie Levinson, the New Formalism attempts to revive what is good about the New Criticism while trying to avoid its failures. What this comes down to is, primarily, a renewed attention to the words on the page. As Fredric V. Bogel says in his survey "Toward a New Formalism" (published in the 2013 volume by Theile and Tredennick, *New Formalisms and Literary Theory*): "For the mode of New Formalism that this chapter describes, a text is principally a linguistic object, a piece of language rewardingly susceptible to various strategies of detailed formalist analysis or interpretation – what is often called 'close reading'" (33). We think this is a very interesting definition of the New Formalism since it equates what in other quarters might simply be called *stylistics* with the practice of close reading, which has always been about the words on the page, but not perhaps about the words on the page *as linguistic objects*.

Levinson's short piece clarifies that the New Formalism grew out of the New Aestheticism (see, for instance, Armstrong 2000; de Bolla 2001; Joughin and Malpas 2003; Attridge 2004; Loesberg 2005); that is, once a renewed interest in aesthetics started to make itself felt, form became one of the concerns of that movement. Thus Levinson's characterization of the articles she summarises is that they all "aim to recover for teaching and scholarship in English some version of their traditional address to the aesthetic" (2007, 559). Interestingly, Levinson sees the New Historicism as the main bone of contention among New Formalists: Rather than defining oneself in relation to the (Old) Formalism or New Criticism, Levinson demonstrates that most proponents of the New Formalism actually try to marry form to New Historicist cultural studies or try to reintroduce a "sharp demarcation" between History and Art (559). (She calls these two camps "activist" and "normative" Formalists.) Even more surprising is the conclusion she comes to in relation to what kind of theoretical focus New Formalists utilize: There is, she finds, in fact little theory and strikingly no theorisation of concepts like "form" (561). Heather Dubrow, who has also written on the New Formalism (2002, 2006), rather lamely identified New Formalism more or less with attention to poetic form and rhetorical devices – an approach to literature that does not seem to go very much beyond the New Criticism. Nor do New Formalists as a rule (W. J. T. Mitchell is a notable exception), Levinson shows, carefully distinguish between different types of formalism, rarely noting the very individual take on form in New Criticism, Russian Formalism, Chicago School Rhetorics, the work of Auerbach, Spitzer, Leavis, or Northrop Frye, etc. (565).

Indeed, what are the negative aspects of the New Criticism that the New Formalists supposedly try to avoid? Noted by Bogel and the editors of the volume, Theile and Tredennick, are New Criticism's obsession with the poem as a unit of meaning and the exclusion of contextual, especially biographical, evidence in the course of interpretation. What the New Formalism seems to amount to, therefore, is a close reading that focuses on formal (metrical, rhetorical) features in the text *but also* reads the text as part of contemporary discourses (ideology) and takes account of generic traditions. In fact, when one goes over the pronouncements by the representatives of the New Formalism, one often has the impression that what is being sold as a new approach is exactly what we have been doing all along. This may of course be a very European perspective on the question, since European universities have, for instance, continued to teach linguistics and narratology as well as rhetoric – despite the influx of theory that partly superseded these skills in North America, as Culler notes in his introduction to *The Literary in Theory* (2007a, 5, 11). Having said that, students do increasingly focus on the twentieth century, thus avoiding exposure to complex formal stanzaic and metrical forms or rhyme schemes (since most post-World War II poets write some kind of free verse); they also tend to learn more about metaphor, which – thanks to Mark Turner and others – is a thriving field under the umbrella of cognitive studies, rather than using rhetorical figures other than metaphor to analyse, say, political speeches. This is particularly odd since ideology has been at the foreground of critical discourse studies in linguistics and particularly since 9/11 has also dominated cultural studies. Nowhere is the link between form and content more intrinsic than in poetry, and the need to scrutinize the import of poetic conventions more urgent: "One wonders whether a more robust poetics would enable different approaches to the literary works, which might, for instance, explore how the conventions or formal conditions of literary works, rather than their themes, make possible certain kinds of critical engagements with institutions of power" (Culler 2007a, 11).

What this session may perhaps achieve, ideally, is a *link* between the formal nature of texts (the various rhetorical strategies or devices) and their meanings, showing how forms and functions interrelate at several levels of analysis. This is, for instance, demonstrated in exemplary fashion by another contributor to *New Formalisms and Literary Theory*. In "Form as a Pattern of Thinking: Cognitive Poetics and New Formalism", Karin Kukkonen (2013) addresses the extensive functionality of formal elements on the example of a comic called *Watchmen* (Alan Moore, Dave Gibbons, and John Higgins, *Watchmen*, New York: DC Comics, 1986) and is able to provide numerous examples concerning the parallelism between form and content. She focuses on anaphora, chiasmus, and hysteron proteron and demonstrates how the comic utilises all of these devices (and many others) to direct the reader's attention towards certain interpretations and towards particular impending plot developments. By taking her example from a comic rather than eighteenth-century poetry, her specialisation, she moreover signals the centrality of form outside the ebony tower of traditional poetic excellence.

It seems to us especially important that departments of literature ensure that knowledge of the rhetorical tradition remains accessible precisely because many of the experiments in the writing of both prose and poetry in the twentieth century are in fact subtle reworkings of more traditional forms. This has been noted most extensively in relation to thematic reappropriations of traditional models (the neo-Victorian novel, the postmodernist fairytale), but less so in connection with poetic form in verse. Besides the easily recognizable figures of apostrophe, metaphor, metonymy, anaphora, and parallelism/antithesis/chiasmus, the rhetoric of modern free-verse poetry that eschews such easy alignments with tradition is a particularly challenging object of analysis, for linguists *and* for literary scholars, as for instance illustrated in Ulrike Pirker's and Marie-Luise Egbert's essays printed below. Echoing Levinson, what we need is a renewed effort to theorize form, particularly in relation to aesthetic effect or affect, and in relation to structure. Levinson (2007, 565-566) summarises some interesting comments by Richard Strier as a revisiting of the issues of function(s), formal redeployments, or adaption, and the testing of the opposition between textual meaning and textual affect (pleasure, jouissance).[1] Hence we see this panel and this section of the *Proceedings* volume as a starting point for further research.

The research constituting this section is varied and multifaceted, giving an impression of what is possible if linguistic and literary scholars approach the topic from their diverse perspectives. The papers have been ordered in a way to give the reader a sense of this diversity, emerging within the framework of a common endeavour. Historically, and seen from a European point of view, this endeavour can tap into a well that has never quite dried up, as rhetoric and its interest in form and structure have never been totally absent from academic study in the first place.

Rhetoric as an art (téchnê) has always been conceptualized as a (more or less circumscribed) system, and hence as an artefact (see Plett 2000, 13-14). Latin rhetoric, largely seen as oratory and persuasive, remained a model within the practical framework of didactics in (post-)Renaissance Europe (see Bender and Wellbery 1990, 17). The Enlightenment brought about a shift in the value judgment of rhetoric – one might think of Kant's much-quoted polemics in his *Critique of the Power of Judgment* here.[2] The eighteenth and nineteenth centuries then saw tendencies to view rhetoric as embellishment, having nothing to do with true poetry and true expression. Prose becomes the dominant form of fiction. Nonetheless, the poetic function of language has continued to draw interest through centuries of criticism; and around the turn from the twentieth to the twenty-first century, with the recent critical approaches elucidated above, rhetoric set out to regain its crucial role. Its appreciation has moved from a prescriptive cat-

---

1   See, for instance, Altieri 2001, 2004, 2006; and Wolfson 2007.
2   For concise overviews, see for instance Plett 2000, 248-250; Plett 2010, 3-31; Bender and Wellbery 1990, 5-22.

alogue of techniques, against which a self-respecting poet is called upon to rebel, towards a descriptive analytical framework, and then, lately, towards a concept with which to grasp the linguistic structuring of cognition: How do we structure and communicate (poetic) meaning? Hence, in a broader sense, rhetoric has to do with questions of language and perception, neither of which can be analyzed without attention to the form they take in a given text. For present purposes, the changes in Plett's standard text on rhetoric are a case in point: In the recent English translation (2010), which is a revised edition of the German text (2000), the chapter "From the Decline of Rhetoric to its Revival" has changed position and is now the first chapter, while it was part of a "Postscriptum" in 2000.

The following essays provide case studies of great diversity and thus correspond to the scope of the present topic, as well as to its diachronic implications. Accordingly, the contributions mirror the sense of the varying fate, the loss and revival of interest rhetoric encountered over time. The textual examples have been taken from different centuries and range from metaphysical poetry via the eighteenth and nineteenth centuries to the late twentieth century. Consequently, the chronological order may be taken as an illustration of continuities, but also of faultlines and breaks occurring in the field.

Jonathan Culler, in his analysis of the uses and functions of the present tense in lyric poetry, also engages in the metadiscourse of the teaching of poetry, which all too often misses a crucial point: the specific qualities that distinguish poetry from (narrative) forms of fiction. The paper by Wolfgang G. Müller also addresses the characteristics of poetic language, as he engages with Roman Jakobson's concept of poeticity and the poetic function in lyric texts. Claudia Claridge's contribution on texts by the metaphysical poet George Herbert scrutinizes the (re-)presentations of the speaker in the poems from a linguistic perspective, employing corpora for quantitative comparison. Depicting his relationship with God, Herbert's speaker conspicuously suppresses the nominative *I*, an effect which can be observed particularly well in frequency analyses. Gero Guttzeit, with his essay on the concepts of eloquence and poetry from 1776 to 1833, addresses a highly significant time in the tense relationship between rhetoric and poetry, and illuminates the shifting ground between the two from the Neoclassical to the Romantic period, with a focus on the Scottish New Rhetorician George Campbell. Alwin Fill, in a linguistic contribution to the panel, gives a close reading of some of D. H. Lawrence's nature poems. In Lawrence's use of metaphors Alwin Fill detects a poetical procedure that blurs the conceptual demarcation lines between humans and animals, animate and inanimate objects, thus questioning implicit cultural assumptions on morality and sanctioned conduct. Eva Ulrike Pirker's textual example of a long non-epic poem by J. H. Prynne is located later in the twentieth century and shows in many ways how intricate the use of rhetoric can be – in poetry that engages with modernism but also sets out to contest some of its tenets. Marie-Luise Egbert's essay on Les Murray's *Fredy Neptune* deals with the most recent text in this collection, a novel-in-verse. Her interpretation sheds light on the linguistic strategies the text uses in order to poetically stage the protagonist's loss of the sense of touch.

The approaches of this section open a horizon reaching across genres as well as across literary periods. Rhetoric and poetry are intertwined with each other, forming strands within structures of meaning. To quote John Bender and David E. Wellbery (1990, 25),

Rhetoricality[3] [...] manifests the groundless, infinitely ramifying character of discourse in the modern world. For this reason, it allows for no explanatory metadiscourse that is not already itself rhetorical. Rhetoric is no longer the title of a doctrine and a practice, nor a form of cultural memory; it becomes instead something like a condition of our existence.

References

Altieri, Charles (2001): "Taking Lyrics Literally: Teaching Poetry in a Prose Culture", *New Literary History* 32: 259-282
--- (2004): "Rhetoric and Poetics: How to Use the Inevitable Return of the Repressed", in: Jost, Walter; Olmstead, Wendy (eds.): *A Companion to Rhetoric and Rhetorical Criticism*. Oxford: Blackwell. 473-493
--- (2006): "Reading for Affect in the Lyric: From Contemporary to Modern", in: Retallack, Joan; Spahr, Juliana (eds.): *Poetry and Pedagogy: The Challenge of the Contemporary*. New York: Palgrave Macmillan, 39-62
Armstrong, Isobel (2000): *The Radical Aesthetic*. Oxford: Blackwell
Attridge, Derek (2004): *The Singularity of Literature*. London: Routledge
Bender, John; Wellbery, David E. (1990). *The Ends of Rhetoric*. Stanford: Stanford University Press
Bogel, Fredric V. (2013): "Toward a New Formalism: The Intrinsic and Related Problems in Criticism and Theory", in: Theile, Verena; Tredennick, Linda (eds.): *New Formalisms and Literary Theory*. Basingstoke: Palgrave, 29-53
de Bolla, Peter (2001): *Art Matters*. Cambridge, MA: Harvard University Press
Culler, Jonathan (2007a): *The Literary in Theory*. Stanford: Stanford University Press
--- (2007b): "Lyric Address", *Litteratura e letteratura* 1, 21-36
--- (2008): "Why Lyric?" *PMLA* 123.1, 201-206
--- (2009): "Lyric, History, and Genre", *New Literary History* 40.4, 879-899
--- (2013): "Theory of the Lyric", Manuscript
Dubrow, Heather (2002): "The Politics of Aesthetics: Recuperating Formalism and the Country House Poem", in: Rasmussen, Mark David (ed.): *Renaissance Literature and Its Formal Engagements*. New York: Palgrave, 67-88
--- (2006): "Guess Who is Coming to Dinner? Reinterpreting Formalism and the Country House Poem", in: Wolfson, Susan; Brown, Marshall (eds.): *Reading for Form*. Seattle, WA: University of Washington Press, 80-98
Joughin, John J.; Malpas, Simon, eds. (2003): *The New Aestheticism*. Manchester: Manchester University Press (Introduction 1-19)
Kukkonen, Karin (2013): "Form as a Pattern of Thinking: Cognitive Poetics and New Formalism", in: Theile, Verena; Tredennick, Linda (eds.): *New Formalisms and Literary Theory*. Basingstoke: Palgrave, 159-175
Levinson, Marjorie (2007): "What is New Formalism?" *PMLA* 122.2, 558-569
Loesberg, Jonathan (2005): *A Return to Aesthetics: Autonomy, Indifference, and Postmodernism*. Stanford: Stanford University Press
Plett, Heinrich F. (2000) *Systematische Rhetorik: Konzepte und Analysen*. Munich: Fink
--- (2010) *Literary Rhetoric: Concepts – Structures – Analyses*. Leiden: Brill
Rawes, Alan, ed. (2007): *Romanticism and Form*. Basingstoke: Palgrave
Theile, Verena; Tredennick, Linda, eds. (2013): *New Formalisms and Literary Theory*. Basingstoke: Palgrave
Wolfson, Susan J. (2007): "Afterword. Romanticism's Forms", in: Rawes, Alan (ed.): *Romanticism and Form*. Basingstoke: Palgrave, 213-222
---; Brown, Marshall (2007): *Reading for Form*. Seattle: University of Washington Press

---

3 Bender and Wellbery use this term to distinguish their use of modern views on discursive rhetoric from the classical uses, see Bender and Wellbery 1990, 25.

JONATHAN CULLER (ITHACA, NY)

The Strange Present Tense of the English Lyric

In this paper I propose to return to a subject that has been out of fashion since the 1970s: poetic language, its distinctiveness. Are there not particular uses of language that are characteristic, even distinctive, of lyric? After some discussion of the problem of a poetics of the lyric, I focus on a special characteristic of the language of lyric in English.

In my *Structuralist Poetics* in 1975, I advocated a poetics that would stand to literature as linguistics stands to language. The task of linguistics is not to provide new interpretations of English sentences, but to reconstruct the elaborate system of rules and conventions that permit utterances to have the form and meaning they do. Similarly, literary studies ought to give priority to understanding the systems of convention and inferential practices that enable literary works to have the meanings and effects they do, rather than seeking to discover new and deeper meanings for the most highly valued works. Hermeneutics rules in literary studies, but – as I still believe – poetics ought to take priority.

What of a poetics of the lyric? Northrop Frye once wrote that "a lyric is anything you can reasonably get uncut into an anthology", emphasizing the central feature of brevity: a poem easily read or spoken in one sitting (1985, 31). I would stress that lyric is characteristically non-narrative, though it effectively subsumes little narratives, assimilating them to a present of articulation. Historically, lyric is bound to voicing, pronounced rhythmic patterning, and a foregrounding of the signifier, especially through rhythm and rhyme. It is important to speak of voicing rather than voice, though many lyrics offer a *figure* of voice: We make sense of the poem by imagining hearing a voice. But in fact the more pronounced the effects of voicing, such as sound patterning, the less there is a mimesis of voice. Modern poetic exploitation of visual form makes it important to stipulate – here is a good rule of thumb – that lyrics are poems for which the *line* rather than the page is a crucial unit. Their effects depend upon lineation, and perhaps the arrangement of lines into stanzas, but not disposition on the page; they need to be read and not just viewed. Lyrics are poems that demand voicing: the lyric is writing shaped to be heard, audibly or inaudibly, often turning on a figure of address. John Stuart Mill famously defined poetry as "overheard", as opposed to rhetoric, which is explicitly addressed to an audience (1833, 348); and Northrop Frye speaks of the lyric poet as pretending to address someone or something – a lover, a friend, or a personified abstraction (1957, 250). I take the underlying structure of lyric to be one of triangulated address: text aimed at an audience of readers through address (implicit or explicit) to an imagined addressee. Apostrophic address is a frequent distinctive feature of lyric.

Poems of the western lyric tradition are extremely varied, but we need to offer students some sort of model for the lyric, parameters of lyric possibilities, or else they will approach poems with whatever implicit model of the lyric they assimilated in secondary school. If we do not tell them what to look for, they will make assumptions about what these literary objects are and operate with some sort of theory of the lyric – doubtless a very unsatisfactory one. In many cases it will be an expressive theory: short poems as the locus of a poet's expression of feeling and rendition of personal experience, a model that offers purchase on some lyrics but is not a useful way into many others (Culler 2008). An alternative model – the one that today dominates the pedagogy of the lyric in the United States – is a reaction against that model. A poem should not be read as the expression of the poet but as spoken by a persona, and to study the poem is to reconstruct why someone might speak thus: in what sort of circumstances, to what end, with what motive. Helen Vendler's influential textbook, *Poems, Poets, Poetry*, begins with this presumption: "Given that each poem is a fictive speech by an imagined speaker" (2010, iii). She urges students to approach poems in this way, to ask what speech act is being performed, what sort of speaker is constructed, what sort of drama of attitudes is enacted, and finally, "under what circumstances would I find myself saying this?" (15). (Frankly, the honest answer to this question is 'Never – unless I am reciting a poem, performing a poetic act.') This conception has a venerable antecedent in the New Criticism: As John Crowe Ransom put it, "The poet does not speak in his own but in an assumed character, not in the actual but in an assumed situation, and the first thing we do as readers of poetry is to determine precisely what character and what situation are assumed. In this examination lies the possibility of critical understanding and, at the same time, of the illusion and the enjoyment" (1938, 254-255). From there it takes only a small leap for Ransom to conclude that the poem "may be said to be a dramatic monologue. [...] Browning only literalized and made readier for the platform or the concert hall the thing that had always been the poem's lawful form" (*ibid.*).

The theory which is now dominant in lyric pedagogy in the United States in effect urges students to treat every poem as a dramatic monologue, with a fictional speaker whose situation and motives must be reconstructed: 'Why would someone say this?'. This approach makes the poem into a mini-novel with a character whose motives are to be analyzed, and thus can be encouraging for students accustomed to fiction; it is pedagogically effective, but has two major flaws. First, in defining a poem as an imitation of a real-world speech act, it treats as ancillary all those aspects of poems – rhythm, sound patterning, intertextual relations – that are most distinctive. Second, it takes a particular case for the norm, ignoring the fact that many poems do not put on stage a fictional character performing non-poetic acts but engage in distinctively poetic acts. Käte Hamburger foresaw the failings of such an approach in insisting, in *Logik der Dichtung* (1957), that lyric does not belong to the system of fictional discourse.

Barbara Herrnstein Smith, who offers the most developed theoretical account of this American model, declares lyrics to be fictional representations of a speech act, of personal discourse (1968, 17), but one thing that confirms for me the dubiousness of her premise is that this notion of lyric as fictional imitation or a real-world speech act plays almost no role in her actual accounts of the structure of poems, for many of which it would be extremely difficult to say what utterance or possible speech act they are representing. Thus, the very first example in her book *Poetic Closure*, introduced to help define notions of formal structure and thematic structure, is Emily Dickinson's poem 536 in the Johnson numbering, "The Heart asks Pleasure – first". What is the real world speech act being represented here? It is hard to say: We would have to invent one and trying to imagine a speaker would be a diversion from engaging with the poem.

> The Heart asks Pleasure – first –
> And then – Excuse from Pain –
> And then – those little Anodynes
> That deaden suffering –
> And then – to go to sleep –
> And then – if it should be
> The will of its Inquisitor
> The privilege to die – (# J 536; 1960, 262)

What we have here is a poetic disquisition on the propensities of the human heart, with a sudden turn at the end, when "Inquisitor" and "privilege" give us a judgment, but one that need not be firmly assigned to some particular speaker. (To say, for example, that it must be spoken by someone so sick at heart that he or she wants to die, and to try to imagine why, would be to go wildly astray.) It is certainly not a poem that produces a fictional speaker or fictional world but offers a poetic observation about this world. Smith rightly makes no attempt to work out what sort of speech event is being imitated or what is the situation of an alleged speaker, and I think there is an important lesson here for the theory of the lyric: There is no need to assume a speaker-character and a projected fictional world.

This lyric of Emily Dickinson's is in the present tense, as are the majority of lyrics – a fact not often noted in critical discourse. Crude statistics are telling. In Baudelaire's *Fleurs du Mal*, for instance, only twelve out of 132 poems are in the past; nine more start in the past but pull into the present, with the *then/now* structure common in lyrics. And four more start in the present and then evoke past events. The present tense is overwhelmingly dominant. In the case of poetry in English, for instance in the anthology of Helen Vendler's *Poems, Poets, Poetry*, where twentieth-century poetry is well represented, the present tense is also predominant: There are 194 poems in the present against 43 in past tenses, with another eleven moving from past to present. In the massive *Norton Anthology of Poetry* (which includes only poetry in English) only 123 of 1266 lyrics are in the past tense, and 21 of these are ballads.[1] The lyric characteristically wants to be itself an event in the lyric present, not the representation of a past event. Suzanne Langer calls the use of the present tense "the most notable characteristic of lyric poetry" (1953, 260). This might be taken to mean that the lyric is a poem in which the poet expresses his or her momentary feelings and thoughts, but in fact, "the present tense proves to be a far more subtle mechanism than either grammarians or rhetoricians generally realize, and to have quite other uses than the characterization of present acts and facts" (*ibid.*). There is indeed a considerable range of possibilities.

This Dickinson poem is not a narrative or an anecdote but a very common sort of lyric that makes general claims, like "Th'expense of spirit in a waste of shame/ Is lust in action" (# 129; Shakespeare 1977, 111). The verb here is the so-called *gnomic present*, of truths asserted, as in *A rolling stone gathers no moss*, or *Water boils at 100 degrees centigrade*. This is a distinct use, definitional, sometimes considered a form of aspect. This present tense is, in fact, far more common in lyric than is imagined by those in-

---

[1] I count as in the past tense a poem without present tense or future tense verbs, except in subordinated positions.

clined to think of fictional speakers and fictional worlds. Ever since Pindar, lyrics have sought to tell truths about this world (and not, *pace* Sir Philip Sidney, to deliver a golden world) – "Water is best, and gold, like a blazing fire in the night, stands out supreme of all lordly wealth" (Pindar 1997, 43) – or, in a very different register:

> They fuck you up, your mum and dad.
> They may not mean to, but they do.
> They fill you with the faults they had
> And add some extra, just for you. (Larkin 1989, 180)

This is not a statement relativized to a fictional speaker – no need to ask who is speaking, or in what situation – but a straightforward declaration, enunciating a general truth.

Though many lyrics *can* be seen as fictional imitations of a recognizable speech act – by a speaker-character – this is best conceived as a special case rather than as a general model, for which we have a name: *dramatic monologue*. Many lyrics, while presenting themselves as voiced or voiceable, do not project a speaker-character. If we ask who is speaking in Blake's "The Sick Rose", we obscure the functioning of the poem, which presents an event of poetic speech:

> O Rose, thou art sick!
> The invisible worm,
> That flies in the night,
> In the howling storm,
>
> Has found out thy bed
> Of crimson joy;
> And his dark secret love
> Does thy life destroy. (1969, 213)

Real-world speakers do sometimes address inanimate objects (cursing computers, for instance), perhaps making a spectacle of themselves; but here we have a distinctive poetic address. Baudelaire wrote that hyperbole and apostrophe are the forms of language that are not only most agreeable but also most necessary to the lyric (1976, vol. II, 164). In Blake's poem the apostrophic address marks this utterance as singular, establishes this speech act as poetic discourse which seeks to be an event rather than a description of an event, and creates a surprisingly strong sense of prophetic revelation, or of stipulation, declaring the rose to be sick. Poems with explicit address situate themselves in a lyric present – the rose is sick now – sometimes with present tense verbs, sometimes with imperatives: "No, no, go not to Lethe!" ("Ode on Melancholy"; Keats 1958, 274); "Devouring time, blunt thou the lion's paw" (# 19; Shakespeare 1977, 19) – though they often, as in the Blake, incorporate verbs in the past, to indicate what has happened to produce the present command, request, question, or assertion.

A good deal of work has been done on present tense narration in fiction. Formerly confined to the historic present, which narrates past events in a present tense for added vividness, and to some instances of *style indirect libre*, present tense narration became more widespread in the late twentieth century, with major works such as Updike's *Rabbit Run* (1960) and Pynchon's *Gravity's Rainbow* (1973) making this their standard tense of narration. Monika Fludernik notes that "most present-tense narratives, however illogical, are easily recuperable as the story of events or as the representation of a mind reliving past experience as present" (1996, 256). But little work has been done on the present tense in lyric, despite its importance. Perhaps because of its predominance, or because people imagine that at bottom the lyric recounts what the poet feels now, it passes without comment, as natural. In English, though, there is an especially distinctive lyric use of the simple present. Generally, to note *occurrences* in the present, we use the present progressive tense: *I am walking*. When we encounter the unmarked non-progressive present tense with occurrences, we know immediately that we are dealing with a poem.

> I sit in one of the dives
> On Fifty-second street,
> Uncertain and afraid ("September 1, 1939"; Auden 2007, 95)

> I taste a liquor never brewed,
> From tankards scooped in pearl (# J 214; Dickinson 1960, 214)

> I wander thro' each chartered street,
> Near where the charter'd Thames does flow,
> And mark in every face I meet
> Marks of weakness, marks of woe. ("London"; Blake 1969, 216)

> I walk through the long schoolroom questioning;
> A kind old nun in a white hood replies
>   [...] the children's eyes
> In momentary wonder stare upon
> A sixty-year-old smiling public man. ("Among School-Children"; Yeats 1958, 212)

If you hear sentences like these – "I fall upon the thorns of life, I bleed!" – you know you are dealing with a lyric. This lyric present offers an unlocated present of articulation and of iteration, for the reader who repeats these words. One way to approach this tense is by looking heuristically at the uses of the simple present attested by grammars; they help illuminate some of its effects but indicate the need for a fuller theory of lyric discourse.

Huddleston and Pullum's authoritative *Cambridge Grammar of the English Language* treats the English present tense as simply non-past. It notes that "the unmarked, non-progressive, version [of the present tense] takes an external view: there is no explicit reference to any internal phase or any feature of the temporal flow (such as whether the situation is conceived as instantaneous or having a duration through time)" (2002, 117). This unmarked non-progressive present tense, or the simple present, "combines freely with states but not with occurrences" (119). It is used both for states that are temporary, *She has a headache*, and those that last or are outside of time, *She is Austrian*. But as Huddleston and Pullum conclude, "The use of the simple present for dynamic situations is thus very restricted" (128).

I want to look at five common uses of the simple present to see how they relate to the lyric present; I think it partakes of some of their qualities but remains different and distinctive.

1. The most common is its use with temporal qualifiers that make the verb in effect designate a serial state more than an occurrence: *I do the Times crossword every morning*. Without such qualifiers, we presuppose them: *I do the Times crossword* means something like, 'I do it every morning', or at least regularly. Note that if we add temporal qualifiers to the lyric examples cited earlier, they become normal usage rather than distinctively poetic: *I walk through the long schoolroom every Thursday*, or *Every*

day after work I wander through each chartered street. But without these qualifiers we have a distinctly odd usage. It is not the so-called gnomic present, of truths: *A rolling stone gathers no moss*; though it does take on some of that quality (more than a simple, single, occurrence). Certainly one effect of the lyric present is to make what is reported something more than a singular event, even though it is clearly that: "I sit in one of the dives/ On 52nd street, /Uncertain and afraid" gives this instance of sitting a different character than *I am sitting*. This comes across as more than a report on what I did once or what I am doing at a particular moment, yet not a state like *I am neurotic*. What "I sit" refers to happens now, but in an iterable now of lyric enunciation, of which I will say more later.

2. Another regular use of the simple present for occurrences is in performative verbs, as in *I promise to pay you back* or *I apologize for being late*. Of course lyrics and epics frequently use performative verbs: Virgil's opening of the *Iliad*, "Arma virumque cano" (262), or Herrick's "I sing of brooks, of blossoms, birds, and bowers, / Of April, May, of June, and July flowers" ("The Argument of His Book"; 1891, 3). But can one go further? Despite J. L. Austin's stipulation that performative language only works if I am "not joking or writing a poem", I think there is some potential relevance here: at least it makes us reflect (1962, 9). The simple test for whether we are dealing with a performative utterance is whether we can add *hereby*: *I hereby promise*. In ordinary English one cannot say *I hereby wander through each chartered street*, – but in Blake's "I wander through each chartered street" is there not something of the implication that I *hereby* wander, by means of the poem? In Gerard Manley Hopkins's "I wake and feel the fell of dark not day", inserting a *hereby* might in fact capture something of the effect of the phrase (1970, 101). And what about *O rose, thou art hereby sick*?

3. Another way we use this present tense is in oral narratives or jokes: "A nun, a priest, an Irishman, a Scotsman, a rabbi and a blonde walk into a bar. The bartender looks at them and asks, 'Is this some kind of joke?'" This is relevant to the lyric use in that we are presented with an unlocated, iterable event, but the present here is clearly a narrative tense, which is not the case with most of our lyric examples. It carries the suggestion of a quasi-mythic narrative with slight claim to reality. If you tell a story about what you did yesterday in this tense – "So I walk into the office and there is George standing at the copy machine" instead of "I walked into the office and there was George standing at the copy machine", the goal is greater vividness but the implication is that this is supposed to be amusing, or at least highly tellable, that is, a story that could be repeated, not just a representation of what happened.

Lyric uses of the simple present in the third person have effects that are slightly different from those in the first person. They are not performative, of course. Byron's

> She walks in beauty, like the night
> Of cloudless climes and starry skies;
> And all that's best of dark and bright
> Meet in her aspect and her eyes. (1978, 11)

has an effect that is somewhat hard to pin down: To walk in beauty is vague enough that we are inclined to take this as definitional, something the woman *is* more than something she is doing. For an event, consider Auden's "The Fall of Rome":

> The piers are pummeled by the waves;
> In a lonely field the rain
> Lashes an abandoned train;
> Outlaws fill the mountain caves. (2007, 188)

The rain lashes the train now, but presumably not always. This stanza gives us an ominous description even though clearly the rain does not always lash an abandoned train: the choice of "lashes" rather than "is lashing" is distinctively poetic.

4. Third person present tenses often take on a more descriptive character than the first-person occurrences. Consider Yeats's "Leda and the Swan", where the non-progressive present does not come until the end of the first quatrain:

> A sudden blow: the great wings beating still
> Above the staggering girl, her thighs caressed
> By the dark webs, her nape caught in his bill,
> He **holds** her helpless breast upon his breast. (1958, 211; ll. 1-4)

The violent action is carried by participles, not the main verb. The definite articles – "*the* great wings", etc. – refer deictically to a presupposed scene that has not been presented, making this seem like the description of a painting, perhaps. But the non-progressive present tense verb of the first tercet undercuts a pictorial perspective:

> A shudder in the loins engenders there
> The broken wall, the burning roof and tower
> And Agamemnon dead. (1958, 211; ll. 9-11)

Describing an event that cannot be depicted, ***engenders*** suggests a different sort of model: what happens in the myth. By convention, we use the non-progressive present tense to describe what happens in works of literature. This is the fourth usage. The *Cambridge Grammar* notes that we talk about authors, works, and characters "from the perspective of their present and potentially permanent existence rather than that of their past creation" (Huddleston and Pullum 2002, 129-130): "Othello kills Desdemona". Is that what is going on in Leda: an account of what happens in the myth? *Hamlet delays* or *Othello kills Desdemona* seem rather more timeless than "A shudder in the loins engenders" but they are at the same time instances of iterated action. The present is appropriate, for the delaying and the killing happen again and again as well as always.

If we move to a poem with a similar action (like "he holds") but which does not recount a known myth that exists prior to it and to which it can deictically refer, what do we find? Consider Elizabeth Bishop's "At the Fishhouses":

> Although it is a cold evening,
> down by one of the fishhouses
> an old man sits netting,
> his net, in the gloaming almost invisible,
> a dark purple-brown,
> and his shuttle worn and polished.
> The air smells so strong of codfish
> it makes one's nose run and one's eyes water. (1969, 72)

Here the sense of a *now* is palpable – the very lack of first person pronouns intensifies the sense of a scene being presented to the reader. The singularity of the scene may be stressed, but it takes on a mythic aspect, as something that happens, not just something that is happening: "he sits netting" rather than *he is sitting netting.*

The end of Keats's "Ode to Autumn" is a fascinating, rather eerie case:

> Hedge-crickets sing; and now with treble soft
> The redbreast whistles from a garden-croft;
> And gathering swallows twitter in the skies. (1958, 273)

Here the vivid yet indeterminate *now* implicit in other examples is made explicit. Perhaps we should call it a *floating now*, repeated each time the poem is read. There is a subtle distinction between *The redbreast is whistling from a garden-croft* and "The redbreast whistles from a garden croft". The former indicates something happening at a particular, locatable time; the latter puts us into this strange iterable time of the lyric now.

In both colloquial and formal English, such action verbs require the progressive form – *I am walking through the long schoolroom questioning, I am sitting netting* –without which they would mark a habitual action and lead one to expect a temporal indication: *I walk to work <u>each morning</u>, The redbreast <u>often</u> whistles, I <u>sometimes</u> fall upon the thorns of life*; and it is that lack of temporal specification that makes this a distinctive tense in English poetry – so much so that as soon as you hear a sentence like these you know you are dealing with a poem.

In *Feeling and Form*, a book from 1953, the philosopher and aesthetician Suzanne Langer notes this distinctive use of the simple present in lyric, which she sees as suspending time, constructing "an impression or an idea as something experienced in a sort of eternal present" (268). George Wright, in a fine paper which is still by far the best discussion of the subject, "The Lyric Present: Simple Present Verbs in English Poems", takes up this distinctive use of the simple present tense without temporal qualification: "I walk through the long schoolroom questioning". We admire such a line, he writes, "as simple, ordinary natural English. It reports an event that has happened – is happening – happens. Such a confusion in our own verbs may show us that the Yeats is not so speechlike as it at first seems" (1974, 563). Wright concludes: "In effect what we find in such verbs is a new aspect or tense, neither past, nor present but timeless – in its feeling a lyric tense". Or again, "It is outside of time but it has duration – a special state but common to all art" (*ibid.*).

While I agree with most of Wright's analysis, I think the allure of the timeless – doubtless because of the assumption that great art should be timeless – leads him to neglect the oddity of the lyric time of enunciation, which is both that of a speaker/poet and that of the reader, who may speak these words also in reading the poem. Wright is thinking in terms of representation, artistic representation, which leads him to timelessness. If we think of the time of enunciation, of the lyric attempt to be itself an event rather than the representation of an event, this changes the perspective on the lyric present, as well as much else. Writing of fiction, Monika Fludernik notes that present tense narration characteristically involves a "deliberate refusal to situate the act of narration" with consequent blurring of the distinction between story and discourse (1996, 253). In the lyric present, which is not a narrative tense, I would say there is no presumption of separation of event and moment of enunciation, but this point of enunciation does seem to be a floating *now*.

5. Classicists studying deixis in the Greek lyric have emphasized the way in which Pindar and others create poems that could be performed on more than one occasion, and indeed, lyric seems constructed for re-performance, potentially ritualistic, with an always iterable *now* (Jones 1995). I think this lyric present is distinctive enough to deserve separate characterization and not assimilated to one of the linguists' cases, especially because of the fusion of enunciation and reception, in a moment that is repeated, every time the poem is read, which gives it a potentially performative effect.

Linguistic accounts of deixis frequently seem to presuppose a perceptually-given *I, here*, and *now* as deictic center: *I* is whoever says "I", and the place and moment of utterance are thought to be given. Then the possibility of deictic shift to the perspective of the decoder is countenanced. But one can argue that, on the contrary, there is in fact no perceptually given *here* and *now*: What counts as here and now is always a function of a situation. In some circumstances – *Don't press the button now but press it now* – *now* is determined in seconds; in other circumstances, *now* might mean nowadays, as opposed to the eighteenth century or pre-human times. *Here* can mean here on earth, or here in this city, or here, this spot on my hand. Perhaps, then, the unusual, unlocated "here" and the "now" of lyric should be seen as a particular literary possibility among other constructions, distinctive certainly, and anomalous, just as address to absent or inanimate others is anomalous, yet in fact part of a distinctive literary situation of utterance. Though distinctive, it still very much participates in the possible effects of our language, whose limits poems push against: effects that it is the task of poetics to spell out.

Looking at the uses of the non-progressive present tense that grammarians identify helps to clarify the distinctiveness of this lyric tense, which does not fit into any of their categories, though a number of them are certainly suggestive of effects that the lyric present can achieve. The usage that seems to me closest to the lyric use is, interestingly, the present we use to talk about writings – what happens in them. But while, as grammars suggest, this seems a special convention (we have to explicitly teach students to use the present tense in this way to talk about authors and works), the lyric present is broader and not something, in my experience, that one has to teach. This suggests that its linguistic import has not yet been properly understood. Above all, I believe that it is temporal rather than a-temporal, not outside of time – iterative but not located anywhere in particular in time, but offering a particularly rich sense of time, of the impossible *nows* in which we, as we read, repeat these lyric structures. It contributes to the sense of lyric as event, not the fictional representation of an utterance. Nor, as I would stress in returning to the issue I took up briefly at the beginning, does lyric project a fictional world: The "Ode to a Nightingale" does not give us a fictional world in which people talk to birds but rather gives us address to a bird in *this* world, in which language repeats as we read and articulate it.

I have argued that a poetics of the lyric should focus on ways in which linguistic elements, such as deixis, structures of address, and the present tense, have effects other than those treated by conventional linguistic accounts. Exploration of all those aspects of lyric that exceed dramatic monologue seem to me crucial to our attempts to promote pedagogically the study of lyric, this central strand of the literary tradition that today seems very much threatened.

References

Primary Sources

Allison, Alexander et al (eds.; 1975). *The Norton Anthology of Poetry*. New York: Norton
Auden, W. H. (2007): *Selected Poems*. Ed. Edward Mendelson. New York: Vintage
Baudelaire, Charles (1976): *Oeuvres complètes*. Paris: Gallimard
Bishop, Elizabeth (1969): *The Complete Poems*. New York: Farrar Strauss
Blake, William (1969): *Complete Writings*. Ed. Geoffrey Keynes. Oxford University Press
Byron, George Gordon (1978) *Byron's Poetry*. Ed. Frank D. McConnell. New York: Norton
Dickinson, Emily (1960): *The Complete Poems*. Boston: Houghton Mifflin
Herrick, Robert (1891): *Works,* vol. I. London: Lawrence & Bullen
Hopkins, Gerard Manley (1970): *The Poems*. Ed. W. H. Gardner; N. H. MacKenzie. Oxford: Oxford University Press
Keats, John (1958): *Poetical Works*. Oxford: Clarendon
Larkin, Philip (1989): *Collected Poems*. New York: Farrar Strauss and Giroux
Pindar (1997): *Olympian Odes, Pythian Odes*. Ed. and trans. William H. Race. Cambridge, MA: Harvard University Press
Shakespeare, William (1977): *Sonnets*. Ed. Stephen Booth. New Haven: Yale University Press
Virgil (1999): *Eclogues, Georgics, Aeneid*. Cambridge, MA: Harvard University Press
Yeats, W. B. (1958): *Collected Poems*. London: Macmillan

Secondary Sources

Austin, J. L. (1962): *How to do Things with Words: The William James Lectures Delivered at Harvard University in 1955*. Ed. J. O. Urmson; Marina Sbisà, Marina. Oxford: Clarendon
Culler, Jonathan (1975): *Structuralist Poetics*. London: Routledge
--- (2008) "Why Lyric?" *PMLA* 123.1, 201-206
Fludernik, Monika (1996): *Towards a 'Natural' Narratology*. London: Routledge
Frye, Northrop (1957): *Anatomy of Criticism*. Princeton: Princeton University Press
--- (1985): "Approaching the Lyric", in: Hosek, Chaviva; Parker, Patricia (eds.): *Lyric Poetry: Beyond New Criticism.* Ithaca: Cornell University Press, 31-37
Hamburger, Käte (1993): *The Logic of Literature* [*Die Logik der Dichtung*, 1957]. Trans. Rose, Marilynn J. Bloomington, IN: Indiana University Press
Huddleston, Rodney; Pullum, Geoffrey (2002): *Cambridge Grammar of the English Language*. Cambridge: Cambridge University Press
Jones, Peter (1995): "Philosophical and Theoretical Issues in the Study of Deixis", in: Green, Keith (ed.): *New Essays on Deixis*. Amsterdam/Atlanta: Rodopi, 28-46
Langer, Suzanne (1953): *Feeling and Form: A Theory of Art*. New York: Scribners
Mill, John Stuart [1833] (1981): "Thoughts on Poetry and Its Varieties", in: Robson, John M.; Stillinger, Jack (eds.): *The Collected Works of John Stuart Mill, Volume I – Autobiography and Literary Essays.* Toronto: University of Toronto Press; London: Routledge and Kegan Paul. <http://oll.libertyfund.org/?option=com_staticxt&staticfile=show.php%3Ftitle=242&chapter=7742&layout=html&Itemid=27> [accessed 21 February 2014]
Ransom, John Crowe (1938): *The World's Body*. Baton Rouge: Louisiana State University Press
Smith, Barbara Herrnstein (1968): *Poetic Closure*. Chicago: University of Chicago Press
Vendler, Helen (2010): *Poems, Poets, Poetry*. Boston: Bedford/St. Martins
Wright, George T. (1974): "The Lyric Present: Simple Present Verbs in English Poems", *PMLA* 89, 3

Wolfgang G. Müller (Jena)

Is There a Special Use of Language in Poetry? Roman Jakobson's Concept of Poeticity and the Relation between Language and Verse

1. The Problem

The problem to be discussed in this article is whether there is a special use of language in poetry. Theorists and critics seem to have reached a consensus on this question, which stands in the tradition of Roman Jakobson's definition of the poetic function. They hold the position that all poetic effects which lyric poetry may produce by its use of language are possible in other genres like narrative prose and drama. From a general perspective they are, of course, right. However, the problem of a generalization of the poetic function for all literary genres is that it does not do justice to some of the specific poetic qualities of the language of lyric poetry. My paper will argue that there is a potential for poetic effects in lyric poetry that is absent in other genres, in other words, that there is something like a specific use of language which is characteristic of lyric poetry.[1]

2. The Poetic Function in Roman Jakobson's Model of the Functions of Language

It is necessary for my argument to have a look at the place Roman Jakobson attributes to the poetic function in his model of the functions of language, which he derived from a communication model. Here is, first, the communication model, which is so well-known that it does not require further comment:

CONTEXT

ADDRESSER → MESSAGE → ADDRESSEE

CONTACT

CODE

Jakobson correlates the following linguistic functions to the six constitutive aspects of communication:

REFERENTIAL

EXPRESSIVE POETIC CONATIVE

PHATIC

METALINGUAL

---

[1] This contribution draws on earlier studies by the author, some of which are listed in the bibliography (Müller 2010, Müller 2011a, Müller 2011b).

The Referential Function states the object of the message by descriptive or declarative statements. The Expressive or Emotive Function refers to the sender's manifestation in the message. The Conative – or, alternately, Appellative – Function refers to forms of address. The Phatic Function is associated with the aspect of contact, the communication channel. The Metalingual or Self-Reflexive Function is the use of language to reflect on itself. The Poetic Function, which is the dominant function in literature, according to Jakobson, is "the set (*Einstellung*) toward the message as such, focus on the message for its own sake" (Jakobson 1981, 356). Having accorded the poetic function a deservedly central position in his model of the functions of literary texts, Jakobson goes on to observe that this function is not exclusive to poetry: "Any attempt to reduce the sphere of poetic function to poetry or to confine poetry to poetic function would be a delusive oversimplification" (Jakobson 1981, 356). In magisterial analyses, he demonstrates the presence of the poetic function in non-fictional discourse, for instance in a political slogan such as "I like Ike". In a general sense Jakobson is right in saying that the poetic function is not exclusively evident in poetry. Many critics and theorists have followed him. Indeed it would be foolish to deny the powerful presence of the poetic function in non-lyric texts such as, for instance, *Beowulf*, John Lyly's *Euphues*, James Macpherson's *Ossian*, Anne Radcliffe's *The Romance of the Forest*, James Joyce's *Ulysses* and *Finnegan's Wake*, Virginia Woolf's *The Waves* and Truman Capote's *The Grass Harp*. Yet in spite of all this evidence and the apparent critical consensus, I believe that it is necessary to insist that there is a special language in lyric poetry that emerges only in this genre. In order to substantiate this claim we have to be aware that lyric poetry consists of verse and that it is the quality of verse that is the basis of poetic and semantic effects that are not possible in non-metrical composition.

3. Jakobson's Poetic Function and the Semantic and Iconic Dimensions of Verse

It is necessary for our argument to take a closer look at Jakobson's definition of the poetic function. In doing so, we hope to approach the core of the problem of the use of language in poetry. A decisive quality of Jakobson's model is that it is based on ideas of Russian Formalism such as alienation (*ostranenie*) and laying bare the device (*obnaženie priema*). This poetological context emphasizes the artistry of the literary text. The formal dimension of the text receives heightened attention.[2] Jakobson's concept of the self-reflexivity of the text implies that by its specific linguistic form an attitude of pointing at itself is inherent in the text, of directing the attention to itself. Jakobson's model has been groundbreaking and innovative in many ways, but his definition of the poetic function as a catalyst of aesthetic sensitization is in two ways problematic:

First, while it is important to realize that the poetic function stresses the 'eye-catching', attention-calling, alerting quality which language may have on account of its aesthetic form, it is at least equally important to be aware of the semantic potential of the formal characteristics of language, in other words, of the iconic potential of form, for semantic emphasis goes hand in hand with aesthetic emphasis.[3] As his whole work, including the famous article "Linguistics and Poetics", shows, Jakobson is an unparalleled mas-

---

2   See Küpper 2008, 70-71.
3   We must, of course, be fair. The deficit of Jakobson's definition of the poetic function concerns only his model of linguistic functions as such, for his demonstration of the semantic function of equivalence relations in verse composition is of incomparable importance.

ter in the elucidation of the semantic implications of form, but in his model on the functions of language the semantic aspect of form remains unconsidered.

Second, Jakobson's definition of the poetic function of language is so wide that it covers all genres and even non-literary uses of language such as advertisements and political slogans. The idea that there is a special form of poeticity, a special language in poetry – i.e. lyric poetry – does not enter his mind, because there is no place for it in his model.

My attempt to characterize the language of lyrical poetry is based on the fact that the metrical form of poetry has a specific semantic potential that is realized when a metrical pattern is filled with language. I will show that metrical form is a signifier, that because of its metrical form the poem has a surplus of meaning that distinguishes it from prose.[4] In order to explain the specific semantic potential of poetic language it is necessary to employ the terms equivalence and iconicity.[5] Iconicity emerges whenever form is used so as to mime and enhance meaning. Roman Jakobson claims that the iconic potential of poetic language is realized largely in the interaction of equivalent and non-equivalent structures. Metrical texts can be regarded as a paradigmatic example for this theory. This is shown in the following two features of verse:

(1) Equivalence, conspicuous in phenomena such as repetition, parallelism, and rhyme.
(2) Non-equivalence, conspicuous in phenomena such as metrical inversion, stress accumulation, enjambement, caesura, change of the length of lines, etc.

Equally conspicuous is the fact that verses that are built in an entirely regular way tend to be monotonous and lack poetic power. On the contrary, because the metrical patterning of verse texts favours evenness, it is the presence of non-equivalent structures such as metrical inversion, stress accumulation, enjambement, caesura, and change of the length of lines that is of the greatest importance for producing aesthetic effects. Such aesthetic effects coincide with semantic emphases and intensifications, a phenomenon that can be regarded as a key to the iconicity of verse.[6] For Küper (1988, 28) "the simultaneous presence of equivalence and non-equivalence" in the poetic text is "a fundamental principle of the discipline of poetics and metrics" (my translation). Referring to the use of iambic pentameter in English literature, he argues that non-deviance would lead to metrical and rhythmic monotony, which would be in blatant opposition to the aesthetic norms of all periods in the history of the English iambic pentameter (Küper 1988, 161).

The following analytical part of this paper will focus on the principle of deviation or non-equivalence, which is realized in such phenomena as metrical inversion and en-

---

4   In doing so, I agree with Lamping 1993, 44, 53.
5   For a more elaborate discussion see Müller 2011a.
6   A recent book with the promising title *Meter and Meaning* by Derek Attridge and Thomas Carper (2003) is disappointing in that it lacks a theoretical foundation and dispenses with a discussion of not only the semantics but also the iconicity of verse. An older study with the same title (Hamm 1954) works with the vague category of "tone" and discusses metre mainly with regard to the reader's reception. An excellent survey of Roman Jakobson's treatment of the relation of metre and semantics is Donat 2003, to which this paper is indebted. My greatest debt is, however, to Christoph Küper's writings on the relation between language and metre, above all his magisterial monograph of 1988, but also his studies of 1973 and 1996 and many others.

jambement. It is important to note that metrical inversion and enjambement are phenomena that do not belong to the same sphere as grammar, syntax, morphology, and the stress system of language. They belong exclusively to the sphere of metrics, even though to be effective they must interact with language.

4. Metrical Inversion

Metrical inversion is especially striking in English poetry at the beginning of iambic verses. In the first verse of the following sonnet by John Keats – "On First Looking into Chapman's Homer" (Keats 1970, 38) – metrical inversion coincides with syntactic inversion.[7]

> **Much have I travelled** in the realms of gold,
> And many goodly states and kingdoms seen;
> Round many western islands have I been
> Which bards in fealty to Apollo hold.
> **Oft of one wide expanse had I been told** 5
> That deep-browed Homer held as his demesne:
> Yet did I never breathe its pure serene
> Till I heard Chapman speak out loud and bold:
> **Then felt I** like some watcher of the skies
> When a new planet swims into his ken; 10
> Or like stout Cortez, when with eagle eyes
> Her stared at the Pacific – and all his men
> **Looked** at each other with a wild surmise –
> **Silent**, upon a peak in Darien.

This poem offers in five of its fourteen verses metrical inversions at the beginning of a line, of which the first three inversions coincide with syntactic inversions. These three instances evince a homology or isomorphism of metrical and syntactical structures, which has an iconic function. In the first case (line 1) the adverb "much" at the beginning of the verse is exposed to give it special emphasis: "Much have I travelled in the realms of gold". This adverb is the cause and simultaneously a component of the inversion structure. Without the inversion, the sentence might look as follows: "I have travelled much in the realms of gold". The iconic function of the inversion can be interpreted in combination with the semantic context of the line. The speaker's considerable travel experiences referred to metaphorically express journeys through the world of literature. It seems as if the exposed adverb "much" and the two following unstressed syllables open rooms that have been traversed. The inversion structure has a considerable gestural impact. When reciting the poem before an audience, the reader may open his or her arms.

In the second case (verse 5) the coincidence of metrical and syntactical inversion occurs in a spatial context as well and accordingly has an iconic function: "Oft of one wide expanse had I been told". Here, too, it is an adverb ("oft") which is exposed and causes the inversion while being part of it. Similarly, in the third case (verse 9) – "Then felt I like some watcher of the skies" – again an adverb, "then", is marked by its initial position.

---

[7] Emphases in this and the following examples are mine.

It is notable that the structurally decisive moments of the sonnet – the beginning of the first quatrain, the beginning of the second quatrain, and the beginning of the sestet – are marked by metrical and syntactic inversion, so that an overarching structure is established. The poetic function of metrical inversion is not limited to special moments in the poem. It informs the whole structure of the sonnet.

We will now look at a line whose special emphasis results from the positioning of a word at the front of a verse that within the sentence stands in the middle. Thus metre can give a word a weight which it would not have as a mere constituent of a sentence:

> Ships, towers, domes, theatres, and temples lie
> **Open** unto the fields, and to the sky;
> (Wordsworth 1968, 38, "Composed Upon Westminster Bridge", ll. 6-7)

An even bolder example can be found in Hopkins's sonnet "I wake and feel the fell of dark" (Hopkins 1967, 101).

> I am gall, I am heartburn. God's most deep decree
> **Bitter** would have me taste [...] (ll. 9-10)

Here the metrical inversion is the outcome of a syntactic dislocation: The word "bitter", the object of the sentence, which grammatically ought to be at the end of the sentence, is put before the predicate, which makes for an expressive description of the 'bitter' self-awareness which the poem articulates.

5. Accumulation of Stressed Syllables

Another departure from the metrical norm occurs when a verse contains more stressed syllables/words than the iambic pentameter allows for, as shown in the following case:

> **Ships, towers, domes, theatres, and temples lie**
> Open unto the fields, and to the sky;
> (Wordsworth 1968, 38, "Composed Upon Westminster Bridge", l. 6)

In this verse there are six words of roughly equal semantic weight, but only five metrical stress positions. This means that one of the semantically important words has to take an unstressed metrical position. A candidate for this position is the first word. Now if "towers" is read as a monosyllabic word, a second stressed monosyllabic word ("domes") moves to an unstressed position. There is no room for a complete analysis of this line, but I hope it has become clear that such a line is characterized by a tension between the metrical system and the natural accent of the words in the sentence, which produces an intense effect of the panoramic fullness of the description of the city. One could argue that such an accumulation of accented syllables is also possible in prose composition. This may be true, but prose would lack the counterpointing of the accent system of language and the stress system of metre which is responsible for the poetic effect of the line in question.

6. Enjambement

Enjambement shall henceforth be understood as a deviation from the metrical norm, as problematic as this definition may be. The principle of parallelism which is characteristic of the structure of metrical composition is especially obvious when the end of the verse and the end of the clause coincide. If the sentence, as is the case with enjambement, runs from one verse to the next one, the principle of parallelism or equivalence which is inherent to metrical composition is disturbed or restricted on another structural level. Thus the interdependence of the principles of equivalence and difference that we have defined as a source for the poeticity of verse is strongly evident in enjambement.

The definition of verse as a metrical pattern that represents equivalence does not include enjambement. Only when the metrical pattern is realized linguistically in a poem does the possibility of enjambement come into play. Different forms of enjambement can be classified according to the place in which a sentence is cut through by the turning of the verse. In the two examples below, verb and object and subject and predicate, respectively, are separated by the turning of the verse:

> Dull would he be of soul who could **pass by**
> **A sight** so touching in its majesty:
> (Wordsworth 1968, 38, "Composed Upon Westminster Bridge", ll. 2-3)
> And the hapless Soldier's **sigh**
> **Runs** in blood down the Palace walls.
> (Blake 1961, 75, "London", ll. 11-12)

In the first example the enjambement represents an aesthetic analogue to the notion of passing by. The enjambement in the second example is even more effective, since it supports the metaphorical (synesthetic) notion of the soldier's sigh running in blood down the palace walls. The iconicity given with enjambement is here intensified by metaphor.

The following remarkable example is taken from Coleridge's "Rime of the Ancient Mariner":

> The fair breeze blew, the white foam flew,
> The furrow followed free;
> **We were the first that ever burst**
> **Into that silent sea.** (ll. 103-106)

In this case the enjambement is a formal analogue of the sudden transition of the voyage of the ship from free, wind-driven locomotion to a sudden stop in a dead calm. Just as the flow of the sentence is impeded, the motion of the ship is stopped in the calm sea as if run against a wall. The effect of the enjambement is here intensified by the internal rhyme "first"/"burst", which gives the line a punch.

Internal rhyme ("so"/"bow", "cross"/"albatross") also contributes to the effect of enjambement in the following stanza from "The Ancient Mariner", in which the action of shooting the albatross is represented iconically by the running of the sentence from one line into another one.

> God save thee, ancient Mariner!
> From the fiends, that plague thee thus! –
> Why look'st thou so?' – **With my cross-bow**
> **I shot the ALBATROSS.** (ll. 79-82)

There is a highly significant contradiction between the line as a complete metrical unit, whose end is marked by rhyme, and the irresistible push of the syntax which forces its way into the next line. *Topicalization*, the front position of a constituent, here, contrary to normal word-order, correlates with enjambement. The violence of the sailor's action finds an aesthetic analogue in the treatment of metre. A similar effect is achieved in the following synesthetic image from William Blake's poem "London", in which the subject (noun) "sigh" is, by enjambement, separated from its predicate, which is here characteristically constituted by the verb form "runs". The running of the blood down the palace wall is iconized by a "run-on line" (Blake 1961, 75).

> And the hapless Soldier's **sigh**
> **Runs** in blood down Palace walls.

Intricate and audacious forms of enjambement are also to be found in Dylan Thomas's poetry.[8] Here is at least one example from "How soon the Servant Sun", where parenthetic insertions occur between subject and verb and the verb then appears displaced as the first word in a new line.

> [...] and the cupboard **stone,**
> (Fog has a bone
> He'll trumpet into meat),
> **Unshelve** that all my gristles have a gown (Thomas 1971, 113)

Let us finally have a glance at the fascinating phenomenon in which the enjambement affects not the sentence, but the singular word in its morphological structure. I will look at a well-known example in terms of its iconic force, the beginning of Hopkins's sonnet about a kestrel ("The Windhover", Hopkins 1967, 36).

> I caught this morning morning's minion, **king-**
>   **dom** of daylight's dauphin, dapple-dawn-drawn falcon, in his riding
> Of the rolling level underneath him steady air, and striding
> High there, how he rung upon the rein of a wimpling **wing [...]**
> (G. M. Hopkins, "The Windhover. To Christ our Lord")

Here the word "kingdom" is split into its two parts by the enjambement, which makes the rhyme "king"/"wing" possible. A marker of the separation is the hyphen in the word "king-dom" which violates the English word-formation rules. Through this audacious dissociative handling of the enjambement the first constituent of the word ("king-") acquires a certain autonomy. The dislocation of the word "king" strengthens the image of kingship, which is implied in words like "minion" ('favourite of a king') and "dauphin" ('oldest son of a king').

A less known example for the innovative linguistic use of enjambement by Hopkins is taken from the poem "The Loss of the Eurydice" (1967, 72-76), which deals with a ship wreckage during a storm. Here the enjambement interferes with the word structures in a way that is morphologically no longer explicable.

> But what black Boreas wrecked her? **He**
> Came equipped, deadly-elec**tric,**
> (G. M. Hopkins, "The Loss of the Eurydice", ll. 23-24)

The rhyme is accomplished by adding the initial letter of the first word of the second of the quoted lines to the rhyme word, the initial consonant of the following word thus being agglutinated onto the preceding one. As a result, the rhyme looks like: "**He/C**" – "elec**tric**". The destructive power of the lightning is mirrored in the linguistic violence of the enjambement, which overrides the rules of morphology. The destruction of a structure through lightning and storm is reflected in the linguistic dislocation within

---

8   I am indebted to Monika Fludernik, who drew my attention to Thomas's use of enjambement.

the rhyme word and the verse line. Hopkins breaks the integrity of a lexeme (rhyme word) and the integrity of the verse line by a forceful dissociative act, as it were, by means of a "poetic lightning".

It is interesting that Dylan Thomas, who like Hopkins has a Welsh background, also uses enjambements that split the morphological structure of words. The following examples are taken from "A Winter's Tale" (Thomas 1971, 190-191):

> the knee- / Deep hillocks and loud (stanza 20)
> in the wake of the she- / Bird through (stanzas 20).
> in the whirl- / Pool at the (stanza 26)

Christoph Küper (1973) points out that in his use of split rhymes Hopkins was influenced by Welsh poetry. The same may hold true for Thomas.[9]

6. Stress Reduction and Reduction of Meaning

A case of stress reduction with a corresponding effect on meaning can be found in a literary ballad by John Keats, "La Belle Dame Sans Merci", which varies the metre of the ballad stanza significantly. In this poem there is no alternation of four-stress and three-stress lines, which is characteristic of the folk ballad, but three four-stress lines are followed by a final two-stress line. Here is the first stanza (Keats 1970, 350):

> O what can ail thee, knight-at-arms,
>   Alone and palely loitering?
> The sedge is wither'd from the lake,
> And no birds sing.

This poem is, as is usual in the literary ballad, written in syllabotonic metre, and its word-music – with its diphthongs and the "l"-sounds, particularly in line 2 – contributes to expressing the solitariness and melancholy of the wandering knight. Thus the shortened last line tends to have an iconic function. It expresses a reduction which tallies with the negatives or negative images which mark the end of several stanzas (Keats 1970, 350-151)

> And no birds sing. (1)
> Fast withereth too. (3)
> On the cold hill side. (9)
> On the cold hill's side. (11)
> And no birds sing. (12)

Metrical reduction – i.e. reduction on the level of metre – coincides with the sense of deprivation expressed in the quoted lines. This is a clear example of metre contributing to the creation of meaning. An analogous effect of the reduction of stresses is produced in Robert Frost's short piece "Fire and Ice" (Frost 1930, 268), which refers to the relative destructiveness of the two elements mentioned in the title, fire standing for passion or ire, and ice for hatred:

> Some say the world will end in fire,
> **Some say in ice**
> From what I've tasted of desire
> I hold with those who favor fire.
> But if it had to perish twice,

---

9   For the phenomenon of split rhymes see also Greber 2002.

> I think I know enough of hate
> To say that for destruction ice
> **Is also great**
> **And would suffice.**

Here the lines which specifically deal with ice contain two stresses fewer than the lines devoted to fire, the metrical reduction iconizing the contraction, the life-killing power of ice. There is irony in the fact that the word "great" occurs in one of the contracted lines.

7. Caesura and Pause

Caesura, a pause or break within a verse line, can also be used with an iconic effect. I follow Katie Wales who observes that "in English verse such pauses are determined by syntax, sense or punctuation rather than metrical form" (Wales 1989, 54). Our first example is the first line from a stanza in Coleridge's ballad "The Rime of the Ancient Mariner" (Coleridge 1967, 186-209):

> **The ice was here, the ice was there,**
> The ice was all around: (ll. 59-6)

The use of caesura, which separates clauses that are almost identical, suggests the perception of the ice in the form of separate images. In the following line, which contains no instance of caesura, the impression is then totalized into a mass of ice with no distinct floes of ice perceptible: "The ice was all around".

Caesura in connection with repetition occurs in an intensified form in another stanza of Coleridge's ballad, producing effects that are alien to the art of the folk ballad:

> **Alone, alone, all, all alone,**
> Alone on a wide wide sea!
> And never a saint took pity on
> My soul in agony. (ll. 232-235)

Here the sense of being alone or isolated is iconized by three instances of caesura (or pauses),[10] which break the flow of the words. The separation of the words in this verse is an analogue of the speaker's radical isolation, his total separation from humanity. It is significant that the separated words "alone" and "all" are connected at the line's end: "all alone". There is again a totalizing effect achieved by the change from caesura to non-caesura, a sense of loneliness as an overwhelming totality: "Alone on a wide wide sea".

8. Conclusion

The iconic potential of phenomena like metrical inversion und enjambement is realized primarily in the interaction of equivalent and non-equivalent structures. While owing to its repetitive structure equivalence or parallelism emerges in metrical composition in a higher degree than in non-metrical language, non-equivalence comes into play through the presence of other structural levels such as the stress system of the language, as well as syntax and morphology. As deviant elements in metrical composi-

---

10 The application of the term caesura to this line is problematic, as Christoph Küper pointed out to me in an oral communication. One should, perhaps, prefer the term pause. An investigation of the relation between caesura and pause would be a useful project.

tion such as metrical inversion, accumulation of stressed syllables, and enjambement have shown, the poeticity of the metrical text is the result of the co-presence of different structural levels. I believe that this paper's argument and analysis leave no doubt that there is a special use of language in poetry written in verse. The approach used here could be widened to include other levels of composition such as style, phonology, rhyme, and stanza which also contain great iconic potential. The exploration of the iconic effects of the interplay of prosodic elements and language could provide a starting-point for a poetics of metre.

References

Primary Sources

Blake, William (1961): *Poetry and Prose*. Ed. Geoffrey Keynes. London: Nonesuch Library
Coleridge, Samuel Taylor (1967): *Poetical Works*. London: Oxford University Press
Frost, Robert (1930): *Collected Poems*. London/New York/Toronto: Longmans, Green
Hopkins, Gerard Manley (1967): *The Poems of Gerard Manley Hopkins*. Ed. W. H. Gardner; N. H. Mackenzie, N. H.. London: Oxford University Press
Keats, John (1970): *Poetical Works*. Ed. H. W. Garrod. London/Oxford/New York: Oxford University Press
Thomas, Dylan (1971): *The Poems*. London: Dent
Wordsworth, William (1968): *The Poetical Works of William Wordsworth*. Ed. Ernest de Selincourt; Helen Darbishire. Vol. III. Repr. Oxford: Clarendon

Secondary Sources

Attridge, Derek; Carper, Thomas (2003): *Meter and Meaning: An Introduction to Rhythm in Poetry*. New York et al.: Routledge
Donat, Sebastian (2003): "Metrum und Semantik bei Roman Jakobson," in: Hendrik Birus et al. (eds.): *Roman Jakobsons Gedichtanalysen: Eine Herausforderung an die Philologien*. Göttingen: Wallstein, 252-276
Greber, Erika (2002): *Textile Texte: Poetologische Metaphorik und Literaturtheorie: Studien zur Tradition des Wortflechtens und der Kombinatorik*. Köln/Weimar/Wien: Böhlau
Hamm, V. M. (1954): "Meter and Meaning," *PMLA* 69, 695-710
Jakobson, Roman (1981): "Closing Statement: Linguistics and Poetics," in: Sebeok, Thomas A. (ed.): *Style in Language*. New York/London: The Technology Press of Massachusetts Institute of Technology/Wiley, 350-377
Küper, Christoph (1973): *Walisische Traditionen in der Dichtung von G. M. Hopkins*. Bonn: Bouvier
--- (1988): *Sprache und Metrum: Semiotik und Linguistik des Verses*. Tübingen: Niemeyer
--- (1996): "Linguistic Givens and Metrical Codes: Five Case Studies of Their Linguistic and Aesthetic Relations," *Poetics Today* 17.8, 9-124
Küpper, Joachim (2008): "Probleme der Gattungsdefinition des lyrischen Textes," in: Hempfer, Klaus W. (ed.): *Sprachen der Lyrik*. Stuttgart: Franz Steiner, 61-71
Lamping, Dieter (1993): *Das lyrische Gedicht*. 2nd edition. Göttingen: Vandenhoeck
Müller, Wolfgang G. (2010): "Metrical Inversion and Enjambment in the Context of Syntactic and Morphological Structures: Towards a Poetics of Verse," in: Conradie, C. Jac et al. (eds.): *Signergy*. Amsterdam/Philadelphia: Benjamins, 347-363
--- (2011a): "Die Sprache der Lyrik," in: Lamping, Dieter (ed.): *Handbuch Lyrik: Theorie, Analyse, Geschichte*. Stuttgart: Metzler, 80-88
--- (2011b): "Meter and Meaning in British Balladry," in: Küper, Christoph (ed.): *Current Trends in Metrical Analysis*. Frankfurt a. M.: Lang, 181-195
Wales, Katie (1989): *A Dictionary of Stylistics*. London/New York: Longman

CLAUDIA CLARIDGE (DUISBURG-ESSEN)

George Herbert's *The Temple*: Positioning the Speaker

1. Introduction

The speaker in the poems of George Herbert's *The Temple* (published 1633) seems to be a vanishing and dissolving entity. His[1] agency and initiative is called into question, superseded by God's instead (see Fish 1970, 486; 1972, 189-191). His struggles are said to end in self-destruction (1970, 479). He is seen as fragmentary, as illustrated by his dialogues with parts of his material or his mental composition, e.g. his heart, body, thought, or happiness (see Rickey 1966, 127). Reading the poems certainly produces the impression of an unstable, somewhat flickering lyrical *I*, but is the outcome truly the unambiguous dissolution of the person? And which means are employed by the author, who was after all a skilled and prominent rhetorician, to create such effects? This paper takes a linguistic approach to these questions. The chosen features for the investigation are deictic choices (first and second person pronouns), the notion of transitivity, as well as meronymy and metonymy. They will help to shed light on, respectively and in combination, (dominant) perspectives or viewpoints in the poems, on agency, and on wholeness *vs.* fragmentation. Comparative evidence will be used where necessary, in particular, John Donne's poems, Early Modern English (EModE) prayers, as well as EModE and modern speech-related data.

2. Pronouns and Perspectives

Poems imply a speaker and a reader and thus are already dialogic in that sense. Some poems additionally have an explicit addressee, either the reader or somebody else explicitly referred to within the poem. Therefore, singular first and second person pronouns, including possessive determiners, are of particular interest. As both *thou* and *you* can have singular reference at the time of writing *The Temple*, they are both included here. The default deictic centre or Bühler's origo is the speaker at the time and place of speaking, marked by the self-reflexive *I*, from whose viewpoint the encoding takes place. This, in essence, most natural perspective can be shifted, however, by choosing alternative formulations lessening or avoiding the *I*-perspective. The Dedication to *The Temple* can illustrate this:

> Lord, my first fruits present *themselves* to thee;
> Yet not mine neither: for from thee *they* came,
> And must return. Accept of *them* and me,
> And make us strive, who shall sing best thy name.
> Turn their eyes hither, who shall make a gain:
> Theirs, who shall hurt themselves or me, refrain. (Dedication)

---

[1] I will use masculine pronouns for the speaker, based on the assumption that a link between the poems' speaker and George Herbert as the author can indeed be made. The poems selected follow the text as given in Herbert 2007.

In contrast to dedications elsewhere, which contain ample numbers of the nominative form *I*, there is not a single instance in these six lines. The first person occurs as *me*, i.e. in object position, which is typically the end or goal, not the origin of the action – thus also not the most typical origin of point of view. The first person is also found as *my/mine*, which is not an independent but a relational use: The *I* is linked to another entity that is seen as more important, as, in fact, the possessive is embedded in a phrase whose head is something else, e.g. *fruits* (l.1). Furthermore, possessive noun phrases, such as *my first fruits*, are grammatically third person (see the anaphoric *themselves, they, them*, l. 1-3) and in subject position produce a more distanced, less subjective speaking perspective – as if things were seen from a disinterested outside. This usage also dilutes agency: It is not the *I* that presents something but the *fruits present themselves*. The negation of *mine* (l.2) even explicitly denies the speaker's agency.[2] Apart from the grammatical forms used, positions and sequences are also of interest. The two instances of *me* stand in second place in coordinated phrases, preceded once by the fruits (*them*, l.3) and once by other people (*themselves*, l.6). Thus, the speaker demotes himself to a less relevant, subordinate position. There is some ambiguity here, however: The final position in lists is seen as the one of most importance to the speaker and clause-final position (as in l.3) usually carries most communicative weight. Also, the first person is actually the most common pronominal choice in these lines (*vs.* three times the second person). And one might even add that the two imperatives (*accept, turn*) strongly imply the first person as the one making the request.[3] Thus, there is a fairly strong presence of the speaker here, but it is somewhat hidden and downgraded by the formal choices.

We find similar strategies in the shaped poem "The Altar". It contains an *I*, but this occurs far into the poem (l.13, of a total of 16) and is preceded by the third person formulation *my hard heart* (l.10). What unambiguously comes first here is the second person, i.e., God, through the two *thy*-phrases (l. 1/3), as well as through the vocative *Lord*, of course. The referent of *thy servant* is the later *I* (the speaker), who is here viewed from a second person perspective and is grammatically third person – the first person is thus submerged by all the other possible persons. This occurs also in other poems, e.g. *thy beggar* ("Gratefulness"), *thy poore debter* ("The Temper"), *thy ill steward* ("Sighs and Grones"). Not always is this to the exclusion of the first person like here, see *I am Thy clay that weeps, thy dust that calls* ("Complaining").[4] In the "Altar", furthermore, in spite of the active sentence structure, the grammatical subject and agent realised by *thy servant* follows two other constituents (the object and a vocative; see also the dedication above). The poem thus begins with a marked theme (Halliday and Matthiesen 2004, 73),

---

2   A related formulation with similar effect is found in "Sighs and Grones" in spite of the initial nominative: *I have abus'd thy stock, destroy'd thy woods, Suckt all thy magazens: my head did ake, Till it found out how to consume thy goods*. Not the speaker, but his head, phrased explicitly in the third person, finds out things.

3   The four clause types highlight the three basic components of the communicative act to different degrees: Declaratives – the message, Interrogatives – the addressee and the (sought-for) message, Exclamatives – the speaker/writer, Imperatives – the speaker/writer and the addressee. Interestingly, imperatives are very frequent in *The Temple*.

4   There is quite extensive objectivisation, however: two second/third person formulations *vs.* one first person, *that* as the only possible relative pronoun here vs. potential *who*, if a more humanised formulation had been chosen.

the direct object *a broken altar*, foregrounding and focusing it extremely as the starting point of the message and pushing the subjecagent into the background.

> A broken A L T A R, Lord, thy servant reares,
> Made of a heart, and cemented with teares:
>   Whose parts are as thy hand did frame;
>   No workmans tool hath touch'd the same.
>   A H E A R T alone
>   Is such a   stone,
>   As   nothing   but
>   Thy pow'r doth cut.
>   Wherefore each part
>   Of my hard heart
>   Meets in this frame,
>   To praise thy Name;
> That, if I chance to hold my peace,
> These stones to praise thee may not cease.
> O let thy blessed S A C R I F I C E be mine,
> And   sanctifie this A L T A R to be thine.

Thy hand, though superficially parallel to *thy servant*, refers to God (metonymically, see below), thus demoting the agency of the speaker even further. Not only is the second person perspective mentioned first, but it also ends the poem (*thine*). *Mine* in the second to last line is doubly linked to the *thou*, first by an equative construction (thy N = mine) and by the rhyme, in this way framing and enveloping the speaker. *Thine* and *mine* by rhyme are almost mirror images of each other, thus calling to mind the biblical "make man in our image, after our likeness" (Gen. 1:26) – but they are also still or again separated by a crucial difference: the one phoneme that makes a difference in meaning. To return to the singular occurrence of *I* in this poem: It occurs both in a conditional context (*if*, further reinforced by the verb *chance*) and in the base of the visual altar. The former may indicate individual existence as being conditional (on God) and thus the general dependence and insecurity of the speaker as man, while the second may paradoxically indicate stability and firmness provided by the *I*. Canning (2012, 160) also pointed to the interesting fact that the poem has the shape not only of an altar but also of the printed letter I. In this sense the speaker *is* the altar and is in this way also extremely foregrounded.

The intimate connection between, and the striving for a unity of *mine* and *thine* (see the final line of "The Altar") are developed to the extreme in "Clasping of Hands". Formally, the poem works on the two words rhyming, but additionally on their both parallel and crossed-over positions across the lines and stanzas, and on quasi-paradoxical assertions (*to be thine* [...] *I now am mine*).

> LOrd, thou art mine, and I am thine,
> If mine I am: and thine much more,
> Then I or ought, or can be mine.
> Yet to be thine, doth me restore;
> So that again I now am mine,
> And with advantage mine the more,
> So mine thou art, that something more
>
> Since this being mine, brings with it thine,
> And thou with me dost thee restore.
>   If I without thee would be mine,
>   I neither should be mine nor thine.

> Lord, I am thine, and thou art mine:
> I may presume thee mine, then thine.
> For thou didst suffer to restore
> Not thee, but me, and to be mine,
> And with advantage mine the more,
> Since thou in death wast none of thine,
> Yet then as mine didst me restore.
>   O be mine still! still make me thine!
>   Or rather make no Thine and Mine!

The two words are the most prominent in this poem of few (different) words, making up 18% of its word-stock (all singular 1p and 2p pronouns even come to a third of the words). Reading the poem, one becomes lost in the seemingly endless repetitions and twists until the difference between *mine* and *thine* indeed becomes blurred in the reader's mind. By making this task of separation difficult, "making no 'thine' and 'mine' is what the poem literally does" as Fish (1970, 477) puts it. In contrast to "The Altar", here *mine* ends the poem, and it also begins it (albeit preceded by *thou*) thus providing a frame; furthermore, *mine* is more frequent than *thine* (16 to 10). If the union is unsuccessful, one might conclude that this is because of a certain dominance/assertiveness of the speaker.

In sum, what seems to be important with regard to pronominal usage in Herbert's poems is (i) which grammatical form of the pronoun – nominative, oblique case, possessive – is used and what this might imply about perspectives; (ii) in which frequency and which positions within the poem, also in what sequence vis-à-vis other pronouns a form occurs and what this says about its relative importance or about the blurring of borders; and (iii) the significance of phonetic form (1p and 2p rhyming in three-quarters of their forms: *me/my/mine – thee/thy/thine*). The first and third of these will now be examined more closely and at the same time more generally, i.e., across the whole of *The Temple*.

How often does Herbert use pronoun forms in *The Temple* and how does this compare to other texts? In other words, how normal or deviant is Herbert's usage, the choices that he has made? Given the lyrical and religious nature of the *Temple* poems, it seems appropriate to choose for comparison other contemporary poetry, EModE prayers, as well as spoken or speech-related data (see footnote 5 for further explanation).

	Herbert	Donne (rel.)	Donne (other)	EModE prayers	CED D2	BNC-KB
Words	38,724	12,064	12,141	280.107	202,510	1,220,856
I	17.1	11.2	15.9	11.8	21.2	38.0
Me	8.2	8.0	10.9	11.4	6.9	3.4
my / mine	19.7	15.3	11.4	12.5	10.8	2.6
Thou	10.6	10.2	8.8	8.5	2.6 (+18.8)	(31.9)
Thee	7.0	6.3	5.4	8.9	1.6	
thy / thine	16.5	14.2	9.2	21.8	1.6 (+6.9)	(3.6)

Table 1[5]: 1p and 2p pronouns in Herbert in comparison (occurrences per 1,000 words)

---

5   John Donne was selected as the closest contemporary poet, and one who allows comparison to both religious poems and poems of a secular nature ("other" in the table). The poems selected follow the text as given in Donne (1968). The Early Modern English prayers from the sixteenth to seventeenth centuries form part of the *Corpus of English Religious Prose* and were kindly provided to me by Thomas Kohnen. CED D2 stands for the *Corpus of English Dialogues* (period D2: 1600-1639), a selection of written but speech-related texts such as trial proceedings, wit-

Compared to speech (CED and BNC), Herbert indeed uses nominative *I* (considerably) less, expressed in per cent only in 38% of all his 1p sg as against 55% (CED) and 86% (BNC). This difference is important for reception, as it contravenes (subconscious) linguistic expectations of readers, which are the result of everyday exposure to language, i.e. based largely on non-specialised textual forms. Both the contemporary as well as the modern reader will notice the reduced occurrence of nominative *I* as a deviant and thus meaningful choice. The difference to the other texts is much less striking, however, indicating a certain unity produced by genre and/or subject matter. Interestingly, Herbert's frequency here is closest to Donne's non-religious poems. Oblique *me* in Herbert is not really outstanding according to the figures; the only clear difference is to modern speech, so that it might strike the modern reader as unusual but not the contemporary reader. Thus, one may conclude that it is only partly the sheer infrequency that so often gives the impression of the speaker as agent receding into the background in the *Temple*. The second point above about positions/sequencing will come into play here again: See also the example in footnote 2, where the initial *I* is 'trumped' by *my heart / it*. Where Herbert's 1p usage does stand out, however, is with regard to his possessive determiners/pronouns. It is higher than in any of the comparison texts, except for Donne's religious poems, with which it is virtually identical. The situation is similar though not identical with 2p determiners/possessives: Again Herbert's frequency is high and similar to Donne (rel.), but here he is outdone by the use in prayers. It is logical to assume that the high frequency in religious poetry is an effect of its closeness to prayer(-style) language. The determiner uses will play a role again in section 4 below.

Table 1 also contains an interesting fact concerning aspect (iii) above: the CED data contains far fewer *thou* than *you* forms, as the latter was in the process of taking over as the default second person pronoun. *Thou* forms were thus by no means the only or even the most obvious choice at the time of writing *The Temple*, see both the CED and Shakespeare's plays showing a clear dominance of *you* in Table 2. Interestingly, religious language is divided, with prose texts moving away from *thou* and prayers upholding this older usage. Religious poetry thus patterns with prayers, as is clearly corroborated also by the difference between Donne's religious *vs.* non-religious poems.

	THOU	YOU
prayers 1/17c	53.0	2.4
Herbert	34.2	3.1
Donne (rel.)	30.7	3.1
Donne (other)	23.4	9.0
Shakespeare	14.2	23.7
CED D2	5.9	26.1
sermons 1/17c	3.9	
rel. treatises 1/17c	2.0	
catechisms 1/17c	0.5	

Table 2[6]: *Thou* and *You* frequencies (per 1,000 words), early seventeenth century

---

ness depositions, dialogic handbooks, comedies. BNC-KB is a section from the spoken part of the modern English *British National Corpus* (file names starting with KB) containing everyday conversation. The figures in brackets in the CED and BNC columns are for *you/your/yours* as the modern reflexes of *thou*-forms, in order to give a feeling for the overall 1p-2p distribution. In all searches spelling variants were considered, of course; thus *mee* or *thyne* are included, for example.

6   The prayers are from Kohnen's corpus, but here only the ones originating in the first half of the seventeenth century have been considered because of the rapid change exhibited by this feature.

While both Herbert and Donne (rel.) use, or avoid, *you* to the same extent, Herbert's use of *thou*-forms is even higher than Donne's. Clearly, the closeness of *Temple* poems to prayers will have played an important role in this choice. Another aspect will have been the connotations of *thou*, namely those of intimacy and trust. The rhyming possibilities, in particular of *mine* and *thine*, should not be neglected here, however: Their exploitation may well have boosted the frequencies in Herbert.

3. Transitivity and Agency

Glancing through the list of verbs co-occurring with the speaker *I*, one is struck by the comparative lack of dynamic activity verbs. The choice of verb and the (corresponding) clausal pattern serve to present a particular encoding of a state of affairs. The important point here is that there is always a choice: A different encoding might have been chosen implying another meaning, another version of reality. This aspect can be systematically approached by using Halliday's concept of transitivity, which charts process types and the corresponding syntactic encoding of participants and circumstances. How active and/or affected entities are will allow statements about agency.

There are six process types (Halliday and Matthiessen 2004, 172), namely processes that are material (happening, creating/changing, doing/acting), mental (seeing, feeling, thinking), relational (having attribute, having identity, symbolising), existential, verbal, and behavioural. More agency is expressed by – in descending order – material, verbal, behavioural, and mental processes (though behavers and sensers can be involved involuntarily), less or none by relational and existential processes (both typically realised by *be* or similar verbs). The processes with the most pronounced and often intentional effect on the world are the material ones of creating/changing and doing/acting; in contrast, mental processes are internal and need not be grounded in reality.

Eighteen finite verbs in "The Collar" occur in 1p contexts (including one *me*-impersonal and three possessive phrases; see underlining), which encode five material, five mental, four relational, two verbal, and two behavioural processes. Material processes are thus already in the minority, although they are more prominent in this poem than in many others. The poem starts with the most prototypical material process (*I struck the board*), i.e. there is visible action, with an animate, intentional actor and an affected object (Goal of the action). After this forceful assertion of the speaker, the material processes become less self-determined: Losing (*what I have lost*) is usually not intentional and with *did drie / drown it* the overt subjects taking the place of Actor are not animate beings at all, but with *my sighs / tears* nominalised semi-mental actions of the speaker. *I grew more fierce and wilde* is taken as material process here, because grow indicates change, but the phrasing could equally be seen as a relational process; the *I* is thus hardly an Actor but rather the Carrier of an Attribute. Two more cases which could be material processes (*I will abroad*) due to their phrasing have to be regarded as mental, i.e., internal, processes instead: the elided motion verb would be material, but *will* on its own expresses simple volition. Thus already in the second and third line

---

The figures for sermons, religious treatises, and catechisms are from Kohnen 2011, who does not provide comparative figures for *you*. THOU and YOU stand for all possible grammatical forms.

(*sigh, pine*) the speaker withdraws into an inner mental world, an internal dialogue with himself. Material processes such as *recover, leave, forsake* are doubly unreal: as part of the imagined dialogue and as imperatives indicating unrealised actions.

> I <u>Struck</u> the board, and <u>cry'd</u>, No more.
>   I <u>will</u> abroad.
> What? shall I ever <u>sigh</u> and <u>pine</u>?
> My lines and life <u>are</u> free; free as the rode,
>   Loose as the winde, as large as store.
>   <u>Shall</u> I <u>be</u> still in suit?
> <u>Have</u> I no harvest but a thorn
>   To let me bloud, and not restore
> What I <u>have lost</u> with cordiall fruit?
>   Sure there was wine
>   Before my sighs did <u>drie</u> it: there was corn
>   Before my tears did <u>drown</u> it.
> Is the yeare onely lost to me?
>   <u>Have</u> I no bayes to crown it?
> No flowers, no garlands gay? all blasted?
>   All wasted?
> Not so, my heart: but there is fruit,
>   And thou hast hands.
> Recover all thy sigh-blown age
> On double pleasures: leave thy cold dispute
> Of what is fit, and not. Forsake thy cage,
>   Thy rope of sands,
> Which pettie thoughts have made, and made to thee
>   Good cable, to enforce and draw,
>   And be thy law,
> While thou didst wink and wouldst not see.
>   Away; take heed:
>   I <u>will</u> abroad.
> Call in thy deaths head there: tie up thy fears.
>   He that forbears
>   To suit and serve his need,
>   Deserves his load.
> But as I <u>rav'd</u> and <u>grew</u> more fierce and wilde
>   At every word,
> <u>Methought</u> I <u>heard</u> one calling, *Childe*:
>   And I <u>reply'd</u>, *My Lord*.

The poem ends with two mental processes (*methought, heard*), one of them indicating uncertainty, and one a verbal (*reply'd*) process. It is noteworthy that the verbal process is not an initiating but a reactive one. Thus, the action of the beginning, however fruitless it might have been, is turned into non-material reaction – the speaker acquiesces. What is apparent in "The Collar" seems to be typical of the *Temple* poems: There are spurts of assertiveness on the part of the speaker, marked by material processes with intentional Actors, but more common – and often following the former – are mental verbs and generally verb phrases indicating reception and reaction. "The Holdfast", for example, contains only verbal and mental verbs. Only the first one of them (*threatened*) is an independent and even 'aggressive' action on the part of the speaker. Passive *was told*, and *heard* put the speaker into the recipient position; *trust, confesse* and *stood amazed* (at this!) all explicitly react, partly echo-like, to an impetus from elsewhere. The first process includes a Sayer, a participant usually endowed with intentionality, and the last (*heard*) involves a Senser, a being who is characterised by being conscious only. The last three lines of the poem do not contain an *I*-process at all (in contrast to the last lines of stanzas 1 and 2); thus, the poet writes himself as an Actor out of the poem.

> I <u>threatened</u> to observe the strict decree
> > Of my deare God with all my power & might.
> > But I <u>was told</u> by one, it could not be;
> Yet I might <u>trust</u> in God to be my light.
>
> Then will I <u>trust</u>, said I, in him alone.
> > Nay, ev'n to trust in him, was also his:
> > We must <u>confesse</u> that nothing is our own.
> Then I <u>confesse</u> that he my succour is:
>
> But to have nought is ours, not to confesse
> > That we have nought. I <u>stood amaz'd</u> at this,
> > Much troubled, till I <u>heard</u> a friend expresse,
> That all things were more ours by being his.
> > What Adam had, and forfeited for all,
> > Christ keepeth now, who cannot fail or fall.

In contrast, object *me* is found more commonly in the context of typical material processes, as the affected Goal of an action carried out by a typical Actor. "Sighs and Grones" can serve as a good example. The Actor is God, though he is only once explicitly indicated (*thou*, l. 3); in standard imperatives, i.e. all the other instances here, the 2p subject remains unexpressed. Interestingly, however, these are unreal contexts: As directives have a world-to-word fit (Searle and Vanderveken 1985), the state of affairs does not (yet) exist in the world, but is supposed to be brought about by the words uttered. However, for the speaker to utter the propositions contained in the directives in the first place, they must represent a mental reality. The speaker perceives himself as an affected entity, touched by God.

> > O Do not <u>use</u> me
> After my sinnes! look not on my desert,
> But on thy glorie! Then thou wilt <u>reform</u>
> And not <u>refuse</u> me: for thou onely art
> The mightie God, but I a sillie worm;
> > O do not <u>bruise</u> me!
>
> > O do not <u>urge</u> me!
> For what account can thy ill steward make?
> I have abus'd thy stock, destroy'd thy woods,
> Suckt all thy magazens: my head did ake,
> Till it found out how to consume thy goods:
> > O do not <u>scourge</u> me!
>
> > O do not <u>blinde</u> me!
> I have deserv'd that an Egyptian night
> Should thicken all my powers; because my lust
> Hath still sow'd fig-leaves to exclude thy light:
> But I am frailtie, and already dust;
> > O do not <u>grinde</u> me!

> O do not <u>fill</u> me
> With the turn'd viall of thy bitter wrath!
> For thou hast other vessels full of bloud,
> A part whereof my Saviour empti'd hath,
> Ev'n unto death: since he di'd for my good,
>   O do not <u>kill</u> me!
>
>   But O <u>reprieve</u> me!
> For thou hast *life* and *death* at thy command;
> Thou art both *Judge* and *Saviour*, feast and rod,
> *Cordiall* and *Corrosive*: put not thy hand
> Into the bitter box; but O my God,
>   My God, <u>relieve</u> me!

At the same time, however, the speaker assumes the right to utter the directives in their strongest possible form, the form with most manipulative strength (Givón 1993, 265). While he is syntactically hidden, he is thus nevertheless present via the performative speech-act dimension.

One may thus sum up the state of affairs in Herbert's *Temple* in the following way: There is a certain ambivalence between a speaker who wants to assert his intentions, his needs, his independence, and who at the same time wants to submit completely to God. Thus, many of the poems contain passages presenting the speaker as a forceful Actor, often to be followed by a retreat into less active process types.

4. Meronomy and Metonymy

I shall now come back to the *my*-phrases mentioned above and to aspects connected with them. In "The Altar" we saw the speaker's heart (*my hard heart*) highlighted, which is a part of the body, by extension of the individual, and thus stands in a relationship of meronomy (part-whole) (see Cruse 1986) to the speaker. Words indicating parts of the body (physical) or the person (abstract) appear prominently in *The Temple*, notably *breast, eye, flesh, hand, head*, but the two most common are *heart* and *soul*. Through this, Herbert highlights the part-like, un-whole nature of humans, or, in the words of "Affliction (IV)", their fragmented state of being *broken in pieces all asunder* (referring to the speaker). The lines *Am I all throat or eye, / To weep or crie? / Have I no parts but those of grief?* ("Complaining") point in the same direction. Noticeably uncommon as referring to the speaker is the body part *face*, i.e. the part that most of all individualises. The quasi-separation into distinct parts is also found in the speaker's addresses to parts or aspects of his body/person in various poems, such as his body/ flesh ("Church-monuments"), and most commonly his heart (e.g. "Easter", "The Dawning", "The Method", "The Discharge") (Rickey 1966, 127). The parts thus acquire a certain autonomy. Perhaps unsurprisingly, one finds a body/soul contrast, as here in extracts from "Church-monuments", with the *I* being clearly aligned with the soul and the body seen as an ultimately expendable part.

> WHile that <u>my soul</u> repairs to her devotion, / Here I intombe <u>my flesh</u>, that it betimes / May take acquaintance of this heap of dust [...]
> Therefore I gladly trust / <u>My bodie</u> to this school, that it may learn / To spell his elements, [...]
> <u>Deare flesh</u>, while <u>I</u> do pray, learn here thy stemme / And true descent; [...]

However, this contrast is not as commonly used by Herbert as one might expect in religious discourse. Other parts are also juxtaposed or even at war with each other in *The*

Temple; in "Affliction (IV)" it is the speaker's thoughts that are fighting against both the heart and the soul, constituting a rational/volitional-involuntary contrast.

> My thoughts are all a case of knives,
>   Wounding my heart
>   With scatter'd smart,
> As watring pots give flowers their lives.
>   Nothing their furie can controll,
>   While they do wound and prick my soul.

While here the soul and the heart seem to be on one side, as it were, in "H. Communion", below, they are on separate levels, the heart being here identified with the physical aspects of the person.

> Yet can these not get over to my soul, / Leaping the wall that parts / Our souls and fleshy hearts;

In "Deniall" the separation of heart and soul is less pronounced, but what is clearly highlighted is the fragmented nature of the speaker. There is no independent 1p in the whole poem (neither *I* nor *me*), only possessive phrases and 3p pronouns referring indirectly to the speaker. The state of the person thus matches the discord of the melody (*untun'd*) and the imperfection of the rhyme, the latter only *mended* in the last two lines. Whether the disintegration of the person is also mended is not resolved here, as it is not clear if God responds.

> WHen my devotions could not pierce
>   Thy silent eares;
> Then was my heart broken, as was my verse;
>   My breast was full of fears
>   And disorder:
>
> My bent thoughts, like a brittle bow,
>   Did flie asunder:
> Each took his way; some would to pleasures go,
>   Some to the warres and thunder
>   Of alarms.
>
> As good go any where, they say,
>   As to benumme
> Both knees and heart, in crying night and day,
>   *Come, come, my God, O come,*
>   But no hearing.
>
> O that thou shouldst give dust a tongue
>   To crie to thee,
> And then not heare it crying! all day long
>   My heart was in my knee,
>   But no hearing.
>
> Therefore my soul lay out of sight,
>   Untun'd, unstrung:
> My feeble spirit, unable to look right,
>   Like a nipt blossome, hung
>   Discontented.
>
> O cheer and tune my heartlesse breast,
>   Deferre no time;
> That so thy favours granting my request,
>   They and my minde may chime,
>   And mend my ryme.

As is visible in several of the examples so far, the meronomies are not simply parts, they also function as metonymies. This is especially clear in those cases where an action is predicated of the named part, see *flesh learns, thoughts wound* or *flie asunder*, and *devotions pierce*. This kind of use thus overtly attributes agency to the part instead of the person as a whole.[7] Van Leeuwen (1996, 60) termed such agentive metonymies "somatisation", which are a "form of objectivisation", i.e. they can have a depersonalising effect. In some cases this may be true, see the *dust/tongue/it* instance in l.16-18. In other cases, involving also slightly different metonymical relationships, this effect is less clear: Some metonymies are rather of the action-for-agent type, e.g. *devotion, thoughts*,[8] or of the instrument-for-action type, e.g. *knee* (Kövecses and Radden 1998, 54). As actions, whether physical or mental, always imply an agent, agency is at least indirectly involved here, even if downplayed. Also, where metonymical vehicles have conventional metaphorical associations, such as the *heart* (seat of emotions), full objectivisation does not apply. *My heart was in my knee*, for example, thus merges feeling, action, and person in an intricate and effective way.

It is also noteworthy here that not only the speaker or humans in general (see "Sepulchre": *so many hearts on earth*) are referred to meronomically/metonymically, but also God, as in *thy silent eares* above. More than half of the *ear*-instances represent God, in fact, and thus highlight him as the aim of the speaker's addresses. *Ear* needs to be seen here as a metaphtonymy (Goossens 2002), meaning 'listening', but also 'understanding' and 'attention'.

Although metonymies, in particular the part-whole type, are very frequent in language generally, those employed by Herbert actually go against a common cognitive principle, namely the preference of human over non-human conceptualisations (e.g. *devotions, knees* vs. *I*). It is especially the persistency of such uses in *The Temple* that make them stand out as marked and highly meaningful. Meronomies and metonymies furthermore present routes of access for conceptualisations. Herbert uses them to highlight those components of people which are important for his purposes: the *heart* and the *soul*, the *body/flesh*, and to a lesser extent *head/mind/thought*. The soul is the goal/purpose of all undertakings, but the heart is both an agent in the pursuit of the goal and also a battling-ground (see Cockcroft 2005), as the recurring metaphors make clear (e.g. in "Nature" HEART IS A WILD BEAST, HEART IS A FORTRESS, HEART IS A STONE, HEART IS A PLANT). These metaphors again mark the speaker not necessarily as weak (as the fragmentation by meronomy might imply), but as forceful and stubborn.

5. Conclusion

According to Fish (1972, 190; 216), Herbert tried to write himself out of his poems, leaving God as their true originator, but did not in fact succeed in this attempt. The visible signs of this attempt are the comparative infrequency of nominative *I*, the particular mine-thine usage, the recurrence of transitivity structures demoting agency, and the fragmented persona, together with highlighting of exactly those parts that are (sup-

---

[7] Compare Canning's (2012: 126) observation on *Macbeth*, where one finds "the weight of agency attributed not to people, but to *parts* of people" (italics original).

[8] Similar instances are *my sighs did drie it / my tears did drown it* in "The Collar" (section 3), *my fears foretold this* ("The Glimpse"), and *let my shame go where it doth deserve* ("Love (III)"). Note that these actions are of the fairly involuntary kind (triggered by emotions) and thus may exhibit even more reduced agency.

posed to be) closest to God. The importance of these aspects is based on their deviance from an implied norm, derived from readers' experience with everyday language use. The above uses simply stand out as marked. In contrast to this, however, one also finds seemingly contradictory aspects, i.e. the repeated reassertion of agentive structures, the forceful imperatives, the not fully conclusive somatisation, and the partly violent metaphors. On the whole, the speaker of *The Temple* is constantly wavering between self-effacement/submission and clear self-assertion.

References

Primary Sources

A Corpus of English Dialogues 1560-1760 (2006): Compiled by Merja Kytö and Jonathan Culpeper, in collaboration with Terry Walker and Dawn Archer

Corpus of English Religious Prose, 1150-1800. Compiled by Thomas Kohnen, University of Cologne (work-in-progress, unpublished)

Donne, John (1968): *The Poems of John Donne*. Ed. Herbert J. C. Grierson. Oxford: Oxford University Press

Herbert, George (2007): *The English Poems of George Herbert*. Ed. Helen Wilcox. Cambridge: Cambridge University Press

Shakespeare, William (1997): *The Riverside Shakespeare*. Ed. Gwynne Blakemore Evans. 2nd edition. Boston: Houghton Mifflin

The British National Corpus, version 2 (BNC World; 2001): Distributed by Oxford University Computing Services on behalf of the BNC Consortium

Secondary Sources

Canning, Patricia (2012): *Style in the Renaissance: Language and Ideology in Early Modern England*. London: Continuum

Cockcroft, Robin (2005): "Who Talks Whose Language? George Herbert and the Reader's World", *Language and Literature* 14.3, 245-258

Cruse, D.A. (1986): *Lexical Semantics*. Cambridge: Cambridge University Press

Fish, Stanley (1970): "Letting Go: The Reader in Herbert's Poetry", *ELH* 37.4, 475-494

--- (1972): *Self-Consuming Artifacts: The Experience of Seventeenth-Century Literature*. Berkeley: University of California Press

Givón, Talmy (1993): *English Grammar: A Function-Based Introduction*. Volume II. Amsterdam: Benjamins

Goossens, Louis (2002): "Metaphtonymy: The Interaction of Metaphor and Metonymy in Expressions for Linguistic Action", in: Dirven, René; Pörings, Ralf (eds.): *Metaphor and Metonymy in Comparison and Contrast*. Berlin: Mouton de Gruyter, 349-377

Halliday, M.A.K.; Matthiessen, Christian M.I.M. (2004): *An Introduction to Functional Grammar*. 3rd edition. London: Hodder Education

Kohnen, Thomas (2011): "Religious Language in 17th-Century England: Progressive or Archaic?" in: Frenk, Joachim; Lena Steveker (eds.): *Anglistentag 2010 Saarbrücken Proceedings*. Trier: WVT, 279-287

Kövecses, Zoltán; Radden, Günter (1998): "Metonymy: Developing a Cognitive Linguistic View", *Cognitive Linguistics* 9.1, 37-77

Rickey, Mary Ellen (1966): *Utmost Art: Complexity in the Verse of George Herbert*. Lexington: University of Kentucky Press

Searle, John; Vanderveken, D. (1985): *Foundations of Illocutionary Logic*. Cambridge: Cambridge University Press

Van Leeuwen, Theo (1996): "The Representation of Social Actors", in: Caldas-Coulthard, Carmen et al. (eds.): *Texts and Practices: Readings in Critical Discourse Analysis*. London: Routledge, 32-70

GERO GUTTZEIT (GIEßEN)

From Hearing to Overhearing? Eloquence and Poetry, 1776-1833

One of the major upheavals in the relationship between rhetoric and poetry is well known to have occurred between the Neoclassicist and the Romantic ages. Put very simply, High Romanticism regarded Neoclassicist poetry as a language without a connection to authenticity or originality and consequently redefined poetry in terms of the poet's expression of feeling, as an essentially uncommunicative communication. This mirrors some of the general characteristics of Romantic ideology, as Jerome McGann has analysed it: "The polemic of Romantic poetry [...] is that it will not be polemical; its doctrine, that it is non-doctrinal; and its ideology, that it transcends ideology" (McGann [1983] 1999, 69-70). What interests me here is the coincidence of this development with the marginalization of rhetoric as a theory of the merely figurative dress of thought, at the end of which rhetoric ceases to be viewed as a theory of communication. In the Romantic age, the concept and practice of poetry changes fundamentally as rhetoric-as-communication is transformed into rhetoric-as-mere-style.

In this article, I shall examine a relatively under-researched field of this transition, namely the explicit critical efforts between the 1770s and the 1830s to define the borders between poetry and what the period calls eloquence as well as between their respective disciplines, poetics and rhetoric. The beginning and end of the time frame in question, 1776 and 1833, are marked by the first publication of the Scottish New Rhetorician George Campbell's *The Philosophy of Rhetoric* on the one end, and, on the other, by John Stuart Mill's famous essay "Thoughts on Poetry and Its Varieties". In his essay, Mill coined the definition that serves as inspiration for the question in the title of this article: Does the reception of poetry in the period change from hearing to overhearing? In Campbell and Mill, we find diametrically opposed positions which are traces of a central development in the theory of the relation between rhetoric and poetry. I shall first survey some of the problematic history of rhetoric and present an argument for the historical identity of rhetorical and poetical discourse.

1. Rhetoric and Poetics

Whether conceived of as a field of research, a methodology, or an institution, rhetoric always invites consideration of the two-and-a-half millennia of its existence, an invitation hard to decline here, since the critical history of rhetoric is closely intertwined with the critical history of poetics. The historical responses to the question of the relationship between rhetoric and poetics can be mapped on a scale that ranges from mutual exclusion to complete identity. But no matter how the distance between the two disciplines is measured, the two language arts remain points of reference for each other. It is important to note again that the Romantic conception of rhetoric is only one of several historical reductions of rhetoric. The repeated effect of these reductions is to negate rhetoric's capacity, through 'discovery' or *inventio*, to arrive at truth; along with this often goes the restriction of rhetoric to the canon of *elocutio*, or style, as lists of figures of speech. Examples include Augustine of Hippo's assignment of rhetoric to the mere presentation of revealed truth (Walker 2000, 322), Petrus Ramus's privileging of dialectic and restriction of rhetoric to style (*elocutio*) and delivery (*pronuntiatio*) (Ong [1958] 2004), and the critique of rhetoric by empiricist philosophers such as Bacon and Locke (Bevilacqua 1968).

The question as to what rhetoric was *before* these reductions has been answered by Jeffrey Walker in his 2000 monograph, *Rhetoric and Poetics in Antiquity*, in a way that is highly relevant for the question of rhetorical and poetic discourse. Rather than affirming one of the standard views that ancient rhetoric is primarily the art of oratory, Walker argues that the ancient rhetorical tradition was from its very beginning poetic, and vice versa: "What came to be called rhetoric was neither originally nor essentially an art of practical civic oratory – rather, [...] it originated from an expansion of the poetic/epideictic domain, from 'song' to 'speech' to 'discourse' generally" (Walker 2000, ix). Based on this Vicoesque argument, Walker views the reductions of rhetoric as the result of a grammaticalization of both rhetoric and poetics in the scholastic tradition, in which both are cut off from notions of argumentation or 'reason':

> 'Rhetoric' tends within this tradition to be formalistically conceived as presentational stylistics and to be identified with a sublunary realm of practical communication, politics, and business. So conceived, it easily comes to be seen as an art of specious ornament, salesmanship, propaganda, and false consciousness at worst and as an art of effective or elegant 'expression' at best. 'Poetry,' for its part, tends to be conceived in terms of a figural mimesis that hyponoiacally signifies moral-philosophical *katholou* [general truths sensu Aristotle] or that dramatistically represents them as models of subjectivity" (Walker 2000, 329).

Walker's reconstruction of the unity of rhetorical-poetic discourse before its grammaticalization is crucial, especially since it serves as a reminder of the rationality that is inherent in rhetorical-poetic discourse. Rather than isolating the political speech as the one and only realm of rhetoric and assigning to poetry only a psychological or didactic function, this argument makes it clear that rhetorical-poetic discourse partakes in argumentation and emotion. I shall now be investigating the cases for the identity and non-identity of rhetorical and poetic discourse in the eighteenth-century New Rhetoric and in Late-Romantic texts.

2. Poetry and Eloquence in the Eighteenth-Century New Rhetoric

In the history of rhetoric, however conceived, the many proclamations of the demise or death of rhetoric were countered by just as many clarion calls for a *nova rhetorica*. The Renaissance, the eighteenth-century Enlightenment, and the twentieth century each have their own New Rhetoric. The importance of rhetoric for poetics in the Renaissance has been widely recognized and the importance of twentieth century New Rhetoricians such as I. A. Richards and Kenneth Burke universally acknowledged; yet with few exceptions (Engell 1995), the group of eighteenth-century British New Rhetoricians is not well-known outside of rhetorical studies.

Yet the importance of this New Rhetoric can hardly be overestimated, both for rhetorical and poetic discourse, as Howell's seminal treatment of rhetoric and logic in the long eighteenth century suggests (Howell 1971). Scholars of rhetoric such as Vincent Bevilacqua mark the period between Adam Smith's Edinburgh lectures on rhetoric (1748-50) and Hugh Blair's *Lectures on Rhetoric and Belles Lettres* (1783) as "the most far-reaching reformation of traditional theory since Peter Ramus's partition of the trivium in the mid-sixteenth century" (Bevilacqua 1968, 191). The most popular of the treatises, Hugh Blair's *Lectures*, was truly ubiquitous: Between 1783 and 1911 at least 283 versions of the *Lectures* appeared, including 112 complete editions, 110 abridged editions, and 61 translations (Carr 2002, 78). While less popular than Blair, George Campbell's *Philosophy of Rhetoric* (1776) saw at least 42 editions, with nearly all editions published in the nineteenth century (Bitzer 1988, vii). Other British treatises such as the Englishman Richard Whately's *Elements of Rhetoric* (1828) also continued the Scottish debate well into the nineteenth century, both in Britain and the United States. In literary criticism, however, the importance of the New Rhetoric is still underrated.

When it comes to the distinction between rhetorical and poetic discourse around 1800, the crucial element is audience. Of the rhetorical theories, George Campbell is most explicit on this score: For him, rhetoric is about the effect on the audience that the speaker or writer wants to achieve. The first chapter of *The Philosophy of Rhetoric* opens: "In speaking there is always some end proposed, or some effect which the speaker intends to produce on the hearer. The word *eloquence* in its greatest latitude denotes, 'That art or talent by which the discourse is adapted to its end'" (Campbell [1776] 1988, 1).

Rhetorical discourse is thus not at all restricted to an orator speaking; for Campbell, rhetoric is "the grand art of communication, not of ideas only, but of sentiments, passions, dispositions, and purposes" (Campbell [1776] 1988, lxxiii). Necessarily, the focus on effective discourse goes hand in hand with a focus on the audience: "The necessity which a speaker is under of suiting himself to his audience, both that he may be understood by them, and that his words may have influence upon them, is a maxim so evident as to need neither proof nor illustration" (Campbell [1776] 1988, 102).

Whilst Campbell is working in the context of rhetorical theory from Adam Smith to Hugh Blair, the scope of his project is unique: His "Philosophy of Rhetoric" falls into an Isocratean or Ciceronian rather than an Aristotelian tradition in that he conceives rhetoric as a universal art of communication grounded in empirical observations of successful oratorical and writerly practice. Campbell's project is not a practical rhetoric, but an examination of the interrelation between rhetorical theory and the Enlightenment philosophy of the human, as theorized especially by David Hume. Seeking the fundamentals of rhetoric in the science of man, Campbell modifies the Ciceronian three types of effect a discourse can have, namely to teach, to delight, and to move, as follows: "All the ends of speaking are reducible to four; every speech being intended to enlighten the understanding, to please the imagination, to move the passions, or to influence the will" (Campbell [1776] 1988, 1).

How does poetry fit into this scheme? For Campbell, poetry mainly has the end of pleasing the imagination and moving the passions, but it can also fulfil the other functions. For Campbell, poetry is one kind of rhetoric, a view for which he argues as follows:

> Poetry indeed is properly no other than a particular mode or form of certain branches of oratory. [...] [T]he direct end of the former, whether to delight the fancy as in epic, or to move the passions as in tragedy, is avowedly in part the aim, and sometimes the immediate and proposed aim, of the orator. The same medium, language, is made use of; the same general rules of composition, in narration, description, argumentation, are observed; and the same tropes and figures,

either for beautifying or for invigorating the diction, are employed by both. (Campbell [1776] 1988, lxxiii)

That Campbell subsumes poetry under oratory/eloquence is no surprise, since he understands rhetoric as a general theory of communication. For Campbell, they form a unit, albeit not as equal partners: Rhetorical and poetic discourse have similar ends, the same general and particular means, and follow the same rules; however, lyric poetry does not figure prominently. The focus of Campbell's theory of literature is clearly on the dramatic and the epic. The word 'poetry', or its variant 'poesy', still refers to all kinds of literature, be it in verse or not. Verse for Campbell is decidedly not a criterion of poetry: "In regard to versification, it is more to be considered as appendage, than as a constituent of poetry" (Campbell [1776] 1988, lxxiii-lxxiv).

That Campbell's approach to poesy is Aristotelian becomes clear in his argument on fiction-as-truth. Campbell states:

> Even in those performances where truth, in regard to the individual facts related, is neither sought nor expected, as in some sorts of poetry, and in romance, truth still is an object to the mind, the general truths regarding character, manners, and incidents. When these are preserved, the piece may justly be denominated true, considered as a picture of life; though false, considered as a narrative of particular events. (Campbell [1776] 1988, 33)

Campbell's strong focus on fictional truth and narrativity is coupled with traditional genres widely associated with the Neoclassicism of the eighteenth century. In a footnote, Campbell offers a table of the genres he classifies as poetry. The table is based on his particular version of faculty psychology[1]:

The object.	Serious.		Facetious.	The end and morals.	The means.		The Poet.	
	Fancy	—Great epic	—Little epic			—Insinuation		Narrator,
	Passion	—Tragedy	—Comedy			—Conformation		Representer,
	Will	—High satire	—Low satire			—Persuasion		Reasoner.

Epic, dramatic, and satirical texts fall into two modes: the serious and the facetious, which aim at the improvement of morals and manners respectively. The schema of object, end, and means is completed with the basic role the poet assumes: "narrator" in the case of epic, "representer" in the case of drama, and "reasoner" in the case of satire.

At first, the absence of the understanding appears somewhat curious. Yet, Campbell repeatedly points out that the dominance of a faculty or function does not mean that the others are completely absent, as the poet's role of "reasoner" in the case of satire shows. Poetry, for the Neo-Classicist Campbell, is thus mainly epic, drama, and satire.

What about the form and content of lyric poetry, then? If lyric poetry might be defined content-wise by the peculiar subjectivity it presents or in formal terms by its phonetic texture,[2] then Campbell only looks at formal characteristics. In a section entitled "Words Considered as Sounds" (Campbell [1776] 1988, 317-329), he examines ono-

---

1   The table is taken from Campbell [1776] 1988, 22.
2   On the problematic of the lyric in generic classifications see Genette 1992.

matopoeia and other phonetic devices. Based on Alexander Pope's precept that the sound be made an echo to the sense, he discusses examples chiefly from Pope and Milton in terms of how they imitate aspects of reality. His discussion encompasses the imitation of sound, motion, size, difficulty and ease, and the agreeable, establishing a typology of possible representative functions of the sound of words.

For Campbell, poetry is thus first and foremost a kind of communication in the traditional genres of epic, drama, and satire. It is capable of truth, but its main appeal is to please the imagination, while it can also move the passions and, to an extent, move the will and enlighten the understanding. Like all rhetorical discourse, it is intended to produce an effect on an audience through particular linguistic means. For Campbell, all discourse, including poetry, is written to be heard.

Though published in the year of the American Declaration of Independence, Campbell's treatise had its strongest influence in the nineteenth century. Students at British and American universities thus regularly came in contact with a rhetorical theory of poetry. In 1828, Richard Whately, the English Archbishop of Dublin, who was also a one-time professor of political economy, wrote the last major treatise connected to the eighteenth-century New Rhetoric, responding mainly to George Campbell. In *Elements of Rhetoric*, Whately is aware of the different possibilities of how to think through the relation of rhetoric to poetry; he states that "some writers have spoken of Rhetoric as the Art of Composition, universally; or, with the exclusion of Poetry alone, as embracing all Prose-composition" (Whately [1828] 2010, 3). In contrast to Campbell's general theory of communication, however, Whately views rhetoric as an "offshoot from Logic": Logic is a monologic process of investigation, whereas rhetoric is "Argumentative Composition" responsible for "*conveying truth* to others" (Whately [1828] 2010, 4, 35). Despite this restriction, Whately discusses a plethora of areas such as science, philosophy, religion, and poetry in his book on rhetoric.

His discussion of poetry builds on Campbell's argument for the truth of fictions and enlarges it with the notion of plausibility as one kind of probability. The second aspect of poetry he mentions is style, which appears when he discusses the elegance of the argumentative composition: "Nor are the considerations relative to Style and Elocution confined to argumentative and persuasive compositions" (Whately [1828] 2010, 40). The third aspect beside plausibility and style is feeling: "The art of addressing the feelings [...] does not belong exclusively to Rhetoric; since Poetry has at least as much to do with the branch" (Whately [1828] 2010, 40). For Whately, poetry is thus an art of addressing the feelings by means of plausibility and style.

Based on Whately's book, or rather using it as a springboard, Thomas De Quincey takes a decisive leap towards Mill's argument in what he himself called an "excursive review" of Whately's *Elements of Rhetoric* (De Quincey [1828] 2010, 81). Indeed, in the review, references to Whately are scarce; De Quincey is much more concerned with synthesizing his own ideas. He no longer speaks about poetic discourse in the way that Campbell and Whately connect it to truth and plausibility; rather, he is concerned with the notion of probability in the context of argumentation, discussing the notion of the enthymeme at great lengths.

De Quincey diagnoses the circulation of two contemporary ideas of rhetoric: "one of which is occupied with the general end of the fine arts – that is to say, intellectual pleasure; the other applies itself more specifically to a definite purpose of utility, viz. fraud" (De Quincey [1828] 2010, 82). In the department of intellectual pleasure, De Quincey finds the highest rhetorical powers in the works of poets from Philip Sidney to John Milton. The decisive distinction De Quincey makes is between eloquence and rhetoric, which are no longer to be viewed as identical as they were in Campbell.[3]

De Quincey separates rhetoric and eloquence by taking up William Wordsworth's definitions of poetry, even echoing his very phrases. De Quincey defines it thus:

> By Eloquence we understand the overflow of powerful feelings upon occasions fitted to excite them. But Rhetoric is the art of aggrandizing and bringing out into strong relief, by means of various and striking thoughts, some aspect of truth which of itself is supported by no spontaneous feelings, and therefore rests upon artificial aids. (De Quincey [1828] 2010, 92)

Artificial aids versus spontaneous and powerful feelings, aggrandizing versus overflow: De Quincey inherits many of the Romantic oppositions, to some extent confirming M. H. Abrams's distinction between the expressive theories of Romanticism that focus on the author in contrast with the pragmatic theories of Neoclassicism that focus on the audience (Abrams [1953] 1971, 3-29). De Quincey's response to Whately is crucial, since he romanticizes eloquence and claims it as the right kind of rhetoric.

There is a development from Campbell's universal theory of rhetoric that includes poetry to Whately's connection of poetry and feeling and to De Quincey's reinterpretation of rhetoric as being opposed to eloquence. This process of gradual reduction or restriction reaches its apex in John Stuart Mill's notion of poetry as discourse that is overheard.

3. John Stuart Mill: Poetry as Discourse Overheard

The opposition of rhetoric and poetry in terms of the effect on an audience is perhaps nowhere as obvious as in John Stuart Mill's essay, "Thoughts on Poetry and its Varieties" (1833). Later, in *A System of Logic*, Mill would in fact define rhetoric along similar lines to Whately: Logic guides one's own thoughts, rhetoric helps communicate them to others (Mill [1843] 1974, 6). Yet "Thoughts on Poetry" reads, in many ways, like a response to the distinction between rhetoric and poetics by the New Rhetoricians, and its central metaphor has become a locus classicus of the relation between poetic and rhetorical discourse.

In the section on the question of "What is Poetry", Mill deals with the *differentia specifica* of poetry in contrast to other aspects of literary texts, comparing it at first to narrative and description. The last aspect from which Mill believes he must distinguish poetry – and the one that he dwells on the longest – is, of course, that of eloquence. Mill writes: "Poetry and eloquence are both alike the expression or utterance of feeling. But if we may be excused the antithesis, we should say that eloquence is *heard*, poetry is *over*heard" (Mill [1833] 1981, 348).

While focusing on feeling, Mill is more than aware of the rhetorical tradition and its classification of effects. "Eloquence", writes Mill, echoing neorhetorical classifications of effects, "is feeling pouring itself out to other minds, courting their sympathy, or en-

---

3   For a detailed account of the "transitional character of De Quincey's rhetorical theory" see Agnew (2012, 2).

deavouring to influence their belief, or move them to passion or to action" (Mill [1833] 1981, 348-49). Mill's and Campbell's enumerations of functions are strikingly similar, as this table shows:

Types of effect	*Docere*	*Delectare*	*Movere*	*(Persuadere)*
Campbell's ends of discourse	Enlighten the understanding	Please the imagination	Move the passions	Influence the will
Mill's ends of discourse	Endeavouring to influence other minds' belief	Courting other minds' sympathy	Move other minds to passion	Move other minds to action

The types of effect are taken from Heinrich Lausberg's reconstruction of ancient rhetoric (Lausberg 1973, 140): As the general aim of rhetorical discourse, persuasion (*persuadere*) governs the other three functions. The ancient classification organizes both the faculties that Campbell distinguishes and the corresponding ends of discourse (Campbell [1776] 1988, 1). Mill's possible ends of discourse seem to differ only with regard to the imagination: pleasing the imagination against courting other minds' sympathy. Yet, as Walter Jackson Bate argued in a seminal essay, the sympathetic imagination was one of the key ideas taken over from the eighteenth century by Romantic authors and critics (Bate 1945).

Of course, Campbell and Mill disagree in their general definitions. Campbell views all rhetorical discourse in a relation of ends and means, defining eloquence as "That art or talent by which the discourse is adapted to its end" (Campbell [1776] 1988, 1). This is where the difference in frameworks lies, since Mill's definition speaks of "feeling pouring itself out to other minds" (Mill [1833] 1981, 348-349). For Mill, even rhetorical discourse thus lies strangely outside of the relation of ends and means. Of course, this is even more true of his definition of poetry: "Poetry is feeling, confessing itself to itself in moments of solitude, and embodying itself in symbols, which are the nearest possible representations of the feeling in the exact shape in which it exists in the poet's mind" (Mill [1833] 1981, 348).

While the poet is central in Mill's definition, the poet is only central in the sense of a space where poetry can happen. It is personified feeling that is engaged in solitary confession and embodies itself in Romantic symbols. Poetry is a soliloquy that hardly needs the poet and must not have an audience. Mill tempers this extreme image in his explanations, but he retains the absolute negation of dialogicity:

> When [the poet] turns round and addresses himself to another person: when the act of utterance is not itself the end, but a means to an end—viz. by the feelings he himself expresses, to work upon the feelings, or upon the belief, or the will, of another,—when the expression of his emotions, or of his thoughts tinged by his emotions, is tinged also by that purpose, by that desire of making an impression upon another mind, then it ceases to be poetry, and becomes eloquence (Mill [1833] 1981, 349)

Overhearing presupposes a discourse that is audible. Consequently, Mill thinks of all poetry as a soliloquy, born in the inner life of the poet and untinged by rules of art. As part of the Romantic ideology, this view is long-lived. What is more, in a certain sense, Mill, who was of course no literary critic, is a purer Romantic than Wordsworth. In the Preface to *Lyrical Ballads*, for instance, Wordsworth states that his habits of meditation formed his feelings in such a way that his poetic descriptions "will be found to carry along with them a *purpose*. If in this opinion I am mistaken I can have little right to the name of a Poet" (Wordsworth [1802] 1991, 237).

While the metaphorical phrase of poetry overheard does not seem to have direct precursors, the rationale behind Mill's argument is strikingly similar to contemporary rephrasings of a classical topos. Both in the neorhetorical treatises and in De Quincey's text there is the notion that art consists in hiding art: *ars est celare artem*. In De Quincey, the identification of rhetoric with an elevated diction is interpreted in terms of the ethos of the speaker: "A man is held to play the rhetorician, when he treats a subject with more than usual gaiety of ornament" (De Quincey [1828] 2010, 81). Therefore, it is necessary to hide the artistry involved in speaking. Whately goes even farther than this and explicitly compares the poet to the orator:

> A Poet, a Statesman, or a General, &c., though extreme covetousness of applause may mislead them, will, however, attain their respective Ends, certainly not the less for being admired as excellent, in Poetry, Politics, or War; but the Orator attains his End the better the less he is regarded as an Orator. If he can make the hearers believe that he is not only a stranger to all unfair artifice, but even destitute of all Persuasive skill whatever, he will persuade them the more effectually, and if there ever could be an absolutely perfect Orator, no one would (at the time at least) discover that he was so. (Whately [1828] 2010, 211-212)

While this rationale might make sense, it still seems that Whately was wrong here. The danger to make an impression of artifice instead of sincerity was not the greatest for the orator; it was far greater for that other language artist: the poet.

4. Conclusion

From hearing to overhearing summarises a certain development in the theory of the relation between rhetoric and poetics that remained in force as part of the Romantic ideology. John Stuart Mill's metaphorical distinction is a result of the romanticising redefinition of eloquence in terms of the overflowing expression of feeling, as found in De Quincey. Whately's *Elements of Rhetoric*, with its strict distinction between logic and rhetoric and its corresponding focus on style and expression, represents a movement in rhetoric itself towards Late-Romantic theory, one that essentially negates Campbell's general theory of communication and his notion of poetry as something that is to be heard.

Roughly two hundred years after Campbell's argument for rhetoric as a general theory of communication, Gérard Genette in his essay on "Rhetoric Restrained" (1982) argued that rhetoric should become a theory of all discourse and no longer be restricted to style only. The possibility to think both rhetoric and poetry in a communicative and dialogical discursive nexus informed by ends and means, by opposition and persuasion, by truth and style, is already given in George Campbell's *Philosophy of Rhetoric*. His argument was that poetry can and should be seen as an integral element of the rhetoric from which it came to be sundered. I suggest we stop overhearing it and begin to listen.

References

Primary Sources

Campbell, George [1776] (1988): *The Philosophy of Rhetoric*. Ed. Lloyd F. Bitzer. Delmar, NY: Scholars' Facsimiles & Reprints

De Quincey, Thomas [1828] (2010): "Rhetoric", in: Burwick, Frederick (ed.): *Selected Essays on Rhetoric*, 81-133: Southern Illinois University Press

Mill, John S. [1833] (1981): "Thoughts on Poetry and Its Varieties", in: Robson; John M.; Stillinger, Jack (eds.): *Autobiography and Literary Essays*. Online Library of Liberty, 341-365. Collected Works of John Stuart Mill 1. Toronto: University of Toronto Press

--- [1843] (1974): *A System of Logic Ratiocinative and Inductive: Being a Connected View of the Principles of Evidence and the Methods of Scientific Investigation. Books 1-3*, Robson, John M.; McRae, R. F. (eds.). *Collected Works of John Stuart Mill 7*. Toronto: University of Toronto Press

Ong, Walter J. [1958] (2004): *Ramus, Method, and the Decay of Dialogue: From the Art of Discourse to the Art of Reason*. Chicago: University of Chicago Press

Whately, Richard [1828] (2010): *Elements of Rhetoric*. Carbondale: Southern Illinois University Press

Wordsworth, William. [1802] (1991): "Preface to Lyrical Ballads (1802)", in: Brett, R. L.; Jones, Alun R. (eds.): *Lyrical Ballads*. 2nd edition. London/New York: Routledge

Secondary Sources

Abrams, Meyer H. [1953] (1971): *The Mirror and the Lamp: Romantic Theory and the Critical Tradition*. London: Oxford University Press

Agnew, Lois P. (2012): *Thomas de Quincey: British Rhetoric's Romantic Turn*. Carbondale: Southern Illinois University Press

Bate, Walter J. (1945): "The Sympathetic Imagination in Eighteenth-Century English Criticism", *ELH* 12.2, 144-164

Bevilacqua, Vincent M. (1968): "Philosophical Influences in the Development of English Rhetorical Theory: 1748 to 1783", *Proceedings of the Leeds Philosophical and Literary Society* 12, 191-215

Bitzer, Lloyd F. (1988): "Introduction", in: Bitzer, Lloyd F. (ed.): *The Philosophy of Rhetoric*, vii-li. Delmar, NY: Scholars' Facsimiles & Reprints

Carr, Stephen L. (2002): "The Circulation of Blair's 'Lectures'", *Rhetoric Society Quarterly* 32.4, 75-104

Engell, James (1995): "The New Rhetoric and Romantic Poetics", in: Bialostosky, Don H.; Needham, Lawrence D. (eds.): *Rhetorical Traditions and British Romantic Literature*, 217-232. Bloomington: Indiana University Press

Genette, Gérard (1982): "Rhetoric Restrained", in: *Figures of Literary Discourse*. New York: Columbia University Press, 103-126

--- (1992): *The Architext: An Introduction*. Berkeley: University of California Press

Howell, Wilbur S. (1971): *Eighteenth-Century British Logic and Rhetoric*. Princeton: Princeton University Press

Lausberg, Heinrich (1973): *Handbuch der literarischen Rhetorik*. 2nd edition. Munich: Hueber

McGann, Jerome J. [1983] (1999): *The Romantic Ideology: A Critical Investigation*. Chicago: University of Chicago Press

Walker, Jeffrey (2000): *Rhetoric and Poetics in Antiquity*. Oxford: Oxford University Press

ALWIN FILL (GRAZ)

Humanizing Metaphors in the Nature Poems of D. H. Lawrence

> She woos the moth with her sweet low word:
> And when above her his moth-wings hover
> Then her bright breast she will uncover
> And yield her honey-drop to her lover.
> (Lawrence 1964: 42)

These four lines from an early poem by D. H. Lawrence ("Love on the Farm", ca. 1910) contain several metaphors in which Lawrence compares animals and plants with humans: "she woos", "sweet low word", "her bright breast", and "her lover" seem to describe a love-scene between a man and a woman. However, Lawrence uses these phrases as poetic metaphors for an insect that enters the blossom of a flower and tries to get honey-drops. "He" is the insect, and "she" is the blossom. These four lines thus form an extended humanizing metaphor in which a natural event (a bee trying to get honey) is compared to a love scene between a man and a woman. A couple making love is the image donor (or, to use another terminology, the 'vehicle') for the bee and the blossom, which are the image carriers (the 'tenor'). Later in the poem, the words *flirt, her lips*, and *stolen kisses* continue the comparison between natural and human processes. One could speculate that in this early poem Lawrence already wanted to show the similarity between human and animal life and thus the equality of humans and animals.

1. *Birds, Beasts and Flowers*

This idea is particularly evident in *Birds, Beasts and Flowers*, a collection of Lawrence's poems which were "begun in Tuscany, in the autumn of 1920, and finished in New Mexico in 1923, in my thirty-eighth year" (from Lawrence's Preface of 1928 [1964, 29]). The poems in this collection are ordered according to the species of plants and animals dealt with. Thus we have groups of poems called "Fruits", "Trees", "Flowers", "The Evangelistic Beasts", "Creatures", "Reptiles", "Birds", "Animals", and "Ghosts". Not all these groups contain humanizing metaphors, but some of them use this device extensively, particularly the seven poems which make up the section "Reptiles".

Titles like "Baby Tortoise", "Tortoise Family Connections", "Lui et Elle", and "Tortoise Gallantry" already make apparent Lawrence's endeavour to put animals on the same level as humans and to show that they belong to the same area of life. In "Lui et Elle" (1964, 358-362), a female and a male reptile are described as a married couple: She is "matronly"; he is called "her husband" and "little old man". In "Tortoise Gallantry" (1964, 362-363), the male tortoise is called a "little gentleman", who "makes advances" on the female. All animals are addressed as *he* or *she*, while for flowers the neutral pronoun *they* is always used. Lawrence wishes to tell us that there is no rift between humans and other living beings. Birds, beasts, and flowers belong to the same area of life as humans, and the processes that play a role in human lives also occur in the lives of animals and plants.

in the wider context of 'anthropomorphism' vs. 'anthropocentrism', in other words, in the light of an ideology which questions the superiority of humans on this earth and particularly the separation of humans from other beings.

4. Metaphor and Rhetoric

At this point, a few words are in order about the extent to which metaphor is part of rhetoric. In connection with rhetoric, one first thinks of hyperbole, litotes, lists of three, and similar figures of speech, but not immediately of literary metaphor. However, describing metaphor as part of rhetoric can be traced to the authority of Aristotle. In book III of his *Rhetoric*, metaphor appears several times as one of the tropes or rhetorical devices with which cognition is supported (see Höffe 2009, 474). Wayne C. Booth, in 1978, wrote an article entitled "Metaphor as Rhetoric: The Problem of Evaluation", in which he argued in favour of seeing metaphor as rhetoric. Heinrich Plett (1973, 80) presents anthropomorphic metaphor as a piece of rhetoric, and in Robert A. Harris's *Handbook of Rhetorical Devices* (2013), metaphor is also among the 60 rhetorical devices discussed.

There seem to be two different functions that rhetorical devices (including metaphor) may have in works of literature:

(1) The first and most obvious one is the aesthetic or poetic function: Rhetorical devices contribute to poetic effects, to showing the world in a poetic light; metaphors, for instance, make us see similarities that would otherwise be invisible. "Using words impressively in speech and writing" is the object of rhetoric, but it is also "designed to persuade" (*OED*, entry for *rhetoric*).

(2) Thus, rhetorical devices also have a second function, which could be called the 'pragmatic' one. This is to help convey a message, which, as we see with Lawrence, is done even in poetry. Works of literature do not, as the New Critics thought, exist only for their own sake; they also contain messages and convey ideas to society, and the rhetorical devices used in literature are meant to support the propagation of these ideas.

Lawrence's humanizing metaphors may be said to fulfil both these functions:

(1) They are poetic elements that uncover similarities that would otherwise be hidden for us, and they show phenomena in a wider context. Reading and understanding them gives us pleasure, and thus they heighten the poetic effect of his poems.

(2) On the other hand, they also support the messages that the writer of this poetry wishes to convey. They are meant to instil a certain idea in people and convince them of the importance of this idea.

In the case of Lawrence, as we have seen, there are two messages that he wishes to express: First of all, humans and animals are on the same level, there is no categorical difference between them. Humans do not live in an *environment* of animals, plants, and inanimate Nature, but there is a '*convironment*' (as it could be called) in which all beings have equal rights.

Secondly, Lawrence wishes to express his view that there is no such thing as sin. Sin was invented by humans, but Nature does not know it; thus for humans as part of Nature talking about sin is "obsolete" (Lawrence 1964, 463).

As I have suggested elsewhere (2006, 172), I would plead for a "Literary Pragmatics" or "Pragmatics of Literature", in which the impact of literary works on society is investigated – or at least the effects intended by the authors of these works. Linguistic Pragmatics has by now existed for about 50 years as a school that investigates the uses and effects of language and of discourse. A pragmatics of literature (or, using another term, 'Impact Criticism') would investigate the impact certain works of literature have had on attitudes in human societies. As far as Lawrence is concerned, Literary Pragmatics would investigate the extent to which the messages shown above (and others, concerning, for example, sex, which will not be discussed here) have found their way into society and perhaps have even contributed to changing traditional views and attitudes.[1]

5. Other Rhetorical Elements in Lawrence's Poetry

Besides humanizing metaphors, Lawrence's poetry also contains a number of other rhetorical elements, such as word repetitions – for example, "on a hot, hot day", "in Sicily the black, black snakes are innocent", and "slowly turned his head, and slowly, very slowly […] proceeded to draw his slow length curving round […]" (all from "Snake", 1964, 349 and 350).

In one of his later poems ("What Is a Man without an Income?"), Lawrence (1957, 280) again uses word repetition:

> What is a man without an income?
> – Well, let him get on the dole!
>   dole, dole, dole
>   hole, hole, hole
>   soul, soul, soul –
>
> What is a man without an income?
> Answer without a rigmarole
>
>   On the dole, dole, dole
>   He's a hole, hole, hole
>   In the nation's pocket.

Lawrence also utilizes the 'list of three', a well-known rhetorical device from political speeches, which we know for instance from Shakespeare's *Julius Caesar* ("Friends, Romans, Countrymen") or Lincoln's *Gettysburg Address* ("of the people, by the people, for the people"). In "Snake", Lawrence uses this device quite extensively. Here are two examples (1964, 350):

> And depart peaceful, pacified, and thankless
> into the burning bowels of this earth?
>
> Was it cowardice, that I dared not kill him?
> Was it perversity, that I longed to talk to him?
> Was it humility, to feel so honoured?

---

[1] The book *Literary Pragmatics*, edited by Roger D. Sell (1991), is not about the impact of literature on society. The contributions deal, among other topics, with the role of the circumstances of the publication of a work of literature and the function of literature as dialogue between the disciplines.

This device is also employed in several other poems from *Birds, Beasts and Flowers*, for instance in "Bibbles" (1964, 399), "Baby Tortoise" (352), "Tortoise Shell" (354) and "Peach" (279). It could be argued that Lawrence, in his unrhymed poems, wished to make up for the lack of rhymes by using these rhetorical elements.

6. Misanthropy

In addition to the two messages discussed so far, there is a third message which Lawrence wishes to convey in his later poems. For this, he also uses metaphor, again comparing humans with animals and plants. However, here he no longer uses humanizing metaphors, but turns the direction of the comparison around: In these poems, he compares humans with animals and plants using the natural beings as the image donors (the 'vehicle' of the metaphor) and humans as image receivers (the 'tenor').

In these later poems (most of them from a collection called *Pansies*, written around 1929), Lawrence's empathy with animals is carried so far that it amounts to a certain misanthropy, or even hatred of humans. For example, in "Mountain Lion" (1964, 401) men are called "the only animal in the world to fear!" In the same poem, the poet says we could easily "spare a million or two of humans / and never miss them". The poem closes with the following exclamation: "Yet what a gap in the world, the missing white frost-face / of that slim yellow mountain lion!" (402).

The poet's misanthropy is directed especially at bourgeois people. There is even a poem that begins with the lines "How beastly the bourgeois is / especially the male of the species –" (1964, 430). Apart from using the word 'beastly', Lawrence here compares bourgeois people, particularly men, to mushrooms (431). He uses three words for mushrooms, in an order which makes them appear increasingly less respectable: *mushrooms, fungus, toadstools*. The comparisons are not metaphors in the strict sense, but similes, since Lawrence spells out the comparisons by using "Like a mushroom", "like a fungus", and "like sickening toadstools". These similes make the bourgeois appear really despicable, as in the following lines (1964, 431):

> How beastly the bourgeois is
> Especially the male of the species –
> Nicely groomed, like a mushroom
> Standing there so sleek and erect and eyeable –
> And like a fungus, living on the remains of bygone life
> Sucking his life out of the dead leaves of greater life than his own.

Later on in the poem, Lawrence compares the bourgeois to "sickening toadstools", which should be "left to melt back, swiftly / Into the soil of England".

In the next poem in this series, called "Worm either Way", Lawrence even writes of bourgeois people who conform to society as worms ("The conforming worm stays just inside the skin / respectably unseen, and cheerfully gnaws away at the heart of life, / making it all rotten inside", 432).

Lawrence's attitude in these last poems is not so much abhorrence of all humans as rather a cutting critique of our social system in which success ("success is a played-out game", 518), getting on (*ibid.*), and triumph are all that many humans care about. One of his poems is actually called "Triumph", and in it, the word *triumph* is repeated six times (519):

> It seems to me that for five thousand years at least
> Men have been wanting to triumph, triumph, triumph,
> Triumph over their fellow-men, triumph over obstacles,
> > Triumph over evil [...]

After this multiple repetition, Lawrence can justifiably write: "Till now the word is nauseating, we can't hear it any more" (519). In a poem called "The Combative Spirit" (1964, 519-520), he even has a list of three (which he repeats) for attitudes that rob us of our freedom:

> We trail behind us an endless tradition of combat, triumph, conquest,
> And we feel we've got to keep it up, keep on combating, triumphing, conquering
> When as a matter of fact, the thought of this endless imbecile struggle of combat
> Kills us, we are sick of it to die.

This is followed by a comparison with the freedom of birds, which ideally we would all possess rather than having to fight for a living: "Living should be as free to a man as to a bird [...]" (520).

7. Conclusion

I have argued that in poetry, rhetorical elements such as metaphors have two functions:

(1) The poetic function, in which creating beauty, making the poem interesting to read, and showing similarities that would otherwise be invisible stand in the foreground.

(2) The pragmatic function, with which an idea, perhaps even an ideology, is propagated.

In Lawrence's poetry, both functions of rhetoric are present. His images create beauty and make us see things in a new light. However, the more important function of the two, it seems, is to express his three messages:

(I)   Animals, plants and even non-living things are on the same level as humans, in the sense of togetherness, a 'convironment' instead of an environment. One could call this his 'ecological' message.

(II) He argues that Nature does not know the concept of sin. All that counts is love – for mountains, animals, and plants as well as for humans.

(III) Finally, in his later poetry, Lawrence uses metaphors in which animals and plants (worms and rotten mushrooms) are the image donors and humans the image carriers. There, he voices a strong critique of western society, which, in his view, is based on a system of grabbing and on the three attitudes of combat, triumph, and conquest.

For the last collection of poems published during his life-time (1929), Lawrence uses a flower metaphor: He calls the poems "pansies", a word in which *pensées* (thoughts) is contained, with an allusion to Pascal and La Bruyère (both of whom he mentions in his foreword to these poems). At the end of this foreword (in the 1957 edition called "Note"), he adds an additional metaphoric extension to this comparison (1957, II, xxxvi, italics original), as follows:

> Anyhow, I offer a bunch of pansies, not a wreath of *immortelles*. I don't want everlasting *flowers*, and I don't want to offer them to anybody else. A flower passes, and that perhaps is the best of it. If we can take it in its transience, its breath, its maybe mephistophelian, maybe palely

ophelian face, the look it gives, the gesture of its full bloom, and the way it turns upon us to depart – that was the flower, we have had it, and no *immortelle* can give us anything in comparison. The same with the pansy poems; merely the breath of the moment, and one eternal moment easily contradicting the next eternal moment. Only don't nail the pansy down. You won't keep it any better if you do.

The metaphoric structure of this paragraph is particularly interesting: The poems are first compared to flowers (pansies), but then for both the poems and the flowers humanizing words are used: *breath, mephistophelian / ophelian face, look, gesture, it turns upon us to depart.*

The rhetorical elements that Lawrence uses, particularly the humanizing metaphors, but also the repetitions and lists of three, show that he aspired to a change in society away from the competitive and combative spirit he saw around him. A Pragmatics of Literature would show whether Lawrence's work has had any effect on the social structures and attitudes of society.

References

Primary Sources

Bloom, Harold et al. (eds.; 1973): *The Oxford Anthology of English Literature*. Volume 2. Oxford: Oxford University Press

Lawrence, David Herbert (1957): *The Complete Poems*. Ed. Richard Aldington. 3 vols. London: Heinemann

--- (1964): *The Complete Poems of D. H. Lawrence*. Ed. Vivian de Sola Pinto and Warren Roberts, 2 vols. London: Heinemann

Secondary Sources

Booth, Wayne C. (1978): "Metaphor as Rhetoric: the Problem of Evaluation", *Critical Enquiry*, 49-72

De Sola Pinto, Vivian (1964): "D. H. Lawrence – Poet without a Mask", in de Sola Pinto, Vivian; Roberts, Warren (eds.): *The Complete Poems of D. H. Lawrence.* Volume 1. London: Heinemann, 1-26

Fill, Alwin (2006): "Literatur und Ökolinguistik: anthropozentrische, anthropomorphe und physiozentrische Sprache in englischen Gedichten", *Anglia* 124/1 (special issue *Literature and Ecology*), 144-174

--- (2007): "'The big mountains sit still...'. Ökolinguistische Interpretation von Gedichten: D. H. Lawrence", in: Fill, A.; Penz, H. (eds.): *Sustaining Language: Essays in Applied Ecolinguistics*. Münster: LIT, 203-214

Goetsch, Paul (1984): "Der gefällte Baum in der englischen, amerikanischen und anglokanadischen Literatur", in: Schläger, Jürgen (ed.): *Anglistentag Konstanz 1983, Vorträge*. Giessen: Hoffmann, 309-344

Harris, Robert. A. ([1997] 2013): *A Handbook of Rhetorical Devices*. <www.virtualsalt.com/rhetoric.htm>

Höffe, Otfried (2009): *Aristoteles: Die Hauptwerke. Ein Lesebuch*. Tübingen: Narr Francke Attempto

Plett, Heinrich F. (1973): *Einführung in die rhetorische Textanalyse*. 2nd edition. Hamburg: Helmut Buske

Sell, Roger D., (ed., 1991): *Literary Pragmatics*. London: Routledge

EVA ULRIKE PIRKER (FREIBURG)

Language and Agency after Modernism: A Reading of J. H. Prynne's "Die A Millionaire (pronounced: 'diamonds in the air')"

Poetry, as a peculiar form of engagement with language, had to redefine itself in the early second half of the twentieth century, a time when language itself had become the object of multifarious scrutiny. Language is a means of orientation in the world, with entrapping as well as liberating qualities, as Leo Spitzer suggested in an essay from the early 1950s, a high time of structuralism and New Criticism, but also a time fraught with the legacy of High Modernism:

> Language is not only a banal mass of communication and self-expression, but also one of orientation in this world: a way that leads toward science and is perfected by science, and on the other hand also a means for freeing us from this world thanks to its metaphysical and poetic implications. (Spitzer 1953, 93)

Poetry, as verbal art, uses language in inventive ways, drawing from, affirming, challenging, or even deconstructing institutionalised uses of language and the language of everyday life. When poets grapple with the question of how to approach through verbal art recurring existential questions such as the question of subjectivity and agency in a globalised, disenchanted world with complex legacies, these poems can be read as a special kind of cultural work. A reading of Jeremy Halvard Prynne's poem "Die A Millionaire (pronounced: 'diamonds in the air')" will help describe the challenges faced by poets writing after Modernism and in the midst of a disenchantment with language that was fuelled by the strongly felt impression of language's limitations, inadequacies, and potential complicity, as rhetoric, with propagandistic or commercial ends. I will explore how Prynne, by developing and following a distinct poetics of language, dealt with these challenges creatively.

In a pun, the title of Prynne's long poem "Die A Millionaire (pronounced: 'diamonds in the air')", which first appeared in the collection *Kitchen Poems* (Prynne 1968, n.p.),[1] draws attention to a tension between materiality, essence, and value on the one hand and relations on the other. Accepting that semantic relations inhere in the visual and phonological qualities of poems is crucial for an understanding of Prynne's oeuvre, which tends to be habitually characterised as "notoriously difficult" (Mellors 2005, 9), but also praised for having appeal and a certain mystic quality.[2] "Die A Millionaire

---

1   Permission to quote consecutive lines of the poem could not be obtained. Since its publication in *Kitchen Poems* (1968) the poem has not been revised for later publications. My references to line numbers can therefore be traced in *Kitchen Poems* and the three editions of *Poems* (Prynne 1982, 13-17, Prynne 1999 and 2005, 13-16 respectively).
2   According to the reviewer Robert Potts, "it appears so alien to our habits of reading [...]. It feels more like a painting or a piece of music, or perhaps a sculpture; something to experience both intellectually and sensually" (Potts 2004).

(pronounced: 'diamonds in the air')" is no exception, although it is one of Prynne's more accessible poems.

The image of a river permeates the poem and is also suggested by its shape, a long body of 161 lines interspersed, at irregular intervals, with half lines that give the impression of bends. Prynne's poem follows an upside down logic, and it draws attention, at the beginning, to the necessity, "to take knowledge / back to the springs", and follow it upstream.[3] Following this cue, it seems productive to begin by considering the poem's last lines, in which the term "purity" occurs twice (ll. 155, 159). In a 2009 lecture given at the University of Chicago Prynne proposed an understanding of "the sounds that poems make [...] as acoustic sonorities, but as semi-abstract representations of relations and ordering between and across sounds within a textual domain" (Prynne 2010, 130). If we take this claim seriously, then the phonological resemblance of the words "purity" (ll. 155, 159) and "poetry", which possess the same consonants in a slightly different order and almost the same vowels, may be highly suggestive of the poet's creation of a semantic relation.[4] The game of sound resemblances evident in the poem's title "Die A Millionaire (pronounced: 'diamonds in the air')" may encourage us to literally pronounce "purity" as "poetry", replace the former with the latter. As a consequence, we will then be treated to a vision of poetry as "a question of names", a process of signification through language, although it is not clear who dominates in this process: the poet or language, the "we" or "the names". Clearly, the "names" obtain more than a signifying function, they can be both signifier and signified. The poetic process, "know[ing] / the names", is a vocation: "We are here to utter them". It is a spiritual engagement, as suggested by the admonition "this is / a prayer". It is sound escaping, physically, perhaps reluctantly, from "between [the poet's] / teeth". It has a visual, even visionary aspect, in that it is locked "between" the poet's "eyes". It is a conviction, is written or imprinted "on [the] forehead". To engage in poetic work, therefore, it is imperative that one should "know / the names", i.e., know the linguistic material and its implications. Knowing the material, however, is not merely an epistemological enterprise; rather, this knowledge seems to be rooted in the realm of intuition, instinct, reflexes, and unmediated experience which is likened to the immediacy of sentiment in the simile "as simple as the purity / of sentiment". In these last lines of "Die A Millionaire (pronounced: 'diamonds in the air')" a sense of immediacy is not

---

3   The necessity of going back to an origin, to "the beginning", is also emphasised in T.S. Eliot's *Four Quartets*, most prominently in "East Coker", which spirals around the speaker's difficulty in carving out an identity in a complex melee of genealogy, experience, perceptions, and knowledge, and whose first line reads "In my beginning is my end" (Eliot 1963, 182). The image of going upstream abounds in poetry of the second half of the twentieth century, e.g. in Robert Duncan's "Poetry, a Natural Thing" (Duncan 1973, 50). Duncan wrote in his Introduction to *The Years as Catches* about his development as a young poet: "I had sought not the poem as a discipline or paradigm of my thought and feeling but as a source of feeling and thought, following the movement of an inner impulse and tension rising in the flow of returning vowel sounds and in measuring stresses that formed phrases of a music for me" (Duncan 1977, i).

4   There is a tradition of poets creatively establishing their understanding of poetry via such sound-relations. In "I dwell in possibility" Emily Dickinson phonologically and semantically ties poetry to the term "possibility": "I dwell in possibility – / a fairer house than prose" (Franklin 1998, Fr 466). Another famous example is Derek Walcott's claim in his Nobel Acceptance speech of 1992, that "in the Antilles poverty is poetry with a V, une vie, a condition of life as well as of imagination" (Walcott 1992, 28).

only conjured up by the physical impact of the "it" on the speaker, but also by the use of such words as "purity" (l. 155, 159), "prayer" (l. 155), "now" (l. 155), "sentiment" (l. 160), and "simple" (ll. 159, 160).

The poem doubly engages with material and value: On the one hand, it emphasises the materialisation of ideas as ideologies that underpin constellations and structures of domination. For such processes and power relations Prynne gives concrete examples: He mentions the endeavour of early medieval monks to spread Christianity in Northumbria (ll. 11-12), he cites imperialism as "just an old, very old name for that idea" (l. 30), "Drang nach Osten" (l. 39) and "Western frontier" (l. 40), i.e., movements in which the spreading of ideas and ideologies went hand in hand with usurpation and domination. Throughout, the complicity of language and narratives (e.g. history, ll. 41-44) with these processes and constellations is invoked. Processes for which the term "expansion" is used are dismantled as processes of "acquisition" (ll. 37-55). Likewise, the expression "spirit [...] of an age" (l. 44), a conversational expression that habitually enters factual realms like history books, is claimed to serve as a disguise for the "need" of the age. Moreover, the word "need" is clandestinely transformed a line later via an internal, masculine rhyme into "greed" (l. 45). The latter term adds a sense of corrupted agency to the passive-receptive notion of "need". Like the entire poem, the section in which these terms occur (ll. 42-46) contains several carefully interwoven sound relations and juxtapositions such as the chiastic structure of "spirit (need) [...] / greed, shielded" (ll. 45-46), alliterations ("head" and "historical" in l. 43, "primary" and "practice", ll. 44 and 46), and the sound resemblances between "primary", "ignominy" and "too many" (ll. 44, 45 and 46). The section literally performs these relations, thereby drawing attention to a central concern of the poem, the materiality of language, its agency *and* its aptitude to be instrumentalised for extralinguistic ends.[5] Furthermore, the claim is established that the domination of a narrative ("historical outline", l. 43) based on faulty or 'improper' assumptions becomes general consensus when habitually repeated by those who go with the flow ("shielded from ignominy by the / like practice of [...] others", ll. 45-46).

Throughout the poem, the semantic field of material and material exchange is exploited. Prynne has woven a dense web of such terms as "need", "demand", "purchase", "acquisition", and "storage", to name but a few, and already the poem's title is steeped in notions of value and material assets that, in themselves, betray complex material qualities: The term "millionaire", although a French term that came to be used in English from the nineteenth century onwards, contains the words "million" and "air" or "aire", the latter of which reappears as isolated word in the parenthesis. "Die" is pho-

---

[5] The idea that language "acts, and sometimes acts against us", i.e., that language has agency in and of itself, is explored in Judith Butler's study *Excitable Speech* (1997, 1). The implications of these insights for poetic language as language that "concentrates attention on language itself" (Jones 2012, 3) have received little scholarly attention. An exception is Derek Attridge's valuable study *The Singularity of Literature*, in which, however, examples from prose texts (see Attridge 2004, esp. chapters 2, 4, and 7, in which the act of creation, the "eventness" of literature and its "performance" are negotiated). In his recent book *Poetic Language*, Tom Jones repeatedly touches on the aspect of language's agency, for instance when he observes that "not all things [...] done by a poem" may have been "done by design" (Jones 2012, 10). My current research project "The Long Poem in Anglophone Literature, ca. 1780-the present" explores the implications of agency in language and form in the poetic process in depth.

netically linked to "diamonds",[6] terms that, together with "Million-" contrast with the lightness suggested by the term "air". The two aggregate states present in the title (the gaseous one in "air" and the solid one in "diamonds") are juxtaposed with that of the river, which permeates the poem and gives it a form, but also with the notion of the "liquid", i.e., solvent millionaire. Like the millionaire, however, we all "die" as marked and measured entities, are "only money" in the words of Ben Watson who wrote in terms not entirely dissimilar to those used in Prynne's poem about the prevalence of a "split consciousness" in a world whose

> economic conditions reduce all life to vicious competition. When the battle's done and the world's been spoiled, they drown us in a [...] pious cant about 'ideals' and 'spirit'. If instead we grasp that we are only money – products of capitalist society – we can locate the social developments that articulate our potential selves. (Watson 1998, 13)

Watson makes reference to Frank Zappa's album *We're Only in It for the Money*, which appeared in the same year as Prynne's *Kitchen Poems* and gives expression to similar concerns. However, Watson's turn "we *are* only money" (my emphasis) and the physical ways in which language, as a vehicle for ideology, impacts the speaker, the "I", the "we", and the diverse invaded spaces of "Die A Millionaire (pronounced: 'diamonds in the air')" are taking matters further than the claim that we are "in it *for* the money". In the latter case, a moment of agency is still on the speaker's side. This agency, Prynne's poem suggests, has been lost and has to be retrieved.

The subject of speaking oscillates between an occasional "I" and a "we", suggesting a metalevel of discourse in which readers are not only addressed in the second person, but sucked into the experience of the speaking subject by way of the first person plural pronoun. The realisation that "we" are caught up in a web only dawns on "us" gradually, because the structures of domination and acquisition are seductive and orderly, they promise orientation and even profit, as the phrases exposed in lines 19-27 suggest: "what the mind / bites on is yours" (ll. 20-21), "the prime joy of control engineering" (ll. 22-23) and "self- / optimizing systems" (ll. 24-25). A disenchantment with ordering has been present in anglophone poetry at least since William Blake's critique of what he perceived as a perverted enlightenment discourse.[7] In Prynne's poem it surfaces not only in the intensive engagement with

---

6   Among other things, the diamond stands for the taintless, inanimate object, for that which will not pass (see for instance Stöcklein 1956, 82), thus forming a contrast with the word "die", which is strengthened by the fact that "diamond" is a noun and "die" a verb. This *contrast* creates a tension with the phonological *link*, which is established by the assonance of "Die a Millionaire" and "diamonds" and further strengthened by the parenthetical note regarding "pronunciation". The implication may be that although the names for objects, actions, and processes may sound alike, they are not necessarily the same. Again, this suggests that language-in-use provides traps that have to be taken into account.

7   An article by James Keery has shed light on some of the ways in which Blake has inspired Prynne (and other writers such as Iain Sinclair), but the connection between Prynne and Blake promises to be an ample field for more in-depth scholarly investigation. Especially Blakean irony, in which rhetorical proficiency and a critique of rhetoric meet, can be made productive in a reading of a variety of Prynne's works. In "Die a Millionaire (pronounced: 'Diamonds in the air')" the middle-section, in which misery narratives around the exploitation of the industrial North are dismantled as complicit with processes of exploitation and domination, is permeated with terms reminiscent of Blake's evocation of the furnaces of hell. An engagement with Saus-

terms and phrases like "control engineering" (l. 23), "self- / optimizing systems" (ll. 24-25), and "plan for the basic / living-unit" (ll. 26-27), but also in the recurring term and image of the "grid" (ll. 60, 61 and 150). A grid is also reproduced on the title of *Kitchen Poems*. Within that grid, the experiencing subject (I/we), as well as entire geographical spaces and landscapes, are marked and defined. The grid is an ordering system which accords everything, including language and narrative, a function that can be measured and sold: it literally has a "grip" on everything and everyone, as is suggested not only by the consecutive exploration of first the "grid" (ll. 60ff.) and then the "grip" (ll. 70-77ff.), but by the phonological closeness evident in the assonant, alliterative relation of those two monosyllabic words.

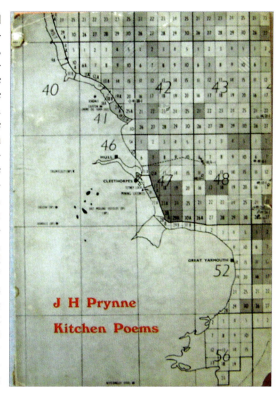

Reproduced with kind permission of J. H. Prynne

By spreading countless semantic, syntactic, and phonological relations such as these, Prynne has visually and aurally (re)produced the notion of a powerful network. Not only are "we", the collective addressee, asked to work hard in order to get back to the springs, behind the names, towards the "purity" of knowledge; the poet Prynne demands of the addressee outside the text, the readers, too, that they engage in hard work when they embark on *their* journey up the "river" in an attempt to make sense of his poem.[8] The poem does not encourage a superficial reading, but set against Prynne's other works (especially later ones for which a consultation of specialist reference works is advisable),[9] it may provide readers with a manual of sorts, "a suitable starting point", as Ian Patterson suggests.

---

sure's notion of arbitrariness and Blake's poetic language was the subject of the William Matthews Lectures Prynne delivered at Birkbeck College in 1992 (Prynne 1993).

8   As N. H. Reeve and Richard Kerridge point out, Prynne's poetry urges its readers to be read with other individuals, other media, other sources, in order to bring it into a dialogue with others. Reeve and Kerridge have conducted their study of Prynne over a decade, because its inception was their exchange of ideas "in an effort to read one poem" which then turned into a prolonged collaborative project (Reeve and Kerridge 1995, viii).

9   An example is "Plant Time Manifold Transcripts" (1972), of which Justin Katko argues that it does not represent a mere mockery of science and scientific jargon, but is a contribution to that 'science' and "must be considered within the terms of its own vocabulary, so that its original

> Fast-moving and insistent, the poem redefines the relation of *I* to *we* in terms of want and need and waste, a process of denaturalisation of the moral by means of a highly ironicised use of econometric terminology where the force of our collusive rejection of [...] 'our polluted history' derives from the poem's argument and sheer emphasis of tone and counter-assertion. It is dense, but apart from the concluding lines, and perhaps the 'poor seventh century Irish monks', it is not difficult. To put it plainly, it makes sense. (Patterson 1992, 234-235)

Nevertheless, "Die A Millionaire (pronounced: 'diamonds in the air')" is not easily categorised in terms of form and genre. It does not comfort (or repel) readers by assuming a recognisable form that would offer immediate clues. In spite of its length it is not (primarily) narrative and cannot be reduced to an analysable 'prose core'. Its length, however, as well as its approach to positions of enunciation and address, its archaeology of sounds, images, and lexemes make it more than a straightforward lyric poem.[10] Yet, its appeal and generic identity as a poem cannot be questioned. It is a poem which pushes its readers deliberately to rethink their definitions of poetry and their ideas about language, offering an innovative approach to poetic discourse after Modernism.

Prynne has been referred to as a poet working in the Modernist legacy, but this claim requires some qualification.[11] "Die A Millionaire (pronounced 'diamonds in the air')" is the second poem in the slim volume *Kitchen Poems*, which was published in 1968. In this axial year, Prynne produced three such volumes: *Kitchen Poems*, *Day Light Songs* and *Aristeas*. They were published by small presses, printed with utmost devotion to aesthetic detail and in small print runs. This is particularly noteworthy, because Prynne had a collection of poems on the market already, *Force of Circumstance and Other Poems* published in 1962 by the more established, commercially successful publisher Routledge and Kegan Paul. Prynne's collections of 1968 break with the poetic discourse established in *Force of Circumstance*, which placed the poet artistically in proximity to the Movement poets,[12] who broke with what they saw as disconnected, intellectualist aesthetics of Modernism.[13]

---

thinking in natural philosophy may be more readily perceived and understood. This kind of close reading has yet to be adopted by the *PTM*'s critics, of which there are few" (Katko 2010, 250).

10 In this context, Eva Müller-Zettelmann's categorisation of another of Prynne's poems, "Of Movement towards a Natural Place", as 'implicit metalyric' has to be mentioned (Müller-Zettelmann 2000, 219ff.). "Die A Millionaire (pronounced: 'diamonds in the air')", too, displays markers of this category. However, Müller-Zettelmann's application of the term 'metalyric' to an extremely wide range of poems raises doubts regarding its usefulness in the description of generic categories. In my view, the term metalyric is more helpful in the description of a mode or attitude that may be more or less prevalent in a poem.

11 See, for instance, Mellors 2005.

12 Among the Movement poets, the foremost influence on the young Prynne was his tutor at Cambridge, Donald Davie. Prynne did not include the poems from his first collection in any of the editions of his collected *Poems* (1982, 1999, 2005).

13 Philip Larkin comes to mind here, who claimed that the writing of a poem "consists of three stages: the first is when a man becomes obsessed with an emotional concept to such a degree that he is compelled to do something about it. What he does is the second stage, namely construct a verbal device that will reproduce this emotional concept in anyone who cares to read it, anywhere, anytime. The third stage is the recurrent situation of people in different times and places setting off the device and re-creating in themselves what the poet felt when he wrote it" (Larkin 1983, 80). Larkin also cultivated his dislike of Modernist art: "No, I dislike such things

The 1968 collections show Prynne's determination to reach out for inspiration and innovation beyond those very British reactions to the modernist project. A year in the United States contributed to his closer acquaintance with the Black Mountain School,[14] an influence which Prynne can be credited with having transported back across the Atlantic in the 1960s and 1970s. The Black Mountain School, too, had issues with the placement of certain High Modernists on a pedestal and questioned what had become the latters' complacent position. To put it bluntly: While the Movement poets went back to using form as a mere medium for content, the Black Mountain School engaged in fields of aesthetic innovation that had been neglected by the Modernists and developed a kind of 'organic' poetics, following such principles as the length of breath as an indicator for ideal ways of structuring poetic texts.[15] While the Movement poets were more bothered by a Modernist diction and intellectualism, the Black Mountain School had issues with the personal cult surrounding especially T. S. Eliot and the conservatism represented by the latter. Eliot did not only inform poetic practice but also criticism and, in Paul de Man's words,

> the perfect embodiment of the New Criticism remains [...] the personality and the ideology of T.S. Eliot, a combination of original talent, traditional learning, verbal wit and moral earnestness, an Anglo-American blend of intellectual gentility not so repressed as not to afford tantalizing glimpses of darker psychic and political depths, but without breaking the surface of an ambivalent decorum that has its own complacencies and seductions. (de Man 1982: 6)

The "ambivalent decorum, its complacencies and seductions" have had a stifling effect on the modernist project in the anglophone poetic world, and the response of the poetic world to modernism has often been characterised by either reverence or rejection of what its monumental figures represented rather than by an open critical engagement with its legacies.[16]

One central legacy is the peculiar Modernist perception of the poet's autonomous relation to language. "I gotta use words when I talk to you", Eliot's Sweeney says at the outset of his terrible tale in "Fragment of an Agon", and he continues: "But if you understand or if you don't / That's nothing to me and nothing to you / We all gotta do what we gotta do" (Eliot 1963: 123). Sweeney's utterance contains three aspects. Firstly, he expresses a need to communicate. Secondly, he addresses the inevitability of having to rely on words in communication. And thirdly, he betrays an attitude of indifference regarding the success of this process. While Sweeney's dilemma is that of the poet, his attitude is not entirely the poet's who in this case has taken pains to evoke or 'communicate' *both* Sweeney's attitude and Sweeney's tale. Put in different terms,

---

not because they are new, but because they are irresponsible exploitations of technique in contradiction of human life as we know it" (Larkin 1970, 11).

14 Named after Black Mountain College in North Carolina, a centre of American avant-garde art and writing which brought forth poets such as Robert Creeley, the aforementioned Robert Duncan, and first and foremost Charles Olson, who was an important influence on Prynne in his formative years.

15 For an exploration of these ideas see Charles Olson's poetological essay "Projective Verse" (1997).

16 As editor and supporter of young poets Eliot helped encourage some careers (e.g. Auden, Hughes) in decisive ways at a time when he had stopped producing innovative work himself. Eliot's continuing influence was divisive. Like Wordsworth a century before him he lived on for a significant period after he had produced his masterpieces.

the poet has the power to evoke both Sweeney's attitude and Sweeney's tale. The Modernist poet has the authority, the vocation, and the autonomy to "do what [*he's*] gotta do".

It is in this aspect, the crucially Modernist legacy of the poet's autonomy, that hero cult and artistic innovation can meet and engage in a highly successful, or highly dangerous,[17] alliance. But if the perceived task of the modernist poet is the evocation, the dismantling, or sometimes the praise of the world he or she inhabits *via* language, for poets writing after Modernism, after Stalin and Hitler, and under the impression of American commercial culture, the certainty of language as a reliable medium has disappeared. Poets have reacted to this state of affairs in diverse ways. The Movement has retreated to an almost spiteful, affirmative use of language as medium. The Black Mountain School has attempted to subject language to new principles of organisation. The L=A=N=G=U=A=G=E poets a generation later have celebrated the opportunities they saw in the liberation of language and its component parts. In the 1960s, several large-scale poetic translation projects[18] were realised. For poets across the globe the idea that language is not a certainty has been a highly productive insight that could be contextualised in the anti-imperialist struggle and could give way to practices of re-writing English literature and "English English" (Rushdie 1982, 8). Although the insight that it was problematic to see language as a means that could be used to represent, portray, and ultimately transcend worldly matter led to crises, the idea that language could be a source of inspiration, a structure with an agency of its own, was also highly invigorating, engendering entirely new approaches to poetic writing and new poetic forms.[19]

By the 1960s, the notion of the poet as autonomous, powerful visionary artist in command of his or her material had clearly given way to a more dialogic understanding of the relation between poets and their material. Prynne's poetry provides abundant evidence of such a dialogic relation. In the words of Andrew Mellors, it

> continually displaces the ground on which sense, reference and value are based, even as it gestures toward a transcendent reality inhering beyond all temporal determinations. While it can be seen to be complicit with the modernist belief in obscurity and fragmentation as the 'surface' signs of a hidden order of aesthetic unity, it radically questions this tradition of determining the indeterminate and unifying the fragmentary. Prynne's poetry complicates notions of order and determination to the extent that the figural metaphysic of an art intended to reveal presence in absence must be rethought. (Mellors 2005, 11)

---

17 The continuity of aspects of High Modernist aesthetics in Fascism, or a Fascist exploitation of Modernist aesthetics, has been the subject of a growing body of research over the past two decades (see, for instance, Hewitt 1993, Huyssen 1995, and Frost 2002).

18 Hughes tended to title his translations as 'versions', perhaps in an attempt to account for this disparity. Together with Daniel Weissbort, who would later edit Hughes's *Selected Translations* (2006), Hughes founded *Modern Poetry in Translation*, a journal designed "to publish poetry that dealt truthfully with the real contemporary world, and to benefit writers and the reading public in Britain and America by confronting them with good work from abroad" (*Ted Hughes Society Journal* 2014).

19 Nevertheless, it has to be remembered that poetry has had a decreasing share of the literary market in the postwar era. The coexistence of many different ways of creating verbal art may have been invigorating to practitioners, but it was a source of confusion to outsiders of poetic schools and movements. Critics tended to side with what they knew and what they had learned at college, so that established voices continued to hold favoured positions.

Poetry, to Prynne, seems to be a kind of practical philosophy of language, exposing what Butler terms the self-dividedness of language:

> The failure of language to rid itself of its own instrumentality or, indeed, rhetoricity, is precisely the inability of language to annul itself in the telling of a tale in the reference to what exists or in the volatile scenes of interlocution. [...] We do things with language, produce effects with language, and we do things to language, but language is also the thing that we do. Language is a name for our doing: both "what" we do (the name for the action that we characteristically perform) and that which we effect, the act and its consequences. (Butler 1997, 9)[20]

The self-dividedness of language and the necessity to question, explore, and understand its "rhetoricity", even if the latter cannot be escaped, is a core concern of Prynne's poem "Die A Millionaire (pronounced: 'diamonds in the air')", and therefore this poem is central to the debates about poetry and rhetoric that the present section investigates. Like the notion of the poet's autonomy, the question of what poetry and rhetoric represent has lost its innocence after modernism, whose towering figures were fascinated by language's potential and sought to expand it for their aesthetic ends.

It almost appears as though a choice had to be made, after Modernism, between poetry and rhetoric: between the investigative, uncertain, creative, perhaps innovative engagement with language on the one hand, and the subjection to an established, agreed-upon, rule-governed, effective use of language on the other. Whereas rhetoric may be defined as the use of language towards an extralinguistic end, a generally agreed-upon definition of poetry seems impossible, except, perhaps, in poetic language, where the question of what poetry is, what it can and should be, is explored time and again. Regarding Prynne's work, Reeve and Kerridge hold that "it is hard to see how anyone could read this poetry without having to consider questions of what poetry, in contemporary culture, is *for*, and what its relations should be to other uses of language" (Reeve and Kerridge 1995, 1).

It would be wrong to deny the existence of earlier poetic expressions of discontent with language. However, whereas this discontent had previously been largely limited to the inadequacy of language as representational *medium*, the notion that we are subjected to, and defined by, language is one that only gained prominence with the advent of structural linguistics and the multifaceted poststructuralist critique thereof. Robert Graves's poem "The Cool Web" gives an inkling of this notion as early as 1927. Here, the healing qualities of "speech", e.g. as a means of blocking out the terrible experience of war, are ironically invoked: speech can "chill the angry day, [...] the rose's cruel scent", and "we" make use of it to "spell away the overhanging night, [...] the soldiers and the fright." "We" let ourselves be soothed by a "cool web of language". The poem ends in a gloomy admonition. Although "we" may be wary of the false solace provided by language, we cannot discard language: "But if we let our tongues lose self-possession / Throwing off language and its watery clasp / [...] / We shall go mad

---

20   Butler makes reference in these reflections to Toni Morrison's Nobel lecture, which thematises the violence of language faced, in particular, by women writers: "[S]he thinks of language partly as a system, partly as a living thing over which one has control, but mostly as agency – as an act with consequences" (quoted in Butler 1997, 6); see also Felman (1983) who explores some implications of this agency for literature. Again, however, it is curious that neither Morrison, Felman, nor Butler include the language of poetry in their explorations. The same gap can be observed in Austinian speech act theory, from which Butler draws repeatedly.

[...] and die that way" (Graves 1959, 56; ll. 5-9, 13-14, 18).[21] Like in Prynne's poem, the suggestion is made that we will all die, regardless of whether we play our part in the game of rhetoric. While Prynne's poem offers the idea of a pure knowledge that has to be regained, Graves warns of the consequences of such an enterprise: madness and (social) death. In Graves's poem, the corrupting agency of the "cool web" remains an abstract power whose domination ultimately provides comfort and security. "Die A Millionaire (pronounced: 'diamonds in the air')" expresses the imperative to question this very domination, expose and dismantle it in search of "the purity", even if the success of this enterprise is doomed, because "right / from the *springs*" the water is spoiled (ll. 112-113; italics original), "the water of life / is all in bottles & ready for invoice" (ll. 114-115) and "to draw / from that well we" have to "put on some other garment" (ll. 115-117).

That "garment" may well be the language of poetry, which, as Prynne insists, follows diverse principles of organisation and thus challenges simple causalities. Poetic language, importantly, is a language that is organised in specific ways not just for the ear, but also for the eye, on the page. The shape of "Die A Millionaire (pronounced: 'diamonds in the air')" immediately triggers a process of signification, even before one has read its words. Although the poem is long, it is not subdivided into 'books', 'chapters', 'songs', or other enumerated parts; it takes several readings to discern sections of the poem that can formally be grouped together.[22] The poem contains full sentences of variable length (one even spanning 15 lines). Some of them are interrupted by parentheses or are complemented by subordinate clauses. It is noteworthy that the final indented unit of the fourth section, i.e., the poem's last lines, discussed at the outset of this paper, breaks with the established pattern of long, nested sentences and consists instead of remarkably short sentence units. Formally, these closing lines serve as a contrast to what came before. The reduction of the length of syntactic units, again, is suggestive of the image of the spring that one has ultimately arrived at, the river narrowed down to its source, leading to the final word of the poem: "that". Or rather, the final line: "As that". It is now up to the readers to decide what may be more important in the process of signification *they* bring to the poem: the sound, the word, the syntactic unit, or the verse line? The tension between the choice "that" (the last word) or the line "as that" (the last line) sums up, in a nutshell, the poet's dialogic relation to language: Is "that", the essence itself, important? Or does significance inhere in "as that", the relation, without which no essence seems conceivable in the first place? In his Chicago lecture on poetry, Prynne said:

> For all the pungent games in which poetry can engage, it comprises at its most fully extended an envelope which finds and sets the textual contours in writing of how things are; while also activating a system of discontinuities and breaks which interrupt and contest the intrinsic cohesion and boundary profiles of its domain, so that there is constant leakage inwards and outwards across the connection with the larger world order. (Prynne 2010, 126-127)

---

21 As has been frequently observed, Graves's poetry sits strangely between a Georgian and a Modernist aesthetic. In "The Cool Web", too, a tension between control and the uncanny, typical of Graves, is evident.

22 These are units that may be said to be closed, stanzaically as well as syntactically, ending with a full stop and ending at the end of a group of verse lines, with the next group beginning after a gap and a non-indented line. Altogether, there seem to be four 'sections' of diverse length, the first containing 60, the second 16, the third 68, and the fourth 17 lines.

Although these remarks were made some four decades after the publication of "Die A Millionaire (pronounced: 'diamonds in the air')", they are, indeed, useful for an understanding of this poem which marks an early stage in Prynne's lifelong engagement with the development of a poetic language and a poetics of language in the service of "ethical seriousness" (*ibid.*, 141). "Language", Prynne closed his Chicago lecture, "is itself an intrinsic fault system, and it is worse than a mistake not to understand this as best ever we can" (*ibid.*, 142).

References

Primary Sources

Duncan, Robert (1973): *The Opening of the Field*. New York: New Directions
Eliot, T.S. (1963): *Collected Poems 1909-1962*. New York: Harcourt, Brace & World
Franklin, Ralph W. (1998): *The Poems of Emily Dickinson*. Vol. I. Cambridge, MA: University of Harvard Press
Graves, Robert (1959): *Collected Poems*. London: Cassell
Prynne, Jeremy Halvard (1968): *Kitchen Poems*. London: Cape Goliard
--- (1982): *Poems*. Edinburgh/London: Agneau 2
--- (1999): *Poems*. Fremantle, W.A./Tarset: Fremantle Arts Centre/Bloodaxe
--- (2005): *Poems*. Fremantle, W.A./Tarset: Fremantle Arts Centre/Bloodaxe

Secondary Sources

Attridge, Derek (2004): *The Singularity of Literature*. London: Routledge
Butler, Judith (1997): *Excitable Speech: A Politics of the Performative*. New York: Routledge
de Man, Paul (1982): "The Resistance to Theory", *Yale French Studies* 63, 3-20
Duncan, Robert (1977): *The Years as Catches: First Poems (1939-1946)*. Berkeley: Oyez
Felman, Shoshana (1983): *The Literary Speech Act: Don Juan With J. L. Austin, Or Seduction in Two Languages*. Ithaca, NY: Cornell University Press
Frost, Laura Catherine (2002): *Sex Drives: Fantasies of Fascism in Literary Modernism*. Ithaca, NY: University of Cornell Press
Hewitt, Andrew (1993): *Fascist Modernism: Aesthetics, Politics, and the Avant-Garde*. Stanford, CA: University of Stanford Press
Huyssen, Andreas (1995): *Twilight Memories: Marking Time in a Culture of Amnesia*. New York/London: Routledge
Jones, Tom (2012): *Poetic Language: Theory and Practice from the Renaissance to the Present*. Edinburgh: University of Edinburgh Press
Katko, Justin (2010): "Relativistic Phytosophy", in: Dobran, Ryan (ed.). *Glossator: Practice and Theory of the Commentary*, 245-293. http://www.glossator.org [accessed 15 January 2014]
Keery, James (2007): "Children of Albion: Blake and Contemporary British Poetry", in: Clark, Steve; Whittaker, Jason (eds.). *Blake, Modernity and Popular Culture*. Basingstoke: Palgrave Macmillan, 100-112
Larkin, Philip (1970): *All What Jazz: A Record Diary, 1961-68 (AWJ)*. London: Faber
--- (1983): "The Pleasure Principle", *Required Writing: Miscellaneous Pieces 1955-1982*. London: Faber, 80-82
Mellors, Andrew (2005): *Late Modernist Poetics: From Pound to Prynne*. Manchester: University of Manchester Press
Müller-Zettelmann, Eva (2000): *Lyrik und Metalyrik: Theorie einer Gattung und ihrer Selbstbespiegelung anhand von Beispielen aus der englisch- und deutschsprachigen Dichtkunst*. Heidelberg: Winter

Olson, Charles (1997): "Projective Verse", in: Allen, Donald; Friedlander, Benjamin (eds.). *Collected Prose*. Berkeley: University of California Press, 239-249

Patterson, Ian (1992): "'the medium itself, rabbit by proxy': some thoughts about reading J.H. Prynne", in: Riley, Denise (ed.). *Poets on Writing: Britain 1970-1991*. Basingstoke: Macmillan, 234-246

Potts, Robert (2004): "Through the Oval Window", 10 April. *The Guardian*. <http://www.theguardian.com/books/2004/apr/10/featuresreviews.guardianreview30> [accessed 15 January 2014]

Prynne, Jeremy Halvard (1993): *Stars, Tigers and the Shape of Words: The William Matthews Lectures 1992 Delivered at Birkbeck College*. London: Birkbeck College

--- (2010): "Mental Ears and Poetic Work", *Chicago Review* 55.1, 126-157

Reeve, N. H.; Kerridge, Richard (1995): *Nearly Too Much: The Poetry of J.H. Prynne*. Liverpool: University of Liverpool Press

Rushdie, Salman (1982): "The Empire Writes Back with a Vengeance", 3 July. *The Times*. Web. [accessed 21 February 2014]

Spitzer, Leo (1953): "Language: The Basis of Science, Philosophy and Poetry", in: Johns Hopkins History of Ideas Club (ed.). *Studies in Intellectual History*. Baltimore: Johns Hopkins University Press, 67-93

Stöcklein, Paul (1956): "Hofmannswaldau und Goethe: 'Vergänglichkeit' im Liebesgedicht", in: Hirschenauer, Ruprecht; Weber, Albrecht (eds.). *Wege zum Gedicht*. Munich: Schnell und Steiner, 77-98

The Ted Hughes Society Journal (2014): "Translations", *Ted Hughes Society Journal*. <http://www.thetedhughessociety.org/translations.htm> [accessed 15 January 2014]

Walcott, Derek (1992): "The Antilles: Fragments of Epic Memory", 28 December. *New Republic*. 26-32

Watson, Ben (1998): *Art, Class and Cleavage: A Quantulumcumque Concerning Materialist Esthetix*. London: Quartet

MARIE-LUISE EGBERT (LEIPZIG)

Poetic and Rhetorical Figurations of Touch in Les Murray's *Fredy Neptune* (1998)

When it came out in 1998,[1] Les Murray's verse novel *Fredy Neptune* earned him the Queen's Gold Medal for Poetry and consolidated his position as one of Australia's most outstanding poets.[2] He had by then already established himself in Australia and beyond as a major English-language poet with several highly acclaimed collections of poetry to his credit.[3] Critical studies dealing with *Fredy Neptune* have to date mostly centred on its generic specialty as a novel in verse on the one hand and on its themes of war and trauma on the other.[4] What will be attempted here is to relate form to content, demonstrating how the poetic and rhetorical features of that text are particularly suited to its subject.

1. A Tale of Trauma

The novel is told by Fredy, born as Friedrich Boettcher to parents of German extraction who have a farm near Dungog, a village north of Newcastle in New South Wales. Shortly before the start of the First World War, fifteen-year-old Fredy finds a job on a German freighter that takes him to the Mediterranean. In the chaos of the incipient war, he boards a war ship on its way to the Black Sea, where he witnesses the battle of Gallipoli, commemorated by Australians today on ANZAC day and associated with Australian soldiers' bravery under adverse conditions. For Fredy, however, who is not a soldier, another event is to take on crucial significance: While on shore leave near Trabzon, he witnesses the burning alive of a group of Armenian women by Turkish men. The event refers to the historical fact of the systematic deportation and killing of an estimated 1.5 to 2 million Armenians during the late Ottoman Empire as the new secular Turkish nation state was beginning to form. This persecution and killing of Armenians under the nationalist regime between 1915 and 1918 is now widely considered the first genocide of the twentieth century (hence preceding the Shoah). Here is how Fredy describes what he sees:

---

1   Before being published as a single volume in 1998, the five books of *Fredy Neptune* had appeared serially in the *Adelaide Review* and in *PN Review* in the UK.
2   For an estimate of his place in English-language poetry, see Coetzee 2011. Murray's poetry has become part of reading lists and the subject of school and university examinations (Clapham 2013), which suggests that the poems are acquiring canonical status within English-language literature.
3   E.g. *Selected Poems: The Vernacular Republic* (1976), *Translations from the Natural World* (1992), *Subhuman Redneck Poems* (1996). Before *Fredy Neptune*, Murray had already written one short verse novel written in stanzas modelled on the sonnet, titled *The Boys Who Stole the Funeral* (1979).
4   For the latter topic, see Lock 2001 and Savage 2008; for generic studies, Henriksen 2001, Clunies Ross 2001, and Egbert 2011.

> [The women] were huddling, terrified, crying.
> crossing themselves, in the middle of men all yelling.
> Their big loose dresses were sopping. Kerosene, you could smell it.
> The men were prancing, feeling them, poking at them to dance –
> then pouf! they were alight, the women, dark wicks to great orange flames,
> whopping and shrieking. If we'd had rifles there
> we'd have massacred those bastards. We had only fists and boots.
> One woman did cuddle a man: he went up screaming, too.
> (Les Murray, *Fredy Neptune*, Book 1:5)[5]

For Fredy, having seen the burning with his own eyes causes a trauma that is somatised in the loss of one of his senses. He becomes entirely incapable of tactile sensation. As a corollary of this, he does not feel pain or exhaustion: "I discovered I was real strong. / When effort doesn't reach pain you can take it much further" (1:25). He can therefore perform superhuman deeds, such as lifting the weight of an engine off a man caught under a car, lifting a ship, or killing a bear with his own hands. This uncommon condition makes him an outsider in more than one way: He cannot physically relate to other human beings (including his inability to feel sexual pleasure), and his abnormal strength causes suspicion ("I had become an alien", 1:25).

Murray has modelled Fredy's disorder on documented psychosomatic effects that trauma can have on the sense of sight,[6] but there is in fact no medical syndrome quite corresponding to the prolonged (but reversible) absence of touch from which the narrator is suffering.[7] In his case, the condition lasts for more than 30 years.

As Robert Savage contends, the protagonist's loss of sensation is not related exclusively to the massacre (2008, 429). It is also the culmination of a development outlined in the two stanzas preceding the scene of the massacre: Having been rejected more than once by women, young Fredy loses belief in his own desirability and lovability. In this sense, he kills part of himself, and the loss of touch is therefore at the same time symbolic of that other loss (*ibid.*).[8]

Fredy, for his part, comes to understand his strange condition as a punishment for having sinned: He considers himself implicated in the crime of killing by his mere presence as a witness. Covering the years from 1915 to 1949, the rest of the plot shows Fredy travelling around the world in search of physical and spiritual healing. However,

---

[5] This and all subsequent parenthetical references are to the American edition of the text (Murray 1998).

[6] Murray has associated this with hysterical blindness (macular anaesthesia), the psychosomatic condition experienced by people who had seen the masses of dead bodies on the battle fields of Cambodia under the regime of Pol-Pot. While their vision was physiologically unimpaired, they were subjectively unable to see (Murray 2007, 272).

[7] For this reason, Lock states: "This is a poetic device, not a medical condition" (2001, 126). There is, however, a known medical condition called CIPA (Congenital Insensitivity to Pain with Anhidrosis), caused by genetic mutation, which manifests itself in the inability to feel temperature and pain.

[8] Savage (2008, 429-31) also makes the case for the existence of a biographical connection with Murray's own emotional humiliation as an adolescent and the lasting effects that was to have on him. Murray himself coined the term 'erocide' for this "killing of the self as a desiring and desirable human being" (Savage 2008, 426, 429). For more details on the biographical background to the writing of the verse novel, see the last part ("1993-") of Peter Alexander's 2000 biography of Murray.

his travels make him see even more of the horrors occurring in the major global conflicts of the first half of the twentieth century. It is when he fully admits to himself what he deems to be his own guilt as an eye-witness to injustice and the horrors of war that Fredy is suddenly able to pray quite sincerely. He prays for forgiveness for himself but also for women – who rejected him – and even for God, who does not prevent evil in this world and hence also appears to be implicated in it. That prayer lifts off the great burden that the past has been for Fredy; he is finally healed and his sense of touch returns (5:254-255).

It is precisely because the novel focuses on a person bereft of tactile sensation that it is an interesting testing ground for the nexus between poetry and rhetoric. While the existence of such a connection seems almost too obvious to require illustration, their precise relationship has undergone fundamental re-evaluations in the course of history. Notably, the idea that poetry might simply have availed itself of the means of 'embellishment' that rhetoric has in store has recently been revealed as untenable.

In his study of the relationship between rhetoric and poetics for the period of antiquity, Jeffrey Walker corrects the prevailing view according to which the primary form of rhetoric, 'pragmatic' rhetoric, derives from practical civic oratory such as was deployed in law courts and political discourse, while 'epideictic' (ornamental) rhetoric is in fact a mere derivative thereof. Epideictic rhetoric, in this view, is considered an application of the principles of practical discourse to literary uses, including epic and lyric poetry, but also panegyric speeches, philosophy and history (Walker 2000, viii, 7). Referring to a key passage in Hesiod's *Theogony* of the eighth century B.C. and further giving evidence from archaic communities throughout the world, Walker contends that the relation was the inverse: Juridical and political eloquence found inspiration in epideictic discourse used in religious ritual and public ceremonies (*ibid.*, 9). Therefore, epideictic rhetoric is in fact in no way derivative but, from a historical perspective, effectively constitutes the primary form of rhetoric (*ibid.*, 10-16).[9] Rather than further engage in the relationship between poetry and rhetoric as such, however, I would like to focus on the case of a text that exploits the combined potential of rhetorical devices with the formal features of poetry.

I aim to demonstrate here that Murray's combination of poetic structures with certain rhetorical means is particularly effective in conveying a real sense of what it means not to be able to feel. These poetic and rhetorical means produce powerful figurations of touch in its absence.[10] One way by which this is achieved is the use of expressions of sight to compensate for expressions of touch. These expressions are frequently realised as metaphors. This is reminiscent of the shift in the relative importance of one sense over another in patients who have partially or fully lost one kind of sensation, as when blindness triggers an acute sense of hearing.

---

9   For an account of the similarly distorting reduction of the discipline of rhetoric to the study of rhetorical figures and tropes and then even to the study of metaphor and metonymy exclusively, see Genette 1982.

10   Both in connection with *Fredy Neptune* and other works of his, Murray has been praised for his "acute sensitivity to sensory impressions and an extraordinary capacity to articulate them" (Coetzee 2011).

2. Poetic Figurations: Stanza Form and Line Break

The long narrative of some 9,600 verses (covering 255 pages) that makes up the novel is subdivided into five books. These roughly correspond to the steps of Fredy's itinerary across the world, which takes him from Australia to the Mediterranean, to Germany, and to the United States. The verses are consistently structured into octets. These do not have a fixed rhyme pattern, though there is the occasional use of a rhyming couplet at the end of an octet.[11] Hence, the stanzas bear a resemblance to *ottava rima*, the Italian form notably employed in English narrative poetry by Byron (see Clunies Ross 2001, 114).[12] Even if there is no consistent metre or set number of syllables per line, there is a tendency for the lines to have six main stresses with a variable number of unstressed syllables, hence forming a kind of sprung hexameter reminiscent of Gerard Manley Hopkins's metrical experiments (Eskestad 2001, 73; see also Padel 1999). While end rhyme occurs only sporadically, other sound effects – like internal rhyme, assonance, consonance, and alliteration – abound in the text.

The effects of enjambments (inside the stanza or even between stanzas) deserve some attention. The novel opens with the speaker apparently referring to a family photograph to introduce himself, his rural upbringing and his partly German background:

> That was sausage day
> on our farm outside Dungog.
> There's my father Reinhard Boettcher,
> my mother Agnes. There is brother Frank
> who died of the brain-burn, meningitis.
> There I am having my turn
> at the mincer. Cooked meat with parsley and salt
> winding out, smooth as gruel, for the weisswurst. (1:3)

In line 6, the statement "There I am", which at first sight seems to be another existential expression just like "There's my father" in line 3, is followed by "having my turn / at the mincer". In this way, "am" turns out to be in fact part of a verb phrase including an adverbial. It is the line break that cuts the construction in two and produces an enjambment. In his fine analysis of the first two octets of the novel, Bruce Clunies Ross shows how the separation of the adverbial "at the mincer" from "turn" produces a pun, as the "turn" placed in line-final position draws attention to the turning of the line itself, so that the movement of the hand that turns the handle of the mincer is, as it were, typographically realised in the poem itself (2001, 115). Yet another dimension of meaning arises from the origin of the term verse itself in the Latin *vertere*, the turning of the text which occurs at the end of each line in verse (*OED*, s.v. 'verse, n.') – analogous to the turn made by a plough when the border of the field has been reached. Occurring as it does in the opening octet of the verse narrative, the pun can be understood as a self-reflexive allusion to the poetic nature of the text.

---

11 Only very rarely does an entire octet follow a specific pattern, such as being organised into rhyming couplets (1:14, stanza 3) or embracing rhymes throughout (1: 14, stanza 4). Clunies Ross interprets the use of the rhymes in these consecutive stanzas – which occur shortly before Fredy reaches Jerusalem – as "a vernacular hymn, at the prospect of Jerusalem" (2001, 117).

12 Clunies Ross characterises the relationship between Murray's octets and *ottava rima* as "tangential" (2001, 113): "Instead of employing the full suite of defining attributes, just sufficient are selected to create the fine balance of formality, intricacy and sprawl which is the hallmark of Murray's poetry" (2001, 114).

Murray's use of this line break exemplifies the way that versified language allows poets to direct readers' cognitive processes in a particular fashion. Concentrating on reader responses to *Paradise Lost*, Stanley Fish has demonstrated the surprise that can result if a poet skilfully handles the semantic and syntactic options of language to lure his readers into expecting a certain continuation of a line, only to deceive them by how that line actually continues. As demonstrated above, the surprise effect can be increased if a syntactic unit is interrupted in an enjambment. Fish identifies three basic principles for the reading process that explain how the surprise effect is achieved: (1) Reading takes place in time so that one word is read after the other (therefore, that which has been perused already establishes an expectation as to how the line will continue); (2) even in the absence of rhyme, a line of verse functions as a structural entity to which the eye will cling; (3) the human mind tends to make sense of the language material that is provided within the first line read, and on the basis of this information, it will make hypotheses about what is going to be said in the following (Fish 1997 [1967], 23).[13]

Working within the framework of cognitive poetics, Margaret Freeman (2002) has illustrated the subtle influence that poets' linguistic choices can exert in an astute analysis of Emily Dickinson's poetry and the notorious editorial changes that her manuscripts underwent at the hands of editors. In Freeman's poignant formulation, "the embodied shape of a text constitutes its cognitive design" (2002, 28, see also 23).

Indeed, in the stanza from *Fredy Neptune*, the use of the deictic pronoun "there" in lines 3 and 4 creates a frame that makes the reader expect another existential expression when "there" opens line 6, but in fact the pattern is broken here, and the assumption of another such expression must subsequently be revised by the reader. Apart from that, the positioning of "turn" at the literal turning point of the verse certainly helps to activate the additional level of meaning elaborated by Clunies Ross: the two lines involved become mimetic of what they describe.[14]

Hence Freeman's term "embodiment", which concerns the typographical shape of lines of verse on the page but also all the levels of linguistic description in which poetry is realised (see 2002, 34 and *passim*), can be fruitfully applied to *Fredy Neptune*. Her emphasis on the cognitive process that is constitutive of the reading process stands in an interesting relation to the concept of embodiment that Les Murray himself uses in his critical writings. In "Embodiment and Incarnation", he writes that

> Two obvious meanings [...] join in the term embodiment [...] the materials in which a work is realized, and [...] its somatic effect upon the beholder. This latter effect, felt in the ghostly sympathy of breath and pulse and muscle, is particularly central to poetry. (Murray 1992, 263-264)

---

13   It should be noted that prose, while it does not have the structural entity of the incompletely filled line, gives occasion for similar effects of surprise. Exploring the syntactic possibilities of prose for such effects, Fish here also underscores the reader's "anticipatory adjustment to his projection of the sentence's future contours" (1970, 124).

14   For an analysis of the opening octet of *Fredy Neptune*, see also Henriksen (2001, 89), who focuses on the use of situational deixis in that octet and draws attention to an ambiguity between situational and textual deixis that can arise when an originally oral epic becomes a written text. She contends that situational deixis in *Fredy Neptune* underscores the vernacular, colloquial quality of the narrative (2001, 92).

In contrast to Freeman, Murray here focuses on the somatic side of the reception process, that is to say, readers' own bodily reactions to poetry that are elicited chiefly by its rhythms and sound effects – and which exert their influence, regardless of whether a poem is performed orally or perused in a silent reading (Clunies Ross 2001, 113). It would be difficult to deny that both cognitive and bodily responses on the part of readers play a significant role in the enjoyment of poetry, even if their subtle interplay usually remains below the level of awareness. That Murray should emphasise the somatic side of reading is in keeping with his general sensitivity to things of the body in a world that privileges ratiocination.

3. Formal and Thematic Foregrounding of Language

It is clear that Murray manipulates the possibilities of verse to his own particular ends, but the devices used themselves are, of course, part and parcel of poetry as such. In a structuralist understanding, the foregrounding (Mukařovský 2000 [1932]) or self-referential function of such poetic devices is part of the definition of poetry inasmuch as poems are understood as texts that draw attention to their own language and structure. From the point of view of the communicative system of language mapped out by Roman Jakobson (1960) in his seminal model, it is the poetic function of language (its orientation toward the message in and of itself) that predominates in literature and poetry in particular.

In *Fredy Neptune*, however, language is foregrounded in two additional ways: First, Fredy's language as the I-narrator is a non-standard variety of Australian English. According to Murray, it is modelled specifically on the socio- and regiolectal variety spoken by small farmers and rural workers in the area where his own father lived as a young man (Murray 2007, 269).[15] The literary variety he has derived from this retains perceptible features of orality such as colloquial expressions, incomplete syntax, and occasionally inconsistent spelling[16] – an interesting device in this scripted text that seems to adumbrate a certain distance from the standardisation entailed by written communication.

Second, thanks to his German mother, Fredy is bilingual, and his vernacular Australian English often contains German loan words (*Weisswurst*) and literal translations such as "I sat around some more / like ordered and not collected, as Germans say" (2:98), to render the German idiomatic phrase *wie bestellt und nicht abgeholt*. Such language hybridity seems to be the result of interference between Fredy's English and his Ger-

---

15 For a brief treatment of Murray's creation of a vernacular, demotic kind of literature (grounded in local traditions and regiolects), which he prefers over "Athenian" literature (observing the standards of a prestigious culture and modelled on classical precedent), see Egbert (2011, 43-44).

16 The most striking inconsistency in the verse novel concerns Fredy's family name, Boettcher: this is spelt in innumerable variants, including Boytcher, Beecher, Bircher, Boettischer, Buttiker, and Boaticher, to name but a few. These different spellings are probably meant to reflect pronunciation variants produced by the many people whom Fredy meets and who find it hard to produce the German *Umlaut* [œ] and the fricative [ç]. The spelling of Fredy with a single <d>, on the other hand, has been accounted for by Murray (2007, 274) himself: this is meant to suggest that Fredy's German mother pronounces the name with a long vowel sound.

man and gives depth to Fredy as a character.[17] But literal translations also often occur when Fredy is quoting in English a dialogue that must have taken place in German, for instance when Fredy is talking to his German fellow-soldiers. One of them tells Fredy: "You do understand Red Welsh. / You're stacking high!" (1:39) – which is a translation of the German *Rotwelsch*, a term for a jargon used among thieves, as well as the verb *hochstapeln*, i.e., to act in the manner of an imposter (Murray 2007, 271). For the passage containing "like ordered and not collected", however, there seems to be a different motivation: Fredy uses this phrase because it seems to him especially apt or expressive. At the same time, he is conveying a piece of knowledge about the German language. The same applies to "their mouths gaped like shop windows offering apes / for sale, as the German saying goes" (4:184). In this case, Fredy is explicitly drawing attention to a rather striking image used in the German idiomatic expression *Maulaffen feilhalten*. In "the Soil Sea, Lake Constance to you English" (4:178), he similarly translates the German designation for the lake.[18]

What emerges from such passages is that Fredy is highly sensitive to language, and that he greatly enjoys expressive words and phrases. This language awareness and linguistic versatility also allow him to express in graphic ways what is not there: his tactile sensation.[19]

4. Rhetorical Figurations: Metaphors and the Sense of Vision

Given his knack for language, it is not surprising that Fredy should resort to rhetorical devices to give graphic expression to his complex and very unusual way of relating to the world. Indeed, the rhetorical tropes of simile and metaphor have a prominent place in Fredy's narrative. The source domain is often the natural world, as in the simile that visualises artillery as "cannons like enormous kangaroos / chained on their timber pallets" (5: 236), where the animals' outward appearance is mapped onto pieces of heavy artillery. Motivated by the need to describe a novel object or experience, these tropes illustrate the narrator's ability to use language creatively and effectively. On board a ship off the coast of Hawaii, Fredy observes the following phenomenon:

> Off Diamond Head, waiting to sail in,
> we sighted this swollen skyscraper lying down in the sky,
> shining like foil, getting huge, coming on over us. (3:115)

---

17 The English spoken by Fredy's mother also clearly shows interference: Fredy quotes her as once using the work "blitz-quick" (1:23) – in a period antedating the Second World War, when *Blitz* as in *Blitzkrieg* had not yet entered the English language.

18 The translation as "Soil Sea" is based on an understanding of the topographical name "Bodensee" as consisting of the components *Boden* ('ground', 'soil') and *See* ('lake', 'sea'). Etymologically, however, the component *Boden* in fact derives from a patronym.

19 Ns Quite apart from the regional and sociolectal features of Fredy's language, such literal translations posed a special challenge for the translation of *Fredy Neptune* into German. That challenge was admirably met by Thomas Eichhorn, whose award-winning translation appeared as part of a bilingual edition of the verse novel (Murray 2004). On some of the strictures of the hybrid language of text, see Eichhorn (2004); Peterssen and Eichhorn (2005). Peterssen (2005, 11-14) offers a brief evaluation of Eichhorn's translation in her study of the German reception of Murray's novel.

The phenomenon Fredy and his comrades have sighted here is deliberately left in the dark as Fredy relays his own amazement at this strange object through verbal descriptions that work by analogy without yet putting a name on it. Somewhat later, another sighting of the same kind of object occasions this description:

> It was a sweet lilac sky, with air so clear the day moon
> looked like a washed potato, up above the phone wires.
>
> Then there was another moon, browner
> with rays like umbrella struts, getting bigger, pointing at us.
> Turning to port, to circle us, it lengthened to a breadroll
> with glass in its chin, with a gallery of all windows
> and its five big growlers beating and smoking. (3:168)

Both "the swollen skyscraper lying down in the sky" and the "[browner] moon" that "lengthen[s] to a breadroll" are metaphors for a zeppelin, an object then seen for the very first time by Fredy and the bystanders. The riddle-like metaphors of "swollen skyscraper" as well as "moon" and "breadroll" are visual approximations to grasp a thing whose name is not yet available either from experience or the lexicon. Fredy paraphrases it to himself by the term 'airship' (3:115), itself a metaphorical usage (and a translation from the German *Luftschiff*). Once the object has properly been designated, its earlier non-technical descriptions appear simply naïve. But both metaphors certainly communicate to readers how strange and novel this thing is to Fredy and his contemporaries.[20]

Significantly, the Zeppelin in its turn becomes a metaphor for Fredy's strangeness as one who is unlike anyone else (just as the airship is unlike anything else, 3:170). His state is grasped in an analogy with the Zeppelin: Fredy is weightless, he hovers in the air like an airship and, even though his body is actually subject to gravity, does not in fact *feel* his being grounded.[21] In this metaphor, then, the common ground between Fredy and the Zeppelin is not their shapes as perceived by the eyes, but their perceived freedom from gravity (which is real for the Zeppelin, but not so for Fredy, see 3:170).

The narrator is most acutely aware of being different when it comes to love: he can neither truly feel sexual pleasure nor any emotional closeness with women. As Fredy hints time and again, not only does he lack tactile sensation, he also is unable to be touched emotionally (see Lock 2001, 126; Kirsch 2000).[22] What is worse, he feels ashamed of this deficiency and finds it difficult to communicate his condition even to someone who loves him:

> [...] how to tell Phyll I was sitting in the middle of the air
> not supported, and touched only in my head. (3:167)

These lines continue the metaphor of Fredy as an airship, and they also make it explicit that Fredy can only react to Phyllis in a cognitive way, he is "touched only in [his] head". The topic of insensation is realised in these two lines by a fusion of a rhetorical

---

20   That this is its chief function transpires from the fact that the second description is offered to the reader long after the first occurrence of the object and its identification.
21   Lock (2001, 127) mentions two scenes in support of this (1:63, 3:163).
22   The double sense of touch as bodily sensation and emotion is pursued in depth by Lock (2001, 126-132), who maintains that in Fredy's case, the Cartesian separation of body and mind does not apply.

trope with the structure provided by versification : In the metaphorical clause "I was sitting in the air / not supported", the line break itself typographically mimes a hovering effect because the word "air" itself is left suspended at the end of the line.

5. Conclusion

In sum, what emerges from these examples is the central importance of the joint means of poetry and rhetoric. Fredy does not become whole again as a person in whom body and mind are fully integrated until, after 34 years, he finally regains his sense of touch. In the long interval, visual imagery and the trope of metaphor in particular serve him to express an experience that no other human being shares with him. The linguistic features with which Murray has endowed the persona of Fredy combine with the poet's unique deployment of poetic and rhetorical devices, creating a powerful narrative of trauma that conveys a sense of a sense that is not there.

References

Primary Sources

Murray, Les (1976): *Selected Poems: The Vernacular Republic*. Sydney: Angus & Robertson
--- (1979): *The Boys Who Stole the Funeral*. Sydney: Angus & Robertson
--- (1992): *Translations from the Natural World*. Paddington: Isabella
--- (1996): *Subhuman Redneck Poems*. Sydney: Duffy and Snellgrove
--- (1998): *Fredy Neptune: A Novel in Verse*. New York: Farrar, Straus, Giroux [first Australian ed. Sydney: Duffy and Snellgrove]
--- (2004): *Fredy Neptune*. Trans. Thomas Eichhorn. Zurich: Ammann

Secondary Sources

Alexander, Peter (2000): *Les Murray: A Life in Progress*. Oxford/Melbourne: Oxford University Press
Clapham, Jason (2013): "Teaching Resources", *LesMurray.org*. English Department, St Edwards, Oxford. 17 November 2013 [accessed 31 January 2013]
Clunies Ross, Bruce (2001): "The Art of Cracking Normal", *Australian Literary Studies*, 20.2, 110-121
Coetzee, J.M. (2011): "The Angry Genius of Les Murray", Review of Les Murray's *Taller When Prone: Poems* and *Killing the Black Dog: A Memoir of Depression*. *The New York Review of Books*, 29 September, n.p. [accessed 31 January 2013]
Egbert, Marie-Luise (2011): "A Novel in Verse: Exploring Narrative Genres through Les Murray's *Fredy Neptune*", in: Brock, Alexander et al. (eds.): *Explorations and Extrapolations: Applying English and American Studies*. Hallenser Studien zur Anglistik und Amerikanistik 14. Münster: LIT, 33-54
Eichhorn, Thomas (2004): "Nachbemerkung des Übersetzers", in: Murray, Les: *Fredy Neptune*. Trans. Thomas Eichhorn. Zurich: Ammann, 514-516
Eskestad, Nils (2001): "Dancing 'On Bits of Paper': Les Murray's Soundscapes", *Australian Literary Studies* 20.2, 64-75
Fish, Stanley [1967] (1997): *Surprised by Sin: The Reader in* Paradise Lost. 2nd edition. London/Houndmills: Macmillan
--- (1970): "Literature in the Reader: Affective Stylistics," *New Literary History* 2.1, 123-162
Freeman, Margaret (2002): "The Body in the Word: A Cognitive Approach to the Shape of a Poetic Text", in: Semino, Elena; Culpeper, Jonathan (eds.): *Cognitive Stylistics: A Cognitive Approach to the Shape of a Poetic Text*. Amsterdam: Benjamins, 23-47

Genette, Gérard (1982): "Rhetoric Restrained", *Figures of Literary Discourse*. London: Blackwell, 103-126

Henriksen, Line (2001): "'Big Poems Burn Women': *Fredy Neptune*'s Democratic Sailor and Walcott's Epic *Omeros*", *Australian Literary Studies* 20.2, 87-109

Jakobson, Roman (1960): "Linguistics and Poetics", in: Sebeok, Thomas A. (ed.): *Style in Language*, Cambridge, MA: MIT Press, 350-377

Kirsch, Adam (2000): "Roves, Tat, Rig, and Scunge", Review of Les Murray's *Learning Human: Selected Poems* and *Fredy Neptune: A Novel in Verse*. *New Republic* 222.24, 52-58

Lock, Charles (2001): "*Fredy Neptune*: Metonymy and the Incarnate Preposition", *Australian Literary Studies* 20.2, 122-141

Mukařovský, Jan [1932] (2000): "Standard Language and Poetic Language", in: Burke, Lucy et al. (eds.): *The Routledge Language and Cultural Theory Reader*. London: Routledge, 225-230

Murray, Les (1992): "Embodiment and Incarnation: Notes on Preparing an Anthology of Australian Religious Verse", *The Paperbark Tree: Selected Prose*. London: Minerva, 251-269

--- (2007): "How Fred and I Wrote *Fredy Neptune*", Afterword to *Fredy Neptune: A Novel in Verse*. Melbourne: Black, 267-276 [first publ. in Craven, Peter (ed.): *The Best Australian Essays 1999*. Melbourne: Bookman, 1999, 364-373]

Padel, Ruth (1999): "Odysseus of the Outback", Review of Les Murray's *Fredy Neptune: A Novel in Verse*. *The New York Times*, 16 May, n.p. [accessed 31 January 2013]

Peterssen, Irmtraud (2005): "'Odysseus from the Outback': *Fredy Neptune* and Its Critical Reception", *Australian Literary Studies* 22.1, 1-28

---; Eichhorn, Thomas (2005): "Translating *Fredy Neptune*: Interview with Thomas Eichhorn", *Australian Literary Studies* 22.1, 29-36

Savage, Robert (2008): "Erocide is Painless: Insensation in Les Murray's *Fredy Neptune*", *Australian Literary Studies* 23.4, 422-433

Walker, Jeffrey (2000): *Rhetoric and Poetics in Antiquity*. Oxford: Oxford University Press

Section 5

Comparison and Comparability in Language Studies

Chairs:

Klaus P. Schneider and Anne Schröder

KLAUS P. SCHNEIDER (BONN) AND ANNE SCHRÖDER (BIELEFELD)

Comparison and Comparability in Language Studies: An Introduction

Comparison in language studies has a long history. If we assume that language studies as an academic discipline emerged in the course of the nineteenth century and is approximately two hundred years old, then comparison has been an integral element of this discipline from its very inception. The paradigm that was dominant for the better part of the nineteenth century is, in fact, known as comparative philology. The insights obtained through work carried out in this paradigm have shaped the way we think about language and languages to this day. Today, both language experts and educated lay persons take the existence of language families for granted. The Indo-European family and its subdivisions of Germanic, Romance, and Slavic (etc.) languages is but one salient example. Comparative philology was mainly focussed on reconstructing the origin, history, and development of individual languages and on establishing genealogical relationships between languages. This was achieved by comparing written manifestations of different languages from different periods in their respective history. In other words, the method employed was diachronic and termed historical-comparative (see, e.g., Schleicher 1861/1862).

Language typology is a more recent field of inquiry in which comparison is essential. Across language families, typologists aim to establish language universals and identify linguistic, specifically morphosyntactic, features shared by languages independently of and beyond their genealogical links. With reference to such features, typological classes of languages are set up. Thus a deeper understanding of the nature of human language and languages is achieved (see, e.g., Comrie 1989). The overall aim of contrastive linguistics, on the other hand, is much more practical. At least in the 1960s and 1970s, the systematic comparison of languages in this area was mainly directed at foreign language teaching and the development of efficient teaching strategies and materials. While in language typology a large number of languages are compared, comparison in contrastive linguistics involves only two languages, namely the native and the target language of foreign language learners. The purpose of contrasting these two languages consists in identifying differences between them and thus being able to predict (according to the so-called strong contrastive hypothesis) or at least diagnose (according to the later and more realistic weak version of this hypothesis) learning difficulties and learner errors (see, e.g., James 1980).

Later, most notably with the publication of John Hawkins's seminal book on *A Comparative Typology of English and German: Unifying the Contrasts* (1986), contrastive linguistics was linked to language typology, aiming at the identification of language patterns and the limits of variation in language. At about the same time, Anna Wierzbicka published her tremendously influential article "Different Cultures, Different Languages, Different Speech Acts" (1985), in which she challenges claims of universality made in speech act theory, conversation analysis, and early politeness theories, attacks them as anglocentric, and postulates the cultural relativity of pragmatic phenomena. This article has sparked a host of contrastive studies in pragmatics and gave rise to cross-cultural and interlanguage pragmatics and later historical, variational, and post-colonial pragmatics (for a brief overview of these disciplines, see Barron and Schneider 2009).

Another much older tradition in which comparison plays a crucial role is dialectology, with its roots in early nineteenth-century Romanticism. In this case, however, it is not different languages, but different varieties of the same language that are examined, usually regional varieties spoken in the same country. Dialect features and dialect boundaries are commonly displayed on maps, ever since Georg Wenker created his *Sprachatlas des Deutschen Reichs* (started in 1888), which was the first linguistic atlas in history. In this tradition, the large-scale multi-volume *Linguistic Atlas of the United States and Canada* (started in 1939 with Hans Kurath's *Linguistic Atlas of New England*) was aimed at facilitating comparison across the regional varieties of North America. The methods in this project changed with the advent of sociolinguistics in the 1960s, with its methodological innovations and its focus on social varieties of a language, for example, comparing working class and middle class speech and, later, female and male speech.

Today, the study and comparison of regional varieties and of social varieties is sometimes subsumed under the term "variational linguistics" or, at least in the United States "(modern) dialectology" (for an overview of dialect geography, sociolinguistics, and atlas projects, see Schneider 2005). The study of national varieties of English, on the other hand, has developed largely independently of dialect geography and sociolinguistics, beginning with overviews that were not based on systematic empirical work (e.g., Trudgill and Hannah 1982). Today, there is a vast number of textbooks as well as handbooks and edited volumes offering overviews of national varieties around the world, based on systematic empirical research, and also monographic in-depth studies of individual first or second language varieties of English as well as textbooks summarising findings on individual varieties (Siemund et al. 2012 is a recent textbook example). In the latter cases, comparison is often implicit, that is, reference is tacitly made to (some) Standard English.

All of the disciplines mentioned above have profited enormously from the creation and the availability of large machine-readable language corpora and corpus linguistic methods, which have broadened the field of inquiry, allowing for more detailed and comprehensive descriptions in contrastive analysis and the various kinds of comparative studies. Furthermore, the last few years have seen the publication of major linguistic atlases advancing the comparison of languages, pidgins and creoles, and varieties of English, including in particular the *World Atlas of Language Structures* (WALS; Dryer and Haspelmath 2013), the *Atlas of Pidgin and Creole Language Structures* (APiCS; Michaelis et al. 2013), and the *World Atlas of Variation in English* (WAVE/eWAVE; Kortmann and Lunkenheimer 2012; 2013). Despite the impressive technological, methodological, and conceptual progress that has been made over the past few decades, a question of central importance is always how researchers involved in linguistic comparison can avoid comparing apples to oranges, as it were, or, in other words, how comparability can be achieved. This is a particularly serious problem for typologists, who often have to resort to using heterogeneous materials and working with outdated or unreliable descriptions of lesser known and understudied languages (see Kortmann, this volume). For the investigation of first and second language varieties of English, on the other hand, the situation has significantly improved with the construction of the *International Corpus of English* (ICE), consisting of twenty-six component corpora, of which fourteen are currently available at least in part. Each component corpus is based on a common design to ensure comparability across corpora. However, the general problem persists and has to be dealt with whenever languages or varieties are contrasted. As König and Gast (2012, 5) remind us, "the problem of establishing comparability and of finding the 'third of comparison' (*tertium comparationis*) is a major issue in any kind of comparative work." To address this problem from a range of different angles, researchers were invited from all fields of linguistics that compare languages or (historical, regional, social, or functional) language varieties to engage in discussions on the issue of the "third of comparison" and further theoretical, methodological, and practical issues evolving around comparison in language studies. The authors of the following six articles accepted the invitation. In all six articles, varieties of English are compared, including historical and present-day varieties, national and regional varieties, first and second language varieties, and pidgins and creoles. All the articles are based on empirical work, using material from larger or smaller corpora of written or spoken language or experimental data elicited by employing different types of questionnaires.

In his article "Comparison and Comparability: The WAVE Perspective", Bernd Kortmann (Freiburg) deals with the problem of comparability in large-scale cross-linguistic (or macro-comparative) and cross-varietal (or micro-comparative) projects focussed on morphosyntactic features. His example is the *World Atlas of Variation in English* (WAVE) mentioned above and its electronic version eWAVE, which together cover 235 morphosyntactic features in 50 first and second language varieties of English and 26 English-based pidgins and creoles. This micro-comparative atlas is contrasted with the also above-mentioned macro-comparative typological atlas projects WALS and APiCS. Problems addressed in this context primarily concern the choice of categories for and the limitations of comparison within and across these three atlases. Kortmann concludes that comparability in large-scale projects increases to the extent that the specific nature of individual languages or varieties is abstracted away.

In her paper "The Comparability of Discourse Features: *I think* in Englishes Worldwide", Daniela Kolbe-Hanna (Trier) contrasts two different approaches for comparing discourse markers across varieties of a language. One approach is purely quantitative and involves the comparison of normalised textual frequencies. The other, more complex approach is based on the notion of linguistic variables as originally proposed by Labov (1966), which, however, has to be modified for the present purposes, as it is not immediately clear what a discourse variable is. Kolbe-Hanna uses the example of *I think* and analyses its occurrences as an epistemic comment clause (or stance marker) across several ICE components, and specifically in ICE Hong Kong and ICE Jamaica. Using the category of adverbial and clausal epistemic expressions as a *tertium comparationis*, the author discusses possible variants and examines their distribution in these two corpora. The approach based on discourse variables is finally considered the more promising method for cross-varietal comparison. The contribution "Comparing Tense and Aspect in Pidgins and Creoles: Dahl's Questionnaire and Beyond" by

Stephanie Hackert (München) and Anne Schröder (Bielefeld) is focussed on an assessment of methods for investigating tense-aspect systems of pidgin and creole languages. It is argued that attempts to describe tense and aspect in these languages with the grammatical categories of Standard English are inadequate, as pidgins and creoles should generally be described on their own terms. A putatively universal creole TMA system is also rejected as unsuitable. As an alternative, the authors suggest employing the TMA questionnaire developed by Dahl (1985) for cross-linguistic studies, which permits language-independent comparison. Using this questionnaire as the third of comparison, tense and aspect in Cameroon Pidgin English (CamP) and Bahamian Creole English (BahCE) are systematically contrasted with tense and aspect in Standard English (StE). This approach is supplemented with semantic maps modelling individual categories of the tense-aspect systems of CamP, BahCE and StE.

In the next chapter on "Comparability and Sameness in Variational Pragmatics", Klaus P. Schneider (Bonn) underlines the importance of comparability in this young discipline, which is interested in pragmatic differences between regional and social varieties of the same language. The author argues in favour of experimental methods involving production questionnaires which warrant systematic control of relevant social factors and provide a degree of sameness needed for identifying pragmatic variables and their variants. Written dialogue data elicited from homogenised populations of native speakers from England, Ireland, and the United States are used to demonstrate how pragmatic variables and their variants can be established on the actional and on the interactional levels of analysis. It is shown that the experimental findings are supported by evidence from corpora of naturally occurring language such as ICE-Great Britain, ICE-Ireland, and the *Corpus of Contemporary American English* (COCA).

The identification of variants is also a key issue in "Comparing Apples and Oranges: The Study of Diachronic Change Based on Variant Forms" by Tanja Rütten (Köln). As her starting point, the author makes the assumption that language change results from a rivalry of competing linguistic forms. This assumption gives rise to the question what exactly counts as competing forms. Re-examining the historical development of the English mandative subjunctive, Rütten discusses a range of constructions which may be considered as variants. Using data from the *Corpus of English Religious Prose*, the frequencies of these variants are established for four fifty-year periods between 1500 and 1700. Diverging frequencies suggest a distinction between core and minor variants. The data further suggest that the subjunctive is highly context-sensitive. These findings may lead to a new assessment of how the subjunctive developed in Early Modern English. They also show that a comparison based on frequencies provides a more accurate picture than a comparison based on proportions.

In the final article, "In Search of Faithful Standards: Comparing Diachronic Corpora across Domains", Thomas Kohnen (Köln) addresses the question of how diachronic corpora covering domains as unrelated as newspaper language, correspondence, and dialogues can be combined and compared. The author suggests basing comparative analyses on text-functional and domain-based parameters. Central categories of functional text structure are text functions, interactive format, and publication format. Central categories of domain structure include hierarchies, sets, and chains of genres. This approach is exemplified in a systematic comparison of the Early Modern part of the *Corpus of English Religious Prose* and the corpus of *Early Modern English Medical*

Texts (Taavitsainen and Pahta 2010). Specifically, the focus is on text functions such as narration, the interactive dialogue format, and the publication format of pamphlets, and on first-, second- and third-order genres. It is demonstrated how each of these parameters contributes to the comparability of corpus data across domains.

References

Barron, Anne; Schneider, Klaus P. (2009): "Variational Pragmatics: Studying the Impact of Social Factors on Language Use in Interaction", *Intercultural Pragmatics*, 6, 425-442
Comrie, Bernard (1989): *Language Universals and Linguistic Typology: Syntax and Morphology.* Chicago: University of Chicago Press
Corpus of Contemporary American English (COCA) <http://corpus.byu.edu/coca/>
Corpus of English Religious Prose (<http://www.helsinki.fi/varieng/CoRD/corpora/COERP/>
Dahl, Östen (1985): *Tense and Aspect Systems.* Oxford: Blackwell
Dryer, Matthew S.; Haspelmath, Martin (eds.; 2013): *The World Atlas of Language Structures Online.* Leipzig: Max Planck Institute for Evolutionary Anthropology <http://wals.info>
Hawkins, John (1986): *A Comparative Typology of English and German: Unifying the Contrasts.* London: Croom Helm
International Corpus of English (ICE) <http://ice-corpora.net/ice/>
James, Carl (1980): *Contrastive Analysis.* London: Longman
König, Ekkehard; Gast, Volker (2012): *Understanding English-German Contrasts.* 3rd and revised edition. Berlin: Erich Schmidt
Kortmann, Bernd; Lunkenheimer, Kerstin (eds.; 2012): *The Mouton World Atlas of Variation in English.* Berlin/Boston: Mouton de Gruyter
--- (eds.; 2013): *The Electronic World Atlas of Varieties of English.* Leipzig: Max Planck Institute for Evolutionary Anthropology. <http://www.ewave-atlas.org>
Kurath, Hans (1939-1943): *Linguistic Atlas of New England.* 6 vols. bound as 3. Providence: Brown University for the American Council of Learned Societies
Labov, William (1966): "The Linguistic Variable as a Structural Unit", *Washington Linguistics Review*, 3, 4-22
Michaelis, Susanne et al. (eds.; 2013): *Atlas of Pidgin and Creole Language Structures Online.* Leipzig: Max Planck Institute for Evolutionary Anthropology (<http://apics-online.info>)
Schleicher, August (1861/1862): *Compendium der vergleichenden Grammatik der indogermanischen Sprachen*, 2 vols. Weimar: Boehlau. (English translation 1874: *A Compendium of the Comparative Grammar of the Indo-European, Sanskrit, Greek, and Latin Languages*, translated by Herbert Bendall. London: Trübner)
Schneider, Klaus P. (2005): "Region and Regionalism in Linguistics: A Brief Survey of Concepts and Methods", in: Hönnighausen, Lothar et al. (eds.): *Regionalism in the Age of Globalism.* Volume 1: *Concepts of Regionalism.* Madison: University of Wisconsin, Center for the Study of Upper Midwestern Cultures, 139-158
Siemund, Peter et al. (2012): *The Amazing World of Englishes: A Practical Introduction.* Berlin: Mouton de Gruyter
Taavitsainen, Irma; Pahta, Päivi (eds.; 2010): *Early Modern English Medical Texts: Corpus Description and Studies.* Amsterdam/Philadelphia: Benjamins, 29-53
Trudgill, Peter; Hannah, Jean (1982): *International English: A Guide to the Varieties of Standard English.* London: Arnold
Wenker, Georg (1888 ff.): *Sprachatlas des Deutschen Reichs.* <http://www.diwa.info/>
Wierzbicka, Anna (1985): "Different Cultures, Different Languages, Different Speech Acts", *Journal of Pragmatics*, 9, 145-178

MIRIAM A. LOCHER (BASEL)

The Relational Aspect of Language: Avenues of Research

1. Introduction

In this theoretical chapter center stage is given to the relational aspect of language and how it has been studied in a number of avenues of research, primarily within the field of politeness research. This overview draws on previously published work on the pragmatic turn (Locher 2012) and on insights from the recent special issue on interpersonal pragmatics in the Journal of Pragmatics (Haugh et al. 2013).

A classic example that zooms right in on the relational side of language is the way in which we use greeting terms in combination with first names/surnames to indicate closeness/distance and power hierarchies. As Holmes (1992, 4) succinctly puts it, "[l]inguistic variation can provide social information". Addressing somebody with their title and surname as opposed to first name thus carries social information. Choosing the title *Ms* over *Mrs* or *Miss* might index social conventions and ideologies on gender.

Within pragmatics, relational issues have been traditionally approached by drawing on politeness research (e.g. Brown and Levinson 1987; Leech 1983; Lakoff 1973). Indeed, the fact that politeness is a topic worth studying is not just exemplified by the abundant politeness literature in linguistics but we can find ample evidence in public discourse as well (see e.g. the many cartoons on politeness published in magazines and online, or publications on (n)etiquette).

In this paper I argue that drawing on classic politeness theories alone might not help us to sufficiently interpret what is going on with respect to the relational side of language more generally. The following example, taken from the Internet social network platform Facebook, is a case in point:

> Back at my desk in Basel after an awesome three and a half months in Vancouver. Thanks to the Basel team for making my leave possible and to the UBC and SJC friends for making it such a special and memorable stay. (December 13, 2012)

This status update was written by myself when I returned home after a sabbatical in Canada. We observe an act of thanking, about which we could raise questions of politeness: Was I polite in thanking my colleagues by posting a message on Facebook in this form? Rather than going for a yes-no answer, it might be more interesting to discuss the relational issues that emerge. There is membership in-group terminology (UBC, SJC) that will be accessible to some people on my friends list but not to others. I am creating in-groups and out-groups and at the same time this has an impact on my own positioning. I am performing the role of an academic in front of "friends" who are fellow academics but also in front of "friends" who do not work in an academic context.

Bucholtz and Hall (2005, 586) argue that "[h]ow one speaks (what style one uses) has an impact on how one is perceived as a person and therefore we can make a link to linguistic 'identity construction', defined here as 'the social positioning of self and other'". There is thus a connection between the relational aspect of language, style, and identity construction, which deserves to be explored in more detail.

This point will become even clearer in the next example. It is taken from a corpus of reflection papers composed by Bachelor students of Medical Science in connection with their communication skills training at a British university (see http://illness-narratives. unibas.ch for a project description). They were asked to write about a memorable encounter with a patient and discuss their own comportment during the encounter.

> While sitting in during a GP visit in my first year of being a medical student, I had to call in a patient, Jane Rosemary (name changed for confidentiality). She was a tall, middle aged woman who walked into the consultation room with her husband. She looked weak and walked slowly in. I noticed that she was not moving her right arm much and she clutched it from time to time, which I believed indicated that she was in slight pain. After greeting her, the GP proceeded to ask her if it was alright for me, a medical student to sit in during the consultation and ask her a few questions about her condition. (N-025)

What we can see here is how a story telling frame emerges when a story world is created and character positioning takes place: We are introduced to the interactants by means of membership categories such as the GP, the medical student, and the patient and her husband. We also see how the student reports on the speech acts of greeting and asking for permission, which are performed by the GP, who is in the hierarchically higher position. Since classic politeness theories are concerned with speech acts as they are performed, it will be difficult to apply them to this extract, in which they are merely named. However, relational issues clearly emerge in the observed positioning and, in the case of the speech acts, we can also see relational concerns in what is narrated.

The examples presented in this introduction demonstrate the pervasive nature of the relational aspect of language and communication. This paper deals with how this aspect has been studied in the field of politeness research and with interpersonal pragmatics more generally. Its aim is to give centre stage to the relational side of language use by sketching the history of politeness research, working with the idea of interpersonal pragmatics, and addressing the potential of research synergies. In order to reach this aim I will first talk about variation in linguistics, before leading over to interpersonal pragmatics and avenues of research on the relational aspect of language.

2. Variation and Interpersonal Pragmatics

It is useful to re-visit the idea of variation in linguistics to position the study of the relational side of language within pragmatics. Variation can be observed at all levels of language from phonology, morphology, syntax, and lexicon to differences in how practices are realised. We find historical, regional, social, and situational variation in language. These different planes of variation cannot easily be separated when looking at naturally occurring language – a point I will return to later. Different research disciplines have tackled variation in different ways, asking different questions about variation and developing different tools for analysis. However, ultimately, all the different disciplines look for patterns and systematic constraints in what they observe (Wardaugh 2002; Coulmas 2005). In a somewhat simplified way, we can posit that historical linguistics asks how the (abstract) language system has changed over time. Dialectology is interested in how regional language varieties differ and can be systematically described and explained. This field can be expanded to the field of Varieties of English, the study of the different Englishes that have developed across the globe.

Variationist sociolinguistics, in the Labovian sense, has found that – in contexts such as the cities in the 1960s – there is not only regional variation, but also systematic language variation that can be linked to social factors such as class, age, or gender. Variationists work with elicited interview data and are interested in how groups of people use language differently. In other words, while intra-speaker variation and style shifts are key starting points for their methodology, they are still interested in the abstract understanding of language and the social impact on its system, rather than in the study of concrete instances of language in use by individuals.

In contrast, research approaches such as Hymes's (1974) ethnography of speaking, conversation, and discourse analysis, interactional sociolinguistics and those concerned with the study of style and audience design have focussed not on the language system per se, but on how language is used for meaning creation by individuals and communities *in situ*. Intra-speaker variation, style shifts, and identity construction emerge as topics. We therefore see a difference in the kind of questions asked about variation. As a consequence, it is not a coincidence that variationist sociolinguistics is also a quantitative approach, while approaches such as discourse analysis or stylistics usually work with qualitative case studies.

Where can we position pragmatics, politeness research, and the study of the relational aspect of language within this rough sketch? First, we need to point out that the definition of pragmatics as the study of language in use is actually not a unified one. According to Taavitsainen and Jucker (2010, 4), there are two traditions in pragmatics. They argue that the Anglo-American tradition of "pragmatics [...] deals with information structure, implicit meanings and cognitive aspects of utterance interpretation" (Taavitsainen and Jucker 2010, 4). This tradition is closely associated with approaches that explain the creation of context-dependent meaning in terms of a pragmatic interface between the language system and acts of language use, often working with constructed examples: Speech Act Theory, developed by Austin and Searle, or other approaches that developed out of the field of philosophy such as Grice's Cooperative Principle (CP; see Langlotz 2011). It is here that the classic politeness theories by Lakoff, Leech, and Brown and Levinson set in, as I will illustrate shortly.

The definition of pragmatics adopted predominantly in Europe is broader (Taavitsainen and Jucker 2010, 4), as can be shown with Verschueren's (2009, 19) definition: Pragmatics is seen as "a general functional perspective on (any aspect of) language, i.e. as an approach to language which takes into account the full complexity of its cognitive, social, and cultural (i.e. meaningful) functioning in the lives of human beings". While the first definition focuses on the language system as it is complemented with a set of rules that aim at explaining language in use, the individual human being engaged in acts of creating meaning is at the heart of explorations in the second research strand. Many of the more recent developments in politeness research adopt this second understanding of pragmatics.

So what about the relational side of language within the study of linguistics? The examples at the beginning of this chapter have shown that the relational aspect of language is hard to ignore. That there is such a relational aspect is of course not new. For example, in 1967, Watzlawick et al. highlighted that "[e]very communication has a content and a relationship aspect such that the latter classifies the former and is therefore a metacommunication" (54). Importantly, the content and relational aspect of language cannot easily be separated, since they co-occur in the same expression (e.g. Fill 1990).

The relational side as a point of interest in itself is not explicitly theorised in variationist theoretical linguistics, sociolinguistics, or dialectology. However, it does occur, for example in the Hallidayan systemic-functional grammar, where the interpersonal is recognized as an important metafunction of language (see e.g. Halliday 1978). The relational component of language is often discussed within discursive approaches to the study of language as diverse as conversation analysis, discourse analysis, interactional sociolinguistics, style, and audience design. However, these approaches might not primarily deal with the construction of relational meaning as such, although some researchers obviously do. Finally, of special interest here is that the relational side of language is given an important role in a number of pragmatic politeness theories, such as Lakoff's, Leech's, and Brown and Levinson's frameworks. I will especially explore the relational component in the politeness field and then move on to some of the discursive approaches within this field.

In general, the label "interpersonal pragmatics" can be used for those studies that focus on the relational/interpersonal in their research endeavours. Studies in interpersonal pragmatics "explore facets of interaction between social actors that rely upon (and in turn influence) the dynamics of relationships between people and how those relationships are reflected in the language choices that they make" (Locher and Graham 2010, 2). What Sage Graham and I propose is not a new theory, but we argue that the *perspective* of interpersonal pragmatics can lead to rewarding research questions and projects without precluding any choice of method (Locher and Graham 2010, 2). Just like Haugh et al. (2013, 9), we find it important that "interpersonal pragmatics be conceptualised first and foremost as offering a pragmatics perspective on interpersonal aspects of communication and interaction [and that it] is conceived of as inherently interdisciplinary or multidisciplinary in nature." Let me now turn to some of the details of how the relational aspect of language has been theorised in that research field that can most generally be labelled as (im)politeness research.

3. Classic Politeness Research and the Relational Aspect of Language

Classic politeness research can now look back on 40 years of research dealing with the relational angle of language. There are three classic theories that all work with Grice's Cooperative Principle (CP): Lakoff (1973), Brown and Levinson (1978/1987), and Leech (1983). Rather than introducing all of these approaches in detail (see Locher 2012 for an overview), I will mainly comment on the theories' stance towards interpersonal issues. Lakoff was the first to link the idea of politeness to 'pragmatic rules' in linguistics. She highlights that while we might consider a sentence in its particular context as grammatically correct, it might nevertheless not be considered well-formed from a pragmatic point of view. For this reason she assumes that there is a set of pragmatic rules forming norms against which deviations are judged. Lakoff thus formulates a set of pragmatic rules that complement syntactic rules (Lakoff 1973, 296). She formulates two "rules of pragmatic competence" that are comprised of "1. Be clear", an early version of Grice's CP, and "2. Be polite" (Lakoff 1973, 296, 298; 1990,

37). The latter rule is split into three rules of politeness in turn: 1. Don't impose; 2. Give options, and 3. Make A[lter] feel good – be friendly. In 1990 these rules were labelled as 1. Distance, 2. Deference, 3. Camaraderie. So, we might use more words than strictly necessary from a content perspective in order to not impose, in order to give options, or to make the addressee feel good. For example, we might say *could you pass me the salt please?* rather than just saying *pass the salt*.

The relational aspect of language is implied in the interpersonal concepts of distance, deference, and camaraderie. Ultimately, Lakoff was in search of universals, just like Chomsky in theoretical linguistics. Her theory is meant to explain how language is used in general by taking relational aspects into account. She argues that these rules are valid across cultures, but that the cultures give different weight to the rules: She claims that Europeans value Distancing strategies, while Asian people are reported to favor Deference and Americans Camaraderie (Lakoff 1990, 35-39).

In 1983, Leech proposed his *Principles of Pragmatics* and has refined the politeness part therein in 2007. Like Lakoff, he argues that what he terms the "Politeness Principle" should be seen in connection with the CP. To understand how meaning is created in actual language use, people interpret deviations from the CP in a certain manner and politeness is one explanatory factor for not expressing yourself as clearly or as briefly as possible etc. from a content point of view. Leech (1983, 132) postulates six maxims (the Maxims of Tact, Generosity, Approbation, Modesty, Agreement, and Sympathy) that together form the Politeness Principle. The maxims all have relational issues at the core, such as how the speaker positions him- or herself towards another person. This can be shown in the sub-maxims that all explicitly mention the role of self or other towards each other. The Agreement Maxim states that people strive to minimise "disagreement between *self* and *other*", while the Sympathy Maxim argues that interlocutors strive to minimise "antipathy between *self* and *other*" (Leech 1983, 132).[1]

In 2007 Leech reformulates the Politeness Principle, drops the maxims, and highlights the fact that the Politeness Principle is a constraint with a particular aim: "The Principle of Politeness (PP) – analogous to Grice's CP – is a constraint observed in human communicative behavior, influencing us to avoid communicative discord or offence, and maintain communicative concord" (Leech 2007, 173). Since offence and concord are concepts that have to do with how people are positioned towards and engage with each other, we once again see a relational element at the core of this theory.

The best-known classic politeness theory is by Brown and Levinson from 1978 and 1987. Like the others, this theory has been influenced by Speech Act Theory and Grice's CP. It is therefore positioned with the other two approaches within the same research thrust that attempted to understand language use as such, moving the theory beyond the sentence to speaker and utterance meaning. By looking at English, Tamil, and Tzeltal, Brown and Levinson especially make a case for universals in their search for pragmatic rules. This interest in the process of creating meaning in general is also visible in the proposed key assumptions. Similar to the idea of the idealised speaker-hearer in Chomskyan syntax, they base their reasoning on an idealised model person who follows

---

[1] Leech's (1983, 132) other maxims come in pairs; for example, the Tact Maxim focusses on the other ("Minimize cost to *other*"), while the Generosity Maxim highlights the importance of the self ("Minimize benefit to *self*").

rational means-ends behavior. Crucially, however, they draw on the Goffmanian idea of face, and develop the idea of the face-threatening act (FTA), which are clearly relational concepts. In fact, we have explicit pointers to the relational effects of language use, namely the creation of social relationships and the explicit mention that language variation can be studied from that angle: "We believe that patterns of message construction, or 'ways of putting things', or simply language usage, are parts of the very stuff that social relationships are made of" (Brown and Levinson 1987, 55).

Brown and Levinson argue that both speakers and hearers systematically take extralinguistic constraints into account when interpreting or shaping a message. These factors are "the 'social distance' (D) of S and H", "the relative 'power' (P) of S and H", and "the absolute ranking (R) of impositions in the particular culture" (1987, 74). Taken together, these aspects make up the "weightiness of the FTA x" (1987, 75), which then lead the speaker to choose one of five main strategies for facework (from bold on record and mitigated strategies to refraining from committing a face-threatening act). D and P are of course relational factors in the way that two independent human beings are set in relation to each other.

In general, the three early theories are meant to be read as complements to existing theoretical thinking on syntax and speech acts of the time by proposing pragmatic rules. These theories have in common that they want to understand variation in language in general (rather than looking at the use of language by individuals[2]) and are looking for explanation of observed variation in patterns by proposing general pragmatic rules. They are thus the result of the pragmatic turn. Furthermore, the combination of all three theories with Grice's CP derived from the philosophy of ordinary language positions the approaches within the Anglo-American understanding of pragmatics, as quoted above. However, in the case of Brown and Levinson we find the addition of ideas on face derived from sociology and anthropology, which broadens their framework. When looking at how the relational component of language is worked into the early politeness theories we can note that they all give it an important position. In the case of Lakoff, the relational component of language is implied in the terms distance/deference/camaraderie. In the case of Leech, his Politeness Principle is a constraint with the aim to "avoid communicative discord or offence, and maintain communicative concord" (2007, 173). This is relational by definition and on a par with the CP in the creation of meaning. Both Leech and Brown and Levinson speak of constraints that influence language choice, such as distance and power differences between interactants. Finally, Brown and Levinson broaden these early theories in that they introduce the idea of "face" and "face-threatening acts", with face being an inherently relational concept.

4. Recent Trends in Politeness Research

The three classic politeness theories – and especially Brown and Levinson's work – have received much attention in the literature and have been applied widely. As discussed in Locher (2012, 2013a), new developments in politeness research have been predominantly developed since the 1990s as a reaction to these still widely used early

---

[2] All three theories work primarily with constructed examples and examples derived from observations that rarely go beyond two speaker turns.

politeness frameworks. This is mainly because the generalisations in the early theories are at the cost of the local, situated meaning of "politeness". It was felt that the perceptions and judgements of the interactants are not sufficiently taken into account there, and that the form-function correlation (for example, indirectness equals politeness, prominent in both Brown and Levinson and in Leech) is problematic. Alternatives were proposed by Fraser (1990), who argued for a conversational-contract view, Watts (1992), who added the notion of markedness within politeness research, and scholars such as Sifianou (1992) or Holmes (1995), who stressed the pro-social, involvement aspect of politeness (see Locher 2004 for discussions). While it is not possible to go into detail here about the particularities of the different frameworks, they have in common that they emphasise the local negotiation of meaning in particular contexts.

There are several trends that started in the 1990s and that are still topical today. The first is about whether we can or indeed should look for universals in relational use of language. We thus find a debate about the theoretical concepts employed in past theories (Eelen 2001). Ultimately this is also a question of how we ask research questions about an abstract system or how meaning is negotiated locally in naturally occurring linguistic data. Once more we find a fundamental split between two different research traditions.

The theoretical linguistics tradition, inspired by Generative Grammar, Speech Act Theory, and Grice's Cooperative Principle, works with theoretical concepts – so called second order or etic – definitions. Politeness then is a theoretical concept rather than a value judgment by interactants *in situ*. The classic politeness theories use the term "politeness" as a shorthand to account for relational considerations that influence linguistic output and interpretation. They add pragmatic rules to syntactic rules, to use Lakoff's (1973) terminology.

Researchers who argue that it would be worthwhile to look at an emic, first order account when one is interested in politeness argue that the term "politeness" refers to a judgment according to the norms pertaining to the specific interaction under investigation. As such the meaning of politeness is negotiable over time and place, and it would be of interest to look at this variability in meaning in its own right. Terms such as *polite, rude, polished*, etc. are then studied in their lay meaning rather than in their theoretical meaning. Crucially, the spotlight is on the negotiation of relational aspects of language within an emerging interaction. Largely as a result of the discussion about universals and the emic/etic discussion, the second trend came about from the nineties to today. Politeness researchers started to look for politeness in contexts where there were no obvious speech acts such as advising, greeting, requesting, and they wondered how then to use the classic theoretical frameworks. It was also argued that theories that have the relational aspect of language at their core should also be useful when analysing data that do not address face-threatening acts (Brown and Levinson 1987, 69) or that are not intended to explain how human beings "avoid communicative discord or offence, and maintain communicative concord" (Leech 2007, 173). Today politeness researchers work on impoliteness, rudeness, and conflict in general, and they are also interested in historical developments of practices. The recent publication by Culpeper (2011) entitled *Impoliteness: Using Language to Cause Offence*, Culpeper and Kádár's (2010) edited collection on *Historical (Im)politeness*, Bousfield's (2008) monograph, and Bousfield and Locher's (2008) edited collection on *Impoliteness in Language* are examples of this trend.

Finally, we can observe that there is a new openness toward mixed methodologies and to combining politeness research with other fields within linguistics in order to approach the relational side of language (see Section 6). Especially the link between judgments on politeness and identity construction (see e.g. Spencer-Oatey 2007; 2011; Locher 2008; 2011) makes it possible to draw on work on style, audience design, or crossing that is also concerned with intra-speaker variation and positioning (see e.g. Bucholtz and Hall 2005; Davies and Harré 1990; Coupland 2007; Rampton 1995).

5. Interpersonal Issues within Relational Work and Discursive Approaches to Politeness

The last avenue of research to be discussed in this chapter is concerned with the discursive approaches that deal with the relational aspect of language (e.g. Haugh 2007; Haugh et al. 2013; Hutchby 2008; Locher 2004; 2006; 2008; 2012; 2013b; Locher and Watts 2005; 2008; LPRG 2011; Mills 2005; Tracy 2008; Watts 1989; 1992; 2003; 2005). While the scholars just mentioned do not present a unified theoretical approach to politeness, there are nevertheless a number of important commonalities. The focus is on practices in the sense that naturally occurring linguistic data is collected and analysed *in situ*. This means that attention is given to context and to the negotiation of relational meaning within emerging interaction. There is also a general interest in interpersonal effects of the entire first order spectrum so that face-enhancing, face-maintaining, and face-aggravating or face-damaging behavior is studied. With some exceptions, the work carried out in this field is primarily qualitative in nature. In what follows, the approach proposed by Richard Watts and myself (Locher and Watts 2005; 2008) will briefly be examined in light of how it treats the interpersonal side of language (for a longer introduction, see Locher 2004; 2012). We propose to use the technical term "relational work" rather than "politeness". The concept "refers to all aspects of the work invested by individuals in the construction, maintenance, reproduction and transformation of interpersonal relationships among those engaged in social practice" (Locher and Watts 2008, 96). This definition highlights that we are interested in more than politeness and in particular in the relational/interpersonal side of language used to create relationships. The research aims are to better understand how people create relational effects by means of language, how this process is embedded in cultural context, and how this is interrelated with historical, social, and cognitive processes. The approach hinges on a number of key concepts, all of which have a relational component: knowledge of frames and norms of different practices, face and identity construction, and judgments of behaviour according to norms. These concepts are all of equal importance and no particular sequence is implied. The key concepts of frames and norms of different practices go hand in hand (see Locher 2012) and are meant to capture the social embeddedness of interaction. In socialisation processes, people acquire knowledge of pragmatic rules that are tied to specific understandings of cultural norms and community of practice norms (see Eckert and McConnell-Ginet 1992). People learn about the rights and obligations of the interactants in particular settings and they acquire knowledge of appropriate action sequences within a practice (frames/scripts/ schemata; see Tannen 1993). It is important to point out that norms are not static but constantly renegotiated through action. This means that norms are at the same time historically embedded and emergent (see also Watts' [1991, 155] useful concept of latent and emergent networks, and Haughet al.'s [2013, 6] observations on "time as infused with historicity").

The second complex of key concepts concerns face and identity construction and the process of judging behavior according to norms. As in many other frameworks, we also adopt the term "face" from Goffman: "The term *face* may be defined as the positive social value a person effectively claims for himself by the line others assume he has taken during a particular contact" (Goffman 1967, 5). This concept is inherently relational since a projected face depends on the update of the addressee for confirmation and face is always at stake (Scollon and Scollon 2001). When people engage in interaction they assess their and other people's contributions in light of the face concerns pertaining to a particular constellation. When doing this, positive and negative emotions[3] play a crucial role and people will label others' and their own behavior with negatively or positively marked first-order lexemes such as *impolite, rude, impertinent, snobbish, refined, cultured, diplomatic, polite*, etc.

Finally, once we have established that people attend to face concerns and take complex considerations of context into account (community of practice norms, knowledge of frames, rights and obligations of the interactants, the history of relationships, etc.), it is a short step to arguing that identity construction is connected to these processes. Ultimately, judging others with emic labels such as *rude, impolite, refined, polite*, or *polished* also adds to the picture that interactants have of the people for whom they have used these labels. In this view, identity is considered dynamic and is defined as "intersubjectively rather than individually produced and interactionally emergent rather than assigned in an a priori fashion" (Bucholtz and Hall 2005, 587; see also Davies and Harré 1990; Spencer-Oatey 2007; Locher 2008; 2012).

People show awareness of different norms of interaction and adopt behavioural and linguistic styles that may maintain, challenge, or enhance their standing towards other interactants in a given situation. As scholars we can describe this pragmatic intraspeaker variation by using terms such as face-enhancing, face-maintaining, and face-aggravating/face-damaging behaviour to describe the relational side of linguistic interaction. The next section points out a number of possible research avenues.

6. Research Synergies and Applications

For scholars interested in the relational aspect of language, the field of interpersonal pragmatics holds many possibilities for interdisciplinarity. I concur with Haugh et al. (2013, 2), who highlight the "inherently interdisciplinary or multidisciplinary" nature of interpersonal pragmatics. For example, they point out the field of "Interpersonal

---

3   In Locher and Langlotz (2008) and Langlotz and Locher (2012; 2013), we discuss the role of emotions in judging as well as the link to relational work and argue that emotions always play a role in questions of face and relational work. Emotions are fundamentally linked to appraisals and to judgments on behaviour even in instances where no linguistic or behavioural surface structure allows the linguist to see evidence of this process (Langlotz and Locher 2013, 91). Haugh et al. (2013, 4) further point out the need to explore the link between interpersonal attitudes, emotions, and evaluations.

Communication", which, while having developed independently from im/politeness research primarily in the United States, is interested in similar linguistic phenomena (Haugh et al. 2013, 1). Within linguistics, there is also a certain overlap of interests with research on identity construction, style, and audience design (see e.g. Bucholtz and Hall 2005; Davies and Harré 1990; Coupland 2007; Rampton 1995). The concepts of positioning, face, and the approach to studying interpersonal communication in different contexts *in situ* is shared by these fields. We can also find overlap of interests with psychology, from which the notion of positioning has been adopted, and with cognitive science/linguistics. The concept of frame, the processes of drawing analogies, of judging according to norms, and the role that emotions play therein are fundamentally also cognitive in nature (see e.g. Culpeper 2011; Langlotz 2010; 2011; Locher and Langlotz 2008; Langlotz and Locher 2012; 2013; Spencer-Oatey 2011). Furthermore, how pragmatic knowledge is acquired when children are socialised (see Scollon and Scollon 1990 for the notion of discourse system) and how adults acquire it in L2 non-immersion contexts, is a thriving field within cognitive and applied linguistics.

When pursuing research within interpersonal pragmatics, there are several options for addressing the field. One possibility is to focus on one or more linguistic strategies that are used for interpersonal effect. In other words, a particular linguistic surface structure is chosen to be studied in detail with respect to what kind of relational effects can be created by using it in different contexts. Examples of such studies are the discussion of mitigation (e.g. Schneider 2010), the study of the multi-functionality of swearing (e.g. Stapleton 2010), and the use of humour (e.g. Schnurr 2010). In contrast, researchers can also choose to focus on particular contexts and practices to explore how the interactants draw on several strategies to create interpersonal effects. Examples of such studies can be found in the chapters of the handbook on *Interpersonal Pragmatics* that explore the settings of the workplace (Vine 2010), courtroom interaction (Cotterill 2010), health discourse (Davis 2010), political discourse (Blas Arroyo 2010), or the discourse of dating ads (Marley 2010). Finally, it is, of course, possible to give centre stage to theoretical considerations and to combine insights from both general trends.

My own recent work in collaboration with Brook Bolander has looked at status updates in Facebook in two focus groups of ten British and Swiss young adults (Bolander and Locher 2010; Locher and Bolander 2014). The strings of brief micro-blogging texts are explored with respect to how language contributes to positioning the self versus others. As the example quoted in the introduction shows, there is a complex creation of in-groups and out-groups happening in front of the direct addressees and the wider reading audience of members of the friends lists. Micro-blogging thus poses interpersonal challenges for the writers that are of interest to scholars. The reflective writing texts of medical students mentioned at the beginning of this chapter can also be explored with a relational lens. The corpus lends itself for studies of linguistic identity construction: How do the students write about themselves in the different roles of students and novice doctors and how do they position the patients, nurses, and doctors in the scenes they describe (see Gygax et al. 2012)? The corpus can also be studied by looking at meta-pragmatic comments on relational issues and concerns. For example, the students give specific importance and value to rapport and empathy (beyond merely mentioning them as communication skills that they were taught in training), and they report that they have become aware of the challenges of communicating appropriately and that the way in which they speak has interpersonal consequences for how they and their fellow colleagues are perceived. Rather than striving for *politeness*, however, the students primarily report that they are worried that they might come across as *rude* or *patronising* (see Culpeper 2011 for similar results). The students also talk about emotions and how challenging it is for them to adequately react to the patients' emotions and their own (Locher and Koenig 2014). These brief pointers have shown that adopting a relational lens when studying interaction opens the research field beyond the study of classic politeness theory.

7. Concluding Remarks

The aim of this chapter was to explore how the relational side of language has been studied in a number of pragmatic approaches over the last forty years. By taking this bird eye's view on the history of politeness research, it has become apparent that the field has been influenced both by the pragmatic turn and by the social turn in linguistics (Langlotz 2011). The pragmatic turn, in its reaction to theoretical linguistics, has inspired work that aimed at discovering universal pragmatic rules that are on a par with syntactic rules. Lakoff, Leech, and Brown and Levinson went for the 'big picture', modelling complex social realities of linguistic communication with a number of constraints (such as differences in distance and power between interactants) that guide linguistic surface structures and their interpretation. That their reduction of complexity – inherent in all modelling work – is meaningful in its own right can be recognised in the fact that hardly anybody would deny that these constraints exist. Criticism about constraints is mainly concerned with their status as universals or the link between linguistic surface structure and relational effect.

Research inspired by the qualitative social turn, i.e., by approaches that analyse language use as a social practice that is performed for social purposes, is interested in how the interpersonal constraints are worked with by interactants in naturally occurring linguistic data. Rather than going for the big, universal picture, this work often offers interpretations of case studies, which can then be used for theory building. A focus on a turn-by-turn negotiation of relational meaning, however, does not mean that quantitative arguments do not have their place in the discursive approaches. For example, if one wants to establish the norms of a particular community of practice, it is important to find means of establishing these norms by looking at the practice over longer periods of time and by repeating analysis in order to discover the patterns. Ultimately, the discursive approaches allow again for more variation (both between groups and within individuals) – variation that had been levelled in the early approaches to politeness.

Ultimately, whether one leans towards one or the other side of the linguistic approaches has to do with what kinds of research questions are posed. The more recent developments in the field have started to look at face-aggravating and conflictual behaviour and by doing this the relational side of language is studied in its entire spectrum. In contrast, the early approaches were intended to theorise how pragmatic meaning is created primarily in situations of cooperation.

It was proposed that the term "interpersonal pragmatics" can be used for all of the discussed frameworks in this paper since the term refers to the particular focus on the interpersonal side of language and communication that they all have in common. My own research path within this field has led me from the early pragmatic theories to thinking of the interpersonal side of language in terms of relational work. The research agenda is then to better understand how people create relational effects by means of language, how this process is embedded in cultural context, and how this is interrelated with historical, social, and cognitive processes. In line with Haugh et al. (2013, 9), I suggest that to achieve these aims, we can work in an interdisciplinary or multidisciplinary manner and draw on past and present politeness research, insights from work on identity and style, cognitive linguistics, communication studies, and psychology.[4]

References

Blas Arroyo, José Luis (2010): "Interpersonal Issues in Political Discourse", in: Locher, Miriam A.; Graham, Sage Lambert (eds.): *Interpersonal Pragmatics*. Berlin/New York: Mouton de Gruyter, 405-434

Bolander, Brook; Locher, Miriam A. (2010): "Constructing Identity on Facebook: Report on a Pilot Study", in: Junod, Karen; Maillat, Didier (eds.): *Constructing the Self*. Tübingen: Narr Francke, 165-185

Bousfield, Derek (2008): *Impoliteness in Interaction*. Amsterdam: John Benjamins

---; Locher, Miriam A. (eds.; 2008): *Impoliteness in Language: Studies on Its Interplay with Power in Theory and Practice*. Berlin: Mouton de Gruyter

Brown, Penelope; Levinson, Stephen C. (1978): "Universals in Language Usage: Politeness Phenomena", in: Goody, Esther N. (ed.): *Questions and Politeness*. Cambridge: Cambridge University Press, 56-289

--- (1987): *Politeness: Some Universals in Language Usage*. Cambridge: Cambridge University Press

Bucholtz, Mary; Hall, Kira (2005): "Identity and Interaction: A Sociocultural Linguistic Approach", *Discourse Studies* 7.4-5, 585-614

Cotterill, Janet (2010): "Interpersonal Issues in Court: Rebellion, Resistance and Other Ways of Behaving Badly", in: Locher, Miriam A.; Graham, Sage Lambert (eds.): *Interpersonal Pragmatics*. Berlin/New York: Mouton de Gruyter, 353-379

Coulmas, Florian (2005): *Sociolinguistics: The Study of Speakers' Choices*. Cambridge: Cambridge University Press

Coupland, Nikolas (2007): *Style: Language Variation and Identity*. Cambridge: Cambridge University Press

Culpeper, Jonathan (2011): *Impoliteness: Using Language to Cause Offence*. Cambridge: Cambridge University Press

---; Kádár, Dániel (eds.; 2010): *Historical (Im)politeness*. Bern: Peter Lang

Davies, Bronwyn; Harré, Rom (1990): "Positioning: The discursive production of selves", *Journal for the Theory of Social Behaviour* 20.1, 43-63

Davis, Boyd (2010): "Interpersonal Issues in Health Discourse", in: Locher, Miriam A.; Graham, Sage Lambert (eds.): *Interpersonal Pragmatics*. Berlin/New York: Mouton de Gruyter, 381-404

Eckert, Penelope; McConnell-Ginet, Sally (1992): "Communities of Practice: Where Language, Gender, and Power All Live", in: Hall, Kira et al. (eds.): *Locating Power: Proceedings of the Second Berkeley Women and Language Conference*. Berkeley, CA: Women and Language Group, 89-99

Eelen, Gino (2001): *A Critique of Politeness Theories*. Manchester: St. Jerome

Fill, Alwin (1990): "Scherz und Streit aus ethnolinguistischer Sicht", *Papiere zur Linguistik* 2.43, 117-125

Fraser, Bruce (1990): "Perspectives on Politeness", *Journal of Pragmatics* 14.2, 219-236

---

4   The examples from the reflective writing texts are taken from research that was funded by the Swiss National Science Foundation in the context of the interdisciplinary project entitled "Life (beyond) Writing": Illness Narratives <illness-narratives.unibas.ch>. I wish to thank Helen Gilroy, Andreas Langlotz, Anne Schröder, and Klaus P. Schneider for their feedback on the oral and written versions of this paper.

Goffman, Erving (1967): *Interaction Ritual: Essays on Face-to-Face Behavior*. Garden City, NY: Anchor Books

Gygax, Franziska et al. (2012): "Moving across Disciplines and Genres: Reading Identity in Illness Narratives and Reflective Writing Texts", in: Ahmed, Rukhsana; Bates, Benjamin (eds.): *Medical Communication in Clinical Contexts: Research and Applications*. Dubuque: Kendall/Hunt, 17-35

Halliday, M.A.K (1978): *Language as a Social Semiotic: The Social Interpretation of Language and Meaning*. London: Edward Arnold

Haugh, Michael (2007): "Emic Conceptualisations of (Im)politeness and Face in Japanese: Implications for the Discursive Negotiation of Second Language Learner Identities", *Journal of Pragmatics* 39, 657-680

--- et al. (2013): "Interpersonal Pragmatics: Issues and Debates", *Journal of Pragmatics* 58, 1-11

Holmes, Janet (1992): *An Introduction to Sociolinguistics*. London: Longman

--- (1995): *Women, Men and Politeness*. New York: Longman

Hutchby, Ian (2008): "Participants' Orientation to Interruptions, Rudeness and Other Impolite Acts in Talk-in-Interaction", *Journal of Politeness Research* 4, 221-241

Hymes, Dell (1974): *Foundations in Sociolinguistics: An Ethnographic Approach*. Philadelphia: University of Pennsylvania Press

Lakoff, Robin Tolmach (1973): "The Logic of Politeness, or Minding Your p's and q's", *Chicago Linguistics Society* 9, 292-305

--- (1990): *Talking Power: The Politics of Language*. New York: Basic Books

Langlotz, Andreas (2011): *Creating Social Orientation through Language: A Socio-Cognitive Theory of Situated Social Meaning*. University of Basel, Habilitation

---; Locher, Miriam A. (2012): "Ways of Communicating Emotional Stance in Online Disagreements", *Journal of Pragmatics* 44.12, 1591-1606

--- (2013): "The Role of Emotions in Relational Work", *Journal of Pragmatics* 58, 87-107

Leech, Geoffrey N. (1983): *Principles of Pragmatics*. New York: Longman

--- (2007): "Politeness: Is There an East-West Divide?", *Journal of Politeness Research* 3, 167-206

Life (Beyond) Writing: Illness Narratives. Universität Basel. <http://illness-narratives.unibas.ch/?Home>

Locher, Miriam A. (2004): *Power and Politeness in Action: Disagreements in Oral Communication*. Berlin: Mouton

--- (2006): "Polite Behavior Within Relational Work: The Discursive Approach to Politeness", *Multilingua* 25.3, 249-267

--- (2008): "Relational Work, Politeness and Identity Construction", in: Antos, Gerd et al. (eds.): *Handbooks of Applied Linguistics*. Volume 2: *Interpersonal Communication*. Berlin/New York: Mouton de Gruyter, 509-540

--- (2011): "Situated Impoliteness: The Interface between Relational Work and Identity Construction", in: Davies, Bethan L. et al. (eds.): *Situated Politeness*. New York/London: Continuum, 187-208

--- (2012): "Politeness Research from Past to Future, with a Special Focus on the Discursive Approach", in: Amaya, Lucía Fernandez et al. (eds.): *New Perspectives on (Im)Politeness and Interpersonal Communication*. Cambridge: Cambridge University Press, 1-22

--- (2013a): "Politeness", in: Chapelle, Carol E. (ed.): *The Encyclopedia of Applied Linguistics*, Oxford: Wiley-Blackwell, n.pag.

--- (2013b): "Relational Work and Interpersonal Pragmatics", *Journal of Pragmatics* 58, 145-149

---; Bolander, Brook (2014): "Relational Work and the Display of Multilingualism in Two Facebook Groups", in: Mass, Christiane et al. (eds.): *Face Work & Social Media*. Münster: Lit-Verlag, in press

Locher, Miriam A.; Graham, Sage Lambert (eds.; 2010): *Interpersonal Pragmatics*. Berlin/New York: Mouton de Gruyter

Locher, Miriam A.; Koenig, Regula (2014): "'All I Could Do Was Hand Her Another Tissue' – Handling Emotions as a Challenge in Reflective Writing Texts by Medical Students", in: Langlotz, Andreas; Soltysik Monnet, Agnieszka (eds.): *Emotion, Affect, Sentiment: The Language and Aesthetics of Feeling*. Tübingen: Narr, in press

Locher, Miriam A.; Langlotz, Andreas (2008): "Relational Work: At the Intersection of Cognition, Interaction and Emotion", *Bulletin Suisse de Linguistique Appliquée (VALS-ASLA)* 88, 165-191

Locher, Miriam A.; Watts, Richard J. (2005): "Politeness Theory and Relational Work", *Journal of Politeness Research* 1.1, 9-33
--- (2008): "Relational Work and Impoliteness: Negotiating Norms of Linguistic Behavior", in: Bousfield, Derek; Locher, Miriam A. (eds.): *Impoliteness in Language: Studies on its Interplay with Power in Theory and Practice*. Berlin: Mouton, 77-99
LPRG - Linguistic Politeness Research Group (eds.; 2011): *Discursive Approaches to Politeness (Vol. 8)*. Berlin: Walter de Gruyter
Marley, Carol (2010): "Interpersonal Issues in the Discourse of Dating Ads", in: Locher, Miriam A.; Graham, Sage Lambert (eds.): *Interpersonal Pragmatics*. Berlin/New York: Mouton de Gruyter, 435-462
Mills, Sara (2005): "Gender and Impoliteness", *Journal of Politeness Research* 1, 263-280
Rampton, Ben (1995): *Crossing: Language and Ethnicity among Adolescents*. London/New York: Longman
Schneider, Stefan (2010): "Mitigation", in: Locher, Miriam A.; Graham, Sage Lambert (eds.): *Interpersonal Pragmatics*. Berlin/New York: Mouton de Gruyter, 253-269
Schnurr, Stephanie (2010): "Humour", in: Locher, Miriam A.; Graham, Sage Lambert (eds.): *Interpersonal Pragmatics*. Berlin/New York: Mouton de Gruyter, 307-326
Scollon, Ron; Scollon, Suzanne Wong (1990): "Athabaskan-English Interethnic Communication", in: Carbaugh, Donal C. (ed.): *Cultural Communication and Interactional Contact*. Hillsdale: Erlbaum, 261-290
--- (2001): *Intercultural Communication: A Discourse Approach*. Oxford: Blackwell
Sifianou, Maria (1992): *Politeness Phenomena in England and Greece*. Oxford: Clarendon Press
Spencer-Oatey, Helen (2007): "Theories of Identity and the Analysis of Face", *Journal of Pragmatics* 39.4, 639-656
--- (2011): "Conceptualising 'the Relational' in Pragmatics: Insights from Metapragmatic Emotion and (Im)politeness Comments", *Journal of Pragmatics* 43.14, 3565-3578
Stapleton, Karyn (2010): "Swearing", in: Locher, Miriam A.; Graham, Sage Lambert (eds.): *Interpersonal Pragmatics*. Berlin/New York: Mouton de Gruyter, 289-305
Taavitsainen, Irma; Jucker, Andreas H. (2010): "Trends and Developments in Historical Pragmatics", in: Jucker, Andreas H.; Taavitsainen, Irma; (eds.): *Handbook of Historical Pragmatics*. Berlin/New York: Mouton de Gruyter, 3-32
Tannen, Deborah (1993): "What's in a Frame?: Surface Evidence for Underlying Expectations", in: Tannen, Deborah (ed.): *Framing in Discourse*. Oxford: Oxford University Press, 14-56
Tracy, Karen (2008): "'Reasonable Hostility': Situation-Appropriate Face-Attack", *Journal of Politeness Research* 4, 169-191
Verschueren, Jef (2009): "Introduction. The Pragmatic Perspective", in: Verschueren, Jef; Östman, Jan Ola (eds.): *Key Notions for Pragmatics: Handbook of Pragmatics Highlights*. Amsterdam: John Benjamins, 1-27
Vine, Bernadette (2010): "Interpersonal Issues in the Workplace", in: Locher, Miriam A.; Graham, Sage Lambert (eds.): *Interpersonal Pragmatics*. Berlin/New York: Mouton de Gruyter, 329-351
Wardhaugh, Ronald (2002): *An Introduction to Sociolinguistics* (4th edition.). Oxford: Blackwell
Watts, Richard J. (1989): "Relevance and Relational Work: Linguistic Politeness as Politic Behavior", *Multilingua* 8, 131-166
--- (1991): *Power in Family Discourse*. Berlin: Mouton de Gruyter
--- (1992): "Linguistic Politeness and Politic Verbal Behaviour: Reconsidering Claims for Universality", in: Watts, Richard J. et al. (eds.): *Politeness in Language: Studies in its History, Theory and Practice*. Berlin: Mouton de Gruyter, 43-69
--- (2003): *Politeness*. Cambridge: Cambridge University Press
--- (2005): "Linguistic Politeness Research. *Quo vadis*", in: Watts, Richard J. et al. (eds.): *Politeness in Language: Studies in its History, Theory and Practice*. Berlin: Mouton de Gruyter, xi-xlvii
--- (2008): "Rudeness, Conceptual Blending Theory and Relational Work", *Journal of Politeness Research* 4, 289-317
Watzlawick, Paul; et al. (1967): *Pragmatics of Human Communication: A Study of Interactional Patterns, Pathologies and Paradoxes*. New York: Norton

BERND KORTMANN (FREIBURG)

Comparison and Comparability: The WAVE Perspective

1. Introduction

Comparability is the key concern of any large-scale comparative enterprise, regardless of whether we are looking at comparative studies in a given discipline or at attempts at making scientific output measurable and, thus, comparable across all academic disciplines.[1] Typically, this means that quantifiable criteria win out over qualitative criteria, so that, for example, in the world of ratings and rankings bibliometric measures are preferred over peer-reviewed quality assessments of selected research papers. In linguistics, the largest-scale comparative enterprises are typological (or: macro-comparative) ones, especially those undertaken with the aim of (literally) mapping linguistic diversity across the globe, as done in the *World Atlas of Language Structures* (WALS; see Dryer and Haspelmath 2013 for its most recent version) and the *Atlas and Survey of Pidgin and Creole Structures* (APiCS; Michaelis et al. 2013), both initiated at, directed from, and electronically hosted by the Max Planck Institute for Evolutionary Anthropology in Leipzig, Germany. The as yet largest-scale comparative enterprise striving to map language-internal (micro-comparative) variation on a global scale is WAVE, which offers ratings, examples, and interactive maps for 235 morphosyntactic features in 50 L1 and L2 varieties of English as well as 26 English-based pidgins and creoles. In print form WAVE comes as *The Mouton World Atlas of Varieties of English* (Kortmann and Lunkenheimer 2012); as an electronic online resource WAVE can be freely accessed as the *Electronic World Atlas of Varieties of English* (eWAVE, last updated in November 2013; www.ewave-atlas.org).

It is from the perspective of (e)WAVE, especially from what it can (and cannot) reveal concerning (dis)similiarities in the morphosyntax across varieties of English and English-based pidgins and creoles, that in this paper some reflections on the central issue of comparability will be offered. In section 2 I begin with a brief review of the typological perspective on comparability and the appropriate choice of categories for macro-comparative (cross-linguistic) comparison, before presenting in section 3 – against the typological background – the WAVE perspective in four steps: A brief introduction to (e)WAVE (3.1) will be followed by a discussion of the nature of the WAVE features (3.2). Next I address the problem that WAVE possibly glosses over important, typically substrate-induced local constraints, as has been pointed out in several recent publications (3.3), before presenting examples of four different types of usage constraints on certain WAVE features (3.4). Section 4, finally, offers some major lessons to be learnt from the WAVE perspective on how much comparability is possible in large-scale comparative studies, and identifies the major challenges and tasks for the

---

[1] For many helpful comments and suggestions the author would like to thank, above all, Alice Blumenthal-Dramé and Klaus P. Schneider.

future design of large-scale mappings of morphosyntactic variation across the varieties of a single language.[2]

2. The Typological Perspective on Comparability

Securing cross-linguistic comparability is the single central premise on which all typological (or: macro-comparative) research rests. As Song (2001, 10) puts it: "Because they study a large number of languages all at once, linguistic typologists must [...] ensure that what they are comparing across languages be the same grammatical phenomenon, not different grammatical phenomena". And Comrie (1989, 134) warns that "[f]ailure to ensure this cross-language comparability would mean that we are not doing language universals research, but are simply analysing each language as an independent unit". But what are the concrete ways of resolving "the apparent paradox of comparability of incommensurable systems" (Haspelmath 2010, 664)? More exactly, which criteria help typologists solving the problem of cross-linguistic identification, which Stassen (2010, 90) formulates as follows: "How can we be sure that the data which we select from the languages in the sample form a coherent body of facts?"

Basically, two types of criteria come to mind in order to identify a given grammatical phenomenon: purely formal or structural criteria (such as certain verbal or nominal markers, determiners, adpositions, complementizers, word order) or "functional – i.e. semantic, pragmatic, and/or cognitive definitions of the phenomenon to be studied" (Song 2001, 10). In the typological tradition established by Joseph Greenberg, the latter type of criteria has been advocated (1966, 74): "I fully realize that in identifying such phenomena in languages of differing structure, *one is basically employing semantic criteria* [sic]". Greenberg's position "has, explicitly or tacitly, been adopted by all authors of major typological studies in the last three decades, and has been canonized in textbooks such as Croft (2003, 13-19)" (Stassen 2010, 92). Thus terms like *Greenbergian typology* and *functional typology* are practically employed as synonyms in the research literature and have largely shaped our understanding of language typology in present-day linguistics. However, to be fair, modern functional typology often also operates with cross-linguistic criteria that are not rooted solely in semantics. "Cross-linguistic criteria that have their basis in pragmatic or discourse-functional notions are also readily permissible" (Croft 2003, 14). Moreover, current typological practice often operates with mixed formal-functional definitions, where "external domain definitions are supplemented by one or more criteria of a formal nature" (Stassen 2010, 95). Take, for example, Stassen's two-part definition of comparative constructions (Stassen 1985, 15), where the semantic foundation – "A construction counts as a comparative construction [...] if that construction has the semantic function of assigning a graded (i.e. non-identical) position on a predicative scale to two (possibly complex) objects" –

---

2   Since (e)WAVE is an outgrowth of the still young research paradigm of producing typologically driven comparative grammars of varieties of a single language, the following account should be seen within the context of a research line that advocates the marriage of language typology and the study of morphosyntactic variation in varieties of English (see especially Bisang 2004; Kortmann 2004; Kortmann et al. 2004; Siemund 2013). Moreover, as the issue of comparability and the "third of comparison" are of fundamental methodological relevance, this paper naturally links up with Anderwald and Kortmann (2013) on the application of typological methods in dialectology.

is coupled with an additional formal criterion: The two compared objects must be expressed by NPs (for the relevant WALS chapter, see <http://wals.info/chapter/121>).

So far we have established the existence of three types of criteria for identifying grammatical phenomena in typological research. Two of these – purely semantic/ functional criteria and mixed formal-functional criteria – are characteristic of typological practice in a Greenbergian or broadly functional tradition and have thus naturally found their way into WAVE. However, purely formal features, too, have been adopted in WAVE (see 3.2 below) even though this is a hotly debated type of identification criterion in typology. This is because formal criteria presuppose the existence of categories whose cross-linguistic validity, let alone universality, is highly controversial in language typology. Which understanding of a typological concept of category has been adopted in WAVE will be made clear below.

In recent years we have witnessed the revival of a debate on the nature of categories to be used in macro-comparative research, which stretches back at least into the late nineteenth/early twentieth century, or to the beginnings of American Descriptivism. Haspelmath has reopened this debate in two relatively recent publications (2007 and especially 2010). In a nutshell, Haspelmath's position can be summarized as follows: There is no such thing as pre-established linguistic categories, which is why "the most important consequence [...] for language typology is that cross-linguistic comparison cannot be category-based, but must be substance-based, because substance (unlike categories) is universal" (2007, 126). Moreover, it is in his 2010 *Language* article on "Comparative Concepts and Descriptive Categories in Cross-Linguistic Studies" that he propagates a return to Boasian categorial particularism, or the view that each language has its own descriptive formal categories, which in turn means that such descriptive categories cannot be compared across languages (2010, 663; see similarly Croft 2001 in his Radical Construction Grammar). Rather what is needed for the purposes of cross-linguistic research on variation in grammar is a special set of comparative concepts exhibiting, among other things, the following properties (Haspelmath 2010, 665): They are (i) created by comparative linguists for the specific purpose of cross-linguistic comparison, (ii) not always purely semantically based concepts, but usually contain a semantic component, (iii) not part of particular language systems, and (iv) they may be labeled in the same way as descriptive categories, but stand in a many-to-many relationship with them (for example, in the grammar of a given language a certain comparative concept may be coded by more than one descriptive category and, vice versa, one descriptive category may code more than one comparative concept). It is this latter property of comparative concepts that leads to two other key statements by Haspelmath on (a) the independence of the enterprises of language comparison and the description of individual languages, and (b) the completely different nature of comparative concepts and (language-particular) descriptive categories. Haspelmath states (2010, 673-674):

> Comparative concepts allow linguists to identify comparable grammatical phenomena in different languages, but by identifying a phenomenon in a particular language as a match of a comparative concept, nothing is claimed about the way in which that phenomenon should be analyzed within the language (what kind of descriptive category should be used for it). Comparative concepts and descriptive categories are quite different kinds of entities that should not be confused.

What makes Haspelmath's take on grammatical comparison so attractive in the context of the present paper is that he has overseen not only WALS (a truly macro-comparative survey by and for typologists), but most recently also APiCS (the typologist's excursion into creolistics, created largely by creolists for creolists and typologists). For many decades, pidgins and creoles had been no-go territories for typologists. With APiCS, for the first time a real effort has been made at making the highly complex grammatical structures of pidgins and creoles comparable (a) among each other and (b) with those of other (non-contact, typically older) languages, as for example covered in WALS. It is interesting how Haspelmath (2010, 678) describes his personal experience when, as a typologist, embarking on the adventure of working with creolists:

> In my own research, I came to feel the need for a clear distinction between comparative concepts and descriptive categories when I got involved in the *Atlas of Pidgin and Creole Language Structures* (Michaelis et al. 2012). [...] The editors had to make it clear repeatedly that the comparative concepts used in the definitions of the features should not be equated with the language-particular descriptive categories that the contributors were used to working with. Thus, it is when language experts and typologists work together directly that the need to distinguish the two kinds of grammatical notions becomes clearest.

This point was absolutely relevant for the process of data collection for WAVE, too, not only for the interaction with contributors on pidgins and creoles, but likewise for the communication with specialists on L1 and L2 varieties of English. This also applies to the next statement by Haspelmath (2010, 681), where he makes clear that the basis of comparison in typological work does not lie in a prior analysis of each particular structural system:

> this is not how typology works. In fact, it cannot work this way because systems are language-particular and do not lend themselves to comparison in an obvious way. Comparative linguists are willing, and indeed forced, to disregard the structural coherence of language-particular systems, and just focus on the properties that they see through the lens of their comparative concepts.

What the comparative linguist is willing, and indeed forced, to do is very hard to accept for the descriptive linguist of a given language or, in cross-varietal language-internal (micro-comparative) surveys, of a variety of a language. This is a recurrent experience we have also had in the process of compiling WAVE.

In this section we reviewed some of the most important statements by leading typologists on comparison and, above all, on cross-linguistic comparability and identification, and we did so because it is on the foundation of these statements that the WAVE methodology was designed and the survey itself compiled. In concluding, one further (and rather serious) comparability problem in language typology needs to be addressed that tends to be overlooked by the typological community. Especially when including languages with a literary tradition, typologists need to exercise more care concerning the (partly striking) differences between the grammars of (standard) written and spontaneously spoken varieties of languages. It is standard typological practice that for the purposes of data collection descriptive grammars are used. For languages with a literary tradition, like most of the European languages, this means that grammars will be consulted that are based on the written standard variety of the relevant language. This is not a problem as long as like is compared with like, i.e., grammars of written standards with grammars of written standards. However, it is also part of standard (and proper) typological practice to work with representative samples, which in turn means that these include languages for which only (often meagre descriptions of) spoken data exist. In other words, typologists seem to be largely unaware of a serious comparability problem. Comparing spontaneous spoken structures with structures characteristic of codified written varieties runs the risk of comparing apples and oranges (a point of criticism already voiced by Miller and Weinert 1998, for example). Generalizations, implicational tendencies, and hierarchies across observations based on these two very different data sets need to be taken with more than just a pinch of salt. This is why far more typologically-driven comparative studies of language-internal variation are needed, which then in turn can be made the basis for typological studies, allowing the research community to compare solely spoken structures across the languages in their sample. Typologically-driven dialectology or, more generally, a typological approach to the study of varieties of English worldwide, as advocated, for instance, in Kortmann 2004 and Siemund 2013, may thus deliver descriptions, observations, and generalizations that can be used as input and, possibly even, an important corrective for language typology.

3. The WAVE Perspective

3.1 Introducing (e)WAVE

WAVE maps morphosyntactic variation in spontaneous spoken varieties across the Anglophone world. In its latest, massively expanded version (eWAVE 2.0, launched in November 2013) it offers ratings, examples, and interactive maps for 235 morphosyntactic features in 30 L1 varieties (10 traditional or low-contact and 20 high-contact varieties) and 18 indigenized L2 varieties of English as well as 26 English-based pidgins and creoles in the following world regions: Africa, America (US plus Newfoundland/Canada), Asia (South and South East), Australia, British Isles, the Caribbean, the Pacific, and, as a convenience category not to be considered as a world region proper, the South Atlantic (represented by the small and extremely isolated high-contact L1 varieties Falkland Islands English, St. Helena English, and Tristan da Cunha English). For details of the compilation method, the informants, the individual variety types and varieties, the rating system and, above all, the set of 235 morphosyntactic features, the reader is referred to Kortmann and Lunkenheimer (2012, 1-6) or http://ewave-atlas.org/introduction. eWAVE 2.0 follows exactly the map format and design of APiCS (not surprisingly, since it was programmed by the same team). Compared with the 74 varieties strong print version (Kortmann and Lunkenheimer 2012) two varieties were added in eWAVE 2.0 (the high-contact L1 variety Philippines English and the South African L2 variety Cape Flats English). Moreover, eWAVE 2.0 offers corrections of about 3% of all feature ratings and about 9% of all ratings of attested features. Of the six possible ratings, the three values for attested features are the following: "A" (feature is pervasive or obligatory), "C" (feature exists, but is extremely rare), and the middle ground "B" (feature is neither pervasive nor extremely rare). Table 1 shows which grammar domains are covered in WAVE, and how the 235 features distribute across these domains:

Grammatical domain	Features (number)	Sum features in group	% of total features
Pronouns	1-47	47	20.0%
Noun Phrase	48-87	40	17.0%
Tense and aspect	88-120	33	14.0%
Modal verbs	121-157	7	3.0%
Verb morphology	128-153	26	11.0%
Negation	154-169	16	6.8%
Agreement	170-184	15	6.4%
Relativization	185-199	15	6.4%
Complementation	200-210	11	4.7%
Adverbial Subordination	211-215	5	2.1%
Adverbs and Prepositions	216-222	7	3.0%
Discourse organization and word order	223-235	13	5.5%

Table 1: Domains of grammar covered in WAVE

3.2 Feature Types

One crucial methodological difference between macro-comparative typological studies, such as WALS and APiCS, and micro-comparative studies exploring language-internal variation, like WAVE, is that for the latter enterprise (a) the notorious problems of cross-linguistic identification are largely non-existent, and (b) formal features, down to the very morph level, can be chosen. The latter characteristic is also addressed in the following statement by Haspelmath in the introduction to the four-volume print version of APiCS: "In dialect atlases, one commonly finds maps displaying the distribution of specific morphs. For example, in Kortmann and Lunkenheimer (2011), Feature 1 is '*She/her* used for inanimate referents'. This makes reference to the specific morphs *she* and *her*. Such features are not possible when one compares languages that are not closely related" (Haspelmath 2013b, xxxvii). The 235 features ultimately chosen were the outcome of a long process of going through the relevant descriptive literature on individual varieties of English and English-based pidgins and creoles and many discussions with experts on the different variety types and different parts of the anglophone world. In the end the two WAVE editors ended up with about 350 features, which for reasons of practicability (what linguist informant would be willing to scan the grammar(s) of that variety or set of varieties he/she is the leading expert for with regard to 350 features?) were boiled down to the current (completely arbitrary) number of 235. Features were selected that were either known or could at least be suspected to be recurrent (see Song 2001 on the importance of recurrence as a relevant factor in the selection of categories for typological comparison), or to offer interesting variation across different variety types and world regions.

The bulk of WAVE features can broadly be classified into those three categories known from typological comparison: purely formal, purely functional, and mixed formal and functional features. The crucial difference (and advantage) in a micro-comparative survey like WAVE is, of course, that it can take a significant "shortcut", as it were: All of its features are formulated relative to (forms and form-function mappings in) Standard English grammar, in order to document a formal and/or functional difference compared with the morphosyntax of Standard English.[3]

Purely formal criteria relating to Standard English forms maintained in non-standard varieties and English-based pidgins and creoles are exemplified in the following features: F8 (*myself/meself* instead of *I* in coordinate subjects), F45 (insertion of *it* where StE favours zero), F48 (regularization of plural formation: extension of *-s* to StE irregular plurals), F68 (*them* instead of demonstrative *those*), and F216 (omission of StE prepositions). However, quite a number of formal WAVE features relate to non-Standard English forms, e.g. F155 (*ain't* as the negated form of *be*), F156 (*ain't* as the negated form of *have*), F157 (*ain't* as generic negator before a main verb), F136 (special inflected forms of *be*), or F137 (special inflected forms of *do*).

Another group of features captures *purely functional criteria* in the sense that the same form or construction is used as in Standard English but with a different meaning or function. Relevant examples include F1 (*she/her* used for inanimate referents), F88 (wider range of uses of progressive *be* + V-*ing* than in StE: extension to stative verbs), F89 (wider range of uses of progressive *be* + V-*ing* than in StE: extension to habitual contexts), F95 (*be sat/stood* with progressive meaning), F108 (*ever* as marker of experiential perfect), F122 (epistemic *mustn't*), F159 (*never* as preverbal past tense negator), F186 (*which* for "who"), or F218 (affirmative *anymore* "nowadays").

Mixed formal and functional features include F211 (clause-final *but* = "though") and F212 (clause-final *but* = "really"), but also features relating to the neutralization of semantic contrasts between different formal categories in Standard English, such as F99 (levelling of the difference between present perfect and simple past: simple past for StE present perfect) or F100 (levelling of the difference between present perfect and simple past: present perfect for StE simple past). The overall effect of having selected the WAVE features along the lines sketched above is a much higher degree of granularity in a cross-varietal survey like WAVE both compared with a cross-linguistic survey like WALS and with the first, much smaller 2004 WAVE forerunner compiled for Kortmann et al. (2004). But, of course, no survey can cover all observable variation. Nor can a survey of this large scope be as fine-grained as (often corpus-based) studies of individual features or form-function mappings in varieties or pidgin/creole languages in natural discourse.

3.3 Limitations and Criticism of WAVE and its 2004 Forerunner: Neglecting the Local Conditions

A crucial point anyone consulting large-scale comparative surveys must keep in mind is that there are (a) strong limits to the variation they allow to capture, and (b) limits to the interpretability of the available data in the relevant survey. Take, for example, the pervasiveness ratings by field workers or informants for the individual features or, related to this, the obvious and perhaps more fundamental problem that each language or variety is represented by a single data point. The latter means that the different degrees of heterogeneity in the individual speech communities are largely glossed over, at least in all that information which can be visualized by way of maps. Put more simply,

---

[3] The relevant formulations are couched in purely descriptive terms, of course, and not in a diction suggesting deviation from the norm.

large-scale comparative surveys may allow us to see the forest for the trees, which is indeed their prime function, but they cannot possibly do full justice to the individual trees (including the special conditions holding for the climate and territory where they grow). Therefore it follows almost naturally that WAVE (and its much smaller 2004 forerunner) has variously received criticism, as will briefly be illustrated below. My point simply is that foregrounding such limitations of WAVE is absolutely justified, but that it is only within narrow confines that any future version of WAVE (or similar endeavour on the horizon) can remedy these drawbacks – largely because this would need to happen at the cost of comparability, probably even at the cost of having to throw overboard the typological approach to language-internal variation altogether. Rather, more local or regional studies on morphosyntactic variation based on corpora or extensive (including ethnographic, sociolinguistic) fieldwork should complement the overall picture that a large-scale survey like WAVE is able to draw. Doing full justice to the local happens at the expense of the global, and vice versa. Thus we should strengthen the documentation, interpretation, and motivation of observable variation within and across varieties of English and English-based pidgins and creoles by (creating and) combining different empirical sources. In other words, we should adopt a multi-methodological complementary approach rather than reshape a given research tool (like WAVE) into one that supposedly captures all variation (even much of the variation on the local level). In my view, the latter approach would lead rather to a weakening of WAVE or similar large-scale typology-driven comparative surveys in linguistics, such as APiCS or WALS.

A frequently made point of criticism concerns primarily (but not exclusively) L2 varieties, pidgins and creoles, namely the neglect of the influence of indigenous local languages on their morphosyntax. For pidgins and creoles, in particular, the danger in motivating the presence of individual morphosyntactic features or even their overall typological profiles is that superstrate-based explanations (i.e., for the anglophone world: certain non-standard varieties of English serving as input varieties) or universalist explanations (i.e., arguing on the basis of psycholinguistically or functionally motivated L2 acquisition universals) are prone to push back the role of the local substrate(s). Recently, this danger has fervently been addressed by Faraclas (2012, 426) for Nigerian Pidgin with regard to the Niger-Congo languages of Southern Nigeria.

Issues like (a) the crucial role of the substrate, often as the source of (b) local constraints on (the form, function, and use of) morphosyntactic categories in the relevant Englishes or pidgin/creole languages, (c) the strongly simplified nature of information available from large-scale cross-varietal surveys like WAVE or, in the following cases, its 2004 forerunner, and (d) the caution with which generalizations across varieties, especially "angloversals" or "vernacular universals" postulated for the anglophone world, need to be treated have repeatedly been addressed in publications on high-contact L1 and L2 Englishes in recent years. For example, in a comparison of Indian English and Singaporean English, Sharma (2009) investigates the 2004 WAVE forerunner features "zero past tense forms of regular verbs", "wider range of uses of progressives", and "deletion of *be*". She identifies strong local constraints on the semantics and use of these features, which in turn she attributes to the impact of Hindi on Indian English and Chinese on Singaporean English. Sharma (2009, 191) concludes that "Surface similarities across New Englishes can be skin deep, diverging dramatically upon closer examination, due to substrate systems or substrate-superstrate interaction. [...] The degree and distribution of a given feature must be understood in relation to the substrate before any universal claims can be made".

The same line of argument can be found in publications by members of the Hamburg team of typology-driven World Englishes research (e.g. in Davydova et al. 2011). Among the morphosyntactic phenomena they have investigated are the present perfect in (different mesolectal varieties of) Indian English and embedded inversion (as in *You know what is Casanova?*) in Indian English, Jamaican English, East African English, Singaporean English, and Irish English. Very much like Sharma (2009), they reach the conclusion that

> careful analysis not only reveals to what extent varieties display interesting similarities, but also, on closer inspection, shows how much real difference can sometimes be hidden below apparent surface similarity. Identical or near-identical surface structures may often hide phenomena that are structurally and historically quite different: what looks the same may not in fact be the same. [...] We feel [...] that much more remains to be done in the field of more detailed analysis of individual varieties, or detailed comparative analysis of small individual domains of grammar across varieties, until conclusive answers about the nature of the universal patterns can be given. (Davydova et al. 2011, 317-318)

Such detailed analysis of individual varieties may also include the analysis of different registers or genres. For some types of discourse, speech communities may prefer their own local style (notably spontaneous narratives), while for others a (mesolectal, upper mesolectal, acrolectal) variety approximating Standard English. I could not agree more on the danger of neglecting local constraints on form, meaning, and use of morphosyntactic elements or constructions, which in turn are often substrate-induced. As Tagliamonte (2009, 127) correctly points out, "even if a feature is universal, it will be subject to constraints. Such constraints reflect universal tendencies as well, but they will manifest differently – by pattern, contrast, and strength – according to the varying constellation of influences in the local setting". In section I look at some examples of local usage constraints drawn from WAVE.

3.4 Usage Constraints on WAVE Features

Broadly, four types of usage constraints – all manifesting local conditions – can be distinguished: (i) constraints within the morphosyntactic system of the relevant variety or pidgin/creole, (ii) constraints restricted to a certain social or ethnic group; (iii) constraints restricted to a certain geographical area, and (iv) stylistic constraints. For each type of constraints some examples will be given from the WAVE data set, drawing especially on the examples and comments provided by the (often native speaker) expert informants. Note that none of the features mentioned below has received an "A" ("pervasive") rating; all features are either rare or at best moderately frequent in the relevant variety.

System-internal constraints: In Liberian Settler English, F30 (non-coordinated subject pronoun forms in object function) is found only with the pronoun *we*. In Sri Lankan English, F77 (omission of genitive suffix; possession expressed through bare juxtaposition of nouns) is possible only when the possessor is human (especially a family member), as in *My friend blog says they broke up recently*. Two other examples of system-internal constraints can be observed in the tense and aspect subdomain of habituality. Thus both in Liberian Settler English (LibSE) and the mesolectal variety of Vernacular Liberian English (VLibE), F90 (invariant *be* as habitual marker) is attested only in temporal or conditional clauses.

Social or ethnic constraints: The following instances of social constraints are again taken from West Africa, more precisely from Ghanaian English and the two WAVE varieties spoken in Liberia. For example, F19 (subject pronoun forms as (modifying) possessive pronouns: first person) is highly stigmatized in both Liberian varieties, being confined to speakers with little formal schooling in LibSE and to the basilect of VLibE. In the latter, the same applies to F32 (distinction between emphatic vs. non-emphatic forms of pronouns). A kind of prestige feature, on the other hand, is F78 (double comparatives and superlatives), the use of which in LibSE indicates settler membership. Largely restricted to another social group, namely younger speakers, is the use of F235 (*like* as a quotative particle) in Ghanaian English. There are no clear examples of ethnic constraints documented in the WAVE material, although such constraints may very well exist.

Regional constraints: Some WAVE features display a regional distribution within individual parts of the anglophone world. Again, for Liberia the use of F68 (*them* instead of demonstrative *those*) in LibSE seems to be restricted to the "upriver area" and is stigmatized as "country". In Hawaiian Creole F112 (anterior *had* + bare root) appears to be restricted to the island of Kaua'I, while F121 (double modals) in Scottish English seems to be restricted to southern varieties, allowing for different collocations in individual varieties.

Stylistic constraints: It goes without saying that the bulk of the WAVE features attested in the 76 data sets qualify as highly informal or colloquial. In the data there is also occasional reference made to a given feature being restricted to a certain genre, as is the case, for example, for F100 (levelling of the difference between present perfect and the simple past: present perfect for StE simple past). In Australian English, it is especially in vivid narratives that one may find the present perfect with reference to specific situations in the definite past. Another large, and as yet largely unexplored, group of instances falling into the broad category of stylistic constraints on morphosyntax deserves to be investigated from the perspective of the emerging field of variational pragmatics, which "investigates macro-social variation, i.e., differences across regional and social varieties of the same language on all levels of pragmatic analysis" (Schneider 2012, 465; see also Schneider and Barron 2008). Especially variational pragmatics phenomena are bound to show the importance of the substrate and entire local habitat of a given variety of English or English-based pidgin or creole, and are thus prime candidates for strengthening the geographical signal of the relevant features.

4. Conclusion and Future Perspectives

Comparison and comparability, key to any comparative enterprise and even more important the larger the scale, come at a price. What we gain in breadth, we are bound to lose in depth. The more we aim to do justice to the specific facts and feature constellations of individual variety types, world regions, areas within them, and individual varieties (ultimately, even, individual speech communities in all their heterogeneity), however, the more comparability is at risk, increasingly limited, and ultimately lost.

Another facet of this problem is that an increase in comparability often comes at the price of abstracting away from the individual language/variety and, at the same time, from its "local habitat". Especially (but not exclusively) for transplanted L1 Englishes, L2 varieties, pidgins, and creoles this means that the influence of indigenous local languages must be neglected. This applies, too, to attempts at motivating or explaining the presence of individual features and observable feature constellations in a certain part of the anglophone world. Especially for pidgins and creoles, the danger in motivations of morphosyntactic features and overall typological profiles is that superstrate-based explanations or universalist explanations push to the background the role of the local substrate(s).

A related point, which underlies much of the skepticism concerning generalizations and, especially, the postulation of angloversals or vernacular universals based on WAVE data (recall the discussion in part 3.3), is the following: Of course, descriptive categories play an important role in large-scale cross-varietal surveys for individual languages. The crucial point for anyone consulting such surveys is, however, not to fall into the "same form – same function" trap. There is always the possibility that the same form may have somewhat different functions and may be subject to different constraints (as outlined in part 3.4) within the relevant morphosyntactic subsystem or speech community of a given variety, pidgin, or creole.

The selection and formulation of features in large-scale surveys has an immediate bearing on the degree of comparability the relevant survey can claim to offer. In the domain of morphosyntax, for example, a significant increase in formal or formal-functional features trying to capture a specific lexical or morphological instantiation of a given morphosyntactic category instead of a range of different instantiations, as e.g. by more openly formulated WAVE features like F4 (alternative forms/phrases for dummy *it*) or F39 (plural forms of interrogative pronouns: using additional elements), might well lead to a reduction of comparability. Ultimately, designing feature sets for large-scale comparative surveys is a balancing act, an attempt to secure as much comparability as possible without at the same time losing too much of the distinctive signal (i.e., structural property) of the individual data point.

WAVE attempts to strike this balance by documenting both sets of forms used for the coding of certain grammatical functions and specific lexical or morphological markers for a certain grammatical function. It goes without saying that large-scale comparative surveys mapping intra-lingual diversity typically have as a (more or less implicit) reference point the standard variety of the given language. In the case of WAVE this is of course Standard English. In terms of methodology, this approach offers a most welcome shortcut in the process of identifying the relevant features to be compared. At the same time, though, quite a number of WAVE features emerged from the other, non-standard end, in the sense that certain form-function mappings or morphosyntactic markers known to exist for a couple or handful of varieties, pidgins, or creoles were meant to be explored on a broad anglophone scale, such as F108 (*ever* as marker of experiential perfect), F109 (perfect marker *already*), or F145 (*gotten* instead of *got*).

Let me finally risk a look into the future of large-scale comparative studies in linguistics. Challenging as it is to secure comparability for any individual large-scale comparative survey, it is even more challenging to design large-scale surveys such that there is also comparability (at least to some degree) across different surveys. APiCS, for example, was and is meant to speak to WALS, especially in terms of feature choice (44 of its 107 features are taken from WALS). If this is clearly formulated as a premise right from the beginning of the design process of a large survey, cross-survey comparability can be reached at least to a reasonable extent. From the WAVE perspective, though, cross-survey comparability has never been an issue, apart from the fact that not only specialists of English, but also creolists and typologists should be able to make good use of it and possibly even adapt it for their own purposes. So far, unfortunately, the comparability of the data for the 26 English-based pidgins and creoles in WAVE with that of APiCS is quite limited. One goal for the immediate future is thus to increase the cross-comparability of WAVE and APiCS, for instance by having a closer look at the real language data and the field workers' and native speaker informants' commentaries for the individual features in the individual (not only English-based) pidgins and creoles.

In the long run, similar large-scale intra-lingual surveys such as WAVE should be orchestrated for other world languages like Spanish, French, Portuguese, and Russian, too, all with rich sets of varieties in different parts of the world (representing the full range of variety types: low-contact L1s, high-contact L1s, L2s, pidgins, creoles). Ideally, such surveys should be modelled as much as possible on existing surveys (without, of course, distorting the representation of the overall typological profile of the relevant world language). Just as APiCS by itself and, possibly, in the future via a merger with WAVE, allows creolists to compare structural properties of pidgins and creoles across the different superstrate/lexifier languages, it will be fascinating to explore via cross-survey studies to what extent, for example, WAVE-based findings for L2 Englishes in different parts of the world are confirmed by (or found to be in striking contrast with) findings for L2 Spanishes, L2 Frenches, etc. This appears to be a worthwhile and by no means unrealistic goal to aspire to. It is a goal that would take us a huge step closer to what Haspelmath (2013a) has recently suggested calling *continent-wide typology* as part of the wider field of *diversity linguistics*, which he defines as "the merging of cross-linguistic comparison and language-particular study into a single field, or at least into a community of linguists that are developing a common language and know that they share many interests" (see his blog <http://dlc.hypotheses.org/340>).

References

Anderwald, Lieselotte; Kortmann, Bernd (2013): "Applying Typological Methods in Dialectology", in: Krug, Manfred; Schlüter, Julia (eds.): *Research Methods in Language Variation and Change*. Cambridge: Cambridge University Press, 313-333

Bisang, Walter (2004): "Dialectology and Typology: An Integrative Perspective", in: Kortmann, Bernd (ed.): *Dialectology Meets Typology*. Berlin/New York: Mouton de Gruyter, 11-45

Comrie, Bernard (1989): *Language Universals and Linguistic Typology*. Chicago: University of Chicago Press

Croft, William (2001): *Radical Construction Grammar: Syntactic Theory in Typological Perspective*. Oxford: Oxford University Press

--- (2003): *Typology and Universals*. Cambridge: Cambridge University Press
Davydova, Julia et al. (2011): "Comparing Varieties of English: Problems and Perspectives", in: Siemund, Peter (ed.): *Linguistic Universals and Language Variation*. Berlin/New York: Mouton De Gruyter, 291-323
Dryer, Matthew S.; Haspelmath, Martin (eds.; 2013): *The World Atlas of Language Structures Online*. Leipzig: Max Planck Institute for Evolutionary Anthropology <http://wals.info>
Faraclas, Nicholas (2012): "Nigerian Pidgin", in: Kortmann, Bernd; Lunkenheimer, Kerstin (eds.): *The Mouton World Atlas of Variation in English*. Berlin/Boston: Mouton de Gruyter, 407-432
Greenberg, Joseph (1966): "Some Universals of Grammar with Particular Reference to the Order of Meaningful Elements", in: Greenberg, Joseph (ed.): *Universals of Grammar*. Cambridge, MA: MIT Press, 73-113
Haspelmath, Martin (2007): "Pre-Established Categories Don't Exist: Consequences for Language Description and Typology", *Linguistic Typology* 11.1, 119-132
--- (2010): "Comparative Concepts and Descriptive Categories in Cross-Linguistic Studies", *Language*, 86.3, 663-687
--- (2013a): "Continent-wide Typology: A Recent Trend within Diversity Linguistics", Blog in *Diversity Linguistics Comment*, <http://dlc.hypotheses.org/340> [accessed 12 Aug 2013]
--- (2013b): "Introduction", in Michaelis, Susanne et al. (eds.): *The Atlas and Survey of Pidgin and Creole Language Structures*. Oxford: Oxford University Press, xxxi-xlviii
Kortmann, Bernd (ed.; 2004): *Dialectology Meets Typology: Dialect Grammar from a Cross-Linguistic Perspective*. Berlin/New York: Mouton de Gruyter
---; Lunkenheimer, Kerstin (eds.; 2012): *The Mouton World Atlas of Variation in English*. Berlin/Boston: De Gruyter Mouton
--- (eds.; 2013): *The Electronic World Atlas of Varieties of English*. Leipzig: Max Planck Institute for Evolutionary Anthropology. <http://www.ewave-atlas.org>
Kortmann, Bernd et al. (eds.; 2004): *A Handbook of Varieties of English*. Vol. 2: *Morphology, Syntax*. Berlin/New York: Mouton de Gruyter
Michaelis, Susanne et al. (eds.; 2013): *Atlas of Pidgin and Creole Language Structures Online*. Leipzig: Max Planck Institute for Evolutionary Anthropology. <http://apics-online.info> [accessed 17 February 2014]
Miller, Jim; Weinert, Regina (1998): *Spontaneous Spoken Language: Syntax and Discourse*. Oxford: Clarendon
Schneider, Klaus P. (2012): "Pragmatics", in: Hickey, Raymond (ed.): *Areal Features in the Anglophone World*. Berlin/New York: Mouton de Gruyter, 463-486
---; Barron, Anne (eds.; 2008): *Variational Pragmatics*. Amsterdam: John Benjamins
Sharma, Devyani (2009): "Typological Diversity in New Englishes", *English World-Wide* 30, 170-195
Siemund, Peter (2013): *Varieties of English: A Typological Approach*. Cambridge: Cambridge University Press
Song, Jae Jung (2001): *Linguistic Typology: Morphology and Syntax*. Harlow et al.: Longman
Stassen, Leon (1985): *Comparison and Universal Grammar*. Oxford: Basil Blackwell
--- (2010): "The Problem of Cross-Linguistic Identification", in: Song, Jae Jung (ed.): *The Oxford Handbook of Linguistic Typology*. Oxford: Oxford University Press, 90-99
Tagliamonte, Sali (2009): "There Was Universals; Then there Weren't: A Comparative Sociolinguistic Perspective on 'Default Singulars'", in: Filppula, Markku et al. (eds.): *Vernacular Universals and Language Contacts: Evidence from Varieties of English and Beyond*. London/New York: Routledge, 103-129

Daniela Kolbe-Hanna (Trier)

The Comparability of Discourse Features: *I think* in Englishes Worldwide

1. Introduction

The rise of variational pragmatics as a linguistic discipline in the last decade (see e.g. Schneider and Barron 2008) has entailed the application of variationist sociolinguistic methods in pragmatic studies. It is now common to analyse the use of different variants of pragmatic variables such as THANKS or APOLOGIES. However, it is questionable whether variationist methods are applicable to constructions with a discourse function, such as comment clauses. Differences in the structure of discourse constructions usually entail a difference in meaning and/or function and thus the *tertium comparationis* is difficult to identify. This paper illustrates different ways of examining the use of the comment clause *I think* in the spoken components of the *International Corpus of English* (ICE) to show the benefits and caveats of applying variationist methods in discourse studies. It aims to explore whether it is feasible to describe a well-defined variable context of *I think* and examine whether the calculation of a linguistic variable has advantages over the comparison of normalised frequencies to compare the distribution of this construction in different corpora.

2. The Comment Clause *I think*

According to Quirk et al. (1985, 1112), "comment clauses are parenthetical disjuncts", optional clauses loosely connected to another clause. In the sentence, they can occur parenthetically, i.e., in initial, medial, and final position. They are "either content disjuncts that express the speakers' comments on the content of the matrix clause, or style disjuncts that convey the speakers' views on the way they are speaking". Biber et al. (1999, 864-865) regard them as one particular realisation of stance adverbials, in the case of *I think* expressing epistemic stance, as in examples (1) and (2):

> (1) She's the first English girl I 've spoken to for about three or four years *I think* (ICE-GB, s1a-020)
> (2) But my friend got it, *I think* about twelve years ago (ICE-GB, s1a-071)

In both examples, the speakers use *I think* to qualify the connected proposition epistemically. Example (1) is ambiguous in scope, since out of context it can qualify the whole noun phrase (*the first English girl I've spoken to for about three or four years*) or just the time reference (*for about three of four years*). So in context, as in (3), it becomes clear that *I think* refers to the time frame, since speaker <A> is not sure when he spoke to an English girl for the last time:

> (3) <D>   What sort of a girl is she
> <A>   Well
> <D>   Is she Chinese

<A>   No she's English
<A>   She's the first English girl I've spoken to for about three or four years *I think*
(ICE-GB, s1a-020)

Thompson and Mulac (1991a, b) have coined the term epistemic parenthetical for non-sentence-initial uses of *I think* as displayed in (1) and (2) and state that these are grammaticalised uses of the "epistemic phrase" *I think* without complementiser in sentence-initial position as in (4):

(4) *I think* she's the first English girl I've spoken to for about three or four years

Van Bogaert (2011) accounts for the grammaticalisation of *I think* from a construction grammar approach and thus shows how this expression is embedded in a network of similar expressions (e.g. *I believe*) and a more abstract construction (the Complement-Taking-Mental-Predicate Construction, CTMP Cxn). Dehé and Wichmann (2010a, b) and Kaltenböck (2008) investigate the prosody of sentences in which *I think* occurs and show that *I think that* is not different in function from *I think*.

3. Data

The analyses presented below draw on unscripted spoken data from the *International Corpus of English* (ICE). The spoken components available at the time of this study are: Canada, East Africa, Great Britain, Hong Kong, India, Ireland, Jamaica, New Zealand, the Philippines, and Singapore. The unscripted spoken parts of these components comprise 500,000 words each, which results in a corpus of altogether 5 million words and about 15,000 instances of the collocation *I think*. However, since the spoken data in ICE-East Africa differ substantially from the make-up of other ICE-corpora, because apparently English is not a medium of private communication (Hudson-Ettle and Schmied 1990, 6-7), they are not included in the analyses below.

4. Two Approaches to the Comment Clause *I think*

A widespread measure of frequency in corpus linguistics is to count instances of a linguistic unit per a certain number of words, as set forth in Biber et al. (1998, 263-264). This measure of normalised frequencies is typically applied in current analyses of pragmatic markers, such as Torgersen et al. (2011); Schweinberger (2011). The resulting findings are initially typically high in recall as they manage to find every instance of the search term, but low in precision, as not every instance found is necessarily identical in function. For instance, a search for all instances of *I think* would not only render comment clause usage, but also uses as subject and verb in a simple clause such as *I think of myself as a non-smoker* (ICE-GB, s1a-015). This requires subsequent manual work to reduce the results to only those instances fulfilling the pragmatic function under analysis as in section 4.1 below.

In sociolinguistic variationist studies researchers typically examine the distribution of different variants of a linguistic variable. According to Labov (1966; 1972), good candidates for linguistic variables "are high in *frequency*, have a certain *immunity from conscious suppression*, are *integral units of larger structures*, and may be easily *quantified on a linear scale*" (Labov 1966, cited from 2006, 32; emphasis given). As integral units of larger structures, the variable should be obligatory for the speaker at the moment of speaking. Linguistically, variants are in free variation, namely functionally equivalent and determined by social factors. Sociolinguistic research relies on the quantification of each variant of the variable and further statistical analyses. The state-of-the-art procedure is logistic regression analysis to gauge the influence of linguistic and social factors on speakers' choice of variants (Kolbe-Hanna and Szmrecsanyi to appear; Szmrecsanyi and Kolbe-Hanna to appear; Tagliamonte and Baayen 2012 offer an overview and outlook). Since Labov's early studies, variationist research has primarily focused on phonetic variables, such as his famous study on the use of postvocalic /r/ in New York, which appeared in second edition forty years later (Labov 2006). The identification of phonetic variables in a recording is possible with high recall as well as with high precision. All pronunciations of words containing a phonemically postvocalic /r/ are actual instances of the variable POSTVOCALIC /r/ and a relevant variant (its realisation or omission) is obligatorily chosen. Especially since the 1980s, sociolinguistic studies have continually also dealt with morphosyntax (e.g. Weiner and Labov 1983; Tagliamonte and Smith 2002). The locus of a morphosyntactic variable as the syntagmatic slot at which speakers have to make a choice is typically identified in corpora via the most frequent matrix expressions. This firstly enables researchers to include zero-variants such as the omission of *that* from sentences such *as I 'd probably suggest that we join at the centre* (ICE-GB, s1b-073) without having to search for zero, which would be an impossible task. Searching for *that* is not an option either because of its multi-functionality as, for instance, demonstrative pronoun or relativiser. Secondly, identifying a larger context in which a variable occurs, for instance, the matrix verb and its argument, helps to represent the point at which a speaker actually has to make a choice and does not start with searching for the potential choices. Thus, searching for the matrix expression yields hits that are high in precision, since they automatically fulfil the desired function, but low in recall, because many uses, for instance, after unusual or infrequent matrix expressions, or in fronted position without any preceding matrix, are not found.

Despite an ongoing discussion whether there ever can be such a thing as a discourse variable (Lavandera 1978; Dines 1980; Coupland 1983; Terkourafi 2011), work in variational pragmatics has illustrated in an excellent manner that and how the variationist approach can be extended to pragmatic features (see also Schneider, this volume). Pragmatic units such as speech acts can be required in specific situations (expressing thanks, requests for information) and speakers have a range of locutionary options to choose from (*thanks, thank you, thanks very much*; *Could you...*, *Would you be so kind as to...*, imperatives). Discourse features such as comment clauses are, however, never required or conditioned to occur (see e.g. Kaltenböck et al. 2011, 861). Considering that an essential criterion for a linguistic variable is its obligatoriness (see above), but an essential criterion for a discourse feature is its non-obligatoriness, the incompatibility is thus rather obvious. It is a moot point whether there can ever be different expressions of the same discourse feature that are functionally truly equivalent. However, reformulations of the Labovian criteria for discourse variables exist, for instance that equivalent variants in discourse must be functionally comparable (Coupland 1983, 461) or have the same procedural meaning (Terkourafi 2011).

The following two subsections illustrate the different kinds of results obtainable from comparing normalised frequencies and from the comparison of variants of a variable.

Based on Labov (e.g. 2006, 27-28) the delimitation of a linguistic variable presupposes exploratory work, which will consist of probing potential lexical alternatives of *I think*. The most promising candidates for a variable context are across lexical categories. In previous research, stance adverbials are repeatedly cited as functionally equivalent alternatives of *I think* (Biber et al. 1999, e.g. 861-865, Dehé and Wichmann 2010). Another context refers to collocations or clusters in which *I think* repeatedly occurs (see Aijmer 1997, 26-29; Hunston 2007); in analogy to variationist studies of morphosyntax, it might be possible to identify the slot in which *I think* most frequently occurs in terms of the collocations or clusters including this comment clause. Hunston (2007, 36) notes:

> Put simply, because there is no one-to-one correlation between form and function, counting forms is not the same as counting functions. On the other hand, there are relations between form and function, and the relations become closer the more specific the form is taken to be (e.g., if it is a phrase, or a word in a pattern, rather than a word).

Hence, even though the same form, i.e., *I think*, does not always fulfil the same function, there are relations between this particular form and its function. It can only function as comment clause because the notion of subjective judgement is entrenched in its form by the first person pronoun and the choice of this word-form. Due to the exploratory and illustrative purpose of this study, statistics will largely remain descriptive. The only independent variable is VARIETY OF ENGLISH, as discussing further potential determiners of speakers' choice between comment clauses would distract from this paper's focus on identifying a useful dependent variable.

4.1 Comparing Normalised Frequencies of the Comment Clause *I think*

In the first step, all instances of the collocation *I think* in the unscripted spoken ICE subcorpora were identified via a concordance search in AntConc (results see Table 1).

ICE-component	n *I think*
Canada	1,194
Great Britain	1,564
Hong Kong	3,353
India	1,015
Ireland	1,286
Jamaica	1,066
New Zealand	1,481
Philippines	1,270
Singapore	1,752

Table 1. Raw frequencies of *I think* in ICE components

Strikingly, the number of instances of *I think* is largest by far in ICE-Hong Kong. Elsewhere the frequencies of *I think* range from 1,000 to 1,600 hits. However, a large part of the ICE-Hong Kong corpus consists of extra-corpus material (often utterances by an interviewer). In this case, 805 instances of *I think* had to be removed from the initial findings, contrasting with around 125 instances of extra-corpus instances of *I think* from all other subcorpora. The resulting 2,548 instances of *I think* still represent a considerably higher frequency of *I think* in ICE-Hong Kong than in any of the other corpora. For all following analyses I used a version of ICE-Hong Kong without extra-corpus material.[1]

---

[1] I would like to thank Sebastian Hoffmann for generating this version of ICE-Hong Kong.

The following analyses will focus on data from Hong Kong and Jamaica, since in Hong Kong *I think* is most frequent and the data from Jamaica exhibit the largest distance from Hong Kong both in usage of *I think* and geographically. As several previous studies are concerned with the use of *I think* in ICE-Great Britain (Kaltenböck 2008; Dehé and Wichmann 2010a, b; van Bogaert 2010; 2011), including this variety as a kind of reference standard was not considered necessary.

As regards actual usage, *I think* in initial position is ambiguous between matrix clause, comment clause, and discourse marker (Brinton 2008, 5; Kaltenböck 2008; Dehé and Wichmann 2010a, b). As discussed by Kaltenböck (2008) and Dehé and Wichmann (2010a), not even the retention of the complementiser *that*, as in (5), is a clear indicator of matrix clause function. Based on prosodic criteria (prenuclear accent on the verb, unstressed pronoun) this instance of *I think that* behaves as a comment clause. The cluster *I think that* is a highly frequent cluster (see below, Table 6 in section 4.2.2) and thus can be reanalysed as an inseparable chunk by speakers.

> (5) Uh when at least among uh Christians uhm uh uh modern contemporary Christians **I think that the problem of faith very often presents itself as an individual problem** (ICE-GB, s1b-028, discussed in Dehé and Wichmann 2010a, 59, emphasis given)

Consequently, the functions are distinguishable only through the analysis of prosody (Dehé and Wichmann 2010a), which is not of central interest for the aim of this paper. Hence, the remainder of this section deals with *I think* in medial and final position in a clause, which are both parenthetical positions and thus mostly comment clauses. The positions of comment clauses are generally initial, medial, or final in sentences (see e.g. Quirk et al. 1985, 1112). However, ICE transcripts of spoken data divide speech into "text units", which "as a general rule, [...] should correspond loosely to orthographic sentences" (Nelson 2002, 4). Consequently, the following analyses assume (content) clauses as syntactic anchor to which comment clauses may be attached (in final position) or inserted (in medial position).

The database was reduced to contain instances of medial and final comment clause *I think*, in the following way: When *I think* was preceded by a finite clausal structure that could be interpreted as a subordinating clause, the instance was deleted even if *I think* did not occur at the beginning of the text unit, as in (6). Obvious non-comment-clause usages such as *I think so*, *I think no*, and *I think of / about* were also removed from the original dataset.

> (6) Uhm <,> before looking into the poem that we are reading this year <,> *I think* it may be helpful if we can <,> narrow down <,> several areas (ICE-Hong Kong, s1b-020)

Sometimes, as in (7), *I think* occurs in final position, but before another clause that is itself introduced by a conjunction. This usage is not final in the text unit, but final in the sense adopted here. A typical medial position is illustrated in (8).

> (7) There are clusters one through nine *I think* <,> and each floor has<,> each cluster have three floors (ICE-Jamaica, s2a-060)
> (8) Is it to be a job <,> uh Cecilia Yeung is conducting another so call *I think* job (ICE-Hong Kong, s1b-075)

Table 2 illustrates raw and normalised frequencies of the comment clause *I think* in medial and final position in unscripted spoken English in Hong Kong and Jamaica. As texts in ICE all consist of roughly 2,000 words, this number of words was considered as the appropriate measure of normalisation (see Biber et al. 1998, 263-264). In Hong Kong English the distribution of the comment clause *I think* across medial and final uses is relatively even (44% vs. 54%) with a slight preference for final position, whereas in Jamaican English, medial position is the preferred option (73%). And while medial *I think* is similarly frequent in both varieties, in final position it is less frequent in Jamaican than in Hong Kong English, which illustrates differences in the frequency of the use of this comment clause between these varieties. However, since the position of *I think* depends on the expression that is commented on, these positions are in no way interchangeable and thus cannot be considered as variants of a variable.

	Medial		Final		Sum	
	n	p. 2,000 w.	n	p. 2,000 w.	N	p. 2,000 w.
Hong Kong	130	0.52	165	0.66	295	1.18
Jamaica	95	0.38	36	0.14	131	0.52

Table 2. Frequencies of *I think* in unscripted spoken ICE-Hong Kong and ICE-Jamaica

In sum, Jamaicans use *I think* in speech less often than people in Hong Kong in general and in clause-final position in particular, but the reason for this difference in usage remains unclear. One explanation might be that speakers of Hong Kong English feel a greater need for marking uncertainty about the whole proposition, but if this is the case, the question arises why speakers should react to this need in clause-final position more than in other positions in the sentence. Sentence-final comment clauses often have scope over the whole proposition (Kaltenböck 2008) and are hence not connected to a specific part of the utterance, which could facilitate their development into politeness markers (Dehé and Wichmann 2010b). Another explanation might be that different strategies of signalling uncertainty exist in Jamaican English than in Hong Kong English.

4.2 Variants of *I think* and the Linguistic Variable

4.2.1 Identifying Variants

As mentioned above, three linguistic contexts lend themselves as potential sources of variants of *I think* which could be subsumed in a superordinate variable, in which *I think* is one of the possible realisations of this variable (like a phoneme as a superordinate context that has several allophonic realisations). Since *I think* expresses epistemic stance, the variable would be epistemic expressions signalling a degree of uncertainty by speakers about the current utterance. As this is true for the large majority of instances of the following expressions, their overall occurrence will again be discussed first. A first attempt at naming a variable or *tertium comparationis* is therefore adverbial and clausal epistemic expressions and the analysis will describe which lexical variants are used in which variety.

According to Biber et al. (1999, 861-865), Thompson and Mulac (2001a, b), and Dehé and Wichmann (2010a, b), comment clauses in general and *I think* in particular assume the function of a sentence adverbial such as *probably, maybe, possibly, presumably, apparently,* and *evidently*. The frequencies of adverbial equivalents were counted in a concordance search, in which I added *perhaps* as a synonym of *maybe*. Table 3 displays the frequencies of the sentence adverbials, which are roughly equal to the frequencies of *I think* (see Table 2).

all positions	Jamaica		Hong Kong		Total
	n	p. 2,000 w.	n	p. 2,000 w.	n
probably	352	1.41	193	0.77	545
maybe	233	0.93	605	2.42	838
perhaps	70	0.28	176	0.70	246
possibly	30	0.12	11	0.04	41
presumably	2	0.01	7	0.03	9
apparently	37	0.15	13	0.05	50
evidently	0	0.00	1	0.00	1
sum	724	2.90	1006	4.02	1730

Table 3. Frequencies of epistemic adverbials in the corpora

Another source of variation is the verb in the comment clause. As observed by Biber et al. (1999, 982-983), *I guess* is a well-established alternative of *I think* in American English. In her discussion of the constructional grammaticalisation of *I think* van Bogaert (2011, 320) shows how the use of *I think* should be seen not as a singular construction, but that it serves as a "template onto which [...] other CTMPs [Complement-Taking-Mental-Predicates] are modelled". Thus, the macro-construction *I* + cognitive verb or CTMP Cxn branches out into several combinations of *I* + *think* and other cognitive verbs which themselves may occur in several forms, e.g. *I think, I thought, I would think, I believe, I'd expect*. The cognitive verbs that occur in the same construction as *I think* are *guess, imagine, reckon, suppose, believe, expect, understand*, and *realize*. Since *it seems* and *it appears* are non-personal expressions that may express uncertainty, Dehé and Wichmann (2010b) also include them in their analysis of epistemic parentheticals, or comment clauses. Table 4 illustrates frequencies of these epistemic expressions, again identified through concordance searches.

all positions	Jamaica		Hong Kong		Total
	n	p. 2,000 w.	n	p. 2,000 w.	n
I guess	194	0.78	65	0.26	259
I believe	68	0.27	73	0.29	141
I suppose	19	0.08	31	0.12	50
it seems	40	0.16	76	0.30	116
I imagine	6	0.02	1	0.00	7
it appears	7	0.03	8	0.03	15
sum	334	1.34	254	1.02	588

Table 4. Frequencies of the clausal epistemic expressions in the corpora

In sum, non-*I think* comment clauses are more frequent in Jamaican English than in Hong Kong English, and this is largely due to the higher frequency of *I guess*. In this respect Jamaican English is similar to American English, where *I guess* is used on par with *I think* (Biber et al. 1999, 982-983).

As frequencies of *I think* exhibited a larger varietal difference in final position, the hypothesis was that more non-*I think* variants in Jamaican English were accountable for this difference in usage. So based on using wider context in the concordance files as well as inspection of the corpus files, sentence adverbial and other clausal epistemic markers in final position were used for further analysis. Table 5 exhibits the frequencies of these epistemic expressions as clause-final comments in the two corpora. As these are very low, no normalised counts are shown (all individual frequencies < 0.05 except for *I guess* in Jamaican English = 0.05).

Whether the one example of *probably* in ICE-Jamaica, given in (9), is actually final, is disputable, as the speaker later repeats it in a continuation of the previous utterance. Its occurrence adjacent to *I think* indicates a greater degree of hedging than if only one of the two expressions was used:

(9) <A> So uhm found any university <?> by this</?>
 <B> Uhm yes university Georgia State University I think *probably*
 <B> Yeah
 <B> **Probably** that one
 (ICE-JA, s1a-067)

Example (10) illustrates a typical instance of an epistemic adverbial in final position, which could be replaced by *I think*.

(10) The other possibility of course is to uhm put restraint on wages voluntary restraint *perhaps* (ICE-Hong Kong, s1b-022)

Any speculations that Jamaican English makes up for its lack of comment clause *I think* in final position by the use of sentence adverbials or other comment clauses cannot be confirmed, as overall, epistemic marking is more frequent in Hong Kong English again. Thus, the impression is confirmed that there is a general tendency to use more epistemic markers in Hong Kong English. Only *I guess* and *probably* appear to be more frequently used in Jamaican English, while there seems to be some preference for *I suppose* and *maybe* in Hong Kong English.

Final	Jamaica	Hong Kong	Total
probably	1	2	3
maybe	0	8	8
perhaps	6	6	12
possibly	0	0	0
presumably	1	2	3
apparently	1	0	1
evidently	0	0	0
I guess	12	4	16
I believe	1	2	3
I suppose	0	7	7
it seems	0	0	0
I imagine	1	0	1
it appears	0	0	0
sum	23	31	54

Table 5. Frequencies (n) of final epistemic adverbials in the corpora

4.2.2 *Tertium Comparationis*: A Linguistic Variable?

As mentioned above, a contextual structure that could serve as *tertium comparationis*, or the variable context, is word clusters in which *I think* appears that fulfil a pragmatic function. The most frequent clusters including *I think* in the database are displayed in Table 6. They could all be described as potential utterance launchers (see Biber et al. 1999, 1003-1005). According to the transitional probability measure available in AntConc, only those clusters beginning with a conjunction, *uh(m)*, and *well* show high association in the cluster (marked by *, if the probability was 0.15 or higher). They provide us with an insight into sentence-initial use of *I think* and other epistemic clauses, because they are all used to introduce a statement. As Dehé and Wichmann (2010a) observe, the functions of *I think (that)* and *I believe (that)* in sentence-initial position – matrix clause, comment clause, and discourse marker – are distinct in prosody only. Without discussing the prosody, the following analysis therefore pertains to epistemic clauses in general, which will function as *tertium comparationis*. Since initial position is the most frequent option, it is also most likely to exhibit variation.

I think it n 469	*uh(m) I think* n 257*	*so I think* n 140*
I think that n 365	*I think I* n 241	*I think we* n 140
I think it's n 293	*but I think* n 226*	*because I think* n 82*
and I think n 257*	*I think the* n 208	*well I think* n 70*

Table 6. Most frequent clusters (3-5 grams) in the corpora

These most frequent clusters most readily lend themselves to examine the choice of verb in the cluster, so the last analysis in this paper focusses on the variation in the verb used in epistemic utterance launchers. One advantage of defining the variable as a larger construction is the opportunity to search for verbs in this construction that have not yet been discussed in previous research. Thus, the *tertium comparationis* is an utterance launcher that can accommodate more than one verb.

The 3-word clusters beginning with *and / because / but / so / uh(m/u) / well* were identified in the corpora using AntConc's clusters tool. Table 7 illustrates the variation in the choice of verb based on van Bogaert's (2011) taxonomy of the CTMP Construction.

	Hong Kong		Jamaica	
	n	%	n	%
I assume	3	0.4	3	0.8
I believe	17	2.1	18	4.6
I expect	1	0.1	0	0.0
I guess	18	2.2	71	18.0
I imagine	0	0.0	1	0.3
I realize	4	0.5	1	0.3
I suppose	7	0.9	11	2.8
I think	761	93.5	287	72.8
I understand	3	0.4	2	0.5
Total	814		394	
total ≠*think*	53	6.5	107	27.2

Table 7: Aggregate frequencies of CTMPs in utterance launchers in the corpora

Overall, as is by now no surprise, epistemic utterance launchers are significantly more frequent in Hong Kong English than in Jamaican English. This higher frequency of utterance launchers overall is mostly due to the highly frequent use of *I think*, which accounts for almost all instances (93.5%) of the variable in Hong Kong, and only for 73% of the variable in the Jamaican data. Once more, *I guess* is mostly responsible for this difference in usage. Measured in percentages, *I suppose* and *I believe* make up a larger proportion of utterance launchers in Jamaica than in Hong Kong, while, measured in normalised frequencies, *I suppose* occurs more frequently in the data from Hong Kong. Nevertheless, the predominance of *I think* in Hong Kong English persists, providing more support for the hypothesis that the use of *I think* in this variety is perhaps developing into a politeness marker (see Dehé and Wichmann 2010b). As regards statistical significance, the distributions of the frequencies of verbs in each corpus are not significantly different from each other (Paired t-test, Welch Two Sample t-test, p=0.6)[2]. Given the overall distribution of the data, *guess* is more frequent than expected in the Jamaican data and *think* is more frequent than expected in the Hong Kong data (which is 60 instances of *guess* and 29 of *think*). Standardised residuals indicate how far an observed frequency diverges from an expected frequency, in this case the measure of divergence is 9.86 for *guess* in Jamaica (and -9.86 in Hong Kong), and 9.92 for *think* in Hong Kong (and -9.92 in Jamaica). Measures of (-/+) 2 or larger are considered to be statistically significant (McPherson 2001, 200-201), so that the difference between *suppose* (+2.6 in Jamaica) and *believe* (+2.4 in Hong Kong) is also significant.

The examination of the clusters also showed the following further variants of *think* in utterance launchers: *mean* (89 in Hong Kong, 136 in Jamaica), *figure* (3 in Jamaica), *know* (36 in Hong Kong, 57 in Jamaica), and general variation in the verb phrase such as past tense or use of auxiliaries. Another potential variant of *I think* is also *I would say* (38 occurrences in total in Jamaica, 71 in Hong Kong). Of these, *figure* is closest to the cognitive verbs in the CTMP construction according to van Bogaert (2011) and *I would say* also expresses uncertainty, whereas *I mean* is a well-known discourse marker and *know* expresses certainty.

5. Summary and Conclusion

In order to identify a *tertium comparationis* for the comment clause *I think* two different measures are available: comparing (normalised) textual frequencies and comparing the percentages of speakers' choices of a linguistic variable of which *I think* is one variant. This paper has illustrated the benefits and shortcomings of both approaches by means of sample analyses of unscripted spoken data from Hong Kong English and Jamaican English.

All analyses showed a higher frequency of epistemic marking in Hong Kong English, and a predominance of the cluster *I think*, especially in this variety of English. The preference for *I think* in Hong Kong English has been noted in previous research in an

---

2   The software R was applied for all statistical analyses. As regards statistical significance, a p-value of 0.05 or less is conventionally considered to exhibit statistical significance, which indicates the probability that a result is due to chance as 5% (or less).

analysis of discourse marker use (Fung and Carter 2007). In Jamaican English, *I guess* is a common alternative.

Another potential variable context that is implicitly present throughout this paper is the position of *I think* in the utterance. However, as discussed above, these different positions are associated with different functions and different scope, so they cannot be considered functionally equivalent variants.

The advantage of using a variable in a clearly defined construction is that it facilitates the gauging of the influence of many potential factors on a speaker's choice of verb in utterance launchers, such as the association of individual verbs with a specific connecting device, speakers' age, or speakers' sex. Thus, analyses employing a linguistic variable have more explanatory power. However, the choice of a different verb always implies a change in meaning and qualitative analyses will have to examine whether this always entails a change in function. In addition, these qualitative analyses will provide a more precise view on the negotiation of stance in general, as stance is dialogic in nature and always related to co-text and context (see Du Bois 2007) and they will provide more insight into the potential development of *I think* as a politeness marker.

References

Aijmer, Karin (1997): "I think: an English Modal Particle", in: Swan, Toril; Westvik, Olaf Jansen (eds.): *Modality in Germanic Languages*. Berlin: Mouton de Gruyter, 1-47

Biber, Douglas et al. (1998): *Corpus Linguistics: Investigating Language Structure and Use*. Cambridge: Cambridge University Press

--- (1999): *Longman Grammar of Spoken and Written English*. Harlow, England: Longman

Brinton, Laurel J. (2008): *The Comment Clause in English*. Cambridge: Cambridge University Press

Coupland, Nikolas (1983): "Patterns of Encounter Management: Further Arguments for Discourse Variables", *Language in Society* 12.4, 459-476

Dehé, Nicole; Wichmann, Anne (2010a): "Sentence-Initial *I think (that)* and *I believe (that)*: Prosodic Evidence for Use as Main Clause, Comment Clause and Discourse Marker", *Studies in Language* 34.1, 36-74

--- (2010b): "The Multifunctionality of Epistemic Parentheticals in Discourse: Prosodic Cues to the Semantic-Pragmatic Boundary", *Functions of Language* 17.1, 1-28, DOI: 10.1075/fol.17.1.01deh

Dines, Elizabeth R. (1980): "Variation in Discourse: 'And Stuff Like That'", *Language in Society* 9.1, 13-31

Du Bois, John (2007): "The Stance Triangle", in: Englebretson, Robert (ed.): *Stancetaking in Discourse: Subjectivity, Evaluation, Interaction*. Amsterdam/Philadelphia: Benjamins, 139-182

Fung, Loretta; Carter, Ronald (2007): "Discourse Markers and Spoken English: Native and Learner Use in Pedagogic Settings", *Applied Linguistics* 28.3, 410-439

Hudson-Ettle, Diana M.; Schmied, Josef (1999): *Manual to Accompany The East African Component of The International Corpus of English ICE-EA: Background Information, Coding Conventions and Lists of Source Texts*. Chemnitz: Chemnitz University of Technology, Department of English

Hunston, Susan (2007): "Using a Corpus to Investigate Stance Quantitatively and Qualitatively", in: Englebretson, Robert (ed.): *Stancetaking in Discourse: Subjectivity, Evaluation, Interaction*. Amsterdam: Benjamins, 27-48

International Corpus of English. <http://ice-corpora.net/ice/>

Kaltenböck, Gunther (2008): "Prosody and Function of English Comment Clauses", *Folia Linguistica* 42.1, 83-134

--- et al. (2011): "On Thetical Grammar", *Studies in Language* 35.4, 852-897

Kolbe-Hanna, Daniela; Szmrecsanyi, Benedikt (to appear): "Grammatical Variation", in: Biber, Douglas; Reppen, Randi (eds.): *The Cambridge Handbook of English Corpus Linguistics*. Cambridge: Cambridge University Press
Labov, William (1966): "The Linguistic Variable as a Structural Unit", *Washington Linguistics Review* 3, 4-22
--- (1969): "Contraction, Deletion and Inherent Variability of the English Copula", *Language* 45, 715-762
--- (1972): *Sociolinguistic Patterns*. Philadelphia: University of Pennsylvania Press
--- (2006): *The Social Stratification of English in New York City*. 2nd edition. Cambridge/New York: Cambridge University Press
Lavandera, Beatriz R. (1978): "Where Does the Sociolinguistic Variable Stop?", *Language in Society* 7.2, 171-182
McPherson, Glen (2001): *Applying and Interpreting Statistics: A Comprehensive Guide*. 2nd edition. New York: Springer
Nelson, Gerald (2002): "Markup Manual for Spoken Texts". <http://ice-corpora.net/ice/manuals.htm> [accessed 10 January 2014]
Quirk, Randolph et al. (1985): *A Comprehensive Grammar of the English Language*. London: Longman
Schneider, Klaus; Barron, Anne (2008): *Variational Pragmatics: A Focus on Regional Varieties in Pluricentric Languages*. Amsterdam: Benjamins
Schweinberger, Martin (2011): The Discourse Marker LIKE: A Corpus-Based Analysis of Selected Varieties of English. PhD thesis. Hamburg University, Hamburg. English department
Szmrecsanyi, Benedikt; Kolbe-Hanna, Daniela (to appear): "New Ways of Analyzing Dialect Grammars: Complementizer Omission in Traditional British English Dialects", in: Grondelaers, Stefan; van Hout, Roeland (eds.): *Proceedings of the Workshop New Ways of Analyzing Syntactic Variation*. Berlin: De Gruyter Mouton
Tagliamonte, Sali A.; Smith, Jennifer (2002): "'Either It Isn't or It's Not: NEG/AUX Contraction in British Dialects", *English World-Wide* 23.2, 251-281
Tagliamonte, Sali A.; Baayen, Harald R. (2012): "Models, Forests, and Trees of York English: *Was/were* Variation as a Case Study for Statistical Practice", *Language Variation and Change* 24.2, 135-178, DOI: 10.1017/S0954394512000129
Terkourafi, Marina (2011): "The Pragmatic Variable: Toward a Procedural Interpretation", *Language in Society* 40.3, 343-372
Thompson, Sandra; Mulac, Anthony (1991a): "A Quantitative Perspective on the Grammaticization of Epistemic Parentheticals in English", in: Heine, Bernd; Traugott, Elizabeth Closs (eds.): *Approaches to Grammaticalization, vol. 2*. Amsterdam: Benjamins, 313-329
--- (1991b): "The Discourse Conditions for the Use of the Complementizer *that* in Conversational English", *Journal of Pragmatics* 16, 237-251
Torgersen, Eivind Nessa et al. (2011): "A Corpus-Based Study of Pragmatic Markers in London English", *Corpus Linguistics and Linguistic Theory* 7.1, 93-118, DOI: 10.1515/CLLT.2011.005
Van Bogaert, Julie (2010): "A Constructional Taxonomy of I Think and Related Expressions: Accounting for the Variability of Complement-Taking Mental Predicates", *English Language and Linguistics* 14.3, 399-427, DOI: 10.1017/S1360674310000134
--- (2011): "I Think and Other Complement-Taking Mental Predicates: A Case of and for Constructional Grammaticalization", *Linguistics and Philosophy* 49.2, 295-332
Weiner, Judith; Labov, William (1983): "Constraints on the Agentless Passive", *Journal of Linguistics* 19, 29-58

STEPHANIE HACKERT (MÜNCHEN) AND ANNE SCHRÖDER (BIELEFELD)

Comparing Tense and Aspect in Pidgins and Creoles: Dahl's Questionnaire and Beyond

1. Introduction

Tense and aspect constitute a central area of research on pidgin and creole languages and have been the topic of a number of studies on either particular pidgins and creoles (e.g. Faraclas 1987; Schröder 2003; Hackert 2004) or on pidgins and creoles in general (e.g. Singler 1990b). However, some of the attempts to describe tense and aspect in these languages can be referred to as 'Anglicist,' as "they describe the system in terms of Standard English" (Schröder 2012a, 171), frequently equating pidgin or creole forms with English tenses and thus taking (either explicitly or implicitly) English as a *tertium comparationis*.

Another approach is Bickerton's (1981, 58) creole model of "anterior" tense, "irrealis" mood, and "non-punctual" aspect. It is true that with Bickerton's publications, "TMA [i.e., tense, mood, and aspect] became the pre-eminent site for the discussion of the phenomenon of the shared properties of creoles and for the debate about its explanation" (Singler 1990a, viii); nevertheless, this model, too, has caused tremendous problems in its application to different pidgins and creoles.

The present paper contrasts tense and aspect in Cameroon Pidgin English (CamP) and Bahamian Creole English (BahCE) with tense and aspect in (Standard) English by means of a language-independent method, which is intended to provide "comparable data on the TMA systems of a large number of languages" (Dahl 1985, 2) and has been judged especially suitable for the investigation of creole tense and aspect systems (Winford 1996a, 321). Nevertheless, it has not yet been widely applied in pidgin and creole studies.

By using data elicited with the help of Dahl's TMA questionnaire (1985), we intend to go beyond the simple juxtaposition and possible translation of language structures and to represent correspondences between the three languages in question in a more systematic manner. Finally, we will present a brief discussion of another tool of cross-linguistic comparison, i.e., semantic maps, and evaluate their usefulness for the description of the tense-aspect systems of pidgins and creoles.

2. Contrastive Approaches to Pidgins and Creoles: 'Anglicist' and 'Creolist' Perspectives

With regard to CamP, many of the descriptions of its tense and aspect system describe this language in terms of English. In Ayafor (2000), for example, the various verbal constructions in this language are referred to as 'tenses' and thus the preverbal marker *di* is equated with the English Simple Present and the Present Progressive. As Ayafor elaborates, "the simple present and the present continuous are expressed in the same way in [CamP]" (Ayafor 2000, 6). The fact that *di* may also express habitual meaning is neglected in Ayafor's analysis, as is the HABITUAL altogether – possibly because this is a category not morphologically marked in English (see Schröder 2012a).

Bickerton's model of tense, mood, and aspect marking in creoles, which is based on a comparison of the TMA systems of Sranan, Guyanese Creole, Haitian Creole, and Hawai'i Creole English, consists of two components: an inventory of three categories ("anterior" tense, "irrealis" mood, and "non-punctual" aspect) and an invariant ordering in which the preverbal particles instantiating these categories occur if they do so in combination (tense – mood – aspect). The parameter crucially influencing the meaning of particular verb structures in this putatively "typical" creole TMA system is the stative/nonstative distinction (Bickerton 1981, 58). Unfortunately, even the four creoles that form the basis of Bickerton's generalizations do not, upon closer inspection, conform to the model. Sranan, for example, does not possess only a single tense marker ("anterior") but grammatically marks future time as well. Even worse, not only one but two categories cover the semantic space of future temporal reference. Whereas *o* expresses the speaker's certainty and/or intention about situations to come, *sa* generally refers to dubitative situations (Winford 1996b, 74). The model has proven even more problematic in its application to other pidgins and creoles, and numerous scholars have recognized the need to depart from it in the description of creole TMA systems (see Winford 1996b, 82).

3. Contrasting Tense and Aspect in CamP, BahCE, and English

3.1 The TMA Questionnaire

The data presented here were elicited with the help of a reduced version of a questionnaire originally developed by Östen Dahl (1985). Dahl used this questionnaire to investigate tense and aspect in 64 languages from various genetic groups all over the world and his study has been described as "one of the most influential contributions to the study of tense, mood and aspect" (Bache 1995, 36). The advantage of this questionnaire is that parallel data for different languages can be elicited and that it constitutes a *tertium comparationis* in the true sense. The questionnaire consists of sentences as well as short connected texts in English that are accompanied by indications of the contexts in which these sentences or texts are assumed to have been produced. Informants are asked to translate them into the language under investigation. The verb is always given in the infinitive, which helps to minimize literal translations of English tense and aspect categories (see Dahl 1985, Chapter 2). For CamP, the questionnaire was filled in by fifteen Cameroonians in Cameroon, representing a cross-section of the educated population. In addition, it was completed by four educated native speakers of British English living in Germany as well as nine educated native speakers of American English living in the US. In the Bahamas, the questionnaire was administered to five highly educated bilingual speakers of BahCE: a journalist, a civil servant, a college lecturer, and two employees from the top echelons of the private sector, one of them being an amateur actor in local productions staged in creole. All elicitations were tape-recorded and later transcribed.

In identifying cross-linguistic similarities in TMA systems, Dahl takes as his basic unit of investigation the actual TMA category itself. Individual categories are identified "by their foci or prototypical uses"; consequently, languages can be compared along two dimensions: "(i) which categories they choose out of the set of cross-linguistic categories, (ii) how they reduce the impreciseness that these categories have in choosing among the possible secondary or non-focal uses they have." According to Dahl, the "foci and extensions of categories may be seen as points and regions respectively in a multi-dimensional 'conceptual space'" (1985, 33). Thus, three levels of description must be distinguished: a basic level of semantic space, a second level of cross-linguistic TMA categories, and a third level of language-specific tenses, moods, and aspects. We follow Dahl's (and others') practice of distinguishing between these three levels in typography: initial capitals (e.g. Simple Past) signal language-specific categories; capitals refer to cross-linguistically occurring category types (e.g. PAST); and lower-case spelling denotes a semantic-conceptual value (e.g. past).

CamP and BahCE are the only two pidgin or creole languages whose TMA systems have been investigated with the help of Dahl's TMA questionnaire and for which parallel data are thus available. This choice, albeit by chance, is extremely fortunate, because although both languages are Atlantic English-lexifier contact varieties, in terms of their social history and current status they cover a wide range of variety types: BahCE is a creole, probably a late eighteenth-century offshoot of Gullah, a North American creole that had formed in the first half of the eighteenth century (see Hackert and Huber 2007). In structural terms, BahCE is much closer to English than most other English-lexifier pidgins and creoles (see Hackert 2012; Hackert 2013). CamP is a variety of West African Pidgin English (WAPE) and thus structurally very close to Nigerian Pidgin, Krio, and Ghanaian Pidgin (see Schröder 2012b). It has been put to a wide variety of uses, has developed into a fully-fledged language and is therefore referred to as an extended pidgin. It is highly variable, influenced at the acrolectal end by Cameroon's official languages English and French, and at the basilectal end by indigenous languages (Schröder 2012b; Schröder 2013).

3.2 Results and Evaluation

For this paper, we decided to have a closer look at the categories PROGRESSIVE, HABITUAL, and PERFECT, because we believe these to show the most striking differences between the systems in question. In the following, we discuss the translations provided by the informants for sentences of the TMA questionnaire that, according to Dahl (1985), are likely to elicit prototypical uses of these universal categories.

3.2.1 Prototypical Uses of the PROGRESSIVE and the HABITUAL

According to Dahl (1985, 92), prototypical occurrences of the PROGRESSIVE can be elicited by sentences such as the following (sentence numbers correspond to those in the original questionnaire used by Dahl):

(5) [Q: What your brother DO right now? (= What activity is he engaged in?) A by someone who can see him:] He **WRITE** letters
(6) [Q: What your brother DO right now? (= What activity is he engaged in?) A by someone who can see him:] He **WRITE** a letter
(9) [A: I went to see my brother yesterday. B: What he DO? (= What activity was he engaged in?) A:] He **WRITE** letters
(10) [A: I went to see my brother yesterday. B: What he DO? (= What activity was he engaged in?) A:] He **WRITE** a letter

Basically all of the English-speaking informants used the Present Progressive or the Past Progressive in their translations of these sentences. All Cameroonian informants translated sentences (5) and (6) with simple preverbal *di*. The Bahamian speakers used the *-ing* form of the verb. For sentences with an additional past meaning, i.e., (9) and (10), *di* was used in combination with *bin* by the majority of Cameroonian informants; Francophone informants used a combination of *bin* plus *bi(n)* (see Féral 1989). In the Bahamas, *was* + *V-ing* was used. The results are summarized in Table 1:

Sentence No.	CamP	BahCE	English
(5)	*di*	V-*ing*	Present Progressive
(6)	*di*	V-*ing*	Present Progressive
(9)	*bin+di / (bin+bi(n))*	*was* + V-*ing*	Past Progressive
(10)	*bin+di / (bin+bi(n))*	*was* + V-*ing*	Past Progressive

Table 1: Prototypical occurrences of the PROGRESSIVE in CamP, BahCE, and English

These results suggest that CamP *di* can safely be regarded as functioning as the progressive marker and as corresponding roughly to the English Progressive. As for BahCE, progressive meaning is expressed via the *-ing* form of the verb, just as in English, but the status of the auxiliary is different in that it is absent in sentences with present reference but present in those with past reference.

Prototypical occurrences of the HABITUAL can be elicited by sentences such as the following (Dahl 1985, 97):

(18) [Q: What your brother usually DO after breakfast A:] He **WRITE** letters
(19) [Q: What your brother usually DO after breakfast A:] He **WRITE** a letter
(20) [Q: What your brother usually DO after breakfast last summer? A:] He **WRITE** letters
(21) [Q: What your brother usually DO after breakfast last summer? A:] He **WRITE** a letter
(31) [Of a visible lake, what the water is usually like] It **BE COLD**

For a more generic meaning, sentence (73) elicits prototypical occurrences (Dahl 1985, 99):

(73) [Q: What kind of sounds do cats make? A:] They **MEOW**

Virtually all CamP informants translated these sentences with simple preverbal *di*, combined with preverbal *bin* in past contexts (sentences (20) and (21)). Francophone Cameroonians preferred a combination of *bin* + *bi(n)* in these latter contexts, which has been described as a typical feature of francophone CamP by Féral (1989, 120-121). Sentence (31) triggered a variety of translations, most frequently without any preverbal marker or with preverbal *di*. In BahCE, either preverbal *does* (sometimes reduced to *is* or *'s*) plus verb or an unmarked verb form is used in both habitual and generic contexts. For habitual past contexts, *used to* + V or *was* + V-*ing* is used. The English-speaking informants used Simple Present or Simple Past forms in the contexts.

Sentence No.	CamP	BahCE	English
(18)	*di*	V or *does*/*is*/*'s* + V	Simple Present
(19)	*di*	V or *does*/*is*/*'s* + V	Simple Present
(20)	*bin+di*/ *(bin+bi(n))*	*used to* + V or *was* + V-*ing*	Simple Past
(21)	*bin+di*/ *(bin+bi(n))*	*used to* + V or *was* + V-*ing*	Simple Past
(31)	*O* / *di* / *(bi)*	*does*/*is*/*'s be* + ADJ	Simple Present
(73)	*di*	V or *does*/*is*/*'s* + V	Simple Present

Table 2: Prototypical occurrences of the HABITUAL in CamP, BahCE, and English

These results suggest that preverbal *di* is the preferred marker for expressing habitual and generic meanings in CamP, and that it corresponds to the English Simple Present in this function. In BahCE, non-past habituals and generics may be expressed by means of either the unmarked verb or the preverbal marker *does*/*is*/*'s*; in past contexts, the preferred marker of habituality is *used to*, but other forms exist as well.

3.2.2 Prototypical Uses of the PERFECT

Prototypical occurrences of the PERFECT are to be expected in sentences such as the following (see Dahl 1985, 131-132):

(42) [Q:] You **MEET** my brother (any time in your life until now)?
(53) [A: I want to give your brother a book to read, but I don't know which. Is there any of these books that he READ already? B:] (Yes,) he **READ** this book
(54) [A: It seems that your brother never finishes books.] (That is not quite true.) He **READ** this book (=all of it)
(56) [Q: Is the king still alive? A:] (No,) he **DIE**

The data elicited for these sentences show that the CamP informants preferred simple *don*, although some informants additionally combined *don* with *bin*. In BahCE, either the unmarked verb or *done* + V occurred. The English native speakers almost exclusively used the Present Perfect in sentences (42) and (53). With regard to sentences (54) and (56), the British English (BE) speakers used the Present Perfect, whereas American English (AE) speakers translated using the Simple Past.[1]

Sentence No.	CamP	BahCE	English
(42)	*don*/ *(bin+don)*	V	Present Perfect
(53)	*don*/ *(bin+don)*	V or *done* + V	Present Perfect
(54)	*don*/ *(bin+don)*	*done* + V	Present Perfect/Past Tense
(56)	*don*/ *(bin+don)*	*dead*	Present Perfect/Past Tense

Table 3: Prototypical occurrences of the PERFECT in CamP, BahCE, and English

As can be seen from the summary of the results in this table, CamP *don* clearly correlates with prototypical perfect contexts and with the English Present Perfect in most cases. In BahCE, either the unmarked verb or *done* + V occurs in these sentences.

However, this account neglects the fact that the PERFECT is usually associated with four different, context-dependent meanings. These are: 1. the perfect of result, 2. the experiential perfect, 3. the perfect of recent past, and 4. the perfect of persistent situa-

---

1   This is a well-known difference between American and British English (see e.g. Leech 2004, 43).

tion (see Dahl 1985, 132; Comrie 1976, 56ff.). According to Dahl, a typical example of the perfect of result is sentence (54), which constitutes an instance of preferred *don* use in CamP and *done* + V in BahCE. The English-speaking informants used Present Perfect and Past Tense forms, depending on the variety of English used (see Table 3 above). Sentence (42) is said to be a typical example of the experiential perfect (Dahl 1985, 132); this sentence constitutes another instance of preferred *don* use in CamP and triggered the unmarked verb form in BahCE and the Present Perfect among English speakers (see Table 3 above).

The perfect of recent past can be elicited with sentence (133):

(133) [The speaker has just seen the king arrive (no one had expected this event)] (Have you heard the news?) The king **ARRIVE**

Unfortunately, this sentence did not figure in the reduced version of the TMA questionnaire used for CamP and English, but experience suggests that most CamP speakers would translate it by means of *don*. One would also expect the Present Perfect in (British) English. The Bahamian informants used unmarked verbs.

Finally, the perfect of persistent situation could have been triggered by sentence (148), but this sentence did not figure in the reduced version of the questionnaire used for CamP and English either.

(148) [Of a coughing child:) For how long has your son been coughing?] He **COUGH** for an hour

However, in CamP *don* use seems very unlikely in this context, and *di* seems to be the more probable translation, especially because of the time adverbial provided in the original sentence, but one would definitely expect Present Perfect Progressive forms in the English translations. In BahCE, *been* + V-*ing* occurred in such contexts if the verb in question was dynamic (*He been coughing for a hour*); stative verbs were used in their base form (*She know me long time*). This suggests that CamP *don* cannot express all meanings of the PERFECT. The same holds for BahCE: There is no single PERFECT category; rather, different perfect meanings are expressed by means of different forms, at least two of which function in other contexts as well.

If these results are summarized, we obtain the following fine-grained and systematic overview of tense and aspect categories in CamP, BahCE, and English.

	Category	CamP	BahCE	English
IMPERFECTIVITY	HABITUAL/ GENERIC	*di* *I di rait leta dem.* *Cat dem di miau.*	V or *does/is/'s* + V *He (does/is/'s) write letter(s).* *They (does/is/'s) meow.*	Simple Present *He (always) writes letters.* *Cats meow.*
	PROGRESSIVE	*di* *I di rait leta dem.*	V-*ing* *He writing letter(s).*	Present Progressive *He is writing letters (right now).*
	PAST HABITUAL	*bin di / bin bi(n)* *(Las sama), i bin di (olweis) rait leta dem.* (CamPA)[2] *(Las sama) i bin bi(n) (olweis) rait leta dem.* (CamPF)[3]	*used to* + V *He used to write letter(s).*	Simple Past or *used to* *He (always) wrote letters.* *He used to write letters.*
	PAST PROGRESSIVE	*bin di/ bin bi(n)* *I bin di rait leta dem.* (CamPA) *I bin bi(n) rait leta dem.* (CamPF)	*was* + V-*ing* *(When I been to see my brother yesterday:) He was writing letter.*	Past Tense Progressive *(When I went to see my brother yesterday:) He was writing letters.*
PERFECT	PERFECT OF RESULT	*don* *I don rid dis buk.*	*done* + V *He done read that whole book.*	Present Perfect/ Simple Past *He has read this book.* (BrE) *He read this book.* (AmE)
	EXPERIENTIAL PERFECT	*don* *Yu don mit ma broda?*	V *You ever meet my brother before?*	Present Perfect *Have you met my brother?*
	PERFECT OF RECENT PAST	*don* *De king don kom.*	V *The king just reach.*	Present Perfect *The king has arrived.*
	PERFECT OF PERSISTENT SITUATION	*bin di* *I bin di koffo wan awa.*	*been* + V-*ing* *He been coughing for a hour.*	Present Perfect Progressive *He has been coughing for one hour.*

Table 4: Tense and aspect contrasts between CamP, BahCE, and English

3.3 Semantic Maps

We will now use the data described above and represent correspondences between the tense-aspect categories of the three languages under investigation by applying the semantic map methodology. This methodology has been used "for a wide variety of linguistic phenomena, particularly in the typology of grammatical semantics" (van der Auwera and Temürcü 2006, 131), and "it has become increasingly clear that these attempts to map out linguistic categorization provide an empirically testable tool for the study of semantic variation across languages" (Cysow et al. 2010, 1).

---

[2] Anglophone CamP.
[3] Francophone CamP.

Taking the results for the HABITUAL and the PROGRESSIVE and combining them into an IMPERFECTIVE category (Comrie 1976, 25),[4] we can visualize the realizations of the conceptual space IMPERFECTIVE in BahCE, CamP, and English as follows:

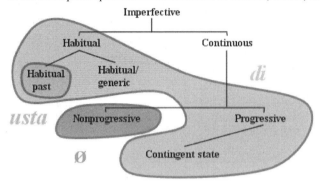

Semantic map 1: The IMPERFECTIVE in CamP

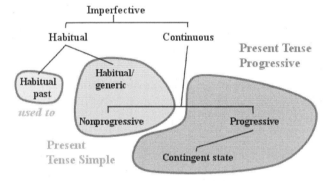

Semantic map 2: The IMPERFECTIVE in English

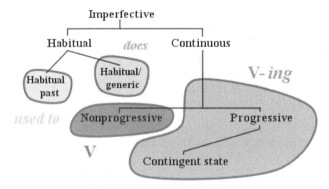

Semantic map 3: The IMPERFECTIVE in BahCE

---

4   For the sake of completeness, we added so-called "contingent state" situations, as in *I am living in London (for the time being)* (see Dahl 1985, 93), as well as non-progressive ones, as in *John knows a lot* (Comrie 1976, 25).

As these visualizations illustrate, the conceptualizations of the IMPERFECTIVE are very different in the three languages in question: CamP has a categorical marker of imperfectivity, whereas in English only progressives are marked morphologically. Habitual-generic and nonprogressive situations are marked by the same form in English (the Simple Present). Past habituals necessitate a separate marker (*used to*) in English and BahCE. A similar marker (*usta*) is described for CamP, but this form was not used by the informants in the elicitation experiment (see sentences (20) and (21) above). In both CamP and BahCE the continuous non-progressive is morphologically unmarked.

With regard to the PERFECT, it is interesting to note that the semantic space covered by this category is cut up in only two different ways in the three varieties. Surprisingly, it is not the two creoles which make the same distinctions but CamP and English:

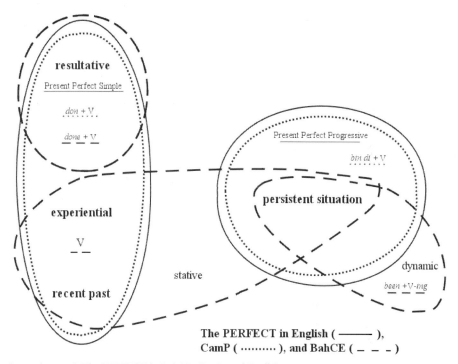

Semantic map 4: The PERFECT in BahCE, CamP, and English

Of course, if we take form into account, we notice that in English we are really dealing with a single grammatical category, realized by the Present Perfect, which may or may not be combined with the Progressive, whereas in CamP we are looking at two quite distinct categories, one of which denotes resultative, experiential, and recent past meanings, the other persistent situations. In BahCE, only resultatives take *done*; persistent situations involving dynamic verbs are marked by means of *been* + V-*ing*; and experientials, recent pasts, and stative persistent situations occur with unmarked verbs. This is not surprising, because these are the three perfect meanings that are closest to the other meanings expressed by the unmarked verb in BahCE, which – as shown in

Hackert (2004, 66) – may be seen as a fairly prototypical instantiation of the PERFECTIVE (PFV). According to Dahl (1985, 78), a "PFV verb will typically denote a single event, seen as an unanalyzed whole, with a well-defined result or end-state, located in the past."

The question is, of course, how bounded situations of this type go together with perfect ones, which, after all, are defined as being linked to the present moment. There are three points to take into account here. First, the experiential is defined as referring to a situation that has obtained at least once in a period of time leading up to the present. Obviously, speakers can place the focus either on the past situation described or on the fact that it took place in a period leading up to the present – and speakers of BahCE, it seems, focus more on the former than on the latter. Second, basically the same holds for recent pasts, or the "hot news" category, as it is sometimes called: we are dealing with situations that are construed as having happened just now, so again the focus can be on the past situation or on the fact that it is barely completed. Finally, stative persistent situations (*I know him long time*) are similar to other non-past statives (*He love me*), and in BahCE, they take the same form, too.

To sum up, in order to postulate the existence of a grammaticalized perfect category, we need to look at how the four typical meanings or uses of that category are expressed in the language under investigation. Whereas English possesses a single, unified perfect (even though typically the progressive aspect is added when persistent situations are described), CamP employs two entirely different forms. Interestingly, BahCE is not even listed as possessing a perfect at all in some of the typological literature, such as the *World Atlas of Language Structures* (WALS) (Dryer and Haspelmath 2013), as it does not express resultative and experiential meanings by means of a single form – which, however, was the requirement for a particular construction to be treated as an instantiation of this category (Dahl and Velupillai 2013).

4. Conclusion

In this article, we have compared (parts of) the tense-aspect systems of two English-lexifier creoles, CamP and BahCE, with that of English by means of data elicited with the help of Dahl's TMA questionnaire (1985). This questionnaire constitutes a language-independent method of obtaining information on TMA categories and thus avoids the pitfalls associated with contrastive endeavors based either on the categories found in a particular language (the 'Anglicist' approach) or on an abstract, putatively universal system (the 'creolist' approach). The need to depart from the Bickertonian model in the description of creole TMA systems has been recognized by a number of researchers but advocated most explicitly by Winford (1996b, 82), who demands "that we must stay in tune with scholars in the fields of semantics and language typology who have contributed so much to our understanding of TMA systems in the world's languages." In view of this, we are surprised that so few creolists have made use of Dahl's questionnaire despite the fact that it provides researchers precisely with typologically valid and thus truly comparable data.

One of the most noticeable findings that emerged from our cross-linguistic comparison is that CamP may be said to possess a true imperfective marker with *di* occurring in both progressive and habitual/generic contexts, whereas BahCE marks these two situation types by means of different forms. As for the perfect, CamP and BahCE were again found to differ substantially in that the former possesses a grammaticalized perfect, *don*, which is employed for three of the four perfect meanings generally recognized, whereas BahCE *done* only occurs with resultatives, which would preclude viewing this form as a grammaticalized perfect marker.

As for the wider implications of our contrastive study, there has been much and at times even acrimonious debate about whether pidgins and creoles actually constitute a linguistic type different from languages that did not emerge in high-contact situations. The only way to resolve this debate is to systematically compare these languages to others and see if they actually pattern differently or if they are only treated differently because of their peculiar sociohistorical origins. Again, even if on a very small scale, comparative studies such as the one presented here could help resolve the issue. This endeavor will be made much easier now by the publication of large-scale databases such as the WALS and the *Atlas of Pidgin and Creole Language Structures* (APiCS; Michaelis et al. 2013), both of which are typological projects that map hundreds of linguistic features for scores or even hundreds of languages. Even though only some of the features covered in APiCS overlap fully with the features covered in WALS, the two projects finally permit valid cross-linguistic comparisons based on language-independent standards of comparison. For varieties of English, the *World Atlas of Varieties of English* (WAVE) does the same job (see e.g. Kortmann, this volume). The data provided by these projects, like our TMA data, could be combined fruitfully with the semantic map approach for cross-linguistic comparisons of conceptual spaces in tense-aspect systems as well as in other grammatical subsystems.

References

Ayafor, Miriam (2000): "Kamtok: The Ultimate Unifying Common National Language for Cameroon", *The Carrier Pidgin*, 28, 4-6
Bache, Carl (1995): *The Study of Aspect, Tense and Action: Towards a Theory of the Semantics of Grammatical Categories*. Frankfurt: Lang
Bickerton, Derek (1981): *Roots of Language*. Ann Arbor, MI: Karoma
Comrie, Bernard (1976): *Aspect: An Introduction to the Study of Verbal Aspect and Related Problems*. Cambridge: Cambridge University Press
Croft, William; Poole, Keith T. (2008): "Inferring Universals from Grammatical Variation. Multidimensional Scaling for Typological Analysis", *Theoretical Linguistics* 34.1, 1-37
Cysow, Michael et al. (2010): "Introduction to the Special Issue 'Semantic Maps: Methods and Applications'", *Linguistic Discovery* 8.1, 1-3
Dahl, Östen (1985): *Tense and Aspect Systems*. Oxford: Blackwell
---; Velupillai, Viveka (2013): "The Perfect", in: Dryer; Haspelmath (eds.). <http://wals.info/feature/68A#2/25.5/148.2> [accessed 8 January 2014)]
Dryer, Matthew S.; Haspelmath, Martin (eds.; 2013): *The World Atlas of Language Structures Online*. Leipzig: Max Planck Institute for Evolutionary Anthropology. <http://wals.info> [accessed 8 January 2014]
Faraclas, Nicholas (1987): "Creolization and the Tense-Aspect-Modality System of Nigerian Pidgin", *Journal of African Languages and Linguistics* 9.1, 45-59
Féral, Carole de (1989): *Pidgin-English du Cameroun: Description Linguistique et Sociolinguistique*. Paris: Peeters/Selaf
Hackert, Stephanie (2004): *Urban Bahamian Creole: System and Variation*. Amsterdam: Benjamins

--- (2012): "Bahamian Creole", in: Kortmann, Bernd; Lunkenheimer, Kerstin (eds.): *The Mouton World Atlas of Variation in English*. Berlin: De Gruyter Mouton, 180-196

--- (2013): "Bahamian Creole", in: Michaelis, Susanne Maria et al. (eds.): *The Survey of Pidgin and Creole Languages*, Volume 1: *English-based and Dutch-based Languages*. Oxford: Oxford University Press, 127-138

---; Huber, Magnus (2007): "Gullah in the Diaspora. Historical and Linguistic Evidence from the Bahamas", *Diachronica* 24, 279-325

Leech, Geoffrey (2004): *Meaning and the English Verb*. 3rd edition. Harlow: Pearson Education

Michaelis, Susanne Maria et al. (eds.; 2013): *Atlas of Pidgin and Creole Language Structures Online*. Leipzig: Max Planck Institute for Evolutionary Anthropology. <http://apics-online.info> [accessed 8 January 2014]

Schröder, Anne (2003): "Aspect in Cameroon Pidgin English", in: Lucko, Peter et al. (eds.): *Studies in African Varieties of English*. Frankfurt: Lang, 83-100

--- (2012a): "Tense and Aspect in Cameroon Pidgin English", in: Anchimbe, Eric A. (ed.): *Language Contact in a Postcolonial Setting: The Linguistic and Social Context of English and Pidgin in Cameroon*. Berlin: De Gruyter Mouton, 165-190

--- (2012b): "Cameroon Pidgin", in: Kortmann, Bernd; Lunkenheimer, Kerstin (eds.): *The Mouton World Atlas of Variation in English*. Berlin: De Gruyter Mouton, 441-458

--- (2013): "Cameroon Pidgin English", in: Michaelis, Susanne Maria et al. (eds.): *The Survey of Pidgin and Creole Languages*, Volume 1: *English-based and Dutch-based Languages*. Oxford: Oxford University Press, 185-193

Singler, John (1990a): "Introduction: Pidgins and Creoles and Tense-Mood-Aspect", in: Singler, John (ed.), vii-xvi

--- (ed.) (1990b): *Pidgin and Creole Tense-Mood-Aspect Systems*. Amsterdam/Philadelphia: Benjamins

van der Auwera, Johan; Temürcü, Ceyhan (2006): "Semantic Maps", in: Brown, Keith (ed.): *Encyclopedia of Language and Linguistics*. Oxford: Elsevier, 131-134

Winford, Donald (1996a): "Creole Typology and Relationships", *Journal of Pidgin and Creole Languages* 11, 313-328

--- (1996b): "Common Ground and Creole TMA", *Journal of Pidgin and Creole Languages* 11, 71-84

KLAUS P. SCHNEIDER (BONN)

Comparability and Sameness in Variational Pragmatics

1. Introduction

Variational pragmatics is the study of pragmatic differences between regional or social varieties of a language, e.g. Irish English and English English or African-American English and European-American English. For this type of study, comparability is a crucial issue. Questions of central concern include the following: How can patterns of language use be compared across language varieties? How can pragmatic 'sameness' be established, which is a prerequisite for such comparison? What kind of sameness is required to identify the variants of a pragmatic variable? These questions are addressed in the present paper.

The following part provides an outline of the analytical framework of variational pragmatics, while part 3 deals with methodological issues, particularly with comparability as one of the methodological principles observed in this discipline. In part 4, the notion of 'pragmatic sameness' is discussed in the context of current controversies about pragmatic variables. Thereafter, in part 5, material from an ongoing research project at the University of Bonn is presented to illustrate how problems associated with comparability and sameness can be solved in empirical work in variational pragmatics, and how pragmatic variables and their variants can be determined. The paper ends with a summary of the major tenets and their consequences for future research in the field of cross-varietal pragmatic variation.

2. Variational Pragmatics: The Basic Framework

Variational pragmatics is conceptualised as an interface between two disciplines in linguistics. As the name suggests, it can be defined as the intersection of pragmatics with variational linguistics (for more details on the basic framework, see Schneider and Barron 2008; Schneider 2010). It is important to note that the term 'variational', and not 'variationist', is used in this context, indicating that the approach adopted for investigating pragmatic variation is not the Labovian paradigm, but a more liberal approach, as will be shown below. To avoid misunderstandings, variational pragmatics is perhaps better characterized as the intersection of pragmatics with dialectology. What is meant is, however, not traditional dialect geography, but the broader contemporary notion of dialectology as that part of sociolinguistics that examines both social and regional varieties of a language and thus integrates dialect geography into the study of sociolects, ethnolects, and genderlects. This understanding of dialectology, which seems to be especially popular in the United States of America, is exemplified for instance in Wolfram and Schilling-Estes's *American English: Dialects and Variation* (2006), which includes chapters on regional variation as well as social class, ethnic and gender variation.

The origin of variational pragmatics derives from the observation that neither dialectology nor pragmatics had taken much notice of one another. Dialectology had focussed almost exclusively on pronunciation, vocabulary, and grammar, but had neglected pragmatic differences. Pragmatics, on the other hand, had initially focussed on universals of verbal communication, but had neglected linguistic variation. If variation was an issue at all, then it was variation between different languages, and also, albeit to a much more limited extent, variation between different situations. These two complementary gaps are addressed in variational pragmatics by adding pragmatics to the study of pronunciation, vocabulary, and grammar in dialectology, and by adding the study of cross-varietal (or macro-social) variation to the study of inter-lingual and situational (or micro-social) variation in pragmatics.

In its standard version, the analytical framework of variational pragmatics comprises two component parts. In one component, five types of macro-social variation are distinguished, and in the other component, five levels of pragmatic analysis are specified. The types of macro-social variation are regional, socioeconomic, ethnic, gender, and age variations. This list, however, is of course not exhaustive. In some projects, occupation is preferred over socioeconomic status or social class, and sometimes distinguished from the level of education (see e.g. Plevoets et al. 2008). Problems with the theoretical status of social class will not be discussed here, nor differences between gender- and sex-based variation (see Haugh and Schneider 2012; Barron and Schneider 2009).

The five levels of pragmatic analysis currently specified are called formal, actional, interactional, topic, and organizational levels. On the formal level, the communicative functions of linguistic forms are analysed, for instance of discourse markers such as *well*, *look*, or *I mean*. On the actional level, the linguistic forms of communicative functions are examined, specifically the realisations of illocutionary acts such as requests, apologies, or insults. Analysis on the interactional level focuses on the combination of communicative functions in discourse, for example, on adjacency pairs and longer sequences of speech acts such as remedial sequences or conversational openings, as well as on aspects of relational work and the negotiation of identities. Work on the topic level examines the selection and management of topics in discourse, such as permissible or taboo topics in small talk between strangers and aspects of topic development. Finally, on the organisational level turn-taking phenomena are dealt with, including types of interruptions, simultaneous talk, or silence. Again, no claim is made that this list is exhaustive. Discourse type or genre and discourse domain may be further relevant levels of analysis (see Schneider 2007; Jucker and Taavitsainen 2012; Esser in press). Moreover, as variational pragmatics has so far concentrated on spoken communication, but will be extended to written communication, the current inventory of pragmatic levels of analysis will have to be modified accordingly.

3. Comparability and Other Methodological Issues

While variational pragmatics is not restricted to any particular data type or method, three general methodological principles have to be observed. These are the principles of empiricity, contrastivity, and comparability, which can be summarized as follows: a) real rather than intuitive data are used, b) varieties have to be explicitly contrasted, and c) relevant social factors have to be controlled (see Schneider 2010, 252-254; 2012a, 1029).

Ad a), the empiricity principle: The term 'armchair linguistics' is used for investigations in which researchers do not work empirically, but rely on their intuitions about (their native) language and on their own communicative experience. This term usually has negative connotations. However, it must be remembered that some of the most important linguistic theories in the twentieth century, including Saussure's and Chomsky's as well as Austin's and Searle's, are in fact 'armchair theories'. Work in variational pragmatics, by contrast, is not a type of 'armchair pragmatics', but based on empirical work. Not intuitions, but real language data are analysed, as language use cannot be invented, but has to be observed in populations of language users. Suitable material may be field data or laboratory data, i.e., naturally occurring or elicited (see Jucker 2009 on the metaphors 'armchair', 'field', and 'laboratory').

Empirical work in variational pragmatics has predominantly used two types of data, namely naturally occurring discourse from machine-readable corpora of spoken language, and experimental data elicited by questionnaires. Corpora that have been employed include large published corpora such as the British National Corpus (BNC) or the Santa Barbara Corpus of Spoken American English (SBCSAE), as well as small self-recorded corpora. Corpus data have mostly been used for studies of the formal level (see part 2 above), as words and set phrases such as discourse markers can easily be searched for in a corpus. Searches for illocutions, by contrast, are, as a rule, not equally possible since pragmatically annotated corpora do not yet exist. SPICE-Ireland, an annotated version of ICE-Ireland, i.e., the Irish component of the International Corpus of English (ICE), is a rare exception (see Kirk 2013). Given this situation, the preferred method of data collection for studies of the actional level (see part 2) is the production questionnaire with discourse completion tasks (DCTs). Interviews and role plays have also been employed, but only to a limited extent, and there are recent innovative studies of speech acts that are based on field notes or participant observation (Bieswanger 2011; Rüegg 2012). The actional and the formal levels are the two levels of analysis which have received more attention in research than the other three, namely, the interactional, the topic and the organizational level (for an overview, see Schneider 2012b).

Ad b): The contrastivity principle, which was first formulated by Barron and Schneider (2009, 429), can be summarized as follows: Macro-social variation can only be adequately studied if at least two varieties of the same type are contrasted. For instance, regional, ethnic, or age variation can only be adequately studied if the language use in two or more regions, ethnic communities, or age groups is contrasted respectively. Variety-specific pragmatic features cannot be properly identified without explicit contrast. Indeed, this applies more generally to any research aimed at identifying variety-specific features on any level of language.

In different areas of variety studies, there is a tradition of making claims about variety-specific features without any explicit comparison. For instance, Lakoff, who is credited with initiating gender studies in linguistics, lists a number of features she considers characteristic of women's speech, for example the use of specific colour terms and the frequent use of question tags (Lakoff 1973). These features have, however, not been established in empirical work. The author relies on her own intuitions, and she describes women's speech as diverging in a number of features from a norm that seems to correspond to male language use. Today research into gender variation is usually based on explicit comparison (see e.g. Murphy 2011), yet this is not equally true for research into age variation. Investigations into specific features in the language use of children or adolescents often lack explicit comparison with adult speakers (see e.g. Georgakopoulou and Charalambidou 2011). Finally, in research into individual first or second language varieties of English, such as Irish English, New Zealand English, or Indian English, researchers often tacitly assume that the identified patterns diverge from Standard English, although it may not be clear what the relevant standard may be.

In conversation analysis, it has been pointed out that focusing on one variety alone is not sufficient to establish specific features of this variety. Schegloff and Sacks (1973), working exclusively with American English data, emphasisze that there is no guarantee that the patterns they identify are specific to this particular variety. They write: "That the materials are all 'American English' does not entail that they are RELEVANTLY 'American English' …" (1973, 291; original emphasis). Whether or not, or to what extent, their materials are "RELEVANTLY 'American English'" can only be established by contrasting these with materials that are taken from another variety such as British English. Thus, the establishment of variety-specific linguistic features and patterns of language use presupposes explicit contrast.

Ad c), the comparability principle: Even if varieties are contrasted, this does not necessarily mean that what is compared is in fact comparable. In other words, researchers investigating pragmatic variation must take good care that they do not compare apples to oranges. It is not sufficient to contrast material from one variety to any material from another variety. Since the central claim of variational pragmatics is that macro-social factors such as region, gender, or age impact language use in interaction, these macro-social factors have to be systematically controlled in order to ensure comparability. Thus, a question of central methodological concern is how this is best accomplished. While many researchers in pragmatics prefer naturally occurring data over experimental data, systematic control of relevant social factors is not easily achieved. If, for example, naturally occurring data are taken from large machine-readable corpora, then demographic information about the interactants may be incomplete or unavailable. Furthermore, even if such information is sufficiently available, then the situations in which the interactants use language may be very heterogeneous and not immediately comparable at all. This may be different for self-recorded corpora, but these corpora tend to be relatively small, and recording spoken discourse in comparable situations may not be trivial, especially when everyday conversation is the focus of analysis (it may be easier e.g. for institutional discourse, but in this case there may be legal obstacles). Moreover, recording spoken discourse and transcribing the recordings is very time-consuming.

In the light of these difficulties, it seems a wise strategy to employ experimental methods that permit the efficient gathering of comparable data. A tool which can be used for this purpose is the discourse completion task, which has been extremely popular especially in empirical pragmatic work for applied purposes. As Ogiermann (2009, 67) maintains: "The only data collection instrument that provides sufficiently large samples of comparable, systematically varied data is the discourse completion task

(DCT)". Like all methods, the DCT has advantages and disadvantages. One obvious disadvantage is that informants do not write down what they would actually say in real life situations, but what they think they would or should say in a particular type of situation. This more schematic version of verbal behaviour is, however, ideal for the study of pragmatic variation, because the many accidentals of real life situations that render comparison problematic are abstracted away. As Blum-Kulka et al. (1989, 13), who employ DCTs for comparing speech acts across languages and cultures, put it: "It is precisely this more stereotyped aspect of speech behavior that we need for cross-cultural comparability."

To compensate for the respective shortcomings of methods, it is advisable to triangulate data from one source with data from another source. DCT data can, for instance, be combined with corpus data. This procedure is also suggested by Jay (2009, 160), who writes: "Research and conclusions will be valuable when they are drawn from a combination of naturally observed public behavior in conjunction with laboratory-based studies of those behaviors." For the purpose of investigating pragmatic variation, it seems fruitful to start with the more manageable DCT method, which provides 'searchables' for corpus searches, i.e., words, phrases, and constructions that facilitate the identification of e.g. speech act realisations in large corpora of naturally occurring spoken discourse and circumvent the difficulties which exist due to the general unavailability of pragmatically annotated corpora. This procedure is illustrated in section 5. Section 4, by contrast, deals with pragmatic variables and pragmatic sameness, two notions that are immediately relevant to issues of comparability and to the discussion in section 5.

4. Theorising Pragmatic Variables and Sameness

As pointed out above (section 1), among the research questions addressed in variational pragmatics, questions of central concern are these: How do social factors impact language use, which pragmatic phenomena are affected, and how are they affected? More technically, these questions can be phrased as follows: Which pragmatic variables can be identified on each level of pragmatic analysis, which variants exist of these variables, and in which contexts are these variants used?

Currently, there is an ongoing discussion in variational pragmatics and related disciplines about pragmatic variables and their variants, and how they can be established. The original idea of linguistic variables goes back to Labov (1966), for whom linguistic variables were phonological variables. A typical textbook example of Labov's concept are the forms *fishing* and *fishin'* (as they are conventionally represented in writing), which illustrate the two phonological variants of the variable -ING, i.e., the pronunciation of the present participle marker of English verbs. Labov's criterion for classifying different forms as variants of a variable was sameness of meaning. According to Labov (1972, 271), the variants of a variable are options "of saying 'the same thing' in several ways: that is, the variants are identical in reference and truth value, but opposed in their social and/or stylistic significance." Sameness of meaning in this particular sense was later considered too limiting, especially for language levels other than phonology, and replaced by functional equivalence (see Lavandera 1978). However, as 'function' is an ambiguous term, it is not clear how functional equivalence can actually be established (see Terkourafi 2011, 355-356).

Elsewhere, I have argued that variationist notions of 'variable' and 'variant' have to be modified for the purposes of variational pragmatics (Schneider 2010). Specifically, I have suggested that "a pragmatic variable is 'that which varies' on the pragmatic level across varieties of the same language, and the respective variants are the options available of which different social groups of speakers make use" (Schneider 2010, 251). For example, every speech act can be realized in a number of different ways. A request, for instance, can be performed by employing a range of different realisation strategies, which include 'mood derivables' (e.g. *Close the door!*), 'suggestory formulae' (e.g. *How about closing the door?*), 'preparatory queries' (e.g. *Could you close the door?*), and 'hints' (e.g. *Cold in here.*) (see Blum-Kulka et al. 1989). In this case, the pragmatic variable is the request, its variants are different realization strategies, and the relevant criterion is illocutionary sameness. Similarly, Jucker and Taavitsainen (2012, 301), while finding it problematic to assume that different realisations of the same speech act are "different ways of saying the same thing", admit that these realisations "share a core of functional equivalence", which, more specifically, would be sameness of illocutionary point ("trying to get the addressee to do something that he or she might not have done without the request").

This approach is challenged by Terkourafi (2012), who in an earlier paper had come up with a relevance-theoretic definition of pragmatic variables based on procedural sameness (Terkourafi 2011). She criticizes that variational pragmatics "relies on the assumption that the analysts can define what constitutes, for instance, a request *outside of particular contexts*" (Terkourafi 2012, 302; original emphasis). More generally, Terkourafi objects that pragmatic phenomena such as speech acts as well as macro-social factors such as age or gender are treated as given rather than discursively constructed. As a remedy, she suggests a definition of speech acts that is based on hearer uptake, that is, on how the addressee understands a speaker's utterance (Terkourafi 2012, 305-307). However, as Barron (forthcoming) has demonstrated, hearer uptake is "not always necessary to establish an utterance as a realization of a particular illocution"; context plays a more crucial part. Context is, in fact, also included in my proposal of variables on the actional level of analysis, for which sameness should "be defined in functional (i.e., illocutionary), propositional and situational terms" (Schneider 2010, 251). As regards the role of macro-social factors, Terkourafi (2012, 308-313) rejects the idea of examining the influence of individual factors and advocates the notion of 'minimal contexts' that are jointly co-constituted by these factors. It is in relation to such contexts that pragmatic phenomena should be analysed. Despite all apparent differences, this proposal corresponds to a distinction Jucker and Taavitsainen draw between realizational pragmatic variables and contextual pragmatic variables. The former are defined as dependent and the latter as independent variables (2012, 296-297).

While much of the discussion centres around speech acts, variables have also been suggested for other levels of pragmatic analysis, and also different types of sameness. For instance, Pichler (2010, 591), discussing discourse markers, comes to the conclusion that "functional comparability" may only be relevant to some classes of markers, whereas "structural commonality" may be more relevant to others. Accordingly, "identity of form" (Schneider 2010, 252) does not seem to be a sufficient criterion for establishing sameness on the formal level of analysis. Furthermore, it has been argued that variables on the interactional level could be defined positionally. Examples include how conversations are opened or closed in a specific type of situation (see Schneider 2010, 251-252). Finally, pragmatic variables on the level of discourse domains are examined in Jucker and Taavitsainen (2012, 302-303). On this level, genre plays a key role.

So far, the discussion of pragmatic variables and sameness has been largely theoretical, or, in other words, an armchair discussion. In the following section, examples from systematic empirical research will be presented to illustrate how the methodological principles of variational pragmatics can be met, how sameness can be achieved, and how variables and their variants can be identified.

5. Some Empirical Evidence

To substantiate the claims made about comparability, sameness, variables, and variants in the preceding sections, material is used from a large-scale study of small talk across national varieties of English (see Schneider 2012a for some of the findings and further references). The varieties initially covered are the native language varieties spoken in England (EngE), Ireland (IrE), and the United States of America (AmE). The original sample included thirty speakers of each of these varieties (later samples were larger). All speakers were female and, on average, fifteen years old. In their respective countries they lived in the same location and went to the same school. The instrument employed for data collection was a dialogue production task (DPT) administered in writing. While in a DCT informants are requested to provide a single turn-at-talk in a short discourse extract, informants completing a DPT are requested to produce an entire dialogue. The DPT used for the present purpose was included in a mixed-task multi-focus questionnaire, consisting of a total of fifteen situations. It was one of two DPTs, while in the remaining thirteen situations either DCTs or multiple-choice questions were used (hence 'mixed-task' questionnaire). In the fifteen situations of this questionnaire, data are elicited on nine different pragmatic phenomena (hence 'multi-focus' questionnaire). Examples are request, complaint, apology, response to compliment, and response to insult. Some of these phenomena occur more than once to provide insights into situational variation. The DPT in question was included to collect data on party small talk between strangers. The instructions read as follows:

> *A conversation between strangers. At a party, one person (A) sees another person (of the same sex) who looks friendly (B). Write a short dialogue that represents language which would typically be used in this situation:*

The participant constellation in this situation is characterized by maximal social distance, meaning that there is no shared history that could be referred to. The participants are supposed to be of the same sex to avoid eliciting stereotypical "chatting-up" discourse, which in our experience is commonly produced by young male informants if the relationship is not specified as in the instructions quoted above. The event type is a social event, specifically a party. The utterances produced by the informants in their dialogues were coded for four parameters: illocution, proposition, conditional relevance, and discourse position. Examples of illocutions (in all capitals) are GREETING, REMARK, and QUESTION. Different illocutions may occur with the same proposition (with capital initial), e.g. QUESTION Identity versus DISCLOSE Identity, i.e., asking the interlocutor's name versus disclosing one's own name. As this example shows, the term 'proposition' is used here in rather a broad sense to refer to the content of an utterance. Conditional relevance pertains to the interactional status of an illocution, e.g. whether a GREETING is initiating or reacting, or whether a DISCLOSE Identity is volunteered or explicitly requested. Finally, discourse position refers to the place of a speech act in a dialogue, e.g. whether a DISCLOSE Identity occurs in the opening turn or in a (much) later turn.

By and large, the speakers of the three varieties use essentially the same speech acts, i.e., utterances with the same illocutions and the same propositions. First and foremost, these speech acts include:

GREETING, e.g. *Hi!*
COMPLIMENT Appearance, e.g. *I really like your top.*
QUESTION Host, e.g. *How do you know the hostess?*
QUESTION Identity, e.g. *What's your name?*
DISCLOSE Identity, e.g. *I'm Ashley.*
REMARK Party, e.g. *Great party, isn't it?*

What differs are the frequencies of these speech acts, their distribution in terms of discourse position and their lexico-grammatical realisation.

One of the most frequent speech acts in all three varieties is REMARK Party, i.e. an assertive act referring to the event. The following examples show that there is a preferred realization pattern (original spelling and punctuation are retained):

1   *Deadly party isn't it?* IRE1F1
2   *Great party isn't it?* IRE1F21
3   *great party isn't it?* IRE1F24
4   *It's a great party isn't it* ENG1F5
5   *cool party isn't it?* ENG1F46

In all of these examples, essentially the same construction type is used, which is a positive assessment phrased as a declarative sentence in the present tense, with the dummy subject *it* and the verb *be* contracted to *it's*, followed by a noun phrase consisting of indefinite article, positively evaluative adjective and the noun *party*. While full versions of this construction do occur (see examples 4), they are by far outnumbered by elliptical versions in which the subject-verb contraction and the article are omitted. To this clause, a question tag is attached. Thus, the most frequent construction can be described as [ADJ $_{EVALpos}$ + N$_{party}$] + question tag. While this construction is employed in all three varieties under study, there are significant cross-varietal differences in the choice of question tag. Speakers of IrE and EngE use the canonical tag *isn't it?*, as in the above examples, whereas speakers of AmE use the invariant tag *huh?*, as can be seen in the following examples.

6   *Cool party, huh?* USA5F8
7   *Fun party, huh?* USA3F6
8   *Nice party huh?* USA2F28
9   *Great party, huh?* USA1F32
10   *Good party, huh?* USA1F50

Thus, the two question tags *isn't it?* and *huh?* appear in complementary cross-varietal distribution. *Isn't it?* occurs exclusively in the two European varieties of English. There is not a single occurrence of *isn't it?* in the dialogues produced by the American informants. *Huh?*, by contrast, is used exclusively in the AmE dialogues, with only one occurrence in the IrE dialogues.

These findings can be summarized as follows: All informants were females in the same age group, and all informants completed the same questionnaire and responded to the exact same instructions. These factors render the dialogues produced by the informants immediately comparable. REMARK Party, which is one of the most frequently used speech acts in this context, is realized in much the same way in all three varieties. There is a clear preference for an elliptical construction with a question tag that is shared across varieties. What varies is the choice of question tag, with speakers of EngE and IrE consistently using one tag and speakers of AmE consistently using another.

Based on these findings, we can say that the question tag in the speech act REMARK Party used in party small talk between strangers is a pragmatic variable, or, more specifically, a pragmalinguistic (as opposed to sociopragmatic) variable on the actional level of discourse. Under identical circumstances, comparable speakers of one variety use one variant, speakers of other varieties use another variant. Given that these findings were arrived at under very particular conditions, the question arises to what extent they can be generalized. For example, whether we can say that all Americans use *huh?* where EngE and IrE speakers use *isn't it?*, or whether this is a specific feature of the language use of fifteen year old school girls from the American South who fill in a written questionnaire about spoken discourse under laboratory conditions. Similarly, we can ask whether the observed distribution of variants is particular to the speech act REMARK Party or party small talk between strangers.

At this point, three answers can be given to these questions. First, *huh?* in REMARK Party was not only found in the relatively small AmE sample used in the research reported here (N=30), but in the overall population of informants from the USA who completed the questionnaire (N=215). Among these informants are male as well as female speakers from different age groups and different regions in the United States. Thus, the observed use of *huh?* does not seem to be particular to the language behaviour of fifteen year old girls. Second, a corpus search of *isn't it?* and *huh?* as question tags (and in no other functions, as established manually) shows no occurrence of *huh?* in ICE-GB (direct conversations) and ICE-Ireland (spoken part), but 1,761 occurrences in COCA (spoken part). *Isn't it?*, on the other hand, appears 850 times in ICE-GB (direct conversations) and 187 times ICE-Ireland (spoken part), but only 0.2 times in COCA (spoken part) (normalized frequencies per million words), and about fifty per cent of the few occurrences of *isn't it?* in COCA were actually produced by speakers from England appearing in a TV documentary. These results support the experimental findings and show that they are not an artefact of the laboratory method employed. Third, the examples from the three corpora demonstrate that *isn't it?* and *huh?* are used more generally in speech acts expressing a positive assessment by employing the same construction type, e.g. *Very organized house isn't it* (ICE-GB), *Beautiful dish, huh?* (COCA).

The complementary distribution of its variants makes the question tag in (elliptical) assessments a clear case of a pragmatic variable, specifically a pragmalinguistic variable on the actional level. Other cases may appear to be less clear. Using the criterion of positional sameness for identifying variables on the interactional level yields patterns that also vary systematically across the three varieties, but do not occur in complementary distribution. For instance, approximately three quarters of the IrE speakers (73.3%) used REMARK Party in their opening turns, whereas just under two thirds of the AmE speakers (60.0%) favour DISCLOSE Identity (i.e., self-identifications) in the same position. Given these relative frequencies and distribution, it seems justified to consider these two speech acts as variants of a sociopragmatic variable on the interactional level. In this case, however, the variants are variety-preferential and not variety-exclusive.

6. Conclusion

In variational pragmatics, which aims at examining cross-varietal variation of language use in (inter)action, comparability can be achieved by employing experimental methods such as dialogue production tasks (DPTs). Such tasks permit systematic control of relevant contextual features and thus warrant situational sameness. Furthermore, these experimental methods provide sameness of tasks, which makes language produced in response to these tasks immediately comparable across populations of speakers of different varieties of the same language. Ideally, the populations which are compared are homogenized to a high degree, e.g. by including speakers of the same sex and in the same age group living in the same place, as in the example from a study of regional variation discussed in part 5.

Observing similarities in the language used in the same situation by speakers of the same variety and differences between speakers of different varieties helps to identify pragmatic variables. Thus it was found that the question tag used in remarks assessing a party in small talk between strangers is a pragmalinguistic variable on the actional level, of which two variants are *isn't?* and *huh?* These two variants seem to be variety-exclusive as the former is used exclusively by comparable groups of speakers of the European varieties of English, i.e., Irish English and English English, whereas the latter is invariably used by a matching group of speakers of U.S. American English. Support of this result is found in corpora of naturally occurring spoken discourse, which also demonstrates that the variants identified occur in a wider range of contexts. To give a further example, what is said to open small talk between strangers at a party can be considered a sociopragmatic variable on the interactional level, as the selection of initial utterances displays a high degree of similarity within each variety, while it varies markedly across varieties. The variants that have been identified seem, however, to be variety-preferential rather than variety-exclusive. Further research is needed to support this finding.

The examples discussed in this paper have shown that it is possible to empirically establish different kinds of pragmatic variables and their respective variants and that the degrees of comparability and sameness that can be achieved by employing experimental methods are a good starting point for studying pragmatic variation in naturally occurring spoken discourse. It is hoped that more studies will be conducted in this field to provide a more comprehensive and differentiated picture.

References

Barron, Anne (forthcoming): "Variational Pragmatics", in: Barron, Anne et al. (eds.): *Routledge Handbook of Pragmatics*. London/New York: Routledge.

---; Schneider, Klaus P. (2009): "Variational Pragmatics: Studying the Impact of Social Factors on Language Use in Interaction", *Intercultural Pragmatics* 6, 425-442

Bieswanger, Markus (2011): "Variationist Sociolinguistics Meets Variational Pragmatics", Paper presented at the *Second Conference of the International Society for the Linguistics of English (ISLE2)*, Boston University, June 2011

Blum-Kulka, Shoshana et al. (1989): "Investigating Cross-cultural Pragmatics: An Introductory Overview", in: Blum-Kulka, Shoshana et al. (eds.): *Cross-Cultural Pragmatics: Requests and Apologies*. Norwood, NJ: Ablex, 1-34

Esser, Jürgen (in press): "Taxonomies of Discourse Types", in: Schneider, Klaus P.; Barron, Anne (eds.): *Pragmatics of Discourse*. Berlin/Boston: De Gruyter Mouton, 443-462

Georgakopoulou, Alexandra; Charalambidou, Anna (2011): "Doing Age and Ageing: Language, Discourse and Social Interaction", in: Andersen, Gisle; Aijmer, Karin (eds.): *Pragmatics of Society*, Berlin/New York: De Gruyter Mouton, 31-52

Haugh, Michael; Schneider, Klaus P. (2012): "Editorial: Im/politeness across Englishes", *Journal of Pragmatics* 44, 1017-1021

Jay, Timothy (2009): "The Utility and Ubiquity of Taboo Words", *Perspectives on Psychological Science* 4, 153-161

Jucker, Andreas H. (2009): "Speech Act Research between Armchair, Field and Laboratory: The Case of Compliments", *Journal of Pragmatics* 41, 1611-1635

---; Taavitsainen, Irma (2012): "Pragmatic Variables", in: Hernández-Campoy, Juan M.; Conde-Silvestre, Juan C. (eds.): *The Handbook of Historical Sociolinguistics*. Oxford: Blackwell, 293-306

Kirk, John M. (2013): "Beyond the Structural Levels of Language: An Introduction to the SPICE-Ireland Corpus and Its Uses", in: Cruikshank, Janet; McColl Millar, Robert (eds.): *After the Storm*. Aberdeen: Forum for Research on the Languages of Scotland and Ireland, 207-232

Labov, William (1966): "The Linguistic Variable as a Structural Unit", *Washington Linguistics Review* 3, 4-22

--- (1972): *Sociolinguistic Patterns*. Oxford: Blackwell

Lakoff, Robin T. (1973): "Language and Woman's Place", *Language in Society* 2, 45-80

Lavandera, Beatriz R. (1978): "Where does the Sociolinguistic Variable Stop?", *Language in Society* 7, 171-182

Murphy, Bróna (2011): "Gender Identities and Discourse", in: Andersen, Gisle; Aijmer, Karin (eds.): *Pragmatics of Society*, Berlin/New York: De Gruyter Mouton, 53-78

Ogiermann, Eva (2009): *On Apologising in Negative and Positive Politeness Cultures*. Amsterdam/Philadelphia: Benjamins

Pichler, Heike (2010): "Methods in Discourse Variation Analysis: Reflections on the Way Forward", *Journal of Sociolinguistics* 14, 581-608

Plevoets, Koen et al. (2008): "The Distribution of T/V Pronouns in Netherlandic and Belgian Dutch", in: Schneider, Klaus P.; Barron, Anne (eds.): *Variational Pragmatics: A Focus on Regional Varieties in Pluricentric Languages*. Amsterdam/Philadelphia: Benjamins, 181-210

Rüegg, Larssyn (2012): *Offers and Thanks Responses: A Varational [sic] Pragmatic Perspective*. Unpublished M.A. Thesis, University of Zurich

Schegloff, Emanuel A.; Sacks, Harvey (1973): "Opening up Closings", *Semiotica* 8, 289-328

Schneider, Klaus P. (2007): "Genre Matters: Textual and Contextual Constraints on Contemporary English Speech Behaviour", *Anglia* 125, 59-83

--- (2010): "Variational Pragmatics", in: Fried, Mirjam et al. (eds.): *Variation and Change: Pragmatic Perspectives*. Amsterdam/Philadelphia: Benjamins, 239-267

--- (2012a): "Appropriate Behavior across Varieties of English", *Journal of Pragmatics* 44, 1022-1037

--- (2012b): "Pragmatic Variation and Cultural Models", *Review of Cognitive Linguistics* 10, 346-372

Schneider, Klaus P.; Barron, Anne (2008): "Where Pragmatics and Dialectology Meet: Introducing Variational Pragmatics", in: Schneider, Klaus P.; Barron, Anne (eds.): *Variational Pragmatics: A Focus on Regional Varieties in Pluricentric Languages*. Amsterdam/Philadelphia: Benjamins, 1-32

Terkourafi, Marina (2011): "The Pragmatic Variable: Toward a Procedural Interpretation", *Language in Society* 40, 343-372
--- (2012): "Between Pragmatics and Sociolinguistics: Where does Pragmatic Variation Fit in?" in: Félix-Brasdefer, J. César; Koike, Dale (eds.) *Pragmatic Variation in First and Second Language Contexts: Methodological Issues*. Amsterdam/Philadelphia: Benjamins, 295-318
Wolfram, Walt; Schilling-Estes, Natalie (2006): *American English: Dialects and Variation*. 2nd edition. Malden, MA: Blackwell

Tanja Rütten (Köln)

Comparing Apples and Oranges: The Study of Diachronic Change Based on Variant Forms

1. Introduction

In historical linguistics, it is often observed that language change results from the rivalry of competing linguistic variants, single forms as well as more complex constructions, of which one eventually predominates over the other(s). The resulting change can be neatly documented in an S-Curve pattern, where the spread of the dominant form at the cost of the rival form(s) is charted. But what exactly counts as a rival form of a given linguistic item? What range of variation is permissible, for example, how many variants and of which kind? In other words, how do we know that we are not comparing apples and oranges when investigating diachronic change that seems based on (apparently) variant forms?

In this paper, I would like to address the assumptions that we make about such comparisons. Re-examining the well-documented evolution of the English mandative subjunctive, I will discuss the following issues: Do two, or more, variant forms necessarily provide identical linguistic options (e.g. modal verbs, *to*-infinitives, and indicative forms as variants of the mandative subjunctive)? Is it feasible to permit variants with only partial overlap of form, function, and/or meaning in the comparison (e.g. *to*-infinitives vs. inflected forms)? How will this affect the results obtained by the comparison? What range of divergent forms, functions, and meanings is indeed desirable in empirical investigations in order to comprehend the process of linguistic change?

The English subjunctive offers a good case in point because it is a linguistic structure with a rather long history, dating back to Old English times. Its attested "non-existence in PDE" (Harsh 1968, 99), and subsequent "revival" (Leech et al. 2009, 52) in the late twentieth century is a striking phenomenon, considering that linguistic change is often thought irreversible. I would like to suggest that we find a plausible answer to this puzzle when we reconsider the comparison and comparability of the subjunctive and its variants in the history of English, following the line of questions posed above.

In the next section, I will comment briefly on the S-Curve Model, which is a basic tool in diachronic comparative studies. Against this background, my major aim is to examine the English mandative subjunctive. After a diagnostic overview of common assumptions about its rivals, I present an alternative study where I consider a more extensive set of variants for the Early Modern English period. I will show that the range of alternatives considered for inflected subjunctives influences the degree to which we perceive its decline over time quite considerably. I will conclude this paper with a short discussion of what counts as a permissible variant in comparative (historical) studies and why.

2. Language Variation and Change – The S-Curve Model

In historical (corpus-) linguistics, the S-Curve Model (see Labov 1994; also Bailey 1973) is a popular tool when comparing competing variant forms that are thought to be involved in language change.[1] Charting such forms, the resulting S-Curve pattern neatly illustrates the chronological substitution of one form by the other. This pattern predicts that linguistic change will be slow at the beginning, rapid in midpoint, and slow again in its final stage with a certain amount of residue of the older form. Change is thus fastest when exposition to both forms is greatest, i.e., when there is contact between many language users of the old and the new form (see Labov 1994, 65).

Figure 1 shows the application of the S-Curve Model in an investigation of the distribution of incoming *you* versus traditional *thou* as a second person singular pronoun in Early Modern English religious discourse (see Kohnen et al. 2011).

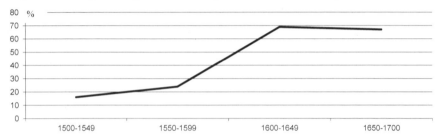

Figure 1. *you* vs *thou* in sermons, catechisms, controversial treatises, and religious biographies: percentages of *you* (based on Kohnen et al. 2011)

Clearly, *you* is chosen only infrequently at the beginning, then shows a rapid increase in frequency of usage. At the end of the Early Modern period we find a distribution of 70:30 in favour of *you*, with considerable residue of traditional *thou*, found in citations from the Bible and as a marker of identity in various non-conformist groups, as in the well-known "Quaker-thou".

This is a straightforward model with a high predictive potential and great explanatory power, but it has one major drawback: It captures binary choices only. It therefore works well here, because for most of its recorded history, English has only had two second person personal pronouns. But how do we know that there are only two rival forms when we look at other instances of variation and change? And what happens when we consider more than two variants?

This leads me to the English subjunctive, which offers a good example because it is generally assumed that it has been substituted by modal verb periphrasis (e.g. in Harsh 1968; Leech et al. 2009; Moessner 2010), so that it does look like a candidate in language change that involves a binary choice.

3. The English Mandative Subjunctive: A Diagnostic Overview

The English subjunctive is a very old linguistic structure, dating back to a comparatively full morphological paradigm in Old English. Its assumed demise has attracted

---

[1] Nevalainen and Raumolin-Brunberg (2003) were among the first to apply this model comprehensively in their seminal study of developing standard forms in Early Modern English.

much scholarly attention in historical studies. In varieties studies, it also commonly occurs as a relevant linguistic structure in both inner and outer circle varieties, and it seems to be a significant determinant for the description of World Englishes. Varieties studies in particular have drawn our attention to the fact that inflected subjunctives have enjoyed a rather unforeseen "revival" in the late twentieth century (see Leech et al. 2009, 52). My attention in this section will therefore be on the historical development of inflected subjunctives with particular emphasis on this unexpected inconsistent and contradictory evolutionary pattern. I will restrict my observations to inflected subjunctive forms in dependent mandative constructions, since the revival seems most prominent here. These constructions are marked by an overt triggering expression of a suasive verb (of commanding, suggesting, ordering, etc.) and a nominal *that*-complement with a finite verb in the subjunctive, as in example (1):[2]

(1) I thinke it necessary now **to admonish** the Reader, **that he expect not** any ample discourse of the liues and actions of the Bishops ... (preface to biography, 1601)

The linguistic life of this construction has been described as one of decline and revival. While its "neglect" had already been lamented by eighteenth-century grammarians (see Auer 2006, 40), Henry Fowler famously pronounced it "moribund" at the beginning of the twentieth century (Fowler 1926/1965, 595), and Harsh ultimately claimed it "nonexisten[t] in PDE" (Harsh 1968, 99), at least in the drama texts on which he bases this judgment. However, the construction seems to be on the rise from the mid-twentieth century onwards (see Övergaard 1995; Leech et al. 2009) and since then has been "enjoying an active retirement" (Peters 1998, 101).[3]

Some of these judgments suggest an S-Curve pattern as discussed in section 2, claiming that the inflected subjunctive is replaced by modal verb periphrasis (i.e., *I admonish the reader that he should not expect...*). This prediction seems to be borne out by its historical development. Moessner (2010), in her study on mandative subjunctives in Middle English, already notes a decline of inflected subjunctives in favour of *should*-periphrasis. This development is confirmed by Fillbrandt's (2006) study for the Early Modern period.

However, in the twentieth century, we observe a rise in subjunctive forms to which different varieties of English react differently (Quirk et al. 1985, 157; Huddleston and Pullum 2002, 995). In a recent investigation, Leech et al. (2009, 53) have shown that while modal verb periphrasis decreased, inflected mandative subjunctives rose from 12.6% in LOB and 85.9% in BROWN to 38.3% and 90.3%, in the course of only thirty years, respectively. Studies on other varieties of English come to similar results for the same period of time (e.g. Peters 1998).

At the same time, and in the very same book, Leech et al. investigate the use of the central modals in the twentieth century and find that "putative, quasi-subjunctive"

---

2   All examples are taken from the *Corpus of English Religious Prose* (currently being compiled at the University of Cologne; see www.helsinki.fi/varieng/CoRD/corpora/COERP/index.html for details).

3   A similar revival has been claimed for inflected subjunctives in adverbial clauses after triggers such as *if, although, lest*, and others, e.g. in Auer (2008, 160), who notes that "the *lest*-subjunctive [...] was in use in the Early Modern English period but then disappeared. After a hibernation period of 250 years, we were able to observe a slow increase starting in the 1960s and then an extremely sharp rise between 1985 and 1994".

should in particular is used less frequently (2009, 87). Unfortunately, they do not bring these two observations together, but one cannot avoid the suspicion that the observed decline of the modal verbs in general, and of putative *should* in particular, may in part be responsible for the return of the subjunctive. So the question is, to what extent has the behaviour of *should* influenced the evolution of the inflected subjunctive? Are mandative subjunctives and *should*-periphrasis really a binary choice? And how can we find out?

Let us start at a different end and consider the variants that are commonly identified as viable alternatives for inflected subjunctives in mandative constructions in the studies quoted above. Usually, they include the following:

mandative verb (e.g. *to admonish the reader~*)	
+ dependent clause with finite VP_{subj}	~ *that he expect not...*
+ dependent clause with finite $VP_{modal\ aux}$	~ *that he should not expect...*
+ dependent clause with finite VP_{ind}	~ *that he does not expect...*
+ infinitival complement (*to-* or bare infinitive)	~ *not to expect...*

Table 1. Mandative constructions: common inventory of variant forms in relevant literature

From a distributional point of view, it is generally claimed that complements in the indicative mood do not figure prominently and may safely be neglected (e.g. Huddleston and Pullum 2002, 995). Infinitival complements are often mentioned but not necessarily taken into consideration in the statistics (e.g. in Leech et al. 2009, 70), or are judged to be of minor importance when contrasted with nominal *that*-complements as an alternative complementation pattern (e.g. in Moessner 2010, 157).

From a structural point of view, however, the issue of the inventory becomes more acute. Most of the variants in Table 1 are dependent nominal clauses with variation in the finite verb phrase. Only the last variant is a non-finite complement, which raises two questions: Does this matter? And: Are there other non-finite constructions that we should consider? Or, more plainly speaking: What counts as a variant form?

In the relevant literature, this question has hardly been asked, and it seems a tacit assumption that only morphological alternatives in the dependent VP are viable variant forms of the inflected mandative subjunctive. It seems surprising that this should be so, since the subjunctive paradigm in mandative constructions is usually explained by the functions that it fulfils rather than by its structural characteristics. So the interest seems to lie first and foremost in alternative constructions that fulfil the same *functions*. In the following section, I will therefore attempt a description of mandative constructions that does not stop at a self-imposed morphosyntactic barrier but considers alternative forms from the perspective of functional equivalence.

4. Variant Forms in Dependent Mandative Constructions in the *Corpus of English Religious Prose* (1500-1700)

Core variant forms of inflected mandative subjunctives are those forms in dependent structures that take a suasive verb as their governing matrix verb, since it is this matrix verb that triggers the mandative subjunctive in the first place (Quirk et al. 1985, 156; Huddleston and Pullum 2002, 999). As was seen in Table 1 (above), these forms may or may not be marked for modality in different ways. They include:

inflected subjunctives

(2) Q. What is the general dutie here **required**? A. **That** the whole Sabbath or Lords day, **be set apart** from al common vses, as holy to the Lord ... (Ball's catechism, 1630)[4]

modal verb periphrasis

(3) Q. What is the generall dutie **required** in this Commandement? A. **That we should vse** the titles ... & ordinance of the Lord, with knowledge ... & sinceritv... (Ball's catechism, 1630)

indicative forms (i.e., not identifiable as subjunctive on morphological grounds)

(4) Q. What is **required** in this commandement? A. **That we worship** God as himselfe hath appointed ... (Allein's catechism, 1631)

to-infinitives

(5) A. The first Commandement **requireth us to know and acknowledge** God to be the onely true God, and our God; (Westminster Shorter Catechism, 1647)

This emphasis on the matrix verb as the centre of mandative constructions seems to invite direct objects in the form of gerunds, nominalizations, and proper NPs into the circle of alternative forms as well, albeit as marginal or minor forms. Nevertheless, one might argue that they are "triggered" by the matrix verb, too. These minor variant forms are illustrated in examples (6) to (8) and summarised in Table 2 (below):

gerunds

(6) Q. What is required in the fourth Commandement? A. The fourth Commandement **requireth the keeping holy** to God such set time as he hath appointed in his word, expressely one whole day in seven, to be a holy Sabbath to himself. (Westminster Shorter Catechism, 1647)

nominalizations

(7) Q. What is required in the seventh Commandement? A. The seventh Commandement **requireth the preservation** of our own and our neighbours chastity, in heart, speech, and behaviour. (Westminster Shorter Catechism, 1647)

substitution by a noun phrase

(8) Q. What doth God require of us, that we may escape his wrath and curse, due to us for sin? A. To escape the wrath and curse of God due to us for sin, **God requireth of us Faith** in Jesus Christ ... (Westminster Shorter Catechism, 1647)

Note that all examples (2) to (8) are taken from the same genre (catechism) and that they are contemporaneous (first half of the seventeenth century). They thus occur in identical extra-linguistic contexts. As direct objects "triggered" by a suasive verb, they also, in a way, provide identical linguistic co-texts.

Another interesting pattern is that of a coordinated declarative-imperative clause in the following example, where the imperative *forgive them* is triggered by the suasive verb *beseech*:

---

[4] Note that the proposition in this and other examples is distributed across two turns, where the matrix clause is dropped in the answer turn (see Halliday and Hasan [1976] for ellipsis as a cohesive device). This is a common feature of catechisms and both question and answer turns are usually fairly close together so that the processing as a single syntactic unit is not impeded (see Rütten [2011, 55-57] for a fuller treatment of this phenomenon as a mnemonic device in didactic contexts).

(9) When the Defeat of Lambert and his Party ... was told him, his onely triumph was that of his Charity, saying with tears in his eyes, Poor Souls! **I beseech God forgive them**. (biography, 1661)

This pattern, even though it does not match the definition of a mandative construction provided above, indicates the fuzzy edges of real language data: An alternative reading in effect suggests that this is a dependent construction with a bare infinitive (*I beseech God [to] forgive them*).

This variety of complementation patterns is by no means exceptional and indicates that all forms are viable alternatives for the authors of these texts. The consistent variability in the Westminster Shorter Catechism in the consecutive treatment of the Decalogue illustrates quite clearly that these variants are a conscious stylistic choice.[5] From a functional perspective, it therefore seems a rash decision to discard non-finite and deverbal variants on the ground that they are not part of a morphological paradigm in the dependent VP. Quite obviously, they do form practical alternatives for contemporary language users. This variability is most likely stylistic and does not involve language change in apparent-time. My point is simply that it gives us a cue as to what constitutes an alternative form for inflected mandative subjunctives apart from morphological likeness.

These alternatives may be grouped according to the status of the verb in the complement clause. This results in a morphosyntactic cline (illustrated in Table 2, below) ranging from inflected subjunctives in the dependent nominal clause and related finite variants, over non-finite forms to deverbal complementation patterns such as gerunds, nominalizations, and substitution by an NP. However, this cline needs further qualification.

First, gerunds are, of course, also non-finite forms. They are singled out as a category in its own right because they form the linking element between fully verbal and fully nominal forms. As such, they incorporate the fact that the more central core variants of the mandative subjunctive are morphological verbal alternatives in a dependent clause, while the minor variants form NPs within a main clause. These are thus one additional structural step removed from the subjunctive paradigm and its core variants in the dependent clause.

Secondly, the coordinated declarative-imperative clauses form an exception in the finite variant set. Here, we find yet another clause structure, i.e., clausal coordination, that also serves quite a different purpose, as will become clear below.

---

5   Compare example (5) first commandment: *to*-infinitive, example (6) fourth commandment: gerund, example (7) seventh commandment: nominalization, and example (8) resumptive requirement of God to mankind: substitution by NP.

		mandative verb (e.g. *the commandment requireth~*)
finite	+ dependent clause with finite VP$_{subj}$	~ *that the Lords Day **be set apart*** (1630 Ball)
	+ dependent clause with finite VP$_{modal\ aux}$	~ *that **we should use** the title of the Lord with faith* (1630 Ball)
	+ dependent clause with finite VP$_{ind}$	~ *that **we worship** God* (1631 Allein)
	[coordinated imperative clause]	?*I beseech God **forgive** them* (1661, biography)
non-finite	+ infinitival complement	~ *us **to acknowledge** God to be the onely true God* (1647 Westminster)
deverbal	+ gerund	~ ***the keeping** holy to God set times* (1647 Westminster)
	+ nominalization	~ ***the preservation** of our chastitiy* (1647 Westminster)
substitution	+ NP	~ ***faith** in Jesus Christ* (1647 Westminster)

Table 2. Mandative constructions: extended inventory of variant forms

Is this comparing apples and oranges? To answer this question it may be worthwhile to identify the resulting distributional pattern first. For this reason, I conducted a study with the Early Modern English part of the *Corpus of English Religious Prose* (COERP). There are two reasons for this choice of database. First, both Moessner (2010) and Fillbrandt (2006) suggest that the Early Modern period is where contact between language users of the (supposedly) old and new forms is greatest and therefore where variability should be most clearly visible (compare the discussion in section 2). Secondly, Moessner (2010, 166) claims that religious language (genres of religious instruction and Bible translations), because of its inherent didactic and authoritative character, is likely to adopt a higher frequency of relevant items than other registers and may, consequently, show the greatest variability of form.

From the *Early Modern English Sampler* of COERP, I selected catechisms, biographies, sermons, and controversial treatises as core genres and prefaces to biographies, catechisms, and sermons as associated genres.[6] Table 3 gives an overview of the dataset:

	catechisms	biographies	sermons	treatises	prefaces	total
1500-1549	7.282	40.408	24.837	43.535	14.567	**130.629**
1550-1599	35.632	40.204	35.377	43.737	13.950	**168.900**
1600-1649	40.405	35.202	34.288	50.191	9.958	**170.044**
1650-1700	40.336	46.310	30.290	50.775	13.139	**180.850**
total	**123.655**	**162.124**	**124.792**	**188.238**	**51.614**	**650.423**

Table 3. The corpus used in the analysis

In this dataset, all variant forms identified in Table 2 were retrieved in a semi-automatic search for triggering expressions. The triggering expressions are taken from Visser's list of verbs that take the mandative subjunctive in their nominal complement in the Early Modern English period (see Visser 1963, 827ff). In total, I investigated 80

---

6   Core genres in COERP are defined as the most central genres in the discourse domain; associated genres, by contrast, are not genuinely religious in nature, but eventually become associated with writings in the domain. For a more detailed description of these categories and the general design of COERP see Rütten et al. (2008) and Kohnen (2010).

verbs and related nominal and adjectival expressions, having excluded all matrix verbs relating purely to mental or locutionary acts (e.g. *to think, to say*, etc.).[7]

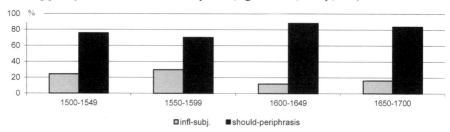

Figure 2. Percentages of infl-subj. vs *should*-periphrasis in COERP

Figure 2 shows that the traditional view that the inflected subjunctive is substituted by modal verb periphrasis in the Early Modern English period seems fairly obvious in religious language, too, when the data are mapped accordingly in a chart. Contrasted in this binary fashion, the prediction that mandative subjunctives decline in favour of the *should*-variant seems justified indeed. Modal verb constructions are by far the preferred choice in religious genres (nearly 80 percent in the first subperiod; over 80 percent at the end of the seventeenth century). This situation seems to have already been established at the beginning of the Early Modern period and proves to be relatively stable (see Moessner's 2010 findings).

However, Figure 3 (below) tells quite a different story. Here the distribution and diachronic development of all variants from Table 2 are given in terms of normalized frequency counts. Each vertical bar indicates the normalized frequency of the variant in a sub-period of fifty years in the Early Modern section in COERP.[8] Note that this is a different representation of the data than in most other studies on the mandative subjunctive. Usually, the focus is on the proportionate arrangement of the core variants. By contrast, Figure 3 shows actual *frequencies* of usage for *all* alternatives. This has important methodological consequences which I will discuss in the conclusions section, below.

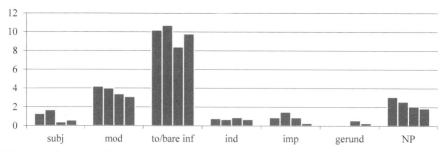

Figure 3. Distribution of *infl-subj* and alternative forms in four 50-year subperiods in COERP. Frequency per 10,000w

---

7   These verbs relate to mental processes and the act of uttering rather than to directive acts, even though one could argue that, if uttered by someone of greater power (e.g. a bishop to a congregation), the communication of mental processes may be taken as a directive.

8   The category *gerund* comprises both gerunds and nominalizations. None are attested for the first two subperiods in the relevant construction.

First of all, Figure 3 shows that the subjunctive is indeed in decline. Figures are roughly cut in half from 1.3 per 10,000w in the first subperiod to 0.6 in the last. Also, modal verb constructions are, in fact, more popular, as proportionate representations have suggested (see Figure 2 and the discussion in section 3, above). But they likewise decrease from 4.2 to 3.1 per 10,000w over the four subperiods. Note that this change is actually obscured by the proportionate arrangement of the data in Figure 2, where the rise from 75 to 83 percent suggests a growth of the modal variant, when quite the opposite is true in terms of frequency.

Other results are noteworthy, too. Modal *should*-periphrasis is certainly not the most immediate rival of inflected subjunctives, since infinitival complements are by far the preferred choice in all four subperiods (averaging around 9 per 10,000w). Quite obviously, this is obscured as well if we only consider finite *that*-complements (again, compare Figure 2). Interestingly, this competition between inflected subjunctives and infinitival complements has been discussed for Early Middle English already in studies on the rise of the *to*-infinitive (see Los 2007, 41). Should we therefore calculate an S-Curve rather on the comparison of the inflected subjunctive and infinitival complements? I will return to this point in my conclusions. It is important to note here that infinitival complements, as the most popular variant, do decline as well during the course of the Early Modern period (from 10.2 in the first subperiod to 9.8 in the last, with a more pronounced dip in the third subperiod). The last of the core variant forms, indicatives, is rather inconsequential in terms of frequency, averaging just below 1 per 10,000w in all periods. This finding, for once, is consonant with the predictions that rely on the proportionate array of the core variants (e.g. Moessner 2010; Leech et al. 2009).

Ignoring coordinated clause constructions with an imperative for the moment, the minor variant forms tell an interesting story. The high frequencies of NP-substitution (averaging around 2 per 10,000w) again testify to the fact that nominal *that*-complementation was not necessarily the primary choice in mandative constructions. May we conclude then, that inflected subjunctives are highly sensitive to co-text, and that part of their demise is due to more overarching changes in complementation patterns?

Also, it is noteworthy that the minor forms decline in quite the same way as the core variants do (NP-substitution decreases from 3.1. to 1.9; gerunds are cut in half from 0.6 to 0.3 per 10,000w). So even though there may be good reason to reject the minor variant forms on morphosyntactic grounds, they do here complete our understanding that mandative constructions in general do decline. This behaviour is consistent in all variants in Figure 3.

Does this development have to do with the nature of religious language in the seventeenth century?[9] A provisionary answer must be in the affirmative. Religious language in the seventeenth century is much less directive and exhortative but much more concerned with persuading and convincing people of the right faith (see Rütten 2011). A general decline of mandative constructions would thus fit in very well with the changing patterns of religious instruction in the seventeenth century.

---

9   This question indicates a pitfall of comparison and comparability on a different level, namely that of genre. On the influence of genre, register, and domain in comparative historical studies see Kohnen (this volume).

Yet perhaps this change also occurs in other domains and genres, and we may be unaware of it because we have not looked at the issue from this angle before. Moessner (2010) discusses the influence of genre on the distribution of mandative constructions in Middle English. While she detects differences in the extent to which a certain variant is used in proportionate terms (that is, compared to the rest of the inventory of variants in a given genre), she does not supply an overview in terms of frequency of usage. Ultimately, therefore, the question of the influence of genre, register, and domain on the frequency of mandative constructions, in general, and on mandative subjunctives, in particular, must as yet remain undecided.

As for imperative forms, they consistently occur after *beseech, bid, command,* and *pray*. In constructions with *beseech* and *pray*, the utterance is less of a complex mandative construction but rather a request in the form of a simple imperative clause involving *beseech* and *pray* as discourse markers. This places the whole utterance more in the vicinity of evolving negative politeness phrases such as *if it please you* than as variants of inflected subjunctives in mandative constructions:

> (10) Dear sirs, **I beseech you with beseeching, consider** well of these things; (preface to sermon, 1663)

In combination with *bid* and *command*, the mandative construction frequently involves direct or reported speech, which may explain the use of an independent imperative clause here. Often, the imperative clause forms part of a quotation from the Bible:

> (11) Again, whereas **our Lord commandeth**, Mk 10 **Suffer** litle children to come unto me & forbid them not. (treatise, 1645, Pagitt)

> (12) If a man should **bid** his servant **goe sheare** all my sheepe and mark them: if that servant should shere all his sheep, and marke them only that he had shorne, and not marke his Lambs because hee could not shere them: doth that servant fulfill his Masters command? (treatise, 1645, Pagitt)

These four verbs form a rather obvious exception and indicate the boundary of functional equivalence. Even though suasive verbs are used, they function as politeness markers in the former case and as reporting verbs in the latter. This brings us back to the general question brought forward in section 1: What counts as a variant form and why? I will try to give a balanced answer in my conclusions section now.

5. Conclusions

I hope to have shown that I have not compared apples and oranges in this paper. In fact, the discussion of the varied set of core and minor alternative forms in mandative constructions may have important consequences for how we judge the evolution of the mandative subjunctive and on how we proceed methodologically in comparative historical studies. I will treat each issue in turn.

The Evolution of the Mandative Subjunctive

A revision of the evolution of the subjunctive along the lines that I have tried to sketch here seems desirable. First of all, we need to give an explicit account of the variant forms and structures of the mandative subjunctive that we include in a comparative study. We need to inquire in more detail into the ways in which these variants interact with one another. Only then can we identify the factors that are decisive in the evolution of the subjunctive. Los's (2007) claim that the subjunctive is losing out to infinitival complements may have to be extended as to include finite nominal *that*-complements in general, affecting modal verb constructions, as well as those that take the indicative form.[10]

Secondly, this study has revealed that the subjunctive is highly sensitive to both co-text and context. With the substitution of *that*-complements by infinitival complements, the prime co-text of mandative subjunctives is lost. Likewise, with the general demise of mandative matrix clauses observed in this study, the crucial trigger for mandative subjunctives is lacking. As a consequence, the "disappearance" and "revival" of mandative subjunctives that was observed in earlier studies may, in fact, be a "phantom change" of what really are secondary repercussions induced by failing co-texts and failing contexts.

In light of these findings, we need to ask again whether the subjunctive did, does, or will decline. Also, we need to ask whether the observed residue is stable. Finally, it seems desirable to consider other forms of (morphological) mood marking, e.g. tense shifts, in our discussion of the subjunctive (for this idea see Rissanen 1999), to arrive at a more accurate picture of its role and evolution in the history of English.

Finally, as a footnote to the evolution on the mandative subjunctive, I would like to make the point that religious language is not as traditional as we generally like to think, in the sense that it does not preserve the old morphological subjunctive paradigm. Instead, it seems to adopt the "incoming" infinitival complementation pattern at a very early stage already.

Consequences on Methodology in Comparative (Historical) Studies

I have shown that a comparison that is based on frequency reveals a much more accurate picture of the evolution of the mandative subjunctive than a comparison that is based on proportions. For one thing, a proportionate arrangement of the data at best obscures and at the worst distorts actual frequencies of a given variant form. Also, normalized frequencies make much more substantial claims on norm-based behaviour, for example, about the conceived standard and permissible (stylistic) variation.

Concerning "sameness" of variant forms, I have shown that there is a morphosyntactic cline of which the discourse-pragmatic mandative meaning, however, remains largely unaffected.

1. Finite Forms

An analysis that includes only variants of the same morphosyntactic kind, i.e., finite forms in dependent VPs, certainly comes closest to identical linguistic options. For mandative subjunctives, these options are provided by the core finite alternatives (inflected subjunctives, modal verb periphrasis, and indicative forms). We have seen that they may fall short of explaining the diachronic evolution of the subjunctive.

---

10 On the correlation of nominal *that*-clauses with *should* and the *to*-infinitive see also Quirk et al. (1985, 1062-63), who note that "the nominal *to*-infinitive clause often indicates that the proposition it expresses is viewed as a possibility or a proposal rather than something already fulfilled. The infinitive clause is then closest semantically to a *that*-clause with putative *should*."

2. Finite / Non-finite Forms

An analysis that extends the set of finite variants to include infinitival complements, and possibly also gerunds, provides "sameness" on the syntactic level, even though it neglects sameness of morphological form. There is thus only partial identity of linguistic options. This perspective has certainly widened our perception on the evolution of mandative subjunctives since it showed that the general change of verb complementation patterns in English is in part responsible for the decline of mandative subjunctives. This, in turn, may help to solve the puzzling, and seemingly inconsistent, behaviour of the "return" of the subjunctive.

3. Verbal / Deverbal Forms

Here, the set of variant forms is further extended to deverbal and nominal forms. This widens the syntactic environment to include simple coordinated sentences of an SVO_{NP}-structure alongside the complex subordinate clause structures with nominal *that*-complements (i.e., SVO_{comp}). The triggering expression alone is common to all variant forms. As a consequence, one accepts a rather mixed bag of alternatives alongside different clause patterns. While this is certainly an uncomfortable idea, in the present study this approach has revealed that the demise of the subjunctive is only in part explained by morphological impoverishment. The limits of this approach are clearly shown where triggering expressions no longer serve mandative contexts but adopt completely different functions, for example, as politeness markers or reporting verbs.

In sum, from a functional perspective, e.g. in an analysis of coding directive modality in the history of English, a great variety of variant forms is no inherent evil, but adds to the full comprehensibility of a functional change. It seems desirable therefore that studies that are interested in function should overcome self-imposed morphological boundaries. From a more strictly formal perspective, e.g. concerning morphological mood marking, there are obviously fewer options to be considered, but they will yield different results.

References

Auer, Anita (2006): "Precept and Practice: The Influence of Prescriptivism on the English Subjunctive", in: Dalton-Puffer, Christiane et al. (eds.): *Syntax, Style and Grammatical Norms: English from 1500-2000*. Frankfurt/Bern: Peter Lang, 33-53
--- (2008): "*Lest* the Situation Deteriorate: A Study of *lest* as a Trigger of the Inflectional Subjunctive", in: Locher, Miriam; Strässler, Jürg (eds.): *Standards and Norms in the English Language*. Berlin: de Gruyter, 149-173
Bailey, Charles-James N. (1973): *Variation and Linguistic Theory*. Washington D.C. Center for Applied Linguistics
Fillbrandt, Eva-Liisa (2006): "The Development of the Mandative Subjunctive in the Early Modern English Period", *Trames* 10. 60/55, 135-151
Fowler, Henry (1926/1965): *A Dictionary of Modern English Usage*, 2nd edition. rev. by Ernest Gowers. Oxford: Clarendon
Halliday, M.A.K.; Hasan, Ruquaiya (1976): *Cohesion in English*. London: Longman
Harsh, Wayne (1968): *The Subjunctive in English*. Tuscaloosa: University of Alabama Press
Huddleston, Rodney; Pullum, Geoffrey (2002): *The Cambridge Grammar of the English Language*. Cambridge: Cambridge University Press

Kohnen, Thomas (2010): "Religious Discourse", in: Jucker, Andreas H.; Taavitsainen, Irma (eds.): *Historical Pragmatics: An International Handbook*. Berlin: de Gruyter, 523-548

--- et al. (2011): "Early Modern English Religious Prose: A Conservative Register?", in: Rayson, Paul et al. (eds.): *Methodological and Historical Dimensions of Corpus Linguistics (VARIENG e-journal)*. <www.helsinki.fi/varieng/series/volumes/06/kohnen_et_al/>

Labov, William (1994): *Principles of Linguistic Change. Volume 1: Internal Factors*. Oxford, UK/ Cambridge, USA: Blackwell

Leech, Geoffrey et al. (2009): *Change in Contemporary English: A Grammatical Study*. Cambridge: Cambridge University Press

Los, Bettelou (2007): "*To* as a Connective in the History of English", in: Lenker, U.; Meurman-Solin, A. (eds.): *Connectives in the History of English*. Berlin: de Gruyter, 31-60

Moessner, Lilo (2010): "Mandative Constructions in Middle English", *ICAME Journal* 34, 151-168

Nevalainen, Terttu; Raumolin-Brunberg, Helena (2003): *Historical Sociolinguistics: Language Change in Tudor and Stuart England*. London: Longman

Övergaard, Gerd (1995): *The Mandative Subjunctive in American and British English in the 20th Century*. Stockholm: Almquist & Wiksell

Peters, Pam (1998): "The Survival of the Subjunctive: Evidence of its Use in Australia and Elsewhere", *English Worldwide* 19.1, 87-103

Quirk, Randolph et al. (1985): *A Comprehensive Grammar of the English Language*. London: Longman

Rissanen, Matti (1999): "Syntax", in: Lass, Roger (ed.): *The Cambridge History of the English Language, Volume III: 1476-1776*. Cambridge: Cambridge University Press, 187-331

Rütten, Tanja (2011): *How to Do Things with Texts: Patterns of Instruction in Religious Discourse 1350-1700*. Frankfurt am Main: Peter Lang

--- et al. (2008): *The Corpus of English Religious Prose: Introduction*. <www.helsinki.fi/varieng/ CoRD/corpora/COERP/index.html>

Visser, Frederik Theodoor (1963): *An Historical Syntax of the English Language. Part One: Syntactical Units with One Verb*. Leiden: Brill

THOMAS KOHNEN (KÖLN)

In Search of Faithful Standards: Comparing Diachronic Corpora across Domains

1. Introduction

The aim of this paper is to raise the question of comparison and comparability from the perspective of corpus-based diachronic studies. The availability of different diachronic corpora stemming from quite distinct, often unrelated domains of language use opens up the possibility of comparing and combining them in order to gather an even larger collection of data and thus to improve possible results. However, it is problematic to simply 'add up' different domain-based corpora, because here 'more data' does not necessarily mean 'better data'. Rather, researchers should be able to select and link suitable parts of existing corpora that meet the specific requirements of their studies.

In this paper I will present a method of comparing diachronic corpora that employs text-functional and domain-based parameters as bases for comparison (on a basic outline of text-functional and domain-based parameters, see Kohnen 2012). First, I will look at general text functions, for example, narration, in texts and genres from different domains. Then the focus will be on the interactive format and the publication format of texts. I will analyse texts from different domains that employ the dialogue form and look at the publication format of pamphlets. Among the domain-based parameters, hierarchies of genres (first-, second-, and third-order genres) are the most important dimensions. Here I will especially look at the status of the first-order rank of genres.

In order to test these parameters as bases for comparison, I will analyse the frequencies and distributions of selected morphosyntactic and pragmatic items in genres from different domains. My focus will be on the question of what kinds of comparisons and comparability are involved and what standards of comparison can be achieved by such an approach.

The data I analyse are selected genres from the *Corpus of English Religious Prose* and the *Corpus of Early Modern English Medical Texts*; in addition I will include texts from other domains (for example, the administrative domain) from the *Helsinki Corpus* and data from the *Corpus of English Dialogues*.

2. General Text Functions

General text functions are functions of texts that recur inside texts and that may be typically associated with sections of texts (see Kohnen 2012; Rütten 2011; Werlich 1983). So, in a sermon we can find sections that attempt to change the addressee's behaviour (exhortation), sections devoted to the explanation of the doctrine of the church (exposition), and sections with stories about exemplary conduct (narration). General text functions (like exhortation, exposition, narration, and argumentation) may be called 'general' because they can be found in many texts in all domains. They are important for the linguistic profile of a text because the predominant text function determines the frequency and distribution of many linguistic features in a text. At the same time, different genres from different domains tend to have similar text functions, resulting in similar frequencies and distributions of such features. Text functions therefore seem to be an important standard of comparison.

I would like to illustrate this point with excerpts from fifteenth-century petitions, sermons, and letters. These all contain large narrative sections. In the excerpts I have highlighted some typical narrative features (following the factor "narrative versus non-narrative concerns" in Biber's [1988] multi-feature analysis): verbs with past tense / present perfect and present participle forms, third-person pronouns, and public verbs. Example (1) below is from a Chancery petition (Fisher et al. 1984, 235). Here the narrative section depicts all the details of the case.

(1) A Roy nostre souerain seigneur Besechen humbly youre Comunes of this present parliament. that where one Iohn Carpenter of Brydham in the Shire of Sussex husbund-man the vii daye of Fevever the yere of youre noble reigne the viiite **saying** to Isabell **his** wijff that **was** of the Age. of xvje. yere and had be maried to **him** but xv dayes. that **they** wolde go to gedre on Pilgremage and **made** to arraye **hir** in **hir** best arraie and **toke** hir with **hym** fro the said Toun of Brydham to the Toun of Stoghton in the said Shire. And there in a woode **he smote** the said Isabell **his** wijff on the hede that the brayne **wende** oute and with his knyff yaf **hire** many other dedly woundes.

Example (2) is from a letter by Margaret Paston in which she tells her husband about an extraordinary incident.

(2) Ryght worshipfull husbond, I recomaund me to yow, and prey yow to wete þat on Friday last passed be-fore noon, þe parson of Oxened **beyng** at messe in our parossh chirche, [...], Jamys Gloys hadde ben in þe tovne and **come** homward by Wymondams gate. And Wymondam **stod** in **his** gate and John Norwode **his** man **stod** by **hym**, and Thomas Hawys **his** othir man **stod** in þe strete by þe canell side. And Jamys Gloys **come** with **his** hatte on **his** hede betwen bothe **his** men, as **he was** wont of custome to do. And whanne Gloys **was** a-yenst Wymondham **he seid** þus. (*Helsinki Corpus*)

Example (3) stems from a sermon, a fifteenth-century revision of John Mirk's *Festial* collection, with a story about the Roman emperor Augustus.

(3) Thus not allonely for bewtye but also for bonyte, euery man hath mater and cause to do hym reuerence. As **dyd** þat noble and high myghti emperoure, Octauianus, which emperoure had bilded **hym** a place many yeris or Criste **was** borne, in þe citee of Rome. And in this paleys **he regnyd** worshipfully and **lovyd** of the Romayns, that **þei wolde** worship **hym** and accept **hym** for **theire** god because **he plesyd** so moch þe peple of **his** empyre. So this emperoure, Octauyan, **was** wise and discrete. **Thinking** and **knowing** that **he** was but a man as oþir men be, **he durst** not take vpon **hym** þe name of God, but anon **he sende** aftir Sibilla, a sage and a wise profetyse, holy and wellavysed. (Powell 1981)

The sheer number of the highlighted elements in examples (1)-(3) shows how much the narrative function shapes the linguistic profile of these texts. Although they belong to quite different genres and cannot necessarily be called 'narrative' in nature, they seem to be quite similar in their linguistic structure. However, this similarity may be 'evened out' by other dissimilar sections in the texts, for example, exhortation and exposition in sermons or petition and thanksgiving in letters.

By contrast, the difference in the frequency and distribution of typically narrative elements in narrative and non-narrative genres can be quite dramatic if there is no mixture of the predominant text function. This can be seen from the frequencies of third-person pronouns in extracts from statutes and scientific treatises, on the one hand, and fiction, biographies, and chronicles, on the other. These data were chosen from the last sub-period of the Early Modern section in the *Helsinki Corpus* (see Figure 1 below). Here the contrast is quite extraordinary if not categorical.

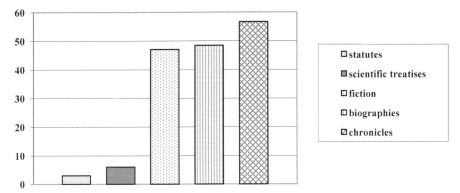

Figure 1. Third-person pronouns (*he, she, they*) in non-narrative and narrative genres (E3, Helsinki Corpus; freq. per 1,000 words)

To sum up some preliminary results: What kind of comparison and comparability do general text functions like narration provide? Basically, it seems that prevailing text functions shape the linguistic profile of texts. Thus, we are dealing with a similarity of textual function, which results in a similarity of linguistic form. Such comparisons are, of course, relevant to studies focussing on the frequency and distribution of morpho-syntactic features in texts and genres. The problem for such studies is, however, that genre designations do not necessarily include reliable information about the prevailing text functions of the respective texts. In addition, some genres seem to have changed their predominant text functions across the centuries (see, for example, Rütten 2011 on sermons). Therefore, especially diachronic studies comparing genres from different corpora must check predominant text functions in the text files.

3. Interactive Format: Dialogue Form

Now let us turn to the interactive format of texts as a basis for comparing genres from different domains. A major dimension in the interactive format of texts is whether their setting is dialogic or monologic, that is, whether the text represents an interaction between speakers or whether only the voice of the author of the text is present. The Early Modern period shows many dialogue settings in genres where we would not expect them today, and these genres belong to a wide variety of domains, for example, medical, religious, and political treatises, as well as handbooks from various sections of life (marriage, horticulture, fishing, and so on).

Thus, the dialogue form qualifies as a basis for comparison. Treatises and handbooks stemming from different domains but sharing the dialogue format should have certain linguistic features in common. At the same time, these texts would differ from 'regular' treatises and handbooks that have no dialogue setting, and one could claim that Early Modern dialogic and monologic genres, although they carry identical designations like treatises and handbooks, should not actually be compared if the focus is on linguistic features that are typical of dialogue.

One set of features that may be considered typically interactive are first- and second-person pronouns because they are used by interactants to refer to themselves and to their conversational partners (in Early Modern English the relevant forms are *I, me, we, us, ye, you, thou, thee*). Figure 2 below shows the frequencies of first-person and second-person pronouns in medical treatises, handbooks, and catechisms with dialogue format and in scientific and educational treatises in the second part of the sixteenth and the first part of the seventeenth century.[1]

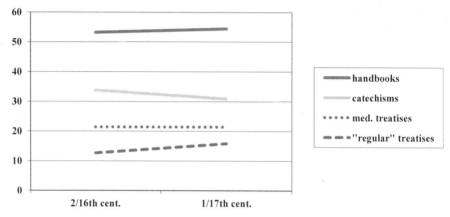

Figure 2. First- and second-person references in medical treatises, handbooks, catechisms (dialogue format), and 'regular' treatises (freq. per 1,000 words)

Figure 2 above shows a quite consistent picture, which, however, does not necessarily fulfil our initial expectations. The four genres cover different ranges of frequencies, with consistently decreasing levels. The handbooks in dialogue format contain more than fifty references in 1,000 words, catechisms slightly more than thirty, medical treatises about twenty, and the 'regular' treatises between twelve and fifteen. This distribution suggests that, among the dialogic texts, medical treatises are the least interactive and that handbooks show the least expository nature, whereas catechisms take up a medial position. The 'regular' treatises do not differ much from the (least interactive) dialogic medical treatises. Thus, it seems that the dialogue format in handbooks and treatises does not necessarily result in a similar frequency of interactive features. Rather, we find a cline of 'interactivity' that ranges from the most dialogic to the most

---

1 The handbook texts were taken from the *Corpus of English Dialogues* (33,210 words for 2/16th century and 30,540 words for 1/17th century), the catechism texts stem from the *Corpus of English Religious Prose* (43,642 words for 2/sixteenth century and 40,192 words for 1/seventeenth century), the medical treatises come from *Early Modern English Medical Texts* (30,939 words for 2/sixteenth century and 31,438 words for 1/seventeenth century), and the non-dialogue treatises are the educational and scientific treatises contained in the *Helsinki Corpus* (23,320 words for 2/sixteenth century and 18,720 words for 1/seventeenth century). Among the educational treatises of the *Helsinki Corpus*, CEEDU2A was not included since this text is presented in a dialogue format.

monologic genres but that does not impose a categorical difference between the linguistic profiles of dialogic and monologic genres.

This cline of 'interactivity' also seems to reflect the general outline and the aims of the texts. The handbooks are fairly informal and full of lively interaction; they want to entertain their readers. By contrast, both catechisms and medical treatises seem to preserve the expository nature of the texts, where different paragraphs are simply assigned to alternating speakers. Here the prevailing aim is the coherent communication of information.[2]

It is quite instructive to see what place 'real' contemporary conversational interaction has on this cline of 'interactivity'. Biber et al. (1999) note in their *Grammar of Spoken and Written English* that the frequency of first- and second-person pronouns in contemporary conversation is about 80 in 1,000 words. This frequency would constitute one extreme on the cline of the frequencies of first- and second-person pronouns, far away from monologic written texts, but still reasonably close to the Early Modern English written dialogic handbooks.

When comparing texts with dialogue format we assume, as we did in the case of general text functions, that a similarity of function results in a similarity of form. Texts sharing the dialogue format seem to contain more first- and second-person pronouns, or, generally speaking, more deictic elements (in particular person deixis). However, quite in contrast to narrative and non-narrative texts, differences between dialogic and non-dialogic texts and differences among dialogic texts seem to be much more subtle, forming a cline between the extreme points of face-to-face interaction and strictly expository texts. Even in purely expository texts (such as the 'regular' scientific and educational treatises in Figure 2), though, reference to addressor and addressee may be common to a certain extent.

It is likely that there are other linguistic items whose frequencies and distributions depend on the dialogic nature of texts (for example, discourse markers and certain cohesive means). But here, as with deictic elements, more research is necessary in order to get a clearer picture of the dimension of variation found in different genres.

4. Publication Format: Pamphlets

The publication format (or compilation format) of texts may serve as another basis for comparison. The publication format of a text refers to its 'neighbourhood', the company it keeps with other texts. Is a text part of a collection of articles or part of a newspaper? Is it published as a pamphlet, in a journal, or simply as a book? Here again, we may assume that texts sharing the same publication format will show certain similarities.

This is most conspicuous with the publication type 'pamphlet'. In the Early Modern period pamphlets served as a popular platform for publishing a wide variety of genres (for example, sermons, petitions, letters, and treatises). It seems that the publication type had an impact on the form and function of the respective genre. Groeger (2010) found out that the publication type of pamphlets made petitions and letters less interac-

---

2   The slightly higher frequency in catechisms seems to be due to the fact that the longer contributions of the pupil usually contain many first-person pronouns, which is in turn due to the 'acts of faith' (for example, *I believe that*) that contain such references.

tive and less formulaic. The primary audience is addressed less often and the formulaic beginnings and endings of letters and petitions are less frequently found in pamphlets. Figure 3 below shows that the frequencies of address forms are significantly lower in pamphlets than in their 'original' genre format.

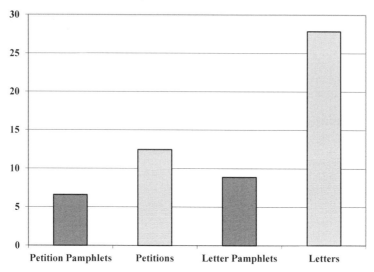

Figure 3. Frequencies of address forms to the (primary) audience in pamphlets and original genres (freq. per 1,000 words) (following Groeger 2010)

Comparisons based on the publication format also assume that similarity of function results in similarity of form, or, in other words, that transformations to identical publication types bring about similar linguistic changes in the source texts, resulting in a similar frequency and distribution of forms and constructions. Here, the most interesting cases will be those where 'host' texts and genres bring together texts from different domains and different publication formats (for example, pamphlets or a newspaper). Existing research so far suggests that the publication format pamphlet modifies the interactive format of the source text or source genre.

5. Domain Structure: Hierarchies

The genres of a particular domain often form a network that can be captured in a systematic fashion (on network structures of genres see also Swales 2004). One important parameter in this domain structure is formed by hierarchies. Genres may be said to develop certain hierarchies in their respective domains, depending on the basic constellations of the discourse participants involved in the communication (Kohnen 2010; 2012). Here we may distinguish first-, second-, and third-order genres.

The first-order sphere contains texts issued by a superior, binding body or authority and directed at all the members of the discourse community. Typical examples are statutes and laws in the administrative domain and the Bible (seen as God's word) in the religious domain. In the second-order sphere the basic constellation of the discourse participants is inverted. Here it is the members of a discourse community that address a superior authority or institution. Typical examples in the administrative domain are petitions to higher institutions and in the religious domain different forms of prayer. In the third-order sphere no superior body is involved in the communication. Members of a discourse community communicate with each other, more or less at the same level, with no higher institution involved. Typical examples are letters among fellow citizens, handbooks, treatises, etc.

Now, it seems promising to employ the hierarchies as bases for comparisons across domains. For example, we can compare first-order genres from three different domains: prestigious medical text books from the domain of science, statutes from the administrative domain, and vernacular Bible translations from the religious domain. The similarities of the three genres as members of the first-order sphere are obvious. They enjoy a high prestige in their domain and they form a fundamental point of reference and basis for justification. In addition, these texts are cited in other texts and they are not likely to change quickly.[3] Are these similarities also reflected in a common linguistic profile of the texts?

When we look at statutes, established medical treatises and Bible translations from the sixteenth century, we find that these texts do not have much in common. Rather, there are quite a few idiosyncratic features that seem to shape the characteristic 'style' of each genre. In the following I will illustrate three typical idiosyncratic features for each genre. The point of this illustration is not to give a comprehensive account but rather to show that in each genre there are features that are incompatible with the features in the other genres and that are to a large extent responsible for the linguistic profile of the genre.[4]

In the statutes I focus on postmodifying constructions with the past participle, so-called absolute infinitives and doublets / triplets involving *and* and *or*. Initially, postmodifying constructions were employed in administrative texts to make the description more precise and comprehensive. Laws and regulations should be accurate and complete, attempting to cover every possible contingency. Thus, in example (4) below, the description of *Clothes* is made more precise and comprehensive through the postmodifying participles *geven, lymyted*, and *assigned*. In addition, the past participles usually lack a description of the agent and thus render the account more 'objective'. All this serves the basic purposes of statutes. Excerpt (4) illustrates how common postmodifying past participles are in statutes.

(4) And be it furthermore ordeyned and enacted by thadvyse and auctoritie **aforesaid** that the Kyng our Sov~ayn Lord or eny other p~sones take not any advantage or p~fuyt of any penalties of forfaitures by an Act **made** in the p~liament **holden** at Westm~ the xxiij day of Januare in the first yere of the Reign of Richard the third … conc~nyng the makyng and drapyng of wollen Clothes **geven lymyted** or **assigned** for eny cloth **made** or hereafter to be made but oonly accordyng to the seid orden^anc~ and statut~ nowe **made** in this p~sent p~liament, Eny acte statute orden^ance or p~vysion to the cont^ary hertofore **made** notwithstondyng. (*Helsinki Corpus*)

---

3   The basic text of the Bible is usually not changed in a new translation, statutes change only when a new law is passed, and in science established authors and theories may only slowly lose their prestige and be replaced.
4   The data for the statutes were taken from the *Helsinki Corpus* (18,440 words), the medical treatises stem from *Early Modern English Medical Texts* (24,492 words), and the Bible translations (Tyndale) come from the *Helsinki Corpus* (21,230 words).

Absolute infinitive constructions are similar to absolute participle constructions in that they are loosely attached to the matrix clause (note the full stop after *agree* in example (5) below) and in that the subject is expressed separately (for example, *the cappe* [...] *to be marked* in example (5)). In the statutes such constructions are often used to refer to the consequences of an enacted law (for example the 'marking' of hats in example (5)). Since the infinitives are usually passive infinitives, the expressed subject is the object of the action and the agent is left out. Thus, absolute infinitives serve the basic purposes of statutes because they express obligation in a compact and objective way.

(5) Ferthermore be it enacted by the said auctorite that no Capper nor Hatter nor other p~sone selle nor putt to sale any cappe ... And that all other cappes and hattes of other woll to be sold at suche price as the bier and seller may resounably agree. **The cappe** made of the seid fynest Leemynster woll **to be marked** in the lynyng of the same cappe with a l~re L.; **The cappe** made of the seconde sorte of the same Leemynster woll **to be marked** with this mark Lr; **The cappe** made of the fynest Cotteswold woll **to be marked** with a l~re C. in the lynyng therof; And **the seconde cappe** of the seconde sorte of Cotteswold woll **to be marked** wyth this marke Cr.; (*Helsinki Corpus*)

Doublets and triplets can already be found in administrative prose of the late Middle English period (see Burnley 1986). They are coordinated phrases (sometimes including even more than three items) that often comprise related or synonymous terms (for example, *knowledge and experience* or *diseases sores and maladies* in example (6) below). Such constructions are usually used for the same purpose as postmodifications with a past participle. For example, *practyse use and mynistre in and to any* [...] *outwarde swelling or disease* in example (6) gives a fairly comprehensive (though hardly elegant) description of the activity on which the law focuses.

(6) Be it ordeyned establisshed **and** enacted by thauctorytie of this p~nt parliament, that at all tymes from hensforthe, it shalbe lefull to everye p~sone being the King~ Subject having knowledge **and** experience of the nature of herbes rotes **and** waters **or** of the operac~on of the same by speculac~on **or** practyse, within any parte of the Realme of Englande, **or** within any other the King~ Domynions, to practyse use **and** mynistre in **and** to any ... outwarde swelling **or** disease, any herbe **or** herbes oyntement~ bathes pultes **and** emplasters, according to theyre cooning experience **and** knowlege in any of the diseases sores **and** maladies aforesaide **and** all other lyke to the same, **or** drinkes for the stone strangurye **or** agues, without sute vexac~on trouble penaltie **or** losse of theyre good~. (*Helsinki Corpus*)

Figure 4 below shows the frequencies of the three features in sixteenth-century statutes, medical treatises, and Bible translations. The most striking result is an almost complementary distribution. Whereas the three features are very common in the statutes, they are hardly found in the other two genres. There are no absolute infinitives in medical treatises and Bible translations, and the frequencies of the other two features in the two genres are minute in comparison to the statutes. It seems that doublets are used to a limited extent in the medical treatises in order to give additional terms for Latin designations, while postmodifying participles are employed to show comprehensiveness and scientific accuracy. The emergent scientific prose of the fifteenth and sixteenth century often exhibits features of the administrative 'curial style' in order to be associated with its prestige and authority. The few doublets in the Bible translations are mainly due to Tyndale's faithful translation of the original Hebrew and Greek texts. But all in all, the overwhelming impression is a nearly complementary distribution.

The three features I selected in the second genre, prestigious medical treatises, are enumeration devices, expressions used for citing authorities, and expanding devices. These features are part of the traditional style of exposition in medical prose of the late 15th and the 16th century, which has also been called 'scholastic' style (see Taavitsainen 1999; Taavitsainen and Pahta 2010).

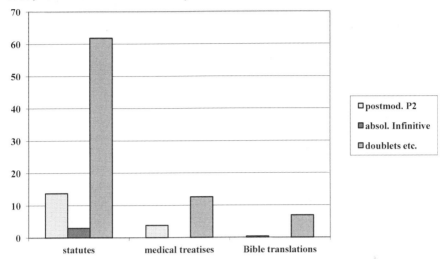

Figure 4. Selected features of sixteenth-century statutes in statutes, medical treatises, and Bible translations (freq. per 1,000 words)

Enumeration devices are those expressions that organise the text by enumerating the individual items under discussion, usually using ordinal numbers (other expressions that sometimes occur are *one, other*, and *then*). In my analysis I restricted my search to the expressions used for referring to the first four items in a description. Example (7) below shows how the ordinal numbers give a clear, though sometimes inflexible structure to the text, which is typical of scholastic exposition.

(7) These be they that haue ther **firste** respect vnto the heape of accidentes, and begynneth their cure of them, wythout any knowledge ether of the disease, … **Secundarilye**, they obserue, and marke, in the cummynge to gether of Accidentes, Medicines which they know to be mete for the disease, onlye by vse and experience. **Thyrdely** they lerne remedies of the historie, of suche as they haue before proued: **fowerthly** they goe from lyke, to lyke. (*EMEMT*)

The second feature includes the linguistic means for introducing citations from other medical handbooks. These are mostly verbs, e.g. *saith, declareth, witnesseth*, and others. Basing one's arguments on established medical authorities was a necessary requirement of the traditional scholastic style. Example (8) below illustrates the extent to which such citations from medical authorities (for example, Galen and Avicenna) shape the text.

(8) There bene two maner of ligamentes, some growe or descende oute of chordes, as we haue declared afore of muscles, **as Galene recyteth**. Howe be it, **Guido is not of that opinion**, whych semeth to vary from the truth, **sayenge** that all the ligame~tes growe out of the bones. I haue founde no doctour of that opinion. There is a nother maner of ligamentes, whych growe out of the bones, **as Auicenna sayeth** in the chapitre De resolutione continuitatis neruorum. And moreouer **Auicenne sayeth** that ligamentes whyche growe out of the bones bene insensyble

membres, and that a man maye laye to them, stronge medicines. And this is the cause why **Guido said** that all the ligamentes growe out of the bones. And **Auicenna sayeth** in the same chapitre y^t the synnowes whych ben ioyned with the muscles take part of them, and **Haliabbas is of the same opinion.** (*EMEMT*)

'Expanding devices', the third feature covered here, include expressions that add more information about the term or topic under discussion, for example, *that is to say, as, viz., namely*, etc. Giving additional detail and providing further explanation is, of course, proof of the high scientific standard these texts claim, which may be illustrated by example (9) below.

(9)   The thyrde election is, of the membres animale, **that is to say** of the heade, and hys partes. The fourth of the extremities of the bodye, **as** of the armes, the legges, and theyr partes. And in euery membre of mans bodye, after the opinion of Auerroys, and Alexandrinus, and other Anatomistes, nyne thynges are to be consydered, **that is to wete**, the composition, the substaunce, the complexion, the quantite, the nombre, the fygure, the combination or knyttynge together, theyr naturall effectes and vtilities, and what dyseases may happen to the sayd membres. (*EMEMT*)

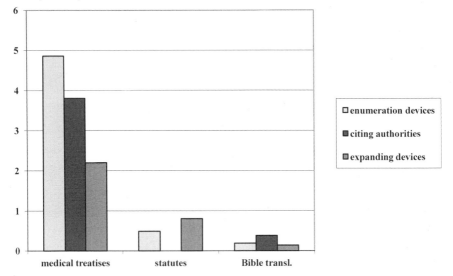

Figure 5. Selected features of sixteenth-century medical treatises in medical treatises, statutes, and Bible translations (freq. per 1,000 words)

It goes without saying that all these features serve the common purpose of proving that these medical texts belong to the established and prestigious scholastic tradition of texts and that they meet the requirements of a high contemporary scientific standard. Figure 5 above shows the frequencies of these three features in the medical treatises, the statutes, and the Bible translations. Again it reveals a nearly complementary distribution. The frequencies in the statutes range between 0 and 0.8, in the Bible translations between 0.1 and 0.4., as opposed to 2.2 to 4.9 in the medical treatises. So, again it seems that the three selected features very much shape the specific style of the genre but can hardly be found in the other two genres.

The three features I selected in Bible translations comprise first, a construction involving verbs of saying (V*ed and said* or V*ed saying*, for example, *Iesus answered and* *sayd* in example (10) below), secondly, a construction where the verbs *say* or *speak* are followed by the preposition *unto* (for example, *Nathanael sayd vnto him* in example 10) and, thirdly, the translation of Greek *αμέν* ('amen') with *verily*. These features seem to be quite specific to Biblical English, but seen from the perspective of (early) sixteenth-century English, they were fairly common (except for the first feature, which reflects Tyndale's faithfulness to the original Hebrew and Greek texts). Example (10) illustrates all three features (and the extent of their frequency) in one short excerpt from St John's Gospel.

(10) Nathanael **sayd vnto him**: where knewest thou me? Iesus **answered, and sayde vnto him**: Before that Philip called the, when thou wast vnder the fygge tree, I sawe the. Nathanael **answered and sayde vnto him**: Rabbi, thou arte the sonne of God, thou arte the kynge of Israel. Iesus **answered and sayd vnto him**: Because I **sayde vnto the**, I sawe the vnder the fygge tree, thou belevest. Thou shalt se greater things then these. And he **sayde vnto him**: **Verely, verely**, I **saye vnto you**: herafter shall ye se heven open, and the angels of God ascendynge and descendynge over the sonne of man. (*Helsinki Corpus*)

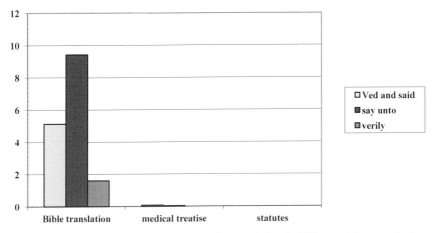

Figure 6. Selected features of sixteenth-century Bible translations in Bible translations, medical treatises, and statutes (freq. per 1,000 words)

Figure 6 above shows again the familiar pattern of a complementary distribution seen in Figures 4 and 5. Only medical treatises contain a minimal frequency of the first and the second feature (0.04 and 0.08).

What do these findings tell us about the nature of the first-order rank of genres used as a basis for comparison? Our short analysis of first-order genres from the sixteenth century reveals that they are quite incompatible in terms of their prominent linguistic features. They show idiosyncratic linguistic profiles that overlap only to a very small extent. These profiles seem to be basically shaped by a few typical features that occur in nearly complementary distribution. Now it seems to me that the high frequency and notorious overemphasis of these genre-specific features (which initially may have had a straightforward function, like comprehensive coverage and precise description) now only serve the purpose of building up the authority associated with the first-order genre and contributing to the high prestige of administrative, scientific, and (in the course of the sixteenth century) religious language. Hence comparisons on the basis of the first-order rank of a genre in a domain hierarchy are likely to reveal distinct linguistic profiles and the reason for this incompatibility seems to lie in the institutional requirements of the first-order rank.

What about the second- and third-order rank of genres as a basis for comparison? Second-order genres (for example, petitions or prayers) could be compared on the basis that they all address a superior institution and would thus share formal and functional features. For example, they would typically include a petition section, address forms and other features which would reflect the manifestations of negative and positive politeness. They would also, since they address a superior institution, adhere to established traditional linguistic forms and be resistant to innovations. The third-order rank comprises a large number of genres in all domains, with no superior institution involved in the communication. Thus, it is unlikely that we would find idiosyncratic genre styles (unless they are copied from first-order genres) but rather the broad linguistic basis of 'common' language use and, probably, a greater disposition for innovation and language change. However, these assumptions need to be corroborated by further corpus-based studies.

6. Conclusions

The aim of this paper was to present a method of comparing domain-based diachronic corpora and to test text-functional and domain-based parameters as bases for comparison. The focus was on the question of what kinds of comparisons and comparability are possible and what standards of comparison can be achieved by such an approach.

Looking back at the several case studies presented in the previous sections, one basic distinction that emerges is the difference between parameters that result in linguistic similarity and parameters that result in linguistic distinctness. Text-functional parameters clearly contribute to a similarity of the linguistic profile. This could be shown for texts with a focus on narration. Similar general text functions result in fairly similar linguistic profiles. The interactive format and the publication format of texts seem to involve more subtle distinctions. Different dialogue genres differ in small degrees and the publication format of pamphlets seems to strengthen or diminish existing formal tendencies of the interactive format of a genre.

Within domain-based parameters, the first-order rank of genres clearly results in greater linguistic distinctness. The authority of the genre (laws, textbooks, the Bible) has to be maintained by a specific style, which is incompatible with the styles of the first-order genres in other domains. It was hypothesised that second-order genres would share similar functional profiles (which may result in similar formal profiles) and that third-order genres may provide a common linguistic basis and are likely to form the locus of language change. Here, however, further research is necessary.

This study has thus, at least to a certain extent, shown what kinds of comparisons and comparability the text-functional and domain-based parameters provide. Yet can they be called faithful standards? I think they can, if the similarities and differences they reveal can actually be associated with the relevant functional dimensions. This association is plausible and can be substantiated in many different examples (as as been shown above). In the end, faithful standards of comparison should allow the researcher to distinguish between those aspects of variability (and change) in language that depend on text functions and domain structure and those that depend on other factors, especially those that seem to be intrinsic to language and linguistic structure.

References

Primary Sources

Corpus of English Dialogues <http://www.engelska.uu.se/corpus.html>
Corpus of English Religious Prose <http://www.helsinki.fi/varieng/CoRD/corpora/COERP/>
Early Modern English Medical Texts, see Taavitsainen and Pahta (2010)
Helsinki Corpus: The Helsinki Corpus of English Texts. 1991. Helsinki: Department of English <http://www.helsinki.fi/varieng/CoRD/corpora/HelsinkiCorpus/>

Secondary Sources

Biber, Douglas (1988): *Variation across Speech and Writing.* Cambridge: Cambridge University Press
--- et al. (1999): *Longman Grammar of Spoken and Written English.* Harlow: Longman
Burnley, David (1986): "Curial Prose in England", *Speculum* 61, 593-614
Fisher, John H. et al. (eds.; 1984): *An Anthology of Chancery English.* Knoxville: University of Tennessee Press
Groeger, Dorothee (2010): *The Pamphlet as a Form of Publication: A Corpus-based Study of Early Modern Religious Pamphlets.* Aachen: Shaker
Kohnen, Thomas (2010): "Religious Discourse", in: Jucker, Andreas H.; Taavitsainen, Irma (eds.): *Historical Pragmatics.* Berlin: Mouton de Gruyter, 523-547
--- (2012): "A Toolkit for Constructing Corpus Networks", in: Suhr, Carla; Taavitsainen, Irma (eds.): *Developing Corpus Methodology for Historical Pragmatics.* VARIENG e-journal, Volume 11
Kytö, Merja (comp.; 1996): *Manual to the Diachronic Part of the Helsinki Corpus of English Texts: Coding Conventions and Lists of Source Texts.* 3rd edition. Helsinki: Department of English, University of Helsinki
Powell, Susan (ed.;1981): *The Advent and Nativity Sermons from a Fifteenth-Century Revision of John Mirk's Festial.* Heidelberg: Winter
Rütten, Tanja (2011): *How to Do Things with Texts: Patterns of Instruction in Religious Discourse 1350-1700.* Frankfurt: Peter Lang
Swales, John (1990): *Genre Analysis: English for Academic and Research Settings.* Cambridge: Cambridge University Press
--- (2004): *Research Genres: Exploration and Applications.* Cambridge: Cambridge University Press
Taavitsainen, Irma (1999): "Dialogues in Late Medieval and Early Modern English Medical Writing", in: Jucker, Andreas H. et al. (eds.): *Historical Dialogue Analysis.* Amsterdam/Philadelphia: Benjamins, 243-268
---; Pahta, Päivi (eds.; 2010): *Early Modern English Medical Texts: Corpus Description and Studies.* Amsterdam/Philadelphia: Benjamins, 29-53
Werlich, Egon (1983): *A Text Grammar of English.* 2nd edition. Heidelberg: Quelle & Meyer

WVT Handbücher zum literaturwissenschaftlichen Studium
Herausgegeben von Ansgar Nünning und Vera Nünning

**17 Dystopia, Science Fiction, Post-Apocalypse:
Classics – New Tendencies – Model Interpretations**
Ed. by Eckart Voigts and Alessandra Boller

Contents: *E. Voigts:* The Dystopian Imagination – An Overview · *R. Nate:* Dystopia and Degeneration: H. G. Wells, *The Time Machine* (1895) · *R. Tripp:* Biopolitical Dystopia: A. Huxley, *Brave New World* (1932) · *E. Voigts:* Totalitarian Dystopia: George Orwell, *Nineteen Eighty-Four* (1949) · *R. Heinze:* Anti-Humanist Dystopia: Ray Bradbury, *Fahrenheit 451* (1953) · *N. Wilkinson, E. Voigts:* Mechanistic Dystopia: E. M. Forster, "The Machine Stops" (1909) and K. Vonnegut, *Player Piano* (1952) · *R. Brosch:* Dystopian Violence: *A Clockwork Orange* (A. Burgess 1962/S. Kubrick 1971) · *C. Houswitschka:* Dystopian Androids: P. K. Dick, *Do Androids Dream of Electric Sheep* (1968) and R. Scott, *Blade Runner* (1982) · *R. Borgmaier:* Surrealist Dystopia: J. G. Ballard, *The Atrocity Exhibition* (1970) · *J. Cortiel:* Feminist Utopia/Dystopia: J. Russ, *The Female Man* (1975), M. Piercy, *Woman on the Edge of Time* (1976) · *R. Borgmaier:* Ambiguous Utopia: U. K. Le Guin, *The Dispossessed* (1974) · *J. Wilm:* Postcolonial Dystopia: J. M. Coetzee, *Waiting for the Barbarians* (1980) · *D. and M. Vanderbeke:* Graphic Dystopia: *Watchmen* (Moore/Gibbons, 1986-1987) and *V for Vendetta* (Moore/Lloyd, 1982-1989) · *L. Schmeink:* Cyberpunk and Dystopia: W. Gibson, *Neuromancer* (1984) · *K. Schmidt:* Religious Dystopia: M. Atwood, *The Handmaid's Tale* (1985) and its Film Adaptation (Schlöndorff/Pinter, 1990) · *S. Georgi:* Posthuman/Critical Dystopia: O. E. Butler's *Parable* Series (1993, 1998) and *Xenogenesis* Trilogy (1987-1989) · *V. Richter:* Dystopia of Isolation: W. Golding, *Lord of the Flies* (1954) and A. Garland, *The Beach* (1996) · *D. Mohr:* Eco-Dystopia and Biotechnology: M. Atwood, *MaddAddam*-Trilogy (2003, 2009, 2013) · *U. Horstmann:* Post-Nuclear Dystopia: R. Hoban, *Riddley Walker* (1980) · *N. Glaubitz:* Eugenics and Dystopia: A. Niccol, *Gattaca* (1997) and Kazuo Ichiguro, *Never Let Me Go* (2005) · *J. Petzold:* Dystopia of Reproduction: P. D. James, *The Children of Men* (1992) and A. Cuarón, *Children of Men* (2006) · *M. Pietrzak-Franger:* Virtual Reality and Dystopia: L. and A. Wachowski, *The Matrix* and D. Cronenberg, *eXistenZ* (1999) · *O. Lindner:* Postmodernism and Dystopia: D. Mitchell, *Cloud Atlas* (2004) · *J. Hollm:* Post-Apocalyptic Dystopia: C. McCarthy, *The Road* (2006) · *S. Domsch:* Dystopian Video Games · *E. Voigts, A. Boller:* Young Adult Dystopia: S. Collins' *The Hunger Games* Trilogy (2008-2010)

ISBN 978-3-86821-565-6, 436 S., kt., € 37,50 (2014)

16 New Theories, Models and Methods in Literary and Cultural Studies
Ed. by Greta Olson and Ansgar Nünning

This book offers readers compact information about advances in literary and cultural theory. Each essay presents an application of a recent theoretical innovation in order to demonstrate how it may be put into practice. The volume thus gives students a reliable and informative overview of innovative approaches to Literary and Cultural Studies that will facilitate their research. – Separated into four sections, the first part comprises a discussion of theory itself. The second section opens with a description of the lasting critical achievements of New Historicism and Cultural Materialism and continues by describing the pertinence of these methods to Media Ecology and Performance Studies. The third part offers descriptions of methodologies that have developed out of political concerns, including Queer Theory, Ecocriticism, and Critical Media Studies. Finally, the last section is devoted to theoretical developments that position themselves as critical and social practices. It includes chapters on literary studies as a life science and translation as a critical practice.

ISBN 978-3-86821-473-4, 248 S., kt., € 25,00 (2013)

Wissenschaftlicher Verlag Trier · Bergstr. 27 · 54295 Trier
Tel.: 0651/41503 · Fax: 0651/41504 · www.wvttrier.de · E-Mail: wvt@wvttrier.de